POLITICS : CANADA

third edition

mcgraw-hill series in canadian politics

Paul W. Fox, *General Editor*

POLITICS: CANADA

third edition

CULTURE AND PROCESS

PAUL FOX

Toronto
McGraw-Hill Company of Canada Limited
Montreal
New York
London
Sydney
Mexico
Johannesburg
Panama
Düsseldorf
Singapore
Rio de Janeiro
Kuala Lumpur
New Delhi

POLITICS:

CANADA   **third edition**

Cover design by Arjen F. de Groot.

To Andrew R.

Library of Congress Catalog Card Number:
74-141017
  567890 BP-70 98765
Casebound edition   ISBN 0-07-092662-X
Paperbound edition   ISBN 0-07-092663-8
Printed and bound in Canada

PREFACE TO THE THIRD EDITION

The third edition of *Politics: Canada* has been altered very markedly. A great deal of fresh material has been added and many of the items in the first and second editions have been revised and brought up to date or in some cases omitted. Once again the size of the book has been increased substantially. A more contemporary approach has been adopted by arranging the new and former contents under the two general headings of culture and process. Several new chapters have been added on English Canada and Nationalism, Regionalism, Voting Behaviour, and Civil Rights.

The new material appearing in this third edition originates from two sources. In the first place it consists of selections in whole or in part of a number of leading articles and items which have been published in academic journals, government sources, books, magazines, and newspapers since the second edition was produced in 1966, and secondly it contains several original articles which are appearing here for the first time.

I wish to thank all contributors, but I owe a debt of particular gratitude to those authors who have allowed me to publish originally here their work which in some cases was prepared especially for this volume. In this connection I would like to single out Mr. Juris Dreifelds for his article on nationalism and socialism in French Canada, Professor David Surplis for his article on Canada's press, Professor Jerry Hough for his study of voter turnout and its implications in a recent municipal election, and Professor Ronald Blair for his charts on the organization of the Prime Minister's Office and the Privy Council Office. I would like to repeat my thanks to the authors of other articles which appeared for the first time in earlier editions of this book, especially to Professors Brian Land, Denis Stairs, and Hugh Whalen who have taken the time and trouble to revise and update for this edition their original contributions.

Once again the bibliographies at the end of each chapter have been brought up to date and have been made reasonably inclusive of recent major Canadian material, although they are not meant to be exhaustive, of course. I have entered most items only once, in the bibliography of the chapter where they seem most appropriate, but there are some repetitions when that appeared to be especially useful. Where a reference is given in a footnote, I have not repeated it in a bibliography. The only abbreviations used in the bibliographies are for sources that occur frequently. *C.J.E.P.S.* stands for *The Canadian Journal of Economics and Political Science, C.P.A.* for *Canadian Public Administration, Q.Q.* for *Queen's Quarterly,* and *C.J.P.S.* for the new *Canadian Journal of Political Science.*

A point made in the second edition should be repeated here; a number of titles of selections are entirely my invention, designed often to relate one article to another, and for such licence the original author or publisher should not be held responsible.

Finally, I have omitted from this edition certain material which appeared in earlier editions because this book is now part of a new series which contains studies in depth of some of the topics touched on formerly in *Politics: Canada.* A complete list of the works appearing in the new McGraw-Hill Series in Canadian Politics is given elsewhere in this edition. Since the Series is open-ended, further items will be added to it continually. Several are already well advanced in preparation. The intention is to have eventually an extensive collection of relatively brief and inexpensive paperbacks on many different aspects of Canadian politics.

Paul Fox
August 7, 1970
Toronto, Ontario

PREFACE

This is not meant to be a text book. It began very simply as a collection of supplementary readings for university students in courses in Canadian government, and then it was realized that the selections might have considerable interest for the general public also.

So far as students are concerned, *Politics: Canada* is intended to be a supplementary collection of readings bringing up to date and amplifying some of the subjects dealt with in standard texts, such as R. M. Dawson, *The Government of Canada,* Toronto, University of Toronto Press, 3rd ed., revised, 1959, and J. A. Corry and J. E. Hodgetts, *Democratic Government and Politics,* Toronto, University of Toronto Press, 3rd ed., revised, 1959. This has made it possible to keep to a minimum the introductory remarks to each section in this book. No effort has been made to repeat the background to contemporary developments though, where necessary, those developments themselves have been explained briefly.

For the same reason—since the book is an addition to a regular text and not an alternative—a lively sympathy for the student's purse has kept the volume to a modest length. This has caused the editor most of his headaches. There was such a wealth of excellent material which might have been included that omitting part of it was a painful necessity, particularly since some of it had to be eliminated in the final re-arrangement of the book. I apologize sincerely to those authors whose important articles had to be sacrificed to the economy of space. To those authors whose works are included I should like to express my thanks for granting me the right to edit their material. I have had to make the unpalatable decision to eliminate all footnotes and to reduce in length virtually every selection. I have tried to wield the blue pencil with care and discrimination, being faithful, I hope, to the author's meaning and to the order of importance he attached to his arguments. Deletions, insertions, and ellipses have been noted with the customary editorial symbols, except in a very few instances where excessive profusion would have disrupted the reading of the text. Some selections have been retitled but in each case the original title has been noted in the reference to the source, which may be consulted also for the original text and footnotes.

vii

The need to save space also led to the decision to exclude some important articles because they are available in other books of readings. Two of these in the field of public administration contain some material relevant to broader aspects of Canadian government; they are J. E. Hodgetts and D. C. Corbett, (eds.), *Canadian Public Administration: A Book of Readings,* Toronto, Macmillan, 1960, and D. C. Rowat, (ed.), *Basic Issues in Public Administration,* New York, Macmillan, 1961. The late Professor R. M. Dawson's *Constitutional Issues in Canada, 1900-1931,* London, Oxford University Press, 1933, is the only other book of readings concerned with the general field of Canadian government. It contains much excellent material on earlier aspects which I have not repeated here. As in the case of the text books mentioned above, I have merely attempted to supplement it and to bring it up to date.

Almost all the selections in *Politics: Canada* deal with the federal government. Material referring to provincial or municipal governments is included only for the light it casts on the central government or because of its general applicability. This is not meant to imply that the other levels of government are not important, merely that they are fields which require separate treatment.

A bibliography to facilitate further reading has been appended to each section of this book. These lists of additional material are not exhaustive, of course. They do not repeat necessarily, for instance, all the references contained in the standard works previously noted. The only abbreviation used in the bibliographies which might require explanation is *C.J.E.P.S.* for *The Canadian Journal of Economics and Political Science.*

I wish to express my gratitude to all the authors and publishers who have permitted me to reprint their material here. Without exception their response has been generous, cooperative, and courteous. I am especially indebted to Mr. Peter Russell and Mr. Brian Land of the University of Toronto for allowing their articles to be printed here for the first time. To my colleagues and others who have given me advice, encouragement, and assistance in planning this book and suggesting material for it, I am also greatly indebted. I shall not mention names but those responsible will know to whom my thanks are particularly directed. Finally, I would like to thank Mr. Neil Patterson of McGraw-Hill for his major role in bringing this book to publication.

Paul W. Fox
University of Toronto
August 7, 1962

CONTENTS

POLITICS: CANADA
third edition

I CULTURE

ONE
POLITICAL SCIENCE

Professor Dahl's article is a useful introduction to the study of political science. It touches on most of the basic questions that arise in connection with political science and outlines the major aspects of the discipline. The bibliography includes references to some recent works in the analysis of political systems and some general works dealing with behavioural aspects of political science, though specific Canadian political behavioural studies are noted in the bibliography to Chapter 10.

WHAT IS POLITICAL SCIENCE?*

ROBERT A. DAHL

What is political science?

To begin, political science is, of course, the study of politics. One might better say, it is the *systematic* study of politics, that is, an attempt by systematic analysis to discover in the confusing tangle of specific detail whatever principles may exist of wider and more general significance.

At the very outset, then, we must distinguish political science as the systematic *study* of politics from the *practice* of politics.

The same person may of course both study and practise politics. The student of politics may serve as an adviser to the political practitioner. Plato, the great Greek philosopher and political theorist, is said to have gone to Syracuse, in Sicily, in 367 B.C. to advise the ruler of that city—who, I am sorry to say, was a tyrant. . . .

Sometimes, though less often, a political scientist may be not only an adviser but also an active practitioner of the political arts. That astounding man of the Italian Renaissance, Niccolo Machiavelli, served as a secretary of the Republic of Florence for fourteen years. . . . [He also wrote] such masterpieces of political science as *The Prince* and *The Discourses* and even a great comic and rather scabrous play, *La Mandragola*. Machiavelli's descriptions and prescriptions are so lacking in ordinary standards of morality that his name has come to be associated with notions of ruthless egoism in politics. To many people, I imagine, he represents the essence of political evil. Yet the man himself loathed despotism and believed devoutly in the virtues of republican institutions. . . .

Machiavelli began his career as a politician and became a political scientist when his political career ended; with Woodrow Wilson the sequence was just the reverse. Wilson was a historian and political scientist long before he began the political career that propelled him into the White House. . . . It has sometimes been said that Wilson himself unfortunately ignored his own advice when he became President. But the practising politician often does ignore the political scientist — even, as in Wilson's case, when the political scientist happens to be himself.

I mention these examples less to show that political scientists are typically involved in politics than the contrary. I want to emphasize that actually engaging in politics is not at all the same thing as studying politics in order to develop principles of general relevance. Political science means the study, not the practice, of politics.

* From *American Politics and Government,* the Forum Lectures broadcast and published by the Voice of America, Washington, D.C., 1965, pp. 1-19. By permission.

AN ANCIENT STUDY

As you may have noticed from these examples, the study of politics is an ancient field of learning. It is also a study that has received unusual emphasis in those Western cultures that derive from the worlds of Greek and Roman civilization. For the Greeks and Romans were immensely concerned with political things.

The modern study of politics, in fact, can be traced to that magnificent and unbelievably creative people, the Greeks of the fifth and the fourth centuries before Christ and, most of all, to the Athenians. It was in Athens that Socrates, Plato, and Aristotle raised to the highest level of intellectual endeavour the kinds of questions about politics that concern thoughtful men down to the present day. I have in mind such questions as:

How do we acquire knowledge about politics and about political life? How do we distinguish politics from other aspects of human life? In what ways are political systems similar to one another? In what ways do political systems differ from one another? What is the role of authority and power in political systems? How do men behave in politics? What are the special characteristics, if any, of *homo politicus,* political man? What kinds of conditions make for stability, for change, or for revolution in a political system? What is required if social peace is to be maintained and violence to be avoided? What sort of political system is the best? How should we and how do we decide questions about what is "the best" in politics?

Every age has produced one or two men who provide great answers to these great questions . . . [such as] the three Greeks: Socrates, Plato, and Aristotle. Let us consider several others. Cicero, who was both witness to and participant in the death agony of the Roman Republic; St. Augustine, born in North Africa in the fourth century; St. Thomas Aquinas, born near Naples in the thirteenth century; Machiavelli, born in Florence in the fifteenth century; Thomas Hobbes, the Englishman, born in the next century; John Locke, also an Englishman, born in the seventeenth century; at the end of the seventeenth century, a Frenchman, Montesquieu, who greatly influenced the men who drafted the United States Constitution; in the eighteenth century, another Frenchman, Rousseau; in the nineteenth century the Germans, Hegel, Marx, and Engels, the Englishmen Jeremy Bentham and John Stuart Mill, the Frenchman Alexis de Tocqueville. . . .

WHAT IS POLITICS?

What is politics? This innocent question is rather like asking a biologist, "What is life?" Biology, it is said, is the science of life or living matter in all its manifestations. Very well. But what is living matter? It turns out that this question is extremely difficult to answer and that biologists do not exactly agree on·the answer. Yet they are quite confident that some kinds of matter—one-celled animals, for example—are clearly at the centre of biology, while others—a piece of granite, for example—are clearly outside the field. So, too, in political science. We pretty well agree on the kinds of things that are definitely political. Thus the governments of the United States, the Soviet Union, and any other nation, province, state, city, town, or colony are unquestionably political and therefore in the domain of political science. The government of an ant colony is not; at any rate I have not noticed any of my colleagues writing about party politics or imperialism in ant colonies. Yet if we can say with confidence what lies at the centre of politics, we are, like the biologist confronted with the question of life, not so sure of the exact boundaries.

Let me therefore describe what is at the centre. To begin, wherever we find politics, most authorities agree, we necessarily encounter human beings living together in some kind of an association. . . . Wherever we find politics we encounter some special relationship among the human beings living together, a relationship variously called "rule," "authority," or "power". To refer once again to Aristotle, the very first page of the *Politics* contains references to different kinds of authority, what distinguishes the authority of the statesman from the authority of the head of the household or of the master over his slave, and the like. Wherever we find politics we discover conflict and ways in which human beings cope with conflict. Indeed, when human beings live together in associations and create rules, authorities, or governments to deal with these conflicts, the very attempts to rule also help to generate conflicts. Which comes first, power or conflict, need not detain us; we find both conflict and power wherever human beings live together. Politics arises, then, whenever there are people living together in associations, whenever they are involved in conflicts, and wherever they are subject to some kind of power, rulership, or authority.

These phenomena exist everywhere, therefore politics is everywhere. But not all associations have equal power. You can very easily test this—though I strongly urge you not to try—by having your family, which is one association, attempt to take over your neighbour's property, which, I am sure, happens to be protected by a more powerful association, the national state in which you reside. The state is the association that has the greatest power within some particular territory. Thus the *government* of the state is obviously at the very centre of politics, and therefore of political science. And the various organized institutions that make up the government of a state—the executive, the legislature, the judiciary, regional organizations, provinces, and local governments—all involve politics.

There are associations, organizations, and institutions that help to determine what the organs of government actually do; what rules the government adopts and enforces. In the modern world the most important are obviously political parties, such as the Republican and Democratic parties in the United States, Conservatives, Labourites, and Liberals in Britain, the Communist party in the Soviet Union, and so on. In many countries the political parties are so influential that one can consider them as a kind of informal government that rules the rulers. Thus political parties are pretty clearly at or near the centre of politics and therefore of political science.

In addition to the parties, other organizations help to determine what the state does, even though they may not run candidates in elections and are not directly and openly represented in parliament. These associations are sometimes called interest groups; any association that tries to secure from the state policies favourable to its members or followers is an interest group. In the United States interest groups include such organizations as the American Medical Association, which represents physicians and has been involved in the struggle over a national program of medical care; labour unions, including the great national organization, the AFL-CIO, which frequently descends on Congress in an attempt to secure legislation favourable to trade unions in particular and the working people in general; farm organizations, which seek to gain favourable treatment for farms. One could go on endlessly simply listing examples of interest-group organizations in the United States. Not long ago the United States House of Representatives debated and passed a bill increasing the legal authority of the federal government to protect the rights of Negroes. A recently published list of the groups who were activelv working in Washington to persuade congressmen to support the bill shows: six civil rights organizations, fifteen labour unions, nineteen religious organizations, and ten other groups.

Neither can we ignore ordinary citizens. Election, voting, and other forms of participation by citizens in civic life are also elements of politics.

Have we now reached the boundaries of politics? Hardly. In fact some political scientists would extend the meaning of politics to include *any* activity involving human beings associated together in relationships of power and authority where conflicts occur. In this sense, politics truly does exist everywhere: within trade unions, within the interest-group organizations of doctors or farmers, in business organizations, even in private clubs, indeed anywhere that human beings assemble together. Viewed in this way, the domain of politics and therefore of political science does not stop simply with the institutions of the state, or even with such familiar political institutions as political parties and organized interest groups, but extends to an enormous range of human activity. The question of how far the boundaries of political science extend is a lively one among political scientists at the present time, but we need not linger over it any more. For it is perfectly obvious that no matter how they draw their boundaries, political scientists have more than enough to do.

IS POLITICS A SCIENCE?

. . . In what sense is the study of politics a science? In what sense *can* it be? Even if it can be, should it be a science? These questions, as you might imagine, are also the subjects of a great deal of discussion; it is not too much to say that the discussion has gone on for a very long time, if not, in fact, from the time of the Greeks.

The term "science" has, of course, many meanings. And the word does not mean quite the same thing in one language as it does in another. In some countries, scholars do not consider that political science is a single subject, like biology, but many subjects. Some scholars speak not of political science but of the political *sciences*. In France, until recently, one heard of *les sciences politiques* and in Italy *le scienze politiche*—that is, the political sciences. What do we mean, then, by the *science* of politics? To some people the word "science" simply means any systematic approach to human knowledge; so that one could speak of the science of physics, the science of mathematics, or perhaps even a science of theology. To others, and this is a good deal more common in English-speaking countries nowadays, the word "science" tends to be restricted to the natural sciences, studies that involve the observation of nature and the development of laws and theories explaining the phenomena of nature such as chemistry, physics, and the biological sciences. In recent years, particularly in the United States, we have come to speak of the social and behavioural sciences, that is, those that seek by observation to develop explanations of human behaviour.

To confuse the matter even more, science is thought of sometimes as an achievement in being, sometimes as a method, and sometimes as a goal.

Physics is a science in the first sense. When one speaks of physics as a "real" science, he probably does not mean that physicists are simply hoping to develop theories that someday will explain the nature of physical reality; he means that they already have such theories, and they are of impressive power to explain the physical world.

But science also refers to the *methods* by which scholars investigate their subject. One might say that a century ago medicine was not very "scientific" because its methods were extremely crude; it was difficult to distinguish the charlatan from the honest inquirer after medical knowledge. Today, on the contrary, medical research in the most advanced laboratories uses highly sophisticated methods of inquiry very much like those used in physics, chemistry, and biology. Yet almost everyone would agree that in its laws, theories, and explanations medicine is not so far advanced as, say, physics.

One might also think of science as a goal, as something to be arrived at by rigorous methods of inquiry, even if present knowledge is somewhat sparse.

In which of these three senses is the study of politics a science? Despite the fact that the best minds of every age have tended to turn their attention to the study of politics, as I pointed out above, certainly the study of politics is not an already achieved science like physics. We simply do not have a body of theories about political systems that enables us to predict the outcome of complex events with anything like the reliability that a physicist, a chemist, or even a biologist generally can predict the outcome of complex events in his field. If you believe that there is such a theory in politics, I am bound to say that you are, in my opinion, deluding yourself. It is true that from time to time a writer, sometimes even a great writer, has claimed that he possesses a full-fledged predictive science of politics. So far, however, no comprehensive theory of politics that undertakes to predict the outcome of complex events has stood the test of experience. The most notable modern example of failure is, I think, Marx. If you examine his predictions carefully and test them against actual developments, he proves to be wrong in so many cases that only those who regard Marxism as a kind of religion to take on faith, and against all evidence, can remain persuaded that it is a truly predictive scientific theory.

Nonetheless, political scientists do have an enormous amount of knowledge about politics, much of it extremely reliable knowledge.

•   •   •

We can say, then, that political science is the study of politics by methods and procedures designed to give us the greatest reliability in a highly complex world. As a body of knowledge, modern political science is definitely not a highly perfected science like physics or chemistry. Our knowledge of politics is continually and rapidly growing; however, this knowledge is of varying degrees of reliability, for some of it is highly speculative and about as reliable as anything one is ever likely to learn about human beings.

MATTERS STUDIED

What objects or phenomena do we actually study in political science? I have already mentioned most of these when I discussed the boundaries of politics, but let me now enumerate the main phenomena, the "objects" of political science. First, we study individual citizens, voters, leaders. Strange as it may seem, study of the ways in which individuals actually behave in politics is one of the newest developments in the field. It is true, of course, that the behaviour of individuals in politics has never been ignored. Machiavelli's *The Prince* describes how many Renaissance political leaders did act and prescribes how they had to act if they were to succeed in the ruthless and tempestuous political jungle that was Renaissance Italy. Even though few writers had as much to say about the seamy side of political life as did Machiavelli, insights about man's political behaviour are scattered in works over the centuries.

Our understanding of man has made a quantum jump since Sigmund Freud and the advent of modern psychology, psychoanalysis, and psychiatry made us all acutely aware of man's capacity for irrational, nonrational, impulsive, neurotic, and psychotic action—in politics, unfortunately, as much as elsewhere. Partly as a result of this change, in the last several decades political scientists have begun to observe individuals and politics with a concern for detail and accuracy that, if not entirely new, is at least highly uncommon. What is new, perhaps, is a search for reliable generalizations. We are no longer content to observe a few individuals engaged in politics and to describe their behaviours, to investigate a few great, unusual leaders or a few simple yet possibly rare citizens. Rather, we want to know how widely our generalizations apply.

. . . [For instance] the independent voter is often thought to be, at least by comparison, a model citizen, rational, thoughtful, responsible, open-minded, in contrast to the partisan who, it is often thought, is less reflective, less thoughtful, and perhaps even less interested in a campaign because he made up his mind long ago and nothing will budge him. The view is, surely, plausible. Beginning with the presidential election of 1940, however, studies by American social scientists began to destroy this happy picture of the independent voter. In one study after another it was discovered that, far from being a thoughtful, attentive, responsible citizen, a person who lacks any spirit of partisanship more than likely has no great interest in politics, is quite ignorant about politics, does not pay much attention to political campaigns, and makes up his mind at the last possible moment, frequently on the basis of rather trivial or accidental influences. . . .

This finding has forced us to do some rethinking of our notions about the roles of the partisan and independent in American politics and perhaps in democratic systems in general. We cannot yet be sure how widespread this phenomenon is. Some studies indicate that it holds in certain European countries, in nations as different, for example, as Britain and Italy. But it may not hold in others. A recent analysis suggests that perhaps our model citizen, the thoughtful, reflective, interested man who does not make up his mind until he has tried to hear both sides of the argument, does actually exist in the United States and may play no negligible role in elections, even though his numbers are pretty tiny.

A second phenomenon studied by political scientists is the private or semipublic associations to which many individuals belong. The most visible of these, as I suggested earlier, are political parties. There are a vast number of studies of political parties throughout the world: how they are organized, how nominations are made, what the parties do in campaigns and elections, the characteristics of party leaders, members, and followers, and differences and similarities in the party systems of various countries.

Perhaps the most significant development during the last several decades has been the discovery of the tremendous importance of interest groups, particularly in the United States. Because class lines are rather weak, vague, and uncertain in this country, despite considerable differences in social standing, prestige, and income, and because our political parties, unlike many European parties, are neither tightly organized nor highly centralized, it was natural, I suppose, that American political scientists were the first to turn their attention to interest groups. It is fair to say, in fact, that they pioneered investigation in this area. In the last decade, however, concern with the role of interest groups in politics has spread to European political scientists, who have also begun to demonstrate that social classes and political parties are by no means the only significant political forces in European politics and that a variety of interest groups are active in the political parties and influence cabinet ministers, the civil servants, and other governmental officials. It would be impossible to understand the operation of any democratic system if one ignored the decisive role often played by representatives of the party of interests that exists in a modern industrialized and urbanized society.

A third focus for study is, of course, the political institutions themselves—the parliaments, the cabinets, the courts, the civil service, and the like. These are such obvious and familiar subjects for political science, therefore, that I will not comment on them further.

A fourth focus is a political system as a whole. A lively question of enduring interest to American political scientists is how to distinguish democracies from other systems and, perhaps more important, what conditions are required for the stability of democratic institutions. As political scientists learn more about the actual operation of democratic political systems, it becomes obvious that the gap between the ideals formulated by classical spokesmen for democracy, such as Locke, Rousseau, and Jefferson, are not only a long way from achievement (a fact that in itself would hardly be a new discovery) but may even have to be reformulated for fear that, as unattainable and utopian goals, they serve merely to discredit democracy as an ideal.

The existence of many new nations only recently liberated from colonial rule and still struggling with problems of independence, internal peace, and self-government presents as great an intellectual challenge to political scientists as they have ever faced: to discover the conditions under which these countries can develop stable constitutional governments based on the consent and support of the bulk of the population and capable of an orderly solution to staggering problems of economic growth and social development. It is fair to state that the study of politics in its 2,000-year development in the West has been rather parochial.

Now that we are confronted by the need for moderately reliable knowledge about the political systems developing in Africa, Asia, and even in Latin America, we find that facts and theories drawn from the experience of European and English-speaking countries are inadequate. As a consequence, during the last decade or so tremendous efforts have been made in the United States to develop scholars with an understanding of the problems and politics of the non-Western world. . . .

I must discuss one other focus of political science that is so painfully important to all of us that it might even be placed at the very centre of the stage. I have in mind, of course, the relation among political systems, that is, international relations. Here, too, the challenge strains our capacities to the very limit if not, indeed, beyond. In their attempt to grapple with the portentous and enormously complicated problems of international politics, political scientists in recent years have resorted to an amazing variety of techniques of inquiry and analysis, not excluding even the use of electronic computers to simulate negotiation and conflict among several countries in international politics. Although some of these efforts might seem absurd and unrealistic, my view is that we are so desperately in need of solutions that we can ill afford to mock any serious intellectual effort to discover them; and help may come from quite unexpected quarters.

METHODS OF STUDY

These, then, are some of the phenomena studied by modern political scientists. You might want to know *how* we study these things? To answer this question properly would require many chapters. Politics, as everyone knows, is not something one can directly observe in either a laboratory or a library. Indeed, direct observation of politics is often extremely difficult or downright impossible. Consequently, we often have to study politics by indirect observation, through historical materials, records, papers, statistical data, and the like. This process, I have no doubt, conveys the customary image of nearsighted scholars consulting the works of one another without ever emerging from the library into the heat and turmoil of political life. Yet one of the oldest though often neglected traditions of political science is the tradition of direct observation.

It is worth recalling that the great Greek students of politics, Socrates, Aristotle, and Plato, were able to and did observe politics in the compact laboratory of the city-state. They did not make the sharp division that modern scholars often make between the world of books and study and the world of affairs. Eighteen centuries later, Machiavelli was able to observe the political life of Renaissance Italy from his post in the Republic of Florence. I rather think there are many scholars today who believe that their fragile dignity would be damaged should they leave their libraries to mingle with the ordinary folk in the noisy byways of politics. Nonetheless, a most interesting development over the last several decades has been the growing insistence that wherever possible the scholar should observe as directly as he can the objects of his study. As a result, never before in history have there been so many scholars seeking to interview politicians, civil servants, and ordinary citizens.

. . . This development is, in my view, an enormously healthy one, for just as the biologist is no less a biologist, but a good deal more, because he observes in his laboratory the organisms with which he works, and just as the physician gains knowledge from studying patients and not merely from reading what others have written about disease, so too the study of political science has gained from the growing conviction that one cannot know politics merely by traversing the path between the classroom and the library. Yet to observe politics directly is much more difficult for us than it was for Aristotle or for Machiavelli; for the world we study is larger and more complicated, the population is greater, and the slice of the world we see—we now know—is not likely to be truly representative of the world.

The political scientist's laboratory, then, is the world—the world of politics. And he must work in that laboratory with the same caution and the same rigorous concern for the accuracy and reliability of his observation that is true of the natural scientist in his laboratory; with a good deal less chance, nonetheless, of succeeding. Because direct observation is no simple matter of casual and accidental interview, the political scientist finds that for every hour he spends observing politics he may have to spend a dozen analyzing his observations. Raw observations are all but useless, so the scholar still must work at his desk, in the silence of his study, reading and reflecting, trying to pierce the veil that seems always to keep truth half-hidden. Now that we have brought our political scientist back to his desk, far from the hurly-burly of politics, let us leave him there. But if he is to study politics he cannot stay there long. You may run into him at the next political meeting you attend.

BIBLIOGRAPHY

Alker, H. R., Jr., *Mathematics and Politics,* Toronto, Collier-Macmillan, 1965.

Almond, G., "A Development Approach to Political Systems," *World Politics,* Vol. XVII, No. 2, January, 1965.

Backstrom, C. H., and Hursh, G. D., *Survey Research,* Chicago, Northwestern University Press, 1963.

Benson, O., *Political Science Laboratory,* Columbus, Charles E. Merrill, 1969.

Bergeron, G., Painchaud, P., Sabourin, L., Tournon, J., *L'état actuel de la théorie politique,* Ottawa, 1964, Vol. I, Cahiers de la Société Canadienne de Science Politique.

Bluhm, W. T., *Theories of the Political System: Classics of Political Thought and Modern Political Analysis,* Englewood Cliffs, N.J., Prentice-Hall, 1965.

Charlesworth, J. C. (ed.), *A Design for Political Science: Scope, Objectives, and Methods,* [A Symposium], Monograph 6 in a Series sponsored by The American Academy of Political and Social Science, Philadelphia, 1966.

Connery, R. H. (ed.), *Teaching Political Science: A Challenge to Higher Education,* Don Mills, Burns & MacEachern Ltd., 1965.

Dahl, R. A., *Modern Political Analysis,* Englewood Cliffs, N.J., Prentice-Hall, 1963.

Dion, L., *Le statut théorique de la science politique,* Montréal, le centre de documentation et de recherches politiques, Collège Jean-de-Brébeuf, 1964.

Duverger, M., *The Idea of Politics, The Uses of Power in Society,* Toronto, Methuen, 1966.

Easton, D., *A Framework for Political Analysis,* Englewood Cliffs, N.J., Prentice-Hall, 1965.

Easton, D., *A Systems Analysis of Political Life,* New York, Wiley and Sons, 1965.

Easton, D., *The Political System, An Inquiry Into the State of Political Science,* New York, Knopf, 1953.

Golembiewski, R. T., Welsh, N. A., Crotty, W. J., *A Methodological Primer for Political Scientists,* Chicago, Rand McNally, 1969.

Gould, J., and Kolb, W. L., (eds.), *A Dictionary of the Social Sciences,* New York, The Free Press, 1964.

Isaak, A. C., *Scope and Methods of Political Science: An Introduction to the Methodology of Political Inquiry,* Illinois, Dorsey Press, 1969.

Merritt, R. L., and Puszka, G. J., *The Student Political Scientist's Handbook,* Cambridge, Mass., Schenkman, 1969.

Polsby, N., Dentler, R., Smith, P., *Politics and Social Life: An Introduction to Political Behaviour,* Boston, Houghton Mifflin, 1963.

Ranney, A., *The Governing of Men: An Introduction to Political Science,* New York, Holt, Rinehart, and Winston, 1966, rev. ed.

Sorauf, F. J., *Political Science, An Informal Overview,* Columbus, Charles E. Merrill, 1965.

Strum, P., and Shmidman, M. D., *On Studying Political Science,* California, Goodyear, 1969.

Wallis, W. A., and Roberts, H. V., *The Nature of Statistics,* New York, The Free Press, 1965.

Wiseman, H. V., *Political Systems, Some Sociological Approaches,* London, Routledge, Kegan, Paul, 1966.

TWO
ENGLISH CANADA
AND NATIONALISM

It is a curious fact that although many English-speaking Canadians since Confederation have supported the cause of Canada as an independent, sovereign country, there actually has been very little written on the subject and, until only recently at any rate, there has been virtually no attempt to work out a doctrine of Canadian nationalism. This deficiency on the part of English-speaking Canadians stands in sharp contrast, of course, to the plethora of particular nationalist thinking and writing which has emanated continually from French Canada.

Some French-Canadian nationalists are inclined to take the lack of English-Canadian nationalist literature as self-evident proof of the non-existence of a significant English-Canadian national spirit. That such an assumption is unwarranted is obvious from the facts of Canadian history which amply demonstrate that many of our English-speaking public figures, such as, for example, Prime Ministers Macdonald, Borden, and King, as well as many Anglophonic journalists, academics, and ordinary citizens, have devoted themselves to the building of a Canadian nation with its own distinctive identity.

For the most part, however, their efforts have been defensive rather than aggressive. In the first half century of our national existence they were directed in the main towards emancipating Canada from its colonial position within the British Empire. That goal was attained by the achievement of Dominion status in 1931. Since then English-Canadian nationalists have found themselves engaged in a second phase of defensive action, this time directed against the absorption of Canada by an omnipresent and almost overwhelming American culture, which is both national and continental. As the political power of the United States has waxed mightily in the post-war period and the pull of North American economic continentalism has grown even more pronounced, English-speaking Canadian nationalism has reacted by becoming increasingly strident. Its substance, moreover, is usually negative rather than positive, long in criticism and short in the development of any theory of Canadian nationalism, unless it is Marxist. The country still awaits the birth of a doctrine of Canadian nationalism, although there are now those, such as Prime Minister Pierre Trudeau and Professor Ramsay Cook, who believe that such an event should be aborted.

Professor Kenneth McNaught's essay on the national outlook of English-speaking Canadians is one of the best discussions available of this whole problem. An excerpt from his contribution to one of the rare books dealing with this subject, *Nationalism in Canada,* edited by Peter Russell, is contained in this chapter. It is followed by a brief passage from Professor John Porter's classic work on Canadian society, *The Vertical Mosaic.* His stimulating perception adds another dimension to the pungent comments by Professor McNaught.

The items noted in the bibliography indicate the extent to which Canadians have become caught up by the subject of nationalism in the past few years, and especially by the threat to it from the United States in various forms, political, economic, and cultural.

A sub-section of the bibliography lists some of the publications which are beginning to appear in rapidly increasing number on related Canadian social issues.

THE NATIONAL OUTLOOK OF ENGLISH-SPEAKING CANADIANS*

KENNETH McNAUGHT

TWO FOUNDING RACES?

Probably because the alternative is so clumsy, the terms "English-Canadian" or "English" are used interchangeably in Quebec to signify those people in the rest of Canada who do not speak French or who are not of French descent. Yet these terms are wildly misleading. They imply the existence in Canada of only two races, and thus that any revision of Confederation must be based upon a dialogue or bargaining process between these two races. Each term also carries the suggestion that the words "Canada" and "Canadian" have come to mean "English

*From Peter Russell, (ed.), *Nationalism in Canada,* Toronto, McGraw-Hill Company of Canada Ltd., 1966. By permission of the author and publisher.

Canada" and "English Canadian." Thus the problem in Quebec eyes concerns the relations between the "two nations"; and it is a striking fact that "nation" and "race" are virtually interchangeable terms in Quebec.

Under the hammer-blows of *nationaliste* theoreticians and the preconceptions of the Bilingualism and Biculturalism Royal Commission, these notions have become widely accepted in journalistic and intellectual circles outside Quebec. Professor Charles Taylor, for example, began a discussion of co-operative federalism in the influential Quiet Revolutionist journal, *Cité Libre,* with the words, "Les Canadiens et les Québécois. . . ." Such usage is now common in the French-Canadian press and few spokesmen for the New Wave pause to reflect that the whole concept of two nations is false. Certainly they have not dwelt upon the startling internal contradiction which more often than not pervades the Quebec argument.

Having established that Canada is composed of two races (or nations, or cultures), the argument goes on to say that only the French nation is really conscious of its own identity and destiny and that without Quebec Canada would become balkanized. The "English" race or culture is so amorphous that it depends upon the French-Canadian nation to keep it from falling into the arms of the United States or from breaking up into regional fragments. At the same time, it is this enfeebled English-Canadian race which has triumphantly imposed its image on Canada and made necessary the French-Canadian revolution. Strange argument.

The illogic springs from a failure to understand the meaning attached to nationality by English-speaking Canadians. And the confusion is deepened by the fascination with which English-speaking Canadian intellectuals, journalists and politicians regard the sophisticated theorizing of French-Canadian spokesmen. In Quebec the battle of ideas and refinement of logic are more highly valued than is generally the case elsewhere in the country. English-speaking Canadian intellectuals, impressed by the progress of the Quiet Revolution's ideological conquest of Quebec, are strongly tempted to reply in kind with counter ideologies of English-Canadian nationalism.

This is a dangerous exercise, as may be seen from a brilliant example of it in a recent issue of *Canadian Dimension* [Vol. 2, No. 5, July-August, 1965]. There, a young political scientist from McGill, Gad Horowitz, pleads for the creation of a specifically English-Canadian nationalism as a necessary counterpoise to the new, extreme French-Canadian nationalism . . . Horowitz is right when he calls for a careful consideration of English-speaking concepts of nationalism in this country. He is dead wrong when he follows out the logic of the French-Canadian *nationaliste* view of two racial nations. And this matter of the English-speaking view of Confederation is now of crucial importance.

The most striking facts about the English-speaking view of Canada are that it rejects racial nationalism and is the product of a deep commitment to slowly evolved historical tradition. There are good reasons why both these aspects of the English-speaking view are less well publicized and less widely discussed than the racial nationalism of French-Canadian spokesmen. There are even better reasons why the English-speaking view should be much more precisely understood at the present time. For that view, in the developing crisis of Confederation, will assert itself with increasing vigour.

•   •   •

At the time of Confederation, indeed, all the supporters of the movement, French- and English-speaking alike, talked of the founding of a new nationality. No amount of quibbling about the different meanings attached by "English" and "French" to the word "nation" can obscure the fact that in the 1860's a political nationality was being founded. The debate and conferences leave absolutely no room for doubt on the matter. Nor is there room to doubt that English-speaking Canadians, then and even more now, thought of Canadian nationality as something that included people of French, British and other origins and which would move steadily toward its own sense of identity. That identity was not to be homogeneous in the American sense, but diverse. It would, and has guaranteed to various minorities (especially the French-speaking minority) particular rights with respect to language, religion, land-holding, military service, hunting and fishing.

Yet, while local differences of culture and law were to be guaranteed (especially in Quebec), there was never any question of an "equality of two founding races." The "races" were, in fact, not equal. A central purpose of Confederation was to recognize this fact and to avoid the frictions which the "two nations" idea had created during the unhappy political evolution under the 1841 Act of Union.

In order to maintain minority rights within Quebec and the other provinces, without at the same time permitting Quebec to become a state within a state, the predominance of Ottawa and the rights of the Canadian majority there (however it might be composed) had to be accepted. . . .

Any survey of Canadian political history reveals that the idea of two "founding races" (each with the expectation of its own developing nationality) has been and must be destructive of the idea of Canada. Moreover, even if one wishes to call the political settlement of 1867 a "compact" or "entente," it is still crystal clear that the "entente" is being broken today by the leaders of the Quiet Revolution and not by any "English-Canadian" view of Confederation. Strange, because of all Canadians the Quebeckers refer most frequently to history as their master.

PRAGMATISM AND "THE COMPACT"

A large part of contemporary Quebec's distrust of "English Canadians" stems from a fixed belief that they are inveterate centralizers. In fact, of course, centralization has never been a fixed goal of English-speaking Canadians. At the time of Confederation Macdonald encountered stiff opposition to an overblown central government from the Maritime Provinces and, in some respects, from the Grit elements within the coalition government of the united province of Canada. Indeed, it was one measure of his pragmatism and of his faith in the idea of a political nationality that he abandoned his preferred goal of legislative union as opposed to a federal pattern of government. Again, the great political-legal battles of the 1880's and '90's between Mowat and Macdonald, the "better terms" campaign in the Maritimes with its peak in the secession resolutions presented by W. S. Fielding in Nova Scotia, and the near-rebellion in Manitoba over the C.P.R. monopoly, all attest to a jealous regard for provincial rights on the part of a majority of English-speaking Canadians.

It is certainly true that English-speaking Canadians have also frequently turned to the central government for the fulfillment of some of their aspirations. But very often this has been for the protection of regional rights or opportunities. In the struggle over Manitoba Schools, for example, the division of Canadian opinion was not simply Quebec against the rest. A very large number of English-speaking Canadians believed that the remedial power of the federal government should be used to sustain minority rights within a province. Furthermore, in many of the instances of apparent English-speaking Canadian support for centralization, a major purpose has been that of using the economic powers of Ottawa to equalize provincial opportunities—not for the purpose of producing a bland national conformity but for the purpose of preserving viable provincial or regional differences of culture. This has been illustrated particularly in the various phases of the Maritimes Rights movement and in the western Progressive movement.

The point is that English-speaking Canadians have always seen the Canadian political state as one in which there is a necessarily shifting balance between the central and provincial powers. Their willingness today to undertake a major redressing of that balance is simply one of many historical examples of a continuing process. Nor is the process always dictated by reasons of ideology or politics. Frequently it has had a strong material basis. In the 1880's, the 1920's and the 1960's, the almost independent prosperity of Ontario and British Columbia has been a considerable factor in these provinces' ready acceptance of "co-operative federalism."

Yet despite the cyclical provincial-rightism of English-speaking Canadians, there is an equally consistent reassertion of the validity of the nation, and it is this that seems most to irritate the *nationalistes* of Quebec. It does so because they vastly underrate the complexity and change in the idea itself. . . . Much of the reason for this change—an acceptance of multi-racialism, or multi-culturalism—is to be found in the confidence produced by the simple fact of Canadian survival. And since that survival has clearly depended upon a flexible response to regionalism, racial feeling and religious differences, tradition has planted firmly in the minds of English-speaking Canadians the idea that their national loyalty is to national diversity. Unhappily this seems trite only to English-speaking Canadians.

Quebec, despite these facts of the English-speaking Canadian development, still charges that in the past English-speaking Canadians have broken "the compact"— by refusing to honour the guarantees to the French language in Manitoba, by refusing to extend language privileges to French-Canadian minorities in other provinces, by imposing conscription for overseas service in the interests of British imperialism and by excluding French Canadians from a fair share of the senior positions in the federal civil service. Less convincingly, but with even greater heat, Quebec charges that the English-speaking power élite has used its combined political-economic domination to exclude Quebeckers from managerial and owner-ship status in the province's industry. The result of this arrogant domination, argue the Quebeckers, was to render their province a "reservation" or "colony" to be exploited by the English-Canadian and American capital, which adroitly financed such unsavoury politicians as Maurice Duplessis and used demagogic pseudo-nationalism as a blind behind which to extend their economic control. The answer to such colonialism was, of course, revolution.

Again we find inconsistency in the Quebec argument—inconsistency with which many English-speaking Canadians have found it either difficult or distasteful to grapple. From declaring that the Quiet Revolution is justified because "English Canada" broke the compact, the ideological directors of Quebec pass to the assertion that the original agreement never was good enough. Now it is not enough merely to undo the grievances within the original framework. It is necessary to break the structure altogether and establish two racial states. Even the most moder-ate spokesmen of the revolution (as can be seen by a glance at *Le Devoir* or *Cité Libre*) find it agreeable to talk of the "states" or the "provincial states" rather than the presently constituted "provinces."

In dealing with this nimble logic English-speaking Canadians are both baffled and resentful. But to say that they have not drawn up any thin red line of verbal battle, that they have generally preferred the familiar paths of compromise and conciliation, is not to say that they have no convictions. I have already noted that the English-speaking Canadians have a very definite concept of Canada—an historic amalgam of the original and undoubted purposes of Confederation plus modifications enjoined by the facts of immigration and growth. Reluctance to contend directly with the ever more extreme racial nationalism of Quebec (except by way of concession) is also explained by a compound of causes.

First, strangely, is acceptance of much of the case put forward by Quebec. Most English-speaking Canadians agree that there has been injustice along the way. In the Manitoba schools question that injustice was a specific and unconstitu-tional denial to French Canadians of rights and expectations spelled out in 1867 and 1870. In the case of conscription in 1917 there was extremely bad political management of the policy itself, and Quebec opinion was still further inflamed by the contemporaneous and deliberate prohibition by Manitoba and Ontario of teaching in the French language in public schools. There has also been admitted injustice in the appointments policy in the federal civil service—not unconstitu-tional injustice, but human and political injustice. On all these counts English-speaking Canadians feel guilty. Indeed, many of them who are Liberals have a positive guilt complex which has led them into a position which might be called the counterpart of those French Canadians who are called *vendus*.

THE PRESENT CONDITION

Beyond the English-speaking *vendu* (perhaps "sold out" is the accurate translation) most Canadians sympathize entirely with the feeling of exclusion which is the basis of the Quiet Revolution's triumph. Indeed, most English-speaking Canadians who have followed Quebec affairs (and there are many more such people than Quebeckers care to admit) admire the new and forthright willingness to use the government of Quebec to achieve collective purposes: to broaden the base of social welfare and to halt the takeover by American capital. But these are purposes which are agreeable to most Canadians, and they are repelled by the new Quebec insistence that such goals can be achieved only through virtually independent "provincial states." That insistence is bound to render difficult or impossible the achievement of similar goals at the national level since it will rob Ottawa of the essential powers of economic planning—indeed it has already placed grave impediments in the path of such planning.

But guilt-feelings and admiration for the new positive approach to the use of government are only half of the explanation of the English-speaking Canadian reluctance to spell out its mounting resistance to racial nationalism and to a new straightjacket constitution. The non-French Canadians know that they have attained a genuine sense of Canadian independence and that the growth of this feeling is not the result of logic-chopping and perpetual rewriting of constitutional formulae. It is the result of deep belief in growth by precedent and the converse suspicion that it is dangerous to commit to words the inner nature of human or social relationships. Since these two facts of feeling and philosophy lie at the heart of the matter, they are worth a further word.

First, independence. Since the enunciation in the 1860's of a new nationality, and despite the chronic outcropping of British loyalties, English-speaking Canadians have moved steadily towards independence. From one precedent to another down to the separate declaration of war in 1939 and the notably "un-British" stand taken at the time of the Suez crisis [in 1956] they gradually severed the constitutional and, to a considerable extent, the emotional ties with the "mother country." Not infrequently, as the career of Mackenzie King amply demonstrates, this process was hastened by an almost too sensitive recognition of Quebec's anti-British creed. Even with respect to the Commonwealth, as opposed to specifically British interest, it would take exceptional daring to assert that the English-speaking majority does not place its primary loyalty with the United Nations or with Canada itself before its concern for things British. The plain fact is that non-French Canada has experienced a sense of independence extending much further beyond the constitutional aspect than has Quebec. It is not without reason that some English-speaking Canadians begin to suspect Quebec of frailty in its protestations of independent goals. . . .

Canadians of British descent have always regarded the political process as essentially pragmatic-experimental. They have shied away from detailed and comprehensive definitions of political and social relationships, preferring to see change come by the establishment of precedents which then become the justification of future decisions. That is why they have continued to hold to the English common law, and that is why civil liberties in English-speaking Canada have been more carefully cherished than they have in Quebec. That is why, too, they adjust more easily to multi-racial nationality than does Quebec. A broadening of rights by precedent—such as the instituting of simultaneous translation in Parliament, the proliferation of dominion-provincial consultations, revision of the appointments policy in the federal civil service and crown corporations, or such other possibilities as special Supreme Court panels of judges trained in the Quebec Civil Code to hear cases arising under that Code—it is this method of change that appeals to English-speaking Canadians.

By contrast, French Canadians prefer to systematize and codify the law, the constitution and, indeed, a broad range of social relationships. Because of these philosophic characteristics and a natural proclivity to verbalization, French Canadians mistake the nearly silent and the usually flexible English-speaking attitude as an absence of conviction or determination. No misunderstanding could have more disastrous and predictable consequences. The point has been well taken by some of the very originators of the Quiet Revolution—by those, in particular, who saw that revolution not only as a movement for social justice but also for the liberalization of Quebec. Of these, Pierre-Elliott Trudeau is perhaps the outstanding example.

. . . It was to stem the now common habit of looking upon and treating Ottawa as a foreign power that this brilliant and essentially non-political sophisticate plunged into the icy waters of federal politics in Quebec. For his pains he has been smeared as a *vendu,* and there is little doubt that he shares what I have called the English-speaking view of Canada. His political fate will likely be the political fate of Canada. . . .

NATIONAL UNITY: CANADA'S POLITICAL OBSESSION*

JOHN PORTER

Canada has no resounding charter myth proclaiming a utopia against which, periodically, progress can be measured. At the most, national goals and dominant values seem to be expressed in geographical terms such as "from sea to sea,"

* Reprinted from *The Vertical Mosaic* by John Porter, by permission of the author and of the University of Toronto Press. © University of Toronto Press, 1965.

rather than in social terms such as "all men are created equal," or "liberty, fraternity, and equality." In the United States there is a utopian image which slowly
over time bends intractable social patterns in the direction of equality, but a
Canadian counterpart of this image is difficult to find.

•   •   •

It would probably be safe to say that Canada has never had a political system
with this dynamic quality [emerging from the polarization of the right and the left,
such as is found in Talcott Parsons' analysis of the American political dynamic
or in British experience or in Marxism]. Its two major political parties do not
focus to the right and the left. In the sense that both are closely linked with
corporate enterprise the dominant focus has been to the right. One of the reasons
why this condition has prevailed is that Canada lacks clearly articulated major
goals and values stemming from some charter instrument which emphasizes progress and equality. If there is a major goal of Canadian society it can best be
described as an integrative goal. The maintenance of national unity has overridden any other goals there might have been, and has prevented a polarizing,
within the political system, of conservative and progressive forces. It has never
occurred to any Canadian commentators that national unity might in fact be
achieved by such a polarization. Rather a dissociative federalism is raised to the
level of a quasi-religious political dogma, and polarization to right and left in
Canadian politics is regarded as disruptive. Consequently the main focus of Canadian politics has been to the right and the maintenance of the *status quo*. The
reason that the Liberal party in Canada was in office so many years until 1957
was not because it was a progressive party, but because it served Canada's major
goal of national unity.

The major themes in Canadian political thought emphasize those characteristics,
mainly regional and provincial loyalties, which divide the Canadian population.
Consequently integration and national unity must be a constantly reiterated goal
to counter such divisive sentiments. The dialogue is between unity and discord
rather than progressive and conservative forces. The question which arises is
whether the discord-unity dialogue has any real meaning in the lives of Canadians,
or whether it has become, in the middle of the twentieth century, a political
technique of conservatism. Canada must be one of the few major industrial societies
in which the right and left polarization has become deflected into disputes over
regionalism and national unity.

Canada's major political and intellectual obsession, national unity, has had its
effect on the careers of men who take on political roles. It has put a premium on
the type of man whom we shall label the administrative politician and has discounted the professional political career in which creative politicians can assume
leadership roles. Creative politics at the national level has not been known in
Canada since before World War I when the westward thrust to Canada's empire

was still a major national goal. Since the empire of the west was secured national goals of development have not been known.

Creative politics is politics which has the capacity to change the social structure in the direction of some major social goals or values. By mobilizing human resources for new purposes, it has the initiative in the struggle against the physical environment and against dysfunctional historical arrangements. Creative politics requires a highly developed political leadership to challenge entrenched power within other institutional orders. It succeeds in getting large segments of the population identified with the goals of the political system and in recruiting their energies and skills to political ends.

BIBLIOGRAPHY

Berger, C., (ed.), *Imperialism and Nationalism, 1884-1914,* Toronto, Copp Clark, 1969.

Canada, *Foreign Ownership and the Structure of Canadian Industry* (Watkins Report), Ottawa, Queen's Printer, 1968.

Canada, *Report of the Royal Commission on National Development in the Arts, Letters, and Sciences* (Massey Report), Ottawa, Queen's Printer, 1951.

Cook, R., and McNaught, K., *Canada and the U.S.A.,* Toronto, Clarke, Irwin, 1963.

Cross, M. S., (ed.), *The Frontier Thesis and the Canadas: The Debate on the Impact of the Canadian Environment,* Toronto, Copp Clark, 1970.

Dickey, J. S., (ed.), *The United States and Canada,* Englewood Cliffs, N.J., Prentice-Hall, 1964.

Godfrey, D., and Watkins, M., (eds.), *Gordon to Watkins to You,* Toronto, New Press, 1970.

Johnstone, J. C., *Young People's Images of Canadian Society,* Studies of the Royal Commission on Bilingualism and Biculturalism, No. 2, Ottawa, Queen's Printer, 1969.

Lipset, S. M., *Revolution and Counter-Revolution,* New York, Basic Books, 1968, chapter 2, "The United States and Canada."

Lloyd, T., and McLeod, J. T., *Agenda 70: Proposals for a Creative Politics,* Toronto, University of Toronto Press, 1968.

Lumsden, I., (ed.), *Close the 49th Parallel, etc.: The Americanization of Canada,* Toronto, University of Toronto Press, 1970.

McCaffrey, G., (ed.), *The U.S. and Us,* Proceedings of the 37th Couchiching Conference, Toronto, Canadian Institute on Public Affairs, 1969.

Morton, W. L., *The Canadian Identity,* Toronto, Madison, 1961.

Purdy, A., (ed.), *The New Romans: Candid Canadian Opinions of the U.S.,* Edmonton, Hurtig, 1968.

Safarian, A. E., *Foreign Ownership of Canadian Industry,* Toronto, McGraw-Hill, 1966.

Smiley, D. V., *The Canadian Political Nationality,* Toronto, Methuen, 1967.

Tupper, S. R., and Bailey, D., *One Continent, Two Voices: The Future of Canada-United States Relations,* Toronto, Clarke, Irwin, 1967.

Wise, S. F., and Brown, R. C., *Canada Views the United States: Nineteenth Century Political Attitudes,* Toronto, Macmillan, 1967.

Social Issues

Adams, I., *The Poverty Wall,* Toronto, McClelland and Stewart, 1970.

Canada, *A Survey of the Contemporary Indians of Canada,* (Hawthorn-Tremblay Report), Ottawa, Queen's Printer, 1966.

Cardinal, H., *The Unjust Society: The Tragedy of Canada's Indians,* Edmonton, Hurtig, 1969.

Chretien, J., *Statement of the Government of Canada on Indian Policy, 1969,* Ottawa, Queen's Printer, 1969.

Lithwick, N. H., *Canada's Science Policy and the Economy,* Toronto, Methuen, 1969.

Lloyd, T., and McLeod, J. T., (eds.), *Agenda 1970,* Toronto, University of Toronto Press, 1969.

Rea, K. J., and McLeod, J. T., (eds.), *Business and Government in Canada: Selected Readings,* Toronto, Methuen, 1969.

Rotstein, A., (ed.), *The Prospect of Change,* Toronto, McGraw-Hill, 1965.

THREE
FRENCH CANADA

In recent years there have been two major aspects to the problem of French Canada: the external, which has concerned the place of French-speaking Canadians within Canada as a whole and their position and role within federal governmental institutions in particular, and the internal, which has been concerned with the development of events inside the province of Quebec itself.

Since the second edition of this book appeared in 1966, the critical nature of the external dimension of the problem has been defused somewhat by the publication of the four volumes of the final *Report of the Royal Commission on Bilingualism and Biculturalism* and a number of its associated research studies (for references to these, see especially the bibliography in Chapter 4), by the actions of the Trudeau government in implementing many of the *Report's* recommendations to provide greater opportunities for French-speaking Canadians both within Canada at large and in the federal government itself (see, for example, the statute in the next chapter establishing two official languages), and by the commencement of the process of wholesale constitutional review (see again the following chapter) which was a response in part to Quebec's demands. For two articles dealing with the former external phase of the problem, see in the second edition of *Politics: Canada*, Tim Creery, "What French Canada Wants," pp. 57-59, and Eugène Therrien, "Lack of Bilingualism in the Federal Administration," *ibid.*, pp. 59-61.

By 1969 the focus of "the French-Canadian problem" had shifted to Quebec. General de Gaulle's famous cry "Québec libre!" in Montreal in 1967 had stimulated the cause of separatism and René Lévesque, a former minister in the Lesage Liberal cabinet, had welded together the two small separatist parties that had acquired modest support in the election of 1966 into a potent movement for independence, the Parti Québécois. The provincial election of April, 1970, merely reinforced concentration on the internal, Quebec aspect of the total problem. The Union Nationale government, which under both Premiers Johnson and Bertrand had been inclined to indulge in "la politique de grandeur" externally at international and federal-provincial confer-ences, was repudiated humiliatingly at the polls and replaced by a Liberal government led by Robert Bourassa, who personally had laid great stress in the campaign on the improvement of economic conditions in Quebec. At the same time, the separatist Parti Québécois won an astonishing increase in the percentage of the popular vote in comparison to the support for the independence parties in 1966, receiving 23 percent of the ballots cast.

This chapter, therefore, concentrates on the Quebec scene. Professor Brady's article sets the stage for present events by outlining the background during the period of the Quiet Revolution in the nineteen-sixties. Mr. Dreifelds' excellent, original article makes a valuable contribution by giving an account not available elsewhere of the compli-cated developments, twists and turns, and interrelations of the most recent nationalist and socialist factions in Quebec. Marcel Chaput's spirited depiction of why many Québécois feel so strongly about independence is still as relevant today as it was when it was written first nearly a decade ago. The editor hopes that his reply is equally relevant. The next item contains a series of answers by René Lévesque to many of the questions which are asked usually about the aims of his separatist Parti Québécois. Since many of M. Lévesque's ideas are similar to the proposals contained in the Brief of the Montreal section of the St. Jean Baptiste Society submitted to the Quebec Legislative Committee on the Constitution in 1964, the latter item, which appeared in the second edition of this book, pp. 67-70, has not been carried over into this edition. The answers given by M. Lévesque are enlarged upon by the platform of the P.Q. in the election of 1970, which is reproduced here in company with the leading planks from the Liberal party's platform in that election. A final table provides in a compara-tive form the results of the four most recent Quebec provincial elections. Since the table gives both the percentage of the popular vote won and the number of seats secured by each party, it is also useful as an illustration of the peculiar effects of our voting system. (See also in this connection both Professor Cairns' article in Chapter 8 and several items in Chapter 9.)

The bibliography is long but by no means complete since the number of books and articles on this subject is very extensive, especially in French, and keeps growing almost daily. In this writer's opinion the most useful basic book is still Ramsay Cook's *Canada and the French-Canadian Question,* noted in the bibliography. One should see also Professor Cook's very useful anthology of French-Canadian nationalist writings, referred to in the bibliography. It goes without saying that Mr. Trudeau's reflections on the subject, noted in the bibliography, are primary reading as well. Chapter 3 of Professor D. V. Smiley's book, *The Canadian Political Nationality,* Methuen, 1967, is very pertinent too. The best criticism of separatists' economic argu-ments is contained in an article by Professor André Raynauld reviewing the Parti Québécois's publication, *La souveraineté et l'économie,* published in *Le Devoir,* April 24, 1970. This daily newspaper undoubtedly is the best source of information and judicious commentary on the continually changing Quebec scene.

THE TRANSFORMATION OF QUEBEC*

ALEXANDER BRADY

Quebec has always differed from other provinces. From the outset its special character was evident among other things in its civil law, the role of the Roman Catholic church in education, health and welfare, the traditional customs that for generations had accumulated in the countryside, and the tight social integration of the French parish. Some provisions in the B.N.A. Act recognized the distinctness of the province. Section 94, for example, contemplated that with provincial consent laws relating to property and civil rights should in all provinces except Quebec be unified by the national parliament, thus in effect giving a special protection to the French law of property and civil rights.

In 1960 Quebec's distinctiveness entered a new phase. The electoral victory of the Liberals in that year was followed by something more than another variant of traditional French-Canadian nationalism, with its constant emphasis on cultural survival. It was a far-reaching programme of reform and development that augmented the activities of the Quebec government, carved out a large new public sector in the economy, accelerated the exploitation of provincial natural resources, encouraged new industries under French-Canadian control, increased and diversified employment, established hospital insurance and welfare services, made remarkable strides in promoting educational reform, and generally quickened the rhythms of social change. Hitherto Quebec more than Ontario had depended on industries with a low level of wages and a high level of protection. The government was determined to alter this, to invigorate stagnant parts of the economy, to quicken mobility in the labour force, and to diminish the pronounced regional disparities in income that hitherto had existed. The implementing of these plans necessitated institutions and devices new for the province, such as the public ownership of electricity, the General Investment Corporation, the Deposit and Investment Fund, the Mining Exploration Corporation, the steel complex of Sidbec, and the recruitment of a new and vigorous civil service.

The replacement of private by public ownership of hydro power was intended to create a power grid across the province as a firm base for economic development and a tool for returning to the Quebec people the benefit of their natural resources. A similar role is intended for other public agencies.

It would be a simplification to assume that these far-ranging plans are merely the product of nationalism, but they are certainly influenced by it. Although we find here many policies of development like those in the other large provinces, they are launched with a special emotional support and are designed to give a new prestige to French Canadians. Leaders in the province are confident that in

*From an unpublished paper written in 1966 by Dr. A. Brady, Professor Emeritus of the University of Toronto. By permission of the author.

their own provincial stronghold the French-speaking people can by suitable means cast off their former economic backwardness, rehabilitate their community, and assert their own distinctness as a people in control of their destiny. "We are not defending the autonomy of the province," said Mr. Lesage at the federal-provincial conference of 1963, "simply because it is a question of a principle, but rather because autonomy is to us the basic condition, not of our survival which is assumed from now on, but of our assertion as a people."

Apart from rhetoric, this feeling is expressed in mundane practices. It is characteristic that the Quebec Hydro, in seeking to satisfy its mechanical requirements for expansion, introduced a fixed preference for local producers over competitors from outside the province, a practice now widely followed by other public agencies. The apparent indifference of the Quebecers to the rest of Canada's economy is derived from an absorbing concern for their own problems and rebuilding their own society.

The new political energy in Quebec has immediate consequences for Canadian federalism, although the major actions of Mr. Lesage's government, like those of other provincial governments, were confined to the area of its competence under the British North America Act. In federal-provincial relations it pursued two major objectives: it endeavoured to secure from the government in Ottawa a larger share of the direct tax field for the provinces, and sought to reduce and ultimately to eliminate joint-cost programmes as an improper intrusion on provincial jurisdiction and an impediment to effective economic planning. In these policies it aimed to preserve its financial independence as well as its legislative and administrative autonomy. In the first of these policies Quebec's position was scarcely different from that of Ontario, whose constant theme in the federal-provincial conference since 1955 has been the urgency for securing larger tax resources for the provinces, which now have to meet heavier expenditures. . . .

To conditional grants and shared cost programmes Quebec was usually implacable in opposition, and throughout the years its arguments have varied little. Its chief case is elaborated in the *Tremblay Report* of 1956, where conditional grants are condemned as insidious forms of centralisation, threatening to undermine provincial autonomy. Mr. Lesage's government inherited these views, although at the outset it accepted some grants previously rejected by Mr. Duplessis. But on formulating and maturing its economic plans, the government became increasingly impatient with policies, whether they embraced conditional or unconditional grants, that involved federal interventions in the provincial field of jurisdiction, especially when incompatible with its own plans.

Its chief criticism of national programmes was their inadequate recognition of the peculiar features and problems of Quebec's society with its sharp regional contrasts. Its views were forcibly expressed and illustrated in Mr. René Lévesque's submission to the War on Poverty Conference in December 1965. Quebec's Minister of Family and Social Welfare argued that some recent federal programmes tended to distort Quebec's own economic and social policies, disrupt their priorities, and hamper the integration imperative for their success. Quebec has inherited two unfortunate situations that current policies of Ottawa fail to remedy. First, an excessively large proportion of its labour force is in old industries, such as tobacco, leather, rubber, textiles, clothing and furniture, which lack the dynamism of new growth and the power to pay employees adequately. Secondly, the immense expansion of the Montreal metropolis (with two-fifths of the population and three-fifths of the industries of Quebec) imposes such a drastic drain on provincial resources and skilled manpower as to impoverish and reduce to virtual stagnation other areas. Consequently the income per head for labour in Montreal might sometimes be four times that for labour in remote regions of the hinterland, thus seriously threatening the social cohesion of the French-Canadian community.

The federal Designated Area Programs of 1963 and 1965, encouraging the establishment of industries in certain high unemployment areas by tax concessions, were criticized by the Quebec authorities on the ground that they conflicted with their own plans on the drawing-board to regroup and invigorate regional economies by choosing carefully a number of growth centres related to natural resources and capable of rapid and permanent industrial expansion. The Quebec plan is ambitious and contemplates more than a temporary palliative for unemployment; it is specially tailored to achieve a balance in the demographic and industrial development of the province and get rid of some persistent pockets of poverty. It is not surprising that the government sponsoring it criticized a national plan that failed to select industries rigorously enough or exhibit any real solicitude for the peculiarities and hazards of the Quebec situation. Similarly Quebec found unsatisfactory certain federal programmes concerned with direct loans to municipalities, winter works, and housing, because they conflicted with its own plans for securing municipal amalgamations and public works on a cooperative and regional basis. It asserted that its aims were frustrated by municipal capital invested on different lines. It complained also about conflicts between its labour and social policies and those of the federal government and emphasized again that differences in aim and purpose made difficult anything like a satisfactory co-ordination.

The meaning of Quebec's so-called Quiet Revolution is reasonably clear. It mainly results from the emergence of a fresh and vigorous political consciousness in the province, expressed by the influential figures in Mr. Lesage's Liberal party and by the corps of able civil servants they recruited. These leaders and officials appreciate the plain fact that the only way to maintain the powers of government is to govern. By employing abundantly the wide authority that the constitution permits, they give a new and more solid significance to Quebec's autonomy.

●　　　●　　　●

It may be perhaps that the Liberals employed the powers of government too much and too rapidly in some sections of the society and inadequately in others. At any rate their electoral defeat in June, 1966, suggested that they had failed to satisfy certain discontented elements of the public in the rural hinterland, in small towns and villages, and in the more impoverished areas of the cities. Their educational reforms were particularly in dispute. They had created a public school system in which a regional composite high school, by-passing the private classical colleges, was to play a crucial part in providing education from the primary to the university stage. Apart from being expensive and increasing taxes (a result deplored by many frugal citizens), this educational venture disturbed many tradition-minded Québecois because it threatened to transform the character of the society and diminish the influence of the old local elites based on the parish. At the same time the farmers as well as the unskilled workers competing in an unstable labour market were not convinced that the Quiet Revolution for all its welfare facilities was of much direct benefit to them. The disgruntled were sufficiently numerous and sufficiently well distributed in the constituencies to give the Union Nationale a majority.

Mr. Lesage stressed how much more federal in spirit Quebec was and how much less prone it was to capitulate to the centralizing pressures of Ottawa. He and his colleagues looked on their province, not as one among ten, but as a cultural or national entity apart, the homeland and stronghold of the French Canadians. They believed, as Quebecers have always done, that federalism in Canada is important primarily because it helps to guarantee the survival of their culture. In effect, French-Canadian nationalism explains the greater intensity of Quebec's provincial spirit compared with that of any other province, as it also helps to explain the single-minded zeal with which it now strives to create a modern, integrated, state-directed economy combined with a vigorous culture.

In thinking of the province, Quebec leaders remember the French-Canadian community within it, to which they credit the attributes of a genuine nationality that claims their loyalty. They can never forget that the government of Quebec is the only one in Canada unmistakably controlled by a French-Canadian electorate, and naturally they want to preserve intact its present constitutional power. Some want to augment it.

A significant symptom of this nationalist thinking is the emphasis on what is called "a special status for Quebec". The phrase has different meanings for different people. It is primarily convenient for expressing sentiments, and may imply little or much in any political context. For some it means no more than formalizing the rights and powers that Quebec already has and the peculiar influence it commands in representing the bulk of the French Canadians. For others it refers to something that Quebec at present lacks but should have—a very special constitutional position that would enlarge its stature and distinguish it from all other provinces. Mr. Lesage once reflected his conception of a special status in saying that "it would be the result of an evolution, during which Quebec would want to exert powers and responsibilities which the other provinces, for reasons of their own, might prefer to leave with the Federal government." This was the characteristic position of a pragmatic politician, cautious and unwilling to commit himself beforehand to explicit objectives. He saw progress achieved through a succession of administrative compromises. For the future he left himself free to test opinion and yield to it as he thought necessary.

Mr. Daniel Johnson, when leader of the Opposition in the Quebec legislature, was less cautious and pragmatic in defining goals and more emphatic in declaring what Quebec's special status should be. In his opinion, the central fact about Canada was its two distinct nations; the French-Canadian in Quebec, and the English-speaking in the nine other provinces. These two communities combined successfully for a hundred years within the federal state because then some sort of equilibrium was feasible between the forces of unity and those of diversity. But since 1945 circumstances have destroyed this equilibrium, and the only satisfactory solution now is to overhaul the constitution and adapt it to the fact of two nations. Thus Quebec should receive a special status with all the larger powers of individual self-rule it wants, making it possible for the English-speaking provinces at the same time to achieve the greater collective unity they apparently want. In Mr. Johnson's view the kind of federation that the British North America Act established is obsolete and should be replaced by a wholly new constitution permitting his two nations to govern themselves and fulfill their destiny with such institutional links between them as their common interests dictate.

Other variants of the special status idea are current in Quebec, and all pivot on the two-nation thesis. Thus early in 1964 Mr. René Lévesque, an impulsive phrase-maker, gave currency to the term "associate state in Confederation". Although he did not explain his idea, it is clear that he sought for Quebec wide economic, fiscal, and political powers to enable it to fulfill its role as the equivalent of a natural state for French Canadians. Others carried the same idea to more doctrinaire and radical lengths, as in the brief of the St. Jean Baptiste Society of Montreal, published some months earlier and submitted in November 1964 to the Constitutional Committee of the Quebec Legislature. It would transform the present federation into a confederation, Quebec and English Canada being recognized as two sovereign states, associated for specific purposes by confederate institutions and treaties subject to revision every five years.

A confusing feature of this debate on Quebec as an associate state is the absence of adequate and precise details on the legal, economic, and social implications of the proposal. The discussion is lacking in depth. Proponents seldom give the impression that they come to grips with the ultimate meaning or real costs of what they propose for Quebec and Canada. Yet they exhibit one predominant motive: they want their community to have in the structure of Canada an accepted equality with the English-speaking people. They reflect the mood and aspirations of French-Canadian intellectuals, university students, and younger politicians. They ardently seek a clear political recognition of their nationality, and see the idea of two distinct nations as basic to everything else. The more radical they are, the more they reject the possibility of an adequate bilingualism and biculturalism under the present constitution, and write off as lost the French-speaking communities outside Quebec. That they can exert a practical influence on events was illustrated in the discarding of the Fulton-Favreau formula by Mr. Lesage in January 1966. In 1964, when the formula was drafted, Mr. Lesage strongly supported it. But subsequently he was influenced by dissidents in his own ranks and by a powerful campaign mounted against it by Mr. Daniel Johnson, who enlisted the support of nationalists of every kind, separatists and neo-separatists, not normally ·aligned with the Union Nationale party. The critics attacked the formula because it treated all provinces as equal and ignored the special status of Quebec and the bi-national idea that such status was designed to express. Mr. Johnson was convinced that under the formula Quebec would be unable to secure the larger constitutional status it needed. To the Government's argument that since Quebec sought a veto on constitutional changes, it was only fair that the other provinces should also have one, he replied: "This is once again a proclamation that Quebec is a province like the others. This is a denial that it is the principal home of a nation. This perpetuates one minority state in a Confederation formed of eleven governments in which English Canada has ten voices and Quebec has one alone". In the current climate of opinion Mr. Lesage evidently found this argument embarrassing and difficult to meet.

Although the bi-national idea with all its implications has manifest support in Quebec, one cannot assume that it must necessarily take the constitutional form prescribed by its present proponents. Political thought in the province remains fluid; it has not hardened into a monolithic shape. There is a variety of opinions in the public and no convincing evidence that the great body of citizens are firmly committed to any one type of constitution, or even have any clear ideas on the matter. They are as likely to be persuaded by the cool pragmatism of Mr. Lesage as by the inflexible logic of Mr. Johnson. At the same time the current of nationalist sentiment still flows strongly and dissatisfaction with the existing federal institutions continues to be vigorously expressed by individuals and groups able to exert influence on the electorate. French-Canadian nationalism will not conveniently go away, although it may change its clothes. Its long history and present strength suggest its survival as a potent force. . . .

NATIONALISM AND SOCIALISM IN FRENCH CANADA*

JURIS DREIFELDS

Quebec's political culture changed drastically in the 1960's . . . . Socialism, which for a variety of reasons never received much electoral support in Quebec, has become much more popular. Nationalism, which has been a recurring phenomenon

*Written in April, 1970, and published here for the first time with permission of the author who is a postgraduate student in the Department of Political Economy, University of Toronto.

in Quebec, has also grown more acute. The first and major force that initiated the change was the extremely rapid dissolution of the power of the Roman Catholic Church which lost much of its relevance and hold especially in the urban areas. Some indicators of this diminishing relevance can be gauged from the figures for recruits to the priesthood. In 1965 there were still 270 theology students at the Grande Seminaire of Montreal. In 1969 there were only 70. In 1966 about 80 students entered the seminary but a year later only 37. In September 1968 the number had dwindled to 23. Moreover, while one of the main points of contact with the population for the Church had been the schooling system, the new law of 1964 establishing a lay Department of Education spelled the end of the Church's control of this vital area.

This decline of the Church also created a monumental crisis of identity. In terms of reference theory, the French Canadians are having trouble finding a perspective on which to base their attitude and values. Many French Canadians have now displaced their primary loyalty to the state of Quebec or to the "nation"; others have found a replacement of their world view in the all-encompassing theories of Marxism and socialism.

SOCIALISM

The political scene in certain areas of Quebec presents several left-inclining factors if viewed in terms of traditional political analysis. Seymour Martin Lipset and other political and sociological researchers have found that manual workers in one-industry towns exhibit high rates of communist support in most countries. One-industry towns, both in mining and lumbering, have become common in Quebec and although they have not shown traditionally any preference for left-wing parties, they now present a potential for radicalism since the ideological hold of the clergy has been rapidly dissipated. However, it could be that this void has been filled by the Social Credit party which has found its strongest support in such one-industry towns.

Trade unions are one of the indicators of political change. Their history in Quebec is consonant with the general political atmosphere. In that province trade unions began under the auspices of the French-Canadian Roman Catholic Church and were set up more as defensive mechanisms against the "alien" international unions. The first national trade union federation was named very appropriately the Confédération des Travailleurs Catholiques du Canada. The period of crisis occurred from 1939 to 1949 when the union had to expand into the new industries generated by the war. The new leaders who emerged from this crisis were not of the same mold as their predecessors. The Asbestos Strike of 1949 radicalized them and placed them in contact with more militant international unions. By 1960 the Church had also retreated in this area.

The new union, now called Confédération des Syndicats Nationaux (C.S.N., or C.N.T.U. in English), evolved into a worker-oriented and more radical body. According to one commentator, A. J. Boudreau, "this union adopts the most anticapitalist position in the North American continent." However, there appears to be more than one tendency in this union since the Telegram-Canada '70 Team has estimated that less than one-third of its members could be classified as radical left-wing while about 40 percent would back traditional or what is seen as right-wing unionism. The remainder would be somewhere in between these two; it is represented by the majority of the present executive which, however, yearns to move left but is held in check by the right wing. The leader of the left-wing faction, Michel Chartrand, defines the role of unions as one that must "crush capitalist fascism" and replace it with socialism.

A poll taken before the 1963 federal election also indicated a certain polarization, although not of a very marked degree, within the working class. It appeared that 6 percent of the union skilled workers and 9 percent of the non-union skilled workers expressed support for the New Democratic Party. This, of course, is not a very high percentage when compared to a province such as British Columbia, but nevertheless, the figures represent an increase over the results of a poll in Quebec in 1953 which showed that this group's interest in the democratic socialist party at that time was virtually zero.

The Church itself has lost its monolithicity. If at one time it looked askance at parishioners who voted for such midly socialistic parties as the N.D.P., now it apparently tolerates a wide divergence of views even within its own ranks. Thus, the periodical review *Maintenant*, which was founded by clerics and which still has several brothers on its staff, proposes socialism as the true answer for Quebec's problems. Its approach is very low key; it tries to bring socialism back into the French-Canadian fold by seeking to integrate it with national aspirations. The Jesuit publication *Relations* has also opted for socialist measures. An editorial appearing in it in 1959 stated that "the nationalization of a certain number of large enterprises is necessary and inevitable."

Socialism, in effect, has become an acceptable part of the political culture of French Canadians. This does not mean that many people would opt for it in elections but it does mean that being a socialist will no longer put anybody outside the pale of French-Canadian society. This in itself is a giant gain for that ideology since its adherents can now engage in public discourse legitimately and be listened to without a priori rejection.

One of the ways that socialism has gained entry into French-Canadian society has been through the articulate stand on nationalism and "souveraineté" propounded by certain factions within the socialist group; for instance, P. Saucier wrote in *Maintenant* in 1967 that "l'idée socialiste enregistre tout de même des gains *en liaison avec un nationalisme très québecois*." People who would normally have discarded socialist arguments as heretical now approach them with less trepidation and even consider them as one alternative among many. Gilles Grégoire, who was deputy leader of the Social Credit and later Créditiste party, exemplifies this change of attitude. M. Grégoire is now a member of the Parti Québecois, but as early as November 1967 he stated: "I believe in strong intervention by the state. I believe that socialism has meaning in Quebec for the separatists today." His version of socialism, however, does not envisage full-scale nationalization until it becomes "relevant in the contemporary world." To him it implies, as he has stated later, "social security measures like Medicare and free education."

This recent change of climate for socialism has become visible in other areas. Student syndicalism and especially U.G.E.Q. (Union Générale des Etudiants de Québec) have opted for left-wing radicalism. U.G.E.Q. has organized sit-ins and demonstrations against American imperialism, big business and the "English." Many new fringe groups and publications that have appeared recently have also embraced left-wing socialism. Thus, all of *Parti Pris,* Révolution Québecoise, Mouvement de Libération Populaire, Front de Libération Québecoise (F.L.Q.), Front de Libération Populaire (F.L.P.), Mouvement des Etudiants de l'Université de Montréal, Ligue des Jeunes Socialistes, and Ligue de Jeunesses Communistes du Québec have opted for extra-parliamentary, left-wing activism.

The N.D.P., although not a truly socialist party, might be taken as one weather vane of leftist political opinion in Quebec. While in the 1950's it obtained a maximum of only 2.5 percent of the vote, by the 1965 federal election it could claim 11.8 percent and several ridings where its candidates placed in second position. The election of 1968 corroborated this trend despite the fact that Trudeau's appeal cut down the N.D.P.'s percentage of the popular vote.

NATIONALISM

Although the decade of the 1960's is the only period in Quebec's history, with the possible exception of the revolt of 1837, in which there has been some resurgence of left-wing strength, nationalism, on the other hand, has historically found far more fertile ground. Far from being a very recent phenomenon like socialism, it has emerged as a strong force almost with cyclical regularity. Paradoxically, the periods between these cycles have been almost devoid of nationalist feelings.

The first nationalist period of this century developed during and after the Boer war from 1900 to 1907. It fundamentally was associated with Henri Bourassa and his fight against imperialism. Bourassa was not a separatist but he evinced a special concern for French Canada and the Roman Catholic Church. He was a racist in the sense of believing that each race had a "voix de sang" and particular instincts and tendencies which gave it an identifiable character. Thus, the French race was characterized by honour, probity and perseverance. Moreover, he felt that God had destined each race for a certain mission and that French Canadians could boast of a certain intellectual superiority whereas the English were instinctively good businessmen. That these myths persisted and were absorbed by French Canadians is undeniable. The schooling system, crowned by the collèges classiques, imbued the participating students until recently with the same idea that French people were destined to be great thinkers rather than businessmen.

The second wave of nationalism was of a more radical nature. It followed the conscription crisis of 1917 and lasted until about 1924. It was initiated by the founding of *L'Action Française* in 1917. This nationalist review discussed French language rights as well as more theoretical and utopian concepts, such as the "revenge of the cradle" introduced by Father Louis Lalande. The guiding force of this entire nationalist period was Abbé Groulx, a historian who was one of the editors of its monthly voice, *L'Action Nationale*. Groulx felt that Confederation was destined to fail and that only the time of its death was as yet unclear. His creation of a new nationally oriented brand of history left its mark on future generations who were to rekindle French-Canadian nationalism. His orientation was more historical than economic, as can be judged from the titles of his articles "Si Dollard revenait" (1919), "Chez nos Ancêtres" (1920), and "l'Appel de la race" (1922). The anti-Confederation stand was later obviated by a seemingly increasing threat of Americanization—i.e. American economic imperialism, American films, and French-Canadian immigration to the U.S.A.

The third period, from 1933 to 1944, coincided with the years of the depression and the second conscription crisis. Its first overt expression was the nationalism of the student publication, *Quartier Latin*. Later, many nationalist groups emerged under the ideological direction of Paul Bouchard and his publication *La Nation*. There were also more militant youth groups such as Jeunesses Patriotes, Jeune-Canada, Front Corporatif, and Jeunesses Laurentiennes.

These various groups proposed several changes in the existing system. They criticized rural emigration and wanted to reinstitute a new policy of a "return to the land." They initiated certain economic campaigns, mostly to support small enterprises—e.g. "une campagne d'achat chez nous." They also wanted to eliminate foreign control from Quebec institutions, mainly though the establishment of corporatism. One of the main figures of nationalism in 1934, D. Dansereau, claimed that Confederation was only a transitory stage leading either to complete unitary consolidation or else to the creation of several new states. In 1935, the idealized state of an independent Laurentie was first presented. The war dampened the nationalist fervour somewhat but the conscription and referendum crises resulted in a nationalist political coalition—the Bloc Populaire party. It gained over 15 percent of the vote in the Quebec provincial election of 1944 and won four seats in the Legislative Assembly. Yet, because of its contradictory political tendencies of left and right, it collapsed quickly as a viable force.

Throughout these three periods of heightened nationalism there was a common belief that the Church formed an integral part of the French-Canadian nation. To be a nationalist then was tantamount to being a devout Catholic. Even before the turn of the century the Church had consolidated its position within the nationalist ideology of French Canada by standing out as the sole defender of "La Survivance." Its position was further strengthened when such men as Frechette and Abbé Casgrain grafted a universal religious mission to the calling of French Canada. Abbé Casgrain wrote that "French Canadians would lead back under the Aegis of Catholicism the errant peoples of the New World." Such messianic purposes managed to integrate admirably the sacred with the secular.

If this merging of French-Canadian nationalism with religion constituted the common bond throughout the past half century, it has become now the single great point of departure for modern nationalism in Quebec. At first it appeared that the trend of religiosity would continue when l'Action Laurentienne, the first separatist group in 1956, preached its great attachment to the Church. However, the trend of events has forced religion into a different position not attached to nationalism. It could also explain in part the fact that nationalism in Quebec today exhibits signs of various ideologies including socialism and Marxism.

Many students of French-Canadian nationalism before 1960 have tended to classify the ideology as a conservative, right-wing phenomenon. This description, however, was not universally true. Henri Bourassa, in the early 1900's, was one of the main champions against imperialism. Although he cannot be classified as a social radical, he did show some sympathy for the socialist C.C.F. party and for its leader, J. S. Woodsworth. The Bloc Populaire, founded in 1942 by Maxime Raymond, was also ambiguous in its political sentiments. It contained right-wing nationalists as well as left-wing elements. The "almost socialist" wing was led by André Laurendeau who had evolved from a conservative nationalist to a more leftist sympathizer after his sojourn at the University of Paris. He opposed economic "dictatorship" by attempting to set up cooperative movements, by advocating the regulation of trusts and, if need be, by even nationalization.

But the political ideology of many nationalists was equally opposed to international socialism as well as to international monopolies. Even Duplessis was considered a reforming nationalist in his first years of political office. It is also true that many French-Canadian nationalists displayed certain sympathies for Mussolini and the Axis powers. But they did not approve of their external politics so much as of the idea of a charismatic leader. They saw the answer to their own divisions and to the creation of a unified collectivity in adoption of the "führerprinciple."

NATIONALISM AND SOCIALISM, 1950-1970

The new nationalism of the late fifties began as a movement closely parallel to that of the 1930's. In 1956, Raymond Barbeau, a young student, picked up the strands of nationalism which had been neglected for some years. He resurrected the idea of a republic of Laurentia in which religion would play an integral part. As he put it, "Le Laurentien est avant tout un chrétien." Gérard Gauthier, one of the editors of the first nationalist publication in this period, *La Laurentie*, again emphasized the stand against internationalism which was thought of as utopian and even "anti-human." Both international capitalism and international proletarian syndicalism were castigated for their disintegrative effects on morals, culture and religious sentiment. The French-Canadian nation was seen as a corporate whole united by the bonds of blood. Confederation was considered an impossible union of sovereign states acting against the best interests of French Canada. This nationalism was of a crusading type, not dependent on logical argument so much as on emotional appeal, intensity of feeling, belligerence, and mystification.

These nationalists seemed to glorify anti-democratic thought. Their ideal state would not be a parliamentary democracy but would be led by a "disciplined and energetic, coherent unity and comprehensive power." Classes would not be merged, yet there was to be a certain class mobility for children of workers and peasants who showed talent and aptitude for command posts. Social salvation was to come through hierarchic and stable organizations which had to be in conformity with ethnic, racial and national aspirations.

This wing of nationalism, organized into the Alliance Laurentienne, was the strongest faction of the separatist movement until 1961. It had youth sections, women's leagues and representatives in many parts of Quebec. Although its paid membership by 1961 amounted to only about 2,000, the publicity it received through its actions of defiance against the Queen and Confederation increased its stature in the separatist milieu. Raymond Barbeau's book, *J'ai choisi l'indépendance*, was widely read before Marcel Chaput's *Pourquoi je suis séparatiste* was even published.

Almost as fanatical, but stemming from the opposite extreme of the political spectrum, was the first truly socialist separatist party or faction. It did not have as many adherents as the Alliance, yet it was more articulate and seems to have had more people writing articles than did *La Laurentie*. It was the reassertion of the left-wing which had been found in milder form within the Bloc Populaire but which had been totally dissipated after the war. The leader of this movement, which was called Action Socialiste pour l'Indépendance du Québec, was Raoul Roy, a former communist and businessman. He edited the journal, *La Revue Socialiste*, which fought for "l'indépendance et la libération proletarienne nationale des Canadiens Français." The publication was also anti-internationalist and opposed the totalitarian version of communism in the Soviet Union. It did sympathize openly with Castro's Cuba, and the Cuban consul in Montreal, Carlos Herrerro, who helped the group organize and delivered speeches whenever necessary.

M. Roy's version of socialism was very intolerant of other brands of leftism in Canada, which were all called "pseudo-gauche" and were accused of living in a dream world of their own because they refused to admit the importance of national liberation. He was also wary of the other left parties because of their centralizing aspects. To him a leftist government in power seemed as much of a threat as a bourgeois type of government. He concluded that mere separatism was not as yet (in 1959) propitious because it would only throw Quebec under the increased domination of foreign monopolists and the old decadent and ultra-conservative Quebec bourgeoisie. His tactical solution was to fight a battle both against capitalist and nationalist exploitation.

The Rassemblement pour l'Indépendance Nationale (R.I.N.) was founded by André d'Allemagne, a young Montreal advertising copywriter, on September 10, 1960. Together with Marcel Chaput and thirty other sympathizers, he worked out the fundamentals of its ideology. At first, it was meant to be only a non-political educational association which would propagate the idea of Quebec's separation and independence. However, by 1962 it had developed greater ambitions and it posited certain reforms which should accompany national independence.

The main outlines of the 1962 program contained in its publication, *L'Indépendance*, indicated the direction of its reforms. Thus, the sole language of the State of Quebec was to be French, schooling was to be free, and cooperatives were to be established both for producers and consumers. Moreover, it envisaged economic planning based on the interests of all the elements of the population. It recognized the need for foreign investments but the state was going to have greater powers of intervention in guiding this investment so that local capital could participate and local personnel could be employed.

When the R.I.N. became politicized, it suffered internal schisms and finally some factions broke away to form new groups. Marcel Rioux, after polling some of the R.I.N. supporters in 1966, found that there was a continual conflict between the pure nationalists and the socialist nationalists. In December 1962, Marcel Chaput, for example, decided to form his own faction after he was replaced as president of the R.I.N. by Guy Pouliot. Chaput's Parti Républicain du Québec was more right wing than the R.I.N. Paradoxically, this same P.R.Q. metamorphosed into another group which was again more leftist oriented. The R.I.N. also gave birth to the Rassemblement National (R.N.) which was created just before the 1966 Quebec election by dissident Créditistes and right-wing, middle class separatists who had walked out of the R.I.N. in 1964 because they opposed the party's "socialism."

To "true" socialists, such as those writing for *Parti Pris,* a radical journal founded by students at the University of Montreal in 1963, the R.I.N. and especially its leader, Pierre Bourgault, were an ideological enigma. In September 1967, they noted that Bourgault had declared his belief that if he lived in the United States he would be politically on the right. Yet, during the assembly of the R.I.N. after De Gaulle's famous pronouncement of "Québec libre!" in Montreal in 1967, Bourgault reaffirmed that French Canadians were fighting the same battle as the blacks of America. In the same year he criticized the "fascists of the left" within the R.I.N., but at different times Bourgault has stated that "pour faire l'indépendance il faudrait bien que ça passe par le socialisme."

The left faction of the R.I.N. finally did separate. Led by Mme Andrée Bertrand-Ferretti, it formed a new grouping, the Front de Libération Populaire (F.L.P.), in the spring of 1968 because it would not compromise with Bourgault's policy of rapprochement with René Lévesque's Mouvement Souveraineté Association (M.S.A.) Lévesque himself had once joined the R.I.N. but broke away after members of the R.I.N. indulged in street riots in Montreal.

Although the R.I.N. was the most successful of the separatist parties during the 1966 provincial election, achieving 5.5 percent of the vote compared to the R.N.'s 3.2 percent, it finally voted to disband and join Lévesque's Parti Québecois because Lévesque was a "valuable instrument who can sell the separatist movement to a majority of Quebec voters." The R.I.N. members who voted to switch parties did so with the resolve that "we are joining the P.Q. without compromising our principles. We will be able to play the same role in that party that René Lévesque used to play in the Liberal Party."

PARTI QUEBECOIS — MEMBERSHIP, POLICIES, CRITICS

Whatever may have been the rationalization of the R.I.N. members in joining the new P.Q., the fundamentals and the direction of the latter party were set by the two founding groups: Lévesque's M.S.A. and Gilles Grégoire's R.N.

There was no question about the political sentiments of the Ralliement National, which were clearly right-wing. There was far more ambiguity about the M.S.A. and its relative position on the political spectrum. Several factors should be considered here. The focus of power within the M.S.A. lay in the hands of Lévesque's followers from the Liberal Party of Quebec: Gérard Belanger, Marc Brière, Reynold Busson, and M. Boivin. However, many of those forming the basic membership were certainly more radical and revolutionary, having come from quite leftist socialist groups. Yet as the leftists themselves openly acknowledged, their numbers were not great and their bargaining power in the M.S.A. was very limited. The R.I.N.'s influence in the M.S.A. was also limited because the R.I.N. refused to join as a constituent body and therefore its members who joined subsequently did so as individuals.

Having emerged from this sort of confused but predominantly cautious background, the Parti Québecois has not tended to favour radical socialist revolutionary measures. Its program, published just before the 1970 Quebec election, corroborates this point, although the verbiage in many cases is very nebulous and unclear. Some of the statements from the Programme P.Q. are indicative of this trend. Thus, "l'entreprise privée conservera son rôle dans les champs où elle est efficace et bénéfique." But "l'Etat québecois s'efforcera de préciser aussitôt et pour aussi longtemps que possible les domaines qui seront réservés à la propriété publique et d'indiquer clairement les règles du jeu." While "le Québec souverain continuera d'accueillir les capitaux étrangers . . . , l'un des soucis primordiaux de l'Etat sera de rendre à la population une maîtrise raisonnable de sa vie économique et de lui assurer, dans ce domaine comme dans les autres, une participation à tous les niveaux du pouvoir." One of the more ambiguous and possibly dangerous paragraphs is the one dealing with radio and television: "l'Etat devra faire du réseau de télévision et de radio un instrument de l'éducation permanente et de la culture populaire ainsi qu'un moyen de diffuser dans la population l'esprit de service et le désir constant du progrès." The statement raises the question of who is to define the nature of "progress."

Judged by the political experience of other Canadian parties, party programs are not necessarily the only determinant of future tactics. Because they are trying to obtain political power, parties have to compromise to obtain the support of the majority of the electorate. This statement would be true of most brokerage type parties, but perhaps not as applicable to an ideological party such as the P.Q. where the guiding ideology is "sovereignty."

The main reason that the P.Q. will not move very much further left than the "Swedish type" of welfare-statism lies in the social characteristics of those supporting independence. In its issue of November 2, 1963, *Maclean's* magazine published a very extensive analysis of separatism. It was found that 13 percent of French Canadians in Quebec were in favour of secession. The most interesting phenomenon relevant to the present analysis was the fact that the greatest percentage of support came from those earning more than $6,000 a year and from those who had finished university or had special or technical training. Since such groups in general are economic conservatives and provide the backbone of all free enterprise parties, it is not likely that if such separatists are members of the P.Q. they will be very ardent socialists.

It is possible, however, that the attraction of the P.Q. has broadened because of Lévesque's personal appeal among the workers and because of the R.N.'s support in rural ridings in Quebec. One left revolutionary has endorsed this opinion unequivocally: "Lévesque a la sympathie d'une grande partie des mouvements syndicaux." The intrusion of Lévesque's personality is certainly a very strong factor in the support of the P.Q. Even in 1963 the *Maclean's* study found that 23 percent would support a party in favour of separatism if it were led by René Lévesque, who was then a Liberal provincial minister; 17 per cent were unsure and only 36 percent declared opposition. The rest of the sample, interestingly enough, had never heard of separatism. This fact leads to another hypothesis. It seems that there has been a polarization on the subject of separatism and that the group which in 1963 was ignorant about it has opted almost entirely on the side of Confederation.

A more recent study carried out by a professional public opinion and research group from Montreal and published in the weekend magazine *Perspectives* on March 28, 1970, showed that six years after the first poll in 1963 there was still only the same percentage of French Canadians in Quebec favouring separatism (13 percent) while the proportion of those opposing it had increased from 43 percent to 70 percent. Against this, however, must be set the fact that 23 percent of Quebec's electors voted for the separatist P.Q. led by Lévesque in the provincial election of 1970. Whatever the reasons for such support, it is interesting that this percentage is identical to the percentage of the 1963 poll's sample who said they would vote for a separatist party if it were led by Lévesque. Certainly, Lévesque has attracted a large following. By October, 1969, the P.Q. had acquired 26,000 paid-up members and the party won about 650,000 votes in the election of 1970.

The P.Q. is not, of course, the only party in Quebec at present favouring separatism. There are a number of other factions, most of which are more radical and revolutionary than the "péquistes." The most militant of these groups, the Front de Libération Populaire (F.L.P.), contains the break-away faction of the R.I.N. which was led into the F.L.P. by Mme Andrée Bertrand-Ferretti, who, however, subsequently quit the F.L.P. The latter also attracted members of the defunct Mouvement Syndical Populaire (M.S.P.). The F.L.P. has been the most visible of all groups on the Quebec political leftist scene. It has organized various demonstrations against McGill University, the Union National Convention, the Société St. Jean Baptiste, and the English language groups in St. Leonard. The F.L.P. believes that independence led by the P.Q. would only perpetuate capitalism.

It has formally renounced any possibility of cooperation or alliance with nationalists of the "S.S.J.B. variety" who, they feel, form a major part of the Parti Québecois. The F.L.P.'s plan of action is to develop an extra-parliamentary, mass, revolutionary movement through the establishment of cells in unions and universities. It has decided to shun "opportunists" and revolutionary "stars" such as Michel Chartrand of the P.Q. and Raymond Lemieux, who founded and led the Mouvement pour l'Intégration Scolaire (M.I.S.), the unilingual French movement in St. Leonard.

Another faction, the Front du Libération du Québec (F.L.Q.), has always been the most terroristic of all separatist groups. It rejects the idea that an electoral party can ever attain independence or national liberation. In its view the P.Q. will have to make compromises with the financiers of rue St. Jacques and Wall Street. To win elections, parties need money and one day the P.Q. will succumb to pressures of necessity and its members will become profiteers. The F.L.Q.'s idea of how to bring about the real revolution rests on something akin to the "workers' soviets" of the 1917 vintage in Russia. These "liberation committees" will bring power to the people and once this happens "committees of defence" will consolidate the proletarian gains against "reaction." Charles Gagnon, one of the leaders of the F.L.Q. and a former professor of sociology, wants total liberation for Quebec—both economic and political. Another leader, Pierre Vallière, who was charged in connection with a fatality caused by a bombing in a shoe factory, is the author of *Les nègres blancs,* which tries to draw a parallel between French Canadians and American Negroes.

The main publication of radical students in Quebec is the *Quartier Latin,* which is distributed to most C.E.G.E.P.s (Collèges d'enseignement général et professionnel, i.e. Quebec's "community colleges") and universities in the province. It too has failed to embrace the P.Q. but its rejection is more reasoned and less vehement than that of some other publications like *La Masse.*

Some radical students tried to join and work within the confines of the Parti Québecois, but a faction of them broke away in March, 1970. Led by the former vice-president of the defunct Union Générale des Etudiants de Québec (U.G.E.Q.), Gilles Duceppe, this splinter group is now trying to form an organization which would stand somewhere between the P.Q. and pure terrorism.

Some members of the extreme left are opposed to the entire concept of an electoral system and therefore also to the P.Q. which is part of it. Others who are just as radical support the P.Q., for example, Claude Charron, an ex-vice-president and international affairs "minister" of U.G.E.Q. who has been elected to the P.Q. executive and is at present in charge of student recruitment and agitation. He was also elected to the Quebec legislature as a P.Q. member in 1970. According to Pierre Bourgault, Charron's election to the executive was a hollow victory for the left because the Grégoire wing of the party allowed it only as a sign of conciliation after Bourgault's defeat in the election for the executive. Nevertheless, it has created the necessary atmosphere within the P.Q. to attract many Quebec students.

A poll taken at Laval University in March, 1970 indicated that more than 55.1 percent of the students were in favour of the P.Q., 29.1 percent opting for the Liberals, 2.6 percent for the U.N., 2.3 percent for the Créditistes, and 1.1 percent for the N.P.D. These statistics fail to indicate the enthusiasm and active support found for the P.Q. within the universities and other student institutions. It is tempting to ask whether any other party could have collected, as the P.Q. did, $1,000 from the science students at the University of Montreal or a like amount from the C.E.G.E.P. at Rosemount and the arts division of the University of Laval. The devotion and complete involvement of students seems to parallel the populist appeal of the Social Credit party in 1962, which, of course, was aimed at a different section of French-Canadian society.

There are also other splinter groups which have taken a stand against the P.Q., such as the Maoists, who just recently started their own publication at Sherbrooke, *l'Estrie Rouge,* and the Trotskyites, more commonly called La Ligue Socialiste Ouvrière. There may also be an undefined, amorphous group of avant-garde artists, poets and writers, who have already taken independence for granted and now want something more—a socialist revolution à la Gagnon and Vallière. Nevertheless, as one French-Canadian journalist stated: "Les étudiants voteront P.Q. C'est la plus grande certitude."

However, not all of the leftist militants have shunned the P.Q. There are diffuse signs that fragments of them, seeing some benefit in upsetting the status quo, have joined the P.Q. In June 1969, when Lévesque was speaking to a P.Q. rally in the east end of Montreal which consisted mainly of New Left bearded types, he uttered the word "revolution" and immediately received a loud cheer. Lévesque quickly explained that what he had meant was social revolution not violence. The Telegram Canada '70 team, which did an intensive study of conditions in Quebec, reported that there was a "grab-bag" of the left in the Parti Québecois. "This group includes Maoists, Castroites, adulators of Che, pure New Leftists of the Students for a Democratic Society type, a clutch of Trotskyites, and even a few neo-Stalinists."

The Nouveau Parti Democratique (N.P.D.), which ran a few candidates in the Quebec provincial election in 1970, has manifested its disillusionment with the P.Q. At first, it wanted to support the P.Q. by not placing candidates in ridings where this party had a chance of winning. Later Roland Morin, the head of the N.P.D., made it clear that the P.Q. was politically closer to Bertrand's Union Nationale. Scorning the P.Q.'s opportunistic, chameleon-like characteristics, he remarked, "ils sont socialistes avec les socialistes, indépendantistes avec les indépendantistes, fédéralistes avec les fédéralistes et de droite avec les gens de la droite." Moreover, the N.P.D. is not interested in political independence for Quebec, but wants to create better conditions for increased economic development. The N.P.D., however, is not a very important factor in the French-Canadian equation. Most of its support is English Canadian, as can be deduced from the fact that Morin had to speak in English after being nominated for the leadership of the party.

The publication *Socialisme* also represents a certain sector of the French-Canadian, leftist intelligentsia which is divided over the question of Quebec separatism. According to Maurice Lamontagne, *Socialisme* was founded in 1964 and represented the culmination of a radical revolution at the University of Montreal. It was influenced strongly by the members of the University's department of philosophy. Although Robert Pouliot of *Sept Jours* has argued that *Socialisme* replaced the political void left by the defunct *Revue Socialiste* of Raoul Roy, the magazine's actual direction, especially on independence, is far more ambiguous than the latter's.

One journalist, having spent several months talking to all factions of the non-P.Q. left, has written that *Socialisme* will become the main information organ for a newly reconstituted leftist front which will include such diverse elements as the Maoists and the Trotskyites. However, in view of the frequency of the formation of this type of leftist coalition and its subsequent fragmentation, there is no reason to think that this front will finally be the "real thing." Nevertheless, it seems clear that whether united or separated, some parts of these various factions of the left have refused to become absorbed by the P.Q. and will continue to lead the same kind of ineffectual fringe politics that they have indulged in for so long. That is why so many of the more articulate and intelligent leaders on the left, such as Jean-Marc Piotte and Raoul Roy, have been faced with an almost insurmountable dilemma—either to join the P.Q. and become absorbed or co-opted within the deradicalizing mainstream of Quebec politics or to stay out "in the cold" and continue without having any real effect on French-Canadian society. They must be aware of what happened to the ex-radicals Pierre Trudeau, Gérard Pelletier, Jean Marchand, Jean-Luc Pepin and Jean Drapeau once they became recognized leaders within the confines of the existing society. They are afraid that once they start to play the game, they too inevitably will have to accept the rules of that game. These rules are exactly the things they want to change.

One other celebrated publication should be mentioned. *Cité Libre* started out in 1949 as an anti-clerical and anti-nationalist review because both of these forces were allied to its main opponent, the Duplessis regime. This anti-nationalist trend in *Cité Libre* has become modified somewhat and the word nationalism has become, in effect, what the word socialism appears to be to many French Canadians, not a pejorative term but also not a very relevant factor in present problems. For a few brief months in 1964, *Cité Libre*'s traditional direction was reoriented radically by a new team of nationalists chosen in error by P. E. Trudeau himself. The new group tried to turn *Cité Libre* into the chief organ of separatist sentiment. This trend was tolerated by Trudeau and Pelletier, the magazine's founders, for only four months and then Pierre Vallière (of F.L.Q. fame) together with ten other staff members were dismissed or departed. Thus *Cité Libre* still stands as one of the chief moderate leftist and anti-separatist forces in Quebec.

Some of the founders of *Parti Pris,* have also indicated their support of Lévesque's type of "independence." André Brochu, one of the founders of *Parti Pris,* eulogized the P.Q. in April, 1970 in the following words: "Le parti québecois c'est la renaissance et la transformation en volonté d'action populaire, de ce que fût, pour nous, parti pris. C'est le parti du Québec, pris par tous les Québécois. C'est notre tranquillité, l'infini de nos patiences faits revolution."

Brochu's statement in the press shows a very definite ideological evolution from an elitist revolutionary position several years ago to a more emotional and sentimental identification with all the streams of Quebec society. There is no trace left of the impatience and the ideological rigidity of former years. On the contrary, there seems to be a return to the veneration of a "chef" who has managed "to channel our most fundamental desires which in reality cannot be claimed by any single generation, any social milieu nor by any ideological sect or particular group."

There have been even more spectacular changes within the left on the question of separatism. A case in point is Michel Chartrand, the Montreal leader of the Confédération des Syndicats Nationaux. Having withstood all the separatist disputes within the N.P.D. and having also on many occasions made eloquent speeches stating why separatism was only a smoke screen to cover the true lines of conflict between the classes, he recently has been instrumental in agitating within the Montreal section of the C.S.N. to obtain full backing for the P.Q.

It would seem that Chartrand does not fear the possibility of another "nationalist reactionary" French-Canadian government. This obvious fact is perhaps the key to much of the change of attitude towards nationalism and separatism evinced by many individuals on the left. Nationalism is no longer a weapon exclusively held by what appeared to them "re-actionary classes." This neo-nationalism, a term presently in vogue to differentiate it from the previous version, is a progressive force which can rectify many of the iniquities in Quebec society. Jean-Marc Piotte has gone to great lengths to dissociate the term from its right-wing connotations. He notes, for instance, the obvious international links between the great leaders of industry and the large monopolies. Piotte's arguments on strategy are probably the most succinct and representative of the leftist-separatists' position and their reasons for opting for Lévesque's party.

The "nationalists" or those who consider Quebec's sovereignty to be the major priority of politics display ambiguity in their attitude towards socialism. A publication like *Action Nationale* stands on the "right side" of politics but some of its directors, such as Jean-Marc Leger, are associated with socialism. Its editor, Jean Genest, sees no evil in using the state to equalize the imbalance of ownership in the Quebec economy but he becomes an anti-statist of the American variety when contemplating the intrusion of the state in education.

The economist Jacques Parizeau, who is one of the main intellectual bulwarks of the P.Q., does not shy away from contemplation of nationalization. His comparison of nationalization to the hammer of a carpenter, viewing it merely as a tool, would certainly not offend any socialist; yet he has been the main economic adviser to two Quebec governments and has advocated very orthodox methods for dealing with fiscal and economic problems. Gilles Grégoire's stand, as noted before, is also extremely ambiguous on the relationship of separatism to socialism.

One of the surprising facets of nationalism is the position of the Union Nationale party. The promise by Premier Bertrand in the 1970 election that a referendum on independence would be held before 1974 was not a radical departure from the previous trend of the party leaders. The late Premier Daniel Johnson's "Egalité ou Indépendance" was complemented by the preference of a large fraction of U.N. members of the Quebec Legislative Assembly for political independence. A poll taken in 1967 by Dominique Clift and Normand Girard for the *Toronto Daily Star* indicated an astounding 64.7 percent of the U.N.'s M.L.A.'s were in favour of political independence, whereas among the Liberal members of the Legislature only 4.8 percent supported this position. The ease with which one U.N. minister, Marcel Masse, spoke in the election about a possible alliance between the U.N. and the P.Q. indicates a tremendous flux and fluidity in political orientation. Probably this was best illustrated by the U.N. candidate in Champlain in 1970, Paul Rochelieu. He was one of the original founders of the right-wing separatist Alliance Laurentienne, then joined the R.I.N., and later went along with Marcel Chaput in forming the Parti Républicain. His brother, Marcel Rochelieu, was a P.Q. candidate in Maskinonge in the same election.

The Créditistes, although cast in the role of anti-separatists and pro-federalists, cannot be counted as very reliable on this matter. Réal Caouette, the federal leader, may be an avid federalist but Camil Samson, the new provincial leader, is definitely not. All indications point to a future split between the federal and provincial wings of the party. Even the disputes in many ridings as to who should choose candidates, the federal M.P.'s or the provincial organizations, has taken on dimensions of confrontation. Caouette's failure to back any one of the provincial hopefuls for the leadership and his naive and incompetent presentation of Yvon Dupuis, a former federal Liberal cabinet minister, as the best candidate created more lines of rupture. However, the greatest obstacle to their cooperation and the reason why the provincial Créditistes can also be considered nationalists lies in the fact that Samson was one of the chief founders of the separatist Rassemblement National and that he ran as an R.N. candidate in Temiscamingue in 1966. Samson, a nationalist, has not budged in his dislike of socialists and his main reason for leaving the new coalition of the M.S.A. and R.N. was the former's socialist direction. This opposition to socialism alone should not hide the fact that the Créditistes have also a deep vein of anti-capitalist feeling. Denunciations of exploitation of the working class and of the enjoyment of the benefits by only a handful of rich persons are the foundation of Créditiste rebellion.

CONCLUSION

The common link between the nationalists and the socialist nationalists is their view of the state and its function in French-Canadian society. Contrary to the right-wing conviction now popular in the U.S. that the state governs best which governs least and the equally strong stand against the expansion of government and bureaucracy, French Canadians have embraced a radically different trend. The state of Quebec has taken over many of the functions of the clergy in assuring "la survivance" and, as such, has been accorded much more confidence by both the left and the right. Professor Louis Sabourin, former dean of the Faculty of Social Sciences at the University of Ottawa, has noted this distinction: "In the past anti-statism was one of the dominant facts of political life. Today the situation has changed considerably. The French Canadians believe that only the State, which they can control, can assure their development in all areas."

This anti-statism of the past should not be taken as opposition to the idea of a strong state. French Canadians did not expect much previously from their provincial legislature and therefore their anti-statism was passive rather than active. For French-Canadian nationalists, however, the ideal of a powerful state is a recurring theme in the present century. Abbé Groulx did not pray for a charismatic wilful leader to lead a weak state. Neither was the idealized "Laurentie" a state where individual rights would flourish at the expense of collective rights. The state, whether the corporatist dream of the right or the instrument of nationalization of the left, has a unique and forceful position in French-Canadian nationalist ideology. It is only during the last decade that the idealized "state" has coincided with an actual "state."

The "dialectic" between the nationalists and socialists is still continuing. This dialectic has affected many pure nationalists as well as many revolutionaries. The situation is still very much in flux since the final political lines have not yet been drawn. Lenin once coined the phrase "kto kovo," meaning "who to whom." It will be interesting to see which tendency becomes dominant in Quebec and in the P.Q. especially—kto kovo, "bourgeois nationalism" or "bourgeois socialism"? If the P.Q. were to take power, or at least to obtain a large representation in the legislature, its direction would be towards nationalism. If, however, the P.Q. is denied any power, then the pressures for radicalization will be increased. However, the end result will certainly be far from socialism because of the inherent non-worker composition of its members. Although Lenin utilized Marx's ambiguous legacy on nationalism for tactical reasons, he also stated that "There is not the slightest doubt that every nationalist movement can only be a bourgeois-democratic movement."

THE SECESSION OF QUEBEC FROM CANADA*

MARCEL CHAPUT

Contrary to previous, or some actual, French-Canadian societies, the secessionist movement is not a new reception committee calling for more national unity. It does not even plead for a greater recognition of French-Canadian rights in Con-

*From *Canadian Commentator,* July-August, 1961. By permission of the author and publisher.

federation. It places the discussion on an entirely different plane: it assumes simply and brutally that French Canadians do not want any more to be a MINORITY; that, instead, they have decided to become masters in their own house.

English-speaking Canadians who are preoccupied by American infiltration of Canadian life, or who demand the repatriation of the constitution to elevate Canada to the rank of a fully sovereign country, will no doubt understand the feeling of the French Canadian. If it is legitimate and desirable that English Canada be politically different from the United States, in spite of the near-identity of language, religion, culture and social institutions between the inhabitants of these two neighbouring countries, it is *a fortiori* legitimate and imperative that French Canada, with unique traits in America, be the sole master of its own destiny. They will understand that it is just as much a necessity for French Canada to be sovereign as it is for Mexico to avoid becoming another star on the American flag.

When the time comes, this necessity will take the shape of a Quebec sovereign unilingual state of French language, just as Mexico is a sovereign unilingual state of Spanish language, just as the rest of Canada will become, if it so desires, a sovereign unilingual state of English language, and so forth with the other one hundred sovereign unilingual states of the world. Having attained sovereignty, Quebec will THEN, and only THEN, sign any treaty, engage in any negotiations, enter any commonwealth, community, market, organization or confederation that HER interests and responsibility will demand. . . .

[Quebec secessionists] believe that a country, like Quebec, which is three times as large as France, five times as large as Italy, thirteen times as large as Cuba, that such a country which stands among the first producers in the world of hydro-electric power, wood, pulp and paper, iron ore, minerals of all kinds, that this country which is linked to the ocean by one of the main seaways in the world, can live by itself and prosper.

Isolation, you say? You will then have to prove that the forty nations which have become independent since the end of the last war did isolate themselves. If so, the self-determination article of the UNO Charter was a huge trap.

Granted, all nations are actually evolving in the direction of big ensembles. But all these large international formations—commonwealths, communities, continental organizations, and so forth—were based on free entry of sovereign states. Moreover, and most important, these sovereign states adhered to a group because of economic or defensive reasons, not for political ones. . . .

But where is isolation, I dare ask? In the formation of a French, independent, Quebec state which would decide her own associations, establish cultural links with the 25 French-language countries of the world, be represented by French-Canadian ambassadors in all capitals, speak for herself, in French, at the United Nations assemblies?—or along the 4,000 miles of so-called bilingual Canada, where, after 94 years of Confederation, French Canadians of nine provinces are still fighting for an odd hour of French teaching and religion in schools that they paid for themselves, in addition to paying for the public ones; where French-Canadian soldiers cannot even be ordered in their own language to die for Canada that is said to be their own; where in the majority of cases, French Canadians have to take off, like their hat and coat, their mother tongue every working morning, in order to earn a living; where French Canadians are kept at the lower echelons of Canadian life . . . what do you expect us to do? Lie down quietly and die? . . .

SEPARATISM — CANADA'S DEATH WISH*

PAUL FOX

The first thing to be noted about Quebec's current separatist movement is that it is not new. It is no exaggeration to say that the history of Canada as a nation is the story of one long-running battle against divisive forces which would split it apart. In Freudian terms, Canada's attempts to fulfil its urge to national life have been accompanied by a contrary destructive death urge.

As a people we have had to fight not only against climate, which has kept us isolated in pockets (especially in winter), but against geography as well. The dividing lines in North America run north and south rather than east and west along the Canadian-American border.

With their backs against the Appalachian mountain range, Maritimers have found traditionally that they have had far more in common—in trade, in industries, in outlook—with New Englanders than with "Upper Canadians", as they still call the residents of central Canada. The latter find that they look south for business and pleasure rather than east or west. Montrealers and Torontonians will visit New York, Lake Placid, Buffalo, or Detroit, often before they visit even each other, let alone Halifax, Calgary, or Vancouver. Prairie folk drift across a border created by men rather than by nature when they go to Chicago or the Midwest; and British Columbians, on the far side of the forbidding Rocky Mountains, feel much closer to the American Pacific states, as they are, than to the rest of Canada.

These natural obstacles have bred strong local sentiments in Canada, and it is against these tendencies that the nation has had to struggle ever since its birth on July 1, 1867.

Confederation brought together three scattered, undeveloped and under-populated British colonies, Nova Scotia, New Brunswick, and "Canada", as the union

*Revised in July, 1970, from an article which appeared originally in the *Family Herald,* March 15, 1962. By permission.

of what are now Ontario and Quebec was called. Though two other Atlantic colonies were included in preliminary consultations, they would not join in forming the new dominion. Prince Edward Island pursued its separate way for another six years and Newfoundland did not enter until 1949.

Meanwhile, many of the citizens in two of the three charter Confederation colonies wanted to withdraw. So serious was the opposition to union by the New Brunswick government that it had to be virtually pushed out of office by the British governor, to make way for a more favourable government whose election was secured by financial contributions from Upper Canada. Nova Scotia was no more enthusiastic. Halifax celebrated Canada's first national birthday by draping its main street in black, and in the federal election which followed the province as a whole elected 18 out of 19 MPs pledged to repeal the act of union.

Out west, in what was to be Manitoba, Louis Riel led a rebellion against encroachment from Ottawa and set up a short-lived republic. Sixteen years later he made a second attempt in the North-West Rebellion. British Columbia entered as a province in 1871 but haggling over the terms of union and threats to secede continued for years.

Here were examples of genuine separatism, expressed in deeds, not just in words. And the spirit is not dead yet. A ludicrous illustration occurred a few years ago when a tiny municipality in Northern Ontario threatened to withdraw from the province if it did not get the road it wanted.

Thus separatism as a sentiment in Canada is common. It is the obvious form of protest of local groups which feel their interests are being threatened by the larger national entity. It is the outlet psychologically for the frustrations of a minority which recognizes rationally that it must buckle under to the majority but cannot accept the inevitability of it without a desperate kick, like a child lashing out against an overwhelming parent.

This is not said to deride the cause of separatism, merely to explain it. On a broader scale, many Canadians today express the same emotion in fighting off the encircling embrace of the United States.

French-Canadian separatism is accentuated by differences in language and religion. The Gallic tongue and Roman Catholic faith mark off French Canadians distinctively from the Anglo-Saxon Protestant majority. But these are only attributes of their fundamental differences, and despite all the hullabaloo to preserve them, they are not the cause of Quebec's separatism. The fight is nothing less than an endeavour to maintain a way of life which is 350 years old, a separate and distinctive French identity in a sea of North American Anglo-Saxonism.

The depth and intensity of this distinctive culture is what has made separatism in Quebec the prototype of such movements, and the most traditional, enduring, and serious of its kind. The nearest analogy that comes to mind is the successful persistence for centuries of the Jewish people in preserving their Hebraic separateness in a world with Gentiles.

Separatism in Quebec therefore is not new. It is a theme which has often been voiced in French-Canadian history, especially at critical moments, such as 30 years ago by the Abbé Lionel Groulx and those who dreamed of an independent republic of "Laurentie" . . . .

But it would be a mistake for English Canadians to dismiss the current song of protest as one more turn on the same old gramophone record. It is the old refrain, but something new has been added also—a modern, accelerated tempo.

A revolution has occurred in Quebec recently. In the last few years Quebec has commenced going through a transformation which is more significant and shattering than anything that has occurred in French Canada since the conquest. Industrialization, urbanization, and modernization have arrived in French Canada with a bang. In the short space of a few years Quebec has entered into a transition that has taken half a century to run its course in other parts of Canada. For years these forces were blocked by the traditionalist patterns of thought of church and state. This Old Regime, as it might well be called, was personified by the late Premier Maurice Duplessis. With his death in 1959 and the fall of his Union Nationale party from power in the election of June, 1960, the dam burst. New ideas, new forces came surging to the surface. Most of these poured into courses more constructive than separatism, but the general spill-over of energy revived separatism in some quarters and gave it fresh grounds to feed upon.

Thus the present separatist movement in Quebec is old and new at the same time, and still challenging. In the provincial election in Quebec on April 29, 1970, René Lévesque's separatist Parti Québécois won 23 percent of the vote, compared to 20 percent for the Union Nationale which had formed the government from 1966 to 1970, and 45 percent for the Liberals who formed the new government.

If the separatists succeeded and Quebec split off from Canada, could it maintain itself for long as a progressive, dynamic national state? Is it not a backward step to split into a smaller unit? The trend of evolution is from the single cell to the multi-cellular. The path of economic and political development in the world is towards integration, not disintegration. Witness the growth of corporations, trading blocks, and regional groupings of nations in Europe and elsewhere. This does not mean that individuality is lost sight of. We do not necessarily all become identical because we become more interrelated. There is still room for diversity in unity— the two are not mutually exclusive. In fact, integration may promote individual development. Is the average modern Frenchman, German, and Englishman not a more developed and distinctive human creature living at a higher level in contemporary integrating Europe than his ancestor was in a more divided and primitive medieval Europe?

The challenge for French Canadians is to retain their distinctiveness while still remaining Canadians in an expanding world. It is a challenge that English Canadians also face in their relationship to the United States. The feat for French Canadians is admittedly more difficult and they are deserving of sympathy and assistance in their attempt to be themselves while moving ahead together. Many of the separatists' complaints against English Canadians are justified. But the solution is not to reverse the process of history. Should Ontario depart from Canada because Ontario pays more taxes into the federal treasury than other provinces (which is one of Dr. Chaput's arguments for Quebec's withdrawal)? Should Anglo-Saxon Protestants in Montreal become Separatists and withdraw from Quebec if French Canada becomes a separate state? Many of the Separatists' arguments can be turned against them. Separatists should remember that not all the penalties for bi-culturalism are paid by the minority; English Canadians as well as French Canadians make sacrifices in the interest of national unity. . . .

ANSWERS TO QUESTIONS
ABOUT QUEBEC AS A SEPARATE STATE*

RENE LEVESQUE

What is the primary purpose of the Parti Québécois?
The Parti Québécois wants Québec to be a sovereign state! A country that will be politically independent from Canada though linked to it economically.

Will that settle the unemployment question?
Unemployment is one of the problems that neither Ottawa nor Québec, nor any of the established parties have been able to solve. Québec presently accounts for about 40 percent of all the unemployed in Canada. Most of Québec's unemployed are French-speaking. The present constitutional system is hardly advantageous to us. At this moment, 8.7 percent of the Québec population is out of work. If Québec were able to negotiate directly with other countries including Canada and the United States; if it could use its taxes as it wishes, it could take advantage of its geographical situation (the St. Lawrence river is a door that opens onto the whole world), develop its natural resources and encourage the establishment of industries which would, each year, create thousands of jobs. All this can only be done if Québec becomes a sovereign state.

Yes, but can Québec achieve independence?
Certainly. Both natural and international law recognize that every nation in the world, large or small, rich or poor, has the right to independence. The fate of any given territory belongs solely to the inhabitants of that territory. No one can prevent Québec from becoming independent.

Can Québec exist alone?
There has never been any question of Québec existing alone. No country can exist alone. Even the United States needs other countries to trade with. After independence Québec, instead of being a simple province will become a nation

*From the Parti Québécois' election leaflet, April, 1970.

open to the world, and will be able to negotiate according to its interests with every country in the world, including Canada.

Suppose Québec became a sovereign state tomorrow — what difference would it make to the present situation?

Québec's independence is not an end in itself; it is a means, and the best one, to bring about the social and economic changes that the country needs.

Will the standard of living in Québec drop after independence?

It will surely not be as low as it is under the present government. The standard of living in Québec within the confederation is 54 percent lower than that of the United States and 27 percent below that of Ontario. Such a situation is unacceptable . . . .

What will happen to national defence?

It is out of the question for us to continue spending 500 million dollars a year, as is now the case, on a system of defence which defends nothing. We shall have a reasonable budget for a force oriented towards peace, not towards war . . . .

Can you explain in greater detail the formula of a SOVEREIGN QUEBEC with ECONOMIC ASSOCIATION?

We suggest the following formula: Québec and Canada would form two SOVEREIGN states which would be associated within the framework of an economic alliance on a contractual and renewable basis.

Essentially do you want a sort of common market like the one that exists in Europe?

Rather like that. West Germany, Italy, France, Belgium, Holland and Luxembourg, all sovereign states, decided about ten years ago to form an economic association. They did not, however, give up their political sovereignty. France is still France with its Frenchmen; Germany is still Germany with its Germans.

All that is a little complicated for a layman. Could you explain the terms one by one?

(a) TWO SOVEREIGN STATES:

Internal and external sovereignty for the state of Québec in all areas is an essential characteristic of this option. Québec alone will decide its policies. It will no longer have to ask Ottawa for permission.

(b) IN ASSOCIATION:

There is no question of our denying the necessity and utility of certain links with the rest of Canada. From a geographic and economic point of view, Québec must continue a good neighbour policy with the rest of Canada and the United States.

(c) WITHIN THE FRAMEWORK OF AN ECONOMIC AND ADMINISTRATIVE ALLIANCE:

Certain agreements will have to be negotiated, in such areas, for instance, as economic exchange, currency, postal services etc. All these will be covered by regulations set up in collaboration. What we want in fact, is to deal with Canada as equals and not as from an inferior to a superior.

(d) ON A CONTRACTUAL AND RENEWABLE BASIS:

This option is clear. Any contract between Canada and Québec can, upon expiration, be amended, modified, terminated or renewed according to circumstances and necessity. This agreement will be formulated by contract and not by a constitution because we wish to make it possible to renew it from time to time.

Is a sovereign Québec economically viable?

The economic growth of a society depends upon its potential and how it is utilized. First of all, its potential is its territory. Of the 145 sovereign states recognized by the U.N. in 1965 a sovereign Québec would rank 16th for its area. On the basis of its population it would rank 63rd. Insofar as education is concerned we are already highly qualified, comparable on that score to Sweden. As to natural resources it is no secret that we are well endowed . . . .

Where will the money come from?

Among ourselves. No one will give it to us. Actually it is our taxes and our savings which now finance the bulk of the investments essential to our development. The public sector in Québec at this time finances itself to a large extent through the Deposit and Investment Fund. And once the Bank of Québec will have been set up, the province, exactly as is the case with Canada, will be less dependent upon capital markets because it will finance much of its debt through this Bank, thereby releasing the funds of the Deposit and Investment Fund for industry.

As to the private sector, its capital will come from the profits realized by businesses operating in Québec and from the savings of Québecers in banks, credit unions, insurance companies, pension funds etc. . . . Capital will also come from foreign countries, for ours is an extremely lucrative market . . . .

What will be the nature of our association with the rest of Canada?

Commercial and monetary union.

Why associate with the rest of Canada?

The Québec and Canadian economies complement each other. Canada is by far Québec's main customer (63.5 percent of its exports). 35 percent of the Québec's manufacturing manpower is dependent on it. Association is in our interest. Furthermore a joint Canada-Québec customs policy would be more advantageous for us if we negotiate it as full partners.

Will the remainder of Canada agree to associate with a sovereign Québec?

Québec imports much from Canada, especially from Ontario—we are among Ontario's best customers. By refusing a commercial union Canada would lose its main market and reduce its own prosperity.

What would happen to our currency?

The dollar currently in use and recognized in world markets will remain. This would be an advantage to both partners, because our interlocking economies need monetary co-ordination. This is what the Common Market countries have come to realize and it explains their search for a common monetary unit.

What portion of the federal debt will we have to assume and through what procedure will we become owners of federal assets?

This will have to be negotiated. We simply point out that because Québecers have paid for them through their taxes, they have become co-owners of the federal properties. They could give up their interest in the Toronto airport just as the Canadians would give up theirs in the Montreal airport. As for the federal debt, it is obvious that we will shoulder our share . . . .

Why build a wall around Québec when common markets are being built elsewhere?

The economist J. K. Galbraith points out that there is currently a tendency in the world to build large economic communities, but not large political communities. This corresponds exactly to the PQ position . . . .

Would there be a reaction from investors?

A government having a clear-cut program, elaborated by a competent task force and operating along stable rules, will not frighten foreign capital. The Americans continue investing in the Middle-East . . . .

THE P.Q. PROGRAM, 1970*

PARTI QUEBECOIS

TAXES

Political sovereignty means first and foremost the full recovery and absolute control of all the taxes we pay each year. It means the power to devote these fiscal resources to the ends that we, and we alone, consider most important.

This power of choice has been denied to those who have the best claim to it, the tax-paying citizens of Québec. Its exercise by Quebecers would put an end to present confusions in which two governments, Federal and Provincial, each set their own priorities without considering the other's activities, each deciding to increase spending or taxes, while we, the tax-paying citizens, never really know where our money is going.

ROLE OF THE STATE

In modern economies, the State stimulates and co-ordinates economic development.

*From the Parti Québécois' election leaflet, April, 1970.

After Québec has achieved independence the state will aim to:
—strengthen the public sector;
—develop a private enterprise policy;
—attain economic democracy.

In the **public sector,** the State will aim at ensuring full employment and accelerating industrialization and technological development. It will do so by creating new businesses, governmental financial "reservoirs" and management bodies, and by working in mixed enterprises with private business.

The State will also assume some control over **private enterprise** by using its taxation powers and by offering incentives to the private sector to enter into the government's over-all plan for Québec's economy. The State will treat both foreign and domestic private enterprise according to rules clearly established beforehand . . . .

PLANNING

To play its part efficiently as prime mover of the economy, the Independent State of Québec will concentrate on three main bodies:
—a Department of Finance and Revenue;
—a Department of National Economy;
—a Planning Board.

The **Department of Finance and Revenue** will be responsible for preparing budgets and collecting taxes. But it will also supervise all financial institutions, both public and private, in order to prevent Québec financial institutions from falling under the control of foreign powers, and to prevent groups of private individuals from gaining control of our financial system. The government will set up as large a reservoir of capital as possible in the public sector. It will set up a Consumer Credit Board to put an end to finance companies' systematic abuses. Finally, a central Bank of Québec will act as the government's financial and fiscal agent.

To end confusion and futile overlapping of jurisdiction, the **Department of National Economy** will regroup existing economically-oriented departments such as Natural Resources, Lands and Forests, Agriculture, Commerce and Industry, Tourism, Fish and Game.

The **Planning Board** will prepare an over-all development plan for the whole of Québec, co-ordinate the main features of state policy, and ensure that citizens have a voice in evolving these policies. More specifically, the Planning Board will establish government priorities as to its investments, will prepare a complete regional development plan, and will co-ordinate industrial research.

MODERN ECONOMY

One of the main objectives of sovereign Québec will be the modernization of its economic activity. On the one hand, the State will establish a specific buying policy in both public and mixed sectors, so that its enormous buying power will serve to create or stimulate employment. On the other hand it will channel the development of existing bodies such as the General Investment Corporation (SGF), the Industrial Credit Bureau, and the Quebec Mining Exploration Corporation (SO-QUEM) . . . .

—The State will ensure public ownership and maximum profit by regrouping railways and airlines.

—-Québec's merchant and fishing fleets are ill-equipped and decrepit; Independent Québec will initiate a vast shipbuilding program, in order to render these industries profitable and to improve the living conditions of those living by them.

In addition, the St. Lawrence will be made navigable all year long.

AGRICULTURE

After Independence has been achieved, the government will apply a coherent agricultural policy, putting an end to the old parties' semblance of action that never has been able to pull agriculture out of its doldrums; the Parti Québécois will establish an over-all policy based on two principles: that agriculture is an industry like any other and consequently must adapt to concentration and modern food commerce techniques; secondly, that the cooperative formula is one of the prime movers of tomorrow's agriculture . . . .

ASSOCIATION WITH CANADA

A **Common Market** offers undoubted advantages: by increasing partner-countries markets, it allows each to specialize in particular fields.

Common Currency means that Quebecers and Canadians will use the same currency. One of the advantages of this formula is the fact that it ensures more stable currency, because more widely used and resting on a broader economic base.

However, agreement on details of an association with Canada is not an essential condition of Québec's accession to its sovereignty. In fact, if negotiations were to fail, or if the agreement outlined was not really to Québec's advantage, a sovereign government would negotiate a fair distribution of federal institutions, forge its own monetary tools and, eventually, enter into economic agreements with other countries . . . .

WAGES AND TAXES

Decent salaries and a fairer taxation . . . The minimum wage will be raised to $2 an hour for all categories of employees throughout Québec. Later, this minimum wage will be adjusted annually, taking into account gains made by unions and the best-organized sectors. In order to meet the real needs of the under-privileged, sovereign Québec will provide a guaranteed minimum income for all.

Independent Québec will also correct present fiscal injustices inflicted on those earning small and medium salaries.

Consequently:

—the sales or consumer tax will be abolished on all basic essential products and will apply only to luxury items and services;

—the school tax will be abolished: the government will finance most school services;

—capital gains will be taxed: moreover, a special tax will be imposed on land speculation profits;

—spouses' income will be taxed as single income but money spent for children's nurseries will be tax deductible.

FAMILY POLICY

—A new family legislation will be enacted and family courts established.

—A new family allowance system will be created with rates varying according to the number and the ages of the children.

As citizens of Québec, women will have equal rights, specifically with regard to wage parity; equal salary for equal work.

—The State will pay an allowance to married women without paid jobs, as well as to widows, unwed or deserted mothers.

—Community nurseries and training for family aids will be encouraged.

—Family planning services wil be supported.

Older citizens will be granted allowances enabling them to live decently.

—Home care service for the sick will be organized.

LABOR

Legislation will be amended in order to ensure complete protection of the worker. Steps will be taken to help solve the unemployment problem. An inventory will be regularly and systematically kept of available manpower and student population, as well as of the needs of the labor market. A radical reorganization of employment offices will be undertaken. . . .

The government will encourage labor organizations and ensure full protection of the right of association.

HOUSING

—Construction of low-rent family housing will become a priority.

—Progressive nationalization of urban land to ensure an effective housing policy.

—Relocation of displaced tenants in urban renewal projects.

—Extension of the Rent Board jurisdiction to all municipalities.

HEALTH

A Public Board will be set up to administer a complete, universal and compulsory health insurance scheme that will cover all medical and surgical, dental, eye and psychiatric care, as well as the purchase of drugs and prothesis.

Moreover:

—All hospitals will become non-profit institutions.

—Community clinics, regional hospitals and specialized treatment centres will be set up.

—Doctors will be paid on a salary basis, taking into account the cost of living and the services rendered.

—Manufacturing, distribution, advertising and prices of pharmaceutical products will be controlled by a state board.

CONSUMER'S PROTECTION

After independence the State will intervene vigorously to stop any practice that threatens to increase unduly the cost of day-to-day consumer products, and to check abuses from finance and advertising companies. . . .

—A public board will be created to administer a complete and compulsory system of automobile insurance.

LANGUAGE

In independent Québec, French will become the only official language. A law will make the use of French obligatory in all business. Collective agreements will be negotiated and written in French.

Immigrants will be required to pass an examination in French to obtain their citizenship and will have to send their children to French schools.

On the other hand, the Parti Québécois will respect the rights of English-speaking citizens who settled in Québec before independence by maintaining an English public school sector which will receive grants on a percentage of population basis. French will be taught efficiently in English schools.

EDUCATION

To complete the school reform so dearly undertaken, the public system will be free up to and including university level. A system of living allowances for students and eventually a pre-salary plan will be set up.

Regional school boards will administer both primary and secondary schools. The Parti Québécois favors creation of a network of unified school boards on the Island of Montréal, responsible for religious and neutral education in French and English, co-ordinated at the top by a representative school development council.

POPULAR CULTURE

. . . the State will establish a national broadcasting network, independent of government, whose standards will be high. It will create a national centre responsible for encouraging film production. It will constitute a special court to deal with questions related to mass media operations, objectivity of information and freedom of expression.

POLITICAL REGIME

In order to strike a balance between efficient government and genuine democracy, independent Québec will be a presidential parliamentary republic. The head of State, the President, will be elected by universal suffrage for five years and the Prime Minister will be chosen from among National Assembly members.

The present voting system will be corrected so as to elect some representatives to the National Assembly by proportional balloting.

National, municipal and school electoral laws will be standardized, the electoral map will be revised regularly, and voters will have a voter's card to identify them accurately at the polls.

As for political parties they will be taken away from big business and patronage promoters: political parties will be required to submit public annual financial statements and reveal their sources of income.

PUBLIC ADMINISTRATION

The government will form its own efficient democratic public administration so that citizens will be able to participate fully in developing national policies. Regional communities will be set up with elected directors, and decentralized government offices opened in all regions. A civil service re-organization will be undertaken to meet acceptable standards of cost and efficiency.

JUSTICE

Changes will be brought to the administration of justice to render it modern, equal for all and available to all. A continuing commission to revise laws will be created to adapt legislation periodically to social change.

—Creation of family courts dealing with questions of marriage, children and deliquency.

—Creation of a Superior Council of Justice that will, among other duties, prepare a list of candidates for appointment as judges.

—Creation of a public judicial service that will provide individuals with lawyers' assistance for both civil and criminal cases, free of charge.

—The government will compensate victims of criminal acts.

FOREIGN POLICY

On attaining independence, Québec will reaffirm its rights to all our territory, including Labrador and islands off the coast of New Québec. The nation will take its place among the free nations of the world and will seek admission to the United Nations. It will pursue a policy of peace and enter into economic and cultural relationship with other nations.

THE LIBERAL PLATFORM, 1970*

ROBERT BOURASSA

Here is what our team wants to do for you . . .
   —first priority: create 100,000 new jobs in 1971
   —reduce the school tax
   —have a scaled sales tax aiming at exempting consumer goods
   —pass a law permitting the annulment of contracts entered into under pressure
   —reduce income tax on small wage-earners
   —abolish the law allowing municipalities to tax tenants
   —construct low-cost housing
   —increase payments to widows and disabled persons
   —create community centres for families
   —inaugurate maternity-leave and establish children's care centres.
   These are only some extracts from our program. . . .
Quebec: To work! Vote Liberal!

*Translation by the editor of an advertisement for the Liberal Party, April 25, 1970.

QUEBEC — PROVINCIAL ELECTION RESULTS, 1960, 1962, 1966, 1970

Party	1960 Popular Vote	1960 Percent of Popular Vote	1960 Seats Won	1962 Popular Vote	1962 Percent of Popular Vote	1962 Seats Won	1966 Popular Vote	1966 Percent of Popular Vote	1966 Seats Won	1970 Popular Vote	1970 Percent of Popular Vote	1970 Seats Won
Liberal	1,077,135	51.4	52	1,205,253	56.4	63	1,095,212	47.4	50	1,298,386	45	72
Union Nationale	977,318	46.6	42	900,817	42.2	31	943,778	40.8	56	563,331	20	17
RIN	—	—	—	—	—	—	128,275	5.5	0	—	—	—
RN	—	—	—	—	—	—	73,015	3.2	0	—	—	—
Parti Québécois	—	—	—	—	—	—	—	—	—	645,488	23	7
Créditiste	—	—	—	—	—	—	—	—	—	336,602	10.6	12
Others	42,144	2.0	1	30,711	1.4	1	72,284	3.1	2	20,293	1.4	
Totals	2,096,597		95	2,136,781		95	2,312,564		108	2,864,100		108

Compiled by the editor from newspaper returns, on the basis of 99.9 percent of the polls having reported in 1966 and 1970. RIN is the abbreviation of le Rassemblement pour l'Indépendance Nationale, and RN for le Ralliement National. The turnout of voters was 79.6 percent in 1962, 74 percent in 1966, and 82 percent in 1970. Results in 1966 adjusted to include corrections from recounts up to June 20, and in 1970 to include corrections from recounts up to May 5.

BIBLIOGRAPHY

(N.B.: The *C.J.P.S.* commenced publishing in its issue of Vol. I, No. 1, March, 1968, pp. 107-118, an extensive Bibliography on "Contemporary Quebec" which it said would be continued in subsequent issues.)

Allard, M., *The Last Chance, The Canadian Constitution and French Canadians,* Quebec, Editions Ferland, 1964.

d'Allemagne, A., *Le colonialisme au Québec,* Montréal, Editions Renaud et Bray, 1966.

Barbeau, R., *Le Québec, est-il une colonie?* Montréal, Editions de l'homme, 1962.

Bergeron, G., *Le Canada français après deux siècles de patience,* Paris, Seuil, 1967.

Bonenfant, J. C., "Le bicaméralisme dans le Québec," *C.J.E.P.S.,* Vol. XXIX, No. 4, November, 1963.

Bonenfant, J. C., and Falardeau, J. C., "Cultural and Political Implications of French Canadian Nationalism," *Canadian Historical Association Annual Report,* Ottawa, 1946.

Bourgault, P., *Québec Quitte ou Double,* Montréal, Ferron, 1970.

Brady, A., "Quebec and Canadian Federalism," *C.J.E.P.S.,* Vol. XXV, No. 3, August, 1959.

Brichant, A., *Option Canada: The Economic Implications of Separatism for the Province of Quebec,* Montreal, The Canada Committee, 1968.

Canada, *A Preliminary Report of the Royal Commission on Bilingualism and Biculturalism,* Ottawa, Queen's Printer, 1965.

Canadian Broadcasting Corporation, *Quebec: Year Eight,* Glendon College Forum, Toronto, C.B.C., 1968.

Chaput, M., *Why I am a Separatist,* Toronto, Ryerson, 1962.

Chaput-Rolland, S., *My Country: Canada or Québec,* Toronto, Macmillan, 1966.

Cook, R., *Canada and the French-Canadian Question,* Toronto, Macmillan, 1966.

Cook, R., (ed.), *French-Canadian Nationalism,* Toronto, Macmillan, 1969.

Corbett, E. M., *Quebec Confronts Canada,* Toronto, Copp Clark, 1967.

Cohen, R. I., *Quebec Votes,* Montreal, Saje Publications, 1965.

Desbarats, P., *The State of Quebec,* Toronto, McClelland and Stewart, 1965.

Dion, G., "Secularization in Quebec," *Journal of Canadian Studies,* Vol. III, No. 1, February, 1968.

Dooley, D. J., "Quebec and the Future of Canada," *The Review of Politics,* Vol. XXVII, No. 1, January, 1965.

Dumont, F., et Martin, Y., *Situation de la recherche sur le Canada français,* Québec, les Presses de l'Université Laval, 1962.

Forsey, E. A., "Canada: Two Nations or One?" *C.J.E.P.S.,* Vol. XXVIII, No. 4, November, 1962.

Forsey, E. A., "The B.N.A. Act and Biculturalism," *Q.Q.,* Vol. LXXI, No. 2, Summer, 1964.

Garigue, P., *L'option politique du Canada français,* Montréal, Editions du lévrier, 1963.

Garigue, P., *Bibliographie du Québec, 1955-1965,* Montréal, les Presses de l'Université de Montréal, 1967.

Gélinas, A., "Les parlementaires et l'administration publique au Québec," *C.J.P.S.,* Vol. I, No. 2, June, 1968.

Gérin-Lajoie, P., *Pourquoi le bill 60,* Montréal, Editions du jour, 1963.

Gow, J. I., "Les Québecois, la guerre et la paix, 1945-60," *C.J.P.S.,* Vol. III, No. 1, March, 1970.

Grant, D., (ed.), *Quebec Today,* Toronto, University of Toronto Press, 1960.

Guindon, H., "Social Unrest, Social Class, and Quebec's Bureaucratic Revolution," *Q.Q.,* Vol. LXXI, No. 2, Summer, 1964.

Groupe des Recherches Sociales, *Les électeurs Québecois,* Montréal, 1960.

Gzowski, P., "This is the True Strength of Separation," *Maclean's,* Nov. 2, 1963.

Johnson, Daniel, *Egalité ou indépendance,* Les éditions renaissance, 1965.

Jones, R., *Community in Crisis—French-Canadian Nationalism in Perspective,* Toronto, McClelland and Stewart, 1967.

Jutras, R., *Québec libre,* Montréal, Les éditions actualité, 1965.

Keyfitz, N., "Canadians and Canadiens," *Q.Q.,* Vol. LXX, No. 2, Summer, 1963.

Kwavnick, D., "The Roots of French-Canadian Discontent," *C.J.E.P.S.,* Vol. XXXI, No. 4, November, 1965.

Lamontagne, L., *Le Canada français d'aujourd'hui,* Toronto, University of Toronto Press, 1970.

Laurendeau, A., *et al., Proceedings of Seminar on French Canada,* Montreal, Montreal Star, 1963.

Laurin, C., *Ma traversée du Québec,* Montréal, Les éditions du jour, 1970.

Lévesque, R., *Option Québec,* Montréal, Les éditions de l'homme, 1968. (English edition, Toronto, McClelland and Stewart, 1968.)

Lévesque, R., *La souveraineté et l'économie,* Montréal, Les éditions du jour, 1970.

Lévesque, R., *La solution: le programme du Parti Québécois,* Montréal, Les éditions du jour, 1970.

Levitt, J., (ed.), *Henri Bourassa on Imperialism and Biculturalism, 1900-1918,* Toronto, Copp Clark, 1970.

MacRae, C. F., (ed.), *French Canada Today,* Report of the Mount Allison 1961 Summer Institute, Sackville, 1961.

McRae, K. D., "The Structure of Canadian History," in Hartz, L., *The Founding of New Societies,* Toronto, Longmans, 1964.

Marier, R., "Les objectifs sociaux du Québec," *C.P.A.,* Vol. XII, No. 2, Summer, 1969.

Meyers, H. B., *The Quebec Revolution,* Montreal, Harvest House, 1964.

Oliver, M., "Quebec and Canadian Democracy," *C.J.E.P.S.,* Vol. XXIII, No. 4, November, 1957.

Orban, E., *Le conseil législatif de Québec,* Montréal, Bellarmin, 1967.

Orban, E., "La fin du bicaméralisme au Québec," *C.J.P.S.,* Vol. II, No. 3, September, 1969.

Paré, G., *Au-delà du séparatisme,* Montréal, Collection les idées du jour, 1966.

Parti Pris, *Les Québecois,* Paris, Maspéro, 1967.

Premier Congrès des Affaires Canadiennes, *The Canadian Experiment, Success or Failure?,* Québec, Les Presses de l'Université Laval, 1962.

Québec, *Le rapport de la commission royale d'enquête sur l'enseignement,* (le rapport Parent), Québec, L'imprimeur de la reine, 1963-1966, 3 vols.

Québec, *Le rapport de la commission royale d'enquête sur la fiscalité,* (le rapport Bélanger), Québec, l'imprimeur de la reine, 1966.

Quebec, *Report of the Royal Commission of Inquiry on Constitutional Problems* (Tremblay Report), Quebec, 1956, 4 vols.

Rassemblement pour l'indépendance nationale, *Programme politique,* Montréal, 1965, (mimeographed).

Raynauld, A., "Les implications économiques de l'option Québec," *Le Devoir,* 24 avril, 1970.

Rioux, M., (ed.), *L'église et le Québec,* [Les textes du réunion de l'Institut Canadien des affaires Publiques, 1961], Montréal, Les éditions du jour, 1961.

Rioux, M., and Martin, Y., *French-Canadian Society,* Toronto, McClelland and Stewart, 1964.

Scott, F., and Oliver, M., (eds.), *Quebec States her Case,* Toronto, Macmillan of Canada, 1964.

Séguin, M., "Genèse et historique de l'idée séparatiste au Canada français," *Laurentie,* no. 119, 1962.

Siegfried, A., *The Race Question in Canada,* with an Introduction by F. H. Underhill, Toronto, McClelland and Stewart, 1966, (reprinted from 1906).

Sloan, T., *Quebec, The Not-So-Quiet Revolution,* Toronto, Ryerson, 1965.

La Société St. Jean Baptiste de Montréal, *Le fédéralisme, l'acte de l'amérique du nord britannique et les Canadiens français,* Mémoire au comité parlementaire de la constitution du gouvernement du Québec, Montréal, Les éditions de l'agence Duvernay, 1964.

Troisième Congrès des Affaires Canadiennes, *Les nouveaux Québecois,* Québec, les Presses de l'Université Laval, 1964.

Trudeau, P. E., "Some Obstacles to Democracy in Quebec," *C.J.E.P.S.,* Vol. XXIV, No. 3, August, 1958.

Trudeau, P. E., *Federalism and the French Canadians,* Toronto, Macmillan, 1968.

Vallières, P., *Nègres blancs d'Amérique,* Montréal, Editions Parti Pris, 1968.

Wade, M., (ed.), *Canadian Dualism: Studies of French-English Relations,* Toronto, University of Toronto Press, 1960.

Wade, M., *The French-Canadian Outlook: A Brief account of the Unknown North Americans,* Toronto, McClelland and Stewart, 1964, (reprinted from 1946).

Wade, M., *The French Canadians,* Vol. I, 1760-1911, Vol. II, 1912-1967, Toronto, Macmillan, 1968.

FOUR
FEDERALISM

The Canadian federal system of government has been undergoing major transformations in recent years, as this chapter and Chapters 5 and 6 (on Regionalism and Federal-Provincial Financial Relations) will demonstrate. The fact that an additional chapter has been added to this edition on regionalism gives some indication of the increasing importance of local growth.

The recent period has been characterized by a series of Federal-Provincial Constitutional Conferences, brought on in large part by Quebec's demands for a new constitution but also by pressure from other provinces to modify the constitution to suit their new needs. One change that has been accomplished already is the Trudeau government's enactment of French and English as the two official languages of Canada. The statute passed in 1969 creating two official languages and providing for bilingual districts and a languages commissioner is reproduced here in its relevant parts. Not all of the provinces greeted this alteration with enthusiasm. To date only New Brunswick has declared itself to be bilingual also in provincial respects. Some premiers had strong and reasoned criticisms of the Act, and Premier Bennett's objections are reprinted here as a sample of such provincial reserve.

Professor Brady's article points out that there have been contradictory trends in Canadian federalism since the Second World War towards centralization and decentralization. For an article on this subject by J. A. Corry, see the first edition of this book, pp. 26-40. The Hon. Jean-Luc Pépin, who was formerly a professor of political science and is now a minister in the federal government, outlines in his article the major premises, as he sees them, of the concept of "cooperative federalism." This theme is carried over in the passage quoted here from the federal government's working paper submitted to the Second Constitutional Conference held in February, 1969. In this paper the federal government under the prime minister's name gives its views on the desirable nature of a new Canadian constitution. The synopsis from the *Report on Intergovernmental Liaison on Fiscal and Economic Matters* proposes the creation of certain specific machinery to make cooperative federalism a reality. Finally, the speech by Mr. Trudeau, which was given first in March, 1966, sums up his philosophy — and to a large extent the philosophy of the era — on the subject of federalism. It is a spirited defence of federalism rather than of centralization.

These selections, which are, of course, only a sample of the writing of the period on the subject, indicate that the major trend in federalism in recent years has been away from centralization towards localism of various kinds: provincial, regional, and municipal. This development is reflected in the bibliography, which also lists separately the federal government's working papers submitted to recent constitutional conferences (Current Constitutional Documentation). The provincial sources are too numerous to list, but should be consulted as well. One should note too the bibliography in the following chapter on regionalism.

TWO OFFICIAL LANGUAGES*

17-18 ELIZ. II, C. 54

[Assented to 9th July, 1969]

An Act respecting the status of the official languages of Canada.

Her Majesty, by and with the advice and consent of the Senate and House of Commons of Canada, enacts as follows:

Short Title

1. This Act may be cited as the *Official Languages Act*.

Declaration of Status of Languages

2. The English and French languages are the official languages of Canada for all purposes of the Parliament and Government of Canada, and possess and enjoy equality of status and equal rights and privileges as to their use in all the institutions of the Parliament and Government of Canada.

Statutory and Other Instruments

3. Subject to this Act, all instruments in writing directed to or intended for the notice of the public, purporting to be made or issued by or under the authority of

*From the *Statutes of Canada, 1969*, Ottawa, Queen's Printer, 1969. By permission.

the Parliament or Government of Canada or any judicial, quasi-judicial or administrative body or Crown corporation established by or pursuant to an Act of the Parliament of Canada, shall be promulgated in both official languages.

•   •   •

Duties of Departments, etc., in Relation to Official Languages

9. (1) Every department and agency of the Government of Canada and every judicial, quasi-judicial or administrative body or Crown corporation established by or pursuant to an Act of the Parliament of Canada has the duty to ensure that within the National Capital Region, at the place of its head or central office in Canada if outside the National Capital Region, and at each of its principal offices in a federal bilingual district established under this Act, members of the public can obtain available services from and can communicate with it in both official languages. . . .

10. (1) Every department and agency of the Government of Canada and every Crown corporation established by or pursuant to an Act of the Parliament of Canada has the duty to ensure that, at any office, location or facility in Canada or elsewhere at which any services to the travelling public are provided or made available by it, or by any other person pursuant to a contract for the provision of such services entered into by it or on its behalf after the coming into force of this Act, such services can be provided or made available in both official languages. . . .

11. (1) Every judicial or quasi-judicial body established by or pursuant to an Act of the Parliament of Canada has, in any proceedings brought or taken before it, and every court in Canada has, in exercising in any proceedings in a criminal matter any criminal jurisdiction conferred upon it by or pursuant to an Act of the Parliament of Canada, the duty to ensure that any person giving evidence before it may be heard in the official language of his choice, and that in being so heard he will not be placed at a disadvantage by not being or being unable to be heard in the other official language.

(2) Every court of record established by or pursuant to an Act of the Parliament of Canada has, in any proceedings conducted before it within the National Capital Region or a federal bilingual district established under this Act, the duty to ensure that, at the request of any party to the proceedings, facilities are made available for the simultaneous translation of the proceedings, including the evidence given and taken, from one official language into the other except where the court, after receiving and considering any such request, is satisfied that the party making it will not, if such facilities cannot conveniently be made available, be placed at a disadvantage by reason of their not being available or the court, after making every reasonable effort to obtain such facilities, is unable then to obtain them.

(3) In exercising in any proceedings in a criminal matter any criminal jurisdiction conferred upon it by or pursuant to an Act of the Parliament of Canada, any court in Canada may in its discretion, at the request of the accused or any of them if there is more than one accused, and if it appears to the court that the proceedings can effectively be conducted and the evidence can effectively be given and taken

wholly or mainly in one of the official languages as specified in the request, order that, subject to subsection (1), the proceedings be conducted and the evidence be given and taken in that language.

(4) Subsections (1) and (3) do not apply to any court in which, under and by virtue of section 133 of *The British North America Act, 1867,* either of the official languages may be used by any person, and subsection (3) does not apply to the courts of any province until such time as a discretion in those courts or in the judges thereof is provided for by law as to the language in which, for general purposes in that province, proceedings may be conducted in civil causes or matters. . . .

Federal Bilingual Districts

12. In accordance with and subject to the provisions of this Act and the terms of any agreement that may be entered into by the Governor in Council with the government of a province as described in section 15, the Governor in Council may from time to time by proclamation establish one or more federal bilingual districts (hereinafter in this Act called "bilingual districts") in a province, and alter the limits of any bilingual districts so established.

13. (1) A bilingual district established under this Act shall be an area delineated by reference to the boundaries of any or all of the following, namely, a census district established pursuant to the *Statistics Act,* a local government or school district, or a federal or provincial electoral district or region.

(2) An area described in subsection (1) may be established as a bilingual district or be included in whole or in part within a bilingual district if

(a) both of the official languages are spoken as a mother tongue by persons residing in the area; and

(b) the number of persons who are in the linguistic minority in the area in respect of an official language spoken as a mother tongue is at least ten percent of the total number of persons residing in the area.

(3) Notwithstanding subsection (2), where the number of persons in the linguistic minority in an area described in subsection (1) is less than the percentage required under subsection (2), the area may be established as a bilingual district if before the coming into force of this Act the services of departments and agencies of the Government of Canada were customarily made available to residents of the area in both official languages.

•   •   •

Commissioner of Official Languages

19. (1) There shall be a Commissioner of Official Languages for Canada, hereinafter in this Act called the Commissioner.

(2) The Commissioner shall be appointed by Commission under the Great Seal after approval of the appointment by resolution of the Senate and House of Commons.

(3) Subject to this section, the Commissioner holds office during good behaviour for a term of seven years, but may be removed by the Governor in Council at any time on address of the Senate and House of Commons.

• • •

25. It is the duty of the Commissioner to take all actions and measures within his authority with a view to ensuring recognition of the status of each of the official languages and compliance with the spirit and intent of this Act in the administration of the affairs of the institutions of the Parliament and Government of Canada and, for that purpose, to conduct and carry out investigations either on his own initiative or pursuant to any complaint made to him and to report and make recommendations with respect thereto as provided in this Act.

OBJECTIONS TO THE ACT*

W. A. C. BENNETT

British Columbia recognizes that the English and French cultures and languages are the predominant ones in Canadian society today, and every effort should be made to encourage, cultivate, and foster them—not from the point of view that Confederation consisted of a union of two founding races or cultures, because British Columbia does not believe history supports that view, but rather because of their intrinsic worth and the benefits to nationhood to be gained by doing so. Having said that, we also recognize that there are six million Canadians whose ethnic origin is neither English nor French. We do not intend to see these people made second-class citizens by constitutional means.

The question, then, is: What are the best means to foster and develop those ethnic and cultural diversities with which Canada is blessed? The cold legal language of a constitution would not, in British Columbia's opinion, be the means at all. In point of fact, the constitution has little effect on how people live in so far as language and culture are concerned. Our linguistic and cultural attitudes are tempered not by legal considerations embodied in a constitution, but in the final analysis reflect the personal habits, attitudes, and practical necessities of the population of the nation. To the extent the first report of the Royal Commission on Bilingualism and Biculturalism reflects these attitudes, we are in agreement with it.

. . . The action the Commission recommended in the first report was not, for the most part, to take the form of constitutional amendment, but rather was to take the form of legislative action in those particular jurisdictions in which the number of French-speaking Canadians made action appropriate. In British Columbia there are

*From *Proposals of the Province of British Columbia on the Constitution of Canada,* December, 1968, submitted to the Second Meeting of the Constitutional Conference, Ottawa, February 10-12, 1969. By permission of the Premier of British Columbia.

fewer citizens *per capita* whose mother tongue is French now than there were when British Columbia entered Confederation in 1871. There are other Provinces in similar circumstances. To provide as a constitutional guarantee the right to speak English and French is as inappropriate in those parts of Canada as to have a requirement that all Canadians speak the language of the native Indians, who were the original founders of the country. . . . Out of approximately forty Superior and County Court Judges in our Province I doubt whether any could conduct a trial in French, and out of a practising legal profession of fifteen hundred, not more than a handful could plead their case in French. Moreover, the lack of sufficient interpreters is also a very real problem. . . .

British Columbia is concerned about other implications of [the Official Languages Act]. We fear that its provisions will "close the door" to unilingual English-speaking Canadians from entry into the Federal Civil Service and its agencies and considerably curtail the promotion possibilities of present-day unilingual English-speaking Civil Servants. It is perhaps too early to support those fears with firm statistics, but it is reported from the statistics that are available that there has been a sharp increase in the number of bilingual appointments at the upper levels of the Civil Service. For example, among a sample of 401 Civil Service appointments in the $10,000 to $15,000 range last year, the percentage of bilingual appointments was 24 percent. So far this year the percentage is 31 percent. Above $15,000 the percentage has jumped from 25 percent last year to 33 percent this year. A much more significant trend is visible among "administrative trainees," usually university graduates, in training for senior positions in the government service. In 1965, out of 108 such trainees hired, only 17 percent were bilingual, whereas so far this year, 171, or 46 percent, are bilingual. Since the majority of the residents of Western Canada do not speak French, nor do they have the opportunity to do so, it is obvious that they are placed at a decided disadvantage from entry into the Federal Civil Service. . . .

CONTRADICTORY POST-WAR TRENDS IN CANADIAN FEDERALISM*

ALEXANDER BRADY

Since 1945 the Canadian federation has undergone more constant and profound change than in any two decades of its history. Its present problems derive from varied political and social forces generated largely by the Second World War and its aftermath: industrialization quickened by war and technology, the accelerated rate of population growth, the wider acceptance of the positive state in economic life, rapid exploitation of natural resources throughout the provinces, and the dynamism of a fresh and potent French-Canadian nationalism.

*From an unpublished paper written in 1966 by Dr. A. Brady, Professor Emeritus of the University of Toronto. By permission of the author.

An immediate effect of the Second World War was to magnify the ambition and multiply the tasks of the national government in achieving economic stability and social welfare. The wartime leaders in Ottawa acquired and exercised decisive power in marshalling human and material resources for national survival. Their authority then resembled that of men ruling a unitary state. Without ignoring the fact of federalism, they were under less necessity than in peacetime to accept its restraints. They could promptly match plans with revenue, for in the emergency they leaped over obstacles that hitherto had hampered federal ministers. In 1914, the national government acquired with provincial consent the exclusive right to impose the lucrative personal and corporate income taxes as if, in the words of Finance Minister Ilsley, "the provinces were not in these fields".

It was doubtless inevitable that leaders who had successfully geared a government for national goals in war should also want to gear it for national goals in peace. The current climate of opinion encouraged them. Everywhere in the western world the concept of national economic planning was in the air. Keynesian ideas on contra-cyclical budgets appealed to practical policy-makers seeking economic stability. The new bureaucracy fashioned in wartime Ottawa perceived that rising productivity elevated the standard of living and increased the capacity of the public to pay for extra welfare measures. It diligently worked out plans to distribute throughout the country, under federal direction, the expected increments of income. Likewise pressures from a host of varied interest groups furthered the same end. Federal politicians quickly appreciated the electoral advantages of employing the national treasury to satisfy the new and avid appetites for welfare services. Aware that federalism imposed restraints on what parliament at Ottawa could accomplish they hoped nevertheless to establish for themselves a more active role in economic and social policy. Even before the end of the war (in 1944) they initiated family allowances, the boldest and most costly welfare venture hitherto attempted in Canada. Soon they were sponsoring a proliferation of federal conditional grants and shared-cost programs to further national standards and circumvent the limits on federal legislative powers. These new projects involved the expansion of federal activity into areas of exclusive provincial jurisdiction, such as natural resources, social welfare, local government, highway construction, and education.

This vigorous post-war initiative of the national government, although at first encouraged by the less affluent provinces, soon came under provincial challenge. The attempt of the government after 1945 to operate a renewable rental system for the basic taxes on personal income, corporations, and inheritance failed to achieve a satisfactory fiscal equilibrium. Quebec repudiated the rental device. Up to 1952 Ontario did likewise, eventually accepted it as a stop-gap, but still remained convinced that it was too inflexible for a time of peace and dynamic change. Whenever the agreements were up for renewal all provinces out of hard necessity eagerly contended for higher payments from the federal treasury. Rapid provincial development and population growth made rental arrangements unstable. Under the compulsions of an industrial society the provinces were driven to ever greater expenditures on the many services for which under the British North America Act they were accountable. They needed augmented revenues to meet the soaring costs of education at different levels, the medley of health and welfare expenditures in the burgeoning metropolitan areas, the constant demand for highways and more highways, and the urgent requests for projects of conservation and water control. It now seems ironic that some fathers of Confederation had viewed provincial powers as relatively unimportant. . . .

COOPERATIVE FEDERALISM*

JEAN-LUC PEPIN

To my mind, cooperative federalism is the best answer to the two main political problems which Canada must solve to guarantee her political future: the problem of relations between the central government and the regional governments, that of Quebec in particular; the problem of relations between French-speaking and English-speaking Canadians. These two problems are intimately related.

Any political system involves: 1) a philosophy that is a concept of man, society and political action . . .; 2) a technique of government. Technique is useless without philosophy . . . and vice versa.

Cooperative federalism does not escape this rule.

THE PHILOSOPHY OF COOPERATIVE FEDERALISM

. . . First of all, . . . I would like to warn my fellow French Canadians against the *cult* (I mean the excessive concern) for the particularities of race, language, culture, nation and state. . . . All these particularities which some people delight in over-stressing, in dramatizing (to such an extent that we are given the impression that, for example, between the French culture and the English culture there is a gap which cannot be bridged, that English institutions are totally incompatible with the French mentality), . . . have their importance, but only a relative one: they are useful only inasmuch as they serve man. . . . There should be no question of opposing cultures, languages, and nations within Canada. We should rather seek

*From a translation in *The Canadian Forum,* Vol. 44, No. 527, December, 1964, pp. 206-210 of a speech to the Conference de l'Institut Canadien des Affaires Publiques, September 12, 1964, by the author, who was then the Member of Parliament for Drummond-Arthabaska and Parliamentary Secretary to the Minister of Trade and Commerce, and who is now the Minister of Industry, Trade and Commerce. By permission of the author and the publisher. Italics are the author's.

to link them, achieving a synthesis mindful of the rights and obligations of each of them.

•   •   •

May I also raise my voice against "Quebec sovereignty", a concept which stems from the old principle of nationalities of the nineteenth century according to which every nation, every association which is sociologically homogeneous is entitled to political independence. . . .

One last excerpt from my creed. It has almost become fashionable in our province to denounce in the name of purity, compromises, pragmatism, package deals, "constitutional laxity" and "political horsetrading," to quote Jean-Marc Léger, as if all this were immoral and disgusting.

You know as well as I do, ladies and gentlemen, that politics, in a federal state as in a unitary state, in a state with a mainly written constitution as in a state with a mainly customary constitution, in a Latin society as in an Anglo-Saxon society, yesterday in Athens and Rome and today in Istanbul and in the Vatican, politics, I say is the art of achieving the greatest possible common good for the whole community by applying wisdom, caution, and also charity, to the solution of conflicts which are *unavoidable,* since we are all stained by the original sin, in the relations between individuals and groups.

Under these conditions, the political man, the politician, . . . improvises, must improvise and cannot help improvising. . . . He is constantly looking for equilibrium, the immediate solutions which do not contradict long-term objectives, the happy medium (where Aristotle places virtue) between equally inaccessible extremes. Negotiation, haggling, compromise, package deals . . . are his stock in trade. As every good craftsman, he is proud of his tools. . . .

•   •   •

THE TECHNIQUE OF COOPERATIVE FEDERALISM

Cooperative federalism is also a set of rules, techniques, and government institutions.

1. Economic decentralization and bi-nationalism.

Cooperative federalism can be defined on the basis of a few forceful ideas. Some of them are *philosophical*: . . . Others are related to *economy*. For example, there is no doubt that the recent popularity of economic decentralization helps to justify cooperative federalism, which advocates a much greater dose of political decentralization. In the *cultural* field, the vitality of French culture in general (I am thinking especially of technology) and the progress of science, arts and letters in French Canada contribute towards supporting the political arguments of Quebec.

In the *socio-political* field, *the theory of two nations,* whether true or false in the eyes of history, is now recognized by the best Canadian constitutionalists and political leaders in both nations; Mr. Pearson first, Mr. Diefenbaker, somewhat behind. Canadian society is bi-national; the Canadian state is the result of at least a moral agreement between the two founding nations.

Here is a fact which, if not new, has at least been recently accepted. Henceforth, the question runs as follows: *How shall we transpose to the Government level this socio-political reality of bi-nationalism?* In other words, how will the presence of a French-Canadian nation affect the rules, the techniques and the political institutions of Canada?

Some people do not want such a transposition: the *separatists,* English- and French-speaking; some deny it partially: the bi-statists and the *confederalists*; some believe that this transposition is possible within the framework of a revised Canadian federal state: these are the *cooperative federalists.* We note that there are among the defenders of this idea varying views as to the methods and amount of economic and political decentralization which are possible and the methods and desirable amount of recognition of the French reality and the Quebec reality.

2. *"To each level of Government according to its aptitudes"*

As "Canada is a vast continental domain—too big, too spread out, too cut up to be governed exclusively, or even dominantly, from one centre" (Mr. Pearson, May 26, 1964), cooperative federalism proclaims, against separatists and centralizers alike, *the necessity of two orders of government in Canada.* But how shall be divided the responsibilities between them?

The traditional *criterion*, the 1867 criterion, of the division of functions—that is, matters of general interest will be attended to by the central government and matters of local interest, by the provincial governments, is not worth much. Everything can in some way be of general interest: agriculture, highways, education . . . temperance!

We must therefore replace the former criterion with two others drawn from common sense and from the Act of '67: *1) the criterion of aptitude*: We must allot to each order of government what it is particularly able to do well in principle and in the present situation. . . . *2) the criterion of agreement between the two nations*: we must not assign to the central government matters over which there is clear-cut dissension between the two nations. The Report of the Tremblay Commission also stated this principle, extrapolating it from the Act of 1867. . . .

3. *Unavoidable overlapping, interdependence*

Without denying the usefulness of dividing as accurately as possible the duties between Ottawa and the provinces, we must observe the unavoidable overlapping of central and regional authorities in most segments of government activity, especially in a period of interventionism like the present one and the next one. I hear Messrs. Lesage, Kierans and others assert that the provinces should participate in the determination of Canada's tariff policies, in her transportation policy and even her monetary policy, her trade policy, her tax policy, etc. I agree wholeheartedly. Cooperative federalism leaves room for consultation, cooperation and coordination even in these traditionally federal fields. I could read you, only as an example, a speech made by Mr. Sharp and speak to you of the Federal-Provincial conferences on international trade promotion, where the participation of the provinces is not only accepted but solicited. However, the provinces, especially Quebec, cannot claim a kind of right to be consulted in sectors of jurisdiction which are considered as "exclusively" *federal* (i.e. monetary policy) while refusing a similar right to Ottawa in sectors of jurisdiction which are considered to be "exclusively" *provincial* (i.e. highways).

The inevitable overlapping, the overall interdependence, is thus a reality which has to be acknowledged.

Hence, it is not possible anymore, in my view, to divide clearly and once and for all the fields of activity. *The sharing of power* between Ottawa and the provinces is no longer the sole major problem of Canadian federalism. The true key problems are: 1) the establishment of *priorities of action*: the decisions as to what must be done first and how, it being understood that everything cannot be done at the same time; 2) *pre-consultation and continuous cooperation* in the establishment of priorities of action as well as the implementation of measures which have been adopted jointly.

4. Provincial priorities

Another key proposition of cooperative federalism: the claim by the provinces, especially Quebec, and the acknowledgment by Ottawa of the priority, not in principle, but "actual" . . . i.e. in the social, economic and political situation in which we Canadians are now living, *of certain provincial requirements*: education, social security, highways and economic development. Once again I repeat, these priorities are essentially relative; the situation could change (unfortunately, a world war is not impossible), the order of priority also. But we can say that cooperative federalism *is essentially a decentralizing force,* that it brings about a certain decrease in Ottawa's role, at least the gradual withdrawal by the central government from essentially provincial sectors. Ottawa's offer to hand over to the provinces a large number of joint plans, announced today, is but one of several proofs.

5. The division of income: "to each according to its needs"

. . . *Tax decentralization is already a reality.* The provinces have recently obtained a large share of the individual income tax and of the estate tax. The equalization formula has been improved. Other federal laws: assistance for technical and vocational training, assistance to municipalities, youth allowances, the submission of federal crown corporations to provincial taxes, student loans, especially the transfer to the consenting provinces of certain *joint plans* with a corresponding share of the powers of taxation and, what is more important, the capitalization now contemplated for the pension fund, which will apparently make no less than $4 billion (and probably more) available to the provinces within the next ten years, . . . all this is contributing not only towards making funds but also additional powers available to the provinces. . . .

6. The repatriation of joint programs

Few commentators deny the theoretical unconstitutionality and the practical difficulties of several joint plans, although most of them recognize the past and future usefulness of the device "in certain circumstances" (Mr. Lesage). We have just said so: cooperative federalism recommends "that the provinces which so desire be entrusted with the full responsibilities of certain well-established programs which at any rate are presently administered by the provinces" (Mr. Gordon) and "which entail relatively stable, annual expenditures," with of course, the equivalent financial resources or better still the equivalent powers of taxation.

This very day, it was announced that twelve joint plans will be offered to the provinces.

Cooperative federalism also recommends that Ottawa should not introduce any more joint plans unless it has the provinces' consent.

7. *Cooperation and coordination*

As a result of all that we have said, cooperative federalism proclaims the necessity of consultation, cooperation and coordination on a permanent basis between the two levels of government. You will tell me that this principle was violated in some cases. That is true, and by both sides. However, the overall progress is no less evident. Mr. Lesage has acknowledged that there has never been so much cooperation between Ottawa and the provincial capitals as now. Agreed, but we must do better still. . .

In the event of irreparable conflicts of ideology or interests, cooperative federalism acknowledges that the provinces have: 1) a right of *option*, i.e., to a different method, more respectful of provincial autonomy, of putting into practice a law which stems mainly from the federal government; 2) the right of *contracting out*: i.e., the right to waive all participation in a federal-provincial plan (i.e. assistance to universities), without being penalized.

Instruments of coordination are already in place and others will be created to make common action more efficient: a federal-provincial secretariat, a joint economic committee, etc.

8. *The particular status of Quebec*

Cooperative federalism acknowledges the right of the French Canadians, a "minority not like the others," the right of Quebec "a province not like the others," to a particular status.

All we have just set forth makes possible a particular status for *Quebec* within Canadian federalism if, for example, it wants to take advantage of options, "contracting out," and withdrawal from joint plans.

Other questions will arise. I agree for my part that the lieutenant-governor could be appointed by the provincial governments; I am sure that the right of the provinces, especially Quebec, to diplomatic or quasi-diplomatic action within the purview of its traditional jurisdiction will soon be acknowledged.

The rights of *French Canadians* are partially acknowledged by the text of 1867; the only thing to do is to make the facts comply with this Act . . . and to draw from its texts certain implications. It is the purpose of the Laurendeau-Dunton Commission to have the French language acknowledged everywhere in Canada where this is possible; it is the objective of the Pearson government to have bilingualism recognized within the federal civil service. If they succeed, as I think they will, major constitutional amendments will have been achieved since Section 133 of the Act of 1867 does not go so far.

9. Constitutional pragmatism

A study of Canadian federalism shows that *circumstances* explain its original formulation as well as the subsequent changes, and that judicial interpretation, conventions of the constitution, ordinary legislation and in rare cases, formal amendment, have been used in the past to *legalize changes.*

From now on, we cannot rely too much on formal amendments and judicial interpretation; major changes present and future, are and will be legalized by constitutional practice and by ordinary acts adopted by the federal and by the provincial governments following consultation and federal-provincial agreements. For example, it should be observed that the recent tax arrangement between Ottawa and the provinces constitutes a *de facto* revision of sections 102 to 120 of the British North America Act.

At this time, a complete redrafting of the Act of 1867 seems to me, considering the present discussions and the nebulousness of the situation, not only impossible but dangerous even if cooperative federalism does not discard it for the future.

You will tell me that I am anglicized, that cooperative federalism is an Anglo-Saxon philosophy and technique. I will reply that even some great jurists of France do not think otherwise about the usefulness of written constitutional documents. We could benefit from reading the article written by George Burdeau in *Les Etudes en l'honneur d'Achille Mestre*, an article entitled: "A Survival: the Idea of a Constitution." . . . For Burdeau real powers exist which are infra, supra and para-constitutional, but which it is not possible to integrate perfectly in a constitutional text. He writes:

> Considering the forces of this type, it would seem that *the idea of the constitution is outmoded.* Politics is similar to an instinctive or internal function in that it admits only the law of possibility and requirements. The truth is that constitutions do not encompass the manifestations of political life. The latter evolves *independently of their provisions . . .*

Unfortunately, to my mind, too many French-Canadian politicians are suffering from *legalitis,* especially with regard to our constitution. They seem to want to settle problems by fabricating legislation. Fortunately, in practice, the pragmatism of the majority overrides them.

CONCLUSIONS

Thus, here are the key propositions, which I might use to define Canadian co-operative federalism:

(1) profitability, even from the economic standpoint, of economic and political decentralization;

(2) the existence of two nations and the necessity of transposing this fact to the political level;

(3) the division of taxation between the central and regional governments according to the principle "to each according to its ability" to find a better solution for such and such a problem;

(4) the unavoidable overlapping of activity between the two levels of government;

(5) the present "actual" priority of provincial authority in certain fields;

(6) the distribution of tax income and taxation powers between Ottawa and the provincial capitals according to the principle "to each level of government according to its requirements";

(7) the necessity of constant cooperation and coordination between the central and the regional governments;

(8) the particular status of the French Canadians and of Quebec;

(9) pragmatism, empiricism, in the legal formulation of the new system.

THE CONSTITUTION AND THE PEOPLE OF CANADA*

PIERRE ELLIOTT TRUDEAU

• • •

The first objective of Confederation should be to ensure that the community we have created in Canada is of a kind and a character which is consistent with the essential values and traditions of our people. This means, first and foremost, the maintenance through the Constitution of a democratic society, a society in which the ultimate sovereignty of Canada is to be found in the people which comprise it. It means that the whole of the Constitution and the institutions of government it creates ought to reflect and to protect those concepts of freedom, equality, and the dignity of the individual which surely characterize Canada.

This implies that the Constitution must also preserve the federal character of our country. For federalism has been devised for the very purpose of enabling the kind of diversity one finds in Canada to flourish within the bosom of a single and a united country. Federalism also protects the individual citizen from an undue concentration of power in the hands of a single government—a concentration such as to create the danger that individual fulfilment will be subordinated to some kind of monolithic authority.

*From the Federal Government's Working Paper of the same title, submitted under the Prime Minister's name to the Second Federal-Provincial Constitutional Conference, February 10-12, 1969, and published by the Queen's Printer, Ottawa. By permission of the Queen's Printer.

The first objective of Confederation the Government of Canada would propose, then, is:

To establish for Canada a federal system of government based on demo-cratic principles.

How this objective will be realized is to be judged by the character of the institutions of government which are created by the Constitution. The kind of federalism the governments of Canada favour will be reflected in their proposals as to the institutions of federalism in the central government, the division of the power to govern between the federal and provincial governments, and the role to be assigned to the respective governments in representing the interests and expectations of Canadians in different regions and linguistic communities of our country. The kind of democratic institutions wanted will be reflected in the character of the institutions of government proposed in a revised constitution—both those of the central government and those of the provinces. The democratic values of our society will also be reflected in the kinds of constitutional guarantees which are proposed for ensuring that government will remain an expression of the public will. The mechanics for achieving this end are taken for granted by most of us—universal suffrage, periodic elections, and annual meetings of legislative bodies—but they should surely be the subject of constitutional guarantees if this objective of the Constitution is to be achieved.

The second objective which the Government of Canada believes should be reflected in the Constitution has to do with the rights of individual Canadians, both in their relations to their governments, and in their relations to one another. The Government of Canada has already stated in its first statement of policy on the Constitution, and again affirms, its conviction that there should be constitutional guarantees ensuring that society, through its governments, will respect the rights of individual citizens. These should include the right of the individual to use English or French as he chooses in essential relationships with public institutions.

The second objective of Confederation should be, then, in the view of the Government of Canada:

To protect basic human rights, which shall include linguistic rights.

The third objective, in the view of the Government of Canada, should be the creation, the preservation, of a society in which the fulfilment of the individual is a primary goal. This goal, if it is to have any meaning, must embrace all aspects of individual development—economic, social and cultural—and it must apply to *all* Canadians.

The development of a country is usually thought of in global terms—in terms of the economic growth of the whole country and of its several sectors, and in terms of the social and cultural development which characterizes a flourishing society and gives it its special identity. In our view, however, economic, social and cultural development should be thought of primarily as the creation of opportunity for individual Canadians—the opportunity to realize their full potential. Secondly, this goal should be thought of in terms of the equalization of opportunity as among the regions of Canada. There is no room in our society for great or widening disparities —disparities as between the opportunities available to individual Canadians, or disparities in the opportunities or the public services available in the several regions of Canada.

It is with this perspective that the Government of Canada is proposing as the third objective for Confederation:

> *To promote national economic, social and cultural development, and the general welfare and equality of opportunity for all Canadians in whatever region they may live, including the opportunity for gainful work, for just conditions of employment, for an adequate standard of living, for security, for education, and for rest and leisure.*

This third objective, like the others, must find its realization through the institutions which are provided for in the Constitution. In this case we must look to the division of legislative power between the two orders of government, to provisions for effective intergovernmental consultation, and to the protection of language rights.

The Government of Canada must be given sufficient powers in the Constitution to enable it to stimulate and expand the economy, and to manage the economy in such a way as to maintain high levels of employment. It must have the power to co-operate with industry and labour so as to maximize the efficiency of the common Canadian market. It must be able to promote growth in all of the sectors and regions of the economy, if disparities in income and in rates of economic growth are to be diminished. It must have the power to redistribute income and to maintain reasonable levels of livelihood for individual Canadians, if the effects of regional disparities on individual citizens are to be minimized. The provincial governments in turn must have the power to promote and to rationalize the development of provincial or regional economies, in the context, of course, of the interests of other regions and of the economy as a whole. They must be able to provide an adequate standard of public services to their citizens and to support the incomes of those who are in need.

Similarly the Constitution should divide the powers to govern in such a way as to enable the Parliament of Canada to contribute to the social and cultural development of the country. The ties of nationhood, the bonds which unite Canadians, must constantly be renewed. New institutions of unity may be needed to replace those which brought Canadians together in the last century. The Government of Canada must have a role in such ventures of Canadian achievement and Canadian unity, if the election of a common Parliament by all Canadians is to have any meaning at all.

Provincial governments will contribute to this venture at the same time as they are contributing to the social and cultural development of their provinces and regions. For these two are not conflicting goals. As the several regions and cultures of Canada flourish, as her two main linguistic communities flourish, so Canada will flourish as well. It is necessary, therefore, that there be strong and effective provincial governments and that they have the capacity for providing those services which contribute most intimately to the direct development of their provinces.

. . . We recognize, of course, that in this complex age both orders of government will be involved, and that new approaches to intergovernmental co-operation will be required if Canadians are to be better served in their search for achievement and for excellence. The Constitution cannot provide all the detailed procedures for intergovernmental co-operation, though perhaps regular meetings of the federal and the provincial heads of government might be provided for constitutionally. What is required in addition is a new orientation to intergovernmental co-operation—a clearer definition of the roles of the two orders of government may well help to achieve this—a new orientation which would focus the attention of governments on the whole complex of public services and the whole of Canada's tax system, *as they affect the citizen*. This new orientation, this focus, is what federal-provincial relations must come to mean to the citizen, instead of the unhappy disputes which have persisted between governments during the post-war period as to the share of certain taxes which each government ought to get.

The fourth objective of Confederation has to do with Canada's place in the international community, and with the concern which Canadians are prepared to express for the well-being of people around the world. . . .

•   •   •

In this process of definition, we have proposed setting forth in the Constitution the relationships between the Head of State, the Governor General, the Prime Minister, the Privy Council, the Cabinet, and the Houses of Parliament. The conditions and means by which the Governor General, the Prime Minister and the Ministers assume and leave office would be defined for the first time. (Indeed, the very mention in the Constitution of the office of Prime Minister and of the Cabinet would be an innovation, as one may at present look in vain for any constitutional reference to them.) The principles of responsible government—including the requirement that every minister be or become a member of one of the Houses of Parliament, and that a ministry can survive only so long as it enjoys the confidence of the House of Commons—are also spelled out in our constitutional proposals. At the same time we would maintain those provisions which ensure representative government: the requirement of an annual session of Parliament, of universal suffrage in election of the House of Commons, and of elections at least once every five years. These are essential to the preservation of the democratic rights of all Canadians. . . .

We have also examined the existing Constitution to see if the institutions of the central government adequately reflect the equally important principles of federalism. We have given particular attention to the Senate and the Supreme Court: the former because it was originally designed in part to protect regional interests, the latter because it is the final interpreter of the Constitution whose decisions frequently affect both federal and provincial interests. . . .

REPORT ON INTERGOVERNMENTAL LIAISON ON FISCAL AND ECONOMIC MATTERS*

INSTITUTE OF INTERGOVERNMENTAL RELATIONS, QUEEN'S UNIVERSITY

A two-part continuing conference of the Prime Minister of Canada and provincial premiers should constitute the top level of the liaison structure between the federal and provincial governments.

The first ministers should meet in closed session at least once a year to examine matters of high policy. Regular open meetings should also be held to discuss broad matters "of principle and opinion."

Plenary conferences of prime ministers and premiers have become cumbersome in size. Discussions with both levels of government indicate strong support for smaller confidential meetings, "especially where negotiations are involved."

> . . . the advantages of public involvement in fundamental matters of national importance warrant further experience with direct access. There may be an additional bonus in that given such a forum, participants may feel less impelled to provide the public through the press with their own views for political purposes regardless of the effect such statements may have on the course of the discussions. We repeat, however, that we do not believe public meetings are the appropriate media for specific and detailed negotiations between interested parties.

The existing committee of finance ministers and provincial treasurers should operate primarily as a staff arm of the conference of first ministers.

Its basic purposes would be to advise on the harmonization of fiscal and economic policies and to deal with matters referred to it for action or advice.

It would examine fiscal and monetary problems, project long-term revenues and expenditures, develop long-term budgeting, and discuss expenditure control and effective revenue collection, public borrowing, budgetary accounting and financial statistics practices.

These responsibilities would encompass work of the existing Tax Structure Committee, which would cease to exist in separate form.

A further series of supporting "functional" committees of ministers from both levels of government would deal with these areas: Agriculture and rural development; labour, manpower and training; health; welfare; national resources; education, including manpower and training. Ministerial committees in some of these areas already exist.

At the official level, the most senior policy advisers of federal and provincial government departments would form a continuing committee in support of the first ministers' conference.

Duties would be altered for the existing continuing committee of officials on

---

*From a Synopsis provided with the Report of the same title as above, published by the Queen's Printer, Ottawa, 1968. By permission of the Queen's Printer.

fiscal and economic matters; it would be the working arm of the finance ministers' committee, becoming a clearinghouse for all technical matters of a fiscal and economic nature. The functional committees would be served by a structure of sub-committees.

A new federal-provincial secretariat should be established to resemble the existing secretariat working on the review of Canada's constitution. It would co-ordinate activities of all federal-provincial conferences "as a trusted intermediary, as a vehicle for the communication of information and as an agent in the promotion of understanding and co-operation among member governments."

The secretariat should preferably have an administrative connection with the federal government which would be responsible for its financing. It would be staffed by officers seconded from both levels of government.

Federal legislation should establish a research body like the U.S. Advisory Commission on Intergovernmental Relations, which represents national, state and local interests. The provinces would have an effective voice in selecting members. Other research on fiscal and economic matters should be commissioned by the secretariat, and governments individually and collectively should continue to support research by independent individuals and organizations.

Because the Economic Council of Canada is a creation of Parliament and is solely the responsibility of the federal government, the provinces feel no substantial or direct involvement in its activity. The structure and status of the council should be examined with a view to converting it into an intergovernmental advisory council.

Standing committees of Parliament and the legislatures should study intergovernmental relations. Task forces would have a useful role to play in examining economic problems that involve the federal government and one or a few provinces.

Governments have not always been well organized internally to handle relationships with other governments. In the federal government, a strong co-ordinating unit for this purpose should be established as part of the Prime Minister's organization.

Procedural improvements in federal-provincial relations should include conferences by closed-circuit television to save travel costs, personnel exchanges between governments, better preparation of agendas and documents, and a new look at sharing conference costs.

The machinery proposed for liaison and consultation would be more effective but no more elaborate than existing structures, and might in fact save money.

But the form of the machinery itself is secondary to a fundamental need for governments to "give up some freedom of action" as the price of co-operation.

The frustrations and delays of negotiation must be accepted.

Political authority and political power are important constraints on smooth and efficient liaison. Regional ties and involvements create conflicts.

"Administratively there are vested interests on the part of officials as well as ministers which act to preserve or create divisions when co-operation is clearly required."

Provinces have rarely acknowledged a place for themselves in fiscal activity, which in its largest sense is concerned with managing government revenue and expenditure in the interests of stable economic growth.

Responsibility in the field of economic policy has been more broadly shared between the levels of government. But there is increasing evidence of interprovincial competition, and growing concern "lest uneconomic measures should result in disorganized development contrary to the best interests of Canada's economic growth."

"The need for interprovincial co-ordination is clear. The need for federal leadership may be even more important."

IN DEFENCE OF FEDERALISM*

PIERRE ELLIOTT TRUDEAU

. . . Strictly from the point of view of economic objectives, the question is not to determine whether Quebec will govern itself by means of a sovereign state, or remain integrated with Canadian society, or will be joined to the United States. . . . What is important, in the last analysis, is for it to make sure that its *per capita* income will increase at the fastest possible speed; and, to achieve that, Quebec's economy must become extremely efficient, tchnologically advanced, fairly specialized, and capable of putting the best products at the best price on all the world's markets.

In fact, our province has too limited a population to support *alone* a modern industrial development, based on mass production and benefitting from the great economics of scale. By necessity, we have to depend on non-Quebec markets, and for that reason we have to be able to meet all competition.

In concrete terms that means that Quebec's economy must in no way be isolated, but rather integrated in a wider complex where we will find at the same time both markets and competitors.

Now it is very important to note that, whatever one says, most of the constitutional uproar at present in vogue in our province leans towards isolation. Thus some people are proposing to give to the government of Quebec jurisdiction (more or less exclusive) over banks, immigration, the employment of labour, foreign

*Translation by the editor of a portion of speech entitled "Le réalisme constitutionnel," given by the author to the founding Convention of the Quebec section of the Liberal Federation of Canada (QLF), in Quebec City, March 26, 1966. By permission of the author, who at the time of writing was the Member of Parliament for Mount Royal, P.Q., and a Parliamentary Secretary to the former Prime Minister Lester B. Pearson, and who is now the Prime Minister of Canada.

trade, tariffs and customs, and many other things. This may be a praiseworthy goal—seizing one's economic destinies—but from all the evidence, it also indicates a desire to use legal instruments to protect our capital, our business men, and our higher ranks of management from foreign competition. That's a sure way to make our factors of production inefficient, and to ensure that our products will be rejected by foreign markets. Quebec will then have to require its consumers to "Buy at home" to dispose of its products, and finally it will be the workers and farmers who will have to pay the dearest for them (either in prices or in subsidies). This line of reasoning applies just as well to steel as to blueberries, and it's erroneous to think that working people have some long run advantage in being converted into a captive market.

•   •   •

In a general way, the present constitution gives to the provinces, hence to Quebec, wide jurisdiction over matters that will permit them to obtain the objectives [they want]. The provinces have complete jurisdiction over education, and it is above all by that means that labour and management can acquire the scientific and financial knowledge that will enable them to act efficiently in an industrial age. . . .

•   •   •

Welfare objectives sometimes conflict with economic objectives. . . . It would be too simple if one could merely say: welfare first, economics second. But one must be careful: scarcely any state can transgress with impunity the laws of economics and technology. Any state that would try to do it, for praiseworthy welfare objectives, would impoverish its economy and by the same act make the welfare goals unattainable. In fact, a determinedly progressive welfare policy can be devised and applied only if the economy is fundamentally sound. All social welfare measures, from children's allowances to old age pensions and forthcoming free education and health insurance, will be dead letters if the economic infrastructure is not capable of carrying the load and paying the cost of such programmes. . . . In short, it is necessary to oppose the dislocation of the country because it would have the effect of weakening our economy and consequently of making it less able to pursue the welfare objectives and to pay for their cost.

Moreover, the Canadian constitution recognizes the widest provincial responsibility for social welfare matters. It allows each provincial government to apply in its own area the social philosophy that best suits its population. The diversity that results from this can provoke a healthy emulation among the provinces in the taxes and the benefits that will thus fall upon their respective taxpayers. Canadian federalism offers its citizens multiple choice, which adds to their democratic liberties. Within the whole Canadian economy, labour and capital will tend to move towards the mixture of fiscal burdens and social services that suit them best. Obviously, for reasons of language, the French-Canadian taxpayer will be relatively less mobile, but this is all the more reason for the Quebec government to choose with care and as democratically as possible its welfare and fiscal policies. . . .

•　　•　　•

. . . I would prefer to safeguard in every possible way the freedom and diversity that are offered by the decentralization of federalism. That is why I think it is urgent to negotiate agreements among provinces for the purpose of establishing at least in the large industrial provinces certain minimal standards of welfare legislation.

In this connection I can only see as incongruous and premature the preoccupation in certain quarters with constitutional reforms that would permit the provinces to conclude by themselves foreign treaties. As long as Quebec, for example, has not concluded with other Canadian provinces agreements on trade union legislation, is it very urgent, is it even economically wise to bind itself by conventions in respect to standards established in other countries? Moreover, Quebec is always invited to have representatives on Canadian delegations to the International Labour Organization, and our province has never grasped how to field a team that could ensure continued and serious participation.

In an analogous realm, the province just recently has been able to enter into certain agreements with France, without overstepping constitutional legality. I agree obviously with this sort of formal arrangement whereby Quebec can gain the greatest benefits; but I am not otherwise overwhelmed by "the image" that Quebec can project on the international stage. I think, for instance, that Quebec has better things to do than to appear at all the UNESCO meetings, while serious negotiations have not been undertaken with a neighbouring province relative to the education of the French-speaking minority there.

My second remark involves those provinces that are too poor to be able by themselves to reach minimal standards of social welfare. Under the existing constitutiton the central government can mitigate these inadequacies by means of equalization payments, and this arrangement has to remain. From this point of view, I regret the quarrel last year between Quebec and Ottawa about the sharing of federal tax revenues. A theory of taxation that doesn't take into account the needs of the recipients, and which seems to claim that a given group of taxpayers must receive in return at least the equivalent of what it pays in taxes, repudiates the whole redistributive functions of taxation, and declares itself to be irrevocably reactionary.

My third remark concerns the concepts of planning and counter-cyclical policy which both involve a kind of intervention by the state in economic processes, on behalf of welfare goals like full employment and planned development. . . . Under the Canadian constitutional system both sorts of policies assume a certain collaboration between the central government and the provincial governments. The first is no doubt chiefly responsible for the overall economy, but its actions can't be effective if they are not coordinated with those of the second. . . . This paper suggests, not constitutional changes, but a more systematic recourse to consultation and agreements between the federal and provincial authorities. . . .

[In regard to cultural aims] let us propound first that what creates vitality and value in a language is the quality of the group that speaks it. The question which arises then is whether the French-speaking people in Canada must concentrate their efforts on Quebec, or whether they should take the whole of Canada as the base of their operations.

In my opinion, they must do both, and I believe that for this purpose they couldn't find a better device than federalism.

For cultural values, in order to be disseminated fully, require a nice blend of protection and non-interference by the state. On one hand, the state has to ensure the protection of cultural values which without it would run the risk of being engulfed by a flood of dollars, but on the other hand, cultural values, even more than those based on economics, wither away quickly if they are removed from the test of competition.

That is why, in the matter of cultural aims, Canadian federalism is ideal. While requiring French Canadians, in the federal sector, to submit their way of doing things (and especially their political forms) to the test of competition, the federal system allows us at the same time to provide for ourselves in Quebec the form of government and the educational institutions that best suit our needs.

•   •   •

That is the reason that I am for federalism. . . . With the exception perhaps of marriage and of radio and television broadcasting, federal jurisdiction applies almost exclusively to those areas where the cultural aspect is reduced to a minimum. . . .

The provinces, on their side, have jurisdiction over all those matters that are purely local and private—over education, natural resources, property and civil rights, municipal institutions, highways, welfare and labour legislation, and the administration of justice. . . .

At one extreme, Quebec has to flee from the temptation of isolation, where one could certainly feel safe from all danger, but would also be barred from progress. At the other extreme, I would be opposed to Quebec taking its stand in a unitary Canadian state, or annihilating itself in a bigger American melting-pot. Nationalism for nationalism, I don't think that a kind of pan-Canadianism or a pan-Americanism is less imbued with chauvinism than the French-Canadian sort! . . .

I can only condemn as irresponsible those who would like to see our people invest undetermined amounts of money, time, and energy in a constitutional adventure that they have not yet been able to state precisely, but which would consist more or less vaguely in scuttling Canadian federalism in order to substitute for it hazy designs of sovereignty from which would emerge something like an independent Quebec, or associated states, or a particular status, or a Canadian common market, or a confederation of 10 states, or something else to be invented in the future—that is after political, economic, and social chaos will have been guaranteed.

Canadian federalism must evolve, of course. But it certainly has been evolving, very substantially, in the last hundred years without the constitution requiring wholesale changes. Periods of great decentralization have alternated with periods of intense centralization in the course of our history, that is, according to the conjunction of social and economic forces, external pressures, and the strength and astuteness of our politicians. Now if there is any immediate basic fact in politics—and at the same time a verifiable proposition in most industrial countries, it is that the state is obliged today to devote a continually increasing portion of its continually increasing budget to those areas which, in the Canadian constitution, fall under the jurisdiction of the provincial governments. In other words, Canadian federalism is evolving at present towards a period of great decentralization.

This reality becomes most obvious if one looks at the total of governmental expenditures apart from transfer payments between governments. The "final" expenditures for the federal government have increased from $4.198 billion in 1954 to $6.550 billion in 1964, an increase of 56 per cent. But during the same period provincial and municipal expenditures have mounted from $2.652 billion to $8.065 billion, an increase of 204 percent.

Thus, demographic, social and economic forces are in the process of transferring to provincial governments an enormous addition in power, without having to change a single comma in the constitution. The fact that some of our French-Canadian politicians and intellectuals have chosen this precise moment to demand imperatively that the country provide itself with a new constitution seems to us to be extraordinarily untimely. . . .

BIBLIOGRAPHY

Aitchison, J. H., "Interprovincial Co-operation in Canada," in Aitchison, J. H., (ed.), *The Political Process in Canada,* Toronto, University of Toronto Press, 1963.

Angers, F. A., "La phase du mouvement dans les relations fédérales-provinciales," *L'Action nationale,* Vol. LIV, novembre, 1964.

Black, E. R., and Cairns, A., "A Different Perspective on Canadian Federalism," *C.P.A.,* Vol. IX, No. 1, March, 1966.

Bonenfant, J. C., "Les projets théoriques du fédéralisme canadien," *Cahiers des dix,* Vol. 29, 1964.

Bonenfant, J. C., et aussi Tremblay, J. N., "Le concept d'une nation canadienne est-il un concept équivoque?" *Culture,* Vol. XXV, No. 2, juin, 1964.

Brady, A., "The Meaning of Canadian Nationalism," *International Journal,* Vol. XIX, No. 2, Summer, 1964.

Breton, A., Breton, R., Bruneau, C., Gauthier, Y., Lalonde, M., Pinard, M. Trudeau, P. E., "Manifeste pour une politique fonctionnelle," *Cité libre,* Vol. XV, No. 67, mai, 1964. English translation in *Canadian Forum,* Vol. XLIV, No. 520, May, 1964.

Canada, *Dominion-Provincial and Interprovincial Conferences from 1887 to 1926,* Ottawa, Queen's Printer, 1951.

Canada, *Dominion-Provincial Conferences, 1927, 1935, 1941,* Ottawa, Queen's Printer, 1951.

Canada, *Dominion-Provincial Conference, (1945),* Ottawa, Queen's Printer, 1946.

Canada, *Proceedings of the Conference of Federal and Provincial Governments, 1950,* Ottawa, Queen's Printer, 1953.

Canada, *Proceedings of the Federal-Provincial Conference, 1955,* Ottawa, Queen's Printer, 1955.

Canada, *Dominion-Provincial Conference, 1957,* Ottawa, Queen's Printer, 1958.

Canada, *Proceedings of the Federal-Provincial Conference, 1963,* Ottawa, Queen's Printer, 1964.

Canadian Union of Students, *A New Concept of Confederation?,* Proceedings of C U S Seventh Seminar held in Quebec City, 1964, n.p., n.d.

Caplan, N., "Some Factors Affecting the Resolution of a Federal-Provincial Conflict," *C.J.P.S.,* Vol. II, No. 2, June, 1969.

Cheffins, R. I., *The Constitutional Process in Canada,* Toronto, McGraw-Hill, 1969.

Creighton, D. G., *The Road to Confederation: The Emergence of Canada, 1863-1867,* Toronto, Macmillan, 1964.

Crépeau, P. A., and Macpherson, C. B., (eds.), *The Future of Canadian Federalism; l'Avenir du fédéralisme canadien,* Toronto, University of Toronto Press, Montréal, les Presses de l'Université de Montréal, 1965.

Croisat, M., "Planification et Fédéralisme," *C.P.A.,* Vol. XI, No. 3, Fall, 1968.

Dehem, R., *Planification économique et fédéralisme,* Montréal, Les presses de l'Université Laval, 1968.

Dubuc, A., "Une interprétation économique de la constitution," *Socialisme 66, Revue du socialisme international et Québecois,* No. 7, janvier, 1966. English translation in *Canadian Forum,* Vol. XLV, No. 542, March, 1966.

Gallant, E., "The Machinery of Federal-Provincial Relations: I," and Burns, R. M., "The Machinery of Federal-Provincial Relations: II," *C.P.A.,* Vol. VIII, No. 4, December, 1965.

Gelinas, A., "Trois modes d'approche à la détermination de l'opportunité de la décentralisation de l'organisation politique principalement en système fédéral," *C.P.A.,* Vol. IX, No. 1, March, 1966.

Hawkins, G., (ed.), *Concepts of Federalism,* Proceedings of 34th Couchiching Conference, Toronto, Canadian Institute on Public Affairs, 1965.

Hawkins, G., (ed.), *The Idea of Maritime Union,* Report of a Conference sponsored by the Canadian Institute on Public Affairs and Mount Allison University, Sackville, N.B., 1965.

Johnson, A. W., "The Dynamics of Federalism in Canada," *C.J.P.S.,* Vol. I, No. 1, March, 1968.

Kear, A. R., "Co-operative Federalism: A Study of the Federal-Provincial Continuing Committee on Fiscal and Economic Matters," *C.P.A.,* Vol. VI, No. 1, March, 1963.

Lamontagne, M., *Le fédéralisme canadien,* Québec, Les presses universitaires Laval, 1954.

Leach, R. H., "Interprovincial Co-operation: Neglected Aspect of Canadian Federalism," *C.P.A.,* Vol. II, No. 2, June, 1959.

Leach, R. H., (ed.), *Contemporary Canada,* Toronto, University of Toronto Press, 1968.

Lederman, W. R., "The Concurrent Operation of Federal and Provincial Laws in Canada," *McGill Law Journal,* Vol. IX, 1963.

Livingston, W. S., *Federalism and Constitutional Change,* Oxford, Oxford University Press, 1963.

Lower, A. R. M., Scott, F. R., *et al., Evolving Canadian Federalism,* Durham, Duke University Press, 1958.

McRae, K. D., *Switzerland: Example of Cultural Co-existence,* Toronto, Canadian Institute of International Affairs, 1964.

McWhinney, E., *Comparative Federalism, States' Rights and National Power,* Toronto, University of Toronto Press, 1962.

May, R. J., "Decision-making and Stability in Federal Systems," *C.J.P.S.,* Vol. III, No. 1, March, 1970.

Meekison, J. P., (ed.), *Canadian Federalism: Myth or Reality,* Toronto, Methuen, 1968.

Muller, S., "Federalism and the Party System in Canada," in Meekison, J. P., *Canadian Federalism: Myth or Reality,* Toronto, Methuen, 1968.

Ontario Advisory Committee on Confederation, *Background Papers and Reports,* Toronto, Queen's Printer, Vol. I, 1967; Vol. II, 1970.

Plumptre, A. F. W., "Regionalism and the Public Service," *C.P.A.,* Vol. VIII, No. 4, December, 1965.

Riker, W. H., *Federalism: Origin, Operation, Significance,* Boston and Toronto, Little, Brown, 1964.

Russell, P., (ed.), *Nationalism in Canada,* Toronto, McGraw-Hill, 1966.

Ryerson, S., (ed.), *et al.,* "The Two Canadas: Towards a New Confederation?" A Symposium, *The Marxist Quarterly,* No. 15, Autumn, 1965.

Smiley, D. V., *The Rowell-Sirois Report,* Carleton Library, Toronto, McClelland and Stewart, 1963.

Smiley, D. V., "Public Administration and Canadian Federalism," *C.P.A.,* Vol. VII, No. 3, September, 1964.

Smiley, D. V., "The Two Themes of Canadian Federalism," *C.J.E.P.S.,* Vol. XXXI, No. 1, February, 1965.

Smiley, D. V., *The Canadian Political Nationality,* Toronto, Methuen, 1967.

Smiley, D. V., "Rationalism or Reason: Alternative Approaches to Constitutional Review in Canada," Paper delivered at the Progressive Conservative Priorities for Canada Conference, Niagara Falls, Ontario, October 12, 1969.

Soucy, E., "Confédération ou 'fédéralisme co-opératif'?" *L'Action nationale,* Vol. LIV, octobre, 1964.

Trudeau, P. E., *Federalism and the French Canadians,* Toronto, Methuen, 1968.

Underhill, F. H., *The Image of Confederation,* Toronto, Canadian Broadcasting Corporation, 1964.

Wheare, K. C., *Federal Government,* London, Oxford University Press, 4th ed., 1963.

Bilingualism and Biculturalism

Albiniski, H. S., "Politics and Biculturalism in Canada: The Flag Debate," *Australian Journal of Politics and History,* Vol. XIII, No. 2, August, 1967.

Canada, *A Preliminary Report of the Royal Commission on Bilingualism and Biculturalism,* Ottawa, Queen's Printer, 1965.

Canada, *Report of the Royal Commission on Bilingualism and Biculturalism,* Ottawa, Queen's Printer, Book I, *General Introduction and the Official Languages,* 1967; Book II, *Education,* 1968; Book III, *The Work World,* 2 vols., 1969.

Gibson, F. W., (ed.), *Cabinet Formation and Bicultural Relations: Seven Case Studies,* Studies of the Royal Commission on Bilingualism and Biculturalism, No. 6, Ottawa, Queen's Printer, 1970.

Lalande, G., *The Department of External Affairs and Biculturalism,* Studies of the Royal Commission of Bilingualism and Biculturalism, No. 3, Ottawa, Queen's Printer, 1969.

Russell, P., *The Supreme Court of Canada as a Bilingual and Bicultural Institution,* Documents of the Royal Commission on Bilingualism and Biculturalism, No. 1, Ottawa, Queen's Printer, 1969.

Constitution

Bissonnette, B., *Essai sur la constitution du Canada,* Montréal, Editions du jour, 1963.

Brossard, J., *L'immigration: Les droits et pouvoirs du Canada et du Québec,* Montréal, Presses de l'Université de Montréal, 1967.

The Canada Committee, *Declaration by English and French-Speaking Canadians,* Montreal, 1966.

Corry, J. A., "The Prospects for the Rule of Law," *C.J.E.P.S.,* Vol. XXI, No. 4, November, 1955.

Dicey, A. V., *Introduction to the Study of the Constitution,* London, Macmillan, 10th ed., 1960.

Driedger, E. A., *A Consolidation of the British North America Acts 1867 to 1952,* Ottawa, Queen's Printer, 1957.

Faribault, M., and Fowler, R., *Ten to One, The Confederation Wager,* Toronto, McClelland and Stewart, 1965.

Jennings, W. I., *The Law and the Constitution,* London, University of London Press, 5th ed., 1959.

La Forest, G. V., *Natural Resources and Public Property Under the Canadian Constitution,* Toronto, University of Toronto Press, 1969.

La Société St. Jean Baptiste de Montréal, *Le fédéralisme, l'acte de l'amérique du nord britannique et les Canadiens français,* Mémoire au comité parlementaire de la constitution du gouvernement du Québec, Montréal, Les éditions de l'agence Duvernay, 1964.

O'Hearn, P. J. T., *Peace, Order and Good Government: A New Constitution for Canada,* Toronto, Macmillan, 1964.

Pepin, G., *Les Tribunaux Administratifs et La Constitution: Etude des articles 96 à 101 de l'A.A.N.B.,* Montréal, Les presses de l'Université de Montréal, 1969.

Tremblay, A., *Les compétences législatives au Canada et les pouvoirs provinciaux en matière de propriété et de droits civils,* Ottawa, Edition de l'Université, 1967.

Current Constitutional Documentation

Canada, *Constitutional Conference, Proceedings of First Meeting, February 5-7, 1968,* Ottawa, Queen's Printer, 1968.

Canada, *Constitutional Conference, Proceedings of Second Meeting, February 10-12, 1969,* Ottawa, Queen's Printer, 1969.

Canada, *Constitutional Conference, Proceedings of Third Meeting, December 8-10, 1969,* Ottawa, Queen's Printer, 1970.

Canada, (Benson, E. J.), *The Taxing Powers and the Constitution of Canada,* Ottawa, Queen's Printer, 1969.

Canada, (Martin, P.), *Federalism and International Relations,* Ottawa, Queen's Printer, 1968.

Canada, (Pearson, L. B.), *Federalism for the Future,* Ottawa, Queen's Printer, 1968.

Canada, (Sharp, M.), *Federalism and International Conferences on Education,* Ottawa, Queen's Printer, 1968.

Canada, (Trudeau, P. E.), *A Canadian Charter of Human Rights,* Ottawa, Queen's Printer, 1968.

Canada, (Trudeau, P. E.), *Federal-Provincial Grants and the Spending Power of Parliament,* Ottawa, Queen's Printer, 1969.

Canada, (Trudeau, P. E.), *Income Security and Social Services,* Ottawa, Queen's Printer, 1969.
Canada, (Trudeau, P. E.), *The Constitution and the People of Canada,* Ottawa, Queen's Printer, 1969.

Provinces and Territories
Beck, J. M., *The Government of Nova Scotia,* Toronto, University of Toronto Press, 1957.
Canada, *Report of the Advisory Commission on the Development of Government in the Northwest Territories,* (Carrothers' Report), Ottawa, Queen's Printer, 1966.
Donnelly, M. S., *The Government of Manitoba,* Toronto, University of Toronto Press, 1963.
Krueger, R. R., "The Provincial-Municipal Government Revolution in New Brunswick," *C.P.A.,* Vol. XIII, No. 1, Spring, 1970.
MacKinnon, F., *The Government of Prince Edward Island,* Toronto, University of Toronto Press, 1951.
Manitoba, *Report of the Royal Commission on Local Government and Finance,* (Michener Report), Winnipeg, 1964.
Mayo, H. B., "Newfoundland's Entry into the Dominion," *C.J.E.P.S.,* Vol. XV, No. 4, November, 1949.
New Brunswick, *Report of the Royal Commission on Finance and Municipal Taxation,* (Byrne Report), Fredericton, Queen's Printer, 1963.
Zaslow, M., "Recent Constitutional Developments in Canada's Northern Territories," *C.P.A.,* Vol. X, No. 2, June, 1967.

Municipal
Crawford, K. G., *Canadian Municipal Government,* Toronto, University of Toronto Press, 1954.
Feldman, L. D., and Goldrick, M. D., (eds.), *Politics and Government in Urban Canada: Selected Readings,* Toronto, Methuen, 1969.
Kaplan, H., "Politics and Policy-Making in Metropolitan Toronto," *C.J.E.P.S.,* Vol. XXXI, No. 4, November, 1965.
Kaplan, H., *Urban Political Systems: A Functional Analysis of Metropolitan Toronto,* Toronto, Copp Clark, 1967.
Lithwick, N. H., and Paquet, G., (eds.), *Urban Studies: A Canadian Perspective,* Toronto, Methuen, 1968.
Lorimer, J., *The Real World of City Politics,* Toronto, James, Lewis and Samuel, 1970.
McRae, K. D., *The Federal Capital: Government Institutions,* Studies of the Royal Commission on Bilingualism and Biculturalism, No. 1, Ottawa, Queen's Printer, 1969.
Plunkett, T. J., *Urban Canada and its Government: A Study of Municipal Organization,* Toronto, Macmillan, 1968.
Rowat, D. C., *Your Local Government,* Toronto, Macmillan, reprinted in paper-back 1962.
Rowat, D. C., *The Canadian Municipal System: Essays on the Improvement of Local Government,* Carleton Library, Toronto, McClelland and Stewart, 1969.
Rowat, D. C., "The Problems of Governing Federal Capitals," *C.J.P.S.,* Vol. I, No. 3, September, 1968.
Whalen, H. J., *The Development of Local Government in New Brunswick,* Fredericton, 1964.
Young, D. A., "Canadian Local Government Development: Some Aspects of the Commissioner and City Manager Forms of Administration," *C.P.A.,* Vol. IX, No. 1, March, 1966.

FIVE
REGIONALISM

In recent years there has been an outburst of interest in regionalism, as Professor Hodgetts notes in the selection from his excellent article which commences this chapter. The federal government has sparked much of this enthusiasm by its own interest, and what is even more important, by making available some hundreds of millions of dollars in grants for regional redevelopment projects. Under federal legislation such as ARDA (the Agricultural and Rural Development Act), FRED (the Fund for Rural Economic Development Act), and MMRA (the Maritime Marshland Rehabilitation Act), various extensive programs have been undertaken for the economic and social improvement of entire regions. Often these projects have involved the cooperation and joint effort of all three sectors of government. Perhaps the best example of this kind of regionalism is the BAEQ project under which the province of Quebec requested ARDA funds to cover 50 percent of the cost of preparing a comprehensive development plan for the whole Lower St. Lawrence, Gaspé, and Iles-de-la-Madeleine region. Quebec established an agency called the Bureau d'Aménagement de l'Est du Québec (BAEQ) to prepare a thorough study of the area. The massive ten-volume report that resulted in 1966 then became the basis for a redevelopment plan for the region which was worked out cooperatively by the participation of provincial, federal, and local personnel and which was financed by Quebec and by Ottawa through use of FRED funds. This is only one example, of course, of such regional redevelopment projects which have also occurred elsewhere, for instance, in Manitoba and New Brunswick.

The provinces have demonstrated considerable interest in regionalism in other forms too. Ontario, for example, has created within its own geographical area a number of different regions for different functions, such as regional municipal governments, ten intra-provincial economic regions, etc.

A good deal of literature, including a number of valuable, commissioned, specialized studies, has been produced by this new interest in regionalism. Since it is too voluminous to be noted item by item in the bibliography appended to this chapter, students seeking further information should consult both federal and provincial sources for references, in particular, for instance, the publications under the imprimatur of the former federal Department of Forestry and Rural Development, which was responsible for many of the programs and studies. (It should be noted in this connection that the Department of Forestry and Rural Development was replaced in 1969 by the creation of the federal Department of Regional Economic Expansion, to which much importance has been attached by the Trudeau government and to which very substantial funds have been allocated to continue this sort of regionalism.) The bibliography in this chapter does refer, however, to many of the more general articles and books on regionalism that have appeared recently.

The emergence of this new conception of regionalism and the devotion of great attention to it have not extinguished the traditional tendency of Canadians to think of regionalism in terms of a province or a group of provinces. As Professor Hodgetts remarks in his article in this chapter, when Canadians talk about regions in Canada, they still are inclined to think of "the regions" as the Atlantic provinces, the Prairies, British Columbia, Quebec, and Ontario. Thus, while new experiments with different regions have been under way lately, there is still considerable interest in the hoary argument about the advisability of amalgamating the Atlantic provinces into one government and the Prairie provinces into another consolidated government. This idea has always had a special appeal for Central Canadians but what is now of additional interest is that at least some residents in each of these two regions have begun to consider it seriously also. Premier Louis Robichaud of New Brunswick has expressed himself in favour of the idea of Maritime union and has engaged his fellow premiers in discussion of the subject. A commission has been appointed to study and report upon the feasibility of such a union. This chapter contains a submission to the commission from the Atlantic Provinces Economic Council (APEC) arguing in favour of amalgamation while the article in this chapter by Professor John Graham offers some arguments against it. In 1970, a conference was held in Lethbridge, Alberta, to consider the pros and cons of the union of the Prairie provinces. Premier W. A. C. Bennett of British Columbia was already on record in favour of such a plan, with an improvement which would extend the borders of the five new provinces that would emerge. An excerpt from his views is included within this chapter. At the Lethbridge Conference one federal minister, the Hon. James Richardson from Manitoba, offered an appraisal of the proposal that did not commit the federal government but left the clear impression that he personally approved the idea. A selection from his address follows in this chapter. The Premier of Alberta, the Hon. Harry Strom, was somewhat less enthusiastic about the proposal for Prairie union, as the extract from his speech to the conference quoted here indicates.

HOW APPLICABLE IS REGIONALISM IN THE CANADIAN FEDERAL SYSTEM?*

J. E. HODGETTS

Almost overnight, regionalism in Canada has become the current fashion and a subject for much intellectual speculation as well as administrative experimentation. This symposium is but one of many testimonials to the growing interest in the subject. In 1964, the Committee on Statistics of the Canadian Political Science Association considered the problem. Early in 1965, Queen's University sponsored a conference on areas of economic stress that was the forerunner to a much larger conference on regionalism convened by the Province of Ontario. The Institute of Public Administration of Canada selected regionalism as the theme for its autumn conference. Recent reports of a royal commission in New Brunswick and of a legislative committee in Ontario are implicitly concerned with regionalism in so far as they propose basic remodelling of the local government services in their respective provinces. The Resources Ministers Council is grappling with the concept, as are also the federal departments of Industry and of Agriculture. On the international plane, the St. Lawrence Seaway and the Columbia River development have projected more grandiose conceptions of regionalism. In short, regionalism, with concomitant regional administrative structures, is being advanced as an answer to the new problems of interdependence that cut across traditional political boundary lines, whether they be municipal, provincial, or national.

The title chosen for this symposium suggests that regional interests are, indeed, a reality within the Canadian federal structure and that policy must accommodate itself not only to the familiar strains of dominion-provincial tensions but to the newer cross-currents of regionalism. . . .

•   •   •

In Canada . . . we are far less clear [than they are in the United States] about the existence of regions with identifiable interests separate from the interests historically contained in and expressed through provincial units. In the First Annual Review of the Economic Council, under a Table labelled "Level and Growth of Personal Income per capita by region," we find the "regions" entitled Atlantic (with a footnote to say Newfoundland is excluded), Quebec, Ontario, Prairies, and British Columbia. This nomenclature, which is quite typical, reveals how quickly we exhaust the regional concept when applied across the nation: once the

*From *The Canadian Journal of Economics and Political Science*, Vol. XXXII, No. 1, February, 1966. By permission of the author and the publisher. This paper is a revision of a contribution made to a Symposium on "Regional Interests and Policy in a Federal Structure" sponsored jointly by the Association of Canadian Law Teachers and the Canadian Political Science Association, University of British Columbia, June 1965.

Maritimes and the Prairies have been mentioned we immediately fall back on the standard political, provincial boundaries. As for that region called the Canadian North, experienced observers are the first to proclaim its heterogeneity and the consequent impropriety of viewing it as a single entity. At the federal level positive administrative recognition of this restricted regional concept is to be found only in such agencies as the Atlantic Development Board, the Prairie Farm Rehabilitation Administration and the Northern Affairs Branch in the Department of Northern Affairs and National Resources.

Thus, if we are defining our region in national terms and thinking of it as an identifiable area having sufficiently common interests that they can be articulated and aggregated and urged on the federal government as part of the demand inputs of our political system, we really have nothing to compare with the American situation. The explanation for this difference may lie in the lack of party discipline in the U.S. Congress and the popular nation-wide election of the Chief Executive. The fluidity of party lines in Congress permits bloc voting across party lines to take place without undermining the parties or the completely separate office of the presidency. In Canada, the rigour of party discipline imposed on MP's virtually eliminates the possibility of bloc voting in the name of the Prairies, the Maritimes, or any other region of trans-provincial dimensions. We have no "cornbelt" or "cotton bloc" voting. Indeed, the only way a regional interest can be assembled is through the political party processes *within* each province, by which means a Social Credit rump from Alberta or a New Democratic party bloc from Saskatchewan may consolidate a minority voice in the House of Commons—but, once again, it should be noted, we are compelled to equate so-called regional interests with the separate provincial interests.

The popular election of the President under a system in which the majority winner takes all of the electoral vote in each state has made it possible to identify regional groupings of states that either hold the balance of power or have a species of veto power in the determination of the presidential winner. In Canada, while we now recognize that a national election tends to turn on the prime minister and the opposition leaders and thus becomes more like a U.S. presidential election, in place of the concentration of support by identifiable blocs of states, the process is splintered into individual constituency contests that prevent us from identifying a genuine regional influence on the final outcome.

If the concept of region viewed from the national perspective in Canada lacks the substance and political influence that may be claimed for it in the United States, at the provincial level it is clearly emerging as a significant working concept. The increasing emphasis placed on region within the provinces derives from two complementary pressures. First, it has long been apparent to students of local government that the traditional political units are proving increasingly unsatisfactory in meeting the costly demands of urbanization, industrialization, and secularization. The problem is that functions have spilled out over the political boundaries, while authority to perform the functions remains legally chained to the traditional units of local administration. And, as functional responsibilities grow in number and expand in scope, the financial, technical, and manpower resources required for adequate performance need to be pooled across political boundaries. Over the last decade or so these deficiencies have become more marked under the impact of rapid social and technological change. The solution, reiterated in one official report after another, is amalgamation to form larger units, or, at a minimum, a merger to perform specific functions.

Further support for the stress on region comes from a more recent acknowledgement by the provinces that there are actually elements missing from their existing organizational apparatus; there is a growing awareness that new functional needs and programs cannot be handled either by the long-standing departmental machinery of the province or even by the merging of present units of local government. One can think here, specifically, of the conservation authorities in Ontario or the more ambitious regional development associations in the same province. The increasing respectability of government planning and the urgent demands for conserving and purifying our soil, water, and air all add to the pressures for a regional approach to these problems. The recently created Saskatchewan Water Resources Commission is an excellent example of a new agency for investigation, planning, co-ordination, and regulation of the development and use of water and related land resources—a multi-purpose assignment with which no single existing department could cope. And, it should be added, not only are provincial and local authorities responding to these pressures, the federal government, too, is making its contributions through such legislation as the recent Agricultural Rehabilitation and Development Act which has fostered regional projects like the one for the Gaspé and has relied on two other regionally based federal agencies—the Prairie Farm Rehabilitation Administration and the Maritime Marshland Rehabilitation Administration—for its "operational arm." The new Department of Industry, under Part II of its authorizing statute, visualizes yet another range of designated development areas.

The proliferation of new agencies, the amalgamation of old agencies, and the recombining of divisions pulled out of existing agencies would appear to provide ample testimony for the thesis that "regional interests" now constitute a significant element in the demand inputs to which the Canadian political system is clearly responding. This conclusion is nevertheless suspect on two counts. First, as already indicated we must discount the influence of regionalism of the American type that rallies interests and demands other than those that have always been expressed through traditional provincial political units. Second, one can go further by asserting that regionalism, at any level one wishes to take it, does not generate spontaneous demands that thrust themselves on the political system and are instrumental in influencing the policy outposts of the system. The region, in this particular stage of development at any rate, is not so much the creator of policy as the creature of policy.

Rephrasing this contention in terms of systems analysis, it can be argued that regionalism is not part of the demand inputs entering the system, but is a creation of the political system itself. David Easton, one of the founding fathers of the systems approach, has anticipated this possibility by coining the expression "within-put" to apply to the not-uncommon situation where events and conditions within the political system may be as significant as any environmental inputs in shaping the ultimate outputs.

Obviously, there has to be a region if we are to think of a regional interest which, in turn, we visualize as shaping or influencing the control of public policy. What is argued here is that in most instances the region is, so to speak, the natural outcome of the adoption of a particular program or policy. The execution of the policy entails the creation of administrative units that must be set up on a regional basis in order to provide the most appropriate combination of functions and resources. In short, the policy, by defining the function or program, explicitly or implicitly creates a concept of the region required for the particular purposes envisaged.

One or two illustrations may serve to buttress what may appear to be a perverse attempt to put the cart before the horse. In the case of "the areas of slow economic growth" to which the Department of Industry was authorized to direct its services, it is clear that the regions might properly be called "bureaucratic constructs." The Minister explained, in 1964, how the initial designation of the areas was based on thirty-five national employment service areas "to bring about quick results and meet an emergency situation." He went on to say that his department was "presently engaged with the departments of finance and labour in making a detailed and exhaustive review of criteria for designating areas . . . which will enable us to single out those areas where special efforts will be required over the years if they are to participate more fully in the general prosperity of the country." In this operation we find little evidence of pre-existing regional interests urging their demands on government; rather, we see the areas "designated" initially on the most convenient, available criteria and ultimately on the basis of more sophisticated statistical data processed within the public service itself.

The regional development program in the Province of Ontario affords a less extreme but perhaps more typical example. While stressing the element of partnership between "province, local municipal governments, and public-spirited local groups and individuals," the official pronouncement goes on to state quite frankly: "In initiating and financially supporting regional development through legislation, the Government of Ontario in the 10 Development Associations has officially recognized both the real need of, and the great potential benefits which stem from this Provincial-Municipal partnership." It would not be unfair to claim that the Government of Ontario, and more precisely the Regional Development Division of the Department of Economics and Development, has, in effect, said to the municipalities: "Look, whether you know it or not, you have certain common regional interests in such matters as promoting tourism, industry, research and conservation and community planning; we, as a Department, can deal with you best if you organize in regional groups; we are prepared to go half way in financing such organizations; and we confidently expect 'regional interests' will soon cluster around the organizations to which we shall be happy to respond in formulating subsequent policies." Again, we may conclude that the political system and not the environment has initiated the input in order to facilitate the conversion process and so trigger a policy output.

In my view this is the normal flow of events as they bear on the alleged forces of regionalism. Parenthetically, it is worth nothing that this particular sequence has not been uncommon in the development of pressure group relations with the political system. The government has found it more convenient to respond to an organized pressure rather than attempt to negotiate with individuals or isolated groups. Thus, in 1906 the Department of Agriculture sponsored the meeting of the Canadian National Live Stock Association, and in 1914 helped finance the Sheep Breeders Association. H. H. Hannam, once president of the Canadian Federation of Agriculture, claimed that the Federation was brought into being because the first Bank of Canada Act called upon "organized agriculture" (then non-existent) to nominate members to the Bank's board of directors. And, just as advisory committees have been popular devices for giving official recognition to organized functional groups in the political system, so too, we almost invariably find provisions for setting up advisory adjuncts to the newer regional organizations.

A final example, drawn from the Province of Quebec, illustrates one further aspect of the positive contribution of the political system to regionalism. The significant reorganization of the educational system of that province has apparently followed the path already described; that is, the political system has produced a global educational program and the ministry has designed the administrative apparatus which they think will permit the most effective implementation of the general goals. Decentralization was necessary and areas had to be designated for administrative purposes. One of the marked features of this development has been the extent to which political and permanent officials alike have had to carry the appeal to the regions in order to enlist their interest and participation. Some senior civil servants—and not merely those in educational administration, for much missionary work has had to be undertaken in other fields as well—have been perturbed by their inevitable public identification with a particular policy. This had its parallel in the Province of Saskatchewan two decades ago and perhaps Quebec civil servants, witnessing the recent exodus from that part of the West after a change in government, may fear that history will repeat itself in this province. In any event, reverting once more to systems analysis, we find that this particular experience in Quebec illustrates not only how the political system can generate its own demands but can at the same time take positive action to create its own supports by manipulating the regional environment in the way just described. The reliance on advisory committees, in conjunction with such programs, shows that in the absence of spontaneous regional interests to create demands and provide supports, the government itself has had to create the organizational framework in which such demands and supports might be expected to germinate. These examples of a pervasive and universal development also buttress an earlier contention; our traditional techniques for aggregating demands and supports—the geographic constituency, the political party, and Parliament itself—have had to be supplemented and possibly even by-passed by these more direct and deliberately constructed tools.

It would be tempting to extend this paper to take into account more specific bureaucratic responses to the forces of regionalism. One might, for example, describe in detail the particular organizational pattern developed by each federal department and agency to resolve the problem of administering a federal domain where three-quarters of the work force has to be employed outside the head-quarters area. On the whole, however, such a detailed story would simply reinforce the main conclusions of this paper, namely, that there are few genuinely spontaneous regional interests in Canada that have an independent impact on policy; and where they do exist our political system, working through disciplined parliamentary parties, only permits them to be aggregated and articulated within conventional provincial boundaries. Thus the growing recognition of regions is basically an artifice of administrators who, working within the political system, play a creative role in constructing regions appropriate to the functions entrusted to them; in some cases, this positive initiatory role may even compel public servants to desert their neutrality in order to generate support from a sometimes indifferent environment which has to be alerted to the task of formulating its own interests around the regional construct. Finally, it may perhaps be argued that, once over the present formative stage, the genuine need for a regional approach to policy-formation and implementation will in itself begin to create self-generating demand and support inputs which will no longer be bureaucratically inspired.

It remains to be seen whether parties can retain their role as aggregators of demands based on new regional interests that are not necessarily tied to the traditional provincial units or whether, along with the proliferation of advisory committees, we will need to design new mechanisms for this purpose. The larger question of Parliament's capacity to convert such regional demands into acceptable policy outputs also constitutes a major challenge to our ingenuity. Meanwhile, at the present intermediate stage of growth, governmental agencies are all energetically throwing themselves into the breach and we are already faced with such a maze of special regions that we may be unable to co-ordinate disparate regional entities. If this development persists we must abandon any hopes we have of gearing our institutions and policies to the conception of a single Canadian political system.

SHOULD THE ATLANTIC PROVINCES UNITE?*

JOHN F. GRAHAM

The question of union of two or more of the Atlantic provinces comes up from time to time. A recent surge of interest in it was generated by Premier Louis Robichaud of New Brunswick at an Atlantic Premiers' Conference at Charlottetown in the fall of 1964, when he proposed that union be seriously considered. Earlier in the year, study of political union of the Atlantic provinces was urged in

*From an article written for this book in 1965 by the author, who is Professor and Head of the Department of Economics, Dalhousie University, Halifax, N.S.

the foreword of the *Report of the Royal Commission on Finance and Municipal Taxation in New Brunswick,* by the Chairman, Edward G. Byrne. Premier Robichaud's proposal initially received a cool reaction from the premiers of the other three provinces, but, subsequently, Premier Stanfield of Nova Scotia, in a public letter to Premier Robichaud, suggested that their two governments appoint committees to study the feasibility and desirability of union of the two provinces, if such a study were the general, non-partisan wish of the respective legislatures.

To the Canadian outsider, union of these small adjacent provinces appears to be a simple matter with obvious advantages to the region. In fact, it is not much simpler than union of the Prairie provinces or even of Ontario and Quebec would be. Certainly, the four Atlantic provinces are clearer geographical entities than they are.

The three Maritime provinces are small in population and in size compared to the other provinces but they have much in common in their history, their resources, their location, and their maritime aspect. Newfoundland too has much in common with the other three, even though its location would inhibit, if not necessarily preclude, its inclusion in a full political union. Table 1 shows that union of all four provinces would give them the third largest population, but that they would still have the smallest area, even when Labrador (112.8 thousand square miles) is included.

Although the current reaction to the idea of union is less parochial than it would have been even ten years ago, the achievement of full political union does seem most unlikely. Provincial loyalties are deeply rooted; it is difficult to see how agreement could ever be reached on a single provincial capital or to believe that the several provincial legislatures would preside over their own liquidation.

The dismantling of the present four civil services and their reconstitutiton into a single civil service are also formidable, though not insuperable, impediments. So also is the problem of assuring the large (40 percent) French Canadian population of New Brunswick that their interests would be adequately safeguarded.

Moreover, there are good grounds for scepticism about the common contention of advocates of union that such a move would enhance the region's political influence in Ottawa since it could then speak with a single united voice. Three governments, or four with Newfoundland, can probably exert more influence than one could. Four premiers at federal-provincial conference tables would undoubtedly carry more weight than one. Probably the number of members of parliament and senators from the region would be reduced and, more important perhaps, so also would the number of ministers from the region in the federal cabinet.

It is true that the present over-representation of the Atlantic Provinces is conducive to debilitating and degrading grass roots federal patronage that might at least be lessened with a reduction in the number of members of parliament and senators. Moreover, there is not much evidence that the members of parliament from any of these provinces have represented its interests in a concerted way. They have generally tended to fall into line with national party policy and discipline. Yet there is no reason to believe they would act differently if the region were a

TABLE 1

1963 Population and Area of Canada by Provinces

	Population (in thousands)		Area (in thousands of sq. miles)	
Newfoundland (incl. Labrador)	481		156.2	
Prince Edward Island	107	1,958	2.2	208.1
Nova Scotia	756		21.4	
New Brunswick	614		28.3	
Quebec	5,468		594.9	
Ontario	6,448		412.6	
Manitoba	950		251.0	
Saskatchewan	933		251.7	
Alberta	1,405		255.3	
British Columbia	1,695		366.3	
Yukon	15		207.1	
Northwest Territories	24		1,304.9	
CANADA	18,896		3,851.8	

single province. In spite of a strong Maritime rights sentiment of long standing, no new parties dedicated to the fight for Maritime interests have emerged, in marked contrast to the rise of vigorous new parties of protest in the western provinces.

Despite strong grounds for scepticism about the political feasibility of union, it is still worthwhile to undertake a thorough study of full political union, for such a study would almost certainly reveal opportunities for fruitful cooperation that a more limited study would fail to do.

The economic aspects of union, wherein lie most of the advantages, can be considered under three headings, those relating to: (1) economic development; (2) administrative and legislative economies; and (3) problems arising from differences in per capita incomes and from the necessity of providing common levels of public services.

There is little doubt that union would greatly facilitate the formulation and execution of a more effective federal-provincial programme of economic development for the region and that, partitcularly, it would enhance the effectiveness of federal agencies concerned with regional development, such as the Atlantic Development Board, the Agricultural Rehabilitation and Development Act, and the Area Development Act. If the region were a single province, it would be easier to develop integrated policies for it in those sectors of the economy which have most in common, such as agriculture, fishing, and tourism, without inhibiting development in sectors that are peculiar to particular parts of the region.

It would also be possible to plan the present drive for secondary manufacturing industry more rationally, particularly in relation to the regional market on which most of such industry is likely to be largely dependent. The duplication and competition in the present promotional activities could be eliminated and a concerted effort made to attract industries to those parts of the region best suited for them. It should also be possible to develop a more powerful package of incentives to new industry in concert with the federal government than at present when there are varying provincial views as to what is needed.

At the same time, there is no assurance that the competitive scrambling of different parts of the region for new industry would cease with political union. The present experience *within* the provinces is not reassuring. In fact, the competition might become more bitter than it is now with different political entities that are expected to compete.

There would likely be some small direct savings from the reduction in administrative overhead that would ensue from the consolidation of government departments, such as having one department of highways instead of three (or four if we consider Newfoundland). The savings of unified administration would be partly offset by the larger size of departments, by the additional costs of administering a larger geographical area, and by the extra costs to citizens of dealing with a more distant government.

One of the main advantages of union would be the possibility of establishment of a first rate civil service, for with a large single administration it would be feasible to build a corps of able adequately paid administrators with considerable specialization of tasks. This alone could contribute greatly to the economic and social development of the region. Whether or not there were any direct savings, there could be considerable economics in the form of better results from the expenditure made.

These results would only be possible with completely consolidated departments operating in a single capital. There would be no point in proceeding with union if the different administrative areas were parcelled out among the present provincial capitals. It is highly likely that initially employment would have to be found for all of the civil servants employed by the four provinces and that it would be a number of years before significant reductions in costs or improvements in the quality of administration could be expected.

There would likely be some reductions in the cost of the legislature, although the single legislature would have to be quite large to represent adequately the sections of a united province, and the stipend of the legislators would likely be increased. Of particular significance is that it should be possible to attract an abler group of legislators to the larger political arena with the greater scope for exercise of ability it would afford. Undoubtedly the number of members of cabinet calibre would be larger in a single large legislature than in each of the four separate provincial legislatures.

Full political union would inevitably require providing common levels of public services throughout the united province. Presumably each public service would have to be provided at the highest level prevailing in any of the present provinces, since it is almost unthinkable that the citizens in any of the component provinces would have the level of any service reduced as a result of union. This constitutes one of the most formidable obstacles to union, for there are considerable differences in average income and therefore in fiscal capacity among the provinces, as Table 2 shows.

TABLE 2

Per Capita Personal Income on the Average for 1961-63

		Percentage of Canada	Percentage of Nova Scotia
Newfoundland	$ 982	59	79
Prince Edward Island	1025	62	83
Nova Scotia	1239	75	100
New Brunswick	1108	67	89
Quebec	1442	87	
Ontario	1930	117	
Manitoba	1615	98	
Saskatchewan	1601	97	
Alberta	1675	101	
British Columbia	1883	114	
CANADA	1652	100	

The provision of common levels of services would require higher taxes throughout the region with least benefits to the wealthiest of the provinces, namely Nova Scotia, which would at the same time be making the largest contribution to the support of the uniform standard of services in the poorer provinces.

This obstacle could only be overcome if the federal government implemented the principle of fiscal equity by making equalization payments sufficient to enable *all* provinces to provide services at the same level as the wealthier provinces, with equivalent tax burdens. If this were done, political union would impose no penalties on Nova Scotia in the form of reduced services or increased tax burdens, and a uniform standard of services could be extended throughout the region.

The union is therefore dependent upon the federal government adopting an equalization policy for which there happen to be very strong ethical and economic arguments that are quite independent of union. The present federal equalization payments fall far short of the amounts necessary to enable the Atlantic provinces to provide services comparable to those of the wealthier provinces with comparable tax burdens. It has been estimated that the Atlantic provinces would have to receive about $148 million *more* in federal transfers than they presently receive in order to provide services comparable to those of the two richest provinces, with comparable tax burdens, and about $84 million more in order to provide services even at the national average, with tax burdens also equal to the national average.

It is essential that any commissions or committees established to investigate union, if their investigations are to be of any value, be composed of well qualified men who will conduct a thorough and careful study. It is worse than useless to charge unqualified political supporters and hangers-on with such a task.

ARGUMENTS FOR MARITIME UNION*

APEC

A few days ago the Atlantic Provinces Economic Council presented its Submission to the Maritime Union Study. In it APEC states that it "fully endorses not only the concept of Maritime Union but also wishes to express deep concern that a single Maritime Province be created as the result of a political union of the provinces."

•   •   •

Three basic arguments for political union of the Maritime Provinces are set forth in the APEC submission. All evolve from fundamental economic reasoning. One is that the reasons for separation of the Maritime Provinces in the nineteenth century now appear to be reasons for union. Another is the increased quality and quantity of services which a single Maritime Province, having one administrative, judicial and economic framework, could provide from the limited provincial government revenues available to the three provinces. Still another basic reason for Maritime Union, the Council contends, is the psychological impact it would likely have on the population of the region.

The acceptance of Union as an instrument for guiding the future should also motivate the region towards acceptance of still other changes—in a rapidly changing world—an attitude and condition regarded by many as a prerequisite for economic growth and development.

(1) If we look at the reasons for the separation of the Maritime Provinces into three separate entities, the state of the economy and the socio-political feeling at that time, a strong argument evolves for union of the provinces at this time. Although Prince Edward Island has always been a separate province since its creation in 1769, the province of New Brunswick was not established until 1784. What is now New Brunswick was originally part of Nova Scotia under British rule but due to numerous

*From the *APEC Newsletter,* Vol. 13, No. 3, April, 1969. By permission. For the full text of the submission, see Atlantic Provinces Economic Council, *Submission to the Maritime Union Study,* Halifax, April, 1969, mimeographed.

pressures at the end of the American Revolution, Nova Scotia was partitioned off at the isthmus so that the peninsula and the mainland became separate provinces.

Although political and social pressures influenced the British to create the province of New Brunswick, the basic underlying reason which gave rise to the move was the existing state of communications. The political motive was to create small enough units so that the British would not receive the harassment they had recently experienced from the Thirteen States. The social problem was that the primarily Loyalist population in New Brunswick feared being governed from Halifax which was both remote and peopled with what they felt were "Republican sympathizers." There was also the problem of geographical, cultural and occupational diversity both between and within the provinces.

The basic reason for separation, however, was that of communications, both in the plain old-fashioned connotation of the word—that of getting from point A to point B—and in the sense of the spread of information and ideas. Today, with relatively good transportation systems and the rapidity of such forms of transportation as air travel; the predominance of radios, televisions and newspapers; and a highly educated public, the population is not only more mobile but much better informed than at any time in the history of the region. Thus, since there has been such a dramatic change in the economy of the region and in life in general, and since the reasons for separation now seem so archaic, it would seem that Maritime Union is the logical step to be taken in an age where a total systems approach is the order of the day.

(2) The Council feels that much of the rationale for Maritime Union is economic in nature. Although Maritime Union is often endorsed on the understanding that the implementation of administrative, judicial and economic co-ordination will ultimately lead to political union, the Council contends that although some informal institutional arrangements may be made towards the creation of a union, the presence and rigidity of present institutions in the region can only be overcome through complete Maritime political union.

. . . APEC believes that the Maritime Provinces are facing a threat today, more serious than in the history of the region.

> The threat, as we see it, is both internal and external. Internally, it is the rapidly rising demand for services in the three provinces and the resultant increases in provincial government expenditures, while increases in revenues needed to pay for these services fail to keep pace. Externally, the threat is that if the three provincial governments do not strive to act together, through union, to increase the level of efficiency (in the pure economic sense of the word — of producing the optimum output at minimum cost) and the quality of services offered, demands for federal funds to cover increased costs in these provincial responsibilities could lead to the provincial governments finding themselves in the unenviable position of becoming mere "colonies" of Ottawa.

One example which shows quite clearly the opportunity for increased efficiency in the region is the excessive number of departmental employees in the three provinces relative to population as compared to other Canadian provinces.

For instance, in 1967, there were 24,106 persons employed in departments of the three provincial governments to cater to a population of 1,486,000. This represents a ratio of one employee per 61.6 of population. These ratios in the three provinces were: Prince Edward Island, 1:50.0; Nova Scotia, 1:56.1 and New Brunswick, 1:73.6. The ratio for the nation excluding British Columbia, and the Atlantic Provinces on the other hand, was 1:106.1 with ratios ranging from 1:71.4 in Alberta to the 1:117.1 in Quebec and 1:114.9 in Ontario. In fact, for the figures available, the ratios for all of the other provinces are higher than those in the Atlantic Provinces with the exception of Alberta's, which was lower than that of New Brunswick.

This, of course, has important implications in dollars and cents terms. If the ratio in the Maritime Provinces (1:61.6) had been the same as that for the rest of Canada, (1:106.1), only 14,006 would have been employed, instead of the actual 24,106. An increase in productivity in this one aspect of government activity would have meant a gross payroll (if paid the Maritime Provinces' average of $3,743) of approximately $52 million in 1967. This increased efficiency then would have been worth almost $38 million—a relative saving of over 40 percent. It must be pointed out that it would probably be unrealistic to expect the ratio to approach that of the nation as a whole, at the present economic state of the region because of the unique factors which characterize it. This is particularly relevant when our smaller total population and our relatively larger rural populations are considered. These and other factors pose a problem since the economics of scale in the provision of public services cannot be called into play. However, even though the suggested savings figure may be high, there is another significant factor. Salary scales for civil servants could be upgraded and greater challenge offered to attract a larger proportion of more highly qualified personnel.

In its Submission APEC analyzes the revenue and expenditure figures of the Maritime Provinces and of the rest of the Canadian provinces for the period 1953-67. The figures used are net figures since these are the closest approximations available on which to make comparisons both on a province-to-province and a year-to-year basis.

This analysis reveals that not only has the composition of each side of the provincial financial accounts changed, but also that growth in some segments far outdistanced that in others over the 1953-67 period. Another observation is that although there are some similarities between all the Canadian provinces on one hand, and the Maritime Provinces on the other, in the direction of changes in components, there are some very marked differences in the magnitude of the changes.

Looking first at total net general revenue, it becomes evident that the revenue of all provinces combined has grown at a faster rate than it has for any of the Maritime Provinces. While the rate for All Provinces was 11.6 percent per year, the rates of the three Maritime Provinces were 10.9 percent, 9.3 percent and 8.4 percent for Prince Edward Island, Nova Scotia and New Brunswick, respectively, for the period. Although there is a significant difference between the rates of increase of All Provinces and the Maritime Provinces in total net general revenue, a more significant difference exists in the composition of the aggregate in the region as opposed to the other provinces.

The most striking aspect of the components which combine to make up total net general revenue is the conspicuousness of the amount and growth of revenue received from other governments by the provincial governments in the region. Firstly, revenue from other governments has increased at more than twice the yearly rate for All Provinces in each of the Maritime Provinces—by 7.9 percent in Prince Edward Island and New Brunswick, and 7.2 percent in Nova Scotia, compared to 3.6 percent in All Provinces. Secondly, the proportion of total net general revenue received from other governments (almost exclusively the federal government) has remained consistently much higher in the Maritime Provinces than for All Provinces, and the gap is widening. Whereas the proportion received by the Maritime Provinces was almost double that of All Provinces in the early 1950s, it is now almost four times as high, at a level approaching 40 percent as opposed to about 10 percent.

The dominance of revenue received from other governments in the Maritime Provinces has, of course, repercussions on the relative size of revenues received by the provincial governments from other sources. For instance, total Tax Revenue for All Provinces increased from 38.7 percent of total net general revenue in 1953 to 68.0 percent in 1967. For the Maritime Provinces it increased from 27.7 percent to 44.3 percent. Both Tax Revenue and Non-Tax Revenue increased at substantially higher annual rates in All Provinces than in any of the three Maritime Provinces.

Looking at provincial expenditures, total net general expenditures of All Provinces increased at an average rate of 12.5 percent per year compared to the lower rates in the Maritime Provinces—Prince Edward Island, 11.1 percent; Nova Scotia, 10.3 percent; and New Brunswick, 8.9 percent. Putting both net general revenue and net general expenditures together, the most obvious conclusion that can be drawn is that spending seems to be growing faster than revenues, not only in the Maritime Provinces, but, also, in most of the other provinces as well. Over the 1953-67 period, the average yearly rates of increase in spending were greater than in revenue for all the entities considered: 12.5 percent as opposed to 11.6 percent for All Provinces, 11.1 percent versus 10.9 percent for Prince Edward Island (inflated by the heavy increase in revenue at the end of the period), 10.3 percent versus 9.3 percent for Nova Scotia, and 8.9 percent versus 8.4 percent for New Brunswick.

Since the tables used were adjusted for comparability, it is probably safe to say that the differences are of a greater magnitude than reflected in the annual rates of increase, even when it is realized that the rates are compounded for every year from 1953 to 1967.

Comparison of the figures for Gross Provincial, Regional and National Products with the respective net general expenditure figures reveal a general movement across the nation towards spending a larger proportion of output. Not only have provincial government expenditures in the Maritime Provinces exceeded increases in output, but also Maritime Provinces' governments continue to spend a significantly higher proportion of output than do All Provinces.

APEC's Submission emphasizes the importance of the increased efficiency which could come about as the result of political union of the three Maritime Provinces.

> Surely, three provinces with combined populations of only 1,486,000 do not require three departments of agriculture, fisheries, forestry, health and welfare, etc. In fact, the population after union, would probably be significantly less than three-quarters of Metropolitan Toronto or Montreal. For instance, in 1966, the total population of the Maritime Provinces was equivalent to about 68 percent of the population of Metropolitan Toronto (2,159,000) and approximately 60 percent of the population of Metropolitan Montreal (2,437,000). With the implementation of political union for the Maritime Provinces, at least some of the economies of scale may come into play.

Not only would political union with the resultant accompanying administrative, judicial and economic unions mean dollars and cents savings for government in the region, but it could also lead to an increase in the quality of services.

(3) The Submission also stresses the value of political union of the Maritime Provinces to the industrial and overall economic development of the region. It points out that the establishment of priorities and the successful implementation of policy can only be achieved by changing the institutions which have been built up to deal with industrial development. Since their establishment, many of them in the last decade, duplication and rivalry has occurred not only between provinces but within provinces as well. . . . It would seem then that it is the institutional framework within which each development and planning agency is set—that of individual provinces—that needs to be abolished before complete co-ordination and co-operation can be achieved. Maritime Union seems to be the most logical answer. . . . By concentrating growth at growth points, the spin-off to the rest of the Maritimes could lead to a faster sustained rate of growth for the entire region.

•   •   •

LET'S HAVE FIVE PROVINCES*

W. A. C. BENNETT

. . . I believe the time has come to recognize that in the interests of economic realities the boundaries of some of the Provinces will have to be altered and the separate existence of some other Provinces will have to be abolished so as to provide five viable and effective political units consonant and in conformity with the

*From *Proposals of the Province of British Columbia on the Constitution of Canada,* December, 1968, submitted to the Second Meeting of the Constitutional Conference, Ottawa, February 10-12, 1969. By permission of the Premier of British Columbia.

five economic regions of Canada. Imagine the increased efficiency and resultant substantial savings to the Canadian taxpayer that would result [from amalgamating the four Atlantic provinces into one and the three Prairie provinces into one and from extending the boundaries of the new five provinces northward].

In keeping with the principle of political units conforming with economic regions of Canada, British Columbia calls for the Federal Government to extend by legislation the boundaries of each of the applicable Provinces northward to the northern limits of continental Canada. Furthermore, the topographical characteristics support communication links and trade patterns running north and south rather than east and west.

For example, in British Columbia, the extension of the Pacific Great Eastern Railway to Fort Nelson and beyond, the construction of the Stewart-Watson Lake Highway with connecting link to the Alaska Highway, and the Alaska Highway itself provide the communication links between British Columbia and the Yukon— the kind of links which are so essential to the economic development of Canada's northern regions. In the light of the tremendous development now taking place in the northern half of British Columbia, sparked by the Peace River power project, now in operation, and the lines of communication to which I have already made reference, it is not only geographically and economically logical, but it would be mutually advantageous for this northern area to be added to the Province so that an integrated development plan could be made to realize to the full the great potential of the whole area.

Ample precedent can be found for the extension of Provincial boundaries northward in the cases of Manitoba, Ontario, and Quebec by legislation of the Parliament of Canada in the years 1912 and 1930.

• • •

AMALGAMATING THE PRAIRIE PROVINCES HAS GREAT ADVANTAGES*

JAMES RICHARDSON

. . . The Eastern regions of our great nation were settled first. This meant, and means, that most centres of influence, the national government itself, and the controlling and administrative offices of almost all national business enterprises, the railways, the banks, and the major industrial and financial institutions were begun in the places of early settlement. There, to this day, their executive and adminis-

*From "Federalism — And the Western Canadians," An Address by the Hon. James Richardson, Minister of Supply and Services, Government of Canada, delivered on May 10, 1970, to the Conference *One Prairie Province? A Question for Canada,* held in Lethbridge, Alberta. By permission of the author.

trative and decision-making centres have remained, but Canada has changed, changed beyond all possible recognition since its establishment in 1867. In the hundred years since Confederation, and at an accelerating pace in recent years, vast natural wealth has been discovered and developed in Western Canada. It is this colossal natural wealth, and the consequent, almost unlimited potential of the West, unknown at the time of Confederation, that is the second fact.

It is the relationship of these two facts, original discovery and settlement from the East across the Atlantic, and the later discovery of Canada's greatest potential in the West, which has created a fundamental imbalance in our country's structure. . . .

It is clearly the responsibility of Westerners to encourage the decentralization of present Government and corporate structures, and at the same time to continue to build strong government and corporate structures in the West. A more balanced industrial and economic growth would, undoubtedly, be beneficial to Canada, and important to Canadian unity.

•   •   •

I want to emphasize that it is too soon for me, or perhaps for any of us, to be committed to this imaginative and forward-looking concept [of Prairie union], but my own knowledge of our country confirms in my mind that there is merit in considering it most carefully. It is my belief that when we have, together, examined some of the merits of a larger and stronger Province in the West, we may well discover that its creation would be a major contribution to federalism and to Canada. . . .

Let us look at some of the merits of a larger and stronger government in the West.

The first is that all the powers and responsibilities now given to the provinces under the Constitution would be legislated and administered evenly in this vast region. The two areas of provincial jurisdiction of greatest importance in this respect would be natural resource development and human resource development, which is, of course, education. Both of these important responsibilities—resources and education—are already under provincial jurisdiction in our Constitution, and it is a question for the people of Western Canada collectively to ask themselves whether or not, in today's world, they could do a better job with a more unified approach to these and other responsibilities, now within provincial jurisdiction.

The second merit of a larger government, from a Westerner's point of view is that, quite apart from the merits of unifying the functions which are already given to the provinces, a larger government, and a stronger government, would be better able to negotiate appropriate changes in the division of powers between the central government and the regional government.

Nothing that the West might propose in the division of powers should undermine the central concept of federalism upon which Canada is built, but it is entirely appropriate that we try to establish a still better structure. We might call it the new federalism designed for Canada's second century, as a federal state. An important consideration to keep in mind in this respect is that the degree to which the West might want to renegotiate the division of powers would depend to some extent on progress made in other areas of Constitutional Review, most particularly the progress made in changing in Senate and the House of Commons to encourage a greater regional influence in both of these institutions.

A third fundamental merit of the "Canada West Concept" is that it would help to achieve the essential balance of Canada which is vital to our on-going confederation. . . . An important purpose which I see for a larger regional government in the West, is that it would be better able to balance the growing power of the central provinces. Of particular attraction to me in this concept is that it, in no way, tries to be harmful to the central provinces. The purpose would be to achieve a stronger West, not a weaker Ontario, or a weaker Quebec. . . .

Yet another reason, and perhaps in some ways the most important reason, for finding merit in a larger and stronger Western Government, is that such a government, and the unity which it could create in the West, would be a reflection of the inherent unity which already exists in this region.

It is my belief that Westerners have an identity, a character, and even a spirit, of their own. To the extent that the West is divided, it is divided more by artificial political boundaries, drawn by remote hands, in remote times; and by provincial administrations of differing political affiliation, than it is by any inherent regional difference. . . .

It should be made clear, in case there is any doubt whatsoever on this matter, that there is no federal government policy, at the present time, either in favour of or opposed to, one Maritime Province, or one Prairie Province. Just as [the Hon.] Jean-Eudes Dubé was giving his personal views when he endorsed political union for the Maritimes, so also my observations on this subject reflect my own thoughts and are not an expression of government policy. . . .

As there is undoubtedly going to be immediate discussion concerning a possible site for the capital, let me, as a start, suggest where it should not be. I believe there are good reasons why the new capital of the Province of Canada West should not be in any one of the present prairie capitals.

. . . It should be possible for Western Canadians in restructuring their political institutions to achieve for the first time in any Canadian province, the best characteristics of both centralization and decentralization. I would visualize that some of the major departments of the new provincial government would be administered, and would have most of their personnel in the present prairie capitals and possibly in other cities as well. For example, and just for example, a new and large Department of Natural Resources might be one of the departments in Edmonton, the Department of Agriculture and other departments could be centered in Regina, and the Department of Education along with other departments, might be located in Winnipeg.

As an additional part of the concept of decentralized government in the West, as well as centralized government, we should aim at constant improvement and strengthening of municipal governments, primarily because of the constantly increasing growth and complexity of our cities. . . .

It is . . . [also] evident to me that at some stage, the Canada West Concept could be widened to consider the possibility of including at least one or two of the regions which immediately surround the three provinces. This possibility, incidentally, gives additional merit to the name, Canada West. . . .

ALBERTA HAS OTHER IDEAS*

HARRY STROM

. . . A number of questions about one prairie province come readily to mind. What would the patterns of imports and exports be? Would we be more likely to gain access to the United States oil market or the Montreal oil market?

Would we be a landlocked entity peddling surplus wheat, consoling ourselves by taking money out of one pocket, putting it in another and saying we were covering the "costs of production"?

If there is a problem with foreign ownership in Canada—would there not continue to be such a problem with a western union?

Our major deficiency in the West has been secondary industry. Would a single prairie province be better able to overcome this deficiency?

Would there be a bilingual problem?

And what of the "equalization payments"?

•   •   •

A full understanding of the one prairie province alternative requires us, I believe, to examine other alternative courses of action.

I discussed one such alternative when I spoke in Vancouver last fall: on that occasion I said:

> Our two Provinces, Alberta and British Columbia, have much in common, we share many ideals and objectives, and a common outlook and a common approach to problems, and, more important than that, we have a fine record of making use of the great opportunities which we have in the West. Realizing the great tradition and appreciating the heritage which we in Alberta and British Columbia share, we ought to be working continually towards greater co-operation between our two Provinces. . . .

*From an Address by the Hon. Harry Strom, Premier of Alberta, delivered on May 11, 1970, to the Conference *One Prairie Province? A Question for Canada*, held in Lethbridge, Alberta. By permission of the author.

There are some very clear practical reasons for an economic union with British Columbia.

British Columbia ports are essential in the export of wheat and coal and other products to the Far East. British Columbia ports are essential to the import of machines and products from the Far East that they must sell to us if trade is to be long term.

The industries of British Columbia are different from those of Alberta. The union of our two Provinces would add a great stability to our economic life and would be beneficial to both.

We know that there is already a great deal of migration between British Columbia and Alberta.

Thus there are good reasons for regarding a British Columbia-Alberta union as a subject as worthy of excellent and stimulating academic analysis. . . .

. . . the Alberta government does not look favourably upon the idea of combining the three provinces. We frankly do not think the people of Alberta would be interested in such a union. . . .

We do think it worthwhile to look at alternatives and I have suggested one such alternative in looking at the two Western provinces of British Columbia and Alberta. . . .

BIBLIOGRAPHY

Brewis, T. N., Paquet, G., "Regional Development in Canada: An Exploratory Essay," *C.P.A.,* Vol. XI, No. 2, Summer, 1968.

Dehem, R., *et al.,* "Concepts of Regional Planning," *C.P.A.,* Vol. IX, No. 2, June, 1966.

Fenton, A., "Resources Ministers' Council: A Model for Government Co-operation," *Canadian Business,* Vol. XXXVI, April, 1963.

Fergusson, C. B., "Maritime Union," *Q.Q.,* Vol. LXXVII, No. 2, Summer, 1970.

Hebal, J. J., "Approaches to Regional and Metropolitan Governments in the United States and Canada," *C.P.A.,* Vol. X, No. 2, June, 1967.

Howland, R. D., *Some Regional Aspects of Canada's Economic Development,* Ottawa, Queen's Printer, 1957.

Krueger, R., Sargent F., deVos, A., Pearson, N. (eds.), *Regional and Resource Planning in Canada,* Toronto, Holt, Rinehart and Winston, 1963.

Lajoie, A., *Les Structures Administratives Régionales: Déconcentration et Décentralisation au Québec,* Montréal, Les Presses de l'Université de Montréal, 1968.

Lemieux, V., "L'analyse stratégique des organisations administratives," *C.P.A.,* Vol. VIII, No. 4, decembre, 1965.

Wade, M., (ed.), *Regionalism in the Canadian Community, 1867-1967,* Toronto, University of Toronto Press, 1969.

Whalen, H., "Public Policy and Regional Development: The Experience of the Atlantic Provinces," in Rotstein, A. (ed.), *The Prospect of Change: Proposals for Canada's Future,* Toronto, McGraw-Hill, 1965.

SIX
FEDERAL-PROVINCIAL FINANCIAL RELATIONS

Federal-provincial fiscal relations is one of the problems that is rarely quiescent in Canadian politics. Controversies between the two jurisdictions over revenue from subsidies, the division of taxation, and the introduction and funding of programs in many different fields, including education, social and welfare services, and income security, have been persistent, vexatious, and often acrimonious throughout the entire history of Confederation. The decades following the second world war have been different only in that they have been characterized by an intensification of the conflicts and complexities in this basic, and perhaps most important, aspect of federalism.

This new phase began in 1940 with the publication of the Rowell-Sirois Report, which endorsed an approach to Canadian federalism that recognized both the need for the establishment of nation-wide minimal standards of social services and the role of the central government in achieving them. The trend was reinforced by the growth of the popularity and scope of the welfare state and the host of additional social services it implied.

While these factors would have been sufficient in themselves to engender much controversy about which jurisdiction was to provide services and how they were to be paid for by very complex arrangements involving tax sharing, equalization payments and stabilization grants, and "opting out" of shared-cost programs, the situation has been complicated further by the commencement of a wholesale review of the constitution, which, beginning in 1968, has resulted in a series of federal-provincial constitutional conferences. By 1970 the latter had focussed on an intensive examination of fiscal relations in the federation. A great deal of literature has been churned out in the process, as the bibliographies in this chapter and in the chapter on federalism attest.

A student interested in this subject would be well advised to begin by reading at least the recommendations of the *Report of the Royal Commission on Dominion-Provincial Relations* (the Rowell-Sirois Report), noted in the bibliography, and some of the numerous articles and monographs which are referred to also in the bibliography. The chapter in Dawson's and Ward's standard text, *The Government of Canada,* dealing with the history of federal-provincial financial relations, provides a good background to the present situation, as do many of the publications by other authors such as Professors D. V. Smiley, J. S. Dupré, and J. H. Perry. The excellent publications of the Canadian Tax Foundation are invaluable, especially the Foundation's annual review, *The National Finances,* and its periodic publication of the *Provincial Finances.* The Foundation also has published a number of very useful studies of specific problems. One should consult also the publications of the Institute of Intergovernmental Relations at Queen's University and the federal government's annual treasury of statistical wisdom, the *Canada Year Book.*

In addition, the reports of the federal Royal Commission on Taxation (the Carter Commission), the Ontario Committee on Taxation (the Smith Committee), the Belanger Commission in Quebec, and the Tax Structure Committee, noted in the bibliography, are very relevant. Professor J. P. Meekison's book of readings, *Canadian Federalism: Myth or Reality,* Toronto, Methuen, 1968, also contains excerpts on this topic.

The literature available has been swelled now since the constitutional conferences began by the numerous working papers, position papers, and speeches on relevant matters produced by the federal government, the provinces, the Continuing Committee of Officials, and the Secretariat of the Constitutional Conference, as well as by the verbatim records of the conferences themselves, published by the Queen's Printer, Ottawa. These are too numerous to be recorded in the bibliography in this chapter. However, a complete list of the government of Canada's working papers presented to the several conferences is given in the bibliography in Chapter 4 on federalism.

The aim of this particular chapter on federal-provincial financial relations is to give in summary form the highlights of recent developments to mid-1970. The selection from the Canadian Tax Foundation's *The National Finances 1969-70* outlines the most recent federal-provincial financial agreements that are to run for the period 1967-72 and it also gives some of the pertinent facts, figures, and problems. For Professor J. S. Dupré's article on the problems of provinces "contracting out" (or more popularly, "opting out") of conditional grants, see the second edition of this book, pp. 168-176, which reproduced a large portion of his article. A reference to the full version of the article is to be found in the bibliography in this chapter. The other two items in this chapter are taken from the federal government's working papers presented to the two constitutional conferences in 1969. They deal with the difficult and complex problems of federal-provincial grants and Parliament's spending powers and income security and social services. They also contain Ottawa's tentative proposals for solutions. For an excellent critique of the first federal paper, see D. V. Smiley's and R. M. Burns' article in the *Canadian Tax Journal,* which is too lengthy to be included here but which is noted in the bibliography to this chapter.

CURRENT FISCAL ARRANGEMENTS, GRANTS, AND PROGRAMS*

The federal government uses three basic methods to transfer fiscal resources to the provinces, territories and municipalities: tax abatements, unconditional grants and conditional grants.

The basic federal abatements of individual and corporate income tax and estate tax are estimated at $2,613.1 million for 1969-70. Unconditional grants to the provinces, principally equalization payments under the *Federal-Provincial Fiscal Arrangements Act,* statutory subsidies, and shares of federal estate tax and income tax on certain public utilities, should amount to $788.2 million in 1969-70. Payments to the territories cover the deficiency on ordinary account, capital needs and amortization of debt. The general payments to municipalities take the form of grants in lieu of taxes on federal property.

The federal government also makes conditional payments or grants-in-aid to the other levels of government for specific purposes such as hospital insurance, assistance to the aged, the blind and the disabled, the Trans-Canada highway, vocational school training, airport development and various resource projects. . . . A summary table showing both unconditional and conditional payments is included . . . . The arrangements under which a province can "opt out" of certain conditional grant programs and receive tax abatements or cash compensation in lieu of grants are also described. . . .

•   •   •

FEDERAL-PROVINCIAL FISCAL ARRANGEMENTS (1967-72)

The Federal-Provincial Fiscal Arrangements Act, 1967 provides for a number of significant changes in the structure of federal payments to the provinces. The federal government increased its abatement of the personal income tax—excluding the abatements under the *Established Programs (Interim Arrangements) Act*—from 24 percent to 28 percent of the federal tax payable in the provinces. The abatement of the corporate income tax, which stood at 9 percent of taxable income in provinces other than Quebec and 10 percent of taxable income in Quebec, was raised to 10 percent in all provinces effective for the 1967 taxation year. The same arrangements hold for estate taxes and succession duties as held during the last year of the previous agreements. For provinces which levy their own succession duties at the same rate as in 1964 (i.e. Ontario and Quebec), the federal government abates its estate tax by 50 percent of the federal estate tax payable, and makes a payment equal to 25 percent of the estate tax payable in the province. For provinces which have increased their succession duty since 1964 (i.e. British Columbia)

* From *The National Finances, 1969-70,* Toronto, Canadian Tax Foundation, 1969, Chapter X. By permission.

the federal government abates its estate tax by 75 percent of the federal tax payable. For provinces which do not levy a succession duty the direct payment is 75 percent of the federal estate tax due in the province.

Whereas earlier abatements of the personal and corporate income taxes by the federal government to provide taxing room to the provinces had usually been unconditional (the exception was the *Established Programs (Interim Arrangements) Act*, which in effect applied only to Quebec), the extra 4 points of personal income tax and 1 percent of corporate income granted to the provinces in 1967 was linked to expenditures for post-secondary education and was in part a substitute for the per capita grants for university costs. The post-secondary education fiscal transfer program was also, partly, to replace federal operating cost contributions to the provinces under the Technical and Vocational Training Agreements which were phased out during 1967-68.

Both the equalization formula and the stabilization formula were expanded by changing their form—relating them to all provincial revenue sources instead of the "standard" taxes and natural resource revenues.

Financing Post-Secondary Education

The federal government in the *Federal-Provincial Arrangements Act (Part II)* changed the form of federal assistance to post-secondary education and increased the extent of its financial commitment. The post-secondary education program provides for a fiscal transfer to each province of equalized tax abatements (4 percent of basic individual income tax and 1 percent of corporation taxable income) and a cash adjustment payment to a total of either 50 percent of post-secondary education operating expenditures incurred in the province, or, at the option of the province, an amount equal to $15 per capita (1967-68 population), escalated annually thereafter at the national rate of growth of post-secondary education operating expenditures. The 50 percent of cost option is irrevocable but a province which has elected to use the per capita option may switch to the other option should this become advantageous. . . .

Conditional grants to the provinces under the *Technical and Vocational Training Assistance Act* were originally scheduled to expire on March 31, 1967 but transitional arrangements have been made whereby capital grants are available, without limit as to time, until they reach, for each province, $800 per capita of its population aged 15 to 19 as of 1961. The federal government has taken over the full cost of training allowances to adults taking occupational training and the full cost of the training programs.

Equalization

In contrast, to the equalization formula for 1962-67 which took into account only the three "standard" taxes and natural resource revenue, the new formula is based on the 16 provincial revenue sources listed below:

Personal income tax, corporation income tax, succession duties and shares of estate tax, general sales tax, motor fuel tax, motor vehicle revenues, alcoholic beverage revenues, forestry revenues, oil royalties, natural gas royalties, sales of Crown leases and reservations on oil and natural gas lands, other oil and gas revenues, metallic and non-metallic mineral revenues, water power rentals, other taxes, other revenues.

For each revenue source a base is chosen which is as close as possible to the actual base of the revenue source in all provinces. Then for each revenue source a "national average provincial revenue rate" is calculated by dividing the total revenue for all provinces by the total base for all provinces. This national average rate is multiplied by the base in each province and divided by the population of the province to give the per capita yield of a "tax" levied at the national average rate. To obtain the equalization payment for the particular revenue source in the province the population of the province is multiplied by the difference between the per capita yield in all provinces and the derived per capita yield in the province at the national average rate. The total equalization payment for the province is the sum of entitlements, positive and negative, for each revenue source.

There is a simpler method of calculating this payment. The percentage of the total base attributed to a particular province is calculated as well as the percentage of the total population in the province. The difference between the percentage of the base and the percentage of the population multiplied by the total revenue in all provinces from a source gives the equalization payment for the revenue source in the province. Again the total payment is the sum of the payments for each source of revenue.

Saskatchewan which had been receiving an equalization payment under the old arrangements appeared likely to lose much, possibly all, of its payments as a result of the new formula. Special provision was made to prevent any sudden year to year declines in Saskatchewan's revenues from this source by five-year transitional arrangements based upon the province's equalization entitlement in 1966-67, the last year of the previous arrangements. The Atlantic Provinces Additional Grants were abolished under the new arrangements but the provinces of Nova Scotia, New Brunswick and Newfoundland are guaranteed an additional equalization payment of $10.5 million while Prince Edward Island is guaranteed an additiona $3.5 million. These are the same amounts as were paid previously in the form of Additional Grants.

Stabilization

The change in the stabilization formula is closely related to the change in the equalization formula. Total net general revenues of a province, including equalization and other unconditional grants from the federal government, are used in determining the size of payment, and not just revenues related to fiscal arrangements with the federal government. In two cases actual revenues are replaced by average revenues: a three-year average of estate tax and succession duty revenue and a five-year average of sales of Crown leases and reservations on oil and natural gas lands are used instead of actual revenue. The stabilization payment is then the amount needed to bring the current year's revenue at the previous year's tax rates up to 95 percent of the previous year's revenue. No payments have been made under the new stabilization arrangements.

"Opting out"

The "opting-out" arrangements are very similar to the arrangements described under 1965 changes in fiscal arrangements. Two changes result from the *Federal-Provincial Fiscal Arrangements Act, 1967*. An agreement entered into for health grants under the *Established Programs (Interim Arrangements) Act* was to be in force only up to March 31, 1967. This terminal date was moved to March 31, 1970, the terminal date for other programs under this Act. The one point abatement of the personal income tax related to the operating costs of certain technical education programs was allowed to expire on March 31, 1967 as scheduled. This change is connected with the federal government's takeover of adult retraining expenses. As a result the total additional abatement received by Quebec for opting out was reduced from 20 to 19 points.

FEDERAL-PROVINCIAL CONFERENCES

In November 1968, two important federal-provincial conference were held. At the meeting of federal and provincial finance ministers, the federal government reiterated its 1966 offer to turn over to the provinces full responsibility for the current shared-cost programs dealing with hospital insurance, health grants and the Canada Assistance Plan. In return, the federal government would cede an additional 17 percent of the personal income tax, the associated equalization plus a final adjusting payment or refund to make the total transfer equivalent to what the federal share of these programs would have been. Again, as in 1966, none of the provinces has accepted this proposal. The conference must be regarded as a preliminary meeting at which both levels of government presented their basic positions; but it did produce agreement to hold further consultations. The Tax Structure Committee, consisting of representatives of the eleven governments, was reactivated to produce forecasts of federal and provincial revenues and expenditures from 1969 to 1972. A committee was set up to study ways of controlling the costs of joint health programs and further consultation will be undertaken to develop similar studies on other shared-cost programs. The present tax collection agreements were renewed for an indefinite period.

The meeting of federal and provincial ministers of health, held at the same time, had much the same theme. The federal government announced that it planned to phase out, over the next three years, certain health grants in such fields as public health and cancer control, retaining only grants for research and professional training. The phased-out grants will be replaced by more flexible grants of an undefined nature. The federal government also announced its intention to abolish hospital construction grants and to hold grants made out of the Health Resources Fund to the present level of $37.5 million.

ESTIMATED PAYMENTS TO THE PROVINCES UNDER THE FEDERAL-PROVINCIAL FISCAL ARRANGEMENTS ACT 1967 FOR FISCAL YEAR 1969-70

(All dollar figures except per capitas in thousands)

	Nfld.	P.E.I.	N.S.	N.B.	Que.	Ont.	Man.	Sask.	Alta.	B.C.	Total
Estimated population April 1, 1969	512,746	110,167	763,851	626,324	5,975,501	7,425,031	977,271	960,649	1,553,247	2,055,519	20,960,306
Provincial revenues											
Individual income tax[b]	17,953	3,255	36,323	32,838	416,453[a]	748,992	78,208	67,838	125,746	190,159	1,717,765
Corporation income tax[c]	10,266	1,269	12,162	9,610	188,710[a]	341,846[a]	29,607	22,051	56,626	72,402	744,549
Estate tax (75% of 3-year average)	456	299	3,737	1,429	37,974	74,334	4,804	3,709	7,409	16,630	150,781
Estimated revenue from all sources	115,561	24,489	195,500	211,885	2,030,590	3,120,213	344,081	342,861	656,748	807,450	7,849,378
Equalization (for all revenue sources)											
Yield at national average rates	106,021	24,399	196,025	151,458	1,894,683	3,032,225	323,829	352,634	846,911	921,193	7,849,378
Per capita yield at national average rates	206.77	221.47	256.63	241.82	317.08	408.38	331.36	367.08	545.25	448.16	374.49
Deficiency from national average ($374.49)	167.72	153.02	117.86	132.67	57.41	—	43.13	7.41	—	—	
Equalization amount from above	85,996	16,857	90,028	83,093	343,069	—	42,147	7,117	—	—	668,307
Guaranteed equalization[d]	48,763	13,885	57,638	54,128	—	—	—	12,261	—	—	186,675
Payments to provinces											
Equalization payment[d]	85,996	16,857	90,028	83,093	343,069	—	42,147	12,261	—	—	673,451
Individual income tax collected	17,953	3,255	36,323	32,838	—	748,992	78,208	67,838	125,746	190,159	1,301,312
Corporation income tax collected	10,266	1,269	12,162	9,610	—	—	29,607	22,051	56,626	72,402	213,993
Share of estate tax collected	456	299	3,737	1,429	12,658	24,778	4,804	3,709	7,409	—	59,279
Share of income tax on certain public utilities	1,297	244	2,017	129	3,031	7,744	969	39	7,599	648	23,717
Statutory subsidies	9,656	657	2,132	1,745	4,023	4,624	2,132	2,144	3,008	1,673	31,794
Total payments	125,624	22,581	146,399	128,844	362,781[e]	786,138	157,867	180,042	200,388	264,882	2,303,546
Value of income tax abatements for post-secondary education included in above											
4% of individual income tax	2,355	465	5,189	3,700	59,493	106,999	9,480	8,223	16,491	27,165	239,560
1% of corporation income tax base	790	127	1,216	961	15,726	28,487	2,691	2,005	5,393	7,350	64,746

(a) Quebec collects its own personal and corporation income taxes and Ontario its own corporation income tax. Quebec and Ontario collect 50% of their shares of estate taxes through their succession duties and British Columbia collects its 75% share through its succession duties. (b) Federal abatement is 28% of federal basic tax. See text. In four provinces the individual income tax rate is 28%. Others are: Newfoundland and Alberta, 30.5%; New Brunswick, 35.5%; Manitoba and Saskatchewan, 33%. Effective January 1, 1970 the rate in Newfoundland and Alberta will change to 33%, in New Brunswick, to 38%, and in Manitoba, to 39%. (c) Federal abatement is 10% of taxable income. See text. In Prince Edward Island, Nova Scotia, New Brunswick and British Columbia the rate is 10%. Others are: Newfoundland, 13%; Quebec and Ontario, 12%; Manitoba and Saskatchewan, 11%; Alberta, 10.5%. Effective January 1, 1970 the rate in Manitoba will be 13%, and in Alberta, 11%. (d) See text for bases of equalization payment. (e) Does not include value of extra abatements to Quebec for opting out of certain joint programs.
Source: Department of Finance.

MEDICARE

The federal government has offered to pay to the provinces one-half of the national average per capita cost of operating a medical insurance plan. . . . At October 1, 1969 all provinces except Quebec, New Brunswick and Prince Edward Island were operating medicare schemes. New Brunswick expects to have a plan in operation by the end of 1969 and Quebec, by July 1, 1970. Prince Edward Island has not yet made any decision.

CURRENT SITUATION

The accompanying table shows how the payments to the provinces under the current fiscal arrangements are calculated and summarizes the estimates of the amounts each province will receive in the form of unconditional payments for the 1969-70 year. The table also contains an estimate of the value of the federal tax abatements in each province, including the value of extra abatements for post-secondary education. It should be noted that this estimate does not include the extra abatements which Quebec will receive as a result of opting out of certain conditional grant programs and operating its own youth allowances program.

The table shows that all provinces except Ontario, Alberta and British Columbia will qualify for an equalization payment in 1969-70. Equalization payments are estimated at $673.5 million and other payments at $442.7 million. The federal government will collect an estimated $1,513.3 million of income taxes on behalf of the provinces with which it has collection agreements.

Quebec is the only province to take advantage of the opting-out alternative under the *Established Programs (Interim Arrangements) Act.* The value of the extra abatements of income tax to Quebec during 1969-70 for the various programs it has opted out of has been estimated by the Foundation as follows:

Program	Tax Abatement	Equali- zation	Operating Cost Adjustment	Estimated Total Value
	(dollar figures in thousands)			
Hospital insurance	14%			
	$208,233	40,375	46,400	295,000
Special welfare programs (old age assistance, blind and disabled allowances, unemploy- ment assistance and Canada Assistance Plan)	4%			
	59,493	11,535	124,666	195,694
Health grants	1%			
	14,873	2,884	—11,757	6,158
Youth allowances	3%			
	44,619	8,652	31,710	21,561

GRANTS TO MUNICIPALITIES

. . . Municipal grants have grown from $1.4 million in 1950-51 to $45.1 million in 1968-69. For the current fiscal year, $49.9 million are provided in the Estimates, including $2.0 million in grants to provinces which impose real estate taxes to finance services usually provided in Canada by municipalities. . . .

GRANTS TO TERRITORIES

. . . The governments of the Territories are gradually assuming responsibility for functions formerly carried out by the federal government. The government of the Northwest Territories at Yellowknife has taken over responsibility for the Mackenzie Region and by April 1, 1970 will also take over responsibility for the Keewatin and Baffin Regions. Pending new financial arrangements between the territories and the federal government the current Estimates authorize interim payments of $6.7 million to the Yukon Territory and $10.4 million to the Northwest Territories, including payments in respect of the amortization of outstanding loans. Another $4.3 million are provided for the Northwest Territories for activities transferred to the territorial government. . . .

TOTAL FEDERAL PAYMENTS TO OTHER GOVERNMENTS

. . . In the accompanying table both conditional and unconditional grants are shown for the fiscal years ending March 31, 1960, and 1968 to 1970. The figures for 1969 and 1970 are estimates only. The table indicates that grants to all levels of government have risen from $931.9 million in 1959-60 to an estimated $2,423.3 million in 1967-68. Data for 1968-69 and 1969-70 conditional grants are not yet available. The last line of the table contains an estimate prepared by the Department of Finance of the value of the abatements granted to taxpayers under the various fiscal arrangements. While these abatements are not paid out as a federal grant to the provinces, they do reduce federal tax collections in the provinces and are therefore an indirect form of grant.

[The last table] provides a breakdown by province of federal contributions to the provinces, municipalities and territories for 1967-68.

SUMMARY OF FEDERAL CONTRIBUTIONS TO THE PROVINCES MUNICIPALITIES AND TERRITORIES

Fiscal years ending March 31, 1960 and 1968 to 1970

($ million)

	1960	1968	1969[a]	1970[a]
A. PAYMENTS TO PROVINCES				
Unconditional grants				
Tax rentals	279.7[b]			
Equalization and stabilization	180.7	547.6	588.7[c]	673.5
Share of federal estate tax	—	55.4	55.5[d]	59.3
Atlantic provinces grants	33.0	—	—	—
Certain public utilities income tax	4.8	6.7	20.8	23.7
Post-secondary education[e]	—	108.0	276.7[f]	328.0
Statutory subsidies	20.7	31.7	31.7	31.8
Total unconditional grants[g]	518.8	749.5	973.4	1,116.2
Conditional grants[h]				
Recreation and culture	1.9	.7	—	—
Hospital insurance	150.6	672.6	792.2[i]	—
Other health, including Medicare	46.1	88.3	112.0[i]	—
Welfare	90.9	406.5	412.4[i]	—
Education	8.4	209.2	—	—
Transportation	65.8	93.2	45.2	—
Agriculture	6.7	3.4	27.6[i]	—
Other natural resources	4.3	44.5	—	—
Civil defence	1.6	4.8	—	—
Municipal winter works	6.6	30.3	—	—
Other	.1	16.7	—	—
Total conditional grants[g]	382.9	1,570.0	1,500.0[j]	—
Total payments to provinces[g]	901.7	2,319.4	2,473.4	—
B. PAYMENTS TO MUNICIPALITIES				
Grants in lieu of property taxes	22.6	43.9	45.1	49.9
Other grants	6.3	46.2	—	—
Total payments to muncipalities[g]	28.9	90.1	—	—
C. PAYMENTS TO TERRITORIES				
Statutory subsidies and tax rentals	1.0	9.4	12.0	21.4
Other grants	.3	4.4	—	—
Total payments to territories[g]	1.3	13.8	—	—
TOTAL FEDERAL PAYMENTS[g]	931.9	2,423.3	—	—
Federal per capita grants to universities	26.1	—	—	—
Estimated value of federal "standard" tax abatements (income and estate taxes)	319.8	1,846.0	2,200.0[j]	2,613.1

(a) Canadian Tax Foundation estimates. (b) Before annual deductions for overpayments under the 1952 tax agreements, totalling $1.0 million. (c) Before deductions for overpayments and interest under the 1962-67 arrangements, totalling $21.2 million. (d) Before additions for underpayments under the 1962-67 arrangements, totalling $4.1 million. (e) Excludes equalization in respect of tax points abated for post-secondary education and value of abatement points, which are included elsewhere in the table. The total value of all components of the post-secondary education program was $348.1 million for 1967-68 and $554.6 million for 1968-69. The $554.6 million figure includes a $52.4 million adjustment in respect of 1967-68. (f) Excludes tax abatements amounting to (a) individual income tax, $175.6 million and corporation tax, $52.0 million and (b) equalization, $21.0 million, included elsewhere. (g) Figures may not add owing to rounding. (h) Conditional grants include value of tax abatements to Quebec plus equalization and operating cost adjustments for those programs from which Quebec has opted out. (i) From *House of Commons Debates*, March 18, 1969. (j) The rounded estimates of $1.5 billion and $2.2 billion will likely be greater than these totals when the final figures are known.

Sources: D.B.S. *Financial Statistics of the Government of Canada, 1959; Public Accounts;* Department of Finance, Dominion Bureau of Statistics.

BREAKDOWN OF FEDERAL CONTRIBUTIONS TO THE PROVINCES, MUNICIPALITIES AND TERRITORIES

Fiscal Year 1967-68

($000)

	Nfld.	P.E.I.	N.S.	N.B.	Que.	Ont.	Man.	Sask.	Alta.	B.C.	Total
A. PAYMENTS TO PROVINCES											
Total unconditional grants	76,254	14,557	80,560	66,187	382,941[a]	26,828	47,523	27,364	14,205	2,242	738,661
Conditional grants											
Agriculture	430	350	1,540	1,205	4,988	5,505	1,965	2,645	2,614	1,465	22,707
Other natural resources	4,973	186	8,185	4,695	527	1,617	5,221	—	—	170	25,574
Emergency measures	90	—	208	121	1,328	1,650	229	203	487	469	4,785
Education	8,442	2,379	19,232	4,694	124,368	79,722	15,274	20,456	26,565	13,389	314,521
Hospital insurance	15,526	3,353	23,975	19,491	—	234,846	30,614	32,296	49,767	57,416	467,284
Other health	1,680	567	10,915	2,738	13,677	28,430	3,545	2,985	5,825	8,205	78,567
Winter works	213	640	420	212	15,083	6,630	754	1,299	2,568	2,495	30,314
Canada Assistance Plan	17,902	1,739	10,264	7,185	—	100,288	15,572	13,404	26,538	32,720	225,612
Other welfare	2,227	1,128	3,235	2,735	−405	6,442	2,829	936	4,058	4,926	28,111
Recreation and culture	700	110	473	343	2,701	2,301	909	421	765	2,544	11,267
Transportation	13,432	3,799	18,142	22,246	23,858	7,585	1,233	1,542	616	902	93,355
Housing	295	—	—	—	—	—	—	—	—	—	295
Total	65,910	14,251	96,589	65,665	186,125	475,016	78,145	76,187	119,803	124,701	1,302,392
B. PAYMENTS TO MUNICIPALITIES											
Grants in lieu of taxes	225	159	2,912	113	8,353	20,595	2,604	1,223	2,278	3,255	[b]43,916
Conditional grants	366	80	2,550	2,231[c]	7,357	21,904	2,600	2,623	3,920	4,316	[d]46,183
Total	591	239	5,462	2,344	15,710	42,499	5,204	3,846	6,198	7,571	90,099

C. PAYMENTS TO TERRITORIES

	Yukon	Northwest Territories
Unconditional grants	3,876	5,494
Conditional grants	1,266	3,141
Total	5,142	8,635

	Nfld.	P.E.I.	N.S.	N.B.	Que.	Ont.	Man.	Sask.	Alta.	B.C.	Total
TOTAL FEDERAL PAYMENTS	142,755	29,047	182,611	134,196	584,776	544,343	130,872	107,397	140,206	134,514	2,144,929

(a) Includes value of abatements and special compensation for opting-out of joint programs. See text. (b) Includes grants to local governments in the territories of $349,000.
(c) Includes special financial assistance to the town of Oromocto. (d) Includes grants to local governments in the territories of $86,000.
Source: Dominion Bureau of Statistics.

FEDERAL-PROVINCIAL GRANTS AND THE SPENDING POWER OF PARLIAMENT*

PIERRE ELLIOTT TRUDEAU

The Constitutional Conference decided, at its February 1969 meeting, to accord priority to "the study of the distribution of powers, in particular the taxing and spending powers", and directed the Continuing Committee of Officials "to give its immediate attention to this aspect of the Constitution." . . .

THE SPENDING POWER: WHAT IT IS AND HOW IT HAS BEEN USED

Ordinarily one thinks of the "spending power" of governments simply in terms of the spending they do on particular programmes, under the authority of legislation passed by their legislative bodies. Constitutionally, however, the term "spending power" has come to have a specialized meaning in Canada: it means the power of Parliament to make payments to people or institutions or governments for purposes on which it (Parliament) does not necessarily have the power to legislate. The best example, perhaps, is the grants to provincial governments to assist in the provision of free hospitalization across Canada: Parliament does not have the power under the Constitution to establish general hospitals or to regulate them or their use; but under its "spending power" it is generally conceded that Parliament can make grants to the provinces to assist them in financing provincially operated hospitalization programmes.

The importance of the spending power in Canada can be illustrated by looking at some of the programmes which are founded primarily upon it (as opposed to being based upon Parliament's regulatory powers). *The equalization of opportunity for individual Canadians*, in the form of income redistribution between persons, has been based in no small measure upon this power. In particular, family allowances are paid to all mothers in Canada ($560 million in 1968-69), and the federal

* From a Working Paper of the Government of Canada bearing the above title, submitted in the name of the Prime Minister to the Federal-Provincial Constitutional Conference, June 11, 1969, and published by the Queen's Printer, Ottawa, 1969. By permission of the Queen's Printer.

government pays to the provinces one half of the cost of social assistance payments to individuals in need (under the Canada Assistance Plan—costing over $400 million). In addition to these measures, Canada Pension Plan payments, Old Age Security payments, and Guaranteed Income Supplements are paid by Parliament under a specific section of the Constitution. Obviously too, the Income Tax Act of Canada, through its higher rates on the rich than on the poor, contributes substantially to income redistribution across the country.

The equalization of provincial public services—including health, welfare, education, and roads—is also accomplished largely because of the existence of the spending power. The Government of Canada makes revenue equalization grants to the governments of low income provinces for this purpose (over $560 million in 1968-69), and it contributes as well to specific provincial or federal-provincial programmes. Health care for individual Canadians is supported through federal grants to the provinces for hospital insurance (nearly $800 million), through a $500 million Health Resources Fund, and now through payments to provincial medical care plans. Higher education is supported, indirectly, through unconditional grants to provinces—grants based upon the total operating expenditures of universities and technical institutes (over $220 million in cash grants, and another $275 million in tax transfers and equalization payments). The Trans-Canada Highway, which finds its constitutional foundation both in the spending power and, because of its interprovincial character, in other provisions of the Constitution, was financed under a joint programme involving both the federal and provincial governments (over $700 million). And there have been other smaller programmes.

Equalization of opportunity for individual Canadians through regional economic development is also achieved in part through federal-provincial programmes involving Parliament's spending power. One example is the $300 million Fund for Rural Economic Development, which is financing a broad range of regional development measures, some of which are based upon the spending power alone. Another is the $125 million ARDA programme (Agricultural Rehabilitation and Development Act) which might have been managed directly by the Government of Canada, but which took the form of a federal-provincial programme. And the new Department of Regional Economic Expansion will have to rely, for its new measures, both upon Parliament's power to legislate and upon its spending power —as did its predecessors, notably the Atlantic Development Board.

Finally, *specific projects of national importance* have been possible, constitutionally, because of Parliament's spending power. Expo is the outstanding example. But many other projects or programmes could be listed (some of which relied in whole or in part upon this power)—Roads to Resources, the South Saskatchewan River Development project, and various other measures within individual provinces.

The scale of the payments made under the spending power of Parliament is another index of its importance. In 1968-69 the Government of Canada spent some $3.4 billion—32 per cent of its budget—on programmes which are based largely upon it, involving payments to persons, payments to institutions, and payments to governments.

	Amounts $ (millions)	% of Federal Expenditures
Payments to Persons	855.2	8.0
Payments to Institutions	77.3	0.7
Payments to Governments		
Conditional Grants	1,616.9	15.0
Unconditional Grants	865.0	8.1
Total	3,414.4	31.8

• • •

. . . Federal governments consistently have taken the position that Parliament's power to spend is clear, while provincial governments generally have limited themselves to criticism of the *use* of the spending power by Parliament—in particular to its use to start new federal-provincial shared-cost programmes, or to terminate old ones, without the consent of the provinces. Only governments of Quebec have advanced the more general proposition that it was constitutionally improper for Parliament to use its spending power to make grants to persons or institutions or governments for purposes which fall within exclusive provincial jurisdiction.

PROVINCIAL GOVERNMENT CRITICISMS

The governments of the provinces have advanced three criticisms of Parliament for its use of the spending power to establish new federal-provincial programmes:
(1) That the Government and the Parliament of Canada are deciding, without the formal participation of the provinces in such decisions, as to when federal-provincial programmes ought to be started.
(2) That shared-cost programmes force upon provincial governments changes in their priorities.
(3) That "taxation without benefit" occurs when the citizens of a province whose provincial government has refused to participate in a shared-cost programme are required to pay the federal taxes which finance the federal share of the programme. . . .
In addition to the arguments which are made concerning federal-provincial shared-cost programmes, the Government of Quebec, as has been noted, has generally argued against the use by the Parliament of Canada of its spending power for the purpose of making payments to persons and institutions. . . .

THE FEDERAL RATIONALE

. . . Programmes which involve payments to persons and institutions and which are excluded from Parliament's jurisdiction under the propositions submitted by the Government of Quebec, include income redistribution measures, possibly certain economic development programmes, contributions to Canada's cultural development, and research and technological development measures—all of which the Government of Canada considers to be important powers of Parliament. This view was advanced by the federal government at the first meeting of the Constitutional Conference, when it was argued that Parliament ought to retain explicit powers in these fields. Secondly, to achieve the programme and fiscal transfers called for in the Quebec propositions relating to these matters would be to weaken very substantially the powers of Parliament across the country, or to call for special status for the National Assembly of Quebec. In either case the structure of Canadian federalism would be fundamentally altered. . . .

The case for a federal spending power for the purpose of enabling Parliament to contribute toward provincial programmes in fields of provincial jurisdiction is to be found in the very nature of the modern federal state—in its economic and technological interdependence, in the interdependence of the policies of its several governments, and in the sense of community which moves its residents to contribute to the well-being of residents in other parts of the federation. . . .

The effectiveness of pollution control, for example, affects the people of neighbouring provinces; provincial educational systems contribute to or fail to advance the economic growth of Canada as a whole; and the equality of opportunity across the country, or the lack of it, affects the well-being of Canadians generally. Moreover the mobility of Canadians—increasing year by year—itself creates a kind of interdependence. . . .

The extra-provincial or national effects of certain provincial public services would pose no problem if the interests of each individual province always coincided with the interests of other provinces and of the country as a whole. In such a simplified state, a provincial government would automatically be serving the national interest when it was doing its job of serving the provincial interest. But this is not always the case. And when it is not—where provincial interests would be better served by one kind of programme and the national interest by another—the provincial legislature which does its job of meeting the needs of its constituents will not be meeting the potential needs of other Canadians. There is nothing new or unusual about this. . . .

It can be argued that the Constitution should be contrived so as to avoid any need for a spending power—that each government ought to have the revenue sources it needs to finance its spending requirements without federal assistance, and further that where the national interest comes to attach to a certain matter within provincial jurisdicion the Constitution ought to be amended to transfer that matter to federal jurisdiction. The difficulty with this "tidy" approach to federalism is that it does not accord with the realities of a Twentieth Century state.

It is quite true that in the ideal state provincial governments ought to have access to enough tax fields that they themselves can discharge their responsibilities. But in fact the tax-raising potential of Canada's provinces differs very markedly across Canada, because of the differing levels of income and economic activity in the country. One percentage point of personal income tax, for example, yields about $3.14 per capita in Ontario, $2.98 in British Columbia, $2.21 in Quebec, $1.89 in Saskatchewan, $1.27 in New Brunswick and 91 cents in Prince Edward Island (1968-69 figures). . . . It is evident from these figures that federal grants to the lower income provinces are essential if these provinces are to provide adequate levels of public services at levels of taxation which are not too far out of line with those in the higher income provinces. . . .

. . . [This] is to suggest that the nationally elected Parliament has a unique and a legitimate role to play in determining the national interest, even where provincial jurisdiction is involved. And it is to suggest, further, that Parliament is the appropriate body to make grants to the provinces for the purpose of equalizing provincial public services and for the purpose of compensating the provinces for adapting their programmes to meet national as well as provincial needs.

Having said this, it must be emphasized that this reasoning does not lead to the conclusion that because Parliament is elected by all Canadians it has or ought to have the power to invade provincial jurisdiction any time it perceives some national interest in a provincial programme. . . . It should play a role, WITH the provinces, in achieving the best results for Canada from provincial policies and programmes whose effects extend beyond the boundaries of a province.

A POSSIBLE APPROACH IN A REVISED CONSTITUTION

(1) The constitutional power of the Parliament of Canada to contribute toward the public services and programmes of provincial governments should be provided for explicitly in the constitution;

(2) The power of Parliament to make unconditional grants to provincial governments for the purpose of supporting their programmes and public services should be unrestricted;

(3) The power of Parliament to make general conditional grants in respect of federal-provincial programmes which are acknowledged to be within exclusive provincial jurisdiction should be based upon two requirements: first, a broad national consensus in favour of any proposed programme should be demonstrated to exist before Parliament exercises its power; and secondly the decision of a provincial legislature to exercise its constitutional right not to participate in any programme, even given a national consensus, should not result in a fiscal penalty being imposed upon the people of that province.

. . . The Government of Canada would suggest the following method for giving effect to these two requirements:

(1) The determination as to when the national interest or extra-provincial interests warranted a new shared-cost programme between the Government of Canada and the governments of the provinces would be arrived at jointly by Parliament and the provincial legislatures, in the manner described below [see original source], instead of by Parliament alone.

(2) Where a consensus had been reached that a new shared-cost programme was desirable, the provincial governments whose legislatures had voted *for* the consensus would receive conditional grants for the programme, once it was started by them. In the provinces whose legislatures had voted *against* the consensus, the people of the province would be paid grants equivalent in the aggregate to the average per capita amount paid to the participating provinces (multiplied by the population of the non-participating province). . . .

Payments to the governments rather than to the people of the non-participating provinces would seem, at first glance, to be a reasonable alternative to the approach here proposed. Upon reflection, however, it is evident that such a suggestion would be inconsistent with the underlying reason for a payment of any kind to non-participating provinces. The basic principle underlying such payments would be this: no provincial government ought to feel obliged to exercise its constitutional powers in a particular way for the reason that a fiscal penalty would be visited upon its people if it took a contrary view. The objective, therefore, clearly must be to keep the *people* of non-participating provinces from paying a penalty: it follows that any payment must logically be made to them. . . .

INCOME SECURITY AND SOCIAL SERVICES*

PIERRE ELLIOTT TRUDEAU

. . . The purpose of this Working Paper is to examine income security and the social services with a view to reaching some preliminary conclusions on the division of powers in these fields.

One of the characteristics of modern industrialized states is the concern of the community as a whole for the security and well-being of the individual and the family. This concern has been variously expressed, and has been manifested in a wide range of public programmes. They include such measures as general income redistribution programmes, payments to persons in need, social insurance schemes, welfare counselling and other services, housing, hospital and medical care insurance, public health clinics and other preventive health measures, vocational training and rehabilitation, urban redevelopment and the development of depressed regions, and other programmes.

* From a Working Paper of the Government of Canada bearing the above title, submitted in the name of the Prime Minister to the Federal-Provincial Constitutional Conference, December 8, 1969, and published by the Queen's Printer, Ottawa, 1969. By permission of the Queen's Printer.

It will be evident that such a broad range of programmes comprehends both social and economic measures. The assurance of adequate levels of income, for example, requires a full-employment policy and the regulation of minimum wages, plus the redistribution of income to lower income families by way of the tax-transfer mechanism (including social assistance payments). The development or redevelopment of urban and rural regions involves both economic measures, such as economic development of various kinds, and social measures, such as housing, the support of the incomes of the poor, and the provision of adequate education services. . . .

. . . We have narrowed the subject matter of this paper to two definable aspects of "social welfare" or "social security", and entitled this Working Paper *Income Security and Social Services*.

INCOME SECURITY

By this is meant the variety of measures which governments have undertaken or might undertake to support or otherwise to maintain the incomes of individuals and families. Such income maintenance may be required either because people are temporarily unemployed, or because they have left the labour force—by reason of age or disability, or because their income is otherwise inadequate.

These measures fall into two general categories. First, there are the public *income insurance* schemes, often called social insurance, under which employed persons insure themselves against losses of income, whether by reason of age or disability (Canada and Quebec Pension Plans), accident (Workmen's Compensation Plans), or unemployment (Unemployment Insurance). Under these plans the employee, and/or the employer on his behalf, contributes a proportion of his income to an insurance fund, and the fund "replaces" his income—usually by a stipulated percentage—when he is injured, unemployed, disabled or retired.

Secondly, there are the *income support* measures, under which the state supports the incomes of everyone who has children (Family and Youth Allowances), or who is past a certain age (Old Age Security), or whose income is insufficient to maintain himself and his dependents (Guaranteed Income Supplement, and social assistance and the Canada Assistance Plan). Beyond the income support programmes presently in operation are the much-discussed "guaranteed annual income" or "negative income tax" plans, under which everyone, or everyone in a designated group, would be entitled to a minimum income, the level of which would be determined by the size of the family's income and the number in the family. Such a plan usually is thought of as a replacement of existing income support programmes, with special needs—such as those of families living in high cost urban centres—being met by supplementary social measures.

SOCIAL SERVICES

By this is meant the services provided by the state to individuals and families, or paid for by the state in their behalf, to ensure their health and social welfare. Again the measures governments have adopted to this end are wide ranging.

The first general category is *preventive, or public health services,* designed to reduce the incidence of illness in the community. Such services include diagnostic clinics, child and maternal health clinics, sanitation programmes, mental health clinics, etc. Secondly, there are the *curative health services.* The most familiar programme is health insurance, under which government pays the hospital and medical and sometimes other health bills of individuals and families. . . .

Thirdly, there are the *social welfare services,* including child welfare programmes, the provision of institutional or custodial care, and the provision of counselling to persons to assist them in coping with their personal or social problems (and thus to assist them to remain active and productive members of the community. . . . Manpower training, placement and mobility measures . . . involve advice and counselling to adults who are seeking to improve their earning capacity. [But] such "services", associated as they are with economic or other "non-social" programmes, are not meant to be included in this definition of social services.

Finally, it must be said that there are, in addition to the general social services programmes described above, special measures for designated groups in the community. For example, the Government of Canada is responsible under the Constitution for the general welfare of Indians, and has established special income security programmes for veterans. While there will be some reference to programmes for these groups in this Working Paper, it will be evident that these responsibilities are of a specialized nature and ought to be discussed in the context of the particular constitutional provisions which empower the Government to act. Consequently, these and other aspects of health and welfare in respect of which there are special constitutional provisions will be dealt with in other Working Papers.

•   •   •

PRESENT PROGRAMMES SUMMARIZED

. . . The principal income security and social services programmes which exist today . . . are substantial—some 10.4 percent of the G.N.P. is now devoted to these measures (1967-68 figures), and they involve all orders of government in their administration—federal, provincial and municipal. A table will indicate both the magnitude of these measures and the extent to which the federal and provincial governments are involved. . . .

Despite the apparent confusion which emerges from a casual examination of this table as to the respective roles of the two orders of government, there is a pattern which emerges when the measures themselves, and how they came into being, are analyzed.

First, income security measures, including both income insurance and income support programmes, have increasingly been recognized as being national in scope, as the sense of community in Canada has broadened. It has become evident that income redistribution between the rich and the poor across the country—the reduction of regional disparities in income and opportunities for individuals and

Estimated Federal and Provincial Expenditures on Selected Income Security and
Social Services Programmes 1969-70

Programmes	Federal Expenditures[1]	Provincial Expenditures[2]	Total
	('000)	('000)	('000)
Income Support Measures			
Family Allowances, Youth Allowances	623,000	104,000	727,000
Old Age Security and Guaranteed Income Supplement	1,760,000	—	1,760,000
Social Assistance (Financial)	350,000	385,000	735,000
Veterans' Pensions and Allowances	325,000	—	325,000
Sub Total	3,058,000	489,000	3,547,000
Income Insurance Measures			
Unemployment Insurance	500,000	—	500,000
Workmen's Compensation	—	220,000	220,000
Canada and Quebec Pension Plans	50,000	16,000	66,000
Sub Total	550,000	236,000	786,000
Social Services			
Health Services	1,540,000	1,920,000	3,460,000
Welfare Services	180,000	200,000	380,000
Sub Total	1,720,000	2,120,000	3,840,000
Total	5,328,000	2,845,000	8,173,000

[1] Federal expenditures include the contributions to Quebec under the Established Programs (Interim Arrangements) Act, 1965.
[2] Provincial expenditures include municipal expenditures.

families—could only be accomplished by the government which is responsible for
the well-being of all Canadians. The acceptance of this point is borne out by the
agreement by all governments to constitutional amendments to this end, and by
the participation of all provinces with the federal government in shared-cost programmes to the same end. This statement must be qualified in respect of the
governments of Quebec: they have generally argued against shared-cost programmes . . . joined in recent years by certain other provinces in respect of specific
programmes. Further, the present Government of Quebec has tentatively proposed
in its Working Paper on the Constitution that all "social security", including both
income security and social services, ought to fall under exclusive provincial jurisdiction. (The exception is unemployment insurance, in respect of which the
Province has not yet made proposals.)

Secondly, it seems also to have been recognized, at least implicitly, that the
mere payment of money by the Government of Canada to the poor or the dis-

advantaged does not in itself constitute an intervention by Parliament into "property and civil rights", nor does it constitute an interference by the federal government into distinctively different provincial or regional approaches to social services. . . .

Thirdly, it seems also to have been concluded, if the federal-provincial programmes adopted by past Parliaments and provincial legislatures are any guide, that there are times when there is a "national interest" in programmes which lie clearly within exclusive provincial jurisdiction. Where this is agreed to be the case, Parliament ought to contribute, and ought to be able to contribute, to the programme involved. The question which has been much debated in Canada is by whom it should be decided that there is such a national interest in a particular provincial programme, and what arrangements should be made in respect of those provinces which refuse to go along with the national consensus. This question was considered in the federal Working Paper entitled *Federal-Provincial Grants and the Spending Power of Parliament*. . . .

A DISTRIBUTION OF POWERS FOR THE FUTURE

Any evaluation of the provisions of Canada's Constitution must be based upon the nature and the objectives of Confederation. The Government of Canada has already expressed its views as to the objectives to which the Constitution ought to give expression. [See *The Constitution and the People of Canada,* p. 6.] . . .

These objectives as applied to the income security and social services fields, ought to result in a distribution of powers which will enable both Parliament and the provincial legislatures to contribute to the well-being of individual Canadians. . . .

SOME GENERAL CONSIDERATIONS

We have already said that in our view it is not possible, in discussing this aspect of the distribution of powers, to use such general terms as "social security" or "social welfare". These terms comprehend too diverse a group of programmes, some of which might properly fall under federal jurisdiction, some under provincial, and some under the concurrent jurisdiction of both orders of government. In particular, it is our view that the income security aspects of what is often called social security differ substantially from the health and welfare services aspects, and ought to be treated differently in the Constitution. It is suggested moreover that the income security field itself is made up of two distinct categories of measures, which also are sufficiently different to deserve differential treatment in the Constitution: first, income insurance schemes under which premiums are contributed by or on behalf of the individual and benefits are paid in proportion to his previous income; and, secondly, general income support schemes under which personal incomes generally are supported without regard to the tax contributed by the recipient, usually with the purpose of increasing the incomes of persons in the lower income brackets. . . .

INCOME SUPPORT MEASURES

It is suggested that Parliament and the provincial legislatures ought to have equal powers to make income support payments to persons, whether in the form of "demogrants" (grants to persons falling into specified age or other population groups), guaranteed income measures, or a negative income tax. This proposition was substantially accepted at the June, 1969 meeting of the Constitutional Conference, where "most delegations agreed that the present power of Parliament to make payments to individuals . . . should not be subjected to any constitutional limitation". However, the rationale for this proposition ought to be recorded, partly to facilitate public discussion of this aspect of the constitutional review, and partly because "one province . . . reserved its position until the question of the distribution of powers had been dealt with . . ."

•   •   •

INCOME INSURANCE

It has already been noted that the provisions of the present Constitution in respect of income insurance differ from those in respect of general income support payments. Here, the Parliament of Canada is empowered to establish certain specific income insurance measures—unemployment, old age, survivors' and disability insurance—while the provinces have the more general power to establish income insurance schemes of any kind (excepting unemployment insurance).

The present constitutional distinction between income insurance and income support generally seems to the Government of Canada to be rather artificial, based as it is on the assumption that government income insurance schemes are of the same character, essentially, as private insurance contracts. In fact, as we now know, public income insurance programmes are rather more substitutes, or substitutable, for general income maintenance measures and vice versa (the suggestion in some quarters, for example, that a guaranteed annual income plan could and ought to replace, in part at least, the present unemployment and workmen's compensation schemes). For this reason it is suggested that the nature of public income insurance schemes ought to be re-examined, as we now know them, with a view to finding a new and better basis for allocating legislative powers in respect of them. . . .

. . . Responsibility for unemployment insurance must be placed with the government which has the power to combat unemployment, and has the capability of meeting the consequences of unemployment—the Parliament and Government of Canada. . . . Responsibility for workmen's compensation ought to remain within exclusive provincial jurisdiction. . . .

The Government of Canada has concluded that the best course would be to put Parliament in a position to provide leadership in the field of public retirement insurance. For this purpose Parliament and the provincial legislatures ought to continue to have concurrent powers in respect of public retirement insurance and associated benefits, but Parliament's powers should be paramount (in the case of conflicts between federal and provincial plans the federal plan would prevail). [Contrary to existing Sec. 94 A, B.N.A. Act.] . . .

Because income insurance schemes generally are substitutable for income support measures, or vice versa, there seems to be no compelling reason for suggesting that the relative jurisdiction of Parliament and the provinces should be different in the two cases. Thus Parliament ought to have concurrent jurisdiction with respect of income insurance measures, analogous to the equal powers it now has and would continue to have to make income support payments to persons. The exceptions would be those noted above.

SOCIAL SERVICES

It was suggested at the outset of this paper that there is an important difference between social services—health and welfare services—and income security. The latter is designed, in essence, to put money into the hands of individuals and families when they need it, whether their needs are occasioned by unemployment, disability, retirement from the labour force, or by any other reason. Income security payments, in short, are not contingent upon the regulation or influence by governments of social or family institutions. But health and welfare services usually are. As we noted at the beginning of this paper social services include preventive and curative health and welfare measures, which necessarily involve the operation of clinics and hospitals, the regulation of these and other institutions, the regulation, training and employment of professional personnel, and the provision of care and counselling (case work) services to individuals and families. It is this distinction which has brought the Government of Canada to propose a different distribution of powers in respect of income security on the one hand, and social services on the other. . . . The Government of Canada would have no wish to become engaged in the regulation of such institutions and professions. . . .

The conclusion of the Government of Canada, then, is that health insurance ought to remain a matter of exclusive provincial jurisdiction, subject to the use of the spending power of Parliament, as proposed above, for the purpose of bringing about an adaptation of provincial programmes to meet agreed national needs. . . .

. . . These are the considerations which have led the Government of Canada to conclude that responsibility for social services ought to remain a matter of exclusive provincial jurisdiction. This is subject to two provisos: first, that Parliament would retain the right to make conditional grants to the provinces wherever it was agreed that the national interest had come to attach to health and welfare programmes (per the proposals in Federal-Provincial Grants and the Spending Power of Parliament); and secondly, that the jurisdiction of Parliament arising out of other heads in the Constitution would remain unimpaired. . . .

. . . It would be for the courts to determine when an income security measure which might otherwise be within Parliament's powers contained a sufficient ingredient of social services (as defined in this Paper), over which the provinces have exclusive jurisdiction, that the whole measure was ultra vires of Parliament—that is, fell within the exclusive jurisdiction of the provinces. Where this was determined to be the case, but where there was thought to be an element of national interest in the programme, Parliament could seek to use its power to make conditional grants to the provinces to persuade the provinces to adapt the programmes to the national needs (see, again, Federal-Provincial Grants and the Spending Power of Parliament).

THE PROPOSALS OF THE GOVERNMENT OF CANADA IN RESPECT OF INCOME SECURITY AND SOCIAL SERVICES

In summary, then, the Government of Canada is advancing the following tentative proposals with respect to income security and social services in a revised Constitution:

(1) That the provincial legislatures ought to have exclusive jurisdiction over social services;

(2) That Parliament and the provincial legislatures ought to have equal powers to make general income support payments to persons;

(3) That Parliament and the provincial legislatures ought to have concurrent powers in respect of public income insurance measures, except that

(a) unemployment insurance ought to fall under the exclusive jurisdiction of Parliament;

(b) workmen's compensation ought to fall under the exclusive jurisdiction of the provincial legislatures; and

(c) in respect of retirement insurance and associated benefits Parliament's powers ought to be paramount.

Where an income security measure contains an ingredient of social services it would be for the courts to decide whether such services were a sufficiently important element of the measure that the whole measure ought to fall under provincial jurisdiction.

The qualifications which attach to these proposals should also be summarized:

(1) The proposals are tentative, and are subject to a distribution of powers which will ensure a strong federal government as well as strong provincial governments;

(2) They are not meant to limit the jurisdiction of Parliament deriving from other specific heads of the Constitution; and

(3) They are based upon the definitions of income support, income insurance and social services employed in this Paper.

It should also be made clear that the proposals in this paper, to the extent that they would alter in future the existing distribution of *legislative powers,* are not intended to prejudice *programmes.* It is intended that their effect should be prospective only, and that laws validly enacted in the past should continue in force at least until transitional measures have been agreed to by the Government of Canada and the governments of the provinces affected.

BIBLIOGRAPHY

Benson, E. J., *The Taxing Powers and the Constitution of Canada,* Ottawa, Queen's Printer, 1969.

Birch, A. H., *Federalism, Finance, and Social Legislation in Canada, Australia, and the United States,* Oxford, Clarendon, 1955.

Breton, A., "A Theory of Government Grants," *C.J.E.P.S.,* Vol. XXXI, No. 2, May, 1965. (See also "Notes," *ibid.,* Vol. XXXII, No. 2, May, 1966; Breton, A., "A Theory of the Demand for Public Goods," *ibid.,* Vol. XXXII, No. 4, November, 1966, and "Notes," *ibid.,* Vol. XXXIII, No. 1, February, 1967.)

Burns, R. M., "The Royal Commission on Dominion-Provincial Relations: The Report in Retrospect," in Clark, R. M., (ed.), *Canadian Issues: Essays in Honour of Henry F. Angus,* Toronto, University of Toronto Press, 1961.

Canada, Minister of Finance, *Report of the Tax Structure Committee to the Federal-Provincial Conference of Prime Ministers and Premiers,* Ottawa, February 16-17, 1970.

Canada, *Dominion-Provincial Conference on Reconstruction; Submission and Plenary Conference Discussion,* Ottawa, King's Printer, 1946.

Canada, *Report of the Royal Commission on Dominion-Provincial Relations* (Rowell-Sirois Report); *Book I, Canada: 1867-1939; Book II, Recommendations; Book III; Documentation;* Ottawa, King's Printer, 1940, 3 vols. (Reprinted in one volume, 1954.) Also Appendices 1-8.

Canada, *Report of the Royal Commission on Taxation,* (Carter Commission), Ottawa, Queen's Printer, 1966, 6 vols. (See also the Commission's individual research studies, Nos. 1-30, especially No. 23, J. H. Lynn, *Federal-Provincial Relations,* Ottawa, Queen's Printer, 1967.)

Canadian Tax Foundation, *Provincial Finances, 1969,* Toronto, Canadian Tax Foundation, 1969.

Clark, D. H., *Fiscal Need and Revenue Equalization Grants,* Canadian Tax Papers No. 49, Toronto, Canadian Tax Foundation, 1969.

Dehem, R., and Wolfe, J. N., "The Principles of Federal Finance and the Canadian Case," *C.J.E.P.S.,* Vol. XXI, No. 1, February, 1955.

Dupré, J. S., "Tax-Powers vs Spending Responsibilities: An Historical Analysis of Federal-Provincial Finance," in Rotstein, A., (ed.), *The Prospect of Change,* Toronto, McGraw-Hill, 1965.

Dupré, J. S., " 'Contracting out': A Funny Thing Happened on the Way to the Centennial," *Report of the Proceedings of the Eighteenth Annual Tax Conference,* Toronto, Canadian Tax Foundation, 1965.

Dupré, J. S., *Intergovernmental Finance in Ontario: A Provincial-Local Perspective,* Toronto, Queen's Printer, Ontario, 1968.

Graham, J. F., Johnson, A. W., Andrews, J. F., *Inter-Government Fiscal Relationships,* Canadian Tax Papers, No. 40, Toronto, Canadian Tax Foundation, December, 1964.

Grey, R., "Conditional Grants in Aid," *Proceedings of the Fifth Annual Conference,* The Institute of Public Administration of Canada, Toronto, 1953.

Hanson, E. J., *Fiscal Needs of the Canadian Provinces,* Canadian Tax Papers, No. 23, Toronto, Canadian Tax Foundation, February, 1961.

Johnson, J. A., "Provincial-Municipal Intergovernmental Fiscal Relations," *C.P.A.,* Vol. XII, No. 2, Summer, 1969.

La Forest, G. V., *The Allocation of Taxing Powers Under the Canadian Constitution,* Toronto, Canadian Tax Foundation, 1967.

Mackintosh, W. A., "Federal Finance (Canada)," in Sawer, G. (ed.), *Federalism: an Australian Study,* Melbourne, 1952.

Mackintosh, W. A., *The Economic Background of Dominion-Provincial Relations,* Toronto, McClelland and Stewart, 1964.

MacNaughton, C., *Ontario's Proposals for Fiscal Policy Co-ordination in Canada,* Budget Papers, Toronto, Department of Treasury and Economics, 1970.

May, R., *Federalism and Fiscal Adjustment,* Ottawa, Queen's Printer, 1968.

Moore, A. M., Perry, J. H., and Beach, D. I., *The Financing of Canadian Federation: The First Hundred Years,* Canadian Tax Paper No. 43, Toronto, Canadian Tax Foundation, 1966.

Nowlan, D. M., "Centrifugally Speaking: Some Economics of Canadian Federalism," in Lloyd, T., and McLeod, J. T., (eds.), *Agenda 1970,* Toronto, University of Toronto Press, 1968.

Ontario, Department of Treasury and Economics, *Intergovernmental Policy Co-ordination and Finance,* Staff Papers, Toronto, 1970.

Ontario, *Report of the Committee on Taxation* (Smith Committee), Toronto, Queen's Printer, 1967, 3 vols.

Perry, J. H., *Taxation in Canada,* Toronto, University of Toronto Press, 3rd ed., rev., 1961.

Perry, J. H., *Taxes, Tariffs, and Subsidies; A History of Canadian Fiscal Development,* Toronto, University of Toronto Press, 1955, 2 vols.

Perry, J. H., "What Price Provincial Autonomy?" *C.J.E.P.S.,* Vol. XXI, No. 4, November, 1955.

Quebec, *Report of the Royal Commission on Taxation* (Bélanger Report), Quebec, Queen's Printer, 1965.

Salyzyn, V., "Federal-Provincial Tax Sharing Schemes," *C.P.A.,* Vol. X, No. 2, June, 1967.

Saunders, S. A., and Back, E., *The Rowell-Sirois Commission Part 1, A Summary of the Report,* Toronto, Ryerson Press, 1940.

Smiley, D. V., "The Rowell-Sirois Report, Provincial Autonomy, and Post-War Canadian Federalism," *C.J.E.P.S.,* Vol. XXVIII, No. 1, February, 1962.

Smiley, D. V., *Conditional Grants and Canadian Federalism,* Canadian Tax Paper No. 32, Toronto, Canadian Tax Foundation, February, 1962.

Smiley, D. V., "Block Grants to the Provinces: A Realistic Alternative?" *Report of the Proceedings of the Eighteenth Annual Tax Conference,* Canadian Tax Foundation, Toronto, 1965.

Smiley, D. V., *Constitutional Adaptation and Canadian Federalism Since 1945,* Document 4 of the Royal Commission on Bilingualism and Biculturalism, Ottawa, Queen's Printer, 1970.

Smiley, D. V., and Burns, R. M., "Canadian Federalism and the Spending Power: Is Constitutional Restriction Necessary?" *Canadian Tax Journal,* Vol. XVII, No. 6, November-December, 1969.

Trudeau, P. E., *Federal-Provincial Grants and the Spending Power of Parliament,* Ottawa, Queen's Printer, 1969.

Trudeau, P. E., *Income Security and Social Services,* Ottawa, Queen's Printer, 1969.

II PROCESS

SEVEN
THE ROLE OF
PUBLIC OPINION

No discussion of the influence of public opinion on politics would be complete these days without some appreciation of Marshall McLuhan's theories about how the media of communication affect our entire world. Harvey Perry has provided a distillation of the essence of McLuhan's thoughts on the subject in a brief article which appropriately commences this chapter.

Public opinion polls also are felt by some to be influential in shaping public opinion. British Columbia has banned the publication of the results of such findings during provincial election campaigns and at least two Members of Parliament have argued that a similar restriction should be adopted during federal campaigns. In any event, polling is now so much a part of public opinion that quite apart from its implications, its methodology needs to be understood fully. Professor Hugh Whalen's article on the subject is an exemplary explanation, analysis, and critique of polling in general and of two Canadian polls in particular, those run by the Canadian Institute of Public Opinion (C.I.P.O., the Gallup Poll in Canada) and those conducted by Professor Peter Regenstreif. In preparing the revision of his original article for this third edition, Professor Whalen has added also some comments on the public opinion polls held in Quebec prior to the provincial election in April, 1970. References alluded to by Professor Whalen can all be found in the bibliography at the end of this chapter.

That lobbying is also now a significant force in shaping public opinion and influencing governments in Canada has been accepted by most observers, but we are still awaiting the appearance of a definitive book on Canadian lobbying and pressure groups. A number of good academic studies of select examples have been published in the form of articles, the most significant of which are referred to in the bibliography in this chapter, but probably the most informative piece about the whole process of lobbying in Ottawa came from the pen of a journalist, Don McGillivray, a few years ago. An extensive, edited version of his five-part series is reproduced here. To pinpoint one example of a lobby, an account of the activities of the Canadian Manufacturers' Association has been included also.

Public opinion is moulded in many ingenious ways. The two classic articles by columnist Ron Haggart, exposing two different methods in the fine art of forming public opinion, are repeated here from the first and second editions "by popular demand," since many readers found them so instructive. It is interesting that although they were written eight years ago, both their subject—the Spadina Expressway in Toronto—and the techniques they describe are still as alive and pertinent today as they were then. For an article illustrating how politicians make use of "trial balloons" to test public opinion, see the first edition of *Politics: Canada*, pp. 16-17.

The question of the relationship between the ownership of the media of communication and the influencing of public opinion, and in particular, the dangers arising from concentration of ownership of media, such as the existence of chains of newspapers, radio and television stations, has been under investigation by the Special Committee of the Senate chaired by Senator Keith Davey. The Committee has unearthed a great deal of information and a variety of opinions from its own research and from the witnesses it has heard. Its report, which is due for publication late in 1970, should be of prime importance since it is expected to provide a good deal of concrete information about such delicate matters as ownership and influence, as well as some interesting recommendations. In the interval Professor David Surplis has supplied a brief original article for this edition which gives a summary of some of the available facts and figures and also makes an interesting, fresh proposal.

At least one prominent publisher, Mr. Beland Honderich, President of the *Toronto Daily Star*, has been urging that Canada should establish a Press Council similar in most respects to that which has existed in Britain for nearly two decades. The gist of his arguments are given here in an extract from a recent speech. Although not all publishers are as enthusiastic as Mr. Honderich about the creation of a Press Council (see, for instance, an editorial in *The Globe and Mail*, Toronto, March 11, 1968, which is opposed to the idea), support for the idea has come from many quarters, including Chief Justice J. C. McRuer's *Report Number One of the Royal Commission Inquiry into Civil Rights*, Toronto, Queen's Printer, 1968, Vol. 2, pp. 767-769. Quebec at least has forged ahead and in mid-1970 is in the process of establishing a provincial Press Council, very similar in structure to the British model. One well-known journalist and political commentator, Douglas Fisher, has offered an alternative. In his submission to the Davey Committee, from which an extract is quoted here, he argues for control by the employees themselves, an expedient which has been tried in both France and West Germany.

The bibliography to this chapter should be consulted for additional material.

McLUHAN — THE MEDIA MOULD OUR WORLD*

J. HARVEY PERRY

... The field of study in which Professor McLuhan has specialized is that of "media". For present purposes the term can be taken to mean the various methods by which humans communicate with one another, (although McLuhan would include all "extensions" of the ability of the stripped down human to influence his environment, a concept not germane to the limited presentation being given here). We communicate mainly through the use of our senses of hearing, seeing and touching, and media are the specific means by which we employ or exploit these senses. Means involving the hearing faculty (the spoken word, music and a variety of other sounds) are aural; those involving the seeing faculty (writing, printing, painting, etc.) are visual; and those involving touch (physical contact of various kinds with materials, other persons, etc.) are tactile. Some media can be solely aural (telephone); others solely visual (book); others both aural and visual (television). It is seldom that one media will combine aural, visual and tactile characteristics, but all our senses, and sometimes also our sense of smell, can be engaged simultaneously by a variety of media to which we are exposed.

On these basic and undeniable attributes of the human as a social animal (if there were no society there would be no need to communicate) McLuhan erects an edifice of astonishing proportions. He comes to this result by attributing the principal characteristics of any given period in man's evolution to the principal media employed in that period. A phase in which the media are mainly aural will have certain characteristics and another in which they are mainly visual will be quite different again. Man's ablity to communicate is crucial, but of equal importance is the effect on him of the means by which he communicates. This results from the way in which particular forms of communication develop one sense as opposed to the others. Whole eras of man's evolution have been given their shape and form by the media then being used. Modern society is not excepted. Today's man is the product of his means of communication, and he is a troubled man because of the violent and rapid changes that are taking place in the media.

McLuhan has demonstrated his theories by tracing man's evolution from the earliest social organisms. Originally media were aural. The faculties of speech and hearing were those first to be developed. Dependence on the spoken and "heard" word gave primitive society some distinctive characteristics. Because of its reliance on "talk" the aural society was a fairly intimate one; aural communication requires physical presence. And because "talk" is the most spontaneous means of communication, the aural society itself was more emotional and less structured in its responses (a sort of continuous village talk-fest).

* From *The Canadian Banker,* Vol. 76, No. 2, March/April, 1969, pp. 2-5. By permission of the author.

There being no reserve of agreed written knowledge to consult, man's judgments at the worst would be based on trivial evidence, or at the best on profoundly original speculation regarding the origins of things. (The Greek philosophers demonstrate the latter point.) His actions were impetuous and his planning short-range.

This phase started to change when the first attempt was made at portrayal on the walls of a cave, and a new "visual" media appeared. A further step was taken with the elaborate use of manuscript and tomb inscriptions by the Egyptians, and the promise of its ultimate full development was apparent in the Grecian and Roman adoption of a phonetic alphabet, (literally the Phoenician alphabet), in which the written characters have both an aural and a visual content, and are used in a pre-determined and orderly way in a line across the page. (This in itself was a massive accomplishment for western man. Some cultures, e.g. the Chinese, have not yet achieved it.) But the ultimate flowering of the visual media came with the invention of movable type by Gutenberg (about 1450), and with it the ability to reproduce the printed page in quantity. From this event there showers the "Gutenberg Galaxy", bringing profound changes to man and society.

The printed line, the printed paragraph, the printed page and the printed book constitute a drastically different media from "talk". Where "talk" is easy, informal and non-structured, the printed book is made up of visual words arranged in a lineal, permanent and structured order from beginning to end. No matter how chaotic or violent its content a book gives the visual impression of organized and orderly presentation, word succeeding word, paragraph paragraph, page page and chapter chapter, to the end. Furthermore, unlike talk, communication through the printed word not only permits but requires isolation. This not only results in the development of the individual as a person detached from the talking group, but also produces a variety of different individuals, since each will have read different books and reacted to them in different ways.

The Galaxy from this development, according to McLuhan, is much of the world as we know it today. The organization of a vast reserve of permanent knowledge has accounted for much of our educational and economic development; the assembly line principle of production was inspired by the orderly lineal progression of the printed page; the emergence of individualism among persons has made possible democracy as a form of government; our cities are organized along the lines of the grid or structured presentation of print, and on and on. We have been living for some centuries in this galaxy. The eye has succeeded to the ear as our leading sense, and the experience has profoundly changed us. But it has not been because of the content of the "message," but the way in which we have received it. This is the sense in which the medium is the message.

Because McLuhan appears to be developing a "field theory" (a theory so broad that it explains and rationalizes all other theories) he has invaded nearly every discipline. As a result he has been greeted either as a prophet or a charlatan by enthusiastic or indignant anthropologists, sociologists, economists, philosophers, political scientists and historians and a few others. The average person might well leave this feud to the academics if it were not that McLuhan's real purpose is to tell us that we are now in the midst of another great period of change that will be more drastic and violent in its effect on our lives than anything previously known in mankind's evolution.

That changes are going on anyone can see. McLuhan again explains (he would say "explores") them in terms of alterations in our media.

For some time we have been unconsciously passing from the Gutenberg Age to the Electric or Marconi Age, as he has called it. This process started slowly with the invention of the wireless, but is now accelerating at enormous speed under the full impact of radio, television, same-day "you are there" reports and illustrations in our press from anywhere in the world, jet travel, the computer and communication satellites. Time and space have collapsed as dimensions in communication. The world comes flooding in on us at full tide every moment of the day. The true pattern of actuality, a complex mosaic of simultaneous and spontaneous events, ideas, happenings, crises, beginnings and endings, now challenges senses that have become attuned to the visual presentation of a message through the sequential arrangement of words across a printed page. Real life is best typified by a newspaper, any page of which is a cross-section—a mosaic—of happenings of only hours before. The total effect of the newspaper is an incredible juxtaposition of information, opinion, drama, commercialism, all assembled at great expense for a life span of a day at the most, to be succeeded on the morrow, or even in the next edition, by another and different mosaic. Television gives us this same effect—that of total involvement in the daily affairs of the "global village".

These are phenomena which all have observed with growing familiarity; not many however have drawn from them the same conclusions as McLuhan. Briefly his thesis is that our media are passing from the visual phase to one in which the aural and tactile (hearing and touch) will again be predominant. This change will bring with it many of the features of an earlier period in our development—a sense of greater participation in actual happenings (involvement); less concern for the precise ordering of our lives and institutions (Gutenberg will go); a more spontaneous expression of judgments on all issues and actual personal contact or combat in support of them (aural and tactile reactions lead to confrontation)—in short a return to the close-quarters intimacy of the village. The big difference will be that this time, with communications instantaneously spanning the world, it will be a "global village".

The practical consequences of the electric age of communications will be profound, according to McLuhan. The generation gap will be a chasm, as generations attuned to visual media and its discipline attempt to understand generations whose senses and attitudes are attuned to different media (McLuhan asks the question, for example, are students rebelling against the book because of the electric age?) Large cities as we know them will become monuments or curiosities, as new generations cease to conceive of design in the orderly grid Gutenberg pattern and as new methods of communication make it possible to run automated businesses from the comfort of one's own home (presumably in the country-side). In any case the computer will mean that the real business of businesses will be moving information and applying it to decision making, a process that will call for entirely different management concepts than those of today. New life for the tactile sense will make shoppers alert to the "feel" of things, and this could mean the end of the packaged merchandise, and on and on—the world of McLuhan is one that few of us would recognize.

To strip McLuhan so completely of his subtleties and his idioms can only be justified by an attempt to get at his basic message in plain language. It will have to be left to the reader, if he wishes to make the effort, to understand the distinction between "hot" and "cool" media; the effect of the incompletely detailed TV image (McLuhan's proposition is that because of the low definition of the TV picture the medium is primarily aural, rather than visual); the implications of advertising as the "mechanical bride"; the full meaning of the (McLuhan) truth that it is not the content of the message that matters but its manner of presentation—"the medium is the message"; the significance of "probes" in his own explorations, and a dozen other fine points. All that has been attempted here is to outline his basic proposition that the manner in which men communicate has profound effects on both individuals and society. This has meant passing up much of the real fun of McLuhan; his *obiter dicta,* many of which bear little on his main thesis, are priceless. As a sample, radio was the perfect vehicle for Hitler's rise to power; on television he would have looked ridiculous.

How much of McLuhan to accept is not a question to be answered in a few words. He does not ask to be taken as a prophet, but rather as an explorer, self-designated to lead along new paths. But one of his purposes is to arouse "visual oriented" people to what might be ahead in the new aural and tactile world of a TV educated generation. Some of what he foresees for the future disturbs him. In an interview he showed strong distaste for the global village—"The global village absolutely insures maximum disagreement on all points . . . It has more spite and envy . . . I don't approve of the global village. I say we live in it"; and of television he said: "I think we would do ourselves a considerable kindness if we closed down TV operations for a few years . . . It is destroying our entire political, educational, social, institutional life. TV will dissolve the entire fabric of society in a short time". (And recall that this has nothing to do with the content of TV programs— merely with the consequences of primary education through ear and touch, rather than eye.) This is almost a cry of despair; the loom-smashers of old could not have spoken more truly from the heart. But is the outlook so bleak? Are we so much the helpless victims of media? Do they truly have so deep and lasting an effect on our lives?

The trouble with McLuhan, as one of his reviewers has said, is that there is always the niggling question—what if he is right? . . .

THE PERILS OF POLLING*

HUGH WHALEN

If the political significance of opinion survey research is to be understood, it must be viewed in its total social setting. For in most countries where it is now undertaken, opinion analysis is only incidentally concerned with the reporting of mass political views and voter intentions. During the last three decades, for better or for worse, attitude measurement and appraisal has become a potent force influencing the decisions taken by corporate leaders, media executives, politicians and civil servants. And in the social sciences attitude surveying is now a key instrument of inquiry. Much survey research is undertaken privately and concerns itself with consumer brand and design preferences, audience rating, market measurement, corporate image, and other commercial matters. The technical foundations which underlie much of this activity have only recently been developed by statisticians, computer technologists, and social scientists in endowed organizations, and government departments. As in most other fields, inter-dependence is everywhere apparent, and devices used successfully in one area have influenced developments in others.

There is little mystery why opinion surveying has appeared to attract more than its share of artful-dodgers and rain-makers. Since its inception in the 1930s, opinion analysis has seldom possessed validity or reliability in adequate amounts. Surveys are valid when they measure successfully those opinion characteristics they are intended to measure; they are reliable when they yield comparable results on different occasions. A perfect validity and reliability may indeed be impossible in practice; but it will not do to suggest, as some apologists of polling have done, that opinion research is scientific merely because it is now widely used. Yet it cannot be denied that much effort in recent years has been directed towards improving the quality of survey methods. What, it may then be asked, is the present state of the art, given its inauspicious beginnings?

METHODOLOGICAL PROBLEMS

Leading American pollers such as Gallup, Roper, and Harris, together with the more important survey research institutions, have experimented steadily with methods based upon statistical inference. The purpose of statistical inference is to estimate the unknown attributes of an entire population (or universe) from the known characteristics of a given sample thereof. Sample design is thus of key importance, for upon it depend the reliability measures of survey estimates.

* Prepared in February, 1966, revised in May, 1970, and published here with the permission of the author who is Professor of Political Science and Chairman of the Department, Memorial University of Newfoundland. For sources alluded to in the article, see bibliography at end of the section.

Various methods of sample estimation and selection can be used to indicate the risk factors associated with sampling error.

Critics of polling have frequently focused their attacks on the use of supposedly undersized samples. Such criticism may sometimes be valid; but often it rests on little rational foundation. Once certain minimum statistical requirements have been met, and a given order of sample error determined, the only justification for increasing sample size is to reduce still further the margin of estimated sample error. Typically, moreover, much greater percentage increases in sample size are required in order to produce small decreases in sample errors.

Let us assume that in a national probability of 100 Canadian voters, 40 percent of respondents indicate a preference for the candidate of Party A. It might be shown statistically that, with a confidence of 99 out of 100, the limits within which the total electorate actually preferred Party A would be from 28 to 52 percent. The error in this case is approximately plus or minus 12 percent in relation to the sample estimate of 40 percent. If the sample were increased to 200 voters, selected at random, the confidence limits might be reduced to, say, between 32 and 48 percent. The range of estimated error in this instance is 8 percentage points above or below the second sample estimate of 40 percent. The following table illustrates hypothetically the inverse relationship between sample size and confidence limits for the entire electorate:

Sample Size	Percentage Confidence Limits
100	28 - 52
200	32 - 48
500	35 - 45
1,000	36 - 44
2,000	38 - 42
5,000	39 - 41

An absolutely correct size for a national opinion sample can never be established authoritatively. Decisions in this matter are bound to reflect accumulated polling experience, the individual poller's judgment, and the given survey's objectives. When surveys, for instance, are concerned strictly with aggregate national election forecasting, and when reliable results are not sought at the regional and provincial levels, it appears that small random samples of the electorate are usually adequate, given the tolerances in errors now accepted by pollers. But when accuracy at various subnational levels is required, when the margin of national survey error must be reduced, and even when elections turn out to be closely contested, larger samples are clearly needed. Herein lies the first of many dilemmas confronting the opinion analyst; for while the cost of polling varies directly with the size of sample, the precision of sample estimate increases only as the square root of the number of respondents interviewed.

A second feature of sample design relates to stratification. When selecting a national sample to measure voting intentions, for example, the various demographic categories of age, sex, rural or urban residence, and the occupation, income, education, religious and ethnic affiliation of the population must be given appropriate representation in the sample. To avoid bias, the sample must be constructed to include the proper proportion of each relevant category of the whole population.

Perhaps the most spectacular instance of sample bias in polling was recorded in the United States during the 1936 presidential election. On that occasion the *Literary Digest* poll, with a massive sample of 2.4 million mailed-in ballots, underestimated Roosevelt's victory by 19.3 percentage points, in large measure because a significant proportion of its respondents were persons listed in *Who's Who*. This polling failure illustrates the inadequacy of large but unrepresentative samples in election forecasting. Results of much greater accuracy have been obtained by the Gallup and other organizations using small stratified samples ranging from two to eight thousand respondents.

There are many different ways of selecting samples that are representative of the universe under study. In the formative years of polling the "quota-stratified" method of selection was widely used. But in recent years the selection of units for inclusion in opinion samples has come to depend increasingly on the principle of "known probability". A probability sample based on random selection is one in which all units of the universe being examined have an equal, and therefore a known, chance of being included. One method of random selection that has gained wide acceptance during the postwar period is "area-probability" sampling, which is described below. Some proponents of this method claim that when properly used it obviates the need for quota procedures since it automatically produces a suitably stratified national sample. Both methods are now generally combined in national opinion surveys.

Quota-stratified sampling involves essentially the following steps: (1) choice of those characteristics of the population to be sampled; (2) the determination of the proportions of the population having such characteristics; (3) the assigning of quotas to interviewers who, largely at their own discretion, select respondents in such a way that the sample is stratified in accordance with the proportions established in (2).

The classic quota method has two deficiencies. First, respondents tend to be selected by interviewers in a manner which prevents knowledge of the probabilities of selection. Thus, according to Hansen and Hauser in Katz's book, "Because the probabilities of inclusion in the [quota] sample of the various classes of elements are unknown, the estimates frequently made of sampling error of quota sample results, supposedly based on sampling theory, usually are erroneous". Second, the latitude given to interviewers may cause serious sample bias. The incorporation of random procedures within quotas has somewhat improved the method, but early surveys frequently underrepresented males, manual workers, and employed females who were not readily available for interview during working hours. Early quota samples for the same reason often gave undue weight to the opinions of middle and upper middle class strata.

The area-probability method of drawing an opinion sample includes the following steps: (1) choice of those characteristics of the population to be sampled; (2) in the case of a national sample, division of the country into classes of the appropriate *areal units,* usually of a politico-geographic nature (e.g., counties, rural municipalities, towns, cities), from which random selections are made; (3) the units so selected, in turn, are arbitrarily divided into smaller *area segments* (e.g., rural areas delineated by rail lines, roads, streams and powerlines; town and city blocks), from which further random selections are made; (4) the area segments so selected, in turn, contain *occupied dwelling units* (each consisting of one household), from which a number are selected by prescribed method; (5) the occupied dwelling units so selected, in turn, contain one or more *adults* (or *eligible voters*), from which a sample of one or more is drawn according to rule.

The first three steps in area-probability sampling are performed in the survey office using maps, aerial photographs, tables of random numbers, and other equipment. The last two steps, however, are undertaken by interviewers in accordance with strict rules intended to prevent subjective bias in selection. The strength of this method of drawing a sample stems from the nature of the selection process which is always verifiable in relation to some known probability, since every adult (or eligible voter) in the population can be associated with but one occupied dwelling unit which in turn can be associated with one, and only one, segment of land. The main practical difficulty with area sampling is its complexity and relative cost. While it does not require extensive pre-listing, it does normally demand greater administrative direction, more skilled interviewers, extensive travel, and time wastage due to "call backs" on respondents.

For these and other reasons most national opinion surveys now combine area-probability sampling with revised quota procedures. The various modes of combination are extremely complex. It seems clear, however, that in practice the pollers have not found methods of selection that guarantee a perfectly random choice of respondents. While progress has undoubtedly been made in that direction, it is known, for example, that interviewers err in applying the rules governing respondent selection and substitution, and that respondents who are to be chosen at random but who are difficult to locate are frequently excluded for budgetary reasons. As we shall see below, errors of this kind are not invariably self-cancelling.

Defects in selection or in size of samples are not the only sources of errors in forecasting. Actual interviewing may be ineffective, even when the respondent uses a secret ballot. Estimation of the proportion and characteristics of eligible voters who will not vote may be wide of the mark. Errors of a similar sort may occur when dealing with "leaning" voters, "undecided" voters, and with electors who refuse to communicate their intentions. Other errors may occur at the coding and data processing stages. Finally, many possibilities for miscalculation arise naturally in the interpretation of the processed data, including the corrections for trends and projections of forecast.

This last factor is of prime importance. Opinion surveys have sometimes failed to detect sharp movements of popular sentiment during the very last days of election campaigns. The classic instance was the American polling debacle of 1948. Gallup, Roper, and Crossley, along with other polling organizations, predicted a Republican victory but the Democratic candidate won with 49.5 percent of the total vote. On the basis of only the ballots cast for the major parties, the following maximum (i.e., positive and negative) percentage point errors of forecast were recorded: Gallup, 9.4 percent; Crossley, 9.5 percent; and Roper, 19.5 percent.

Failure on this occasion to predict the election of President Truman caused gnashing of teeth and much explanation on the part of the polling fraternity, produced extreme joy and chagrin in the respective party camps, and stimulated the most elaborate inquiry of polling error ever undertaken. Sponsored by the Social Science Research Council, and weighing all the evidence—not merely the hypotheses suggested by the pollers, the media pundits and the politicians—the investigating committee reported that the failure was due in large part to important, late, unexpected, and undetected shifts of voter preference to the Democratic candidate. Sample errors of estimate were found to exist, but apparently they did not contribute significantly to the errors of forecast. Additional mistakes included a failure to predict the behaviour of an abnormally large group of undecided voters and an inadequate projection of voter turnout. For the most part, moreover, these errors were additive and did not cancel.

There are various measures of error associated with the sampling of total population characteristics. The poller, for instance, can calculate his chance "standard error" in relation to the number of respondents interviewed. Measures of this kind can be called *statistical errors,* since they emerge from the body of sampling theory and technique and were invented to deal with discrete objects having fairly stable internal and external characteristics. But opinions are not discrete objects exhibiting stability through time. Since pre-election attitudes in relation to the actual voting decision are often evanescent and imperfectly communicated even when the respondent uses a secret ballot, and since a significant part of the electorate (20-25%) never exercises the franchise, there is little necessary congruence between statistical error and what can be called the poller's *error of forecast.*

It appears that the limiting cases involving the relationship between the two kinds of error are these: (1) if the poller exercises correct judgment in appraising the many political, non-statistical variables affecting the election process, he may well achieve minimum forecast error even with substantial statistical error; (2) if, on the other hand, he deals inexpertly with political trends, he may obtain large forecast error even with minimum statistical error. Within these broad limits, of course, there is bound in practice to be much accidental cancellation of error.

ARE THE POLLS SCIENTIFIC?

In addition to the above factors, several other points should be noted before answering the question of whether or not the polls are "scientific". Clearly, the experimental work during the last three decades on opinion sampling has improved the quality of generalizations upon which pollers now base their projections of forecast. As compared with the pre-1948 period, for instance, there is now less tendency to assume that election campaigns do not influence voting intentions. Devices such as more extended interviewing and last-minute telegraphic probes have proved useful in the detection of late election trends. Improvements have also been introduced in areas not strictly related to statistical inference. The evaluations of "undecided" voter behaviour have improved, as have projections of the percentage of voter turnout at elections.

Yet, despite all these developments, V. O. Key's view is undoubtedly still true: "The sample survey is more useful as a means of identifying gross differences in the behaviour of voters and the correlates of these differences than in predicting the outcome of elections. Even with a purely random sample, the odds against predicting the winner when the division is near 50-50 are quite high, an inherent feature of the polls not well explained to the public by the polling organizations." Even Gallup concedes "that at some future date the 'polls will go wrong' again, especially in a close election." But as a justification of opinion surveying he adds that "no other method will be found—apart from sampling of the kind we do— which is more accurate."

There is, of course, little agreement on what constitutes accuracy of polling forecast. Ability to pick the winner is obviously the basic test. In this regard, even in some very close election contests, the polls have recently established a high degree of accuracy. The leading American polling organizations have predicted successfully the winners in eight of the last nine presidential elections. Their record in predicting the outcome of congressional and state elections, however, is much less outstanding. But in the American presidential race of 1960, for instance, Gallup forecast a Kennedy victory with 51 percent of the vote. When the more than 60 million ballots were cast, Kennedy received 50.2 percent as compared with Nixon's 49.8 percent. Using a national sample of approximately 8,000 respondents, Gallup's maximum error thus amounted to only 1.6 percentage points. The record of the Canadian Gallup poll in forecasting national election winners is discussed below.

Apart from accuracy in the prediction of the winning candidates or parties, polling success can be measured in terms of a correct forecasting of the distribution of the popular vote among contesting parties. In the latter case it is possible to distinguish forecast errors expressed in actual votes, in percentages, and in percentage points. These errors, in turn, may be totalled and expressed in simple or weighted averages. Let us assume the following election:

TABLE 1:   Calculated Error of Polling Forecast: An Illustration

Forecast and Vote	Party A	Party B	Party C	Party D	Total
Poll forecast (in millions)	4.5	4.0	1.0	.5	10.0
Poll forecast (in percent)	45	40	10	5	100
Actual vote (in millions)	5.0	3.0	1.5	.5	10.0
Actual vote (in percent)	50	30	15	5	100
Error of Forecast					
Vote Error (million)	—.5	+1.0	—.5	0	±2.0
Percentage Error	—10	+33	—33	0	±76
Percentage Point Error	—5	+10	—5	0	±20

The total error of forecast in this illustration involves ±2 million votes out of a total of 10 million votes cast. The total *percentage error* (i.e., where the actual vote percentage is expressed as 100 and the forecast deviation is measured from that base) stands at ±76 percent. The total *percentage point* error (i.e., the total of the differences between the percentage forecast for each party and the percentage of actual votes cast for each party) is ±20 percent. When these cumulative errors are simply averaged among the four parties, percentage error is reduced to ±19 percent, while the percentage point error falls to ±5 percent.

The Gallup organization has always claimed that its final election forecasts are accurate only to within an average of four percentage points. An allowance for permitted error expressed in this way is, of course, thoroughly misleading; it permits substantial real forecast error while suggesting only minimal failure. But it also gives to polling organizations an important tactical advantage. When questioned about forecast errors, they can usually claim to be well within accepted limits. At that point the discussion tends to shift abruptly from the causes of forecast error to the public's error in appraising polling objectives and methods.

The committee which examined the American polling failure of 1948 made bold to say:

> Too many people had an exaggerated impression of the accuracy of the pre-election polls — in spite of the numerous statements, particularly by Gallup, that poll results were subject to average errors of 3 to 4 percentage points. Too many people seemed to feel that average error meant maximum error, and they did not realize that average error of 4 percentage points can produce errors of 8, 12 or more percentage points. Until readers and users of poll results understand these errors . . . there will continue to be adverse reactions. . . .

The Canadian Institute of Public Opinion (Gallup poll) has conducted nine national pre-election polls since 1945. Since the Institute does not undertake to predict the number of parliamentary seats each party will win, it cannot be expected to name the winning candidate or party as in American presidential elections. It seeks rather to predict the distribution of the total vote among the contesting parties. The Institute's performance in nine Canadian general elections is summarized in Table 2. (Unbracketed figures indicate the poll percentage error; bracketed figures indicate the poll percentage point error.)

In nine federal elections in which the C.I.P.O. has made predictions about the percentage of votes to be cast for party categories, the Institute has correctly predicted the proportions in only six out of 36 instances. In the case of the two major parties, substantial forecast errors occurred in 1957 and in 1965. The Institute grossly over-estimated Liberal strength in each case. In five instances it also mis-calculated CCF-NDP strength by substantial margins, but these errors were slight in relation to the total vote. Average polling error in eight elections was approximately the same for the two major parties, but inasmuch as the publication of poll results has any real effect on the outcome of a Canadian election, the Progressive Conservatives were placed at a disadvantage in 1957 and 1965. Cumulative figures on polling error are set out in Table 3.

TABLE 2: Calculated Error of C.I.P.O. Pre-Election Final Forecasts, 1945-1968

Election	Liberal		Progressive Conservative		CCF-NDP		Others	
1945	—5	(—2)	+6	(+2)	+9	(+1)	—6	(—1)
1949	—3	(—2)	+4	(+1)	+12	(+2)	—19	(—1)
1953	+2	(+1)	0	0	0	0	—9	(—1)
1957	+17	(+7)	—13	(—5)	—7	(—1)	—16	(—1)
1958	0	0	+4	(+2)	—16	(—2)	0	0
1962	—3	(—1)	+2	(+1)	—11	(—2)	+17	(+2)
1963	—2	(—1)	—2	(—1)	+6	(+1)	+6	(+1)
1965	+10	(+4)	—10	(—3)	0	0	—6	(—1)
1968	+4	(+2)	—6	(—2)	+6	(+1)	0	0
Total Error	±46	(±20)	±47	(±17)	±67	(±10)	±79	(±8)
Average Error	±5.1	(±2.2)	±5.2	(±1.9)	±7.4	(±1.1)	±8.8	(±0.9)

Sources: Calculated from Reports of the Chief Electoral Officer and C.I.P.O. Press Releases. Final data for the 1965 election were obtained from a preliminary report of the Chief Electoral Officer as reported in the *Montreal Star*, December 28, 1965. Vote allocations assigned to parties in the first five elections as calculated by H. A. Scarrow, *Canada Votes*, New Orleans, 1962, pp. 118, 132, 146, 162, and 176. Calculations are at slide rule accuracy from actual vote percentages to one decimal place; Gallup poll forecasts are not reported in fractions of percentage points.

TABLE 3: Measures of C.I.P.O. Cumulative Polling Error, Party Vote Plurality, and Electoral Participation Rates, 1945-1968

Election	Total Forecast Error		Unweighted Average Error	Vote Error (000's)	Party Plurality (000's)	Voter Turn-out %
	%	Percentage Point				
1945	26	6	1.5	314.8	721.8	75
1949	38	6	1.5	350.9	1,161.4	74
1953	11	2	0.5	112.8	1,007.0	68
1957	53	14	3.5	964.8	129.8	74
1958	20	4	1.0	291.5	1,460.7	79
1962	33	6	1.5	466.4	7.8	80
1963	16	4	1.0	315.8	510.5	80
1965	26	8	2.0	616.9	599.1	75
1968	16	5	1.2	395.2	1,099.5	76

Sources: Calculated from Table 2 and the Reports of the Chief Electoral Officer.

Various measures of the Institute's maximum and average forecast error are set out in the first four columns above. Total percentage error in column 1 represents the sum of positive and negative percentage polling deviations measured from a 100 percent base of the actual vote proportions received by the four categories of parties. (Although not generally used in the analysis of polling accuracy, these aggregate percentage deviations are nevertheless the purest indicators of election forecasting performance. To illustrate, if it is projected that a given party is to receive 1 percent of the total vote and in fact it obtains only 0.5 percent of all votes cast, the percentage error is —50 while the percentage point error is only one-half of —1 percent.) In the elections of 1949 and 1962, when the Institute's maximum percentage point error was relatively small (6%), its cumulative percentage error of forecast was ±38 and ±33 percent respectively, due to major miscalculations of the minor party vote. In the elections of 1957 and 1965, when the Institute's maximum percentage point error was very large (14% and 8%), its cumulative percentage error stood at ±53 and ±26 percent respectively. The latter figure is relatively small because of the polls's accuracy in predicting the minor party vote in 1965.

It is clear from these comparisons that polling error expressed as an unweighted percentage point average—the measure used by all Gallup organizations—bears little relationship to actual polling competence. Such a measure is obtained by dividing total percentage point error by the number of categories of parties. Hence an average error of ±3.5 percent in 1957, while it remained well within the Institute's permissible error of ±4 percent, involved a total forecast error of 53 percent, or nearly one million votes when the Liberal and Progressive Conservative parties were separated by less than 130,000 votes. Similarly, an average polling error of only ±2 percent in 1965 involved a total forecast error of 26 percent, or almost 617,000 votes when the two major parties were separated by only 599,000 votes. Even when, as in 1962, average polling error was very low (±1.5%) the disparity between the error expressed in actual votes (466,000) and the leading party's plurality of 8,000 votes was spectacularly large.

Table 3 also indicates a somewhat uncertain relationship between polling accuracy and voter turnout in Canadian general elections. Assuming a minimal sampling error and a small proportion of "undecided" respondents, the error of polling forecasts ought to vary inversely with the size of voter participation. But in fact there appears to be little consistent correlation between these two variables. At the level of 74-75 percent turnout, for example, the following C.I.P.O. percentage point errors were recorded: ±6 (1945), ±6 (1949), ±8 (1965), and ±14 (1957). During the three elections when voter participation reached the peak of 79-80 percent, comparable errors ranged between ±4 and ±6 percent. When voter participation was at an all-time low of 68 per cent in 1953, on the other hand, the Institute's error of forecast stood at its lowest point of only ±2 percentage points.

It would seem to be a reasonable conclusion that the Canadian Institute of Public Opinion has not achieved an outstanding record of accuracy in the prediction of Canadian election outcomes. On the basis of nine election forecasts its average percentage error per election has been ±26.7, while its error in percentage points has averaged ±6.1. Moreover in the elections of 1957, 1962, and 1965 the latter error, expressed in votes, was greater than the leading party's vote plurality.

When a relative rather than an absolute comparison is made, however, a different conclusion emerges. With the possible exception of the Australian (Gallup) poll, which at least in its early years attained a consistently high degree of accuracy, the Canadian poll has obtained results that compare favourably with thoses achieved by survey organs in other countries. Following are the percentage point forecast errors recorded in Gallup poll predictions in five countries during and immediately prior to 1965:

Country	Party	Percentage point of Error
Canada	Liberal	+4
	Prog. Cons.	—3
	N.D.P.	0
	Social Credit, etc.	—1
United States	Democratic	—3
	Republican	+3
United Kingdom	Labour	+2
	Conservative	+2
	Liberal, etc.	—4
Australia	L.C.P.	—4
	D.L.P.	—2
	A.L.P.	+4
	Other	+2
Norway	Socialist	+0.1
	Non-Socialist	—0.1

Source: Byrne Hope Sanders, "Gallup Poll Points with Pride to Nov. 8 'Record of Accuracy,'" *Financial Post*, November 20, 1965, p. 25. The British and Australian data have been slightly altered to rectify errors in presentation.

C.I.P.O. POLLING TECHNIQUES

According to a newspaper article in the *Toronto Daily Star* on November 8, 1961, the Canadian Institute of Public Opinion used at that time a force of 600 part-time interviewers to gather its findings. All the interviewers in Canada were women. An average study cost between $4,000 and $5,000. In its early years of sampling voters' opinions, the C.I.P.O. terminated its interviewing 10 days before an election, but after 1957 the date of final questioning was moved up to three or four days before polling day, in order to improve the accuracy of results. The normal sample of 690 persons per survey was also enlarged immediately before elections.

For its final pre-election surveys the C.I.P.O. has for some time drawn a national sample of rather less than 3,000 respondents. Of all the persons interviewed, some are not eligible to vote, some refuse to express their intentions, some are undecided at the time of interview, while a few always claim either to have no party preference or to favour some party other than the four major national parties. Of the 2,700 individuals interviewed prior to the 1962 election, for example, 510 (18.9%) for various reasons did not communicate a clear intention.

The standard question put to respondents is: "If a federal election were held today, which party's candidate do you think you would favour?" Respondents indicate their preferences by marking a "secret" ballot. When there is an expression of indecision, a further question is put: "Will you please mark the ballot to show the way you are leaning at the present time?" For survey purposes the "leaners" are assumed to have expressed adequately their party preferences.

As a general rule, moreover, the relatively large number of respondents unable to express their intentions clearly are presumed as a group to have the same preference characteristics as those who do mark their ballots. The adequacy of such procedures has often been questioned. In some countries behavioural regularities in this area have been observed. American Gallup poll officials claim that, within a two percent tolerance, their undecided voters tend to behave in the same way as voters who have expressed a clear intention, except, of course, in the 1964 presidential election where there is evidence to indicate that an unprecedented number of undecided voters actually cast ballots for Goldwater. An adequate understanding of similar phenomena is lacking in Canada.

In addition to the data on party preference, the Institute's interviewers in final election polls solicit opinions on various political questions and attempt to measure the intensity of voter interest in the campaign. Respondents are asked to rate their own interest in the pending election. From this latter information an attempt is made to project the rate of actual voter participation. With the possible exception of 1962 results, the projections of voter interest have appeared to parallel actual trends of turnout. For subsequent analysis of the correlates of voting preference, interviewers also obtain information on the age, sex, education, occupation, religion, mother tongue, and trade union characteristics of respondents. Finally, in each case socio-economic status is determined by the interviewer in accordance with a prescribed "home and standard of living" scale.

The Canadian Institute of Public Opinion purports to use area-probability sampling methods. But as in other countries a combined quota-area procedure is actually used. The rural component of the Canadian sample, in fact, is not based on area methods at all but rather on a crude geographic quota system which allows the interviewer much discretion in the choice of respondents. The urban part of the sample, however, incorporates some aspects of area-probability technique. The urban census tracts are first stratified in accordance with income and a random sample of units is chosen. From the tracts so selected a further sample of block units is chosen by random selection. Interviewers with given quotas, beginning at any convenient dwelling unit in the urban blocks, then proceed to interview a random selection of adults in every second dwelling. This process continues until all quotas are complete. When the field data are processed the sample is weighted for age by duplicating IBM cards for the age classes requiring greater representation. And the units thus added are assumed to have gross voting preferences similar to those actually interviewed.

A second limitation worth noting is that the Institute, apparently for budgetary reasons, restricts "call backs" on persons not directly available for interview. For this reason the sample is biased against men, employed adult females, and probably low income groups. "The effect of this [bias]", in the words of Professor R. R. Alford who has made extensive use of C.I.P.O. results, "is difficult to estimate".

REGENSTREIF PREDICTIONS

In addition to the forecasts of Canadian elections provided by the Institute, there are the newspaper-sponsored polling activities of Professor S. P. Regenstreif. This poller undertook his first national survey prior to the 1958 election, and during the next three elections his party seat predictions were widely publicized. His national polling record was as follows:

TABLE 4:   Calculated Seat, Percentage, and Percentage Point Error of the Regenstreif Poll in Three General Elections, 1962-1965

Party	1962			1963			1965		
	Seat Error	% Error	% pt. Error	Seat Error	% Error	% pt. Error	Seat Error	% Error	% pt. Error
Liberal	— 5	— 5	— 2	— 7	— 5	— 3	+ 9	+ 7	+ 3
P.C.	—16	—14	— 6	—19	—20	— 7	—18	— 19	— 7
N.D.P.	— 3	—16	— 1	+ 4	+23	+ 2	— 4	— 19	— 2
S.C., etc.	— 6	—20	— 2	— 1	— 4	0*	— 9†	— 56	— 3
Total	—30	—55	—11	±31	±52	±12	±40	±101	±15
Doubtful	30 (11%)			23 (9%)			22 (8%)		

Sources: Calculated from S. P. Regenstreif, *The Diefenbaker Interlude,* p. xi. Seat prediction for 1965 as published in the *Winnipeg Free Press,* November 6, 1965.
* Less than 0.5%.   † Includes two elected Independent candidates.

Certain characteristic features of this poll are apparent. First, Regenstreif has never succeeded in obtaining complete accuracy in his twelve attempts at predicting party seat distributions in the House of Commons. Second, in 10 of the party seat predictions he underestimated the number of members actually elected. In particular, he has consistently failed to predict accurately the electoral fortunes of the Progressive Conservative party. During the three elections under review that party returned 308 members to parliament, whereas Regenstreif's forecasts called for only 255. His total error in this regard stands at — 17 percent. His miscalculations of total party seat distributions have ranged between 30 and 40 seats per election, or from 11 to 15 percent of all parliamentary seats. Regenstreif also designates a number of constituencies as being in doubt. In 1963 and 1965 the numbers left in doubt were 23 and 22 respectively, or slightly less than one-tenth of all constituencies.

These calculations, however, fail to convey the real limits of Regenstreif's polling errors. In spite of allowances for doubtful seats, he was prepared in all three elections to forecast which party would win a majority of seats, or which party would assume or retain office with minority status in parliament. As a justification for the use of his services in 1963 and 1965, the press frequently alluded to his earlier predictions that the Diefenbaker government would not obtain its majority in the election of 1962, and that the Social Credit party would emerge as a potent force in Quebec's federal ridings. The first of these forecasts was very accurate; the second was less accurate, since he had projected only 20 seats for the Caouette party when in fact it secured 26. Prior to the 1965 election, on the other hand, Regenstreif assigned 140 seats to the Liberals, 79 to the Progressive Conservatives, 17 to the N.D.P., and 7 to the Social Credit and *Créditiste* groups when in actual fact Mr. Pearson's government narrowly failed to get its majority and secured only 131 seats while the Progressive Conservatives elected 97 candidates. These errors of forecast had their source in a major underestimation of Mr. Diefenbaker's strength on the Prairies and in the Maritimes, and at least to some degree in a sanguine assumption of *Créditiste* decline in Quebec. The only element in his forecast sustained by the electoral decision was an increased support for the N.D.P.

In sharp contrast to his previous national polling efforts, Professor Regenstreif's predictive performance in 1968 was extremely cautious. For the first time he did not assign a specific seat distribution to the contending parties but limited himself to a range of possible outcomes. The Liberals, he felt, could receive between 128 and 145 of the seats available. In the event, they obtained 155. The Progressive Conservatives were assigned victories in the range 75 to 93. They actually elected only 72 members. The N.D.P. potential was considered to be between 20 and 28 whereas they obtained 22. The *Créditistes* were thought capable of electing between 8 and 12 members when in fact they won 14. While conceding that all signs pointed to a Trudeau victory, Regenstreif said: "The Liberal potential straddles the majority line of 133 seats. The likelihood is that Trudeau will get it, provided most of the uncertainties are resolved in his favor. But political realities require a cautious analysis." (*Toronto Daily Star,* June 22, 1968.) It is apparent that in spite of its more cautious approach the Regenstreif poll in 1968 continued to exhibit the weaknesses described above. In this case its projections failed to capture the magnitude of Mr. Trudeau's electoral sweep — a victory that produced a Liberal party plurality in excess of one million votes. At the same time, it seriously overestimated Progressive Conservative constituency potential. It is worth observing, finally, that the direction of poll forecast errors in 1968 is the reverse of those apparent in 1965.

In his first venture at public polling during a provincial election, Regenstreif's errors were even more substantial. His predictive performance during the Ontario election of 1963 is set out in Table 5.

TABLE 5:   Calculated Seat, Percentage, and Percentage Point Error of the
Regenstreif Poll in the Ontario Provincial Election, 1963

	Conservative	Liberal	N.D.P.	Total
Poll Forecast (Seats)	56	35	5	96
Seats Won	77	24	7	108
Seat Error	—21	+11	— 2	± 34
Percentage Error	—27.3	+46.0	—28.5	±101.8
Percentage Point Error	—19.4	+10.2	— 1.9	± 31.5

Sources: *Toronto Daily Star,* September 23, 1963, p. 1; the *Canadian Parliamentary Guide, 1965,* Ottawa, 1965, p. 709.

Disregarding the 12 seats left in doubt, Regenstreif in this instance failed to forecast accurately 34 out of 96 constituency results. As with the federal polls he underestimated Conservative strength and overemphasized Liberal seat potential. But the margins of error in this poll were greater than in those examined above. Total percentage error due to seat misallocations, for example, exceeded ± 100, while the maximum percentage point error exceeded ± 31. If the 12 doubtful seats were added to those allocated in error, total failure of forecast extended to 46 of the 108 legislative contests. In the Ontario election of 1967, although he did engage in opinion sampling activity, Professor Regenstreif did not hazard a public prediction of party seat allocations.

Regenstreif's original method of polling requires brief comment. It is in no way related to the methods used by the Canadian Institute of Public Opinion. First, eleven main politico-geographic regions of Canada are chosen. The poller then visits each region and conducts interviews using a crude quota stratified in terms of income, residence (urban, suburban, and rural), religious affiliation, and ethnicity. Within these strata requirements the choice of actual respondents is supposedly made at random. Just how random selection is made in these conditions remains obscure. In comparison with other polling organizations, the Regenstreif sample is very small: 210 (1958), 375 (1962), 470 (1963).

Regenstreif's techniques of polling are not amenable to tests of statistical significance since, as he himself has said, he relies heavily on his own powers of judgment:

> . . . most of the surveying done by me is based on what is known as 'judgment' sampling—in other words, the selection of the people to be interviewed was purely a matter of my own personal discretion—and there is no real way of statistically determining how representative of the general population my respondents are. Secondly, such efforts, . . . are not 'scientific' because they are not really replicable by someone else, even if they were to operate on the same set of assumptions that I did. In this sense, this style of research is more in the category of 'art' than of 'science'.

Along with the much greater caution apparent in his polling activity since 1965, Regenstreif's projections in recent years have been based not only on his own personal interviews with voters but as well on the results of national pre-election surveys conducted by private opinion research groups.

MEDIA POLLS: THE QUEBEC ELECTION, 1970

In recent provincial elections there has been a marked increase in polling activity sponsored by newspapers and undertaken by private survey research organizations. In most cases an attempt is made to project proportional vote distributions among contending parties rather than to forecast actual constituency outcomes. The preferred technique of inquiry involves the use of random provincial samples whose voting intentions are sought exclusively through telephone interviews. While some of these studies have succeeded in predicting general trends of provincial voting behaviour, their conclusions have not significantly reduced uncertainties associated with actual election results. During the 1970 Quebec election, for example, Montreal's *La Presse* and the *Toronto Daily Star* commissioned polls both of which detected a massive decline in support for the governing *Union Nationale* party. As indicated in the following table, however, these polls failed to predict much more than the defeat of the Bertrand government.

TABLE 6:   Major Quebec Pre-Election Polls, 1970

Party	La Presse (First Poll)	Toronto Star	La Presse (Second Poll)	Actual Vote	Percentage Point Error	Vote Error
	%	%	%	%		(000's)
Lib.	26	32	37	44	—7	—186.4
P.Q.	25	23	29	24	+5	+133.2
U.N.	13	16	15	20	—5	—133.2
Créd.	12	9	15	11	+4	+106.5
Others	2	1	4	1	+3	+ 79.9
Undecided	22	19				

Source: Poll results and unofficial Quebec election result as reported in the *Toronto Daily Star*, April 18, 24 and 30, 1970. The *Montreal Star* also sponsored a regional poll not summarized in this table.

The *La Presse* polls were conducted by the *Centre de Recherches sur l'Opinion Publique*. That paper's first poll, taken between April 8-12, sampled 776 persons by telephone; its second, carried out on April 23-24 some five days before the election, sampled 1,377 individuals. The *Toronto Star* poll was conducted by Canadian Facts Company during April 13-18 and sampled 820 Quebeckers by telephone. The latter poll results were summarized in the press by Professor Regenstreif.

Because the first two polls listed in Table 6 did not deal with a significant residual category of undecided voters, the analysis here of forecast error is confined to the second *La Presse* poll. That poll underestimated Liberal strength by —7 percentage points. In somewhat smaller measure it overestimated *Parti Québecois* strength by +5 percentage points. Approximate vote error in these projections amounted to 187,000 and 133,000 respectively. All the polls clearly underestimated the governing party's strength while generally overstating actual support for the *Créditistes*, N.D.P., and other candidates. Cumulative percentage point error of the second *La Presse* poll amounted to ±24, which represents about 640,000 votes in a universe of some 2.7 million. A forecast error of such magnitude failed completely to signal the scope of Mr. Bourassa's victory which gave the Liberal party 72 of Quebec's 108 legislative seats and 600,000 more votes than its nearest competitor, the P.Q. party.

It should be emphasized that the forecast error recorded in these Quebec polls exceeds the tolerance limits accepted by most survey organizations themselves. In his analysis of the *Toronto Star* poll, for instance, Regenstreif claimed that the sample was extracted in a manner calculated to insure accuracy within 3 percent 19 times out of 20. But in the case of the second *La Presse* poll, the average percentage point error relating to the four major party categories amounted to ±5.2. It will be recalled that in the federal election of 1957, when the C.I.P.O. recorded its greatest error of forecast (see Table 3, above), the cumulative party average percentage point error stood at only ±3.5. Based upon their recorded performance in Quebec and in British Columbia, these media telephone polls have not demonstrated high reliability.

DO POLLS INFLUENCE PUBLIC OPINION?

During the recent Quebec election Mr. Bertrand told his listeners at one meeting to ignore public opinion surveys published in daily newspapers, especially those conducted by the English-language press. These papers, he asserted, "want the death of the *Union Nationale*." Many pundits and not a few politicians have suggested that so far from having only a disinterested concern with the measurement of opinions, polling activity itself exercises a powerful influence on the opinions that it seeks to measure. It is often held that during election campaigns, for instance, the publication of poll results tends to interfere with what ought to be the autonomous decision-making functions of the electorate. As we should expect, professional pollers have done their best to refute this charge, sometimes by ignoring it entirely. Gallup and others have assembled evidence to disprove the general claim that dissemination of poll results during election campaigns fosters a "band wagon" effect. There are indeed many instances on record of ultimate electoral success, even in the face of unfavourable poll results, by "under-dog" candidates and parties. Similarly there are cases where minority parties often increase their actual vote in spite of the poll showings of stronger competitors.

Instances of this type merely document the obvious. Polls may be in error; and such evidence, by itself, tells very little about the uncertain relation between polling and electoral behaviour in various political cultures. The plain truth is that notwithstanding the findings of particular case studies of opinion formation, the real character of such a mysterious relationship can hardly be known in any fundamental sense. Indeed, the psychology of voting is infinitely complex; and the range of variables potentially important as determinants of electoral behaviour appears to be well beyond human management in any except the most general and imprecise sense. While they were not explicitly developed in its report, considerations of this kind probably induced the (Barbeau) Committee on Election Expenses in 1966 to recommend the prohibition of the publication of public opinion polls during election campaign periods.

PRIVATE POLLS

The Liberal party, and to a lesser extent all major parties, are making greater use of privately commissioned opinion surveys at the national, provincial, regional, and local constituency levels. Indeed, the results of a private national poll supplied by an unnamed American poller were reputed to have been a contributing factor in Mr. Pearson's decision to call the election in 1965. During the campaign the Liberals commissioned a national poll, crosschecked the results of other surveys, and conducted many local opinion studies. These private surveys apparently indicated that the Gallup poll consistently overestimated Liberal party strength. Despite some success at the constituency level, the private polls failed to produce realistic results in the Maritimes, and to a lesser extent in Quebec and on the Prairies. The Progressive Conservatives used no national private polls but claimed to have access to the results of some provincial polls.

It appears clear that the demand for such survey activity cannot be reduced because of supposed failure. There will always be enthusiastic party functionaries willing to commission surveys of the voting preferences and political attitudes of ethnic groups, older citizens, suburbanites, trade unionists, and other important electoral groups. In this area a typical response might well be that of Mr. Keith Davey, the Liberal party's national organizer from 1961 to 1966. In private conversation before the 1965 election he is reported to have said that the party's commissioned studies indicated a Liberal victory of between 160 and 170 seats, when in fact the party won only 131 seats.

It has been suggested that a substantial number of Liberal failures occurred in seats considered safe, and where, accordingly, little survey work was undertaken. If this interpretation has any factual base, it may well stimulate greater rather than reduced polling effort in future elections. One presumes, however, that party leaders are well aware of the main deficiency of private polling: the tendency of some survey organizations to supply only those results which the client is willing to receive.

In spite of their obvious shortcomings it is well known that in practice considerable sums may be spent by parties or candidates on opinion polls that are supposed to have propaganda value toward the end of election campaigns. The Barbeau Committee recommended prohibition of such polls, for public purposes, in federal elections. In the words of the Committee:

Polling surveys of this type are often urged on a candidate, thus increasing his costs, to off-set the purported results of an opponent's polling of public opinion. The committee sees no purpose in prohibiting parties and candidates from using such surveys for their private purposes only, but considers their uncontrolled use for public purposes improper, and thus an unnecessary expense to parties and candidates.

The Committee Recommends that:

The publication for public consumption of the results of any such poll, from the date of the issuance of the election writ to polling day, be prohibited. The prohibition of publication should include not only private polls arranged by parties or candidates, but polls conducted by any other organization during the same period. (*Report of the Commission on Election Expenses*, 1966, p. 51.)

It remains to be seen whether the government will act upon this particular recommendation of the Committee. As far as the public polls are concerned there has been little popular negative response to polling error; and the media demands for election forecasting are clearly increasing not decreasing. It is my own forecast that notwithstanding the threat of prohibition, the pollers will continue to have a secure position in the politics of a democratic society.

LOBBYING AT OTTAWA*

DON McGILLIVRAY

OTTAWA—In the old redbrick houses of downtown Ottawa, in posh new executive suites, in the comradely exclusiveness of the Rideau Club, in the select eateries of the nation's capital and the nooks and crannies of parliament—there is an almost unknown and invisible branch of Canada's government.

It is the Ottawa lobby—a growing army of people whose job it is to find out what the government is doing and to influence policy on behalf of organized interest groups and private companies.

One of the myths of Canadian politics is that this country has no lobbyists, at least, none like those in the United States where the "pressure business" tends to break out into public scandals ranging back from Bobby Baker to the Teapot Dome of the 1920's and beyond. . . .

Most of it is "clean" lobbying—presentation of a case without threats or bribes —rather than "dirty" lobbying, to use current American definitions. But it's still lobbying according to the dictionary definition: "to address or solicit members of a legislative body, in the lobby or elsewhere with intent to influence legislation. . . ."

The Ottawa lobby is different in kind as well as degree. Washington lobbyists con-

---

* From a five-part series by *Southam News Services,* April 9-April 15, 1964. By permission.

centrate on congressmen but in the Canadian parliamentary system, to quote one Ottawa lobbyist, "the power of the individual member of parliament or senator is just about zero."

So the main focus is on the cabinet and the civil service. And because cabinet and civil service decisions are made behind closed doors, finding out what is likely to be done is just as important as, and vital to, the job of influencing decisions.

This is more like the British lobby, described in a recent study as "an anonymous empire" which is in a state of "symbiosis" with the government—a term borrowed from biology, meaning that the two support and feed each other.

Ottawa lobbyists avoid the term "lobby" because they feel it carries an implication of underhanded methods. But, it's being recognized by students of government that lobbying, far from being something sinister which should be stamped out, is a vital part of democratic government.

S. E. Finer, a student of the British lobby, has written that lobbying "embodies two basic democratic procedures—the right to participate in policy making and the right to demand redress of grievances." Without it, he says, government would be "a rigid and ignorant tyranny" and the civil service "a stupid bureaucracy."

"In the age of bigness and technology," he writes, "the lobby tempers the system —it does so by promoting continuous interchange between governors and governed."

The Ottawa lobby provides vital services to the government and parliament at little direct cost to the taxpayers. It conducts research into government proposals, serves as a quick and handy indicator of the feelings of affected groups, suggests projects, turns up flaws in legislation, and checks, balances, advises and warns the public authorities.

Most of Canada's profusion of royal commissions are really little but an extended consultation with affected pressure groups.

But this doesn't mean that the present system of Canadian lobbying hasn't got flaws—and serious flaws. But the system has never been examined by parliament or political scientists. In this, Canada is forty years behind the United States and 10 years behind Britain.

The Canadian lobby is now ripe for study. The number of lobbyists grows daily. The steady year-round back-stage business of lobbying is increasing. And the past year has been a vintage one for examples of open lobbying.

1. *Pressure group lobbying*: In June, the stock exchange lobby led by Eric Kierans forced withdrawal of the Gordon takeover tax and in July, construction industry pressure forced modification of the sales tax on building materials.

2. *Provincial lobbying*: Sustained pressure from Manitoba Premier Duff Roblin played a big part in keeping Trans-Canada Air Lines overhaul base in Winnipeg despite the opinions of consultants that it would cost almost $30 million extra over the next ten years.

3. *Diplomatic lobbying*: The French embassy pulled out all the stops in its lobby for Sud Aviation's Caravelle to be bought as TCA's new jetliner. MPs were wined and dined at the embassy—some of them as many as four times within a month—

and plied with information. Just as the decision was about to be made, the MPs were offered a free Caravelle ride to Montreal to see a French exhibition.

4. *Mass lobbying*: Burly Hal Banks, now-deposed boss of the Seafarers' International Union, brought 2,000 banner-waving seamen to the front steps of parliament October 21 to buttonhole MPs and try to prevent the government putting the SIU under trusteeship.

5. *Grassroots lobbying*: The Canadian Labor Congress has had thousands of postcards—carried post-free under House of Commons franking privileges—mailed to MPs from union members across the country. This was to counter an effort by the insurance lobby to have clients of insurance agents write opposing the Canadian pension plan.

EXTENT

. . . It's a safe bet that there are more full time lobbyists than legislators in Ottawa.

This may involves some double counting because many Senators are both lobbyists and legislators—the one job merges into the other. . . .

But any count of the Ottawa lobbyists would have to include, as a beginning, approximately 100 professional, full-time lobbyists representing business firms in Ottawa.

Some of these are merely manning listening posts or holding sinecures which involve little except making government appointments for the big boss of the company when he comes to the capital.

But others are hard-working men with intelligence, subtlety and inside contacts, well worth the five-figure salaries they are paid.

Then there are lawyers. Ottawa has 322 lawyers in private practice, an oversupply—even counting the bread-and-butter legal end of the capital's real estate boom—if it were not for government work.

What they do ranges all the way from strictly professional services in the Supreme Court, through the quasi-legal work with government boards and commissions, down to the job of lobbying in government departments and among cabinet ministers.

This "parliamentary work" doesn't demand a lawyer but lawyers claim their training and professional standing is an advantage to their clients. One estimate is that half of Ottawa's lawyers do parliamentary work but some lawyers say this is too high. . . .

Lobbyists who claim to be public relations consultants are likely to belong to the National Press Club of Canada, a common meeting ground with newsmen, which moved into new quarters two years ago with the aid of generous gifts solicited from national corporations.

A recent count showed that the press club had 147 active newsmen and 122 associate members, the category into which public relations men fit. They can't belong to the Parliamentary Press Gallery, which once invited a member to resign for lobbying activities, but lobbying the Parliamentary correspondents is a popular procedure, against which the newsmen, as much as the politicians or the civil servants, have to be on guard. Some succeed better than others—"handouts" are common, but they consist of printed propaganda, of which the government itself is far and away the major source.

Any registration of lobbyists would also take in the 187 national organizations which have offices in Ottawa. Some are lobby offices and nothing else. Others have a variety of functions—a national organization has to have an office somewhere—but their main job is often contact with the government.

They represent all kinds of groups — aircraft makers, ban-the-bombers, barristers, bakers, brewers, manufacturers and mushroom growers, trade union and war veterans, to name a few.

Definitely not so welcome are a minority group on the fringes of the business—influence peddlers, fly-by-night contractors with a bankroll out looking for palms to grease, "pressure boys" who try threats when persuasion fails, people who rake-off high fees for "inside dope" which is really information available to all and others who somehow find out about an up-coming policy and collect money on the claim that they engineered something that was going to be done anyway.

Such "dirty lobbying" isn't unknown in Ottawa but it's usually the private client rather than the public interest that gets hurt. And both the lobbyists and the lobbied insist that it's a minor factor in the over-all picture.

Members of parliament think of themselves as the chief targets of the lobbyists but they're not.

"What can a member of parliament do for you?" asks one lobbyist. "He can make a speech in caucus if he's on the government side or in the house if he's in opposition. But that's all."

Different lobbyists are often used to promote the same cause in the civil service and among the politicians.

"With civil servants, confidence is all-important," says an Ottawa insider who has been on both sides of the lobby business. "A senator is no good. They'll run like scared rabbits or clam up if they see any kind of politician coming. But if you're going to lobby politicians you have to have somebody who talks their language."

An Ontario Liberal MP expresses the distaste felt by most members and ministers at lobbying approaches made on the basis of past friendship or by somebody who has a special entree, such as a member of the press.

"They find somebody whom you used to know and he phones and invites you out to dinner to talk over old times. Then, in the middle of the chat, whammo you get the pitch. I always feel like putting on my hat and walking right out."

MPs also become spokesmen for special interests, although Commons rules forbid them taking money for advancing any cause coming before parliament. What they do get is research help which can make them look good in the House of Commons. Many a well-timed question or information-packed speech in the Commons owes much to the invisible lobbyist.

Some of this special advocacy is due to such factors as the natural interest maritime members have in fishing and prairie members in wheat. Tobacco area

MPs speak for the tobacco growers and members from cheese producing ridings become known in the House as cheese spokesmen. . . .

METHODS

. . . Three of the most solid and powerful pressure groups now established in Ottawa are the Canadian Manufacturers' Association, the Canadian Labor Congress and the Canadian Federation of Agriculture.

These groups—and more than 180 like them—have offices in the capital which maintain continuous two-way consultation with cabinet ministers and civil servants. They encourage, advise and warn. They nominate members for bodies like the Economic Council of Canada and dozens of advisory committees in the departments.

They're consulted about legislation when it's still only a gleam in the minister's eye. They see it through parliament and they watch, like proud or anxious parents, its administration.

Consultation with the pressure groups (or "interest groups" as they are now called by some political scientists) is welcomed by ministers.

"If a minister is smart, he'll have them in," says one smart former Conservative minister. "It's one way to neutralize criticism. Have both sides in and let them argue it out before you decide. The minister has to take responsibility for what he brings into the House but he'll be a lot more comfortable if he knows that the people affected have agreed beforehand." . . .

. . . The unwritten rules prevent a group which has been taken into the minister's confidence from starting a public campaign against his bill before it ever reaches the Commons.

They also prevent the group from agreeing privately then raising a public fuss when the minister makes his plan public.

The rules of the game are binding on ministers too. If a minister puts forward a plan a pressure group views as strictly second best, the group may still work with him to make it as bearable as possible.

But it would be a grave breach of lobbying etiquette for the minister to stand up and claim that the plan had been endorsed by the farmers, oilmen, union leaders or whatever the group might be.

Breaking the rules brings a breakdown in consultation, sometimes with recriminations on both sides.

Such a breakdown occurred between the Diefenbaker government and the CLC after the labor congress teamed up with the CCF to form the New Democratic Party. The government felt the CLC had given up its right to be consulted on labor appointments to public bodies. The CLC insisted that labor men appointed should be delegates of the organized labor movement. The final blowup was Claude Jodoin's resignation from the National Productivity Council in 1962.

Different pressure groups work in different ways. The CMA, CLC, and scores of other organizations present annual briefs to governments, comment on public policy in press releases and appear before royal commissions. The federation of agriculture puts its brief before the government and the opposition party caucuses.

Other groups work quietly behind the scenes. Little is heard of the effective work of horticultural groups in Ottawa. The Canadian Bar Association and the chartered accountants have a vital advisory role in each year's budget. The churches never present a brief but their influence is considerable on such questions as Indian affairs, lottery laws and liquor regulations.

One of the slickest, most effective efforts was the quiet behind-the-scenes operation of the oil lobby in 1959 when the national energy policy was in the making. The industry's best minds were moved into Ottawa and kept around for nine months while the oil policy was shaped generally to the industry's satisfaction.

In sharp contrast but no less successful was the angry public protest of the construction industry against last year's sales tax on building materials. E. J. Benson, Mr. Gordon's parliamentary secretary, recently called it "the best organized lobby in Canadian political history."

That takes in a lot of territory, including the tariff and railway lobbies which once dominated government policy. But the builders put constant, pounding pressure on the cabinet and Mr. Gordon for weeks. They piled his office knee-deep with letters and telegrams. Delegations camped in the corridors. In every town the press got solemn warnings of the local effect of the tax. Every day when he walked into the Commons, Mr. Gordon knew the opposition was well supplied with ammunition.

But the finance minister's cabinet colleagues cracked first and forced him to yield, an experience which has made him react against pressure. Just before this year's budget, automobile dealers poured telegrams into Ottawa seeking repeal of the $5,000 ceiling on the value of cars which can be deducted as a business expense. They convinced some Liberal MPs but they just stiffened Mr. Gordon's resistance. . . .

Sometimes lobbying backfires. An outstanding example was the "Coca-Cola lobby" when Hon. Douglas Abbott was minister of finance. One year, Mr. Abbott had decided to take the excise tax off soft drinks, but the soft drink people didn't know about it.

They enlisted clergymen to preach against the evils of strong drink, contrasted with the benign effects of pop. Then these men of the cloth descended on Ottawa to make the same pitch to Mr. Abbott, coupled with a plea for tax removal. This so incensed the finance minister that he left the excise tax on soft drinks for another year.

The Canadian Medical Association is an example of a quietly powerful group. Since 1953, the advisory committee to the department of national health and welfare composed of doctors, has been under instructions to see "that nothing Government may do will thwart" the CMA policy on health insurance. . . .

More and more groups are finding it pays to open an Ottawa office. About 50 such offices have been opened in the past ten years.

One pointed example was the opening, in November 1962, of an Ottawa office for the Canadian Pharmaceutical Manufacturers Association. It was no coincidence that the industry had just come through the thalidomide controversy, that the Commons was about to set up a special committee on drugs and that the report recommending withdrawal of tariff protection from drugs [was in process]. . . .

COST AND PURPOSE

. . . It is estimated that three-quarters of the important "blue-chip" Canadian companies are now represented in the capital, most of them by their own men.

Hundreds of other companies have a representative of some kind—a lawyer, senator, accountant or one of the freelance lobbyists who take on several clients.

There's no way to estimate the cost of Ottawa representation to Canadian firms but it must run into several million dollars.

The rock-bottom cost of having an office in Ottawa at all runs between $30,000 and $40,000 a year. For the fancier setups, the cost is correspondingly higher.

What do they get for their money? Why do they maintain Ottawa offices?

"Fear," is the answer given by one Ottawa insider. "They're afraid they'll be left out or left behind if they don't have somebody here."

"They don't really expect to influence policy or anything. They're just buying insurance against policy that could really hurt them."

But other people in the lobbying business say companies get real benefits from having their own men on the spot.

For one thing, it gives them a guide through the growing jungle of red tape. Companies outside the capital often waste precious weeks and months just writing letters to the wrong civil servants or failing to give all the information the government must have to act.

This is lobbying far below the level of policy making. It involves no bribes or pressure or favoritism. A man on the spot can find out what's holding up a customs case or a contract award with a telephone call. He knows who to call. He knows who has the authority to remove road blocks. Often what he does is simply to get a document moved from the bottom of a pile of papers to the top. . . .

"I'm a salesman," says one big company lobbyist in Ottawa, "and my stock in trade is information."

The typical lobbyist at this level is a very smooth and cultured gentleman, a member of the Rideau Club and the Royal Ottawa Golf Club where he rubs shoulders every day with cabinet ministers and top civil servants.

He may be an executive of his company—some corporations regard the Ottawa assignment as a reward for long service in tougher places. He's very much part of the Ottawa establishment and he knows the people that it's worthwhile for him to know.

His office door probably gives no clue to his real job. His work is often done at the club or over lunch at such restaurants as La Touraine—conveniently near defence headquarters—and the Chateau Laurier.

One such Ottawa lobbyist has premises as functional for their purpose as a

Prairie grain elevator or a fishing wharf. There's a bar with nothing but the best liquor, a board room where delectable meals can be served and a painting moves aside to disclose a screen on which, at a snap of his fingers, a hidden projector begins to show movies of the product the lobbyist is trying to sell to the government.

The most sustained lobbying efforts of this kind are in the aircraft business, an international industry which sells its products principally to governments. One aircraft company has kept a man in Ottawa for years to sell a single type of plane. If he fails to persuade the government, he has lost three or four years out of his life.

For an international company, the services of a top-grade Ottawa lobbyist can be vital. Information he gets during a round of golf or over lunch can tie in with something the company has going in South America or Europe.

If a decision is going to be made by five civil servants, the lobbyists specialized knowledge can pick out the man who will dominate the meeting and any persuasive efforts can be focussed on him. It's no use lobbying people who won't stay lobbied.

In this context, information is as vital as influence. The company that comes up quickest with a project which fits into the government's plans is likely to get the job. In this there's no hanky-panky or sacrifice of the public interest. It's just that knowing the direction of thinking can enable a company to get there fastest with the mostest.

Or where the government is preparing to drop a project, advance information can help a company involved to cut its losses.

Confidence is important if ministers and civil servants are to trust a lobbyist with information. This is why the top-notch lobbyists carefully guard their reputation for discretion and their anonymity.

CONTROL

The House of Commons rule book speaks in majestic, Elizabethan tones about bribery.

"The offer of any money or other advantage to any member of this House, for the promoting of any matter whatsoever depending or to be transacted in Parliament, is a high crime and misdemeanor, and tends to the subversion of the Constitution."

High crime it may be but it's not unknown.

In 1956, when the pipeline bill was under consideration, a Conservative MP, now dead, confided to a friend:

"Offers are being made that make my $10,000 indemnity look like peanuts."

Whatever offers were made or accepted didn't save the pipeline bill from scorching debate. Nor did they save the Liberal government which forced it through by using closure.

Present day Ottawa lobbyists look on the pipeline as a kind of watershed, the last of the old-style, all-out, no-holds-barred lobbies. . . .

In those bad old days, lobbyists would offer all-expense weekends in New York, complete with baseball and theatre tickets. Now, if you're lucky, you can wangle a ride to the Grey Cup game—if it's in Toronto.

Once "party girls" were brought in from Toronto to help entertain susceptible officials. Liquor was unlimited. Pressure and persuasion were applied in varying ways.

Present-day lobbyists, reformed characters to a man, say the Avro Arrow lobby in 1959 was the only one which showed signs of returning to the old standards. Avro used every technique and gimmick possible, including a threat that prominent Conservative newspapers would be turned against Prime Minister Diefenbaker.

But Mr. Diefenbaker cancelled the Arrow anyway, just in time to head off a television show featuring a free film distributed by Avro in which the history of Canadian flight culminated in the Arrow. This kind of pressure has always been bitterly resented by governments.

Ottawa's gentlemen lobbyists now deplore the bare-knuckle tactics used then by Crawford Gordon, Avro president at the time. They see this kind of lobbying as an American import that just doesn't work in Canada. . . .

. . . lobbyists say there are still some juniors who will take $10 or so—although the senior civil servants are incorruptible.

Their present salaries help to keep them that way.

"It used to be a big occasion for a civil servant if you took him and his wife out to the Chateau for dinner," says one lobbyist. "But now it's nothing. He can well afford to go there on his own."

Apart from wining and dining, there's very little attempt at bribery. Sometimes a minister's executive assistant will find a bottle of liquor on his desk but it may be there in genuine gratitude, rather than for ulterior motives. . . .

Even if it's accepted that there isn't much wrong in present day Ottawa lobbying, there is still a danger point where pressure, patronage and political funds meet. The rapidly rising cost of elections has led to decision by the Pearson government to try to find ways of limiting election spending. Perhaps, eventually, all legitimate campaign expenses will be paid from the public purse.

This would cut down the danger that gratitude—which has been defined as "a sense of favors yet to come"—would be used as a lobbying advantage by party fund contributors.

But some members of Parliament feel there should be registration of lobbyists as well.

"If this is a profession," says James Walker, Liberal whip in the Commons, "why shouldn't we consider having them register so it could be recognized as such."

Mr. Walker has been thinking about putting in a private members' bill or resolution calling for registration of lobbyists. . . .

In the United States, lobbyists have been required to register since 1946, stating the interest they represent and the source of their income. But the effectiveness of the law has been called into question. More than 3,000 lobbyists have registered but it has been estimated that three times as many haven't. The financial statements of those who do register fail to tell the complete story of their lobbying income and expenditure.

THE CMA — SPOKESMAN FOR INDUSTRY*

W. D. H. FRECHETTE

The Canadian Manufacturers' Association is a non-profit, non-political organization supported and directed by its 7,300 members who manufacture every sort of industrial product in cities and towns all the way from St. John's, Newfoundland, to Victoria, B.C. We are just two years short of celebrating our hundredth birthday and growing more vigorous with the passage of time. Our member companies are both large and small, but obviously—with that many members—there is a preponderance of small ones. In fact, the great majority of our member companies employ less than 100 people. Yet our total membership is responsible for three-quarters of all the manufacturing production of Canada.

The main objective of the CMA is to encourage the pace of this country's industrialization. But that is far from all. We emphasize the greatest possible employment of Canadians and the maximum use of domestic materials. And side by side with the promotion of manufacturing we exist for the promotion of exports. We have, in other words, been propounding the "Buy, Make and Sell Canadian" philosophy in one way or another for over 60 years.

There are two ways we attempt to achieve our objective. The first is in the legislative field. As the recognized authoritative voice of the most important segment of the economy, the manufacturing industry, we are constantly appearing before all levels of government with submissions on legislation which affects manufacturers. Sometimes our briefs involve laws which we think should be placed on the statute books, sometimes laws that are already there. The second way we work toward our objective is in the area of consultation and individual service to our members through our head office departments and our division and branch offices across Canada. These services cover a wide field of subjects important to industry and over the years we like to think that we have developed them to a fine art.

* From an address delivered in January 1969, by the author, who is the General Secretary of the Canadian Manufacturers' Association. By permission.

Canada, for our purposes, is divided geographically into six Divisions, each under the supervision of a full-time manager, assisted by trained staff. All CMA members are automatically members of the CMA Division in which their place of business is located. The Division is an integral part of the national organization, but has autonomy within its own field of activity. Similarly, most CMA members are now participants in one or other of the Association's 37 branches. Policies are established in a democratic way—by an appropriate committee. We have some 75 committees, on which over a thousand members serve voluntarily right across the country. . . .

Policies involving national matters—such things as unemployment insurance, trade and taxation—are established by a national standing committee, often advised by a subcommittee of top experts on the subject. They are presented for final ratification to the Executive Council, which is the overall governing body and which we call the parliament of Canadian industry. Policies on provincial or purely local matters are similarly formulated by division and branch committees. In this way, the thinking of the best brains in manufacturing industry is utilized to the utmost before policy is adopted.

At our head office in Toronto we have a variety of specialist departments which cover the fields of trade and tariffs, commercial intelligence, industrial relations, legislation, taxation, public relations, economic research and transportation. The consultative personalized services are of a kind to which a price tag may be more readily affixed than to the impersonal services of policing legislation and acting as advocate for the industry, although the latter are of at least equal importance.

Taking the two major areas of Association activity—those of establishing policies in relation to Government action, and those of service—it is appropriate to note that policies are established by Committees, composed of members; services to members are provided by the CMA staff complement of 114 people who man its nine offices across the country. Members of the staff are, of course, involved as well in the committee work as advisers and in carrying out the research on which committee decisions are made besides committing such decisions to the appropriate written words. [The CMA's total income in 1969 amounted to $941,000.]

By its very nature, an organization like CMA has little direct contact with any large proportion of the electorate. Its influence and effectiveness with governments are therefore dependent upon the objectivity and responsible character of its submissions. While its main focus is on the interests of its membership, it has to be well in tune with national goals and the public interest. These submissions range all the way from the presentation of formal briefs and the provision of written and oral evidence at public enquiries to informal discussion and day to day contacts at the more technical level.

The CMA's special contribution to the public policy-making process lies in its ability to foresee and to explain the practical impact on the manufacturing industries of a given line of government policy, a particular piece of legislation or the application of implementing regulations. In its absence, governments would be faced with the alternative of immense additions to their own information-gathering apparatus or resort to a lot of costly experimentation.

To illustrate the depth and variety of subject matters in the CMA hopper, perhaps it will suffice to mention some recent briefs:

— the British Columbia Division has recently submitted its views to the government on new legislation affecting collective bargaining in that province;

— the Newfoundland Branch has been engaged in discussions with the Provincial Government concerning its recent submission reviewing Workmen's Compensation laws and practice;

— the Quebec Division has been waging a prolonged battle against the St. Lawrence Seaway Authority proposal to cut off water service to industry along a part of the Lachine Canal;

— the Ontario Division, having submitted a detailed evaluation of the Rand Commission proposals on labour legislation, invited representatives of the news media to a no-holds-barred news conference at which the CMA position was fully explained and deeply explored;

— the national submission on combines, mergers, monopoly and restraint of trade was the subject of recent discussion with the Economic Council of Canada which has been assigned the task of an exhaustive review of legislation in this field.

Some mention, at least, should be made of the mammoth job of work done by the Tariff Committee in connection with Canada's new anti-dumping legislation and by the Taxation Committee on the Carter Commission's Report and subsequent proposals for tax reform. One further topic which was under examination for a good two years before our recent submission on the subject to the Prime Minister of Canada concerns the highly topical and controversial subject of wages and prices in the context of inflationary pressures. CMA tackled this subject early and in such a manner that our analysis was described by the Minister of Consumer and Corporate Affairs as "a splendid example of industry taking an initiative in the process of consultation which I and my colleagues have been striving for."

While in all these endeavours the CMA certainly concentrates its attention on the effects of public policy on manufacturers, we cannot be other than keenly aware of the views of other responsible organizations whose focus is on non-manufacturing sectors of the business community, to say nothing of our counterparts in other countries.

There is, in fact, a continuous flow of information between ourselves and, for example, The Canadian Chamber of Commerce and the Canadian Construction Association. The effect of these relationships is such that policy positions are harmonized to the fullest extent possible and in many cases become identical. A similarly valuable relationship is cultivated by the CMA through its periodic talks with, among others, representative Japanese organizations, with the U.S. National Association of Manufacturers and through its active participation in regional international business organizations covering the Americas, the North Atlantic and the Pacific Basin. The CMA's extensive international links and activities make a long story in themselves. . . .

THE STRANGE CASE OF THE ALL-ALIKE LETTERS*

RON HAGGART

About the middle of January, it was still extremely doubtful whether the Spadina Expressway would be built. The newspapers were full of gloomy and unfavourable stories reporting the activities of the organized opponents of this $70 million super-highway.

The project was in hiatus. Then, within a period of a few days, all three newspapers in Toronto began receiving letters of a different sort. All of them urged immediate construction of the Spadina Expressway; all of them were clearly and concisely written and bore the stamp of a remarkable professionalism.

They were like capsule editorials. To see if there was any other common thread connecting these letters, I examined the published letters in all three papers, and I asked Royston J. Packard, the expert on questioned documents in the attorney-general's crime laboratory, to help me examine the original copies of the letters published by The Star.

Mr. William Marr had a letter in the Globe and Mail on Jan. 12: "We are amazed that anyone could possibly disagree with the fact that this (Spadina) Expressway is absolutely necessary."

Mr. Marr is employed by Webb and Knapp, the large land developers who have a contract to build a $25 million shopping plaza for Eaton's and Simpson's which will gain an entrance off busy Highway 401 by way of the Spadina Expressway.

V. L. Carrigan, a truck driver who lives in Scarboro, had a letter in The Star Jan. 13. Mr. Carrigan says that William Marr wrote the letter for him. Mr. Carrigan is William Marr's brother-in-law.

D. R. Densmore, a driver-salesman who lives in Scarboro and delivers Pepsi-Cola in the O'Connor Dr.-Kingston Rd. area, had a letter in The Star Jan. 19. Mr. Densmore says that William Marr wrote the letter for him. Mr. Densmore is William Marr's brother-in-law.

Royston Packard says the letters from Densmore and Carrigan were written on the same typewriter—a typewriter equipped with Smith-Corona Presidential No. 77 elite typeface.

B. A. Whalen had a letter in the Telegram Jan. 17 which bore a remarkable resemblance to a letter in the Star of Jan. 18 signed by F. Allin. Whalen's letter

* From *Toronto Daily Star*, March 1, 1962. By permission of the publisher.

in the Telegram was longer than Allin's letter in The Star but their thoughts were almost identical:

It seems unbelievable to us to realize that the Metro Council is now on the threshold of chucking the results of years of work out of the window because of the influence of a short-sighted few.

The whole expressway and rapid transit network was designed as a whole, like a fine machine, and we can't just chop things off as we please without upsetting the balance of the whole thing. The Spadina Expressway is a vital link in this system and is long overdue.—*F. Allin in The Star, Jan. 18.*

. . . It is unbelievable that Metro Council is now on the threshold of chucking the whole thing out of the window because of the influence of a short-sighted few.

The whole expressway and rapid transit network was designed as a whole, like a fine machine, and we can't just chop things off as we please without upsetting the balance of the whole thing.

The Spadina Expressway is a vital link in this system and is long overdue.—*B. A. Whalen in the Telegram, Jan. 17.*

It seems pretty clear that F. Allin and B. A. Whalen had a common source of inspiration.

Royston Packard says that the original copy of Allin's letter "would seem to exhibit alignment characteristics very similar" to the letters from Carrigan and Densmore, but because a different kind of ribbon was used he cannot be definite that the three letters came from the same typewriter.

Still, there is the remarkable coincidence that all three of these letters were written on typewriters equipped with the same kind of typeface. And the words from these letters appeared in a fourth letter, under a different signature, in the Telegram.

A brief submitted to the Metropolitan roads committee from the West Glen Ratepayers' Association in favour of the Spadina Expressway was written by North York councillor Irving Paisley. Mr. Paisley says the stencil for this brief was typed in the offices of Webb and Knapp. It, too, was typed on a machine equipped with Smith-Corona No. 77 Presidential elite typeface.

There were others letters, too.

Miss Dorothy Silverstone had a letter in the Globe and Mail of Jan. 19: "If the Metro Toronto's transit planning computer has definitely shown that by 1980 there will be a 127 percent increase in the use of private cars and only a 60 percent increase in the use of public transit, then surely . . ."

Miss Silverstone went on to support the building of the Spadina Expressway. Miss Silverstone works in the financial section of Toronto Industrial Leaseholds, a Webb and Knapp subsidiary.

Fabio Ridolfi had a letter in both the Telegram and The Star of Jan. 17 supporting the Spadina Expressway. Mr. Ridolfi is a member of the joint staff maintained by Webb and Knapp and John Graham, design consultants, who are working on drawings for the $25 million shopping plaza on the Spadina Expressway.

James Crookes had a letter in The Star on Jan. 18: "The Spadina Expressway is an obvious answer to this desperate necessity. . . ."

The letters from Fabio Ridolfi and James Crookes were both typed on a Remington. Royston Packard says they were probably typed on the same Remington, but since they were both carbon copies it is difficult to make a positive comparison.

Gerald Dixon had a letter in the Globe and Mail Jan. 12 and the Star of Jan. 16 favouring the Spadina Expressway (". . . the result of years of planning and research by various technical staffs").

According to officials of Webb and Knapp, Mr. Dixon is a member of the same staff working on the $25 million shopping plaza as Messrs. Marr and Ridolfi.

Paul C. Ellard had a letter in the Telegram Jan. 26 which began, as did Gerald Dixon's, "It is amazing . . . . "

Mr. Ellard is a consulting engineer with a branch office in the same building at 2 Carlton St. as Webb and Knapp; he was employed on a Webb and Knapp $12 million shopping plaza in London, Ont., and according to Webb and Knapp's public relations director, will probably be employed on the Webb and Knapp plaza on the Spadina Expressway.

This remarkable series of coincidences links together a majority of the letters which appeared in the press during the middle of January in support of the Spadina Expressway. None of it, of course, shows that Webb and Knapp, the shopping plaza builders, had any role in inspiring the letters.

When I consulted Brig. Claude Dewhurst, chief of public relations here for Webb and Knapp, he replied: "Are you suggesting there was a common hand behind these letters? I wouldn't be permitted to do such a thing; after all, we have an interest in the project."

Webb and Knapp's interest is that the Spadina Expressway and its all-important cloverleaf connection with Highway 401 will feed traffic into the $25 million shopping plaza. And Webb and Knapp's design and construction contract with the T. Eaton Co. can be cancelled "if the venture is frustrated through adequate road facilities not being available."

Later, Brig. Dewhurst reported that the employees Marr, Ridolfi, and Dixon, all draftsmen working on plans for the Yorkdale plaza, got together as individuals, wrote letters to the papers and urged others to do so. "They were worried about their jobs," Brig. Dewhurst explained. "They were concerned that they would be laid off if the Yorkdale project didn't go through."

THE BRILLIANT CAMPAIGN TO MAKE PUBLIC OPINION*

RON HAGGART

At the end of last year, things were going rather badly for the Spadina Expressway project. The newspapers, reporting as usual the organized opinion of the community, were full of stories all blackly against another superhighway.

Controllers Won't Back Expressway, reported the Star. Planner Faces Opponents, said another headline. Chaos Feared if Expressways Slice Up Metro, said the Globe and Mail.

Meetings of 12 associations of taxpayers, and then of 85 associations, were reported under headlines like "Shame If It Carries" and "Spadina Results 'Bad As H-Bomb' ".

Suddenly, about the middle of January, the climate of public opinion radically changed. Citizens' associations and ratepayers groups, with all the fervor of an Algerian riot, appeared to be lining the streets, urging the reluctant politicians to hurry up with the Spadina highway.

This new public opinion was recorded in the Telegram of Jan. 12: "New life for the Spadina Expressway . . ." the paper reported, "emerged today with growing public support for the $67 million project. The expressway plan will be revived at Metro roads committee on Jan. 22 by ratepayer groups who are demanding that it be built immediately."

These demands from the citizens were heard at a number of meetings called by the roads committee of the Metropolitan Council, and on Jan. 29 the extent of the swing in public opinion was recorded by The Star: "Champions of the Spadina combined expressway and rapid transit line," it reported, "outnumbered the opposition by better than three to one. . . ."

The single, most important hand behind this magical change in public opinion was a short, sharp bundle of hyperthyroid salesman's energy named Irving Paisley. He runs a prosperous insurance agency near Bathurst and Lawrence and is a councillor in North York.

"There is no doubt about it, that it was going the other way until I took over," Paisley has said of his success in this campaign.

Mr. Paisley's technique was to arrange for masses of approving briefs and statements to descend on the politicians who were making the decision.

Briefs from 25 ratepayer organizations, all enthusiasticaly in favour of the Spadina Expressway, were submitted to the Metropolitan roads committee.

Of these, Mr. Paisley himself wrote at least eight. He was the author of the briefs from the Winston Park Ratepayers' Association, the West Glen Ratepayers' Association, the Blackwood-Ranee Ratepayers' Association, the Joyce Park Rate-

---

* From *Toronto Daily Star*, February 26, 1962. By permission of the publisher.

payers' Association, the Maple Leaf Ratepayers' Association, the Faywood Ratepayers, the Beverley Hills Ratepayers' Association, the Danesbury Ratepayers, and the Hillmount-Viewmount Ratepayers' Association.

An example of Mr. Paisley's genius in the arts of creative public opinion was the brief in support of the Spadina Expressway submitted by the West Glen Ratepayers' Association.

Mr. Paisley describes this association as being "defunct." He went to see Mrs. Dorothy Somers, the secretary of the association, and she agreed that the Spadina Expressway was a good idea.

Mr. Paisley then phoned three members of the executive of the West Glen ratepayers' and they, too, agreed with Mr. Paisley's enthusiastic support of the expressway. Mr. Paisley then wrote a brief which said ". . . I am instructed by the executive of the West Glen Ratepayers' Association to place on record its wholehearted support of construction of the Spadina Expressway." Then followed two pages of well-reasoned argument in favour of the highway.

The brief was signed by Mrs. Dorothy Somers, secretary. Curiously, Mrs. Somers' name was spelled incorrectly, appearing with two m's in this official communication from the West Glen ratepayers.

Another example was the brief from the Winston Park ratepayers. John O'Hagan, who lives on Winston Park Blvd. and publishes a paper in Woodbridge, is listed as president.

Mr. Paisley describes this organization as being "defunct."

Mr. Paisley visited Mr. O'Hagan at his home and got his agreement to the project, although Mr. O'Hagan told him he could not speak for the organization. Mr. Paisley went back to his insurance office on Bathurst St. and phoned a few members of the executive of this organization. Mr. Paisley then wrote the brief of the Winston Park ratepayers and took it back to Mr. O'Hagan for his signature.

The brief began: "I am instructed by the members of the Winston Park Ratepayers' Association to urge your committee . . . . "

In this case, the members represented totalled approximately four.

In the case of the Hillmount-Viewmount Ratepayers' Association ("We endorse this project which should be put under way as quickly as possible"), Mr. Paisley telephoned the president, Albert Glazer, in hospital where Mr. Glazer was recovering from an operation, and repeated the creative process as before.

The brief from the Beverley Hills ratepayers, which was also written by Mr. Paisley, was signed "Isobel Walker, per." Nothing followed the "per," but that, too, was Mr. Paisley.

Twenty-five copies of each of the 25 briefs had to be submitted to the Metropolitan roads committee. Stencils for at least 10 of these were cut in Mr. Paisley's insurance office. He and his staff worked all one Saturday night until 1 o'clock in the morning turning out the material.

They were so overworked they had to send two of the briefs downtown to have the stencils typed by a friend of Mr. Paisley's. These two stencils (the ones from Winston Park and West Glen) were typed in the offices of Webb and Knapp, the land developers who are building the shopping plaza for Eaton's and Simpson's which will get its entrance from Highway 401 by way of the Spadina Expressway.

Almost all of the briefs from the 25 citizens' associations were mailed to the Metropolitan officials from Mr. Paisley's office, or dispatched downtown by taxicab from Mr. Paisley's office.

Mr. Paisley organized a car pool so that citizens could go down and hear the deliberations of the roads committee, and he wrote and mailed out to his constituents 9,076 copies of a leaflet supporting the Spadina Expressway.

He paid for the postage with a cheque for $136.29 drawn on the account of his insurance agency.

This brilliant campaign had the desired results. The Telegram reported on Feb. 5: "The ratepayers appeared to be evenly split, but growing support for the project was indicated as North York councillor Irving Paisley presented letters from 10 more groups in his township, representing 15,000 people."

And The Star on Feb. 6 was able to report: ". . . a 3½-hour session which saw 36 briefs presented—28 of them in favour of the big transportation complex."

"I do have a knack for organization," Mr. Paisley says.

CANADA'S PRESS: WHO OWNS WHAT, WHERE AND WHY*

DAVID SURPLIS

One of the things Canadians have taken for granted, perhaps for too long, is our daily diet of news. We have tended to accept what little we have read in our daily newspaper, or have heard or seen on radio and television newscasts, as a fairly complete record of the events which affect our lives. Too often we have appeared to believe that if Earl Cameron, Walter Cronkite or the Daily Sun-Globe-Intelligencer didn't mention a matter, it can't have been important.

However, recently there has been renewed interest in challenging the veracity of what we are served up by our news sources. Perhaps this phenomenon owes its origins to the famous "credibility gap" that befell former President Lyndon Johnson, but whatever the cause, terms such as "news management" are becoming more important these days. One evidence of this concern is the special committee of the Senate which was established under the chairmanship of Senator Keith Davey to take a hard look at the state of news gathering and dissemination in Canada. The committee is expected to report in the fall of 1970 with some pertinent observations on the ownership, operation, control and management of our mass media.

* Published originally in this book in 1970 with permission of the author, who is a members of the Department of Political Studies, University of Guelph.

Whatever the Davey committee finds and reports, it is difficult to foresee what kinds of curative measures can be prescribed (presuming the committee does not give our media a clean bill of health). It is still more difficult to envisage what kinds of legislative measures can be enacted since the track record of committee and royal commission recommendations being implemented is not too good. Contention abounds when "freedom of the press" and "government" are mentioned in the same context.

There are many different aspects of news gathering, handling, and publishing which might be examined if space permitted. Questions of objectivity, the coverage of "bad" versus "good" news, and the right of the public "to know" as opposed to the individual citizen's right to privacy are all pertinent and important issues. But this article will be confined to examining only a few of the basic facts regarding Canadian news sources.

CONCENTRATION OF OWNERSHIP

The first fact about news gathering and publishing in Canada is that it is a business, a big business. The amount of money required to run a newspaper—especially to start up a newspaper—is staggering. Estimates are that it would require at least ten million dollars to launch a daily newspaper in a major urban area in Canada. Hence newcomers do not tend to break into publishing. On the contrary, the larger metropolitan dailies or the large publishing groups (which dislike the term "chains") are the only ones that can afford to expand their operations. As smaller, independent dailies are sold, often to meet estate taxes, they are frequently swallowed up by the larger groups. Because of a combination of business failures and takeovers by chains, the number of publishers of newspapers is steadily declining, even though the number of newspapers has remained relatively constant in recent years.

There are 113 daily newspapers in Canada today but as the accompanying table shows, about half of them are controlled by a few large publishing groups. Three "chains" alone, Thomson, FP Publications, and Southam, own 49 newspapers which together account for almost half of the 4.5 million papers sold daily in Canada. This situation can be expected to continue (unless some legal barriers are erected); for example, in the past five years four independent newspapers have been taken over by chains, including the influential Toronto paper, *The Globe and Mail*.

It is very difficult to prove or disprove the assertion that group ownership is bad per se. One man who should know more about this matter than anyone else is Canadian-born Lord Thomson of Fleet whose companies own more than one hundred newspapers in various parts of the world. When asked why he purchased more and more newspapers, Lord Thomson replied that he had no desire to control news and opinion, he simply buys papers "to make more money" and he makes more money "to buy more newspapers."

The Davey committee heard statements on both sides of the argument over group ownership. The Senators were told that group ownership can provide the ability to improve coverage (by pooling resources and long-term financial planning) but they were also warned by other witnesses that chain ownership could lead to editorial management and suppression of the news. There is also the problem of the large urban areas which are served by only one local newspaper, such as Edmonton, Regina, Saskatoon, Hamilton and London. Do chains predominate in these areas simply because they produce a better product?

It is true, however, that the mass media field as a whole is quite competitive. For example, on a typical day in January, 1970, Toronto and area residents got their news in a number of different ways: 400,000 listened to Jack Dennett's famous morning newscast on Canada's largest radio station (CFRB); over two million persons read one of Toronto's three daily English-language newspapers (the Canadian Daily Newspaper Publishers Association estimates 2.9 readers for each newspaper printed, on average); and over half a million watched the late newscasts on both national television networks. Moreover, these were not by any means the only news sources available to Torontonians. While there undoubtedly was a lot of overlapping for the sources given, the figures do show that there are alternatives available and that they are utilized by a great many people. Not all Canadians are in the fortunate position of having such a variety of news sources but in virtually all areas where a newspaper is published, television and radio will be competing for the attention of the citizen.

OVERLAPPING OWNERSHIP

Of course, the beneficial results of such "competition" have to be questioned because one man or one chain may have an interest in all three types of media in a given area. The classic case of this combination of interests occurs in London, Ontario where Walter Blackburn publishes the only local newspaper and is also chairman of the company controlling the local television station and the leading radio outlet. Overlapping ownership has become more and more general as proprietors of one medium have sought to expand into the lucrative markets of the others. Toronto Telegram publisher John Bassett, in explaining to the Davey committee how he moved into the cable television business (subsequently disallowed by the Canadian Radio-Television Commission), said that he believed it was a good way to make "lots of dough."

However, it is very difficult to prove that concentration of ownership means detailed control of news and opinion and that it is necessarily bad for the public; the only sure statement is that it leads to questions being asked. Such questions can lead to two results: the public can experience a serious "credibility gap" or publishers can provide better services because they have a heightened awareness of the public's incredulity. Some indication of the extent to which one company has overlapping interests in Canadian media can be found in the example of Southam Press Limited.

SOUTHAM PRESS LIMITED

The interests of this large, public publishing company extend far beyond the 11 newspapers listed in the accompanying table. Southam also has a 49 percent interest in the *Brandon Sun,* 48 percent of the *Kitchener-Waterloo Record,* and 25 percent of London Free Press Holdings Limited, which also controls London's only television station as well as the leading radio outlet. The company has a 50 percent interest in Canada's only oil newspaper, *The Daily Oil Bulletin of Calgary,* and 50 percent of Southstar Publishers Limited (the *Toronto Daily Star* holds the other 50 percent) which publishes the *Canadian Magazine.* This magazine is distributed in Southam papers and those of other subscribers and, with its sister publication, *The Canadian Star Weekly,* has a circulation of well over two million. Southam also publishes the *Financial Times,* a burgeoning weekly financial newspaper.

The company also has preponderant interests in radio and television by virtue of its connections with Selkirk Holdings Limited. By itself and through Selkirk, Southam is involved in radio stations in Calgary, Lethbridge, Edmonton, Grande Prairie, Vernon, Vancouver, Victoria, and Ottawa. Its television interests are located in Lethbridge, Calgary, Hamilton, Victoria, Vancouver, and Kelowna. As well, the company is involved in cablevision outlets in Ottawa, Winnipeg, and Lethbridge, plus a television production company in Toronto.

In testimony presented to the Davey committee, Southam publishers stated flatly that there was no interference by the parent company in their subsidiaries' news and editorial affairs. As for their radio and television interests, Southam at present is attempting to sell all of its holdings to Selkirk—while maintaining a substantial interest in Selkirk. The paradox with Southam is that the company has never founded a newspaper but has often been an innovator in the electronic media.

Other examples of overlapping ownership could be given. There is the case in New Brunswick of industrialist K. C. Irving who controls all of the province's five English-language newspapers, a radio and television station in Saint John, and is reputed to have an interest in a Moncton television station. What is even more noteworthy about these holdings is the fact that Irving dominates the economic life of the province through his diverse interests in oil, timber and services.

There also has been a series of complaints in recent years from French-speaking journalists in Quebec that Paul Desmarais, a Montreal financier, has too much influence in the news industry in that province through multiple ownership of media by means of various companies such as his huge Power Corporation. But this may be changing somewhat since although his companies still own the four important newspapers as noted in the chart, Power Corporation was reported recently to be divesting itself of its electronic media holdings.

POSSIBLE IMPROVEMENTS

The Davey committee heard many pleas for and against the establishment of a press council like the one in Britain. Such a council would hear complaints from the public; however, its only sanction would be moral suasion. What is really required, to avoid arguments both over the proposal of a press council and the acceptable limits of government intervention, is some kind of institute to conduct long-range, continuing studies of all facets of the mass media. The need to know more facts about publishing and readership or listenership grows and changes as the media themselves alter. An institute to conduct pertinent study could be run by the media themselves, perhaps with some assistance from government. The federal government's new agency, Information Canada—whose very formation appears to be an indictment of the mass media—might well play some role here as well.

The plain fact is that both the public and the media themselves do not know enough about the total picture. Publishers protest that the public must be satisfied or its members would not patronize their publications; the public generally state that they "know what they like." But if neither knows the full impact of the media, or the full role the media can play, how can there be improvement? A new institute, sufficiently funded to provide the studies desperately needed, would be a progressive step. Too often complaints about the media fall into the category of Mark Twain's observation about the weather: everybody talks about it but nobody does much about it.

Canada's Major Daily Newspaper Publishing Groups

Paper	Circulation*	Paper	Circulation*
F.P. Publications Limited (G. M. Bell—John Sifton) 8 newspapers			
The Ottawa Journal	81,012	The Globe and Mail (Toronto)	269,698
Winnipeg Free Press	131,919	The Albertan (Calgary)	35,522
The Lethbridge Herald	20,108	The Sun (Vancouver)	254,033
The Daily Colonist/			
Victoria Daily Times	70,662		
Total Average Paid Circulation: 862,954			
Southam Press Limited (Public Company) 11 newspapers			
The Gazette (Montreal)	132,738	The Spectator (Hamilton)	125,524
North Bay Nugget	18,432	The Ottawa Citizen	82,452
Owen Sound Sun-Times	14,325	The Winnipeg Tribune	76,680
The Calgary Herald	95,453	The Edmonton Journal	145,682
The Medicine Hat News	7,803	The Citizen (Prince George)	12,277
The Vancouver Province	115,536		
Total Average Paid Circulation: 826,902			
Thomson Newspapers Ltd. (Lord Thomson of Fleet) 30 newspapers			
British Columbia			
Kamloops Daily Sentinel	9,274	The Daily Courier (Kelowna)	8,496
The Daily Free Press		Penticton Herald	6,398
(Nanaimo)	9,413		
Saskatchewan			
Moose Jaw Times-Herald	8,944	Prince Albert Daily Herald	8,110

Paper	Circulation*	Paper	Circulation*
Ontario			
The Barrie Examiner	10,160	The Daily Standard-Freeholder	
Chatham Daily News	14,777	(Cornwall)	14,516
The Evening Reporter (Galt)	13,413	The Guelph Mercury	17,018
Kirkland Lake Northern News	6,299	The Daily Packet and Times	
The Oshawa Times	23,274	(Orillia)	7,888
The Peterborough Examiner	24,421	The Pembroke Observer	7,592
The News-Chronicle		Daily Times-Journal	
(Thunder Bay)	15,760	(Thunder Bay)	16,951
The Sudbury Star	34,331	The Sarnia Observer	18,565
The Evening Tribune (Welland)	19,202	Timmins Daily Press	11,423
Brampton Times and		The Daily Sentinel-Review	
Conservator	7,590	(Woodstock)	9,971
Quebec			
Quebec Chronicle-Telegraph	4,214		
Prince Edward Island			
The Charlottetown Guardian/			
The Charlottetown Evening			
Patriot	21,218		
Nova Scotia			
The New Glasgow News	9,885		
Newfoundland			
The Evening Telegram		The Western Star (Cornerbrook)	n.a.
(St. John's)	n.a.		

Total Average Paid Circulation: 359,103

Gelco Enterprises Ltd., Gesca Ltee., Trans-Canada Newspapers (Paul Desmarais)

Paper	Circulation	Paper	Circulation
La Voix de L'Est (Granby)	11,332	La Presse (Montreal)	205,158
La Tribune (Sherbrooke)	37,800	Le Nouvelliste (Trois-Rivieres)	44,876

Total Average Paid Circulation: 299,166

New Brunswick Publishing Co. Ltd. (K. C. Irving)

Paper	Circulation	Paper	Circulation
The Daily Gleaner (Fredericton)	16,527	The Moncton Daily Times/	
The Telegraph-Journal/		The Moncton Transcript	32,866
The Evening Times-Globe			
(Saint John)	53,387		

Total Average Paid Circulation: 102,780

Large Independents

Paper	Circulation	Paper	Circulation
Toronto Daily Star	386,013	The Telegram (Toronto)	242,652
The Montreal Star	187,302		

* Circulation Source: Audit Bureau of Circulations, figures for September 30, 1969.

WE NEED A PRESS COUNCIL*

BELAND H. HONDERICH

. . . I seriously doubt if the newspaper industry as a whole, and I include *The Star* in this, has devoted sufficient thought and attention to the improvement of professional standards and the development of a responsible code of ethics for our business. . . .

I submit that the newspaper industry no longer can afford the luxury of indifference. Both from the point of view of the public and our own selfish interests as newspapermen, we must increasingly concern ourselves with the quality of what we do and how we can improve it. . . .

For these reasons, I welcome the recommendation of Chief Justice McRuer, in his Royal Commission report on civil rights, that we establish a press council in Ontario to discipline the press and other news media.

The very thought of a press council that would closely examine what newspapers do and rap us over the knuckles when we err is enough to excite some publishers into a frenzy. Why this should be I don't know. We delight in writing editorials telling other people how to conduct their affairs. Are we so perfect that we cannot benefit from the test of public examination and scrutiny? . . .

. . . I would like, first, to register my disagreement with Chief Justice McRuer's statement that not infrequently publishers take a deliberate risk of libel action in the coverage of bizarre crime news "for the purpose of promoting circulation". Newspapers certainly err at times but I doubt very much if they do so deliberately. . . .

What the Chief Justice overlooks is that newspapers move at a much faster pace than the judicial process. The pressure of deadlines frequently requires reporters and editors to do in minutes what a lawyer or judge would want days to consider.

I do not wish this to be interpreted as an excuse for the mistakes we make. On the contrary, I believe that we must adopt a professional attitude and learn to report the news both quickly and accurately.

At the same time, I would remind you that the theory of a free press in a free society is not that truth will be presented perfectly and instantly in every newspaper account but rather that truth will finally emerge from free reporting and free discussion.

If newspapers were to withhold news until they had time to check and double-check every last detail, the public simply would not know what is happening. And without some knowledge of what was happening, public opinion could not influence the course of public events.

* From a speech given by the President and Publisher of the Toronto Star Limited, April 27, 1968, to the Western Ontario Newspaper 14th Annual Awards Dinner. By permission of the author.

A press council, it seems to me, could render a service to newspapers by helping to educate the public to the real function of the press and the problems it encounters in reporting the news.

I am not as familiar as I would like to be with the operation of the British Press Council but on the basis of what I have read, I would think a similar council would work well in Ontario.

The British Press Council is a voluntary organization consisting of an independent chairman, 20 professional members representing publishers, editors and journalists, and five members of the general public.

The objects of the Council are:

1. To preserve the established freedom of the British Press.
2. To maintain the character of the British Press in accordance with highest professional and commercial standards.
3. To consider complaints about the conduct of the press or the conduct of persons and organizations towards the press, to deal with these complaints in whatever manner seems practical and appropriate, and to record resultant action.
4. To keep under review developments likely to restrict the supply of information of public interest and importance.
5. To report publicly on developments that may tend towards greater concentration or monopoly in the press (including changes in ownership, control and growth of press undertakings) and to publish statistical information relating thereto.
6. To make representation on appropriate occasions to the government, organs of the United Nations, and to press organizations overseas.
7. To publish periodical reports recording the Council's work and to review, from time to time, developments in the press and the factors affecting them.

The Council pursues these objectives by investigating complaints from the public and from newspapers and by publishing its findings. It has no power to compel anyone to do anything. A newspaper can accept or ignore its recommendations but it can only ignore public opinion at its own risk.

Let us consider what a press council might do if it were set up to further similar objects in Ontario.

The first object of an Ontario press council would be to work for the preservation of freedom of the press.

Freedom of the press, I am sorry to say, is a very much misunderstood and abused term in Canada and sorely needs clarification. Some newspapermen interpret it simply as an extension of free speech. Others still regard it as a special privilege conferred on publishers to exercise as they see fit on behalf of their commercial or other interests.

Every time a government passes a law that affects telegraph rates or newspaper revenues you can expect some publisher to urge that we send a delegation or letter to Queen's Park or Ottawa to protest that the tax violates freedom of the press. You will all recall the fuss that was stirred up by some publishers several years ago when Parliament enacted legislation providing for Canadian ownership and control of Canadian newspapers. This was described as a violation of freedom of the press and was so represented at several international newspaper association meetings.

This particular law makes it unattractive for American or other foreign interests to buy Canadian newspapers because Canadian companies that place advertising in foreign-owned newspapers cannot deduct the expense for income tax purposes. Because the highest offers for Canadian newspapers usually come from the United States, the law may well restrict the sales price of newspapers. It may also prompt other countries to enact similar legislation and thus restrict international newspaper operations. It does not, however, restrict freedom of the press and I defy any newspaperman here tonight to cite a single instance in which it has restricted his ability to report the news.

What is freedom of the press? In law, freedom of the press in Canada is nothing more or less than the right of public discussion or free speech. It confers no special rights or privileges on newspapers. We have the same right as other individual Canadians to engage in free speech subject to the laws of libel and other legal restraints enacted for the protection of various public and private interests.

Unlike the United States, there is no constitutional basis in Canada for press freedom. It is a right that evolved over the years in England as part of the development of the parliamentary system and there is no constitutional practice to suggest that it is anything more than the right of the individual to engage in free discussion. . . .

I suggest that a press council consisting of newspapermen and representatives of the public could do much to clarify misunderstanding . . . and also act as a public watchdog in guarding against infringements on legitimate press freedom. . . .

In my experience, the greatest threat to freedom of the press in Canada comes from within and not without. We are not always as diligent as we should be in searching out the significant news and reporting it to the public.

The second object of an Ontario press council would be to maintain the character of the press in accordance with the highest professional and commercial standards. At the moment I know of no organization in Ontario or Canada that concerns itself primarily with the professional standards of our business. In this respect, we lag far behind the other major professions. . . . Individual papers have accomplished a great deal in the last ten years to raise editorial standards. But individual action is not good enough. . . .

I suggest there is an urgent need in both Ontario and Canada today for higher professional standards in both the editorial and commercial sections of our industry. The fact that we have not worked as an industry to promote higher standards may explain why we are not attracting enough bright young people into our business.

Let me deal first with the editorial side. I think newspapers as a whole are doing a fair job of reporting the news. Certainly they are doing as well as radio and television and in some respects a better and more responsible job. But there are many areas in which improvements are sorely needed.

I am not satisfied, for example, that our reporting is always as accurate as it should be. Very few Canadian newspapermen take shorthand and without short-hand or speedwriting I doubt if we can record speeches and public statements accurately enough. Every day we take liberties with things people say and if we are honest with ourselves we must admit that this opens the door to errors and misrepresentation.

I think we should encourage reporters to learn shorthand or speedwriting. Failing this, reporters should be equipped with tape recorders as are radio reporters.

The important financial and economic developments in recent months illustrate another shortcoming. How many newspapermen here tonight who wrote or handled stories on the gold crisis really knew what it was all about? And how many can explain, in the way an ordinary person can understand, the reasons behind the recent run on the Canadian dollar and what it means to the Canadian people? . .

Finally, I sometimes think that we need to broaden our interpretation of the news. A recent *New Yorker* cartoon had an anxious-looking man saying to a news vendor: "I'll tell you what I am looking for. I'm looking for a paper that's honest and realistic but counterbalanced with news of a cheering and optimistic kind. Do you have such a paper?"

To be honest and realistic, newspapers must of course report the grim events of a severely disturbed world—disturbances from which our own fortunate country enjoys less immunity than ever before.

But is not our concept of news too narrowly confined to these four c's: conflict, controversy, contradiction and condemnation? We are zealous to report nearly everything that is going wrong in our society, in our country and in the world—and we should, because it is only by exposure and public debate that ills and injustices can be corrected. But we are not nearly so keen to discover and report the things that are going right.

Let me illustrate. Just before the Middle East war last June, when it appeared that Israel was about to be encircled and confronted by the Arab countries, a group of Christian ministers in Toronto issued a statement of sympathy and concern with the fears of the Jewish community. For some reason, the editors of the news-papers and the other communications media did not consider this newsworthy.

What they did think newsworthy, however, was a later statement by a leading Toronto rabbi bitterly reproaching Christian ministers for failing to offer moral support to their Jewish brethren in their hour of anxiety.

The result of this neglect of the positive and accenting of the negative was predictable: resentment and misunderstanding between the Christian and Jewish community were increased when they could have been allayed.

Conflict was news; co-operation and solidarity were not. And I suggest the press' predilection for gloom and doom adversely influences public attitudes in many important fields.

Has the English-language press of Canada, in general, reported the positive side of the so-called Quebec revolution—the gains in education, social and economic justice—as thoroughly as it has reported the confrontation between Quebec and Ottawa? Have the press and broadcasting media of Quebec kept their public fully informed on the movement toward conciliation, toward the redress of legitimate French-Canadian grievances, in English-speaking Canada? I doubt it. And I doubt if our crisis of national unity would have been as grave as it is if our appreciation of positive news was as strong as our tradition of negative news.

Strikes and picket-line violence always get reported. But how often does the press report and analyze those situations of durable industrial peace based on mutual respect between management and labor, and on a responsible attitude toward the community and the economy in their price and wage policies? . . .

It may be objected that people are not interested in reading or hearing about the things that are going right; that they have a taste for conflict, controversy and disaster. But I submit that positive and constructive developments can be reported interestingly and sometimes even dramatically. . . .

At any rate, the proper test of news is significance, whether the event is of a happy or tragic nature. We should remember that people are at least as inclined to follow good example as they are to be warned by bad ones.

Of course, a press council could not and should not tell newspapers what "positive" news to report. But in a case such as that I mentioned, arising out of the Middle East war, it could point out that ignoring the positive and reporting the negative had caused unnecessary conflict and probably worsened community relations. And it could certainly check up on us when—as sometimes happens— we report some politician's stale or already answered accusations as if they were news. . . .

I can also see an advantage in having a press council concern itself with commercial standards—particularly truthfulness in advertising. Our salaries are paid by advertising and in the long run it seems to me we have a selfish interest in seeing that advertisements mean what they say. Otherwise the public will lose confidence in our integrity.

So much for the need to improve professional standards. An Ontario press council would also consider complaints about the conduct of the press or the conduct of persons and organizations against the press. From time to time newspapers publish information which proves to be inaccurate and which harms the reputation or interests of people even though it may not constitute libel. When this happens we should be big enough to correct our mistakes without the existence of a press council. The fact is, however, that if a newspaper is not willing to make amends there is no recourse for the injured party. The very existence of a press council, to which the public could complain, would, I suggest, help to inspire public confidence in the press and in our willingness to conduct ourselves in a responsible manner.

Not all the complaints registered with the press council would come from the public. Some persons and organizations invite the publication of incomplete or misleading reports by refusing to give the press reasonable co-operation.

Again, the press is sometimes accused of delving into sordid matters (such as the pathology and treatment of sex deviates and sex criminals) for the sake of sensation when in fact such publication is necessary to get public opinion to support enlightened corrective measures. A press council ought to be helpful in drawing the distinction between sensation and education.

The British Press Council concerns itself with the trend towards greater concentration or monopoly in the press and publishes statistical information on this important subject. There is a need for similar information in Canada.

If my figures are correct, three newspaper groups now control 48 percent of the English-language newspaper circulation in Canada. I have been taught to believe that the interests of democracy are best served by having many voices in the field of communications. If this is so, the concentration of newspaper ownership is a matter that would benefit from public review.

I do not wish to imply that group ownership of newspapers is necessarily contrary to the public interest. Indeed, my association with editors and publishers of some group newspapers suggests to me that they conduct themselves in much the same manner as do independent newspapers. In some areas, particularly business management, they are much more efficient than some independent papers.

Editors of some group newspapers are given wide freedom to determine their own policies and it is not unusual to see one group newspaper disagreeing with another on a matter of important public policy. This is healthy and I am glad to see it.

The fact remains, however, that three groups control about half the English-language newspaper circulation in Canada and if they so decided they could determine what each of these newspapers did and said.

Even if one could assume that the present degree of concentration was not harming the public interest, is it a trend that should be allowed to continue?

What about the joint ownership of newspapers and radio and television stations? I must be frank here and say that if a third television channel is made available in Toronto, I would find it necessary, for competitive reasons, to apply for the licence. I am not at all sure, however, that public policy in this area has received the consideration it deserves. A press council could fill a useful function in keeping the public informed on this matter.

Finally, a press council, by publishing periodical reports on developments in the press and the factors affecting them, could contribute to much better public understanding of newspapers. This is particularly true in respect to charges that the press is irresponsible.

The press at times may do things that are irresponsible but at other times things that the public say are irresponsible actually are done in the public interest. I have in mind here stories that expose or draw to public attention some of the sordid aspects of our society. Social progress in this country would be much slower were it not for the fact that newspapers had the courage to print stories about these social and economic ills and injustices. . . .

We hear a lot these days about the millions of people who watch television but what we overlook is the fact that every day of the week almost ten million Canadians read daily newspapers and only rarely are television programs seen by an audience as large as this. Radio and particularly television do an excellent job in reporting certain news stories. But where would the people of Canada be without newspapers to tell them in depth and detail what really happened? . . .

ANOTHER WAY — WORKERS' CONTROL*

DOUGLAS FISHER

. . . One might also go on to explore the idea . . . of expanding the professional status of newspapermen. If one looks only as far as France or Germany, there can be found the comparatively recent phenomenon of part worker control in the running of newspapers.

In France no fewer than 30 newspapers, magazines and press groups have seen editorial staff group themselves into "journalist" associations—small incorporated companies in which each member owns shares. These associations have no direct links with trade unions but their aims go much beyond traditional union objectives.

According to one summary written by Jean-Louis Servan Schreiber, a French magazine publisher, the associations want three things:

(1) The veto power in the choice of the publisher, especially when the publication is sold or when the publisher dies or resigns.

(2) A special professional status for journalists, different from that of other employees of the publishing enterprise, which would reduce the rights of a publisher to alter their articles.

(3) Legislation to require the publisher to sell them 35 percent stock of the companies they work in, so that while participating in the profits they can have a veto right on vital decisions affecting the papers.

M. Servan-Schreiber continues:

Some (the associations) go further and request that information should become a public service protected from the power of money and capital. To achieve that they propose that magazines or newspapers become some part of non-profit foundations. The whole concept will probably seem bizarre or shocking to many. It is however a fact of life which we must live with from now on. And even if the requests of the journalists' associations appear outrageous in their formulation one must admit that they are not without justification.

* From testimony given by the author to the Special Senate Committee on Mass Media, December 16, 1969. By permission of the author.

BIBLIOGRAPHY

Public Opinion and Polling

Adams, J. S., *Interviewing Procedures: A Manual for Survey Interviewers*, Chapel Hill, N.C., 1958.

Albig, W., *Modern Public Opinion*, New York, McGraw-Hill, 1956.

Alford, R. R., "The Social Bases of Political Cleavage in 1962," in Meisel, J., (ed.), *Papers on the 1962 Election*, Toronto, University of Toronto Press, 1964.

Christenson, R. M., and McWilliams, R. O., (eds.), *Voice of the People*, New York, McGraw-Hill, Inc., 1962.

Dion, L., "Democracy as Perceived by Public Opinion Analysts," *C.J.E.P.S.*, Vol. XXVIII, No. 4, November, 1962.

Dion, L., "Régimes d'opinions publiques et systèmes idéologiques," *Ecrits du Canada Français*, Vol. XII, 1962.

Fenton, J. M., *In Your Opinion*, Boston, Little, Brown, 1960.

Gallup, G., *A Guide to Public Opinion Polls*, Princeton, Princeton University Press, 1948, 2nd ed.

Gallup, G., and Rae, S. F., *The Pulse of Democracy: The Public Opinion Poll and How It Works*, New York, Simon and Schuster, 1940.

Katz, D., *et al.*, (eds.), *Public Opinion and Propaganda*, New York, Holt, Rinehart, and Winston, 1960.

Key, V. O. Jr., *A Primer of Statistics for Political Scientists*, New York, Crowell, 1959.

Kish, L., *Survey Sampling*, New York, John Wiley, 1965.

Lane, R. E., and Sears, D. O., *Public Opinion*, Englewood Cliffs, N.J., Prentice-Hall, 1964.

Lippmann, W., *Public Opinion*, New York, Macmillan, 1960.

Lipset, S. M., "Polling and Science," *C.J.E.P.S.*, Vol. XV, No. 2, May, 1949, and *ibid.*, Vol. XVI, No. 3, August, 1950.

Meir, N. C., and Saunders, H. W., (eds.), "The Polls and Public Opinion," *Iowa Conference on Attitude and Opinion Research, University of Iowa*, New York, Henry Holt, 1949.

Mosteller, F., *et al.*, in collaboration with Doob, L. W., *et al.*, *The Pre-Election Polls of 1948: Report of the Committee on Analysis of Pre-Election Polls and Forecasts*, Bulletin 60, New York, Social Science Research Council, 1949.

O'Hearn, W., "Panel Debates Public Opinion Polls," [Panel discussion by Byrne Hope Sanders, Peter Regenstreif, John de B. Payne, Leslie Roberts, Vincent Price], *The Montreal Star*, November 20, 1965.

Qualter, T. H., "The Manipulation of Popular Impulse, Graham Wallas Revisited," *C.J.E.P.S.*, Vol. XXV, No. 2, May, 1959.

Qualter, T. H., *Propaganda and Psychological Warfare*, New York, Random House, 1962.

Regenstreif, S. P., *The Diefenbaker Interlude: Parties and Voting in Canada, An Interpretation*, Toronto, Longmans, 1965.

Rogers, L., *The Pollsters, Public Opinion, Politics, and Democratic Leadership*, New York, Alfred A. Knopf, 1949.

Roper, E. B., *You and Your Leaders, Their Actions and Your Reactions*, New York, William Morrow, 1958.

Schwartz, M., *Public Opinion and Canadian Identity*, Scarborough, Fitzhenry and Whiteside, 1967.

Pressure Groups

Clark, S. D., *The Canadian Manufacturers' Association: A Study in Collective Bargaining and Political Pressure*, Toronto, University of Toronto Press, 1939.

Dawson, H. J., "An Interest Group: The Canadian Federation of Agriculture," *C.P.A.*, Vol. III, No. 2, June, 1960.
Dawson, H. J., "The Consumers' Association of Canada," *C.P.A.*, Vol. VI, No. 1, March, 1963.
Dawson, H. J., "Relations between Farm Organizations and the Civil Service in Canada and Great Britain," *C.P.A.*, Vol. X, No. 4, December, 1967.
Dion, L., *Les groupes et le pouvoir politique aux Etats-Unis*, Québec, les presses de l'Université Laval, 1965.
Dion, L., *Le Bill 60 et la société québécoise*, Montréal, Ed. HMH, 1967.
Dion, L., "A la recherche d'une méthode d'analyse des partis et des groupes d'intérêt," *C.J.P.S.*, Vol. II, No. 1, March, 1969.
Dion, L., "Politique consultative et système politique," *C.J.P.S.*, Vol. II, No. 2, June, 1969.
Dowd, E., "Citizen's Lobby Needles Queen's Park," *The Telegram*, October 11, 1969.
Eggleston, W., et al., "Pressure Groups in Administration," *Proceedings of the Fifth Annual Conference*, The Institute of Public Administration of Canada, Toronto, 1953.
Englemann, F. A., and Schwartz, M. A., *Political Parties and the Canadian Social Structure*, Toronto, Prentice-Hall, 1967.
Fraser, B., "The Facts and Myths about Lobbies," *Maclean's*, February 28, 1959.
Horowitz, G., *Canadian Labour in Politics*, Toronto, University of Toronto Press, 1968.
Kwavnick, D., "Pressure Group Demands and the Struggle for Organizational Status: The Case of Organized Labour in Canada," *C.J.P.S.*, Vol. III, No. 1, March, 1970.
Manzer, R., "Selective Inducements and the Development of Pressure Groups: The Case of Canadian Teachers' Associations," *C.J.P.S.*, Vol. II, No. 1, March, 1969.
"People vs. Pollution," *Maclean's*, January, 1970.
Taylor, M. G., "The Role of the Medical Profession in the Formulation and Execution of Public Policy," *C.J.E.P.S.*, Vol. XXVI, No. 1, February, 1960.
Thorburn, H. G., "Pressure Groups in Canadian Politics: Recent Revisions of the Anti-Combines Legislation," *C.J.E.P.S.*, Vol. XXX, No. 2, May, 1964.

The Media

Braddon, R., *Roy Thomson of Fleet Street*, London, Fontana Books, 1968.
Bruce, C., *News and the Southams*, Toronto, Macmillan, 1968.
Canada, *Report of the Royal Commission on Publications* (O'Leary Report), Ottawa, Queen's Printer, 1961.
Canadian Facts Ltd., *Report of a Study of the Daily Newspaper in Canada and its Reading Public*, Toronto, 1962.
Cater, D., *The Fourth Branch of Government*, Boston, Houghton Mifflin, 1959.
Cook, R., *The Politics of John W. Dafoe and the Free Press*, Toronto, University of Toronto Press, 1963.
Donnelly, M., *Dafoe of the Free Press*, Toronto, Macmillan, 1968.
Eggleston, W., "The Press in Canada," *The Royal Commission on National Development in the Arts, Letters, and Sciences* (Massey Report), Ottawa, King's Printer, 1951.
Ferguson, G. V., and Underhill, F. H., *Press and Party in Canada: Issues of Freedom*, Toronto, Ryerson, 1955.
Gordon, D. R., *Language, Logic, and the Mass Media*, Toronto, Holt, Rinehart, Winston, 1966.
Great Britain, *Report of the Royal Commission on the Press*, London, H.M. Stationery Office, 1949.

Great Britain, *Report of the Royal Commission on the Press, 1961-1962*, London, H.M. Stationery Office, 1962.

Hamlin, D. L. B., (ed.), *The Press and The Public*, Toronto, University of Toronto Press, 1962.

Harkness, R., *J. E. Atkinson of the Star*, Toronto, University of Toronto Press, 1963.

Hocking, W. E., *Freedom of the Press*, A Report from the Commission on Freedom of the Press, Chicago, University of Chicago Press, 1947.

Ickes, H. L., *Freedom of the Press To-day*, New York, Vanguard, 1941.

Irving, J. A., (ed.), *Mass Media in Canada*, Toronto, Ryerson, 1962.

Kesterton, W. H., *A History of Journalism in Canada*, Toronto, Carleton Library, McClelland and Stewart, 1967.

Levy, H. P., *The Press Council: History, Procedure and Cases*, Toronto, Macmillan, 1967.

Lindstrom, C. E., *The Fading American Newspaper*, Garden City, Doubleday, 1960.

McNaught, C., *Canada Gets the News*, Toronto, Ryerson, 1940.

Peers, F., *The Politics of Canadian Broadcasting, 1920-1951*, Toronto, University of Toronto Press, 1969.

Qualter, T. H., and McKirdy, K. A., "The Press of Ontario and the Election," in Meisel, J., (ed.), *Papers on the 1962 Election*, Toronto, University of Toronto Press, 1964

Restrictive Trade Practices Commission, *Report Concerning the Production and Supply of Newspapers in the City of Vancouver and Elsewhere in the Province of British Columbia*, Ottawa, Queen's Printer, 1960.

Seymour-Ure, C., "The Parliamentary Press Gallery in Ottawa," *Parliamentary Affairs*, Vol. XVI, No. 1, Winter, 1962.

Shea, A., *Broadcasting: The Canadian Way, Montreal*, Harvest House, 1963.

Weir, E. A., *The Struggle for National Broadcasting in Canada*, Toronto, McClelland and Stewart, 1965.

Williams, F., *Dangerous Estate: The Anatomy of Newspapers*, London, Arrow Books, 1959.

EIGHT
POLITICAL PARTIES

The subject of political parties is not one of the neglected fields in Canada. A good deal has been written on the topic, as the length of the bibliography in this chapter indicates. One of the most important leading articles that has appeared recently is that by Professor Alan Cairns, with which this chapter commences. He examines several aspects of the connection between the electoral system and the party system in Canada and his insights are so challenging that they undoubtedly will become part of the conventional wisdom on the subject. That this wisdom is mixed and sometimes contradictory is brought out by Professor McLeod in his article in which he performs the useful service of listing and summarizing the various major interpretations of the Canadian party system. An excerpt by the editor attempts to do somewhat the same sort of thing in regard to providing a brief history of each of our major parties.

In the past few years the party system has come increasingly under question. In her paper given to a Conservative conference Miss MacDonald asks whether our parties are not outmoded, while Mr. Roussopoulos, who is identified with the New Left, answers the question point-blank by arguing that the whole political system is outmoded.

The remainder of the chapter attempts to provide answers to those questions which one hears over and over again in Canada, "What is Conservatism? Liberalism? Socialism in Canada?" Professor W. L. Morton gives his interpretation of Canadian Conservatism while former Prime Minister Pearson gives his view of Liberalism. Mr. David Lewis, an NDP MP and long-time prominent executive in both the former CCF party and its successor, the New Democratic party, tackles the subject of assessing the principles of contemporary socialism. At least one section of his own party does not agree with him in one important respect — in the matter of how best to deal with the threat of American capitalism. In 1969 this group, which despite the fact that it took a hard line on the American issue became known as "the Waffle Group," issued its own manifesto at the NDP Convention in Winnipeg. The "Waffle" Manifesto has become sufficiently important within the party, and within the country at large in the editor's opinion, for it to be reprinted here in its entirety. A reply, appropriately enough from Mr. Lewis, is also reprinted because it too represents the opinion of many NDP members and citizens.

THE ELECTORAL SYSTEM AND THE PARTY SYSTEM IN CANADA, 1921-1965*

ALAN C. CAIRNS

This paper investigates two common assumptions about the party system: (i) that the influence of the electoral system on the party system has been unimportant, or non-existent; and (ii) that the party system has been an important nationalizing agency with respect to the sectional cleavages widely held to constitute the most significant and enduring lines of division in the Canadian polity. Schattschneider, Lipset, Duverger, Key and others have cogently asserted the relevance of electoral systems for the understanding of party systems. Students of Canadian parties, however, have all but ignored the electoral system as an explanatory factor of any importance. The analysis to follow will suggest that the electoral system has played a major role in the evolution of Canadian parties, and that the claim that the party system has been an important instrument for integrating Canadians across sectional lines is highly suspect.

•　　　•　　　•

THE BASIC DEFENCE OF THE SYSTEM AND ITS ACTUAL PERFORMANCE

If the electoral system is analysed in terms of the basic virtue attributed to it, the creation of artificial legislative majorities to produce cabinet stability, its perform-

TABLE 1: Percentages of votes and seats for government party, 1921-1965

	% Votes	% Seats		% Votes	% Seats
1921	40.7	49.4(L)	1949	49.5	73.7(L)
1925†	39.8	40.4(L)	1953	48.9	64.5(L)
1926	46.1	52.2(L)	1957	38.9	42.3(C)
1930	48.7	55.9(C)	1958	53.6	78.5(C)
1935	44.9	70.6(L)	1962	37.3	43.8(C)
1940	51.5	73.9(L)	1963	41.7	48.7(L)
1945	41.1	51.0(L)	1965	40.2	49.4(L)

† In this election the Conservatives received both a higher percentage of votes, 46.5%, and of seats, 47.3%, than the Liberals. The Liberals, however, chose to meet Parliament, and with Progressive support they retained office for several months.

Note: The data for this and the following tables have been compiled from Howard A. Scarrow, *Canada Votes* (New Orleans, 1963), and from the *Report of the Chief Electoral Officer* for recent elections.

* From the *Canadian Journal of Political Science/Revue canadienne de Science politique,* Vol. I, No. 1, March/mars, 1968. By permission of the author and publisher.

ance since 1921 has been only mediocre. Table I reveals the consistent tendency of the electoral system in every election from 1921 to 1965 to give the government party a greater percentage of seats than of votes. However, its contribution to one party majorities was much less dramatic. Putting aside the two instances, 1940 and 1958, when a boost from the electoral system was unnecessary, it transformed a minority of votes into a majority of seats on only six of twelve occasions. It is possible that changes in the party system and/or in the distribution of party support will render this justification increasingly anachronistic in future years.

If the assessment of the electoral system is extended to include not only its contribution to one-party majorities, but its contribution to the maintenance of effective opposition, arbitrarily defined as at least one-third of House members, it appears in an even less satisfactory light. On four occasions, two of which occurred when the government party had slightly more than one-half of the votes, the opposition was reduced to numerical ineffectiveness. The coupling of these two criteria together creates a reasonable measure for the contribution of the electoral system to a working parliamentary system, which requires both a stable majority and an effective opposition. From this vantage point the electoral system has a failure rate of 71 percent, on ten of fourteen occasions.

•   •   •

THE EFFECT ON MAJOR AND MINOR PARTIES

Table 2 indicates an important effect of the electoral system with its proof that discrimination for and against the parties does not become increasingly severe when the parties are ordered from most votes to least votes. Discrimination in favour of a party was most pronounced for the weakest party on seven occasions, and for the strongest party on seven occasions. In the four elections from 1921 to 1930 inclusive, with three party contestants, the second party was most hurt by the electoral system. In the five elections from 1935 to 1953 inclusive the electoral system again worked against the middle ranking parties and favoured the parties with the weakest and strongest voting support. In the five elections from 1957 to 1965 inclusive there has been a noticeable tendency to benefit the first two parties, with the exception of the fourth party, Social Credit in 1957, at the expense of the smaller parties.

The explanation for the failure of the electoral system to act with Darwinian logic by consistently distributing its rewards to the large parties and its penalties to the small parties is relatively straightforward. The bias in favour of the strongest party reflects the likelihood that the large number of votes it has at its disposal will produce enough victories in individual constituencies to give it, on a percentage basis, a surplus of seats over votes. The fact that this surplus has occurred with only one exception, 1957, indicates the extreme unlikelihood of the strongest party having a distribution of partisan support capable of transforming the electoral system from an ally into a foe. The explanation for the favourable impact of the

TABLE 2:   Bias of electoral system in translating votes into seats

Year	Rank order of parties in terms of percentages of vote									
	1		2		3		4		5	
1921	Libs.	1.21	Cons.	0.70	Progs.	1.20				
1925	Cons.	1.017	Libs.	1.015	Progs.	1.09				
1926	Libs.	1.13	Cons.	0.82	Progs.	1.55				
1930	Cons.	1.15	Libs.	0.82	Progs.	1.53				
1935	Libs.	1.57	Cons.	0.55	CCF	0.33	Rec.	0.05	Socred	1.68
1940	Libs.	1.43	Cons.	0.53	CCF	0.39	Socred	1.52		
1945	Libs.	1.24	Cons.	1.00	CCF	0.73	Socred	1.29		
1949	Libs.	1.49	Cons.	0.53	CCF	0.37	Socred	1.03		
1953	Libs.	1.32	Cons.	0.62	CCF	0.77	Socred	1.06		
1957	Libs.	0.97	Cons.	1.087	CCF	0.88	Socred	1.091		
1958	Cons.	1.46	Libs.	0.55	CCF	0.32	Socred	0		
1962	Cons.	1.17	Libs.	1.01	NDP	0.53	Socred	0.97		
1963	Libs.	1.17	Cons.	1.09	NDP	0.49	Socred	0.76		
1965	Libs.	1.23	Cons.	1.13	NDP	0.44	Cred.	0.72	Socred	1.51

Independents and very small parties have been excluded from the table.

The measurement of discrimination employed in this table defines the relationship between the percentage of votes and the percentage of seats. The figure is devised by dividing the former into the latter. Thus 1 — (38% seats/38% votes), for example — represents a neutral effect for the electoral system. Any figure above 1 — (40% seats/20% votes) = 2.0, for example — indicates discrimination for the party. A figure below 1 — (20% seats/40% votes) = 0.5, for example — indicates discrimination against the party. For the purposes of the table the ranking of the parties as 1, 2, 3 . . . is based on their percentage of the vote, since to rank them in terms of seats would conceal the very bias it is sought to measure — namely the bias introduced by the intervening variable of the electoral system which constitutes the mechanism by which votes are translated into seats.

electoral system on the Progressives and Social Credit from 1921 to 1957 when they were the weakest parties is simply that they were sectional parties which concentrated their efforts in their areas of strength where the electoral system worked in their favour. Once the electoral system has rewarded the strongest party and a weak party with concentrated sectional strength there are not many more seats to go around. In this kind of party system, which Canada had from 1921 to Mr. Diefenbaker's breakthrough, serious discrimination against the second party in a three-party system and the second and third party in a four-party system is highly likely.

Table 3 reveals that the electoral system positively favours minor parties with sectional strongholds and discourages minor parties with diffuse support. The classic example of the latter phenomenon is provided by the Reconstruction party in the 1935 election. For its 8.7 percent of the vote it was rewarded with one seat, and promptly disappeared from the scene. Yet its electoral support was more than twice that of Social Credit which gained seventeen seats, and only marginally less than

TABLE 3:   Minor parties: percentages of seats and votes

	Progressives		Reconstruction		CCF/NDP		Soc. Credit		Créditiste	
	votes	seats	votes	seats	votes	seats	votes	seats	votes	seats
1921	23.1	27.7								
1925	9.0	9.8								
1926	5.3	8.2								
1930	3.2	4.9								
1935			8.7	0.4	8.9	2.9	4.1	6.9		
1940					8.5	3.3	2.7	4.1		
1945					15.6	11.4	4.1	5.3		
1949					13.4	5.0	3.7	3.8		
1953					11.3	8.7	5.4	5.7		
1957					10.7	9.4	6.6	7.2		
1958					9.5	3.0	2.6	—		
1962					13.5	7.2	11.7	11.3		
1963					13.1	6.4	11.9	9.1		
1965					17.9	7.9	3.7	1.9	4.7	3.4

that of the CCF which gained seven seats. The case of the Reconstruction party provides dramatic illustration of the futility of party effort for a minor party which lacks a sectional stronghold. The treatment of the CCF/NDP by the electoral system is only slightly less revealing. This party with diffuse support which aspired to national and major party status never received as many seats as would have been "justified" by its voting support, and on six occasions out of ten received less than half the seats to which it was "entitled." The contrasting treatment of Social Credit and the Progressives, sectional minor parties, by the electoral system clearly reveals the bias of the electoral system in favour of concentrated support and against diffused support.

DISTORTION IN PARTY PARLIAMENTARY REPRESENTATION

No less important than the general differences in the way the electoral system rewards or punishes each individual party as such, is the manner in which it fashions particular patterns of sectional representation within the ranks of the parliamentary parties out of the varying distributions of electoral support they received. This sectional intra-party discrimination affects all parties. The electoral system consistently minimized the Ontario support of the Progressives which provided the party with 43.5 percent, 39.7 percent, and 29.4 percent of its total votes in the first three elections of the twenties. The party received only 36.9 percent, 8.3 percent, and 10 percent of its total seats from that province. Further, by its varying treatment of the party's electoral support from Manitoba, Saskatchewan, and Alberta it finally helped to reduce the Progressives to an Alberta party.

TABLE 4:   Percentages of total CCF/NDP strength, in seats and votes coming from selected provinces.

	N.S.	Que.	Ont.	Man.	Sask.	Alta.	B.C.
1935 votes	—	1.9	32.7	13.9	18.8	7.9	24.8
seats	—	—	—	28.6	28.6	—	42.9
1940 votes	4.5	1.9	15.6	15.6	27.0	8.9	26.2
seats	12.5	—	—	12.5	62.5	—	12.5
1945 votes	6.4	4.1	31.9	12.5	20.5	7.0	15.4
seats	3.6	—	—	17.9	64.3	—	14.3
1949 votes	4.3	2.3	39.2	10.6	19.5	4.0	18.6
seats	7.7	—	7.7	23.1	38.5	—	23.1
1953 votes	3.5	3.7	33.4	10.1	24.6	3.7	19.7
seats	4.3	—	4.3	13.0	47.8	—	30.4
1957 votes	2.4	4.5	38.7	11.6	19.8	3.8	18.6
seats	—	—	12.0	20.0	40.0	—	28.0
1958 votes	2.7	6.6	37.9	10.8	16.3	2.8	22.2
seats	—	—	37.5	—	12.5	—	50.0
1962 votes	3.8	8.9	44.0	7.4	9.0	4.1	20.4
seats	5.3	—	31.6	10.5	—	—	52.6
1963 votes	2.6	14.6	42.6	6.4	7.3	3.4	21.5
seats	—	—	35.3	11.8	—	—	52.9
1965 votes	2.8	17.7	43.0	6.6	7.6	3.2	17.3
seats	—	—	42.9	14.3	—	—	42.9

Note: Percentages of votes do not total 100 horizontally because the table does not include Newfoundland, Prince Edward Island, New Brunswick, or the territories where the CCF/NDP gained a few votes but no seats.

An analysis of CCF/NDP votes and seats clearly illustrates the manner in which the electoral system has distorted the parliamentary wing of the party. Table 4 reveals the extreme discrimination visited on Ontario supporters of the CCF from 1935 to 1957. With the exception of 1940, CCF Ontario voting support consistently constituted between 30 and 40 percent of total CCF voting support. Yet, the contribution of Ontario to CCF parliamentary representation was derisory. During the same period there was a marked overrepresentation of Saskatchewan in the CCF caucus. The 1945 election is indicative. The 260,000 votes from Ontario, 31.9 percent of the total CCF vote, produced no seats at all, while 167,000 supporters from Saskatchewan, 20.5 percent of the total party vote, were rewarded with eighteen seats, 64.3 percent of total party seats. In these circumstances it was not surprising that observers were led to mislabel the CCF an agrarian party.

The major parties are not immune from the tendency of the electoral system to make the parliamentary parties grossly inaccurate reflections of the sectional distribution of party support. Table 5 makes it clear that the electoral system has been far from impartial in its treatment of Liberal and Conservative voting support from

Ontario and Quebec. For fourteen consecutive elections covering nearly half a century there was a consistent and usually marked overrepresentation of Quebec in the parliamentary Liberal party and marked underrepresentation in the parliamentary Conservative party, with the exception of 1958. For ten consecutive elections from 1921 to 1957 Ontario was consistently and markedly overrepresented in the parliamentary Conservative party, and for eleven consecutive elections from 1921 to 1958, there was consistent, but less marked, underrepresentation of Ontario in the parliamentary Liberal party. Thus the electoral system, by pulling the parliamentary Liberal party toward Quebec and the parliamentary Conservative party toward Ontario, made the sectional cleavages between the parties much more pronounced in Parliament than they were at the level of the electorate.

The way in which the electoral system affected the relationship of Quebec to the parliamentary wings of the two major parties is evident in the truly startling dis-

TABLE 5:   Liberals and Conservatives: Percentages of total parliamentary strength and total electoral support from Quebec and Ontario

	Conservatives				Liberals			
	Ontario		Quebec		Ontario		Quebec	
	seats	votes	seats	votes	seats	votes	seats	votes
1921	74.0	47.1	—	15.5	18.1	26.6	56.0	43.8
1925	58.6	47.4	3.4	18.4	11.1	30.1	59.6	37.8
1926	58.2	44.9	4.4	18.7	20.3	31.7	46.9	33.4
1930	43.1	38.9	17.5	24.0	24.2	33.7	44.0	30.6
1935	62.5	43.1	12.5	24.7	32.4	34.4	31.8	31.5
1940	62.5	48.6	2.5	16.4	31.5	34.4	33.7	31.2
1945	71.6	52.7	3.0	8.3	27.2	34.6	42.4	33.3
1949	61.0	43.6	4.9	22.6	29.0	31.9	35.2	33.2
1953	64.7	44.2	7.8	26.0	29.8	32.6	38.6	34.2
1957	54.5	42.9	8.0	21.7	20.0	31.1	59.0	38.1
1958	32.2	36.2	24.0	25.7	30.6	33.3	51.0	37.8
1962	30.2	36.9	12.1	21.6	44.0	39.2	35.0	28.6
1963	28.4	37.8	8.4	16.0	40.3	39.1	36.4	29.3
1965	25.8	37.4	8.2	17.3	38.9	38.6	42.7	30.0

crepancies between votes and seats for the two parties from that province. From 1921 to 1965 inclusive the Liberals gained 752 members from Quebec, and the Conservatives only 135. The ratio of 5.6 Liberals to each Conservative in the House of Commons contrasts sharply with the 1.9 to 1 ratio of Liberals to Conservatives at the level of voters.

Given the recurrent problems concerning the status of Quebec in Canadian federalism and the consistent tension in French-English relations it is self-evident that the effects of the electoral system noted above can be appropriately described as divisive and detrimental to national unity. . . . The electoral system has placed serious barriers in the way of the Conservative party's attempts to gain parliamentary representation from a province where its own interests and those of national unity coincided on the desirability of making a major contender for public office as representative as possible. The frequent thesis that the association of the Conservatives with conscription in 1917 destroyed their prospects in Quebec only becomes meaningful when it is noted that a particular electoral system presided over that destruction.

The following basic effects of the electoral system have been noted. The electoral system has not been impartial in its translation of votes into seats. Its benefits have been disproportionately given to the strongest major party and a weak sectional party. The electoral system has made a major contribution to the identification of particular sections/provinces with particular parties. It has undervalued the partisan diversity within each section/province. By so doing it has rendered the parliamentary composition of each party less representative of the sectional interests in the political system than is the party electorate from which that representation is derived. The electoral system favours minor parties with concentrated sectional support, and discourages those with diffuse national support. The electoral system has consistently exaggerated the significance of cleavages demarcated by sectional/provincial boundaries and has thus tended to transform contests between parties into contests between sections/provinces. . . .

PARTY SYSTEM AS A NATIONALIZING AGENCY

. . . One of the most widespread interpretations of the party system claims that it, or at least the two major parties, functions as a great unifying or nationalizing agency. Canadian politics, it is emphasized, are politics of moderation, or brokerage politics, which minimize differences, restrain fissiparous tendencies, and thus over time help knit together the diverse interests of a polity weak in integration. It is noteworthy that this brokerage theory is almost exclusively applied to the reconciliation of sectional, racial, and religious divisions, the latter two frequently being regarded as simply more specific versions of the first with respect to French-English relations. The theory of brokerage politics thus assumes that the historically significant cleavages in Canada are sectional, reflecting the federal nature of Canadian society, or racial/religious, reflecting a continuation of the struggle which attracted Durham's attention in the mid-nineteenth century. Brokerage politics between classes is mentioned, if at all, as an afterthought.

The interpretation of the party system in terms of its fulfilment of a nationalizing function is virtually universal. Close scrutiny, however, indicates that this is at best questionable, and possibly invalid. It is difficult to determine the precise meaning of the argument that the party system has been a nationalizing agency, stressing what Canadians have in common, bringing together representatives of diverse interests to deliberate on government policies. In an important sense the argument is misleading in that it attributes to the party system what is simply inherent in a representative democracy which inevitably brings together Nova Scotians, Albertans, and Quebeckers to a common assemblage point, and because of the majoritarian necessities of the parliamentary system requires agreement among contending interests to accomplish anything at all. Or, to put it differently, the necessity for inter-group collaboration in any on-going political system makes it possible to claim of any party system compatible with the survival of the polity that it acts as a nationalizing agency. The extent to which any particular party system does so act is inescapably therefore a comparative question or a question of degree. In strict logic an evaluation of alternative types of party systems is required before a particular one can be accorded unreserved plaudits for the success with which it fulfils a nationalizing function.

. . . The basic approach of this paper is that the party system, importantly conditioned by the electoral system, exacerbates the very cleavages it is credited with healing. As a corollary it is suggested that the party system is not simply a reflection of sectionalism, but that sectionalism is also a reflection of the party system.

The electoral system has helped to foster a particular kind of political style by the special significance it accords to sectionalism. This is evident in party campaign strategy, in party policies, in intersectional differences in the nature and vigour of party activity, and in differences in the intra-party socialization experiences of parliamentary personnel of the various parties. As a consequence the electoral system has had an important effect on perceptions of the party system and, by extension, of the political system itself. Sectionalism has been rendered highly visible because the electoral system makes it a fruitful basis on which to organize electoral support. Divisions cutting through sections, particularly those based on the class system, have been much less salient because the possibility of payoffs in terms of representation has been minimal.

PARTIES AND CAMPAIGN STRATEGY

An initial perspective on the contribution of the parties to sectionalism is provided by some of the basic aspects of campaign strategy. Inadequate attention has been paid to the extent to which the campaign activities of the parties have exacerbated the hatreds, fears, and insecurities related to divisive sectional and ethnic cleavages.

The basic cleavage throughout Canadian history concerns Quebec, or more precisely that part of French Canada resident in Quebec, and its relationships with the rest of the country. The evidence suggests that elections have fed on racial fears and insecurities, rather than reduced them. The three post-war elections of 1921, 1925, and 1926 produced overwhelming Liberal majorities at the level of seats in Quebec, 65 out of 65 in 1921, 59 out of 65 in 1925, and 60 seats out of 65 in 1926. . .'. In view of the ample evidence documented by Graham and Neatby of the extent to which the Liberal campaigns stirred up the animosities and insecurities of French Canada, it is difficult to assert that the party system performed a unifying role in a province where historic tensions were potentially divisive. The fact that the Liberals were able to "convince Quebec" that they were its only defenders and that their party contained members of both ethnic groups after the elections scarcely constitute refutation when attention is directed to the methods employed to achieve this end, and when it is noted that the election results led to the isolation of Canada's second great party from Quebec.

More recent indications of sectional aspects of campaign strategy with respect to Quebec help to verify the divisive nature of election campaigning. The well-known decision of the Conservative party in 1957, acting on Gordon Churchill's maxim to "reinforce success not failure," to reduce its Quebec efforts and concentrate on the possibilities of success in the remainder of the country provides an important indication of the significance of calculations of sectional pay-offs in dictating campaign strategy. The logic behind this policy was a direct consequence of the electoral system, for it was that system which dictated that increments of voting support from Quebec would produce less pay-off in representation than would equal increments elsewhere where the prospects of Conservative constituency victories were more promising. The electoral results were brilliantly successful from the viewpoint of the party, but less so from the perspective of Quebec which contributed only 8 percent of the new government's seats, and received only three cabinet ministers.

In these circumstances the election of 1958 was crucial in determining the nature and extent of French-Canadian participation in the new government which obviously would be formed by the Conservatives. Group appeals were exploited by the bribe that Quebec would get many more cabinet seats if that province returned a larger number of Tory MPs. Party propaganda stimulated racial tensions and insecurities. . . .

The significance of Quebec representation in explaining the nature of the Canadian party system has often been noted. Meisel states that the federal politician is faced with the dilemma of ignoring the pleas of Quebec, in which case "he may lose the support of Canada's second largest province without the seats of which a Parliamentary majority is almost impossible. If he heeds the wishes of Quebec, he may be deprived of indispensable support elsewhere." Lipson describes Quebec as the "solid South" of Canada whose support has contributed at different times to the hegemony of both parties, a fact which is basic in explaining the strategy of opposition of the two major parties. An important point is made by Ward in his observation that Liberal dominance in Quebec contributes to "internal strains in other parties." He adds the fundamental point that it is the electoral system which "by throwing whole blocks of seats to one party" fosters for that party a "special role as protector of the minority," while other parties are baffled by their inability to make significant breakthroughs in representation. Prophetically, as it turned out, he noted the developing theory that opposition parties should attempt to construct parliamentary majorities without Quebec, thus facing French Canadians with the option of becoming an opposition minority or casting themselves loose from the Liberals.

Ward's analysis makes clear that the special electoral importance of Quebec and the resultant party strategies elicited by that fact are only meaningful in the context of an electoral system which operates on a "winner take all" basis, not only at the level of the constituency but, to a modified extent, at the level of the province as a whole. It is only at the level of seats, not votes, that Quebec became a Liberal stronghold, a Canadian "solid South," and a one-party monopoly. The Canadian "solid South," like its American counterpart, is a contrivance of the electoral system, not an autonomous social fact which exists independent of it. . . .

Quebec constitutes the most striking example of the sectional nature of party strategy, electoral appeals, and electoral outcomes. It is, however, only a specific manifestation of the general principle that when the distribution of partisan support within a province or section is such that significant political pay-offs are likely to accrue to politicians who address themselves to the special needs of the area concerned, politicians will not fail to provide at least a partial response. The tendency of parties "to aim appeals at the nerve centers of particular provinces or regions, hoping thus to capture a bloc geographical vote," and to emphasize sectional appeals, are logical party responses within the Canadian electoral framework.

ELECTORAL SYSTEM AND PARTY POLICY

. . . The inquiry can be extended by noting that the electoral system affects party policies both directly and indirectly. The direct effect flows from the elementary consideration that each party devises policy in the light of a different set of sectional considerations. In theory, if the party is viewed strictly as a maximizing body pursuing representation, party sensitivity should be most highly developed in marginal situations where an appropriate policy initiative, a special organizational effort, or a liberal use of campaign funds might tip the balance of sectional representation to the side of the party. Unfortunately, sufficient evidence is not available to assert that this is a valid description of the import of sectional considerations on party strategies. The indirect effect of the electoral system is that it plays an important role in the determination of who the party policy makers will be.

The indirect effect presupposes the preeminence of the parliamentary party and its leaders in policy making. Acceptance of this presupposition requires a brief preliminary analysis of the nature of party organization, especially for the two major parties. The literature has been unanimous in referring to the organizational weakness of the Liberals and Conservatives. Some of the basic aspects and results of this will be summarily noted.

The extra-parliamentary structures of the two major parties have been extremely weak, lacking in continuity and without any disciplining power over the parliamentary party. The two major parties have been leader-dominated with membership playing a limited role in policy making and party financing. Although there are indications that the extra-parliamentary apparatus of the parties is growing in importance, it can be safely said that for the period under review both major parties have been essentially parliamentary parties. . . . Thus, the contribution of the electoral system to the determination of the parliamentary personnel of the party becomes, by logical extension, a contribution to the formation of party policies. Scarrow has asserted that "it is the makeup of the parliamentary party, including the proportional strength and bargaining position of the various parts, which is the most crucial factor in determining policy at any one time." While this hypothesis may require modification in particular cases, it is likely that historical research will confirm its general validity. For example, the antithetical attitudes of Conservatives and Liberals to conscription in both world wars were related not only to the electoral consequences of different choices, but also reflected the backgrounds and bias of the party personnel available to make such key decisions. . . .

The significance of the electoral system for party policy is due to its consistent failure to reflect with even rough accuracy the distribution of partisan support in the various sections/provinces of the country. By making the Conservatives far more of a British and Ontario-based party, the Liberals far more a French and Quebec party, the CCF far more a prairie and BC party, and even Social Credit far more of an Alberta party up until 1953, than the electoral support of these parties "required," they were deprived of intra-party spokesmen proportionate to their electoral support from the sections where they were relatively weak. The relative, or on occasion total, absence of such spokesmen for particular sectional communities seriously affects the image of the parties as national bodies, deprives the party concerned of articulate proponents of particular sectional interests in caucus and in the House, and, it can be deductively suggested, renders the members of the parliamentary party personally less sensitive to the interests of the unrepresented sections than they otherwise would be. As a result the general perspectives and policy orientations of a party are likely to be skewed in favour of those interests which, by virtue of strong parliamentary representation, can vigorously assert their claims.

If a bias of this nature is consistently visited on a specific party over long periods of time, it will importantly condition the general orientation of the party and the political information and values of party MPs. It is in such ways that it can be argued that the effect of the electoral system is cumulative, creating conditions which aggravate the bias which it initially introduced into the party. To take the case of the Conservative party, the thesis is that not only does the electoral system make that party less French by depriving it of French representation as such, but also by the effect which that absence of French colleagues has on the possibility that its non-French members will shed their parochial perspectives through intra-party contacts with French co-workers in parliament. . . .

While a lengthy catalogue of explanations can be adduced to explain the divergent orientations of Liberals and Conservatives to Quebec and French Canada the electoral system must be given high priority as an influencing factor. A strong deductive case therefore can be made that the sectional bias in party representation engendered by the electoral system has had an important effect on the policies of specific parties and on policy differences between parties. Additionally, the electoral system has helped to determine the real or perceived sectional consequences of alternative party policy decisions. . . .

In some cases the sectional nature of party support requires politicians to make a cruel choice between sections, a choice recognized as involving the sacrifice of future representation from one section in order to retain it from another. This, it has been argued, was the Conservative dilemma in deciding whether or not Riel was to hang and in determining conscription policy in the First World War. Faced with a choice between Quebec and Ontario, in each case they chose Ontario. It should be noted that these either/or sectional choices occasionally thrown up in the political system are given exaggerated significance by an electoral system capable of transforming a moderate loss of votes in a section into almost total annihilation at the level of representation. If only votes were considered, the harshness of such decisions would be greatly mitigated, for decisions could be made on the basis of much less dramatic marginal assessments of the political consequences of alternative courses of action.

ELECTORAL SYSTEM AND PERCEPTIONS OF THE POLITY

A general point, easily overlooked because of its elementary nature, is that the electoral system has influenced perceptions of the political system. The sectional basis of party representation which the electoral system has stimulated has reduced the visibility of cleavages cutting through sections. . . .

. . . A hasty survey of political literature finds Quebec portrayed as "the solid Quebec of 1921," western Canada described as "once the fortress of protest movements," since transformed "into a Conservative stronghold," eastern Canada depicted in the 1925 election as having "punished King for his preoccupation with the prairies," and the Conservative party described in 1955 as "almost reduced into being an Ontario party," when in the previous election 55.8 percent of its voting support came from outside that province.

The use of sectional terminology in description easily shades off into highly suspect assumptions about the voting behaviour of the electorate within sections. One of the most frequent election interpretations attributes a monolithic quality to Quebec voters and then argues that they "have instinctively given the bulk of their support" to the government or it is claimed that "the voters of Quebec traditionally seem to want the bulk of their representation . . . on the government side of the House. . . ." Several authors have specifically suggested that in 1958 Quebec, or the French Canadians, swung to Diefenbaker for this reason. . . . A recent analysis of New Brunswick politics argues that the strong tendency for MPs from that province to be on the government side of the House "must be" because "it seeks to gain what concessions it can by supporting the government and relying on its sense of gratitude."

The tendency of the electoral system to create sectional or provincial sweeps for one party at the level of representation is an important reason for these misinterpretations. Since similar explanations have become part of the folklore of Canadian politics it is useful to examine the extremely tenuous basis of logic on which they rest. Quebec will serve as a useful case study. The first point to note is the large percentage of the Quebec electorate which does not vote for the party which subsequently forms the government, a percentage varying from 29.8 percent in 1921 to 70.4 percent in 1962, and averaging 48 percent for the period 1921 to 1965 as a whole. In the second place any government party will tend to win most of the sections most of the time. That is what a government party is. While Quebec has shown an above average propensity to accord more than fifty percent of its representation to the government party (on eleven occasions out of fourteen, compared to an average for all sections of just under eight out of fourteen) this is partly because of the size of the contingent from Quebec and its frequent one-sided representation patterns. This means that to a large extent Quebec determines which party will be the government, rather than exhibiting a preference for being on the government or opposition side of the House. This can be tested by switching the representation which Quebec gave to the two main parties in each of the eleven elections in which Quebec backed the winner. The method is simply to transfer the number of seats Quebec accorded the winning party to the second main party, and transfer the latter's Quebec seats to the former. This calculation shows that had Quebec distributed its seats between the two main parties in a manner precisely the opposite to its actual performance it would have been on the winning side on seven out of eleven occasions anyway. It is thus more accurate to say that parties need Quebec in order to win than to say that Quebec displays a strong desire to be on the winning side.

One final indication of the logical deficiencies of the assumption that Quebec voters are motivated by a bandwagon psychology will suffice. The case of 1958 will serve as an example. In 1957 when there was no prediction of a Conservative victory, Quebec voters gave 31.1 percent of their voting support to the Conservative party. In 1958 that percentage jumped to 49.6 when predictions of a Conservative victory were nearly universal. On the reasonable assumption that most of the Conservative supporters in 1957 remained with the party in 1958, and on the further assumption, which is questionable, that all of the increment in Conservative support was due to a desire to be on the winning side, the explanation is potentially applicable to only one Quebec voter out of five.

In concluding this critical analysis of a segment of Canadian political folklore it is only necessary to state that the attribution of questionable motivations to Quebec or French Canada could easily have been avoided if attention had been concentrated on voting data rather than on the bias in representation caused by the single-member constituency system. The analysis of Canadian politics has been harmfully affected by a kind of mental shorthand which manifests itself in the acceptance of a political map of the country which identifies provinces or sections in terms of the end results of the political process, partisan representation. This perception is natural since elections occur only once every three or four years while the results are visible for the entire period between elections. Since sectional discrepancies between votes and seats are due to the electoral system it is evident that the latter has contributed to the formation of a set of seldom questioned perceptions which exaggerate the partisan significance of geographical boundaries.

ELECTORAL SYSTEM, SECTIONALISM, AND INSTABILITY

Individuals can relate to the party system in several ways, but the two most fundamental are class and sectionalism. The two are antithetical, for one emphasizes the geography of residence, while the other stresses stratification distinctions for which residence is irrelevant. The frequently noted conservative tone which pervades Canadian politics is a consequence of the sectional nature of the party system. The emphasis on sectional divisions engendered by the electoral system has submerged class conflicts, and to the extent that our politics has been ameliorative it has been more concerned with the distribution of burdens and benefits between sections than between classes. The poverty of the Maritimes has occupied an honourable place in the foreground of public discussion. The diffuse poverty of the generally underprivileged has scarcely been noticed.

Such observations lend force to John Porter's thesis that Canadian parties have failed to harness the "conservative-progressive dynamic" related to the Canadian class system, and to his assertion that "to obscure social divisions through brokerage politics is to remove from the political system that element of dialectic which is the source of creative politics." The fact is, however, that given the historical (and existing) state of class polarization in Canada the electoral system has made sectionalism a more rewarding vehicle for amassing political support than class. The destructive impact of the electoral system on the CCF is highly indicative of this point. It is not that the single member constituency system discourages class based politics in any absolute sense, as the example of Britain shows, but that it discourages such politics when class identities are weak or submerged behind sectional identities.

This illustrates the general point that the differences in the institutional contexts of politics have important effects in determining which kinds of conflict become salient in the political system. The particular institutional context with which this paper is concerned, the electoral system, has clearly fostered a sectional party system in which party strategists have concentrated on winning sections over to their side. It has encouraged a politics of opportunism based on sectional appeals and conditioned by one party bastions where the opposition is tempted to give up the battle and pursue success in more promising areas.

A politics of sectionalism is a politics of instability for two reasons. In the first place it induces parties to pay attention to the realities of representation which filter through the electoral system, at the expense of the realities of partisan support at the level of the electorate. The self-interest which may induce a party to write off a section because its weak support there is discriminated against by the electoral system may be exceedingly unfortunate for national unity. Imperfections in the political market render the likelihood of an invisible hand transforming the pursuit of party good into public good somewhat dubious.

Secondly, sectional politics is potentially far more disruptive to the polity than class politics. This is essentially because sectional politics has an inherent tendency to call into question the very nature of the political system and its legitimacy.

Classes, unlike sections, cannot secede from the political system, and are consequently more prone to accept its legitimacy. The very nature of their spatial distribution not only inhibits their political organization but induces them to work through existing instrumentalities. With sections this is not the case.

Given the strong tendency to sectionalism found in the very nature of Canadian society the question can be raised as to the appropriateness of the existing electoral system. Duverger has pointed out that the single-member constituency system "accentuates the geographical localization of opinions: one might even say that it tends to transform a national opinion . . . into a local opinion by allowing it to be represented only in the sections of the country in which it is strongest." Proportional representation works in the opposite manner for "opinions strongly entrenched locally tend to be broadened on to the national plane by the possibility of being represented in districts where they are in a small minority." The political significance of these opposed tendencies "is clear: proportional representation tends to strengthen national unity (or, to be more precise, national uniformity); the simple majority system accentuates local differences. The consequences are fortunate or unfortunate according to the particular situation in each country."

SECTIONALISM AND DISCONTINUITIES IN PARTY REPRESENTATION

It might be argued that the appropriate question is not whether sectional (or other) interests are represented proportionately to their voting support in each party, but simply whether they are represented in the party system as a whole proportionately to their general electoral strength. This assertion, however, is overly simple and unconvincing.

An electoral system which exaggerates the role of specific sections in specific parties accentuates the importance of sectionalism itself. If sectionalism in its "raw" condition is already strong, its exaggeration may cause strains beyond the capacity of the polity to handle. By its stimulus to sectional cleavages the electoral system transforms the party struggle into a struggle between sections, raising the danger that "parties . . . cut off from gaining support among a major stratum . . . lose a major reason for compromise."

This instability is exacerbated by the fact that the electoral system facilitates sudden and drastic alterations in the basis of party parliamentary representation. Recent changes with respect to NDP representation from Saskatchewan, Social Credit representation from Quebec, and the startling change in the influence of the prairie contingent in the Conservative party, with its counterpart of virtually eliminating other parties from that section, constitute important illustrations. The experience of Social Credit since 1962 and more recent experience of the Conservative party reveal that such changes may be more than a party can successfully handle.

Sudden changes in sectional representation are most pronounced in the transition from being an opposition party to becoming the government party. As Underhill notes, it is generally impossible to have more than one party with significant representation from both French and English Canada at the same time. That party is invariably the government party. This has an important consequence which has been insufficiently noted. Not only are opposition parties often numerically weak and devoid of access to the expertise that would prepare them for the possibility of governing, but they are also far less national in composition than the government party. On the two occasions since the First World War when the Conservatives ousted Liberal governments, 1930 and 1957, their opposition experience cut them off from contact with Quebec at the parliamentary level. Even though the party was successful in making significant break-throughs in that province in 1930 and especially in 1958, it can be suggested that it had serious problems in digesting the sudden input of Quebec MPs, particularly in the latter year.

The transition from opposition to government therefore is a transition from being sectional to being national, not only in the tasks of government, but typically in the very composition of the party itself. The hypothesis that this discontinuity may have serious effects on the capacity of the party to govern is deserving of additional research. It is likely that such research will suggest a certain incongruity between the honorific status symbolically accorded Her Majesty's Loyal Opposition, and an electoral system which is likely to hamper the development in that party of those perspectives functional to successful governing.

THE ELECTORAL SYSTEM AS A DETERMINANT OF THE PARTY SYSTEM

Students of Canadian politics have been singularly unwilling to attribute any explanatory power to the electoral system as a determinant of the party system. Lipson has argued that it is not the electoral system which moulds the party system, but rather the reverse. Essentially his thesis is that parties select the type of electoral system more compatible with their own interest, which is self-perpetuation. He admits in passing that once selected the electoral system "produces a reciprocal effect upon the parties which brought it into being."

Lipson's interpretation is surely misleading and fallacious in its implication that because parties preside over the selection, modification, and replacement of particular institutions the subsequent feed-back of those institutions on the parties should not be regarded as causal. In the modern democratic party state, parties preside over the legal arrangements governing campaign expenses, eligibility of candidates, the rules establishing the determination of party winners and losers, the kinds of penalties, such as loss of deposits, which shall be visited on candidates with a low level of support, the rules establishing who may vote, and so on. Analysis is stifled if it is assumed that because these rules are made by parties the effect of the rules on the parties is in some sense to be regarded as derivative or of secondary interest or importance. Fundamentally the argument concerns the priority to be accorded the chicken or the egg. As such it can be pursued to an infinite regression, for it can be asserted that the parties which make a particular set of rules are themselves products of the rules which prevailed in the previous period, which in turn. . . . It might also be noted that parties which preside over particular changes in electoral arrangements may be mistaken in their predictions about the effect of the changes, It is clear that the introduction of the alternative ballot in British Columbia in 1952 misfired from the viewpoint of its sponsors, with dramatic effects on the nature of the provincial party system which subsequently developed.

The only reasonable perspective for the analyst to adopt is to accept the interdependence of electoral systems and party systems and then to investigate whatever aspects of that interdependence seem to provide useful clues for the understanding of the political system.

In a recent article Meisel explicitly agrees with Lipson, asserting that parties are products of societies rather than of differences between parliamentary or presidential systems, or of electoral laws. This argument is weakened by its assumption that society is something apart from the institutional arrangements of which it is composed. It is unclear in this dichotomy just what society is. While it may be possible at the moment when particular institutions are being established to regard them as separate from the society to which they are to be fitted, this is not so with long-established institutions which become part and parcel of the society itself. Livingston's argument that after a while it becomes impossible to make an analytic distinction between the instrumentalities of federalism and the federal nature of the society they were designed to preserve or express is correct and is of general validity. To say therefore that parties are products of societies is not to deny that they are products of institutions. The only defensible view is once again to accept the interdependence of political and other institutions which compose society and then to establish the nature of particular patterns of interdependence by research.

Confirmation of the view that electoral systems do have an effect on party systems is provided by logic. To assert that a particular electoral system does not have an effect on a particular party system is equivalent to saying that all conceivable electoral systems are perfectly compatible with that party system and that all conceivable party systems are compatible with that electoral system. This is surely impossible. Any one electoral system has the effect of inhibiting the development of the different party systems which some, but not necessarily all, different electoral systems would foster. To accept this is to accept that electoral systems and party systems are related.

APPROACHES TO A THEORY OF THE PARTY SYSTEM

This paper has suggested that the electoral system has been an important factor in the evolution of the Canadian party system. Its influence is intimately tied up with the politics of sectionalism which it has stimulated. Sectionalism in the party system is unavoidable as long as there are significant differences between the distribution of party voter support in any one section and the distribution in the country as a whole. The electoral system, however, by the distortions it introduces as it transforms votes into seats produces an exaggerated sectionalism at the level of representation. In view of this, the basic theme of the paper in its simplest form, and somewhat crudely stated, is that statements about sectionalism in the national party system are in many cases, and at a deeper level, statements about the politics of the single-member constituency system.

The suggested impact of the electoral system on the party system is relevant to a general theory of the party system but should not be confused with such a general theory. The construction of the latter would have required analysis of the import for the party system of such factors as the federal system, the relationship of provincial party organizations to the national party, the nature of the class system, the underlying economic and cultural bases for sectionalism, a parliamentary system of the British type, and many others. For this discussion all these have been accepted as given. They have been mentioned, if at all, only indirectly. Their importance for a general theory is taken for granted, as is the interdependencies they have with each other and with the electoral system. It is evident, for example, that the underlying strength of sectional tendencies and the weakness of class identification are interrelated with each other and with the electoral system as explanations of sectionalism in Canadian politics. For any one of these to change will produce a change in the outcomes which their interactions generate. We are not therefore suggesting that sectional tendencies are exclusive products of the electoral system, but only that that system accords them an exaggerated significance.

Concentration on the electoral system represents an attempt to isolate one aspect of a complex series of interactions which is only imperfectly understood and in the present state of our knowledge cannot be handled simultaneously with precision. In such circumstances the development of more systematic comprehensive explanations will only result from a dialectic between research findings at levels varying from that of individual voters through middle-range studies, such as Alford's recent analysis of class and voting, to attempts, such as those by Scarrow and Meisel, to handle a complex range of phenomena in one framework.

We can conclude that the capacity of the party system to act as an integrating agency for the sectional communities of Canada is detrimentally affected by the electoral system. The politicians' problem of reconciling sectional particularisms is exacerbated by the system they must work through in their pursuit of power. From one perspective it can be argued that if parties succeed in overcoming sectional divisions they do so in defiance of the electoral system. Conversely, it can be claimed that if parties do not succeed this is because the electoral system has so biased the party system that it is inappropriate to call it a nationalizing agency. It is evident that not only has the electoral system given impetus to sectionalism in terms of party campaigns and policy, but by making all parties more sectional at the level of seats than of votes it complicates the ability of the parties to transcend sectionalism. At various times the electoral system has placed barriers in the way of Conservatives becoming sensitively aware of the special place of Quebec and French Canada in the Canadian polity, aided the Liberals in that task, inhibited the third parties in the country from becoming aware of the special needs and dispositions of sections other than those represented in the parliamentary party, and frequently inhibited the parliamentary personnel of the major parties from becoming attuned to the sentiments of the citizens of the prairies. The electoral system's support for the political idiosyncracies of Alberta for over two decades ill served the integration of that provincial community into the national political system at a time when it was most needed. In fact, the Alberta case merely illustrates the general proposition that the disintegrating effects of the electoral system are likely to be most pronounced where alienation from the larger political system is most profound. A particular orientation, therefore, has been imparted to Canadian politics which is not inherent in the very nature of the patterns of cleavage and consensus in the society, but results from their interplay with the electoral system.

The stimulation offered to sectional cleavages by the single-member constituency system has led several authors to query its appropriateness for national integration in certain circumstances. Lipset and Duverger have suggested that countries possessed of strong underlying tendencies to sectionalism may be better served by proportional representation which breaks up the monolithic nature of sectional representation stimulated by single-member constituency systems. Belgium is frequently cited as a country in which proportional representation has softened the conflict between the Flemish and the Walloons, and the United States as a country in which the single-member constituency system has heightened cleavages and tensions between north and south. Whatever its other merits, the single-member constituency system lacks the singular capacity of proportional representation to encourage all parties to search for votes in all sections of the country. Minorities within sections or provinces are not frozen out as they tend to be under the existing system. As a consequence sectional differences in party representation are minimized or, more accurately, given proportionate rather than exaggerated representation—a factor which encourages the parties to develop a national orientation.

EXPLANATIONS OF OUR PARTY SYSTEM*

JOHN T. McLEOD

[The] tedious similarity between [our] two major parties may be one reason for the difficulty of formulating any general theory explaining the Canadian party system. In the nineteenth century it was customary to interpret the two-party system in Macaulay's terms as the reflection of the division of mankind into those who exalt liberty above all else and those whose primary concern is social order. This "literary" theory was invoked by Laurier and given lip-service by Mackenzie King, but it is not taken seriously by contemporary scholars. It is also possible to regard

* From "Party Structure and Party Reform," in *The Prospect of Change: Proposals for Canada's Future,* edited by A. Rotstein, Toronto, McGraw-Hill of Canada, 1965. By permission of the author and publisher.

our national parties as mere collections of interest groups in search of power, but the student will search in vain for any satisfactory interpretative theory suggesting how the vague "interests" are brought together or kept together, now by one party, now by another. In more fashionable terms of behaviourism and "images", Professor Mallory has attempted to explain the success or failure of Canada's major parties by stressing a leader's ability to capture the "national mood". Mallory argues that the important factor is "that at any given time only one party is in tune with a national mood—and that party is likely to stay in power until the mood changes and leaves it politically high and dry." However, Mallory fails to enlighten us as to how or why political moods change. Suggestive as the concept may be, it is not clear how "moods" may be created or identified, nor is it clear whether a leader creates the mood or whether the mood calls forth the leader.

How then do we make sense of the Canadian party system? Perhaps Mallory is most helpful when he gets down to fundamentals and insists that "The most important thing about Canadian politics is that they are parochial rather than national." There persists a certain narrowness of viewpoint in the various sections of the Canadian population. The politics of each region tend to be rather introverted. Canada is composed of five major regions: the Maritimes, Quebec, Ontario, the Prairies, and British Columbia. Each of these regions possesses different political traditions and each contends with rather different social and economic problems. Our heterogeneous population is divided not only into segments of rural and urban, rich and poor, United Empire Loyalists and recent immigrants, but also and most important into a dualistic pattern of English and French. These cleavages make Canada an exceedingly difficult nation to govern. Democratic political parties attempt primarily to organize the population into majorities, but majorities are painfully difficult to attain when the electorate is so fragmented.

Faced with these difficulties, our major parties must inevitably be flexible and broadly inclusive if they are to be national. Above all, they must attempt to harmonize and conciliate the various conflicting interests of the society, and to do so they must emphasize the modest but essential virtues of moderation and compromise. In a nation lacking unity or cohesion, the national political party becomes the shock-absorber of domestic conflicts . . . the principal task of the national political party is to discover some means of bringing the various regions and interests closer together. . . .

Thus it is not surprising that our parties are constantly preoccupied with the search for simple common denominators of slogans and policies on which it may be possible to unite enough of the diverse elements of the population to win elections. The search is always a difficult one, and the common denominators may be distressingly low, but such is the penalty that must be paid for the advantages of physical size and cultural diversity. Issues for which no common denominator can be found tend to be evaded or solutions postponed.

. . . Intellectually tempting as it might be, further political polarization into radical and conservative camps seems to be a luxury which Canadians have been unable to afford. The chief function of party in this country has always been to prevent new cleavages and to draw the divergent elements together into a majority by whatever means possible. . . .

All of this is readily understandable and familiar; however, it does not explain why a party may be more successful at one time than at another in working out broadly acceptable policies and controlling the seats of power. What more can be offered toward an explanation of the Canadian party system?

In the absence of a generally accepted theory of party operation, the most helpful informing hypothesis is that of Macpherson and Smiley who have set forth the concept of single party dominance. Macpherson's analysis of the rise of Social Credit in Alberta yields the suggestion that Alberta has never had an orthodox system of two evenly matched parties frequently alternating in office. Instead, Alberta reveals a pattern of one massive party completely overwhelming its opposition and remaining in power for a long period of uninterrupted years. This deviation from the two-party norm is what Macpherson has dubbed the "quasiparty system". Smiley takes American experience as his starting point and quotes Samuel Lubell to the effect that in American national politics the prolonged dominance of one party has been the usual state of affairs. . . . Smiley defines single-party dominance as a system in which "one political party retains such overwhelming strength over a period of at least a decade that the major political issues of the community are fought out and the major conflicts of interest resolved within that party."

When the concept of single party dominance is applied to the Canadian party system its relevance is at once apparent. Our politics since Confederation have normally been dominated by one broad middle-of-the-road party which has so effectively occupied the centre of the stage that the opposition has been squeezed off into the wings. There have been three major periods of such single party dominance in Canada. John A. Macdonald's Tories easily dominated our politics from 1867 until 1896, slipping from office only briefly in the aftermath of the Pacific Scandal. The Liberals under Laurier had things very much their own way from 1896 until 1911. After the interval of the coalition government of 1917, Mackenzie King and his hand-picked successor dominated our political life from 1921 until 1957 with only two short interruptions, and held office for one comfortably undisturbed period of 22 years. Altogether, these three leaders were in power for 56 of the 98 years since Confederation. We have not had frequent alternation between Liberal and Conservative governments, but long periods in which one party was clearly predominant.

Our experience at the provincial level also bears out the importance of the concept of single party dominance. Although the Maritime provinces for the most part seem closer to the classic pattern of the two-party system, most of the other provinces have demonstrated their adherence to the pattern examined by Macpherson and Smiley. Alberta never had a two-party system. The Liberals were in power there from 1905 to 1921 with only negligible Conservative opposition; the United Farmers of Alberta held sway from 1921 to 1935, and Social Credit has been so securely entrenched there ever since, that in the last provincial election the opposition won only three of the sixty-three seats. In Saskatchewan the Liberals were the dominant party from 1905 to 1944, the Tories managing to win only one election during the whole period; after 1944 the CCF held power in the Wheat Province for twenty years. A series of non-partisan coalition governments in Manitoba during most of the 1922 to 1958 period kept that province in the quasi-party pattern, while at present in Ontario the dominant Conservative party shows no sign of faltering after twenty-one years of continuity in office. Other examples could be cited, including the prolonged rule of Mr. Duplessis and the *Union Nationale* in Quebec for twenty years, but already we have ample evidence to establish that single party dominance has been significantly widespread at the provincial as well as the national level of government.

Inevitably, there is a high premium placed on artful leadership. In the absence of binding principles the leader of the party becomes the focal point of the member's loyalty. Personality rather than philosophy is the key to office. That leader succeeds who can best command the support of, and work out accommodations between, the most numerous interests. . . . A successful leader becomes the major symbol of his party; the party stands for what he stands for, and his pronouncements become party dogma. Whether it is Macdonald or Laurier, King or Diefenbaker, "The Chief" is the mainspring of the machine, and absolute power to formulate policy is concentrated in his hands. The most adroit conciliator will be longest in power.

If a party is to stay long in office its leadership must also reflect the duality of the Canadian nation. The most successful prime ministers have appeared to share their power with a lieutenant who represents the other major language group. An English-speaking leader must have an able French Canadian at his side; a French Catholic first minister must have a prominent English Protestant colleague. Macdonald leaned heavily on Cartier, Laurier on Fielding and Sifton, Mackenzie King on Lapointe and St. Laurent. The fundamental importance of this vestige of the pre-Confederation dual prime-ministership is emphasized by the failure of Borden, Meighen, or Diefenbaker to find such a lieutenant from Quebec. The inability of the Conservative party to win a parliamentary majority in any two successive elections in the twentieth century is often ascribed to this failure.

To become dominant, a national party must achieve a considerable degree of support from Quebec. The voters of Quebec traditionally seem to want the bulk of their representation at Ottawa on the government side of the House. This desire to find representation on Mr. Speaker's right is not peculiar to Quebec but appears to be shared by most of the major interest groups of the country. Such interests clamor for representation not merely in the House but in the cabinet where real power is exercised. Their desire for spokesmen in the cabinet helps to promote the "bandwagon" effect which broadens the support of the government party and strengthens single party dominance.

It follows that the cabinet of a dominant party includes a congeries of elements which have little in common except a willingness to support an attractive leader and an eagerness to have a voice in the councils of state. The wide divergences of opinion inside the governing party make conflict the rule rather than the exception within the cabinet. The major clashes of interest within the nation are likely to be expressed not between competing parties but inside the dominant party. . . . Argument between the parties on the floor of the House and on the hustings is superseded by argument behind the closed doors of cabinet and caucus; major issues are resolved mainly in secret, and the fruitfulness of open democratic debate to educate the voter is stultified. Elections do not often decide issues, and a danger arises of public apathy or contempt toward the ordinary democratic processes.

With the normal role of the opposition so greatly diminished, the minority party tends to be preoccupied with mere posturing and manoeuvering, attempting to splinter off dissident groups from the dominant party and waiting to exploit the inevitable schisms within the government ranks. An opposition leader will not usually try to compete with the governing party by emphasizing a sharply different approach to policy-making, but will concentrate on the omissions and shortcomings of cabinet policy in order to persuade groups supporting the dominant party that they would get a "better deal" if the ins and outs were reversed.

Moreover, when a transfer of power does take place, the new administration will alter the emphasis of government programs, but the basic orientation of policy will change very little. The new cabinet, like the old, will be concerned with placating the major interest groups, and one of the most important of these will still be corporate business. . . .

By definition, however, in a system of single party dominance, the ins and the outs do not exchange places very often, and a further characteristic of the system is that the opposition group will be very weak. The opposition may be weak numerically, as in the national parliament during 1958-62 or in Alberta since 1963, but, more often and more important, after a long period out of office, the opposition may be weak qualitatively. It will lack the practical experience of power which would enable it to probe and criticize the technicalities of government more effectively. A former minority party, when it does finally achieve power, may be so accustomed to negative opposition that it finds difficulty in formulating for itself constructive alternative policies. Like a nagging wife, it may know what it objects to but not what it wants. The traditional weakness of the opposition in Ottawa has been suggested as one of the reasons why most of the provincial governments are frequently controlled by the minority party or by third parties. The most effective opposition to the nationally dominant party then comes from the provincial capitals, and the device of federalism helps to redress the political imbalance.

Following a shift of power, a newly elected government may not be able to profit from the technical advice of the civil service if, over two decades or more, the senior civil servants have become intimately identified with the previously dominant party. This was apparent in Ottawa in 1957-58, and in Regina in 1964; in both cases the civil service had become closely linked with the government party over a long period of years and, through no necessary fault of its own, had become compromised in the eyes of the incoming administration. The complexity of modern government and the enormous technical demands on it make it imperative that a highly competent staff of civil service experts be built up, but when single party dominance has been the rule, a change of government may tend to destroy the top echelon of the old bureaucracy or at least make it less useful to the new cabinet. With a lack of experienced administrative advisors, the incoming government will have a harder time to find its feet, and new policy innovations are less likely to be attempted or to be successful.

The resulting stagnation of policy and the fact that most governments bog down in the middle of the road are reasons for the rise of third parties. Sameness of policy creates areas of discontent, and third parties appear as vehicles of protest against the inertia of single party dominance. Professor Pinard has argued that third parties arise not only where dissident feeling against the majority party are strongest, but where the traditional minority party has become so weak as to be discounted as an effective means of expressing protest. The prolonged success of one party may so eviscerate the organization of its customary opponents that only a new party will be regarded as an effective alternative to the government.

The role of third parties in Canada has been not only to express sporadic electoral discontent but also to capture provincial governments, to formulate more concrete ideologies, and to seek a balance-of-power position in the national parliament at times of transition when no party has a clear majority. Most important, third parties like the CCF, and the Ginger Group before it, have served to popularize radical policy innovations and to push the government party off its conservative stance in the political dead-centre. The influence of third parties on policy has far exceeded their power as measured in numbers of seats won. The origins of such positive departures from the middle of the road as old age pensions, unemployment insurance, hospitalization insurance, and medicare can be attributed largely to the influence of third parties.

Why? There is no general agreement among scholars as to why this pattern of politics has been so prevalent in Canada. Although there is no one explanation which is entirely satisfactory, a number of hypotheses deserve consideration.

Macpherson's analysis of the quasi-party system in Alberta rests on the proposition that the conditions necessary for this pattern to emerge are a "quasi-colonial" economy and a "largely *petit-bourgeois*" class structure of independent agrarian producers. The argument is that Alberta's economy produces staples for distant markets, that the producers are dependent upon and united in their resentment of external capitalist interests, and that the independent small farmer gives the prairie society a virtual homogeneity of class consciousness. "The peculiarity of a society which is at once quasi-colonial and mainly. *petit bourgeois* is that the conflict of class interests is not so much within the society as between that society and the forces of outside capital. . . ." Macpherson contends that as Canada's economy becomes increasingly dependent upon that of the United States, our position more closely approximates that of a quasi-colonial nation which is therefore likely to live under a quasi-party system.

Although Macpherson does not explain why the Alberta farmers turned to the political right under Social Credit while their neighbours in Saskatchewan veered to the left under the CCF, his book remains one of the most provocative pieces of social analysis published in Canada. We must weigh seriously the argument that the Canadian economy is a precarious one *vis-à-vis* the American industrial giant, and that single party dominance may be an expression of a Canadian will to bind our people more closely together and consolidate our politics in the face of external threats to our regional or national interest. Macpherson may exaggerate the importance of class as a factor in our politics, but at least it should be evident that the great bulk of our population regards itself as middle-class, that the predominant social ethos in Canada is a *bourgeois* ethos, that our major parties are principally middle-class parties financed by business, heavily influenced by a compact social elite, and led by middle-class men highly sensitive to commercial interests. If Canada does not possess class homogeneity, surely our closest approximation to a prevailing class consciousness is a middle-class consciousness. Can we seriously doubt that the relative absence of sharp class conflict in Canada is a primary factor in the existence of single party dominance?

Canada's preoccupation with the centrifugal forces of regional diversity and English-French duality may lead to a more orthodox interpretation which avoids emphasis on class. Political scientists are fond of referring to regional, economic, ethnic, and religious differences in the population as "structural cleavages". Professor Maurice Pinard has argued that "Such cleavages strongly alienate a region from one of the two major parties and tie it to a single party as the sole [principal?] defender of its interests, hence leading to one-party dominance." It may be possible for the bulk of the population to be persuaded at a given time that only one party possesses the requisite leadership to be able to form a strong majority government and act as the broker of interests, effectively smoothing over the structural cleavages. Many writers have also noted that the single-member simple-plurality electoral system amplifies the number of seats held by the winning party, reduces the seats held by the minority parties, and gives further institutional impetus to the system of single party dominance.

Whatever the reasons for the prevalence of the single party dominance pattern, some of the main implications and results of this phenomenon are apparent. It may be useful to review the most striking corollaries of the system.

First, there will be a deliberate avoidance of ideological issues by the national parties. This tends to render the parties more alike, to narrow the voter's range of choice between them, and to make our politics more gray and dull. Both parties will attempt to gain the dominant position by emphasizing their ability to include and conciliate most of the major contending interests in the nation, and to do so they will exalt pragmatism, compromise, and moderation. They will keep their "principles" as vague and nebulous as possible and avoid divisive philosophizing at all costs. . . . The parties compete not for the political right or left but for the centre. Their supreme role must be as unifying agents, and their chief method of operation must be compromise.

Periods of minority government in the twentieth century can be regarded as periods of transition during which no one party was able to achieve a position of national dominance. The elections of 1921 and 1925 did not give any one party a clear majority, as the Progressives bore witness to widespread agrarian discontent, and neither of the traditional parties could achieve a position of dominance. Similarly, the emergence of minority government in 1957 marked the Liberal fall from dominance and the start of the Conservative resurgence. Diefenbaker's inability to establish the Tories as the dominant party resulted in further minority governments in 1962 and 1963.

There are sound reasons to indicate that minority governments can provide effective administrations, but the old parties both laud "stable" majority governments as infinitely preferable. The persistent re-appearance of minority governments since 1921 might suggest that coalition between a major and a minor party would prove attractive as a means of providing solid majority administrations, but Canada's parties have stoutly resisted coalition except at times of extreme crisis. We have had only two coalition governments in Canada, one at Confederation and one in 1917. Both worked; that is to say, both accomplished things and in neither case did the process of government break down. The Union government of 1917 enforced conscription and, for better or for worse, enabled the majority to govern. The 1864 coalition of Macdonald and George Brown succeeded in bringing about Confederation.

There was a major difference between these two coalitions which is extremely significant. The 1864 arrangement included important representatives of French Canada on the government side, but the Union government of 1917 did not. Cartier was a member of the Macdonald administration, thus placing the leading spokesman of French Canada in a cabinet post, but the 1917 cabinet included no Quebec leader of consequence. The former coalition was effective in that it accomplished its aims and did not divide the English and French; on the other hand, the 1917 administration, by ignoring Quebec, badly split the Liberal party and dealt the Tories a blow from which they did not recover until 1958. This underlines once again that, in the long run, Canada cannot have a stable government which does not rest firmly on the support of both English and French Canada.

At present there appears no immediate prospect of national coalition government. Instead, the foregoing analysis suggests that we are in a period of transition in which neither party is yet able to attain a dominant position. It is a situation of great uncertainty, but one pregnant with possibilities, for transition periods such as this are times when new directions of policy may be sought and fundamental premises re-examined. . . .

POLITICS AND PARTIES IN CANADA*

PAUL FOX

Canadian politics and political parties tend to be characterized by the word "moderate". Like Britain and the United States, to which Canadian political parties owe a good deal in formative influences, Canada is a predominantly middle class nation with middle class values. This is reflected in the fact that radical parties of either the right or the left are virtually non-existent and that those parties which do exist seek the golden mean in order to get the maximum number of votes.

This tends to diminish the differences between parties and to make them difficult to pinpoint. In some cases it is more a matter of history and traditional loyalty that distinguishes them rather than logic or the planks in their platforms. This is very apparent in comparing the two parties which have dominated Canadian politics since the country became a dominion in 1867, the Conservatives and the Liberals.

The Conservatives originated in Canada as the colonial equivalent of the British Tory Party. In pioneer days they were ardently loyal to the Crown and stood for the maintenance of the British connection. Under their first great leader, Sir John A. Macdonald, who was Prime Minister almost continuously from 1867 until his death in 1891, the party broadened its appeal by incorporating some of the opposing Liberals and by devising a "National Policy", which stressed the development of the country from sea to sea, the construction of transcontinental railways, and the fostering of industry and commerce by the adoption of relatively high tariffs.

These elements left their mark on the party for many years, so much so that it was stigmatized by farmers and French Canadians for decades. The farmers complained that it was the party of "big business", sacrificing the agrarian interests of the three wheat-growing prairie provinces to the financial and commercial demands of the large metropolitan centres (Toronto and Montreal) in the more populous and wealthier provinces of Ontario and Quebec. The French Canadians, Roman Catholic in faith and predominant in Quebec, were alienated by the militant Protestantism and pro-British sentiments of some of the leading Conservatives. When one Conservative Government in the nineteenth century executed Louis Riel, a Roman Catholic rebel with French Canadian blood in his veins, and another Conservative Government rigorously implemented universal military conscription during World War I (which French Canadians considered to be a "British" war), the Conservative Party went into an eclipse in Quebec from which, after four decades, it recovered in the elections of 1957 and 1958, but only spasmodically as it turned out.

* From an address by the author on September 26, 1969.

In every general election from 1917 to 1957, with one exception, the Conservatives never won more than half a dozen seats in this French-Canadian province which, because of its size, has approximately one-quarter of the total number of seats in the House of Commons. Conservative weakness in Quebec combined with meagre support in the western agrarian provinces explains to a large extent why the Tories went out of power nationally in 1921 and remained out, except for five years, until 1957.

The two elections within ten months in 1957 and 1958 brought about a striking change. In the former, the Conservatives under Mr. Diefenbaker secured nine seats out of 75 in Quebec, not many but with one exception more than the party had won in the last 40 years. This also provided a bridgehead for future operations. In the succeeding election Quebec, sensing the strong drift in political currents and not wanting to be found on the wrong bank of the stream, gave Mr. Diefenbaker startling support, electing 50 Conservative members of Parliament.

At the same time Mr. Diefenbaker, himself a western Canadian who had practised law in a small prairie town and had sat as a western M.P. for 18 years, was able to revive the cause of Conservatism in that part of the country by the sheer force of his own personality. . . .

The result of the election on 31 March 1958 was the most decisive victory in the history of Canadian federal government; the Conservatives were returned with 208 seats out of a total of 265. It was an astonishing revival for a party which had almost disintegrated during the long period of Liberal ascendancy.

Unfortunately for the party, its fortunes varied with its leader's. Mr. Diefenbaker's popularity and command of the situation waned almost as rapidly as they had waxed. The 1962 election returned the Conservatives to the status of a minority government, and the 1963 election found them defeated by the Liberals.

Like its British forbear, the Liberal Party in Canada commenced as a reform movement. It was a fusion, after Confederation, of small-scale pioneer farmers of British stock and the more radical and progressive elements in the French-Canadian society known as "Rouges". The colours adopted by the party were red and white in contrast to the Conservatives' blue and white, a distinction that was quite valid. From its birth the Liberal Party tended to be more egalitarian, proletarian, and nationalistic. With the advent to leadership of Sir Wilfrid Laurier, a Roman Catholic French Canadian from Quebec, the party became strongly bi-ethnic and succeeded in gaining power in 1896 and holding it till 1911. World War I and the conscription issue split its two wings apart; most French Canadians and Laurier opposed conscription, while many leading Anglo-Saxons abandoned Laurier and entered a wartime coalition government headed by the Conservatives.

From this crisis the party was rescued by the genius of William Lyon Mackenzie King, who, following his election as leader in 1919, set the Liberals on the path towards a broadly based middle-of-the-road social welfare state. By many artful compromises Mackenzie King kept himself and his party in power almost continuously from 1921 until his retirement in 1948, thereby establishing a personal record as the Prime Minister in Canada who had held office the longest, 21 years and five months.

He was succeeded by Louis St. Laurent, the second French Canadian (both Liberal) to be Prime Minister. Though Mr. St. Laurent tried to continue Mr. Mackenzie King's victorious tactics of maintaining the centre-of-the-road policy while moving forward, the process of aging had rendered the Liberal Government less flexible and less dynamic, and in 1957, after 22 continuous years of power, during which it had won what appeared to be very comfortable electoral pluralities, the party was narrowly defeated by Mr. Diefenbaker's resuscitated Conservatives who secured 112 seats to the Liberals' 105. Mr. St. Laurent resigned as Premier and subsequently retired as leader, being replaced by his former Secretary of State for External Affairs, Mr. Lester B. Pearson. But Mr. Pearson and his Liberals were no match for Prime Minister Diefenbaker's Conservatives, who in the 1958 election reduced the number of Liberal seats to 49.

Under Mr. Diefenbaker the Conservatives appeared to take over the mantle of the Liberals as the party of moderate reform and progress appealing to the diverse geographical, economic, religious, and ethnic groups in the country. However, the Liberals regained their ascendancy in 1963, winning a minority-government victory that they repeated in 1965, largely by appealing to the middle and upper middle class voters in large urban centres. The new Liberal leader chosen in 1968, Mr. Pierre Elliott Trudeau, was able to enhance this urban, midle-class support, and to win a majority government by combining it with his general personal appeal throughout the country. The careers of the two main parties thus confirm the point made earlier, that it is difficult to explain other than historically the differences between Canadian parties because of their tendency to seek the broad middle ground which leads to victory.

Additional proof of this is that there is no party in Canada on the extreme right wing and the party farthest to the left is virtually extinct. The Communist Party (formerly called the Labour Progressive Party) never had much success in Canada. It elected on only one occasion a federal member of Parliament and his career ended ignominiously in prison when he was convicted of conspiracy to turn over government secrets to Russia in wartime. This assisted in convincing most Canadian voters, if they needed further evidence, that the party was more interested in serving the Kremlin than the Canadian people, and subsequent events such as the Soviet restrictions on Jews and the repression of the Hungarian revolt created serious dissensions within its own ranks. Party membership has fallen to a few thousand and in the most recent federal election in 1968 only 14 Communist candidates were nominated, and together they received fewer than 4,000 votes out of the 8,125,838 ballots cast, or approximately .05 percent. The trend of electoral support for the party has been steadily down since 1945, till it has now reached almost the vanishing point.

Further proof of the need to seek the middle of the road in Canadian politics is presented by the history of minor parties. Canada has had a number of these but as yet none has been strong enough to form a government at Ottawa. For the most part they have tended to be regional parties representing special interests, in particular western prairie farmers who have been prone to organize their own political movements in protest against the wealthier, more populous "east" (actually central Canada—Ontario and Quebec). Following the discontents of World War I the farmers created their own Progressive Party which, at its zenith in 1921, sent 64 members to the House of Commons and acquired the balance of power. The party quickly dissolved, however, because of the centrifugal nature of its ultra-democratic organization and its lack of firm leadership. In 1935 the Social Credit Party, which espoused unorthodox monetary doctrines and stirred up strong emotional and religious support, elected 17 members to Parliament from Alberta and Saskatchewan, but after reaching a high point of 19 in 1957 it was wiped out completely by the Conservative landslide in the following year. It gained great support in Quebec in 1962, electing 26 MPs from that province alone (for a total of 30) but subsequently the Quebec wing split away, electing nine *Ralliement des Créditistes* in 1965 to five for Social Credit. In 1968, the English-speaking Social Credit party was wiped out in Parliament, winning no seats at all, while the *Créditistes* continued with 14 seats.

A party that attempted to fuse the agrarian interests of the west and the labour forces of the east was born during the depression of the 1930s with the cumbersome title of the Co-operative Commonwealth Federation. Dedicated to the principles of democratic socialism it has tried to become the Canadian equivalent of the British Labour Party but it has not had the success of its model. The number of seats it has won has fluctuated widely, from seven in its first trial in 1935 to 28 in 1945 and back to eight in 1958, though throughout the period its share of the popular vote varied between about eight and ten percent. After reorganizing itself as the New Democratic Party in 1961, its fortunes improved electorally. It received 17 percent of the popular vote in 1968 and elected 22 MPs.

The dilemma of the C.C.F.-N.D.P. is that it has been squeezed into an almost impossible position left-of-centre in politics in which it can scarcely find sufficient unique ground on which to make a stand. It fears moving left lest it be accused of being communist, which it abhors, and it cannot move right into the mixed field occupied by Conservatives and Liberals without losing the identity it desires as a working class party. While it is thus stuck on the horns of a dilemma, the Conservatives and Liberals have appropriated many of its social welfare planks. Its chief obstacle is the hard fact of Canadian middle class democracy; like all radical and sectional parties it can consider broadening its appeal only at the risk of losing its claim to existence. . . .

In the sphere of the provinces each government, whatever its political stripe, finds that its most fruitful tactic is to set itself up as the defender of provincial rights against the central administration, particularly in the fields of taxation and finance. This has become so commonplace that some theorists have suggested that the real opposition to the government of the day at Ottawa comes not in the traditional manner from the benches to the left of the Speaker in the House of Commons but from the provincial regimes, whether or not they are of the same political complexion as the federal government. This may or may not be true but it is undeniable that any provincial administration tends to make much more of an issue out of its wrangles with Ottawa than out of its own party ideology.

Dogma is either ignored or soft-pedalled and the provincial governments seek to become all things to all people—or at least to all voters. Like federal governments the provincial administrations move according to the inexorable fundamental law of Canadian politics towards the centre of the road, or perhaps it would be more precise to say they spread themselves all over the road. Whatever the official label of the party, whatever the planks in its platform before election, it tends to become moderate and eclectic when it obtains power. This has applied to radical parties like the United Farmers, Social Credit, and the C.C.F., but it also works in reverse sometimes with Conservatives and Liberals. Thus, a Conservative Government in Ontario urged the public ownership of a natural gas pipeline and played a leading role in the achievement of national hospital insurance, while the C.C.F. government in Saskatchewan made a determined effort to attain more private capital investment in its natural resources. In Alberta, Social Credit, which drew its strength originally from rural farms, is now the darling of some business men. In Manitoba, the Roblin Conservative government was probably more progressive than the Liberal-Progressive government it replaced. Thus, the party names do not mean too much in Canada, both provincially and federally, and it is often difficult to establish differences clearly. . . .

ARE OUR PARTIES OUTMODED?*

FLORA MacDONALD

. . . Have the parties recognized the fact—are they willing to recognize the fact— that they must adapt to meet the changing needs of society? When a person says to me, as one did recently, "What's a party for and who cares?", I, for one, am concerned that parties are failing to meet the needs of the society they claim to serve.

Should we not be reminding ourselves that because of their special position in the democratic system, a more significant contribution is required of political parties than of other groups?

What is the role of the political party generally seen to be, and what might it become?

The political party is generally assumed to be one among the many voluntary

* From a paper entitled "Electoral and Party Reform" given by the author to the Progressive Conservative Priorities for Canada Conference held in Niagara Falls, October 9-13, 1969. By permission of the author.

associations in society, that is, one of a number of private groups as distinguished from public bodies.

But in effect, the political party differs in degree, as well as in scope, from groups which exist to foster special interests or unite common concerns such as the Canadian Manufacturers' Association, the Canadian Chamber of Commerce or the Boy Scouts' Association.

The political party is a voluntary association insofar as its members are recruited voluntarily from all segments of society, but its interests extend to all aspects of social and economic concern. Its status is quasi-public as compared with the private interest groups one usually associates with the term "voluntary association."

The recommendations I have suggested in preceding sections [of this paper], i.e., disclosure, limitation and subsidization, would have the effect of making the political party an even more public body, and the recommendations for new and extended activities outlined below, emphasizing the social function of the political party, will further serve to distinguish it from other special interest groups.

The political party is generally acknowledged to have two principal functions—political and legislative. I would suggest that the time has come to add a new dimension—the social function.

The political function involves the recruitment of party candidates, and participation in the electoral process. All too often the public impression of the political party association is that its activities begin and end with the nomination of candidates, the provision of election machinery, and the dissemination of party literature. Valuable as these exercises are, party associations deserve to be regarded as something more than robots turned on for action every four years to get their candidates elected, or as mere echo chambers of the party line.

It must be acknowledged, however, that this assumption on the part of the public is based on more than idle speculation. It is true that many constituency associations come alive only during election periods. Between elections they lie dormant, with such activity as does exist centering around small executives which lack the resources to rouse their membership from lethargy.

What I am proposing is that the party association ought not to be regarded simply as a vote-getting machine; it has a special responsibility in its legislative function to ensure the continued well-being of our democratic system.

. . . My concern is with the legislative function of the extra-parliamentary party, and the degree of participation in the decision-making processes accorded the host of Canadians who identify themselves as party activists; for the degree to which they are involved will reflect the viability of the party as an ongoing institution.

The term "participatory democracy," coined long before Mr. Trudeau made his debut on the political stage, has lost some of its impact through over-usage. But this does not diminish the importance of the concept. Conferences such as this one, and similar conferences being held later this year by the New Democratic and Liberal parties, provide unique opportunities for the general membership to become involved in the discussion and formulation of policy. But one is still prone to question the degree to which such conferences represent the varied interests of the party. Policy conferences should be organized not only at the national, but at regional and constituency levels; and they should bring together not just the elite but the so-called "rank and file."

The extra-parliamentary membership must be involved in the discussion and formulation of policy, not only because it will provide them with a raison d'être for existence other than in election periods, but also because it will better equip them to meet their responsibility as political educators. I said earlier that the democratic system imposes on political parties the obligation to inform the electorate of the issues and to propose solutions to domestic and national problems. This would be impossible of realization if the burden were to fall solely on our 264 Members of Parliament. The extra-parliamentary party must shoulder its share of this responsibility.

But this is not possible unless the party officials realistically encourage the development of a communications system which permits the upward as well as the downward flow of information for purposes of decision-making.

The argument can be made that this is not the case at present. Habits of conformity and subservience dominate political gatherings. Dissent, rather than being encouraged as a means of focussing awareness, is equated with disloyalty. The views of the party hierarchy are accepted without question. Authoritarian attitudes inhibit grass roots activity. When was the last time a constituency association spoke out publicly, not as individuals but as a political group, on matters of concern to its community?

And yet, should not the party association be continually aware that as the group responsible for the initial steps in the democratic process, it has a special obligation to take a stand on matters of public concern? Do we fear that public statements, however constructively critical they may be, may result in controversy? We need to remind ourselves that public comment on legislative action or inaction will come, be it from political opponents or the media. Would not governments be equally as well-served if their political associates were as alert as their political opponents in voicing their concern about situations which call for redress, and in pressing for solutions? It is not the charge of creating tensions within the party structure that disturbs me, so much as the fear that by their lack of action within the community political parties will become increasingly irrelevant.

Which leads me to urge that political parties should assume a social function that will facilitate the creation, through involvement and study, of a public consciousness. What I am suggesting is that parties develop a new role at the constituency level as action groups involved in and concerned with all kinds of social issues —poverty, drugs, law reform, housing, penal reform, status of minority groups, etc. . . .

There is a growing danger to political parties that pressure groups, protest movements, student activists, social planning councils, will so establish themselves as agents of social change that parties will have little room to manoeuvre. Many already feel there is so little genuine radicalism inside the party system that anyone wishing to effect change must look elsewhere.

Unless parties adapt to meet the needs of a changing society—unless party associations become more actively involved in the life of the community—unless we recognize that the need is pressing and the time ripe for the role of constituency associations to evolve into something new and uniquely different—then the day may not be far off when the community will question, with some justification, the privilege of small groups, bearing party labels, to foist their choice of candidates on the electorate.

It seems to me that in order to retain this privilege, which is the essence of their being, Canada's political parties must become much more a part of our "aware" society by assuming this whole new function and structure that I have outlined. Change is rendering many practices obsolete, making the need for new functions more obvious. . . .

THE SYSTEM IS OUTMODED — SAYS THE NEW LEFT*

DIMITRIOS ROUSSOPOULOS

Most people in Canada are fed up with "politics"—by which they mean the machinery of political decision-making. At the moment this feeling has no political expression, although anger, despair and frustration expresses itself in many acts of violence.

Our existing political institutions were developed at a time when a far less bureaucratized and centralized society existed. The party system in Canada, for instance, existed before universal suffrage; the parties represented special group interests in existence before the founding of Canada.

Power today is monopolized in immense bureaucracies which have become political institutions by virtue of the role they play in society. The power of the gigantic corporations is informal, to be sure, but there is little doubt that they have drawn off real power from our formal political institutions. Couple this development with the concentration of power at the top of the parliamentary pyramid, and both the legislature and the electorate are reduced to ritual.

This concentration of power, plus the new manipulative methods of conditioning public attitudes and motivation through the mass media, which celebrate the "values" of a society of compulsive consumption, raise in our minds a questioning of the value of the electoral and parliamentary system of representative democracy.

The issues that divided the political parties in this country are artificial—questions of *management* rather than *basic policy*. The important questions of the day —the growth of liberal totalitarianism, the wasteland between people and government, the lack of quality in our lives and the purposelessness of our society,

* From the *Toronto Daily Star*, April 6, 1970. By permission of the publisher.

racialism, the arms race, Viet Nam and so on—are not usually put before the people.

Politicians and opinion makers exert strenuous efforts to fix our attention on ritual, in this case the casting of the vote. Voting, as a result, becomes an isolated, magical act set apart from the rest of life, and ceases to have any political or social meaning except as an instrument by which the status quo is conserved. Electoral pageantry serves the purpose of a circus—the beguilement of the populace. The voter is reduced to voting for dazzling smiles, clean teeth, smooth voices and firm handshakes.

If we could vote for those who really control the country—for example the directors of the Royal Bank of Canada, the governors of universities, social welfare agencies, industrial corporations and the shadows behind the ministries—then the trappings of liberal democracy would soon become transparent. The real power centres lie far beyond the people's influence at elections. They remain constant *whatever* party is "in power." So the only possible argument for participating in electoral politics, for voting during federal or provincial elections, is that marginal benefits may be gained.

This is obviously a serious conclusion to reach and to recommend—or at least to sanction—for it implies that the political parties, without exception, cannot operate within the province of deep political concern. This is not to say that "it makes no difference" who wins an election; it is rather to say that the "difference" is so slight or lies in such relatively trivial areas that one might very well bypass the area of electoral politics as being irrelevant to any fresh and profound issue of political circumstance.

To the New Left the elaborate procedures and structures of "representative" or parliamentary democracy (which is only one form), born in the 19th century and embroidered on since, stand as ossified caricatures. We live in a society where the majority of people passively consent to things being done in their name, a society of managed politics. The techniques of consultation are polished, but they remain techniques and should not be confused by anyone with participation.

Herbert Marcuse reformulated the libertarian insight that in our type of society any conventional opposition group inevitably assumes the values of the system it opposes and is eventually absorbed by it. In Canada as elsewhere this is the fate of socialists and social democrats.

The object of Canada's power elite and its supporting institutions is clear: It is to muffle real conflict; to dissolve it into a false political consensus; to build, not a participatory democracy where people have power to control a community of meaningful life and work, but a bogus conviviality between every social group. Consensus politics, essential to modern capitalism, is manipulative politics, the politics of man-management, and it is deeply undemocratic. Governments are still elected to be sure, MPs assert the supremacy of the House of Commons, but the real business of government is the management of consensus between the powerful and organized elites.

Consensus politics is intended for any large-scale structural change. It is the politics of pragmatism, of the successful manoeuvre within existing limits. Every administrative act is a kind of clever exercise in political public relations. Whether the manoeuvres are made by a Conservative, Liberal or New Democrat hardly matters, since they all accept the constraints of the *status quo.*

The product of this system is an increasing rationalization of the existing sources of power. The banks, corporations, the federations of industrialists, trade union movement are all given a new and more formal role in the political structure. And to the extent that the "public interest" is defined as including these interests it also excludes what, on the other side, are called "sectional" or "local" interests—namely those of the poor, the low-paid and unorganized workers, youth in general and the backward regions. . . .

What we face is not simply a question of programs and ideologies; what we face primarily is a question of institutions. Certain institutions in our society will simply no longer yield fundamental social and political change.

Many people, along with the New Left, are concerned with such issues as: The boredom and conformity of life in the midst of a society of cybernetics; the human need for *creative* work; the continued existence of raw, naked exploitation at the work-place and at home; the power of the state over society, of centralized political entities over community, of the older generation over the younger, of bureaucracy over the individual, of parental authoritarianism over youthful spontaneity, of sexual, racial, cultural and imperialist privilege over the unfettered development of human personality.

At the same time, many of us believe that we have a qualitatively new order of possibilities—the possibility of a decolonialized Canada, of a free, non-repressive, decentralized society based on face-to-face democracy, community, spontaneity, and a new sense of human solidarity. This we believe amidst a technology so advanced that the burden of toil and material necessity could be removed from the shoulders of our people.

In the face of this kind of *revolutionary* change, electoral politics are meaningless, for elections are not won on these grounds; they are won amid tried formulas, old slogans and self-fulfilling prophecies. They are won by proposing changes of degree, not of kind; by working for adjustment not transformation.

So the New Left in this country, as in other industrial-technological societies, has concluded that there is no alternative but to withdraw our allegiance from the machines of electoralism, from the institutions of "representative" democracy, to forgo the magic rite of voting and to create instead an extra-parliamentary opposition.

The idea is to build a coalition of individuals and groups with a common critique of liberal democracy. The coalition will range from radicals to revolutionaries— from those who believe it still useful to support candidates who while campaigning will also criticize the inadequacies of the system of representation, to those who seek to encourage the development of new constituencies of the self-organized powerless, of producers who control what they produce, of people who control their environment and neighborhood *directly*. New forms of freedom need to be experimented with—workers' control, participatory democracy (which means control, not consultation), direct democracy—in a period where technology is laying the basis for a decentralized post-scarcity society. . . .

An extra-parliamentary opposition is primarily an act of negation. To paraphrase the philosopher Kolakowski, it is a wish to change existing reality. "But negation is not the opposite of construction—it is only the opposite of affirming existing conditions."

CANADIAN CONSERVATISM NOW*

W. L. MORTON

One of the first principles of a conservative is respect for authority; not for authority merely as the right to command, but for authority as the expression of that law and order, and that civil decency, without which society dissolves in anarchy.

And the next first principle is a similar respect for tradition, for that which is handed down from the experience of the race, or the wisdom of our ancestors. . . . The conservative subscribes, in short, to Burke's definition of the social contract as a partnership in all virtue, a partnership between the generations, a contract not made once for all time, but one perennially renewed in the organic processes of society, the birth, growth, and death of successive generations.

Authority and tradition, then, are cornerstones of conservative belief. And the quarry from which they are dug is a particular belief about the nature of man. To the theologian this is the belief in original sin, the belief that man is by his nature imperfect and may be made perfect only by redemption and grace. In philosophic terms, it is a denial of the fundamental liberal and Marxist belief that human nature is inherently perfectible, and that man may realize the perfection that is in him if only the right environment is created. And, I need not tell you, this belief in human fallibility, or the opposite belief in human perfectibility, are what unmistakably and for all time separate the conservative from the liberal. . . .

It is because he knows that the individual man is weak, imperfect and limited, that the conservative believes that men need to be sustained by authority and guided by tradition, the formulated experience of society.

This human need of fellowship . . . gives rise to another fundamental conservative principle; that is, loyalty. . . . [The Conservative] gives loyalty not to institutions or abstractions, but to persons, not to the Crown but to Queen Elizabeth, not to the Conservative party but to John Diefenbaker. . . .

* From *Conservative Concepts,* Vol. I, Vancouver, University of British Columbia, 1959. By permission of the author.

Finally, the conservative holds firmly to the need for continuity in human affairs. He does so because he believes in what Coleridge calls the principle of Permanence in society. Today's conservative, however, believes in Permanence while recognizing the fact of change in human affairs. But changes should come, he firmly believes, by way of organic growth, not by deliberate revolution or skilful manipulation. . . . He lives for the simple, organic things: children, dogs, the elm on the skyline, the water lapping at the rock. He is interested in family; he instinctively wants to know who your people were and where you come from. He sees society as persons knit by kinship and neighbourhood. And he endows society and nation with the same sense of organic life and believes that men in their particular communities are members one of another.

That is how I define the conservative.

If that definition will serve to hint at the main characteristics of conservatism, I should now like to ask what are the particular qualities of Canadian conservatism? I raise the question, not because I profess to be able really to answer it, but only because I think it important to raise it. . . ,

It is important to realize that Canadian conservatism is of more than English origin, important though that is, and that it is a blend of so many strains of conservatism that it possesses a distinct national character. . . .

There is first of all the French Catholic tradition, that of the old *bleus* which at the touch of ultramontanism became the ultra-nationalist creed of the *castors*. Not only are there profoundly conservative qualities in Roman Catholicism itself . . . [but] in Quebec this strain of conservative thought worked itself out, superficially not so much an anti-democratic movement as a cultural isolationist one. For Quebec, majority rule has meant English rule. Perhaps its chief manifestation today is M. Duplessis' opposition to centralization. . . .

The next strain of Canadian conservatism was that of the Loyalists. . . . The Loyalists of the American colonies refused to see the king struck from the constitution, to be replaced by an elected democrat; they refused to see the legislature devour the executive and override the courts; they refused, in Chief Justice William Smith's famous phrase, to see "all America abandoned to democracy." . . .

The third strain of Canadian conservatism is that drawn from what Keith Feiling calls the Second Tory party. . . . The constitution of checks and balances of the glorious Revolution is merely an elaboration of the Tudor-Tory ideal of Clarendon, which was the basis of the Restoration. . . .

Canadian conservatism, derived from these many strains, took its Canadian form, of course, in the struggle for responsible government. . . . From this period emerged the Liberal Conservatism of John A. Macdonald, a conservatism inspired through Elgin by the Peelites of the Pittite tradition. It was a conservatism which through responsible government had come to terms with democracy in Canada, and was prepared to move with the times when the need for change was proven. Since that time, if I am not mistaken, the essential character of Canadian conservatism has not changed. It has remained traditional and constitutional, progressive and pragmatic. It has concerned itself with sound administration of existing laws rather than the forming of new laws, and with economic development rather than with political reform.

If the principles of Canadian conservatism have not substantially changed in the last century, what role is there for these principles in mid-twentieth century? . . .

What then is a conservative philosophy for our times and circumstances? . . . That philosophy, as Russell Kirk reminds us in the new American conservative review *Modern Age*, must rest on absolute values, the established norms of our western tradition, both secular and Christian. The relativism of the liberal thinkers of our times must be shunned for the moral infection it is.

It must remember that such values do not practically exist outside of or beyond persons. It follows, therefore, that people are themselves of absolute value; they are never means to any end whatever; they are, themselves, as they exist, the test of justice, of the good life, and all social and economic values.

But as persons they never exist in isolation. Man, said Aristotle, is a political animal, a being who lives in a *polis,* a social order. Men are always members of some group. The conservative philosophy will always cherish all human association —the family, the church, the municipality, the province, the nation.

Because that philosophy has persons as its test of values, it will be mindful of their unfailing weaknesses, their proneness to error, to crime and to sin. But it will also be mindful of how, by the authority of tested institutions, the educative force of tradition and the mutual support of loyalty, men can be made better than they naturally are, more wise, more brave, more gracious.

It will insist, finally, following the lead of those restorers of learning, Hilda Neatby in this country and Allan Bestor in the United States, that among men as endowed by nature there can be no equality if there is to be liberty for men to realize what is in them. But a conservative philosophy will rest assured that there can be justice. Justice is that each should have his own and that each should be what it is in him to be. It will also never doubt that there can be something now almost forgotten, a sense of honour. This men can possess only when they know what they stand for and what is expected of them. This is possible only in a society which recognizes merit, which makes duties the preface to rights, and rights a trust to be discharged, not an opportunity to be exploited.

Such a philosophy would also honour intelligence. . . .

Finally, that philosophy will stress the need for continuity of development, and for time to mature, to test and to adapt, whether it be ideas or hospitalization schemes.

A sound philosophy should always admit of being reduced to a practical program. Can such a program, applicable to present circumstances in Canada, be deduced from the above attempt to sketch a conservative philosophy for our time? I believe so, and here is my statement of it:

1. The frank and loyal acceptance of the welfare state, in order to keep it one humanely administered for people, for people who matter as people. For the welfare state is not in any conflict with conservative principles, of which *laissez faire* and rugged individualism are no part.

2. The reflective development of social and financial policies which will strengthen the family, preserve our local institutions and enable the provinces to discharge their functions under the constitution.

3. The restoration of the balance of the constitution by assuring the continued impartiality and independence of the Queen's representative; by strengthening the Senate through appointment of some Senators by the provinces, with a suspensive veto by the Senate on legislation of the Commons; by dropping reference to the dangerous and improper idea of the electoral mandate; by recreating the tradition of ministerial and parliamentary independence and by these changes reducing the now extravagant power of the office of prime minister.

4. The improvement of government by setting administration above legislation; by re-capturing the spirit of the rule by law; by the institution of appeals to the courts in all cases from the decisions of administrative boards; by replacing the onus of proof on the Crown in all criminal trials.

5. The maintenance in foreign policy of the national interest by all possible forms of international association, the Commonwealth, the United Nations, and in special but limited undertakings with the United States, in order that by organic relationships national independence and international obligation may be reconciled and made mutually supporting.

6. The massive support of the able in education and of research in all fields of knowledge.

7. The re-valuation of democracy, by a dignified ceremony uniform for all conferrings of citizenship; by the forfeiture of the franchise for repeated non-use; by the encouragement of people of first rate ability and genuine distinction to seek public office by election or to accept it by appointment.

8. The cultivation of our traditions by systematic encouragement and public patronage of the arts, letters and history.

9. The creation of a Canadian system of honours that merit may be recognized and distinction acknowledged without the present recourse to the farce of the Q.C. or to the overworked honorary doctorate. . . .

Conservatism is the only alternative to Communism. Liberalism, if anything, has by its encouragement of class war in unrestrained competition prepared the way for it. Socialism at best inoculates against it. Only conservatism can fight it philosophically, for only conservatism, as a political creed, denies the basic postulates of Communism, its materialism and its utopianism, and points to a way of life in which the material is infused with the ideal, and the ideal with the human and the possible. . . .

LIBERALISM*

LESTER B. PEARSON

. . . The Liberal Party is the party of reform, of progress, of new ideas. The Conservative Party, by its very name, stresses conservation and caution. . . .

What, then, are the principles that have inspired and guided the Liberal Party in its service to the Canadian people? The fundamental principle of Liberalism, the foundation of its faith, is belief in the dignity and worth of the individual. The state is the creation of man, to protect and serve him; and not the reverse.

Liberalism, therefore, believes in man; and that it is the first purpose of government to legislate for the liberation and development of human personality. This includes the negative requirement of removing anything that stands in the way of individual and collective progress.

The negative requirement is important. It involves removal and reform: clearing away and opening up, so that man can move forward and societies expand. The removal of restrictions that block the access to achievement: this is the very essence of Liberalism.

The Liberal Party, however, must also promote the positive purpose of ensuring that all citizens, without any discrimination, will be in a position to take advantage of the opportunities opened up; of the freedoms that have been won. . . . Liberalism is the political principle that gives purpose and reality to this kind of progress.

Liberalism stands for the middle way: the way of progress. It stands for moderation, tolerance, and the rejection of extreme courses, whether they express themselves in demands that the state should do everything for the individual, even if it means weakening and destroying him in the process, or in demands that the state should do nothing except hold the ring so that the fittest survive under the law of the jungle.

In other words, Liberalism accepts social security but rejects socialism; it accepts free enterprise but rejects economic anarchy; it accepts humanitarianism but rejects paternalism.

The Liberal Party is opposed to the shackling limitations of rigid political dogma, or authoritarianism of any kind, which is so often the prelude to oppression and exploitation. It fights against the abuse of power either by the state or by persons or groups within the state. . . .

Liberalism, also, while insisting on equality of opportunity, rejects any imposed equality which would discourage and destroy a man's initiative and enterprise. It sees no value in the equality, or conformity, which comes from lopping off the tallest ears of corn. It maintains, therefore, that originality and initiative should be encouraged, and that reward should be the result of effort. . . .

* From Introduction to J. W. Pickersgill, *The Liberal Party*, Toronto, McClelland and Stewart, 1962. By permission of the author and publisher.

But how can freedom ... be made meaningful in the face of today's industrial and economic pressures? Government must keep pace with the changing needs of the times and accept greater responsibilities than would have been acceptable to a Liberal a hundred years ago. That is why the Liberal Party favours social and economic planning which will stimulate and encourage private enterprise to operate more effectively for the benefit of all.

Liberalism must always remember that responsibility is the other side of freedom. . . .

In short, freedom and welfare must be kept in a healthy balance or there will be trouble. This essential balance can be achieved by applying to every proposal for further intervention by the state the question: will it truly benefit the individual; will it enlarge or restrict his opportunity for self-expression and development?

The Liberal purpose remains the creation of opportunity for men and women to become self-directing, responsible citizens. This means, as we have seen, the simultaneous pursuit of freedom and welfare. . . .

For the progress Canada has made, and will make, national unity has been essential. The necessity for doing everything possible to maintain and strengthen this unity has been the cornerstone of Liberal policy from the very beginning of its history. Moreover, Liberalism has understood that national unity must be based on two races, cultures, traditions, and languages; on a full and equal partnership of English- and French-speaking Canadians. . . .

Canada is a federal state in which the constitutional and historic rights of the provinces must be preserved. It is important also that the provinces must not be separated by economic inequality which would make national unity difficult, it not impossible. The Liberal Party, therefore, considers it a duty of the federal government to help equalize the distribution of income and wealth and development among the provinces. . . .

A SOCIALIST TAKES STOCK*

DAVID LEWIS

. . . What are the ends which socialism seeks to achieve? They are, broadly, the following:

(1) A classless or egalitarian society within the borders of a nation. Socialists have proclaimed as their goal a society from which exploitation of man by man and of class by class or of group by group will be eliminated; where every person will have an equal opportunity to share in a rich and varied life and to develop his

* From a pamphlet of this title published by the Ontario Woodsworth Memorial Foundation, Toronto, 1956. By permission of the author and publisher.

talents, whatever they may be, to the full, both at work and during leisure hours. This—the classless society based on equality—is the major aim of democratic socialism.

(2) Equality among all nations, regardless of colour, race, or economic standard. We strive for a world based on the brotherhood of man from which the practices of imperialism and the ignominy of colonialism will disappear; a world in which the more advanced economic societies will assist the less developed ones without the price in human exploitation which has characterized overseas expansion in the last centuries. We want a classless world society based on universal brotherhood.

(3) Human freedom everywhere. The socialist dream is of a society in which the worth and dignity of every human being is recognized and respected, where differences of origin, of religion and of opinion will not only be tolerated, but accepted as desirable and necessary to the beauty and richness of the human mosaic.

(4) Economic and social security. Socialists seek not only equality of opportunity but a constant advance in the opportunities offered and available to mankind; not only a fair division of the cake, but a constantly larger cake. Socialists long ago recognized that modern technological advance has made possible, and will increasingly make possible, an economic standard of living from which material suffering, economic want and the oppression of insecurity can disappear. We know, of course, that meeting the economic needs of mankind will not by itself create the life for which the human spirit strives. But we also know that if we can break the prison walls built by economic pressures and insecurities, the human spirit will be released and our moral and cultural values enriched by new and greater opportunities.

(5) A lasting peace based on freedom and equality within nations and freedom and equality among nations. This end is today shared by all men of goodwill the world over, but socialists have always been among the leaders searching for peace. . . .

Let me say immediately that I am well aware that some of these aims are shared by democratic non-socialists. . . . However, some of the aims which I have described are held by socialists only and all of them together form the fabric of democratic socialist philosophy and do not form the fabric of any other political philosophy.

People who support the capitalist society as a desirable social system believe in a class society and not in a classless one; they believe in inequality and not in equality; they believe in the right of one nation to make profits at the expense of another, just as they believe in the right of one group within a nation to make profits at the expense of the rest; they believe in the right of the sons and daughters of the rich to have greater opportunities than those of the poor; and even as regards freedom they place the rights of property above those of human beings or, at least, on an equal footing. All these concepts the socialist passionately rejects.

At the other extreme, those who believe in the communist society reject in practice all of the aims of socialism, despite their deceitful words and slogans. In every communist land there has been established a new, but no less evil class society. The elite of the communist party, the membership of that party, the civil service in government as well as in the party, the secret police, and the army, form a class or classes which are the top of a social pyramid as clearly defined as the pyramid of wealth to which we are accustomed and, if anything, much more oppressive and evil in its consequences. It is unnecessary to remind you that the communist state stifles freedom and enthrones uniformity and conformity as the absolute duty of every citizen. Domination by the chief communist state over other nations and states, rather than equality among nations, has been the communist practice. . . .

•   •   •

What means has the socialist proposed for building the road to this [socialist] society? Briefly, they are, I think, the following:

(1) We must emphasize, first, the determination of the socialist to pursue at all times only democratic procedures and to base his actions on the consent of the people freely expressed. To use any form of dictatorship to achieve so-called desirable ends is a perversion of our basic ideas of freedom and will in practice also pervert the ends. . . .

(2) A constant and continuing improvement in the existing standards of living and in the social services provided by the state. . . .

(3) The third means which the socialist has proposed, and when he has had the chance, has used, is that of social planning. The socialist rejects the capitalist theory that an unregulated law of supply and demand should control the destinies of a society and its members. He believes that it is both necessary and possible for society collectively to plan at least its economic future and to regulate the production and distribution of goods and services so as to achieve an expanding economy of full employment and fair share for all members of society. . . .

(4) The fourth means which the socialist has proposed is that of public owner-ship, whether it be ownership by the state—federal, provincial or municipal—or ownership by a collectivity of citizens in the form of co-operatives, credit unions or the like. There are three main reasons behind the socialist belief in public ownership.

First and foremost, that the modern concentration of wealth and property places too much power, both economic and political, in the hands of too few people or, what is even worse, in the hands of giant corporations which, by their very nature, are without heart and without soul. . . .

Secondly, nationalization has been proposed by socialists because the job of social planning is made more difficult by the power of private corporations and would be made much easier by public ownership of the key levers in the economy.

Thirdly, the growth and power of private corporations have imposed on society a standard of values which perverts the best ideals of man. . . .

•   •   •

Among democratic socialists there is, and always has been, agreement about the ends. On the other hand, there is, always has been and probably always will be, disagreement about the means. . . .

Perhaps first among socialist controversies is the question of the extent to which the tool of public ownership can or should be used by socialists in modern society. . . .

Until fairly recently it had been accepted by most socialists as axiomatic that nationalization of industry would automatically bring with it greater social and political freedom and a release from the obstacles to the widest liberty which private economic power produces. . . .

The developments in the Soviet Union, in particular, and in other communist states as well, have completely shattered these assumptions and have shown them to have been and to be entirely false. In the communist societies all wealth, or almost all wealth, has been taken over by the state. But, instead of greater freedom, there is actually no freedom at all. . . .

Similarly, we have learned from the actions of the Soviet Union . . . that there are pressures toward aggression and war other than economic ones and that the lust for power and the zeal of fanaticism are at least as powerful forces endangering peace as economic competition and conflicts. . . .

Socialists can, therefore, no longer regard nationalization as an automatic panacea for all ills, but must regard it merely as one tool that is available in appropriate circumstances for the furtherance of socialist ends.

The experience of the Scandinavian countries, the history of the Roosevelt era in the United States and developments during the last war, have all shown that there are available in the modern economy tools of control and of planning which can be effectively applied without actually replacing private with public ownership in all spheres. . . . The use of fiscal and financial policies to influence the volume and direction of investments, to redistribute income, and to stimulate purchasing power, has been demonstrated as a practical tool for economic planning, at least in periods when there is no major depression. . . .

In all modern societies there is growing up a considerable body of social welfare legislation which produces what are known as "transfer payments". These—unemployment insurance benefits, old age pensions, family allowances, farm support payments and the like—provide a constant stream of purchasing power into the hands of large sections of the people. . . .

•   •   •

THE N.D.P. "WAFFLE" MANIFESTO: FOR AN INDEPENDENT SOCIALIST CANADA*

Our aim as democratic socialists is to build an independent socialist Canada. Our aim as supporters of the New Democratic Party is to make it a truly socialist party.

The achievement of socialism awaits the building of a mass base of socialists, in factories and offices, on farms and campuses. The development of socialist consciousness, on which can be built a socialist base, must be the first priority of the New Democratic Party.

The New Democratic Party must be seen as the parliamentary wing of a movement dedicated to fundamental social change. It must be radicalized from within and it must be radicalized from without.

The most urgent issue for Canadians is the very survival of Canada. Anxiety is pervasive and the goal of greater economic independence receives widespread support. But economic independence without socialism is a sham, and neither are meaningful without true participatory democracy.

The major threat to Canadian survival today is American control of the Canadian economy. The major issue of our times is not national unity but national survival, and the fundamental threat is external, not internal.

American corporate capitalism is the dominant factor shaping Canadian society. In Canada, American economic control operates through the formidable medium of the multinational corporation. The Canadian corporate elite has opted for a junior partnership with these American enterprises. Canada has been reduced to a resource base and consumer market within the American empire.

The American empire is the central reality for Canadians. It is an empire characterized by militarism abroad and racism at home. Canadian resources and diplomacy have been enlisted in the support of that empire.

In the barbarous war in Vietnam, Canada has supported the United States through its membership on the International Control Commission and through sales of arms and strategic resources to the American military-industrial complex.

The American empire is held together through world-wide military alliances and by giant monopoly corporations. Canada's membership in the American alliance system and the ownership of the Canadian economy by American corporations precludes Canada's playing an independent role in the world. These bonds must be cut if corporate capitalism, and the social priorities it creates, are to be effectively challenged.

Canadian development is distorted by a corporate capitalist economy. Corporate investment creates and fosters superfluous individual consumption at the expense

* Resolution No. 133 submitted to the Fifth Federal Convention of the New Democratic Party held in Winnipeg from October 28-31, 1969. The Resolution was submitted by the New Democratic Youth Federal Council and several N.D.P. constituency organizations, but has been known popularly as the Watkins' or "Waffle" Manifesto.

of social needs. Corporate decision-making concentrates investment in a few major urban areas which become increasingly uninhabitable while the rest of the country sinks into underdevelopment.

The criterion that the most profitable pursuits are the most important ones causes the neglect of activities whose value cannot be measured by the standard of profitability. It is not accidental that housing, education, medical care and public transportation are inadequately provided for by the present social system.

The problem of regional disparities is rooted in the profit orientation of capitalism. The social costs of stagnant areas are irrelevant to the corporations.

For Canada the problem is compounded by the reduction of Canada to the position of an economic colony of the United States. The foreign capitalist has even less concern for balanced development of the country than the Canadian capitalist with roots in a particular region.

An independence movement based on substituting Canadian capitalists for American capitalists, or on public policy to make foreign corporations behave as if they were Canadian corporations, cannot be our final objective.

There is not now an independent Canadian capitalism and any lingering pretensions on the part of Canadian businessmen to independence, lack credibility.

Without a strong national capitalist class behind them, Canadian governments, Liberal and Conservative, have functioned in the interests of inter-national and particularly American capitalism, and have lacked the will to pursue even a modest strategy of economic independence.

Capitalism must be replaced by socialism, by national planning of investment and by the public ownership of the means of production in the interests of the Canadian people as a whole.

Canadian nationalism is a relevant force on which to build to the extent that it is anti-imperialist. On the road to socialism, such aspirations for independence must be taken into account. For to pursue independence seriously is to make visible the necessity of socialism in Canada.

Those who desire socialism and independence for Canada have often been baffled and mystified by the problem of internal divisions within Canada.

While the essential fact of Canadian history in the past century is the reduction of Canada to a colony of the United States, with a consequent increase in regional inequalities, there is no denying the existence of two nations within Canada, each with its own language, culture and aspirations. This reality must be incorporated into the strategy of the New Democratic Party.

English Canada and Quebec can share common institutions to the extent that they share common purposes. So long as Canada is governed by those who believe that national policy should be limited to the passive functions of maintaining a peaceful and secure climate for foreign investors, there can be no meaningful unity between English and French Canadians.

So long as the federal government refuses to protect the country from American economic and cultural domination, English Canada is bound to appear to French Canadians simply as part of the United States.

An English Canada concerned with its own national survival would create common aspirations that would help to tie the two nations together once more.

Nor can the present treatment of the constitutional issue in isolation from economic and social forces that transcend the two nations be anything but irrelevant.

Our present constitution was drafted a century ago by politicans committed to the values and structure of a capitalist society. Constitutional change relevant to socialists must be based on the needs of the people rather than the corporations and must reflect the power of classes and groups excluded from effective decision-making by the present system.

A united Canada is of critical importance in pursuing a successful strategy against the reality of American imperialism. Quebec's history and aspirations must be allowed full expression and implementation in the conviction that new ties will emerge from the common perception of "two nations, one struggle."

Socialists in English Canada must ally themselves with socialists in Quebec in this common cause.

Central to the creation of an independent socialist Canada is the strength and tradition of the Canadian working class and the trade union movement. The revitalization and extension of the labor movement would involve a fundamental democratization of our society.

Corporate capitalism is characterized by the predominant power of the corporate elite aided and abetted by the political elite. A central objective of Canadian socialists must be to further the democratization process in industry.

The Canadian trade union movement throughout its history has waged a democratic battle against the so-called rights or prerogatives of ownership and management. It has achieved the important moral and legal victory of providing for working men an effective say in what their wages will be.

At present management's "right" to control technological change is being challenged. The New Democratic Party must provide leadership in the struggle to extend working men's influence into every area of industrial decision-making.

Those who work must have effective control in the determination of working conditions, and substantial power in determining the nature of the product, prices and so on. Democracy and socialism require nothing less.

Trade unionists and New Democrats have led in extending the welfare state in Canada. Much remains to be done: more and better housing, a really progressive tax structure, a guaranteed annual income.

But these are no longer enough. A socialist society must be one in which there is democratic control of all institutions which have a major effect on men's lives and where there is equal opportunity for creative non-exploitive self-development. It is now time to go beyond the welfare state.

New Democrats must begin now to insist on the redistribution of power, and not simply welfare, in a socialist direction. The struggle for worker participation in industrial decision-making and against management "rights" is such a move toward economic and social democracy.

By strengthening the Canadian labor movement, New Democrats will further the pursuit of Canadian independence.

So long as Canadian economic activity is dominated by the corporate elite, and so long as workers' rights are confined within their present limits, corporate requirements for profit will continue to take precedence over human needs.

By bringing men together primarily as buyers and sellers of each other, by enshrining profitability and material gain in place of humanity and spiritual growth, capitalism has always been inherently alienating. Today, sheer size combined with modern technology further exaggerates man's sense of insignificance and impotence. A socialist transformation of society will return to man his sense of humanity, to replace his sense of being a commodity. But a socialist democracy implies man's control of his immediate environment as well, and in any strategy for building socialism, community democracy is as vital as the struggle for electoral success. To that end, socialists must strive for democracy at those levels which most directly affect us all—in our neighborhoods, our schools, our places of work. Tenants' unions, consumers' and producers' cooperatives are examples of areas in which socialists must lead in efforts to involve people directly in the struggle to control their own destinies.

Socialism is a process and a program. The process is the raising of socialist consciousness, the building of a mass base of socialists, and a strategy to make visible the limits of liberal capitalism.

While the program must evolve out of the process, its leading features seem clear. Relevant instruments for bringing the Canadian economy under Canadian ownership and control and for altering the priorities established by corporate capitalism are to hand.

They include extensive public control over investment and nationalization of the commanding heights of the economy, such as the key resource industries, finance and credit, and industries strategic to planning our economy.

Within that program, workers' participation in all institutions promises to release creative energies, promote decentralization, and restore human and social priorities.

The struggle to build a democratic socialist Canada must proceed at all levels of Canadian society. The New Democratic Party is the organization suited to bringing these activities into a common focus.

The New Democratic Party has grown out of a movement for democratic socialism that has deep roots in Canadian history. It is the core around which should be mobilized the social and political movement necessary for building an independent socialist Canada.

The New Democratic Party must rise to that challenge or become irrelevant. Victory lies in joining the struggle.

THE DEPUTY LEADER REPLIES*

DAVID LEWIS

Foreign control of our economy has resulted in an inefficient and inadequate industrial structure in our country. It has resulted in an erosion of our political independence and it threatens the very survival of Canada as a national entity.

However, to speak of this as being an instance of American imperialism, as the Watkins Manifesto seems to do, is a fallacy.

The fact is that the industrial and corporate powers in Canada, as well as Federal and Provincial governments, have invited large-scale American investment.

The fact is that Canada is the only country in the Western world which permits foreign investment without rules, without limit and without consideration of the long-run consequences.

It is in this context that anti-Americanism on the question of foreign ownership makes no sense.

In my opinion, the time has come for inspiring appeal to Canadians to stand guard over their own destiny. And when we make this appeal, we must lay blame for our present situation where it belongs, on Canadian authorities and Canadian political and corporate leadership.

The great tragedy of the post-war period is that the future of mankind is in the hands of the military-industrial complex in Washington and the Communist-military complex in Moscow, pursuing ends which every democratic socialist passionately rejects.

But to speak of American imperialism without, at the same time, recognizing the dangers in the ruthless application of Soviet imperialism, is to miss an essential fact of present day history and to mislead the Canadian people.

And to rant against racism in the United States as if we don't have any in Canada and in many other parts of the world, is a form of very questionable self-righteousness.

Another point important to Canadian survival is internal unity.

The so-called Watkins Manifesto talks of the English-French relationship in Canada in a way which is totally unacceptable to me, as one New Democrat. I am deeply convinced that our party will do a great disservice to the Canadian people, both English and French speaking, if it lends any weight to the notion of two Canadas or to the idea that a possible division of our country is acceptable.

We must continue to search for dynamic policies that will give French Canada the fullest opportunities for cultural growth and enrichment everywhere in the country but as part of one united Canada.

* From a speech by David Lewis, M.P., Deputy Leader of the Federal N.D.P., to the Fifth Federal Convention of the party, Winnipeg, October 30, 1969. By permission of the author.

It is our conviction that Canada's position is the result of the corporate values which have controlled our national development in the past century. Liberal and Conservative parties have always been continentalist. Since they have accepted the values of our present society, they naturally welcome foreign investment and control as the easiest way to make a fast buck and to increase material growth.

It is therefore clear that only the NDP is genuinely worried about the future of Canada as an independent nation. And it is also clear that only a democratic socialist party can do anything effective to overcome the threat of foreign ownership.

Only a party which seeks to build a new society in Canada, with new cultural and social values and a new relationship between individual citizen and state, is prepared to challenge corporate power, whether foreign or Canadian. And it is a determined challenge to private corporate power which is essential for building a basis for a genuinely independent Canada.

In my view, it is a form of short-sighted thinking for a socialist to aim his shafts only against foreign-owned corporations.

Many years ago, our party rejected the idea that public ownership is a panacea for all ills. History of the past five decades has shown that you can have full public ownership accompanied by ruthless dictatorship of more than one stripe. This, we do not want for Canada.

Our knowledge of the economy has progressed and there are many more tools available in addition to public ownership. The NDP has proposed the use of all these tools: investment control, fiscal and monetary controls, social planning, the expansion of social capital and ever-increasing public investment to eliminate regional disparities and to improve quality of life in our cities.

We have proposed a Canada Development Fund or Corporation, publicly owned and controlled, to enable large public investment and thus bring effective Canadian control of our economy. This is the sensible road to Canadian independence.

True radicalism does not consist in old-fashioned, fundamentalist rhetoric; it consists in using modern socialist methods to find modern socialist solutions to modern capitalist problems.

BIBLIOGRAPHY

Parties and Politics

Adams, Ian, *The Poverty Wall*, Toronto, McClelland and Stewart, 1970.

Badgley, R. F., Wolfe, S., *Doctors' Strike: Medical Care and Conflict in Saskatchewan*, Toronto, Macmillan, 1967.

Beeching, W. C., and Lazarus, M., "Le socialisme en Saskatchewan—trop ou trop peu," *Socialisme 64, Revue du socialisme international et Québecois*, No. 2, automne, 1964.

Buck, T., *Lenin and Canada*, Toronto, Progress Books, 1970.

Canada, *Report of the Committee on Election Expenses*, Ottawa, Queen's Printer, 1966.

Caouette, R., *Réal Caouette vous parle*, Montréal, Les éditions du Caroussel, 1962.

Carrigan, O., *Canadian Party Platforms: 1867-1968*, Toronto, Copp Clark, 1968.

Cherwinski, W. J., "Bibliographical Note: The Left in Canadian History, 1911-1969," *Journal of Canadian Studies*, Vol. IV, No. 4, November, 1969.

Clark, S. D., *Movements of Political Protest in Canada, 1640-1840*, Toronto, University of Toronto Press, 1959.

Coates, R. C., *The Night of the Knives*, Fredericton, Brunswick Press, 1969.

Comeau, P. A., "La transformation du parti libéral Québecois," *C.J.E.P.S.*, Vol. XXXI, No. 3, August, 1965.

Cook, R., (ed.), *Politics of Discontent*, (Essays on Aherhart, Pattulo, H. H. Stevens, George McCullagh), Canadian Historical Readings, Toronto, University of Toronto Press, 1967.

Dawson, R. M., *The Conscription Crisis of 1944*, Toronto, University of Toronto Press, 1961.

Denman, N., *How to Organize an Election*, Montréal, Les éditions du jour, 1962.

Dion, l'Abbé G., et O'Neill, L'Abbé L., *Le chrétien et les élections*, Montréal, Les éditions de l'homme, 8 me éd., 1960.

Dion, l'Abbé G., et O'Neill, L'Abbé L., *Le chrétien en démocratie*, Montréal, Les éditions de l'homme, 1961.

Dion, L., "The Concept of Political Leadership," *C.J.P.S.*, Vol. I, No. 1, March, 1968.

Dion, L., "A la recherche d'une méthode d'analyse des partis et des groupes d'intérêt," *C.J.P.S.*, Vol. II, No. 1, March, 1969.

Dion, L., "Politique consultative et système politique," *C.J.P.S.*, Vol. II, No. 2, June, 1969.

Easton, D., "The Theoretical Relevance of Political Socialization," *C.J.P.S.*, Vol. I, No. 2, June, 1968.

Engelmann, F. C., and Schwartz, M. A., *Political Parties and the Canadian Social Structure*, Toronto, Prentice-Hall, 1967.

Epstein, L., "A Comparative Study of Canadian Parties," *The American Political Science Review*, Vol. LVIII, No. 1, March, 1964.

Epstein, L. D., *Political Parties in Western Democracies*, New York, Praeger, 1967.

Farr, D. M. L., Moir, J. S., Mealing, S. R., *Two Democracies*, Toronto, Ryerson, 1963.

Fox, Paul, "Early Socialism in Canada," in Aitchison, J. H., (ed.), *The Political Process in Canada*, Toronto, University of Toronto Press, 1963.

Godfrey, D., and Watkins, M., (eds.), *Gordon to Watkins to You*, Toronto, New Press, 1970.

Granatstein, J. L., *The Politics of Survival: The Conservative Party of Canada, 1939-1945*, Toronto, University of Toronto Press, 1967.

Greenslade, J. G., (ed.), *Canadian Politics: Speeches by F. M. Watkins, Stanley Knowles, J. R. Mallory and H. D. Hicks*, Sackville, Mount Allison University Publication No. 4, 1959.

Gwyn, R., *The Shape of Scandal, A Study of a Government in Crisis*, Toronto, Clarke, Irwin, 1965.

Harbron, J. D., "The Conservative Party and National Unity," *Q.Q.*, Vol. LXIX, No. 3, Autumn, 1962.

Heasman, D. J., "Political Alignments in Canada: The Fragmentation of Canadian Politics," *Parliamentary Affairs*, Vol. XVI, No. 4, Autumn, 1963 and Vol. XVII, No. 1, Winter, 1963-64.

Heasman, D. J., "Parliamentary Developments, The Politics of Canadian Nationhood," *Parliamentary Affairs*, Vol. XIX, No. 2, Spring, 1966.

Higginbotham, C. H., *Off the Record: The C.C.F. in Saskatchewan*, Toronto, McClelland and Stewart, 1968.

Hogan, G., *The Conservative in Canada*, Toronto, McClelland and Stewart, 1963.

Horowitz, G., "Tories, Socialists and the Demise of Canada," *Canadian Dimension*, Vol. II, No. 4, May-June, 1965.

Horowitz, G., "Conservatism, Liberalism, and Socialism in Canada: an Interpretation," *C.J.E.P.S.*, Vol. XXXII, No. 2, May, 1966.

Horowitz, G., *Canadian Labour in Politics*, Toronto, University of Toronto Press, 1968.

Horowitz, G., "Toward the Democratic Class Struggle," in Lloyd, Trevor and McLeod, Jack, (eds.), *Agenda 1970*, Toronto, University of Toronto Press, 1968.

Hunter, W. D. G., "The New Democratic Party: Antecedents, Policies, Prospects," *Q.Q.*, Vol. LXIX, No. 3, Autumn, 1962.

Irving, J. A., *The Social Credit Movement in Alberta*, Toronto, University of Toronto Press, 1959.

Knowles, S., *The New Party*, Toronto, McClelland and Stewart, 1961.

Kornberg, K., Smith, J., and Bromley, D., "Some Differences in the Political Socialization Patterns of Canadian and American Party Officials: A Preliminary Report," *C.J.P.S.*, Vol. II, No. 1, March, 1969.

Laponce, J. A., "Canadian Party Labels: An Essay in Semantics and Anthropology," *C.J.P.S.*, Vol. II, No. 2, June, 1969.

Lavau, G., "Partis et systèmes politiques: interactions et fonctions," *C.J.P.S.*, Vol. II, No. 1, March, 1969.

Leslie, P. M., "The Role of Political Parties in Promoting the Interests of Ethnic Minorities," *C.J.P.S.*, Vol. II, No. 4, December, 1969.

Lipset, S. M., *Political Man, The Social Bases of Politics*, New York, Doubleday, 1963.

Lipset, S. M., *Agrarian Socialism: The Cooperative Commonwealth Federation in Saskatchewan*, New York, Anchor Books, Doubleday, 1968.

McGuigan, M., and Lloyd, T., *Liberalism and Socialism*, Toronto, Exchange for Political Ideas in Canada, 1964, [pamphlet].

McHenry, D. E., *The Third Force in Canada: The Cooperative Commonwealth Federation, 1932-1948*, Berkeley, University of California Press, 1950.

Macpherson, C. B., *Democracy in Alberta: The Theory and Practice of a Quasi-Party System*, Toronto, University of Toronto Press, 1953.

MacQuarrie, H., *The Conservative Party*, Toronto, McClelland and Stewart, 1965.

Meisel, J., "The June 1962 Election: Break-up of our Party System?" *Q.Q.*, Vol. LXIX, No. 3, Autumn, 1962.

Meisel, J., "The Stalled Omnibus: Canadian Parties in the 1960s," *Social Research*, Vol. XXX, No. 3, Autumn, 1963.

Meisel, J., *L'évolution des partis politiques canadiens*, Cahiers de le Société canadienne de Science politique, no. 2, 1966.

Meisel, J., *Les transformations des partis politiques canadiens*, Cahiers de la Société canadienne de Science politique, no. 2, 1966.

Meisel, J., "Canadian Parties and Politics," in Leach, R. H., *Contemporary Canada*, Toronto, University of Toronto Press, 1968.

Meynaud, J., *Argent et politique*, Montréal, Le centre de documentation et de recherches politique, Collège Jean-de-Brébeuf, 1966.

Morrison, D. R., *The Politics of the Yukon Territory, 1898-1909*, Toronto, University of Toronto Press, 1968.

Morton, D., *With Your Help, An Election Manual*, Ottawa, New Democratic Party, 1966.

Morton, D., "The Effectiveness of Political Campaigning: The N.D.P. in the 1967 Ontario Election," *Journal of Canadian Studies*, Vol. IV, No. 3, August, 1969.

Morton, W. L., *The Progressive Party in Canada*, Toronto, University of Toronto Press, 1950.

Muller, S., "Federalism and the Party System in Canada," in Meekison, J. P., *Canadian Federalism: Myth or Reality*, Toronto, Methuen, 1968.

Neill, R. F., "Social Credit and National Policy in Canada," *Journal of Canadian Studies*, Vol. III, No. 1, February, 1968.

Neumann, S., *Modern Political Parties*, Chicago, University of Chicago Press, 1956.

Newman, P. C., *The Distemper of Our Times, Canadian Politics in Transition: 1963-1968*, Toronto, McClelland and Stewart, 1968.

Nichols, H. E., *Alberta's Fight for Freedom*, [A History of Social Credit] n.p., 1963, 5 vols.

Nicholson, P., *Vision and Indecision: Diefenbaker and Pearson*, Don Mills, Longmans, 1968.

Nixon, Robert, (ed.), *The Guelph Papers*, (Ontario Liberal Party Conference), Toronto, Peter Martin Associates, 1970.

Oliver, M., (ed.), *Social Purpose for Canada*, Toronto, University of Toronto Press, 1961.

Paltiel, K. Z., "Federalism and Party Finance," Address to the 38th Annual Meeting of the Canadian Political Science Association, Sherbrooke, P.Q., June 8, 1966.

Paltiel, K. Z., *Financing Political Parties in Canada*, Toronto, McGraw-Hill, 1970.

Peacock, D., *Journey to Power: The Story of a Canadian Election, (1968)*, Toronto, Ryerson, 1968.

Pickersgill, J. W., *The Liberal Party*, Toronto, McClelland and Stewart, 1962.

Quinn, H. F., "The Role of the Liberal Party in Recent Canadian Politics," *Political Science Quarterly*, Vol. LXVIII, No. 3, September, 1953.

Quinn, H. F., *The Union Nationale: A Study in Quebec Nationalism*, Toronto, University of Toronto Press, 1963.

Regenstreif, P., "Note on the 'Alternation' of French and English Leaders in the Liberal Party of Canada," *C.J.P.S.*, Vol. II, No. 1, March, 1969.

Richardson, B. T., *Canada and Mr. Diefenbaker*, Toronto, McClelland and Stewart, 1962.

Robertson, H., *Reservations Are For Indians*, Toronto, James Lewis & Samuel, 1970.

Robin, M., *Radical Politics and Canadian Labour, 1880-1930*, Kingston, Queen's University, 1968.

Rodney, W., *Soldiers of the International: A History of the Communist Party of Canada, 1919-1929*, Toronto, University of Toronto Press, 1968.

Rose, W., *Social Credit Handbook*, Toronto, McClelland and Stewart, 1968.

Roussopoulus, D., (ed.), *The New Left in Canada*, Montreal, Our Generation Press, 1970.

Scarrow, H. A., "Distinguishing Between Political Parties—The Case of Canada," *Midwest Journal of Political Science*, Vol. IX, No. 1, February, 1965.

Schindeler, F., Lanphier, C. M., "Social Science Research and Participatory Democracy in Canada," *C.P.A.*, Vol. XII, No. 4, Winter, 1969.

Schultz, H. J., "The Social Credit Back-benchers' Revolt, 1937," *Canadian Historical Review*, Vol. XLI, No. 1, March, 1960.

Smiley, D. V., "The Two-Party System and One-Party Dominance in the Liberal Democratic State," *C.J.E.P.S.*, Vol. XXIV, No. 3, August, 1958.

Smiley, D. V., "The National Party Leadership Convention in Canada: A Preliminary Analysis," *C.J.P.S.*, Vol. I, No. 4, December, 1968.

Smith, D. E., "A Comparison of Prairie Political Developments in Saskatchewan and Alberta," *Journal of Canadian Studies*, Vol. IV, No. 1, February, 1969.

Sullivan, M., *Mandate '68, The Year of Pierre Elliott Trudeau*, Toronto, Doubleday, 1968.

Taylor, Charles, *The Pattern of Politics*, Toronto, McClelland and Stewart, 1970.

Thomas, L. G., *The Liberal Party in Alberta: A History of Politics in the Province of Alberta, 1905-1921,* Toronto, University of Toronto Press, 1959.
Thompson, R. N., *Canadians, It's Time You Knew,* n.p., The Aavangen Press, 1961.
Thompson, R. N., *Commonsense for Canadians: A Selection of Speeches,* Toronto, McClelland and Stewart, 1964.
Thorburn, H. G., *Politics in New Brunswick,* Toronto, University of Toronto Press, 1961.
Thorburn, H. G., (ed.), *Party Politics in Canada,* Toronto, Prentice-Hall, 1961.
Tyre, R., *Douglas in Saskatchewan: The Story of a Socialist Experiment,* Vancouver, Michell Press, 1962.
Underhill, F. H., *Canadian Political Parties,* Canadian Historical Association Booklet No. 8, Ottawa, 1957.
Underhill, F. H., "The Revival of Conservatism in North America," *Transactions of the Royal Society of Canada,* Vol. LII, Series III, June, 1958.
Underhill, F. H., *In Search of Canadian Liberalism,* Toronto, Macmillan, 1960.
Vallieres, P., "Le Parti Socialiste du Québec à l'heure de la révolution tranquille," *Cité libre,* Vol. XV, No. 1, janvier, 1964.
Ward, N., and Spafford, D., (eds.), *Politics in Saskatchewan,* Toronto, Longmans, 1968.
Wearing, J., "Party Leadership and the 1966 Conventions," *Journal of Canadian Studies,* Vol. II, No. 1, February, 1967.
Wearing, J., "A Convention for Professionals: The PCs in Toronto," *Journal of Canadian Studies,* Vol. II, No. 4, November, 1967.
Wearing, J., "The Liberal Choice," *Journal of Canadian Studies,* Vol. III, No. 2, May, 1968.
Wearing, J., "The Trudeau Phenomenon," *C.J.P.S.,* Vol. II, No. 3, September, 1969.
Whalen, H., "Social Credit Measures in Alberta," *C.J.E.P.S.,* Vol. XVIII, No. 4, November, 1952.
Williams, J. R., *The Conservative Party in Canada, 1920-1949,* Durham, Duke University Press, 1956.
Winham, G. R., Cunningham, R. B., "Party Leader Images in the 1968 Federal Election," *C.J.P.S.,* Vol. III, No. 1, March, 1970.
Young, W. D., *The Anatomy of a Party: The National C.C.F. 1932-61,* Toronto, University of Toronto Press, 1969.
Young, W. D., *Democracy and Discontent: Progressivism, Socialism, and Social Credit in the Canadian West,* The Frontenac Library, Toronto, Ryerson, 1969.
Zakuta, L., *A Protest Movement Becalmed: A Study of Change in the C.C.F.,* Toronto, University of Toronto Press, 1964.

Political Biographies

Barrette, A., *Mémoires,* Vol. I, Montréal, Librairie Beauchemin, 1966.
Beal, J. R., *The Pearson Phenomena,* Toronto, Longmans, 1964.
Beck, J. M., *Joseph Howe: Voice of Nova Scotia,* Carleton Library, Toronto, McClelland and Stewart, 1964.
Benson, N. A., *None of It Came Easy: The Story of J. G. Gardiner,* Toronto, Burns and MacEachern, 1955.
Borden, H., (ed.), *Robert Laird Borden: His Memoirs,* Toronto, Macmillan, 1938, 2 vols.
Borden, R. L., *His Memoirs,* Carleton Library, Toronto, McClelland and Stewart, 1969, 2 vols.
Bourassa, A., Bergevin, A., and Nish, C., (eds.), *Henri Bourassa, Biography, Bibliographical Index, and Index of Public Correspondence, 1895-1924,* Montreal, les Editions de l'Action Nationale, 1966.

Bourassa, A., (ed.), *Henri Bourassa, Montréal,* les éditions de l'Action Nationale, 1966.
Careless, J. M. S., *Brown of the Globe,* Vol. I, *The Voice of Upper Canada, 1818-1859,* Toronto, Macmillan, 1959; Vol. II, *Statesman of Confederation, 1860-1880,* Toronto, Macmillan, 1963.
Creighton, D., *John A. Macdonald: The Young Politician,* Toronto, Macmillan, 1952; *The Old Chieftain,* Toronto, Macmillan, 1955.
Dafoe, J. W., *Laurier: A Study in Canadian Politics,* Carleton Library, Toronto, McClelland and Stewart, 1963.
Dawson, R. M., *William Lyon Mackenzie King: A Political Biography, 1874-1923,* Vol. I, Toronto, University of Toronto Press, 1958.
Dempson, P., *Assignment Ottawa,* Don Mills, General Publishing, 1968.
Donaldson, G., *Fifteen Men: Canada's Prime Ministers from Macdonald to Trudeau,* Toronto, Doubleday, 1969.
Drury, E. C., *Farmer Premier: The Memoirs of the Hon. E. C. Drury,* Toronto, McClelland and Stewart, 1966.
Ferns, H. S., and Ostry, B., *The Age of Mackenzie King: The Rise of the Leader,* London, Heinemann, 1955.
Graham, R., *Arthur Meighen,* Vol. I, *The Door of Opportunity,* Toronto, Clarke, Irwin, 1960; Vol. II, *And Fortune Fled,* Toronto, Clarke, Irwin, 1963; Vol. III, *No Surrender,* Toronto, Clarke, Irwin, 1965.
Gwyn, R., *Smallwood, The Unlikely Revolutionary,* Toronto, McClelland and Stewart, 1968.
Hutchison, B., *The Incredible Canadian,* Toronto, Longmans, Green, 1952.
Hutchison, B., *Mr. Prime Minister, 1867-1964,* Toronto, Longmans, 1964.
Institut canadien des affaires publiques, *Nos hommes politiques,* Montréal, Editions du jour, 1964.
La Marsh, Judy, *Memoirs of A Bird in a Gilded Cage,* Toronto, McClelland and Stewart, 1969.
Laporte, P., *The True Face of Duplessis,* Montreal, Harvest House, 1960.
La Roque, H., *Camillien Houde, le p'tit gars de Ste. Marie,* Montréal, Les éditions de l'homme, 1961.
McGregor, F. A., *The Fall and Rise of Mackenzie King: 1911-1919,* Toronto, Macmillan, 1962.
MacInnis, G., *J. S. Woodsworth, A Man to Remember,* Toronto, Macmillan, 1953.
McKenty, N., *Mitch Hepburn,* Toronto, McClelland and Stewart, 1967.
McNaught, K., *A Prophet in Politics: A Biography of J. S. Woodsworth,* Toronto, University of Toronto Press, 1959.
Neatby, H. B., *William Lyon Mackenzie King, 1924-1932: The Lonely Heights,* Vol. II, Toronto, University of Toronto Press, 1963.
Newman, P. C., *Renegade in Power; The Diefenbaker Years,* Toronto, McClelland and Stewart, 1964.
Pickersgill, J. W., *The Mackenzie King Record,* Toronto, University of Toronto Press, Vol. I, 1939-1944, 1960; with Forster, D., Vol. II, 1944-1945, 1968.
Roberts, L., *C. D.: The Life and Times of Clarence Decatur Howe,* Toronto, Clarke, Irwin, 1957.
Roberts, L., *The Chief: A Political Biography of Maurice Duplessis,* Toronto, Clarke, Irwin, 1963.
Schull, J., *Laurier, The First Canadian,* Toronto, Macmillan, 1965.
Schultz, H. J., "Portrait of a Premier: William Aberhart," *Canadian Historical Review,* Vol. XXXXV, No. 3, September, 1964.
Sévigny, P., *This Game of Politics,* Toronto, McClelland and Stewart, 1965.

Shaw, B., (ed.), *The Gospel According to Saint Pierre*, (Trudeau), Richmond Hill, Pocket Books, Simon and Schuster, 1969.

Sherman, P., *Bennett*, Toronto, McClelland and Stewart, 1966.

Steeves, D. G., *The Compassionate Rebel: Ernest E. Winch and His Times*, Vancouver, Evergreen Press, 1960.

Stewart, M., and French, D., *Ask No Quarter: A Biography of Agnes MacPhail*, Toronto, Longmans, Green, 1959.

Thomson, D. C., *Alexander Mackenzie: Clear Grit*, Toronto, Macmillan, 1960.

Thomson, D. C., *Louis St. Laurent: Canadian*, Toronto, Macmillan, 1967.

Van Dusen, T., *The Chief*, (Diefenbaker), Toronto, McGraw-Hill, 1968.

Wallace, W. S., *The Macmillan Dictionary of Canadian Biography*, Toronto, Macmillan, 1963, 3rd edition.

Ward, N., (ed.), *A Party Politician: The Memoirs of Chubby Power*, Toronto, Macmillan, 1966.

Watkins, E., *R. B. Bennett*, Toronto, Kingswood House, 1963.

NINE
THE ELECTORAL PROCESS

This chapter has been altered substantially from the section on Representation that appeared in the second edition. Except for incidental references in other items such as the introductory article, this chapter contains little of the discussion which appeared in the second edition (*vide* pp. 303-315) on the subject of the new method of redistributing seats in the House of Commons that came into effect with the passage of the Electoral Boundaries Readjustment Act of 1964. The reason for this omission is that this subject now has been dealt with quite thoroughly by two other books in the Series of which *Politics: Canada* has become a part. Interested students should consult the following two sources: T. H. Qualter, The Election Process in Canada and W. E. Lyons, One Man, One Vote.

Both books have been published in Toronto in 1970 by McGraw-Hill in their Series in Canadian Politics. Professor Qualter's book is a detailed and unique source of most of the basic information pertinent to the holding of elections in the federal government and in the ten provinces, including the periodic redistribution of seats. Professor Lyons' book is a more specialized study of the new federal method of redistribution and of its impact upon the results of the election in 1968.

The other items in this chapter have been brought up to date. The first article, which explains briefly how a federal election is held, is followed by a table giving the results by party standing of each of the federal elections from 1867 to 1968. A detailed breakdown on the results of the 1968 election, compared to the results for 1965, is then given in terms of both the number of seats won and the percentage of votes gained by parties by province. In the next article the editor takes note of the discrepancy which usually occurs between the percentage of popular votes won and the percentage of seats gained by a party in order to consider the pros and cons of applying to Canada a modified form of the proportional representation system of voting.

The item in the second edition which discussed how elections are financed traditionally in Canada has been omitted from this edition because a special study which examines this topic in detail has appeared now in the McGraw-Hill Series in Canadian Politics. Professor Khayyam Paltiel's *Political Party Financing in Canada* published in

Toronto in 1970 by McGraw-Hill, provides a lucid, documented, and fascinating account of this subject. The editor has added to this edition of *Politics: Canada,* however, a few brief facts about the high cost of winning—and losing—a seat in the federal election of 1968.

The two items from *Le Devoir* which appeared in the second edition explaining and criticizing Quebec's recent legislation on election expenditures are repeated in this edition since they still offer useful information and helpful hints to individuals and other governments contemplating similar reforms. Quebec's original statute in 1963 limited rigorously the amounts of money that could be spent in provincial campaigns and provided for partial repayment by the state of election expenditures. The act also reduced the voting age to 18 years and added the party affiliation of candidates to their names on the ballot. This act can be found in *Revised Statutes of Quebec, 1964,* c. 7, as amended by 13-14 Eliz. II, 1965, c. 12 and c. 13, and 14-15 Eliz. II, 1966, Bill 3. Professor Paltiel gives a fuller assessment of the law in Chapter 8 of his book. Chapter 9 of the same work outlines the recommendations of the recent federal Committee on Election Expenses. As this third edition of *Politics: Canada* goes to press, Parliament is considering a bill to implement some of these recommendations. Peter Thomson's article, with which this chapter concludes, describes the gist of these developments.

The bibliography at the end of the chapter lists some of the relatively few works available on the electoral process.

ELECTING A CANADIAN GOVERNMENT*

One of the most important powers exercised by the prime minister is the right to ask that the Governor General dissolve Parliament and give orders that writs of election be issued. . . .

In this manner the machinery for conducting a general election in Canada is put in motion. On instructions from the Governor in Council (in other words, the cabinet) the Chief Electoral Officer, an independent official chosen by the House of Commons, issues the writs of election to the returning officer in each constituency, or riding. These officers direct the preparation of voters' lists, appoint deputy returning officers for each polling subdivision in the constituency, receive nominations of candidates and provide for the printing of ballots.

The voters' lists are compiled by enumeration of the electors, which begins 49 days before the election. Enumerators [in twos], representing the two opposing

---

* Reprinted originally from the Bank of Montreal *Business Review*, May 29, 1962. By permission. Revised by the editor in July, 1970.

political interests that received the highest numbers of votes in the constituency in the preceding election, make a door-to-door list of urban voters. (Only one enumerator is required in rural ridings.) Preliminary lists of electors are posted in public places, such as telephone poles, so that any voter may protest the inclusion or omission of any name. The official list of eligible voters must be compiled at least 26 days before the election date. Final revision of voters' lists must be completed 16 days before the election. . . .

The returning officer in every constituency designates the locations of the polling stations. In a recent election, the number of polling stations within each riding ranged from 27 to 458, and the number of voters who cast their ballots in each station was between 2 and 350. Each deputy returning officer and his poll clerk supervise the conduct of the polling on election day, under the scrutiny of two agents for each candidate. The Canada Elections Act requires a voter to fold the ballot paper as directed so that the initials on the back and the printed serial number on the back of the counterfoil can be seen without unfolding it, and hand it to the deputy returning officer, who ascertains, without unfolding it, that it is the same ballot paper as that delivered to the elector. If it is the same, the officer is required in full view of the elector and others present to remove and destroy the counterfoil and himself deposit the ballot in the box. After the poll is closed, the ballots are counted by the deputy returning officer in the presence of the poll clerk and party scrutineers, and the ballots, locked in the ballot box, are forwarded to the returning officer. Although the results of the election are usually made public on election night, the official addition of votes for all of the polling divisions in the constituency is made by the returning officer who subsequently issues a declaration of election in favour of the candidate who obtained a plurality; that is, more votes than any other candidate. (In case of a tie, the returning officer who is not otherwise permitted to vote may cast the deciding ballot.) This candidate will become the parliamentary representative for the constituency.

In federal elections in Canada the ballot bears, in alphabetical order, the name, address, and occupation of each candidate for the House of Commons in the constituency. The party affiliation of the candidate is not given, [although that is now being proposed seriously in Parliament].

When a person wishes to become a candidate for election to the House of Commons, he must take certain formal steps in order to have his name appear on the ballot. To assure his candidacy any elector (that is, a person 21 years of age or over, who is a Canadian citizen, or other British subject who has been resident in Canada for the preceding 12 months) must file nomination papers endorsed by 25 other electors and make a deposit of $200 with the returning officer for the constituency within the time prescribed in the Elections Act. It is possible for a candidate to seek election in a constituency in which he does not reside. The deposit of each candidate is refunded if he polls at least half the number of votes of the winning candidate; if less, the deposit is forfeited to the Crown. In a recent election such forfeitures totalled some $75,000.

●   ●   ●

The campaign which follows the announcement that an election will be held usually lasts for a month to six weeks. The facilities of air transport, television, and radio have done little to reduce the pressure on the contestants; on the contrary, they are subjected to increased demands for their presence. The leading

CANADIAN GENERAL ELECTIONS 1867-1968
PARTY STANDINGS IN HOUSE OF COMMONS

DATE OF ELECTION	PARTY STANDING								TOTAL SEATS
	Cons.	Lib.	Prog.	U.F.A.	C.C.F.-N.D.P.	S.C.	S.C.R.	Other	
August 7-September 20, 1867	101	80							181
July 20-September 3, 1872	103	97							200
January 22, 1874	73	133							206
September 17, 1878	137	69							206
June 20, 1882	139	71							210
February 22, 1887	123	92							215
March 5, 1891	123	92							215
June 23, 1896	89	117						7	213
November 7, 1900	78	128						8	214
November 3, 1904	75	139							214
October 26, 1908	85	133						3	221
September 21, 1911	133	86						2	221
December 17, 1917	153*	82							235
December 6, 1921	50	117	64					4	235
October 29, 1925	116	101	24					4	245
September 14, 1926	91	116	13	11				14	245
July 28, 1930	137	88	2	10				8	245
October 14, 1935	39	171			7	17		11	245
March 26, 1940	39	178			8	10		10	245
June 11, 1945	67	125			28	13		12	245
June 27, 1949	41	190			13	10		8	262
August 10, 1953	51	170			23	15		6	265
June 10, 1957	112	105			25	19		4	265
March 31, 1958	208	49			8				265
June 18, 1962†	116	100			19	30			265
April 8, 1963‡	95	129			17	24			265
November 8, 1965‡	97	131			21	5	9	2	265
June 25, 1968‡	72	155			22		14	1	264

* Unionist.
† Figures include results of service vote and deferred election in Stormont held July 16, 1962. C.C.F. became N.D.P. July 31, 1961.
‡ Final figures, including results of service vote and disputed elections.

members of the various parties are presented with schedules well nigh impossible to meet as they cross and re-cross the country, giving speeches, meeting thousands of people, making countless appearances on platforms and before the press, consulting with their campaign managers and advisers, and performing multitudinous other duties. All electioneering must end two days before election day.

[In 1968] nearly eleven million Canadians were given the opportunity to choose the nation's parliamentary representatives and the voters in each of the 264 constituencies [elected one MP each, the turnout across the country being about 75 percent]. By so doing they were choosing not only their own member but also, indirectly, the prime minister and cabinet.

The leader of the group which has the largest number of its candidates elected to the House is traditionally invited by the Governor General to form a government, and to take the office of prime minister. Usually the party which forms the government has a majority of the seats in the House of Commons. But, in point of fact, as may be seen in the accompanying table, there have been seven occasions since Confederation, in 1921, 1925, 1926, 1957, 1962, 1963 and 1965 when the party winning the largest number of seats still had less than half the total number in the House. In these circumstances, the government functions as a minority government.

General elections must be held in Canada at least once in five years. During the [1968] election the Chief Electoral Officer's requirements for staff and supplies involved an estimated expenditure of $14 million and the services of over 150,000 persons. This was entirely apart from the work done by the political parties themselves in order to perform their role of informing the voters. But the ultimate responsibility for the result of this democratic process rests with each Canadian voter who, on election day, gives his mandate to the House of Commons. The importance of each vote cast is underlined by the fact that . . . [it is common for many seats to be won by a plurality of less than a thousand votes each].

1968 FEDERAL ELECTION RESULTS

PAUL FOX

June 27, 1968—Preliminary incomplete returns from the federal election on June 25 indicate that the percentage turnout of voters was approximately the same as in 1965 when 75.4 percent of those eligible voted. The record turnout was in 1958 when 79.8 percent voted.

The following tables give comparative details for the two most recent federal elections and demonstrate once again the recurrent problem of the disparity between the number of seats parties win and the percentages of the popular vote for them.

Seats won by parties in 1968 (1965 results in brackets)

Province	Lib.	PC	NDP	SCR	SC	Ind.
Nfld.	1(7)	6				
P.E.I.		4(4)				
N.S.	1(2)	10(10)				
N.B.	5(6)	5(4)				
Que.	56(56)	4(8)		14(9)		(2)
Ont.	64(51)	17(25)	6(9)			1
Man.	5(1)	5(10)	3(3)			
Sask.	2	5(17)	6			
Alta.	4	15(15)			(2)	
B.C.	16(7)	(3)	7(9)		(3)	
Y.-N.W.T.	1(1)	1(1)				
Totals	155(131)	72(97)	22(21)	14(9)	(5)	1(2)
Percentages of seats	58.7(49.4)	27.3(36.6)	8.3(7.9)	5.3(3.4)	(1.5)	.4(.7)

Percentages of votes for parties in 1968 (1965 percentages in brackets)

Province	Lib.	PC	NDP	SCR	SC	Others
Nfld.	43.0(64.1)	53.1(32.0)	4.4(1)		(2)	(1)
P.E.I.	45.0(44.0)	51.8(53.8)	3.2(2)			
N.S.	38.0(42.0)	55.2(49.0)	6.7(9)			
N.B.	44.0(47.0)	49.7(43.0)	4.9(9)			
Que.	53.6(45.6)	21.3(21.3)	7.5(12)	16.4(17.5)		1.1
Ont.	46.6(43.6)	32.0(34.0)	20.6(22)			.8
Man.	41.5(31.0)	31.4(41.0)	25.0(24)		1.5(4)	
Sask.	27.0(24.0)	36.9(48.0)	35.7(26)		(2)	
Alta.	35.7(22.0)	50.4(47.0)	9.3(8)		1.9(23)	2.7
B.C.	41.7(29.9)	19.4(19.2)	32.9(32.9)		5.8(17)	
Y.-N.W.T.	57.0(52.0)	33.5(45.0)	9.6(3)			
Nationally	45.3(40.1)	31.4(32.4)	17.0(17.9)	4.4(4.6)	.8(3.6)	.9(1.1)

THE PROS AND CONS OF P.R. FOR CANADA*

PAUL FOX

Most voters would probably be quite shocked if they were told that they were seldom ruled by a majority, that there is every chance that a Canadian government will not likely represent a majority of the Canadian people, and that more people will probably vote against a government than for it.

Yet that has been the case in 12 out of the last 15 federal elections. Only twice since 1921 has the winning party got more than 50 percent of the popular vote (the Liberals won 51.5 percent in 1940 and Mr. Diefenbaker about 53.6 percent in 1958).

How do minority wins occur? The winner may get more votes than any of his several opponents, but he may not get more than 50 percent of the total. For example, in a certain Ontario riding recently the Liberal candidate received a vote of 14,035, the Progressive Conservative 11,155, the NDP 8,302, the Communist 1,413, and another candidate 307. The top man thus had 14,035 votes for him and a grand total of 21,177 against him.

When this sort of thing is repeated in constituency after constituency, a party may win an election by obtaining more seats than any other party or all the other other parties combined and still not have had even half the citizens voting for it.

The appearance of important smaller parties, like the NDP and Social Credit, has had a lot to do with this sort of outcome. But the minor parties aren't the real cause of the weakness. The actual defect is in the election machinery. It works in such a way that the party that wins the election ordinarily gets far more seats in the House of Commons than its share of the popular vote entitles it to.

At the same time, the opposition parties usually get far fewer. In every election since 1896 the incoming government has ridden into power with more seats than its portion of the national vote gave it. Sometimes the discrepancies have been really shocking.

In 1930, when the Conservatives won, they polled 48 percent of the vote and secured 56 percent of the seats.

Five years later, after the 1935 election, the shoe was on the other foot. The Liberals won only 44.8 percent of the vote but got 70.6 percent of the seats. That left only a quarter of the desks in the Commons for all the other parties, which had got more than half of all the votes in the country. The result was that the Tories got about half as many seats as they might have expected from the vote, and the CCF got only about a third as many.

These figures also show how our election system multiplies slight shifts in voting at the polls into big landslides for the winner in terms of seats in parliament. In

---

* Reprinted originally from *The Financial Post*, August 8, 1953, with permission of the publishers. Revised in July, 1970.

1930, for example, the Conservatives increased the number of seats from 91 to 137. But there was no landslide in public opinion. The voting showed that they had won only 3.3 percentage points more of the votes.

Five years later the Liberals were swept back into power by something that looked more like an avalanche. They just about doubled the number of their seats, from 91 to 173. Almost a 100 percent increase in seats, but how much of an increase in popular vote? 80 percent? 50 percent? No, it was actually half a percentage point *less* than in 1930!

In 1958, with less than 54 percent of the popular vote, Mr. Diefenbaker won 78 percent of the seats in the Commons. In 1968 with only 45.3 percent of the vote, the Liberals won a majority of nearly 59 percent of the seats.

Absurd results like these bring our present system of voting into question and raise the issue, what can be done to remedy such defects? The answer is: not much, so long as we retain our present election machinery which, in effect, maximizes the importance of the winning party's ballots and minimizes the value of the vote for the other parties.

Should we scrap our present system, then, and try something different? Few Canadians realize that we came close to doing this in the 'twenties.

In 1924, and again in 1925, the federal government introduced a bill to abolish our present method of election and to replace it by Alternative Voting. These bills were never passed. But about the same time, Manitoba and Alberta switched over to the new system, followed by British Columbia in 1952.

The big difference between Alternative or Preferential Voting and our present federal method is that the voter gets as many choices as there are candidates and marks his ballots in order of his preference: 1, 2, 3, 4, 5, and so on. When the polls close, the first choices for each candidate are counted, and if no one has a clear majority, the contestant with the fewest votes is dropped and the second choices on his ballots are distributed. If there's still no majority, the next lowest man is put out and his second choices are distributed. And so it goes until someone finally gets a majority.

The great advantage to this method is, of course, that it ensures that the winner finally gets a majority and that nobody gets in by a plurality. But that's about all it does. It doesn't solve the problem of the wasted votes for the losing parties and it doesn't give the minorities any representation. It can also encourage a little skullduggery because by means of it two parties can cooperate at an election to knock out a third. (Party A and Party B pass the word along to their supporters to vote their own party first and the other party second, but under no circumstances to cast a ballot for Party C.)

The truth is that no system of voting will guarantee equal weight to all votes and fair representation to minority groups so long as we stick to our present method of electing only one member of parliament from each constituency.

The big weakness of single-member districts is that only one man and one party can be chosen to represent all the voters living in that area.

This is unreal if there are many different points of view in the riding. The only sure way of giving them representation is to enlarge the constituency so that it has a number of seats and to fill these seats in proportion to the way the electorate votes.

This, in a nutshell, is the system of voting known as Proportional Representation. It had quite a vogue in Canada about 30 years ago when cities like Winnipeg, Calgary, Edmonton, and Vancouver adopted it, and it is still popular in some cities in the United States, Belgium, Holland, France, Italy, and Scandinavia. Israel and Australia have also introduced it.

There are about as many different systems of proportional representation as there are ideas about government. Somebody once counted 300 varieties, but they all work much the same way. Under the Hare System, which is probably the best known in Canada, electors go to the polls and vote for all candidates in order of preference. There will likely be a large number of candidates, at least as many as there are persons to be elected multiplied by the number of political parties, for each party will want to nominate a full slate. A minimum of five candidates is essential to make P.R. work well.

The quota necessary for election is figured out by dividing the number voting by the number of seats to be filled plus one, the one being added to reduce the quota a bit to allow for such contingencies as spoiled ballots.

The next step is to count the first choices for each candidate. Anyone who has secured the quota is declared elected. If he has more than the quota, his surplus is transferred to the second choices. If none of the hopefuls has a quota, or if too few have it, then the man with the least first choices is eliminated and the second preferences on his ballots are distributed as marked. If this is not enough, the next lowest man is put out and his second choices are allocated. This goes on until the required number of candidates reaches the quota.

The supporters of P.R. say it has been tried in Canada in cities like Winnipeg and that it has worked well. They argue that its greatest asset is that it eliminates the startling discrepancy between the popular vote for parties and the number of seats they win in the legislature.

Representation in parliament of political parties becomes identical to the proportion of votes they get at the polls: no more plurality wins, no more narrow-majority wins for one party in a lot of constituencies and a huge "wasted" vote for the other parties; no more over-representation of one party and under-representation of the others with a small knot of voters swinging an election one way or the other and converting a small shift in votes into a landslide in seats.

Instead, there would be an exact mathematical similarity between proportion of popular vote and proportion of seats and completely unbiased treatment for both minor and major parties. There would also be a seat for any minority that could muster a quota, and as many seats for the larger groups as would be proportional to their voting strength.

If P.R. is such a cure-all, why not adopt it in Canada?

Oddly enough, the best argument for it is also the best argument against it. The fact is that P.R. produces *too* accurate a rememblance between public opinion and representation in parliament.

If we used it across the country, it would be rare for a party to get a majority in the House of Commons, at least judging by the voting since 1921. This would change completely the basis of our system of cabinet government, which depends on the party in power having enough strength to get its legislative programme through parliament. A party without a majority would be forced to battle every proposal through the Commons, or to enter into a coalition with some other party or parties.

There are other arguments against P.R. A favourite is that it multiplies the number of parties because it gives them a better chance of securing representation in the legislature. This is not as true as most people think. In France and Belgium, for example, there are no more parties now than there were before P.R. was introduced.

But there is a danger in a country like Canada, which has strong regional feelings and interests, that P.R. might foster a large number of regional parties in the federal House. Even under the existing system, the tendency in that direction is strong. Another difficulty is that P.R. increases the size of constituencies in thinly populated areas to almost unreasonable dimensions. If P.R. were put into effect in Canada and no riding were to have less than five members, it might well be, for example, that the whole of Manitoba outside of Winnipeg and its suburbs would become one or two gigantic electoral districts. Candidates would have a tremendous and expensive task trying to campaign over such a huge area and the voters might never get a glimpse of their MPs.

Actually, none of the disadvantages of P.R. is really significant except the one overwhelming argument that if it were introduced all across Canada it would jeopardize our system of parliamentary government. And that limitation is so serious that it makes it impossible to recommend the wholesale adoption of P.R. in this country.

Is there no solution then?

The remedy seems to be to mix the two systems together judiciously to get the good effects of each. This could be done quite easily. Our present system of voting could be left for large rural areas and most other places, while P.R. could be introduced in a few densely-populated urban centres. This was first suggested and debated in Parliament 40 years ago.

Vancouver, Toronto, and Montreal might be good places to start. An analysis of the election results in these three places shows a crying need for a fairer method of representation. . . .

THE HIGH COST OF WINNING — AND LOSING — A SEAT*

PAUL FOX

. . . One good example of the high cost of winning—and losing—a seat in Parliament emerges from the figures for campaign costs in the 1968 federal election.

According to the figures filed for candidates' expenses in the riding of Don Valley in Toronto in 1968, the winner, Robert Kaplan, a Liberal, spent $68,369 to beat Dalton Camp, his Conservative rival, who found that losing is a pretty expensive business too. Mr. Camp reported expenditures of $38,400. The NDP candidate in the riding of 63,000 voters reported expenses of $1,740.08. Although Mr. Camp spent more than half as much as the winner, he lost by less than 5,000 votes out of 53,000.

The figures for the two major candidates in the Don Valley riding were not typical, of course, of the reported costs of campaigning in the election. From reports available thus far, the Kaplan figure appears to be the largest yet filed. However, several other candidates in the Metro Toronto area reported expenditures in excess of $20,000. . . .

QUEBEC LIMITS CAMPAIGN COSTS AND PAYS FOR THEM†

Quebec City, April 27, 1966—It will cost Quebec's taxpayers between $8 and $10 million to elect a new government next June 5th, when in the past years the cost of a provincial election rarely exceeded $3 million.

This increase is mainly due to the fact that the June 5th election will be held under the new electoral law adopted during the session of 1963, which provided for radical changes in the financing of a campaign by the candidates entering the lists.

Under the new electoral law, the candidates will be reimbursed by the state for a part of the expense they will incur in attempting to get elected.

The increase is also due to the fact that the number of voters will be slightly increased because of the law that now gives the right to vote in Quebec provincial elections to young persons 18 years of age or more, adding approximately 600,000 new voters.

* From an address on March 15, 1970.
† Translation by the editor from *Le Devoir,* Montreal, April 27, 1966. By permission of the publishers.

The new law now strictly limits the expense candidates can incur for purposes of getting elected.

A candidate will not be allowed to spend more than an amount equal to 60 cents per voter for the first 10,000 voters registered in his constituency. Between 10,000 and 20,000 voters, the permitted amount per elector will be [an additional] 50 cents, and in a constituency where there are more than 20,000 voters, the expense will be fixed at 40 cents per voter for those beyond 20,000. For example, a candidate whose riding has 25,000 voters will be allowed to spend up to a maximum of $13,000.

Because of the distances involved and the remoteness of certain constituencies, the amount allowed for each voter in them will be increased by 10 cents. The ridings where this applies are Saguenay, Duplessis, the Iles-de-la Madeleine, and Abitibi.

In constituencies of up to 10,000 voters, the government will reimburse the candidate for the first 15 cents per elector that he spends.

In ridings with more than 10,000 voters, the government will pay one-fifth of the expenses beyond the basic 15 cents.

Thus, where a candidate runs in a riding with 25,000 voters, he will be reimbursed by an amount equal to 15 cents per elector for the first 10,000, plus seven cents per voter for the number between 10,000 and 20,000, plus five cents per elector for those between 20,000 and 25,000.

A candidate's expenditures will be repaid according to the terms provided by the law, which requires his official agent to send in to the chief returning officer, after the election, his statement of expenses.

To obtain the repayment laid down by law, a candidate will have to get at least 20 percent of the votes cast in his riding.

In the section dealing with electoral expenses, the law is quite precise. All of a candidate's expenditures are considered as electoral expenses except those he makes for transportation, as well as those for food and lodging. The $200 deposit that a candidate has to put up at the time of his nomination is not included as an electoral expenditure either. Neither are the costs involved in holding a convention in his riding, nor his personal costs up to a $1,000.

WEAKNESSES IN THE NEW ELECTORAL LAW*

CLAUDE RYAN

. . . I am not in favour of granting to candidates direct subsidies from the state. Instead, I am in favour of indirect state aid consisting especially of a sharing in the costs of renting accommodation and buying broadcasting time on radio and

* Translation by the editor of an editorial from *Le Devoir*, April 1, 1966. By permission of the publisher.

television. The system devised by Quebec's legislators does not provide for any control over the central electoral funds of each party; because of this omission, it runs the risk of still hiding evil under the cover of a respectability that is more apparent than real. . . .

Notwithstanding the reservations voiced by several citizens and responsible organizations, the Quebec government is ready to embark on a scheme based on the principle of direct, though partial, aid given by the state to candidates.

If it is too late to alter the fundamental principles adopted by the law-makers, there is still time to correct certain serious injustices that the new system threatens to perpetrate.

Bill 13 (1963) has been too narrowly conceived to serve the interests of the two major parties. It hardly gives a chance to third party candidates and to independents.

The law-makers undoubtedly wanted to prevent a proliferation of crackpot candidates. But the evil that it wished to avoid seems likely to be less serious than the one that will be inevitably created: for several foolish candidacies that will be discouraged successfully, one will "punish" unjustly dozens of candidates whose only fault will be that of pursuing their way in other than beaten paths. This sort of handicap is the very opposite to the spirit that underlies our democratic system.

To overcome the weaknesses in Bill 13, the executive committee of the *Rassemblement pour l'Indépendance Nationale* (RIN) has suggested that some simple but effective amendments be made in sections 219 and 375 of the electoral law. These amendments would put on the basis of equality, in the eyes of the law, all the parties that nominate at least 20 candidates in the next general election. These proposed amendments are fair and square. If the law-makers want to make a democratic beginning, they ought to accept them without hesitation. . . .

OTTAWA CASH FOR CANDIDATES AND VOTES FOR 18-YEAR-OLDS*

PETER THOMSON

OTTAWA — Candidates running in the next general election can count on some contributions from the Federal Government to help pay campaign expenses.

The Government paved the way for contributions to election expenses when it introduced legislation yesterday which provides for registration of major political parties and the optional listing of party affiliation on ballots.

The legislation, which is the first major move to overhaul the Canada Elections Act in 10 years, also lowers the voting age to 18 for general elections, adding about 1,250,000 voters to the 1972 voters' list.

* From *The Telegram*, Toronto, May 20, 1970. By permission of the publisher.

Privy Council president Donald Macdonald introduced the bill in the Commons yesterday, where it received routine first reading.

He later told newsmen that the Government "anticipates" payments toward election expenses as a result of the new provision.

A special committee will be appointed to consider the question of election expenses, Mr. Macdonald said, and it will likely recommend the amount of money to be provided by the Government.

The legislation provides that only parties with 75 or more candidates can be registered. Thus, election expense assistance will not be available to regional splinter groups which are unable to field a large team.

Mr. Macdonald said the limit was set at 75 to assure national representation in any party that qualifies for Federal election expense assistance. An all-party Commons committee had unanimously recommended that the figure be set at 20.

He admitted the legislation works against small groups, and declared that this was the Government's intent.

In effect, the Government legislation will make it very difficult for small parties or independent members to compete successfully against candidates from the three major parties.

It means that Canada is unlikely to develop a multi-party system with subsequent coalitions such as exist in France.

BIBLIOGRAPHY

Cairns, A. C., "The Electoral System and the Party System in Canada," *C.J.P.S.*, Vol. I, No. 1, March, 1968.

Daniels, S. R., *The Case for Electoral Reform*, London, Allen and Unwin, 1938.

Hermens, F. A., *Democracy or Anarchy? A Study of Proportional Representation*, Notre Dame, University of Notre Dame, 1941.

Horwill, G., *Proportional Representation; Its Dangers and Defects*, London, Allen and Unwin, 1925.

Humphreys, J. H., *Proportional Representation*, London, Methuen, 1911.

Johnpoll, B. K., "The Liberals Called the Election Too Soon," *Toronto Daily Star*, April 23, 1966.

Lakeman, E., and Lambert, J. D., *Voting in Democracies*, London, Faber, 2nd edition, 1959.

Long, J. A., "Maldistribution in Western Provincial Legislatures: The Case of Alberta," *C.J.P.S.*, Vol. II, No. 3, September, 1969.

Lyons, W. E., *One Man—One Vote*, Toronto, McGraw-Hill, 1970.

McGeachy, J. B., "One Rural Vote Equals 2, 3, or 4 City Votes," *Financial Post*, August 20, 1960.

McGeachy, J. B., "Redistribution Should Abolish the Rural Tyranny at Ottawa," *Financial Post*, December 7, 1963.

McIlwraith, M., "Misrepresentative Government," *Canadian Commentator*, March, 1963.

MacKenzie, W. J., *Free Elections*, London, Allen and Unwin, 1958.

Paltiel, K., *Political Party Financing in Canada*, Toronto, McGraw-Hill, 1970.

Qualter, T. H., "Representation by Population: A Comparative Study," *C.J.E.P.S.*, Vol. XXXIII, No. 2, May, 1967.

Qualter, T. H., "Seats and Votes: An Application of the Cube Law to the Canadian Electoral System," *C.J.P.S.*, Vol. I, No. 3, September, 1968.

Qualter, T. H., *The Election Process in Canada*, Toronto, McGraw-Hill, 1970.

Ross, J. F. S., *Elections and Electors*, London, Eyre & Spottiswoode, 1955.

Schindeler, F., "One Man, One Vote: One Vote, One Value," *Journal of Canadian Studies*, Vol. III, No. 1, February, 1968.

Ward, N., "A Century of Constituencies," *C.P.A.*, Vol. X, No. 1, March, 1967.

Wearing, J., "How to Predict Canadian Elections," *Canadian Commentator*, February, 1963.

TEN
VOTING BEHAVIOUR

The fact that this chapter now appears as a separate section is one indication of the rapid growth of the study of Canadian electoral behaviour in recent years, but the long bibliography at the end of the chapter is even better proof of the extent of interest of Canadian scholars in this field.

Many items might have been reprinted here if space permitted, but since it is limited, two have been chosen as leading examples of excellent and interesting studies. One is a reproduction in major part of an article from the *Canadian Journal of Political Science;* the other is a "Toronto original," appearing in print here for the first time. Both acquaint students with the use of contemporary techniques in analyzing voting behaviour and each leads to distinct and provocative conclusions. Professor John Wilson's study is conducted at the level of federal politics but has significant implications for provincial politics as well. Professor Jerry Hough's article deals with the other sector of Canadian government, the municipal arena, but it too has broader and important implications, in regard to both voter turnout and social action.

POLITICS AND SOCIAL CLASS IN CANADA: THE CASE OF WATERLOO SOUTH*

JOHN WILSON

•   •   •

. . . There is . . . some evidence to suggest that social class may be becoming a more important influence in the electoral behaviour of certain parts of the country than has been the case in the past. An analysis of the result of the federal by-election held in the autumn of 1964 in the southwestern Ontario riding of Waterloo South may throw further light on the kinds of changes which appear to be taking place in Canada.

One of the most obvious consequences of the brokerage doctrine [of parties] is the greater propensity of the party organizations to stress the characteristics of their candidates rather than the party program or the interests of the electorate which a party might seek to serve. If, as the theory requires, a major national party has to behave as a department store—putting everything on sale because it cannot be sure which "line" will "go best" with its customers—then it is only a short step to the belief that it will gain as much through the smile of the counter clerk as it will through the quality of its merchandise.

On the face of things the Waterloo South by-election was typical in this respect of the practice throughout Canada. Each of the three parties nominated candidates who were thought to have a special claim on the loyalties of the electorate. Moreover, when the New Democrat won—breaking a Conservative hold on the constituency which went back almost without interruption to the First World War — it was widely claimed that his special qualities had been the principal cause of his victory, that the circumstances of the by-election were in any case unique, and that Mr. Saltsman would not be able to hold the riding in a general election. Not only does this explanation have very little to do with the more deeply rooted attachments to party which have been found to exist in most other democratic countries, it is not even necessarily internally consistent. If Mr. Saltsman did have a special personal drawing power there would be no reason to suppose that he could not continue to win in Waterloo South in general elections irrespective of the cause of his first victory.

It is, however, comparatively easy to show that such an explanation leaves too much unaccounted for to be acceptable. What was ignored by the analysts was the fact that the same Max Saltsman—in the provincial election only fourteen months earlier—had given the poorest performance of any NDP or CCF candidate in Waterloo South since before the Second World War. Yet he had been living in the

* From the *Canadian Journal of Political Science/Revue canadienne de Science politique*, Vol. I, No. 3, September/septembre, 1968. By permission of the author and publisher.

constituency for nearly seventeen years. It hardly seems likely that his personal following could have mushroomed almost overnight to the extent required to win the by-election.

There were other peculiarities in the result which suggested that it was not to be explained in terms of the candidate's characteristics alone. One of the most intriguing aspects of the campaign was the fact that the Liberal candidate had run as a New Democrat in the two previous federal elections. Although he believed that by switching to the Liberals he could unite the progressive vote in the riding and thereby defeat the Conservatives, the immediate effect of his candidacy was merely to divide the local Liberal association so badly that its ability to mount a campaign at all was in serious doubt. In these circumstances it would not be expected that Liberal supporters who wished to protest the adoption of a former New Democrat as their candidate would do so by voting for the NDP. Yet, on the face of it, that is what happened.

TABLE I: Recent Federal Results in Waterloo South

	1962	1963	1964	1965	1968
Conservatives	Chaplin	Chaplin	Chaplin*	Chaplin*	O'Brian
	10,448	10,143	9,086	8,609	9,993
Liberals	Shaver	Shaver	Stewart	Menary	Epp
	6,759	7,387	4,563	4,758	7,121
New Democrats	Stewart	Stewart	Saltsman	Saltsman	Saltsman
	6,889	7,105	11,856	12,465	10,622
Social Credit	Fast	Bezan			Gervais
	486	328			114
Total	24,582	24,963	25,505	25,832	27,850

* A son of the member whose death caused the 1964 by-election.
Source: Report of the Chief Electoral Officer for Canada and for 1968 the preliminary recapitulation provided by the Returning Officer for Waterloo.

If the votes cast for each party are compared with those for 1963 (see Table I) it appears that the result depended on the defection of roughly a thousand Conservatives and nearly three times that number of Liberals—all to the NDP. In fact, however, the shifts which took place were rather more complex than that. The data in Table II [see original article] show that although a somewhat larger *proportion* of 1963 Liberals switched to the NDP, because there were originally many more Conservatives in the riding the latter made a greater contribution to the NDP victory in absolute terms. The fact that the change which occurred was primarily the result of the defection of former Conservatives raises intriguing questions about the sources of party support in southwestern Ontario. And when it is remembered that Mr. Saltsman maintained his position in the succeeding general election of 1965 (and with somewhat less support in 1968) it seems likely that a more profound change—based, perhaps, on the identification of the parties with specific interests in the electorate—took place in Waterloo South.

RELIGIOUS AFFILIATION, ETHNIC ORIGIN AND THE VOTE

The idea that certain sociological factors may have some influence on the pattern of our voting is given recognition in all the major studies of Canadian electoral behaviour, whether at the constituency, regional, or national level. In these analyses two main observations have been made: first, that the intensity of the influence exercised by any one factor will vary from area to area throughout the country, and second, that whatever the strength of the factor which seems most prominently at work the influence of social class has very little to do with it. Instead, as has already been suggested, the system encourages electors to distinguish between themselves on the basis of their religious affiliation or their ethnic origin, or collectively as residents of a particular region. While such differentiation suggests that the practice of brokerage is not entirely successful it is nonetheless the case that these factors generally cut across class lines and thereby eliminate the possibility that the nation will fall apart in class war.

TABLE III: Federal Electoral Behaviour of Roman Catholics in Selected Areas (horizontal percentages)

Year	Area	CON	LIB	NDP	SC	n
1963	National	19	52	9	20	930
1953	Kingston	2	95	3	*	89
1962	St. John's	53	47	*	*	128
1962	Hamilton	15	78	7	†	91
1963	Sudbury	16	70	11	3	295
1964	Saskatoon	23	60	17	*	203
1964	Waterloo South	14	34	52	*	91

* No candidate.
† Social Credit and Conservative votes combined.
Sources for the data from other studies presented in Table III are, respectively: Peter Regenstreif, *The Diefenbaker Interlude: Parties and Voting in Canada* (Toronto, 1965), 104, calculated from CIPO data in Table IX; John Meisel, "Religious Affiliation and Electoral Behaviour: A Case Study," *Canadian Journal of Economics and Political Science,* 22, no. 4 (Nov. 1956), 486, calculated from Table II; George Perlin, "St. John's West," in Meisel, ed., *Papers on the 1962 Election,* 10, calculated from Table I; Grace M. Anderson, "Voting Behaviour and the Ethnic-Religious Variable: A Study of a Federal Election in Hamilton, Ontario," *Canadian Journal of Economics and Political Science,* 32, no. 1 (Feb. 1966), 30, calculated from Table I; J. E. Havel, *Politics in Sudbury* (Sudbury, 1966), 65, calculated from Table 36; and John C. Courtney and David E. Smith, "Voting in a Provincial General Election and a Federal By-election: A Constituency Study of Saskatoon City," *Canadian Journal of Economics and Political Science,* 32, no. 3 (Aug. 1966), 349, calculated from Table X.

It has become a commonplace of political analysis in Canada that of the influences affecting our electoral behaviour the most significant for many years has been religious affiliation. And few studies which have tested the relationship have failed to find a very strong connection between professing the Roman Catholic faith and a preference for the Liberal party. Table III brings together from a number of recent studies evidence which shows how consistently the connection has been found in most parts of the country. The strength of the relationship is, of course, not absolutely uniform, and Perlin's Newfoundland data as well as those for Waterloo South show that it is not even necessarily the case that the Liberals will be the leading party amongst Roman Catholics everywhere in Canada. But such regional variation as may occur does not affect the possibility that religious affiliation will still be found to be the most important single influence on the way Canadians vote. It may be that the party preference of Roman Catholics is simply a product of the local circumstances in which they find themselves, but it may also be that the fact that an elector adheres to that faith remains the principal element in the choice he makes on election day. In St. John's that tends to make him a Conservative, in Kingston and Sudbury and in other places it tends to make him a Liberal, and in Waterloo South it apparently tends to make him a New Democrat.

In fact, however, before the 1964 by-election the Liberals *were* the dominant party amongst Roman Catholics in the riding, [the percentage distribution among the 75 Roman Catholics in the sample who remembered how they had voted in 1963 was Conservative 29, Liberal 52, and NDP 19], and the magnitude of the shift to the NDP in this group suggests that something other than religious affiliation may have been the principal motivating factor. If this were the case we might expect to find a general shift in all religious groups. Table IV makes it clear not only that this did not happen, but that there were very marked differences in the propensity of particular groups to change the pattern of their vote. Anglicans, Lutherans, and Roman Catholics appeared much more likely to change than others, while adherents of the United Church seemed hardly inclined to change at all. Thus, while the distribution does not conform to the national pattern, it may still be the case that an association exists between religious affiliation and the vote sufficient to account for the behaviour of the riding.

TABLE IV: Some Religious Groups Were More Likely to Change Than Others
(percentages)

Religious affiliation	Switched to the NDP	All voters
Anglican	42	23
Baptist	9	7
Lutheran	15	10
Presbyterian	3	14
Roman Catholic	24	18
United Church	2	18
Other	5	10
N	103	504

In fact there are important differences in party strength in each of the larger religious faiths in Waterloo South. Even though they do not dominate, Table V shows that the Liberals do find greater support amongst Roman Catholics than in any other group. It can be seen as well that the Conservatives appear to be especially dependent upon Anglicans and Baptists for their position in the riding, while the NDP draws disproportionate support from Presbyterians. But while the existence of a general connection between religious affiliation and the vote can easily be shown, that factor alone by no means explains the behaviour of all electors. A closer examination of Table V suggests that since the level of the NDP vote does not vary as sharply from group to group as is the case with the other parties, religious affiliation plays a much smaller part in explaining its strength. In fact, if an association is sought between either seven or three religious groups and a hypothetical two-party vote (Conservatives and Liberals together, and the NDP) no relationship is found to exist at all. Obviously, therefore, religious affiliation only helps to account for the difference between the level of the Conservative and Liberal vote in Waterloo South; it tells us nothing about the NDP.

TABLE V: Religious Affiliation and the Vote in 1964 (percentages)

	Anglican	Baptist	Lutheran	Presbyterian	Roman Catholic	United Church	Other	All voters
Conservatives	48	45	40	35	14	37	34	36
Liberals	5	10	18	9	34	21	16	16
New Democrats	47	45	42	56	52	42	50	48
N	118	33	50	71	91	91	50	504

It is possible, however, since the same kinds of links between religious affiliation and voting are not found in all parts of Canada, that the variation is due not just to local circumstances but to other factors being more important as determinants of electoral behaviour. The religion to which a person adheres is so very often a function of his ethnic origin that it may be the case that the apparent connection between the Liberal party and adherents of the Roman Catholic faith in some parts of the country is in reality an association between that party and the dominant ethnic group in such areas. It has been suggested, for example, that the strong relationship between being Catholic and voting Liberal in Sudbury is probably only a reflection of the more important link between the French minority in that city and the national Liberal party viewed as the special agent of French interests in Canada. If this kind of association were the dominant one we would of course expect to find differences in the intensity of the Catholic-Liberal relationship from region to region depending upon the proportionate strength of particular ethnic groups.

In Waterloo county, of course, a large part of the population is of German origin. While the south riding is by no means as notable in this respect as Kitchener and other areas to the north, it may still be the case that ethnic origin has a more fundamental influence on the vote than does religious affiliation, and that it goes farther in accounting for the support of all three parties. Table VI shows that there are substantial differences in Liberal and Conservative strength among the groups examined but that, again, the level of the NDP vote seems unaffected by such considerations. A general association between ethnic origin and the vote clearly exists irrespective of the group combinations used, but, as with religious affiliation, no association can be found at all when the Liberal and Conservative vote is combined and contrasted to that of the NDP.

TABLE VI: Ethnic Origin and the Vote in 1964 (percentages)

	English	Irish	Scots	German	Other	All voters
Conservatives	43	43	31	32	27	36
Liberals	8	14	16	20	30	16
New Democrats	49	43	53	48	43	48
N	185	44	89	103	83	504

The fact that religious affiliation and ethnic origin are differentiating influences only between Conservatives and Liberals means that by themselves these factors give a rather inadequate explanation of the voting pattern in Waterloo South. If the NDP were an unimportant element in the riding this would perhaps be of less significance, although to the extent that a thorough description of Canadian electoral behaviour is being sought it should be a matter of some concern when the traditional explanations cannot account for any part of that behaviour, however small. In any case it seems probable that our concern with the differences which have been with us since the beginning — together with the fact that it is generally possible to find some sort of relationship between religious affiliation, ethnic origin, and the vote—has served to disguise a development of recent years that needs to be made more explicit.

SOCIAL CLASS AND THE VOTE

It has already been suggested that since religious affiliation and electoral behaviour do not necessarily show the same kind of relationship in all parts of Canada, the varying level of the association may be the consequence of local circumstances. It may also be the case that other, more permanent, societal conditions which vary from one part of the country to another are the real cause of the differential influence which the traditional elements of race, religion, and region have been found to have. Thus, to take one example, the apparently increasing regionalization of Canadian electoral preference, to which Professor Meisel has drawn attention, may in fact be no more than an expression of the comparatively *unequal* growth of urbanization and industrialization in different parts of the country. A comprehensive national study might very well find that these factors are the most fundamental influence at work in our system. It might also find that the older patterns of voting are able to maintain themselves only in areas unaffected by the pressures of an increasingly complex economy, while in Canada's major industrial centres what appears to be a continuing relationship between religious affiliation, or ethnic origin, and the vote is in reality only a reflection of the more permanent influences which city life tends to promote. To put the matter in another way, it may merely be the case that Roman Catholics in some areas do not vote for the Conservative party because as a general rule Roman Catholics are not as well off as some other religious groups.

TABLE VII: There Are Sharp Ocupational Class Differences Between Religions (percentages)

	Anglican	Baptist	Lutheran	Presby-terian	Roman Catholic	United Church	Other	Whole sample
Non-manual workers	42	37	29	42	26	52	32	38
Manual workers	58	63	71	58	74	48	68	62
N	130	40	59	84	110	118	65	606

The extent to which significant differences in wealth between various religious groups exist in Canada is unclear, but it is a fact that in Waterloo South there are important distinctions to be made between the kinds of people who are adherents of each of the larger faiths. Table VII shows how very sharp those distinctions may be. In fact there appears to be a broad connection between the relative class composition of the riding's religious groups and their propensity to shift to the NDP. It was noticed earlier (in Table IV) that Anglicans, Lutherans, and Roman Catholics were the most likely to change their vote and adherents of the United Church were hardly inclined to change at all. It can now be seen that the Lutheran and Catholic groups tend to be substantially more working class in composition than the others, while the United Church is much more heavily middle class in composition than is the riding as a whole. Nothing approaching the same degree of distinction on an occupational class basis can be found among ethnic groups, although this appears to be mainly a consequence of the dominantly British character of the constituency. However that may be, the differential class composition of the leading religious groups—taken together with their varying propensity towards changing their voting pattern between 1963 and 1964—suggests that social class may have more to do with the vote in Waterloo South than any other single variable.

The fact is that while the NDP attracted broadly the same level of support among all religious and ethnic groups, the class composition of its vote makes it clear that it may be characterized—in Waterloo South—as a working class party.

That it also polls a respectable share of the lower middle class vote does not necessarily detract from this interpretation of the data in Table VIII. Such evidence as is available in other English-speaking countries where social class is thought to be the prime determinant of electoral choice suggests that strong support in the lower middle class is not at all uncommon with labour-oriented parties. Nor is the NDP's superior strength among skilled and semi-skilled workers—compared to unskilled workers — necessarily unique: the same phenomenon has been found in both Germany and Sweden. On the other hand, Table VIII shows that the Conservatives and the Liberals are both more heavily dependent upon middle class support than would be expected if social class were of no consequence at all as an influence on the vote.

TABLE VIII: Social Class and the Vote in 1964 (percentages)

	Middle class		Working class		
	Upper middle	Lower middle	Skilled and semi-skilled	Unskilled	All voters
Conservatives	55	45	27	31	36
Liberals	21	20	13	17	16
New Democrats	24	35	60	52	48
N	66	135	261	42	504

Of course, in a riding where three-fifths of the electorate is to be found in the working class any party which is to be successful will have to attract a large proportion of the labour vote. That such drawing power on the part of the Conservatives was an important element in their earlier victories in Waterloo South is made clear by the comparative data for 1963 and 1964 in Table IX. Although it is obvious that an association between class and the vote exists in both elections, the fact that NDP strength in 1963 fell considerably short of dominating the riding suggests that the role played by social class before the by-election was a comparatively minor one. This is not to claim that the changes which occurred were necessarily due to an increase in class-voting. But when a party whose main appeal is to the working class is conspicuously unsuccessful in one election and then manages to capture the constituency in another (while the association between class and the vote is maintained) the very least that may be said is that there appears to have been an increased willingness on the part of the electorate to accept it on the terms on which it offers itself. If that is the case it may be said that social class has become a more important influence.

That acceptance does not, however, mean that individual electors necessarily actively think of themselves as members of distinct social classes. While an association can also be found between self-assigned class and the vote, there is a marked disparity between the subjective and objective assignments of class status,

TABLE IX: Social Class and the Vote in 1963 and 1964 (percentages)

	1963 federal election*			1964 by-election		
	Middle class	Working class	All voters	Middle class	Working class	All voters
Conservatives	64	46	53	48	28	36
Liberals	29	25	27	21	13	16
New Democrats	7	29	20	31	59	48
N	177	254	431	201	303	504

* Excluding five Social Credit voters.

especially in the middle class. This suggests that the kind of association which exists is more probably based on a broad recognition of economic interests rather than on any more doctrinaire view of the matter. That this is the case appears to be confirmed by the data in Table X. Within each objective class the patterns of the vote is not altered at all by variations in the subjective status of respondents. Clearly what counts is where a person finds himself in the social hierarchy whatever label he attaches to the position.

The proposition that social class is now the most important influence on the vote in Waterloo South is further supported by the fact that an association between the two variables can be found irrespective of the manner in which the data are organized. It will be recalled that while religious affiliation and ethnic origin both appeared to affect the three-party vote, when an association between them and a hypothetical two-party vote (Conservatives and Liberals, and the NDP) was sought none could be found to exist. But between social class and the same two-party vote there continues to be a relationship every bit as significant as that found when the three parties are treated as separate entities. It therefore seems probable that the influence of class gives a more all-inclusive explanation of the electoral behaviour of the riding than any other single variable.

TABLE X: Objective Social Class Is More Important Than Subjective Social Class (percentages)

	Objective middle class		Objective working class	
	Subjective middle	Subjective working	Subjective middle	Subjective working
Conservatives	48	47	29	27
Liberals	21	21	10	13
New Democrats	31	32	61	60
N*	105	92	48	246

* Only 491 cases are included because 13 respondents did not know their subjective social class.

THE RELATIVE IMPORTANCE OF RELIGIOUS AFFILIATION, ETHNIC ORIGIN, AND SOCIAL CLASS

Examination of the apparent effect of individual variables on the vote leaves a good deal to be desired. It is obvious that the three influences which have been discussed each have some part to play in determining the pattern of the vote in Waterloo South, but what is most needed is a method of assessing their relative importance.

Considerable support for the interpretation of the riding's behaviour which has been developed so far may be found when the data relating to religious affiliation, ethnic origin, and social class are organized in a multivariate table. When this is done for the 1964 data (Table XI) it can easily be seen that the variation in the level of the NDP vote continues to be a function of social class regardless of religious or ethnic pressures. There appears also to be an influence due to class in the Liberal and Conservative vote, but it is much less precise and evidently interfered with by the effect of religious affiliation and ethnic origin. In order to assess the change which has taken place in the riding the data for the 1963 election are organized in the same fashion in Table XII. But apart from the fact that there are substantially different levels of support for all three parties it can be seen that the direction of the relationship observed in Table XI remains the same.

TABLE XI: The Effect of Religious Affiliation, Ethnic Origin, and Social Class in 1964 (percentages)

	Principal Protestant faiths*				Roman Catholics			
	British		Non-British		British		Non-British	
	Middle class	Working class	Middle class	Working class	Middle class	Working class	Middle class	Working class
Conservatives	53	33	46	40	55	13	15	5
Liberals	14	7	27	7	27	17	69	34
New Democrats	33	61	27	53	18	70	15	61
N†	115	151	44	53	11	23	13	44

* Anglican, Baptist, Lutheran, Presbyterian, and United Church.
† Only 454 cases are included because of the exclusion of 50 adherents of other religions.
Note: Percentages do not always add to 100 because of rounding.

Using Coleman's method of calculating "effect parameters" for each dichotomized variable it is possible to measure the importance of each of the three independent attributes in relation to the others as factors affecting each party's vote. The result of these calculations for both elections is presented in summary form in Table XIII, together with a statement in each case of the probability that the observed effect could have occurred by chance. A number of conclusions necessarily follow from this analysis. First, roughly half of the variation in the 1964

TABLE XII: The Effect of Religious Affiliation, Ethnic Origin, and
Social Class in 1963 (percentages)

	Principal Protestant faiths*				Roman Catholics			
	British		Non-British		British		Non-British	
	Middle class	Working class	Middle class	Working class	Middle class	Working class	Middle class	Working class
Conservatives	71	50	67	59	64	38	23	13
Liberals	24	14	25	19	27	48	69	57
New Democrats	5	36	6	22	9	14	8	30
N†	105	131	36	46	11	21	13	30

* Anglican, Baptist, Lutheran, Presbyterian, and United Church.
† Only 393 cases are included because of the exclusion of 43 adherents of other religions.
Note: Percentages do not always add to 100 because of rounding and the Social Credit vote,
which is not shown.

vote for each party is accounted for by the three factors of religious affiliation,
ethnic origin, and social class acting together. Clearly these are the most influential
sociological determinants of the vote in Waterloo South. However, while religious
affiliation has the strongest effect on both the Liberal and Conservative vote, the
influence of social class is nearly as powerful as, and in the case of the Conservatives is more important than, the effect of ethnic origin. But since class is the only
significant influence among the three factors in the NDP vote it follows that it
explains more of the variation in the riding's electoral behaviour than either of the
other two elements considered.

The effect parameters for 1963 show that this was not the case before the by-
election. For each party in that year the effect of class was less important than in
1964, and the over-all influence of the variable fell considerably short of that of
religious affiliation. In the case of the NDP the difference between the two elections
in the effect of class is particularly striking. It is also worth noticing in this instance
that nearly three-quarters of the variation in the party's 1963 vote is apparently
due to factors which promote support for the other parties—measured by the effect
of random shocks s. What this analysis suggests is that the weakness of the NDP
before the by-election stemmed from its apparent irrelevance to the principal
concerns of the electorate in Waterloo South. That does not necessarily mean that
individual voters did not regard their social status as a relevant electoral consideration; it may be that they did not see the NDP as a party capable of serving that
interest. If that was so, what was required to develop the necessary identification
was an opportunity for the party to spend as much time as possible with every
voter. The by-election offered just such an opportunity by allowing the party to
concentrate its resources in one place, and the evidence is that they were used to
maximum advantage. Whether or not this resulted in an active identification
between working class voters and the NDP cannot be precisely determined from

TABLE XIII: Effect Parameters

	Effect parameters			Significance		
	CON	LIB	NDP	CON	LIB	NDP
1964						
Religious affiliation	.21	.23	.03	<.001	<.001	>.30
Ethnic origin	.12	.18	.06	<.018	<.001	>.10
Social class	.20	.18	.38	<.001	<.001	<.001
r	.06	−.04	.19			
s	.41	.45	.34			
1963						
Religious affiliation	.27	.30	.02	<.001	<.001	>.30
Ethnic origin	.15	.14	.01	<.009	<.013	>.40
Social class	.16	.02	.18	<.006	>.35	<.001
r	.19	.12	.06			
s	.23	.42	.73			

The values associated with each variable in Table XIII are estimates of the effect of each upon the vote of the party in question. These are calculated in each case by averaging the percentage differences in each pair of controlled comparisons shown in Tables XI and XII. The two values r and s represent the total effect of what Coleman calls "random shocks" — r in the direction of the behaviour being examined (i.e., voting for a particular party) and s in the opposite direction (i.e., not voting for that party). In the case of each party all five values aggregate to unity, indicating that all influences have been accounted for even though all are not identified. The probability that the observed effect could have occurred by chance is tested by estimating the variance of each effect parameter, finding the standardized normal deviate, and consulting tables of the standardized cumulative normal distribution. For examples of these particular calculations see Coleman, *Introduction to Mathematical Sociology*, 205-7.

the data available, but it does seem strongly suggested by the differential effect of class on the party's vote between 1963 and 1964.

Such an interpretation obviously depends upon the questionable assumption that a substantial section of the working class in the riding had — for reasons associated with their economic position—been voting Conservative before the by-election, since (as was seen at the outset) the NDP victory depended heavily upon defections from the Tory party. But in Waterloo South there are excellent reasons for supposing that a connection between the Conservative party and organized labour has existed for quite a long time. So much attention has been paid to its almost unbroken record of Conservative victories in federal elections since 1921 that it is often forgotten that the riding not only returned a Labour member to Queen's Park after the First World War but that it continued to return the same man long after the Farmer-Labour government collapsed in 1923. That Karl Homuth's following was not an entirely personal one is shown by the fact of his defeat in 1934. But what is most striking is that the same Karl Homuth went over to the Conservatives in the early 1930s and sat as the federal member for

Waterloo South from 1938 until his death in 1951. His long association with the riding must have helped to promote a belief in at least the national Conservative party's sympathy for the aims of labour.

In Ontario generally, there is also some evidence to suggest that a strong link has existed from the earliest times between the Conservative party and the urban working class. During the long period after Confederation in which the Liberals controlled the legislature at Queen's Park, it was nearly always the case that the Conservatives carried the towns which were buried inside the dominantly rural constituencies on which the government depended for its majority. Such a pattern is, of course, not class politics in the sense in which it is understood today, but it is a fact that the Tory party—both nationally and provincially—made a special attempt to attract working class support. A recent analysis has suggested that Sir John Macdonald's promotion of the National Policy in the last century was the source of a good deal of the labour radicalism of the time, but much of the evidence indicates that a careful examination of the growth of party appeals to labour might show a trend not unlike that which occurred in the United Kingdom. Certainly there is a curious parallel between Macdonald's legislative recognition of the claims of organized labour in the 1870s and Disraeli's successful attempt to cut into Liberal support among British workers in the same period. At the provincial level in Ontario when the Conservatives first came to power in 1905 there was a very marked increase in the amount of progressive legislation which was introduced. After the 1930s it seems clear that the experience of the Hepburn government created for many working class people an image of the Liberal party as deeply hostile to labour, although to suppose that the recollection of that period could be a significant influence in more recent times would require a rather strained belief in the ability of an older generation to pass its troubles on to the young.

But whatever the historical source of the connection between the working class and the Conservative party in Ontario it is clear that in many areas of the province —especially in dominantly British ridings where the effect of ethnic or religious "cross-pressure" is less significant—the level of the party's support is being sharply reduced by the success of the NDP. And since the Conservative party's appeal to the worker has always been couched in the terms required by the brokerage theory the growth of a sentiment favouring an openly labour-oriented party suggests the growth of a class politics. It is possible, therefore, that the behaviour of Waterloo South is typical of what is happening in Ontario.

A CLASS POLITICS FOR CANADA?

The extent to which the evidence of the by-election affects a general account of the role of social class in the Canadian political system is necessarily uncertain. While it seems clear that the NDP has established a hold on the riding which must depend upon the effect of influences more permanent than the attractiveness of its current candidate, the area is by no means a microcosm of the nation. On the other hand, there are many constituencies throughout Canada with social structures similar to that of Waterloo South where the growth of urbanization and industrialization has created conditions in which a class politics might be expected to flourish. As more and more of our people move to the cities the traditional influences of religious affiliation and ethnic origin are likely to become less important in the face of the pressures of an increasingly complex technological society. Nor is there any reason to suppose that the affluence which accompanies this development will result in a decline in the willingness of people to distinguish between themselves on the basis of social class. Lost in any of our sprawling metropolitan areas, the one link which the voter has with those around him is his occupation and the social status which it gives him in combination with related attributes such as income and education.

These considerations all point to a greater potential role for class as a determinant of Canadian electoral behaviour in the future. Whether any of our parties will actively seek to harness that potential remains to be seen, for the electoral success which the practice of brokerage has won for the Liberals, and to a lesser extent for the Conservatives, makes the full acceptance of a different style of political behaviour comparatively unattractive even to the NDP. But the price which the nation pays for that kind of success may well prove to be too great. Gad Horowitz has put the case very simply that a greater influence for social class is necessary in Canadian politics: "The promotion of dissensus on class issues is a way of mitigating dissensus on many non-class issues." While the evidence of Waterloo South is that social class *can* become the principal influence in our electoral behaviour, it remains the case that a substantial proportion of the electorate continues to divide itself on the basis of religious affiliation and ethnic origin. But since these people tend also to be rather more middle class it may be argued that we are approaching the stage — in southwestern Ontario at least — where the middle class persists in dividing itself along racial and religious lines in support of the two older parties at the same time as the working class is turning in increasing numbers to the New Democrats.

This growth in strength is, however, generally not sufficient to permit the NDP to make significant constituency gains, for although it is the leading party in most areas of working class concentration throughout the country its share of the labour vote remains substantially lower than that of social democratic parties in other parliamentary systems cast in the British mould. Its success therefore frequently depends upon the Liberals and the Conservatives dividing the rest of the vote, simply because there are comparatively few constituencies in Canada which are sufficiently working class in character to guarantee an NDP victory on that basis alone. On the other hand, since there is no prospect of a marriage of convenience between the two older parties, and since their division of the vote tends in many cases to be based on their promotion of those racial, religious, and regional differences which have been with us since the beginning, it may be said that if the NDP is allowed to become a major party in the House of Commons it will be because the traditional brokers of the Canadian political system were unable to rid themselves of the doctrine handed down from their fathers. But in that case, if Professor Horowitz' account of the matter is correct, national unity will have been preserved in spite of our traditional political practice rather than because of it.

VOTERS' TURNOUT AND THE RESPONSIVENESS OF LOCAL GOVERNMENT: THE CASE OF TORONTO, 1969*

JERRY F. HOUGH

In politics it is a common general phenomenon that fewer people vote in local elections. In Metropolitan Toronto, for example, 750,000 persons voted in the 1968 federal election, 625,000 in the 1967 provincial election, and 340,000 in the 1969 local elections. The crucial question is—what is the meaning of the relatively low turnout in local elections? Furthermore, is the decline in turnout spread evenly through all socio-economic groups or do the characteristics of the voters in the local elections tend to differ from those in, say, federal elections?

These are not questions of academic interest alone. Today there are widespread calls for decentralization of power, for local self-rule, for power near the people, for citizen participation and governmental responsiveness to citizens' groups. In the past in the United States "states' rights" has normally been the slogan of the conservative, but now both in Canada and the United States decentralization is often advocated by those on the left who term it a vital precondition for increased governmental responsiveness to lower-income groups. The government that is "closest to the people" must be, it is argued, most responsive to the wishes of the people.

Seldom, however, are discussions of the relative responsiveness of different levels of government related to the basic facts of electoral mechanisms and behavior and to traditional democratic theory. In particular, little attention has been given to the differences in the rates of voter turnout. These questions will be explored in this article, which draws its evidence from the municipal election held in the city of Toronto on December 1, 1969. It will focus upon three wards which contain a fairly representative cross-section of the city's population.

The three wards selected out of a total of eleven in Toronto are located midway between the eastern and western boundaries of the city and extend from the waterfront on Lake Ontario to the northern boundaries of the city. The southernmost

* This article, which is published originally here, is based on a class project in Political Science 300 and 2306 in the academic session of 1969-1970 at the University of Toronto. I would like to express my deep gratitude to the students who made the paper possible, to my wife Barbara who obtained a large number of questionnaires from reluctant or hard-to-locate respondents, and to Professor Donald Forbes of the University of Toronto for many helpful comments.

ward—Ward VI—stretches from the waterfront to Bloor Street, which is the major east-west axis of Toronto. The ward contains the downtown business area, and most of it is populated by persons of low income and diverse ethnic backgrounds, including many residents who are not yet citizens. The northeast quadrant of the ward has been the scene of the construction of many high-rise apartment houses—by late 1969 twenty-seven were at least ten stories high. These apartment houses are inhabited predominantly by relatively young professionals, clerical personnel, and students. In 1961 the ward's average annual family income was slightly in excess of $3,500.

The middle ward—Ward V—is located immediately north of Ward VI, between Bloor Street and St. Clair Avenue. Its population tends to be divided into two groups. The southwest quadrant is populated primarily by New Canadians who have begun the movement towards the suburbs and who have family incomes averaging from $500 to $1,000 more a year than the New Canadians of Ward VI. The rest of the ward is largely Anglo-Saxon in ethnic origin and contains a fairly high percentage of people with professional or white-collar occupations. In the ward as a whole, the average family income was somewhat in excess of $5,000 in 1961, but it would be more realistic to speak of an average income of slightly over $4,000 in the southwest quadrant and of slightly over $6,000 in the rest of the ward.

The northern ward—Ward XI is clearly one of the elite wards in the city. In 1961 more than half of the males in the ward held professional, managerial, or technical jobs, and the average family income was in excess of $8,000 a year. More than a third of the ward consists of the former village of Forest Hill—the "Crestwood Heights" described by J. R. Seeley, R. A. Sims, and E. W. Loosley in their sociological study by that title published in 1956—but the ward has also seen much high-rise construction during the past ten to fifteen years. The apartment dwellers in Ward XI tend to be older than those in Ward VI.

The study of the turnout in these three wards is based upon two sources. First, a sample of 921 eligible voters was drawn from the municipal voters' list. Every fourth polling subdivision was selected in each ward, and one voter was taken out of each forty voters on the lists in the chosen subdivision. Thus, a typical subdivision containing 261 to 300 voters would provide seven persons for the sample. Each subdivision list was then divided into equal-sized groups, the number of which corresponded to the number of persons to be provided for the samples. (The groups were formed simply by counting down the list, a 280-voter list, for example, being divided at the 40th, 80th, 120th voter, etc.) A random-number table was then used to select one voter from each group. A similar procedure was followed with respect to the supplemental voting list (those who added themselves to the list after the original list was published).

Each of the persons selected in the sample received a one-page questionnaire which was designed to ascertain the individual's opinions on several leading issues, the degree of his contact with the aldermen in the past, and certain of his socio-economic characteristics. In addition, the assessed value of the individual's house or apartment and further socio-economic data were gathered from the city assessment lists, and the poll books were examined after the municipal election to determine whether these persons had voted in it. Second, in an effort to compare the voter turnout in the three wards in the federal and municipal elections, aggregate federal and municipal turnout data were collected for each polling subdivision within their boundaries. This information was then arranged by census tract so that the relative rates of voter turnout in different income areas could be compared.

I. THE TURNOUT

In the last twenty years the official voting statistics for municipal elections in Toronto have shown a consistently low voter turnout in a range from 30 to 45 percent. The results in 1969 revealed little difference since City Hall reported that 38.5 percent of the electors on the voters' list had gone to the polls. For the three wards in question, each of which had approximately the same total population (within a thousand of 66,000 persons), the turnout was 29.4 percent (12,080 votes cast) in low-income Ward VI, 38.4 percent (15,082 votes) in middle-income Ward V, and 47.3 percent (23,660 votes) in high-income Ward XI.

The traditionally low turnout in Toronto municipal elections has been one of the most discussed aspects of municipal politics. Yet, an examination of the turnout among the 921 voters in this study's sample reveals a situation quite at odds with the traditional preconceptions. If, as indicated in Table 1, one looks at the turnout within the entire sample, one finds results that, reassuringly, are quite close to the official data. However, if the analysis is limited to the 561 electors actually living in the polling subdivision at the time of the election, the turnout was not 38 percent but more than 57 percent.

TABLE 1:   Percentage of Voter Turnout by Ward in the Toronto City Election, December 1, 1969

Ward	Total population — Turnout among all electors on voters' list (official data)	Sample Data — Turnout among all electors drawn from voters' list	Sample Data — Turnout among residents drawn from voters' list	Sample Data — Turnout among "real" residents drawn from voters' list[1]
Ward V	38.4	41	46	55
Ward VI	29.2	30	42	61
Ward XI	47.3	46	49	56

[1] This column excludes those residents who had moved or died prior to the election, as well as those who by reason of citizenship or age should not have been included on the voters' list originally.

Behind the astonishing difference in the left-hand and right-hand columns in Table 1 lie several key facts about municipal elections in Toronto. In the first place, while the federal voters' list is based on an enumeration undertaken shortly before the election, the city voters' list is compiled on the basis of assessment information, the collection of which is begun eleven months before the election. Given the considerable movement of people within the city, the number of "dead souls" on the list is quite high by December, particularly in wards assessed near the beginning of the year or in wards (usually less affluent wards) with a more transient population.

A second explanation for the low turnout rates announced officially can be found in the eligibility rules for voting in a Toronto municipal election. In a federal election any Canadian citizen or British subject with a year's residence in Canada is given the franchise, but the rules of qualification for the municipal election are not so simple. The voters' list historically originated as a list of ratepayers—those who own property or who rent apartments or offices—and those citizens remain the core of the list today. A spouse of a ratepayer is now also usually given the vote, as is a person who lives in a rented room and has resided in the city since January 1st of the year prior to the election, that is, for 23 months because the election is held in December. However, the roomer (in contrast to the apartment tenant) is denied participation in the vote for school trustee, regardless of the length of his residence in the city.

The rules of eligibility for the municipal election mean that its voters' list should contain fewer residents than the federal list, but on the other hand the municipal list includes a significant number of non-residents not found on the federal list. Owners of a business or building, absentee landlords and those who rent offices (e.g., doctors, dentists, and lawyers) are ratepayers and are usually eligible to vote in the municipal election at their place of business. Even if they live outside the city, they still may vote for Toronto city mayor, aldermen, and school trustees— indeed, for aldermen and school trustees in each ward of the city in which they own or rent property. If they live within the city, they may vote for mayor only at their place of residence, but may vote for aldermen and school trustees once in each ward in which they are ratepayers. If a firm or business is a partnership, all partners are granted the franchise at their place of business. The spouse of an absentee land- lord or a business owner is also entitled to vote in the polling subdivision of that property, as is the spouse of a business tenant if he or she lives in the city. As a result, a large partnership has a considerable number of non-resident votes. One downtown law firm, for example, was entitled to 52 votes at its place of business, and 15 of these were cast.

Any analysis of voting participation must not ignore the non-resident voters. They amounted to 11 percent of the eligible voters in the whole city, but con- stituted 29.5 percent of those in Ward VI. An examination of both the voters' lists and the poll books for the three wards under study indicated that the non- residents constituted one percent of the votes in Ward XI, 5 percent in Ward V, and 17 percent in Ward VI. In general, very few (5 percent) of the absentee non- residents in the 921-person sample went to the polls, but 22 percent of the non- residents actually working within the polling subdivision cast a ballot.

Granting the franchise to non-residents had only a marginal impact upon the outcome of the 1969 election in Wards V and XI, but was nearly of decisive importance in the aldermanic election in Ward VI. One of the candidates, an incumbent alderman, had been accused of a voting record that was not responsive to the interests of his poorer constituents, and he finished a fairly distant fifth in the low-income polling subdivisions in which less than 10 percent of the vote was supplied by non-resident electors. He also finished fourth in the subdivisions based exclusively or almost exclusively upon high-rise apartments, but he headed the list of aldermen in the 15 subdivisions in which at least 90 percent of the voters were non-residents. In the overall vote he came within 37 votes of finishing second and of being one of the two aldermen elected in the ward.

In all three wards most of the voters were, of course, residents, and it is their socio-economic characteristics that shape the profile of the voting electorate. The data on these characteristics, drawn from the sample, will appear quite familiar to any student of voting behavior. The following figures are based not on the entire 921-person sample, but on the 561 persons within it who were residents and who still lived in the polling subdivision at the time of the election. Information on whether the person voted is available for all 561 in the sample, while data on socio-economic characteristics is available for over 95 percent of the sample.

Voter turnout by occupation: (As is customary in studies of electoral behavior, married women are classified by the occupation of their husband.) Professionals, 68 percent; managers and officials, 62 percent; shopkeepers, 47 percent; sales personnel, 63 percent; clerical personnel, 50 percent; foremen, technicians, and skilled craftsmen, 52 percent; semi-skilled and unskilled workers, 47 percent; students, 70 percent; retired persons, 58 percent.

Voter turnout by educational background: Public school, 52 percent; incomplete and complete high school, 58 percent; Grade 13 and incomplete college, 63 percent; undergraduate or graduate degree, 76 percent.

Voter turnout by assessed value of house: (Home owners only) Under $2,500, 37 percent; $2,500-$4,500, 62 percent; over $4,500, 62 percent. (A house assessed for $2,500 usually has a market value in the vicinity of $15,000.)

Voter turnout by assessed value of flat or rented house: (Tenants only): Under $2,500, 42 percent; $2,500-$4,500, 61 percent; over $4,500, 69 percent. (The turnout among roomers, those with too little space to be officially assigned a portion of the assessed value of a house or flat, was 42 percent.)

While these statistics show quite pronounced variations in voters' turnout among groups of different socio-economic status, they still overstate the degree of electoral participation by persons in the lower socio-economic position. The figures are based upon the voters' list, and they do not include three groups in which the poor are over-represented.

The first group not on the voters' list were those who moved into the polling subdivision after the completion of the assessment but who did not ask to be added to the list in the autumn. The sample data make clear that the number of electors who had moved by the time of election was considerably greater than the number of persons who added themselves to the list. (In Ward VI, the number who moved was over three times larger, while in Ward XI at the other extreme it was only 70 percent larger.) A comparison of the occupations of persons in the sample who moved and the occupation of persons who were added to list, as well as an examination of the socio-economic characteristics of the areas in which the ratio between the number who moved and those who asked to be put on the list is highest, both show that the more well-to-do elements of the population were far more likely to take the steps necessary for self-enumeration.

A second low-income group not on the voters' list was the transient roomer. While the roomer category includes persons of all status levels, most of the higher-status roomers were living with their parents or other relatives and had resided in the city for some time. The roomers who could not meet the 23-month residence qualification were predominantly either students or persons in low-income occupation.

A third low-income group not on the voters' list was the immigrant. As indicated earlier, Ward VI and Ward XI each had a population of approximately 66,000 persons, but 10,064 resident votes were cast in Ward VI compared with 23,328 resident votes in Ward XI. Part of this difference may be explained by factors already mentioned, but the single most important factor was the tendency for large numbers of low-income immigrants to settle in Ward VI upon first arriving in Toronto. It is perfectly understandable why such immigrants are not granted the vote until they become citizens, but the unavoidable consequence of this practice is that the lowest-income areas—those with the greatest need for various welfare services—have the fewest potential votes per capita in the city.

II. UNORGANIZED AND ORGANIZED CONTACT WITH ELECTED CITY OFFICIALS

Voting is the most widespread form of political participation, but it certainly is not the only type of such activity. A citizen can contact administrative agencies or elected officials. He can join in organized group activity. He can attend citizen meetings and express his views.

The questionnaire distributed in the three Toronto wards contained two questions related to contact with aldermen. One question asked the respondent about his knowledge of the aldermen's names and programs, and the other asked whether he had contacted an alderman during the previous three years. The data collected on this question is, for several reasons, not totally reliable and almost certainly overstates the amount of knowledge and the frequency of contact. The questionnaire did not check the claim of knowledge by asking the names of the aldermen, and the fact that the question was asked at the time of the election sometimes led to confusion between contact with aldermen and contact with candidates. Moreover, the one-sixth of the population whose questionnaires were not received had a level of voters' turnout considerably below that of those completing the questionnaire, and it is likely that their familiarity with the aldermen was also less.

Even if the statistics are accepted at face value, they still suggest rather low levels of knowledge about aldermen among the city's population. Of the respondents in the sample 64 percent admitted not knowing the name of either aldermen in their ward and 22 percent stated that, although they knew the name of at least one alderman, they had not learned much "about their program or the job they were doing." Only 14 percent said that they had learned "a good deal about one or both of the aldermen." The proportion claiming to have written, telephoned, or talked with one of their aldermen "either to complain about something or to make some suggestion" also stood at 14 percent.

The sample data also indicated that there was as much (or more) class differentiation in the degree of familiarity with aldermen as in voting participation. An especially sharp distinction can be drawn between persons of two groups of occupations: 51 percent of the respondents who were professionals, managers, owners, and salesmen (63 percent of the males in these occupations) stated that they at least knew the names of an alderman, while only 22 percent of those who were workers or clerical personnel made such a claim (25 percent of the males in these occupations). Twenty-four percent of the professionals, managers, owners, and salesmen asserted that they had contacted an alderman, compared to 5 percent of the workers and clerical employees.

A similar picture emerges from an examination of citizen participation in more organized political activities. Ward V, for example, had been the scene of considerable activity among ratepayer organizations, nearly a dozen of which functioned within the ward. Yet, all of these organizations were located in the more well-to-do sections of the ward; none had arisen in the southwest quadrant inhabited by lower-income New Canadians.

When the ratepayer groups organized a public meeting at which the proposed construction of an expressway through the ward was to be discussed with the Chairman of the Metropolitan Council, it was possible to distribute questionnaires to those who attended the meeting. The meeting was announced in the newspapers, and approximately 250 persons attended, three-quarters of them from Ward V. Yet, the occupational profile of those from Ward V who returned the questionnaire had little in common with the occupational profile in the ward as a whole. Fully 46 percent of the Ward V residents attending the meeting were professionals, 14 percent were managers and business owners, 18 percent were clerical and sales personnel, 16 percent were retired persons, and 6 percent were students. (As before, married women are classified by the occupation of their husbands.) Skilled, semi-skilled, unskilled, and service workers were represented by one woman, the wife of an electrician.

Ninety-one percent of the Ward V residents at the meeting opposed the expressway, 8 percent approved, and 1 percent marked "Don't know." In the ward as a whole, however, the survey found 42 percent approving the expressway, 38 percent opposed, and 20 percent uncertain. Forty-seven percent of the workers approved the expressway, 30 percent disapproved, and 20 percent were uncertain.

That the meeting should have such an upper-class character was not surprising. As Mancur Olson has convincingly demonstrated in *The Logic of Collective Action*, an individual guided by strictly rational, economic considerations will seldom find that his personal involvement in organized political activity has an impact on his own direct rewards that is at all proportionate to the money and effort expended. (Olson suggests that involvement in interest group activity is usually to be explained by compulsion, as often is the case with trade unions, or by various side-benefits.) Thus, for a person with a professional, managerial, or business-oriented occupation, dues to a ratepayers' organization are of marginal importance, and the social rewards, even the business contacts, may be quite valuable. Yet, if a low-income person has the drive, time, intelligence, and verbal ability to be an effective participant in citizens groups, his life situation could surely be improved much more dramatically if he were to spend his evenings in job-oriented education courses.

III. A COMPARISON OF VOTERS' TURNOUT IN THE FEDERAL AND CITY ELECTION

Greater voter turnout among persons of higher income and status is, of course, not peculiar to municipal elections. It is also present in federal elections, and often for identical reasons. But the question remains, are the socio-economic characteristics of persons who vote in a municipal election similar to those of persons who vote in a federal election?

Although the question is simple, it is not simple to answer. The boundaries of the city wards and the federal ridings do not coincide, and even if only overlapping sections of wards and ridings were considered, a thorough comparison should be based on separate studies undertaken at the time of each election. The people in the present sample could have been asked whether they did, in fact, vote in the most recent federal election, but in the past such questions have not led to reliable results. The percentage of respondents who claim to have voted in any election tends to be consistently higher than the percentage who actually voted.

While it is difficult to compare turnout in the federal and municipal elections on the basis of available sample data, the official reports of turnout by polling sub-division can be arranged in such a way as to produce a revealing comparison. The first step in such an analysis is to ascertain the boundaries of the polling sub-divisions and (in this case at least) to determine which federal sub-divisions lie within the boundaries of the wards being studied. The second step which is necessary if variations associated with socio-economic differences are to be analyzed, is to examine the boundaries of the census tracts within the section of the city being studied and to find out which federal and city polling sub-divisions are located within each. Fortunately, the major streets are frequently used as boundaries for census tracts as well as polling sub-divisions, but often it is necessary to extrapolate the data in order to ensure that identical areas with identical (or virtually identical) populations are being compared. Finally, of course, the non-resident electors on the voters' list and the non-residents who voted must be excluded from the municipal voting data in order to make it comparable with the federal data.

In this study, the numbers of eligible voters and actual voters within each census tract were determined for both the federal and municipal elections, and the census tracts were then ranked by the average family income of their inhabitants as reported in the 1961 census, the most recent reporting such data. The ranked list of census tracts was then divided into four groups in such a way that the groups were as equal as possible in size of population (as reported in the partial 1966 census). The results of this comparison of federal and municipal sub-division data are summarized in Table 2.

TABLE 2:   Voters' Turnout in the 1968 Federal and the 1969 Municipal
Elections, The Territory of Toronto Wards V, VI, and XI

Group of Census Tracts (with the ranges of average income in 1961)	Total Population 1966	1968 Federal Election			1969 Municipal Election[1]		
		Electors on list	Votes cast	%	Electors on list	Votes cast	%
I. ($7,000-$12,000)	49,256	34,596	26,075	75	35,073	17,373	50
II. ($5,500-$7,000)	47,977	31,504	22,788	72	31,673	14,621	46
III. ($4,000-$5,500)	49,151	23,321	15,979	69	22,765	8,944	39
IV. ($3,000-$4,000)	48,557	17,498	10,518	60	17,116	5,097	30
Total	194,941	106,919	75,360	70	106,627	46,035	43

[1] The statistics on the 1969 municipal election exclude the non-resident electors on the list and the non-resident votes cast. They also exclude the returns from 7 apartment houses built between the two elections. The purpose of the latter exclusion was to preserve the comparability of the data in the two elections, and it had little effect on turnout figures for the municipal election. Had the new apartment houses been included, the turnout in the municipal election would have been 31 percent in Group IV and 47 percent in Group II.

Sources: Information on the turnout in polling sub-divisions in the federal election was obtained in the *Report of the Chief Electoral Officer, Twenty-Eighth General Election, 1968*, Ottawa, Queen's Printer, 1969. The boundaries of the sub-divisions were found in the voting lists for the ridings which have territory within the three wards. (In Toronto, these lists are collected and preserved at the Municipal Reference Library.)
Information on the municipal election was obtained from the voters' lists for the three wards and from the poll books for the wards' polling sub-divisions.

As noted previously, the precise turnout percentages (for the federal election as well as the municipal election) will vary depending upon whether or not one excludes electors who moved prior to the election and whether or not one tries to estimate the number of eligible voters who were not included on the list. Whatever adjustments are made in the figures showing percentage of turnout, however, several facts emerge in stark relief from the data of Table 2.

First, in both the federal and municipal elections the number of electors on the list decreased sharply from high-income areas to lower-income areas. The drop would have been much greater if there were not many more "dead souls" on the municipal voters' list in the poorer areas than in the well-to-do areas. The decrease in the ratio of electors to residents can be explained in part by enumeration procedures, but primarily by the larger numbers of non-citizens and the larger number of children in the lower-income areas.

Second, the reduction in the number of actual voters was even more marked than the decline in the number of electors on the list. In both the federal and the municipal elections, the most well-to-do area (Group I) had approximately twice as many electors on the voters' list as the poorest area (Group IV). However, the well-to-do areas had over two and a half times as many votes cast in the federal election and nearly three and a half times as many votes cast in the municipal election.

Third, the decline in voters' turnout from the federal election to the municipal election was greater in the poorer areas than in the well-to-do sections. In the census tracts in Group I, the number of votes cast in the municipal election was only 33 percent less than those cast in the federal election. In the census tracts in Group IV, the number of votes cast was 52 percent less. As a consequence, as Table 3 indicates, the "median" voter in the city election was of higher socio-economic status than the "median" voter in the federal election.

TABLE 3: Comparative Percentages of Actual Voters in Census Tracts in Wards V, VI, and XI in Toronto, 1968 Federal Election and 1969 Municipal Election

Group of Census Tracts (with the ranges of average income in 1961)	Total Population 1966	Actual Votes Cast	
		Federal	Municipal
I. ($7,000-$12,000)	25.3	35	38
II. ($5,500-$7,000)	24.6	30	32
III. ($4,000-$5,500)	25.2	21	19
IV. ($3,100-$4,000)	24.9	14	11
Total	100.0	100	100
N=	194,941	75,360	46,025

Source: *Idem.,* Table 2.

In conclusion, it should be noted that the statistics of Tables 2 and 3 give only a rough indication of the variations in voters' turnout among citizens of different income levels, for there is considerable diversity among the inhabitants of each census tract. For example, 25 percent of the persons in the sample who lived in the lower-income census tracts (Groups III and IV) had professional-managerial occupations, while 9 percent of those in the higher-income census tracts (Groups I and II) were semi-skilled or unskilled workers. The statistical differences shown in Table 2 and 3 would surely have been greater were it not for this fact.

IV. VOTERS' TURNOUT AND THE RESPONSIVENESS OF POLITICIANS ON POLICY ISSUES

Traditional democratic theory, at least that propounded by Jeremy Bentham, assumed that governmental officials in any country are consciously or unconsciously motivated by self-interest. It suggested that for this reason a democratic electoral mechanism would push politicians towards decisions that would maximize the number of votes they receive, or at least that it would lead to the "bankruptcy" of those politicians who failed to follow this rule.

If one takes this assumption seriously, what policy outcomes would one predict in cities with voting patterns like those in Toronto? During a snowstorm the plows must begin on one street rather than another. Is it not more rational for officials to start in the section with more votes cast per street than in the section with fewer votes cast per street? If garbage funds are limited and sacrifices must be made in service, should a rational politician cut services equally or should he decide to retain back-door collection of garbage in the high turnout areas while requiring residents of poorer areas to place the garbage cans on the street curb for collection?

To take another illustration, let us assume that the low-income sections of Ward VI with their large families and numerous working mothers desire governmental day-care centers. Let us assume that the high-income inhabitants of Ward XI want a new Learning Resources Center for their college-bound children, a center in which the library collection is supplemented with records, tapes, videotape television cameras, courses on film-making, and so forth. With four-tenths of a vote being cast for each child under the age of 15 in the low-income census tracts of Ward VI and 1.95 votes being cast for each child in Ward XI, where would Bentham suggest that the intelligent city leader would receive the maximum political return on the dollar spent? (The calculations on both Ward VI and Ward XI exclude census tracts in which high-rise apartment tenants are a predominant element.)

Of course, if the decisions in such cases would produce a massive backlash—a major rise in turnout in the low-income areas—then the calculations of the politician should be quite different. However, the examples chosen are not hypothetical. The Learning Resources Center was built in Ward XI, and the high-income, high voter-turnout areas do receive better snow removal and back-door garbage collection. These decisions, and others like them, have actually produced greater dissatisfaction with city services among the inhabitants of the poorer areas. Forty percent of the respondents in the low-income census tracts (Group IV of Table 2 and 3) rated city services as only fair or poor, as compared to only 22 percent of the respondents in the high-income census tracts (Group I).

Yet, in practice, the important political fact is not the higher levels of dissatisfaction in the poorer areas, but the 59 percent "good" or "excellent" responses to the question. Indeed, when the persons in these areas were asked whether the city provided better services to other areas, only 30 percent answered affirmatively. Nine percent thought their own area was treated better, 25 percent thought that all areas were treated equally, and 36 percent checked the response "I have no idea." Not only was there no surge in voter turnout, but the candidate who carried the low-income areas was the incumbent mayor.

V. WHOM WOULD DECENTRALIZATION BENEFIT?

Given the data on relative turnout in the federal and municipal elections and given the class composition of participation in organized citizen-group activity, why do so many advocates of increased governmental responsiveness to the poor, especially so many young advocates, also call for a decentralization of power to those levels of government at which the political participation and voting power of the poor are at their lowest levels?

Several quite different explanations might be used to answer this paradox. It is possible, for example, that the left-wing advocates of decentralization have understood something fundamentally true about the political system and that their program is quite appropriate. One might argue either that the current inequalities in participation are easily correctable or that the assumptions of traditional democratic theory need to be rethought in a systematic manner. It is also possible that those proposing decentralization have not really understood the inner mechanisms of the Western political systems, that their political program is simply inappropriate for achieving their stated goals. A third possibility is that the advocates of decentralization, themselves of upper and upper-middle class occupations and origins, unconsciously favor political arrangements in which their own basic interests will not be seriously challenged. In such a case their program would be quite appropriate to their unconscious goals.

None of these possibilities should be dismissed lightly. If democratic theory is not wholly inaccurate, however, the data would certainly suggest that decentralization of power is insufficient in itself. If involved, affluent citizens really do want government that is both decentralized and more responsive to the poor (even if this means higher taxes, slower snow removal in their areas at times, and delays in the construction of learning resource centers for their own children), then at a minimum great attention must be paid to the details of the electoral mechanisms. Surely it is vital to deprive the non-resident professional, businessman, and landlord of his extra vote. Surely it is vital to grant first-class citizenship to the roomer. Surely it is vital to bring the system of municipal enumeration into conformity with the federal and provincial practices and enumerate at a time much closer to the election. Surely it is vital to take some step to decrease the number of immigrant non-voters, perhaps by reducing the period required for citizenship.

Even such a factor as electoral boundaries assumes special importance because of the class differences in the rates of voters' turnout. Imagine an area populated in its northern half by 50,000 affluent persons and in its southern half by 50,000 poor persons, an area in which the northern half casts three times as many votes as the southern. If two electoral districts are created and the boundary is drawn along a north-south line, then each district will have 25,000 persons of each income level. It might well be predicted that the representative or representatives in each district would be much more sensitive to the demands of the northern area with its larger number of votes. If the boundary is drawn east-west along class lines, however, then the poor will obtain representation equal to that of the affluent, despite their lower turnout rate. Moreover, in the latter situation, quite unlike the former, there would exist powerful incentives for candidates competing for the vote of the poor to raise loudly questions about differentials in the quality of city services in the two areas.

However, even electoral tinkering is not likely to be enough. Something needs to be done to correct the factors that lead to the citizens (particularly the less affluent citizens) having much less information about local representatives and local governmental affairs than about those at the federal level. Something must be done, if citizens' meetings are to attract a representative cross-section of the population, to ensure that such meetings provide social and psychic rewards to others than the verbally adroit.

Perhaps most important, fundamental changes in the local tax structure may be required. All studies have shown that lower-income voters favor an expanded governmental role in the providing of various welfare services. Yet, in the 1969 municipal election in Toronto these voters favored an incumbent mayoralty candidate whose major theme had been prevention of tax increases. Surely one reason for this contradictory attitude towards increasing local governmental services is that federal services are financed through a progressive income tax while municipal services are financed through a property tax that must be paid even if income drops because of unemployment, underemployment, or retirement—a tax for which there are no exemptions to protect the poor.

If upper middle class citizens are serious about decentralizing power in order to increase responsiveness of government to the needs of the poor, then they must work both for electoral mechanisms designed to produce greater parity in the electoral influence of the affluent and non-affluent and for conditions in which the poor can logically vote for programs that will meet their own needs. If, on the other hand, middle class citizens are not serious about such issues, if they simply advocate decentralization and citizen participation in general terms, then the question raised at the beginning of this section should be posed once more. Is a fundamental rethinking of democratic theory really necessary or are upper and upper-middle classes once more calling for programs that serve their own basic interests—and calling for them in the name of social justice for the poor?

BIBLIOGRAPHY

Aitken, M., *Hey Ma! I Did It,* Toronto, Clarke, Irwin, 1953.

Alford, R. R., *Party and Society: The Anglo-American Democracies,* Chicago, Rand McNally, 1963.

Anderson, G. M., "Voting Behaviour and the Ethnic-Religious Variable: A Study of a Federal Election in Hamilton, Ontario," *C.J.E.P.S.,* Vol. XXXII, No. 1, February, 1966.

Beck, J. M., "Quebec and the Canadian Elections of 1958," *Parliamentary Affairs,* Vol. XII, No. 1, 1959.

Beck, J. M., "The Election of 1963 and National Unity," *Dalhousie Review,* Vol. XLIII, No. 2, Summer, 1963.

Beck, J. M., "The Electoral Behaviour of Nova Scotia in 1965," *Dalhousie Review,* Vol. XLVI, No. 1, Spring, 1966.

Beck, J. M., and Dooley, D. J., "Party Images in Canada," *Q.Q.,* Vol. LXVII, No. 3, Autumn, 1960.

Beck, J. M., *Pendulum of Power: Canada's Federal Elections,* Toronto, Prentice-Hall, 1968.

Blair, R. S., "Electoral Competition in the Canadian Provinces," Address to the 38th Annual Meeting of the Canadian Political Science Association, Sherbrooke, P.Q. June 10, 1966.

Canada, *Report of the Chief Electoral Officer, Twenty-Eighth General Election, 1968,* Ottawa, Queen's Printer, 1969.

Cohen, R. I., *Quebec Votes,* Montreal, Saje Publications, 1965.

Courtney, J. C., (ed.), *Voting in Canada,* Toronto, Prentice-Hall, 1967.

Courtney, J. C., and Smith, D. E., "Voting in a Provincial General Election and a Federal By-Election: A Constituency Study of Saskatoon City," *C.J.E.P.S.,* Vol. XXXII, No. 3, August, 1966.

Davis, M., "Ballot Behaviour in Halifax Revisited," *C.J.E.P.S.,* Vol. XXX, No. 4, November, 1964.

Davis, M., "A Last Look at Ballot Behaviour in the Dual Constituency of Halifax," *C.J.E.P.S.,* Vol. XXXII, No. 3, August, 1966.

Dean, E. P., "How Canada Has Voted: 1867 to 1945," *Canadian Historical Review,* Vol. XXX, No. 3, September, 1949.

Eldersveld, S., *Political Parties: A Behavioural Analysis,* Chicago, Rand McNally, 1964.

Engelmann, F. G., "Membership Participation in Policy-Making in the C.C.F.," *C.J.E.P.S.,* Vol. XXII, No. 2, May, 1956.

Englemann, F. G., and Gilsdorf, R. R., "Recent Behavioural Political Science in Canada: An Assessment of Voting Behaviour Studies," Address to the 38th Annual Meeting of the Canadian Political Science Association, Sherbrooke, P.Q., June 8, 1966.

Eulau, H., *The Behavioural Persuasion in Politics,* New York, Random House, 1963.

Filley, W. O., "Social Structure and Canadian Political Parties: The Quebec Case," *Western Political Quarterly,* Vol. IX, No. 4, December, 1956.

Fox, P. W., "A Study of One Constituency in the Canadian Federal Election of 1957," *C.J.E.P.S.,* Vol. XXIV, No. 2, May, 1958.

Fox, P. W., "Canada's Most Decisive Federal Election," *Parliamentary Affairs,* Vol. XI, No. 3, Summer, 1958.

Gagne, W., and Regenstreif, P., "Some Aspects of New Democratic Party Urban Support in 1965," *C.J.E.P.S.,* Vol. XXXIII, No. 4, November, 1967.

Granatstein, J. C., "The Armed Forces Vote in Canadian General Elections, 1940-1968," *Journal of Canadian Studies,* Vol. IV, No. 1, February, 1969.

Grossman, L. A., " 'Safe' Seats: The Rural-Urban Pattern in Ontario," *C.J.E.P.S.,* Vol. XXIX, No. 3, August, 1963.

Hahn, H., "Voting in Canadian Communities: A Taxonomy of Referendum Issues," *C.J.P.S.,* Vol. I, No. 4, December, 1968.

Hamelin, J. et M., *Les moeurs électorales dans le Québec de 1791 à nos jours,* Montréal, Les éditions du jour, 1962.

Havel, J. E., *Les citoyens de Sudbury et la politique,* Sudbury, Laurentian University Press, 1966.

Hoffman, D., "Intra-Party Democracy: A Case Study," *C.J.E.P.S.*, Vol. XXVII, No. 2, May, 1961.

Jewett, P., "Voting in the 1960 Federal By-Elections at Peterborough and Niagara Falls: Who Voted New Party and Why?" *C.J.E.P.S.*, Vol. XXVIII, No. 1, February, 1962.

Johnpoll, B. K., "Two Aspects of Voter Behaviour in Saskatchewan," Address to the 38th Annual Meeting of the Canadian Political Science Association, Sherbrooke, P.Q., June 8, 1966.

Kamin, L. J., "Ethnic and Party Affiliations of Candidates as Determinants of Voting," *Canadian Journal of Psychology*, Vol. XII, No. 4, December, 1958.

Kim, K. W., "The Limits of Behavioural Explanation in Politics," *C.J.E.P.S.*, Vol. XXXI, No. 3, August, 1965.

Land, B., *Eglinton, The Election Study of a Federal Constituency*, Toronto, Peter Martin Associates, 1965.

Laponce, J. A., *People vs. Politics, A Study of Opinions, Attitudes, and Perceptions in Vancouver-Burrard, 1963-1965*, Toronto, University of Toronto Press, 1969.

Lemieux, V., "Les dimensions sociologiques du vote créditiste au Québec," *Recherches Sociographiques*, Vol. VI, No. 2, May-August, 1965.

Lemieux, V., "L'analyse hiérarchique des résultats électoraux," *C.J.P.S.*, Vol. I, No. 1, March, 1968.

Lemieux, V., "La composition des préférences partisanes," *C.J.P.S.*, Vol. II, No. 4, December, 1969.

Lemieux, V., (ed.), *Quatre élections provinciales au Québec*, Québec, les presses de l'Université Laval, 1969.

Meisel, J., "Religious Affiliation and Electoral Behaviour," *C.J.E.P.S.*, Vol. XXII, No. 4, November, 1956.

Meisel, J., *The 1957 Canadian General Election*, Toronto, University of Toronto Press, 1962.

Meisel, John, (ed.), *Papers on the 1962 Election*, Toronto, University of Toronto Press, 1964.

Pinard, M., "Political Factors in the Rise of Social Credit in Quebec," Address to 36th Annual Meeting of the Canadian Political Science Association, Charlottetown, June, 1964.

Pinard, M., "One-Party Dominance and Third Parties," *C.J.E.P.S.*, Vol. XXXIII, No. 3, August, 1967.

Regenstreif, P., "The Canadian General Election of 1958," *Western Political Quarterly*, Vol. XIII, No. 2, June, 1960.

Regenstreif, P., "Some Aspects of National Party Support in Canada," *C.J.E.P.S.*, Vol. XIX, No. 1, February, 1963.

Regenstreif, P., *The Diefenbaker Interlude: Parties and Voting in Canada, An Interpretation*, Toronto, Longmans, 1965.

Robin, M., "The Social Basis of Party Politics in British Columbia," *Q.Q.*, Vol. LXXII, No. 4, Winter, 1966.

Rothney, G. O., "Denominational Basis of Representation in the Newfoundland Assembly, 1919-1962," *C.J.E.P.S.*, Vol. XXVII, No. 4, November, 1962.

Scarrow, H. A., "Federal-Provincial Voting Patterns in Canada," *C.J.E.P.S.*, Vol. XXVI, No. 2, May, 1960.

Scarrow, H. A., "By-Elections and Public Opinion in Canada," *Public Opinion Quarterly*, Vol. XXV, Spring, 1961.

Scarrow, H. A., "Patterns of Voter Turnout in Canada," *Midwest Journal of Political Science*, Vol. V, No. 4, 1961.

Scarrow, H. A., "Voting Patterns and the New Party," *Political Science,* Vol. XIV, No. 1, March, 1962.

Scarrow, H. A., *How Canada Votes, A Handbook of Federal and Provincial Election Data,* New Orleans, Hauser Press, 1962.

Schindeler, F., and Hoffman, D., "Theological and Political Conservatism," *C.J.P.S.,* Vol. I, No. 4, December, 1968.

Simmons, J. W., "Voting Behaviour and Socio-Economic Characteristics: The Middlesex East Federal Election, 1965," *C.J.E.P.S.,* Vol. XXXIII, No. 3, August, 1967.

Ulmer, S., (ed.), *Introductory Readings in Political Behaviour,* Chicago, Rand McNally, 1961.

Wilson, J., "Politics and Social Class in Canada: The Case of Waterloo South," *C.J.P.S.,* September, 1968.

Wilson, J., "The Myth of Candidate Partisanship: the Case of Waterloo South," *Journal of Canadian Studies,* Vol. III, No. 4, November, 1968.

Wrong, D. H., "Ontario Provincial Elections, 1934-1955," *C.J.E.P.S.,* Vol. XXIII, No. 3, August, 1957.

Young, W. D., "The Peterborough Election: The Success of a Party Image," *Dalhousie Review,* Vol. XL, No. 4, Winter, 1961.

Zakuta, L., "Membership in a Becalmed Protest Movement," *C.J.E.P.S.,* Vol. XXIV, No. 2, May, 1958.

ELEVEN
THE EXECUTIVE PROCESS: THE CROWN

In the past few years the monarchical system of government in Canada has been questioned increasingly. A news item reprinted here from the daily press exemplifies recent criticism. The passage quoted from an article by Frank MacKinnon is a lively defence of the virtues of monarchy for Canada.

In 1947 new Letters Patent accorded to the governor general in Canada virtually all of the powers the monarch could exercise in Canada. Section II of the Letters Patent contains the essence, but the formal document is worth reprinting because of the flavour of royal government it conveys. For Professor Mallory's article on the role Canada played in the appointment of a governor general in 1935, which casts much light on the inner workings of our constitution, see the first edition of this book, pp. 109-115.

The segment reprinted from Dr. Forsey's book delineating the 1926 Canadian constitutional incident illustrates one aspect of the governor general's powers, the vice-regal right to refuse dissolution of parliament to his prime minister, while Professor Mallory's note on the lieutenant-governor's choice of a successor to Premier Duplessis in Quebec raises for examination another power of the crown, namely its right to select a prime minister. A lieutenant-governor also possesses, on paper at least, the discretion to veto legislation outright or to reserve his assent to it. Professor Mallory's second note assesses the most recent case of reservation, which occurred in Saskatchewan in 1961. The bibliography at the end of the section lists some of the recent literature on the federal government's power to disallow provincial legislation.

A short passage from the *Canadian Almanac and Directory* on the granting of honours in Canada is also reprinted here because there seems to be a general lack of understanding of the subject.

WE'RE ON THE ROAD TO REPUBLICANISM*

PETER DEMPSON

Whither the monarchy in Canada? The question of the future of the monarchy was resurrected again last September by State Secretary Gerard Pelletier who, when visiting London, casually predicted that Canada would evolve into a republic in one or two generations. But it soon became apparent he was speaking only for himself.

Prime Minister Pierre Trudeau was quick to issue a mild rebuke to Mr. Pelletier, pointing out that the Crown was still a vital part of the Canadian constitution and would continue to be. . . .

Many Canadians—mainly those under 30—have come to the conclusion, however, that the monarchy is outdated, and that Canada would be better off as a republic. This was pointed up in a poll taken for the Canada 70 series, published by The Telegram.

More than half of the Canadians polled in the study outside of Quebec were either loyal or indifferent to the monarchy. In Quebec, 90 percent expressed the view that the monarchy had outlived its usefulness.

Prince Philip, who isn't one to back away from a contentious issue, was asked when he visited Ottawa in October what he thought the future of the monarchy in Canada was. He promptly replied that it was a matter for Canadians themselves to decide.

"The monarchy exists in Canada for historical reasons," he said, adding that it was considered to be a benefit to the nation. "But if Canadians feel the monarchy has no further role to play in Canada, then for goodness sake, let's end the thing on amicable terms without having a row about it."

The Prince said flatly that the royal couple didn't make periodic trips to Canada "for our health, so to speak. We can think of other ways of enjoying ourselves." . . .

Along with other family benefits, Prince Philip gets £40,000 ($104,000) a year from the British Parliament. . . .

The Queen draws an allowance of $1.3 million a year from the state. It has remained unchanged since she ascended the throne in 1952. Although one of the richest women in the world, she spends more than that amount to meet the demands made on her. She makes up the difference by dipping into her private income, mostly the revenues of real estate.

The Queen is responsible for paying 300 fulltime employees, from the lord chamberlain to the housemaids. A new government employment tax also comes out of her allowance. . . .

Canadian taxpayers bear none of the direct costs of the monarchy in Britain. Canadians, however, contribute to the institution through the upkeep of Crown

* From *The Telegram,* Toronto, December 4, 1969. By permission.

representatives in Canada—the Governor General and the 10 lieutenant governors of the provinces.

Many Canadians are convinced that eventually the monarchy will disappear in Canada and be replaced by a republican form of government, patterned, perhaps, after India or some other Commonwealth countries. But this isn't likely to happen in the foreseeable future.

The ties with Britain remain strong, even though more than half of Canada's population is now of other than Anglo-Saxon descent. . . .

Still, even if a majority of Canadians now favor stripping the trappings of royalty from the constitution, it would be exceedingly difficult to do. Any change in the British North America Act must have the consent of all provinces, hence any provincial government could veto abolition of the monarchy at the outset.

Should Canada become a republic in time, however, it's likely it would retain the parliamentary system of government, modelled on British precedents. It would be necessary, of course, to have a non-partisan head of state on the analogy of the modern Crown. The Governor General would probably be replaced by a president and the lieutenant-governors by governors.

The new system, to be successful, should stem from the constitutional expression that modern monarchs and their viceroys have been stripped of all political power. But in a republic this might be difficult. An elected president could defy Parliament, as Charles de Gaulle did on more than one occasion.

The last two Governments have been whittling away at the monarchy, like tidal waves lashing a rugged shore. Royal Mail on post boxes has become Canada Mail. The royal insignia on buildings and documents has been replaced by the Canadian coat-of-arms. Even in Ottawa's official publication, *The Organization of the Government of Canada,* a key section was rewritten by the Trudeau Administration.

Formerly it contained this passage: "Executive power in Canada is vested in the Queen by the British North America Act, 1867." Reference to the Queen has now been abolished. The new version reads:

"Executive power in Canada is exercised by the Cabinet and carried out in the name of the Governor General, who acts formally on the advice of the Privy Council."

Eugene Forsey, of Ottawa, long regarded as one of Canada's outstanding constitutional experts, has branded these moves as "creeping republicanism." But whether creeping, crawling or bounding, nothing could be plainer or more flagrant than what is happening.

It almost makes a mockery of what Queen Elizabeth said in the fall of 1957 when she opened Parliament and greeted senators and MPs as " . . . your Queen—together we constitute the Parliament of Canada."

It's obvious that those words have now been largely forgotten, despite the reassurances by the Prime Minister that the monarchy still has a vital role to play in Canada.

THE VALUE OF THE MONARCHY*

FRANK MACKINNON

A constitutional monarch protects democracy from some peculiarities of political power. It has been retained in our system because it works. Other reasons, such as nostalgic recollections of the past and sentimental ties with Britain, are secondary — to some, irrelevant — and should not obscure basic facts of government. One of these facts is a tendency of man, whether deep-sea diver or astronaut on the one hand or politician on the other, to suffer from the "bends" during rapid rises from one level of pressure and atmosphere to another.

History clearly indicates how common and serious are the "bends" in government. Even small rises from private citizen to mayor may bring on giddiness while major ascents from backbencher to minister or from minister to head of government can cause acute distress of the equilibrium. Constitutions have prescribed various remedies. Complicated procedures select those who are to make the political climb; ascent by stages is sometimes provided—perhaps by planned pauses in the back benches or the opposition; control of those on high is arranged through established contacts with those below; and, most difficult of all, some arrangement must be made to end the stay in political orbit of those who have been there long enough and can not or will not come back by themselves. A sure cure has not yet been devised, however, and the "bends" remain a major occupational hazard of rulers, which some overcome for varying periods and to which others fall quick and tragic victims.

To relieve this difficulty at the heights of political power is the main purpose of the constitutional monarchy. Some human being must be at the summit of government, and much depends on his stability. Unfortunately great talent, public acclaim and hero worship, and even assumptions of "divine right" have not been reliable stabilizers when the head of state wields power. We therefore place two persons at the top: one is at the very summit and he stays there permanently and is accustomed to living at that level; the other is temporary and he is made to understand that his status is sponsored and may be ended at any time.

The monarch holds power in the state on behalf of the people, and he or she is the personal symbol of authority which man finds necessary in every system. Heredity makes his tenure unquestioned and ensures a rigid training for the job. Pomp and ceremony attract respect and provide the show which people always expect from heads of state. But the monarch is not allowed to wield the power of head of state by himself; the pomp and ceremony are all that he can manage safely at his level and he must wield the power only on the advice of others.

* From *The Dalhousie Review*, Vol. 49, No. 2, Summer, 1969, by permission of the author and publisher.

These others are the sovereign's ministers, especially the prime minister, who is the head of government. A prime minister is almost at the summit but not quite, and that difference is crucial to democracy. He is given no power whatever; he advises the Crown on the exercise of the Crown's power; and that difference is also crucial to democracy. He has no pomp of his own, so that he knows that he is not an indispensable symbol. He is a trustee into whose hands is placed the exercise of power but not power itself.

This separation of pomp and power at the top took centuries to develop and was the result of the mistakes of many sovereigns and ministers. Other arrangements for such separation in other systems did not go so far as the British, who make the monarch so colourful and the prime minister so powerful and responsible an adviser that each, regardless of the personalities concerned, knows his place. . . .

The monarchy therefore serves democracy. It keeps the ministers in second place as servants of the state—electable, responsible, accountable, criticizable, and defeatable—a position necessary to the operation of parliamentary government. The people and their parliament can control the head of government because he cannot identify himself with the state or confuse loyalty to himself with allegiance to the state and criticism with treason. He is discouraged from the common tendency of officials, whether elected or not, to regard and make themselves indispensable, to entrench themselves in expanding power structures, to resent accountability and criticism, and to scoff at the effects of prolonged tenure of office or advancing years. Moreover, such control avoids the charges of treason, executions, assassinations, revolutions, and miscellaneous other expensive upheavals which so often accompany attempts to control and change governments that take themselves too seriously.

The democratic sensibilities of some people are disturbed by the idea of an élite, a symbol, an official who is neither elected nor chosen by someone who is elected. They err if they think the withdrawal of monarchy will remove such elements from government. These elements are characteristic of government itself, whatever its form, and are simply transferred to other institutions when a monarchy disappears. Whatever their system, men will have élites and symbols. Heads of government, elected or not, will take to themselves if they can the prestige and power of monarchs, disguised perhaps, but with the same basic elements; they find them a natural and necessary feature of government authority. The existence of a monarchy protects the prime minister from such temptations. . . .

Monarchal phenomena are common in other activities of society. The cult of the celebrity is as dominant in our day as it ever was in history. How often is "I touched him" heard in a screaming crowd! The élite in athletics have always been admired and well paid. Universities feature academic ceremonial. There are many resemblances between churches and royal courts—the raiment, titles, powers of clergy, even the throne, tiara, and crown. And in the smallest communities the dignities and regalia of fraternal and religious lodges are reminiscent of the potentates and knights of old. These are such natural and acceptable phenomena that it is not difficult to understand government officials taking advantage of them.

Man has found, however, that in government it is hard to criticize and advise a tremendous swell in robes or uniform who also has power, a retinue, and a palace. Our system discourages these things as much as possible for working politicians, but, since they are inevitable anyway, they are placed with the Crown, partly to provide a good show, mainly to strengthen the democratic state.

All systems, including democracy, contain the means for their own destruction. It is in time of crisis, when some serious and unexpected dislocation take place for which there is no normal remedy, that systems break down for good. . . . Parliamentary government presupposes change as required; but such change means orderly alteration of power, not conditions of general panic and destruction. When an electoral system is stalemated, when a parliament breaks down, when a prime minister dies in office and there is no obvious successor, when a leader becomes very ill or insane and everyone knows it but himself and the public—these are among the times when political paralysis is brought on by shock and uncertainty. In such circumstances a constitutional monarch provides a symbol of continuity, order, and authority. He can not, of course, step in and take over; he can only encourage others and sponsor the search for an orderly solution of the difficulties. He is above suspicion and can command confidence because of his prestige, because he is above politics and ambition for personal aggrandizement, and because he does not exercise power on his own initiative. Even in such modest periods of upheaval as elections, he represents the state as a whole while the parties involved, including the government, can oppose each other to even the most vituperative extremes—a process which should never be taken for granted. No political leader can be a symbol of the whole state either in crisis or in elections; nor should he be in a parliamentary democracy. That is the job of a monarch.

There are other purposes of the monarchy: the encouragement of dignity and respect for government, the example of a royal family, the colour of pageantry, the sponsorship of good works and the inevitable social activities of government; the source of honours and awards; a continuing focus of loyalty and emotion; a unifying force among a people; and, in our monarchy, a headship for a family of nations, the Commonwealth. Each of these functions has its own merits and weaknesses. Whether or not we approve of any or all of them, we must remember that none is irrelevant or disposable: each one crops up in some form in every system of government. When a monarchy disappears, other institutions soon take them on. Then trouble begins because of the transfer of such functions to the power structure. Officials and political parties from right to left have found many ways of using them to protect themselves and their powers and prestige from the legitimate operation of democracy. They are in safer hands, and are more effective, with the Crown.

An elected non-political president is often used as an alternative to a monarch. His main problem, aside from the temporary and relatively uninteresting and colourless character of his office, is the ease with which he can be overshadowed by the prime minister and, worse, the ease with which he can compete with the prime minister. Everyone concerned knows exactly where the monarch and his advisers stand in relation to one another and to the people. This arrangement, as already noted, is not so clear in a republic because two elected heads can get in each other's way and trespass on each other's powers.

An elected political president wielding power directly is a completely different institution at the head of a different system of government. He could not function in the parliamentary system as we know it. As every American president has testified, this kind of official also finds burdensome the combination of head of government and head of state.

Which is the "best" system? No one knows; some people tend to think their own is "best" whatever it is; others tend to admire any system other than their own; some are more concerned with the kind of system they have than with how it works. Two things, however, are clear; that systems are not automatically transferable from one place to another—too much depends on the environment; and that any system must allow, not only for logical forms and cherished principles, but also for peculiarities of human nature in government, particularly the hierarchal "bends."

Canadians have retained the Crown as represented by the Sovereign, the Governor-General, and the Lieutenant-Governors. All the reasons for the Crown have applied in both federal and provincial governments, and, on the whole, the relations between the Crown and the Ministers have worked extremely well. The twelve incumbents together cost a little more than two cents per citizen per year. By no stretch of the imagination can the Governors-General or the Lieutenant-Governors be considered to have played any significant role in actual government in our time, or to have obstructed or overshadowed their Premiers. Their job has been to occupy the top levels in their respective jurisdictions and to handle the decorative and emergency functions, while leaving the Prime Ministers and Premiers to handle the powers of government without actually possessing them, and to be electable, responsible, accountable, criticizable, and removable. The Governors-General and the Lieutenant-Governors are something more than constitutional presidents; they have a Sovereign's auspices to signify authority, to enhance their prestige, and to clearly mark the line between pomp and power.

Over the years, Canada's eleven heads of government have been a mixed lot. Some have been everything democratic theory describes, real leaders of a parliamentary system. Some have been virtual dictators; some could control their legislatures personally with an iron hand; some had delusions of grandeur; some would do with their constitutions exactly what they could get away with. Some, on the other hand, have been weak, indecisive, ineffective, or inadequate to the demands of high office. The offices of Prime Minister and Premier, like any office, are only partially what the constitution says they are; they are in large measure what the talents and personalities of the incumbents make them. To all of them, the fact that they were elected gave them a mandate. It did not ensure good government, but it did make them responsible and disposable. The existence of the Crown made sure that they stayed that way. . . .

Those who worry about the monarchy sometimes doubt the relevance in Canada of the Sovereign herself because she is Queen of several countries. Such a situation is common in Canada; many citizens owe allegiance to outside heads of their businesses, churches, unions, international political parties, and other groups. Nevertheless, a shared head of state is controversial. We need to remember that under our constitution the Sovereign is a part of Parliament and is the formal, ultimate source of political power, and the law sets out the facts of power with clarity for all to see and recognize as authentic. Governments in Canada may have quarrelled over which may do what, but power to govern has itself been unassailable and unquestioned from colonial times to the present. This stability of law is by no means universal around the world in an age when constitutions have been unusually short-lived and unreliable and when human rights have enjoyed only modest protection. Governments and their supporters come and go, but the Canadian people know that their rights and the powers of their state enjoy a solid, recognized base and the validations of centuries of usage. The sovereign is the legal expression and permanent non-partisan symbol of that fact.

Canadians may some day have their own resident sovereign. Perhaps, when the Queen's reign ends, Prince Charles could become King of the rest of the Commonwealth while Prince Andrew moved to Ottawa to found a purely Canadian dynasty while continuing the stable heritage of constitutional power. Whatever happens, vague or emotional platitudes about monarchal and democratic theory and principle are unrealistic unless considered with the actual practical operation of government and the political performance of men. When the monarchy makes the constitution work as a plan for humans as distinct from a paper declaration, however grand, then it should be recognized as a bulwark of democracy and of the rights Canadians want to enjoy under their parliamentary system.

LETTERS PATENT CONSTITUTING THE OFFICE OF GOVERNOR GENERAL*

GEORGE R.
  [L.S.]

CANADA

GEORGE THE SIXTH, by the Grace of God, of Great Britain, Ireland and the British Dominions beyond the Seas KING, Defender of the Faith.

To ALL TO WHOM these Presents shall come,

GREETING:

Preamble Recites Letters Patent of 23rd March, 1931

WHEREAS by certain Letters Patent under the Great Seal bearing date at Westminster the twenty-third day of March, 1931, His late Majesty King George the

* From the *Canada Gazette,* Part I, October 11, 1947, pp. 3014-3016. By permission of the Queen's Printer.

Fifth did constitute, order, and declare that there should be a Governor General and Commander-in-Chief in and over Canada, and that the person filling the office of Governor General and Commander-in-Chief should be from time to time appointed by Commission under the Royal Sign Manual and Signet:

AND WHEREAS at St. James's on the twenty-third day of March, 1931, His late Majesty King George the Fifth did cause certain Instructions under the Royal Sign Manual and Signet to be given to the Governor General and Commander-in-Chief:

AND WHEREAS it is Our Will and pleasure to revoke the Letters Patent and Instructions and to substitute other provisions in place thereof:

Revokes Letters Patent of 23rd March, 1931, and Instructions

Now THEREFORE We do by these presents revoke and determine the said Letters Patent, and everything therein contained, and all amendments thereto, and the said Instructions, but without prejudice to anything lawfully done thereunder:

AND We do declare Our Will and pleasure as follows:

Office of Governor General and Commander-in-Chief Constituted

I   We do hereby constitute, order, and declare that there shall be a Governor General and Commander-in-Chief in and over Canada, and appointments to the office of Governor General and Commander-in-Chief in and over Canada shall be made by Commission under Our Great Seal of Canada.

His Powers and Authorities

II   And We do hereby authorize and empower Our Governor General, with the advice of Our Privy Council for Canada, or of any members thereof or individually, as the case requires, to exercise all powers and authorities lawfully belonging to Us in respect of Canada, and for greater certainty but not so as to restrict the generality of the foregoing to do and execute, in the manner aforesaid, all things that may belong to his office and to the trust We have reposed in him according to the several powers and authorities granted or appointed him by virtue of The British North America Acts, 1867 to 1946 and the powers and authorities hereinafter conferred in these Letters Patent and in such Commission as may be issued to him under Our Great Seal of Canada and under such laws as are or may hereinafter be in force in Canada.

Great Seal

III   And We do hereby authorize and empower Our Governor General to keep and use Our Great Seal of Canada for sealing all things whatsoever that may be passed under Our Great Seal of Canada.

Appointment of Judges, Justices, etc.

IV   And We do further authorize and empower Our Governor General to constitute and appoint, in Our name and on Our behalf, all such Judges, Commissioners, Justices of the Peace, and other necessary Offices (including diplomatic and consular officers) and Ministers of Canada, as may be lawfully constituted or appointed by Us.

Suspension or Removal from Office

V   And We do further authorize and empower Our Governor General, so far as We lawfully may, upon sufficient cause to him appearing, to remove from his office, or to suspend from the exercise of the same, any person exercising any office within Canada, under or by virtue of any Commission or Warrant granted, or which may be granted, by Us in Our name or under Our authority.

Summoning, Proroguing, or Dissolving the Parliament of Canada

VI   And We do further authorize and empower Our Governor General to exercise all powers lawfully belonging to Us in respect of summoning, proroguing or dissolving the Parliament of Canada.

Power to Appoint Deputies

VII   And Whereas by The British North America Acts, 1867 to 1946, it is amongst other things enacted that it shall be lawful for Us, if We think fit, to authorize Our Governor General to appoint any person or persons, jointly or severally, to be his Deputy or Deputies within any part or parts of Canada, and in that capacity to exercise, during the pleasure of Our Governor General, such of the powers, authorities, and functions of Our Governor General as he may deem it necessary or expedient to assign to such Deputy or Deputies, subject to any limitations or directions from time to time expressed or given by Us: Now We do hereby authorize and empower Our Governor General, subject to such limitations and directions, to appoint any person or persons, jointly or severally, to be his Deputy or Deputies. . . .

Succession

VIII   And We do hereby declare Our pleasure to be that, in the event of the death, incapacity, removal, or absence of Our Governor General out of Canada, all and every the powers and authorities herein granted to him shall, until Our further pleasure is signified therein, be vested in Our Chief Justice for the time being of Canada (hereinafter called Our Chief Justice).

•   •   •

Coming Into Effect of Letters Patent

XVII   And We do further declare that these Our Letters Patent shall take effect on the first day of October, 1947.

IN WITNESS WHEREOF We have caused these Our Letters to be made Patent, and for the greater testimony and validity thereof, We have caused Our Great Seal of Canada to be affixed to these presents, which We have signed with Our Royal Hand.

GIVEN the 8th day of September in the Year of Our Lord One thousand Nine-Hundred and Forty-Seven and in the Eleventh Year of Our Reign.

BY HIS MAJESTY'S COMMAND,
W. L. MACKENZIE KING,
Prime Minister of Canada.

WAS THE GOVERNOR GENERAL'S REFUSAL CONSTITUTIONAL?*

EUGENE A. FORSEY

In the Canadian Parliament of 1921-5, the Liberal party, under Mr. Mackenzie King, had 117 members, the Conservatives 50, Progressives, Labour and Independents 68. For most purposes, however, the Liberal Government enjoyed the support of a majority of the Progressives, so that it was able to carry on for four years without serious difficulty. By September 5, 1925, Mr. King had become convinced of the necessity of seeking at the polls a clear working majority over all other parties. He accordingly advised and secured dissolution. The election was held October 29. It returned 101 Liberals, 116 Conservatives and 28 Progressives, Labour members and Independents. The Prime Minister and eight other Ministers lost their seats.

On November 5, a month and two days before the new Parliament's legal existence could begin, the Prime Minister issued a statement asserting that three courses were open to him: to resign at once, to meet the new House of Commons, or to advise "an immediate dissolution". He had decided to meet the new House, at the earliest practicable moment.

This proved to be January 7, 1926. From then till the House adjourned, March 2, to allow the Prime Minister to find a seat in a by-election, and again from March 15, when the sittings resumed, till June 25, the Conservatives made repeated efforts to defeat the Government, but without success. The Government's majorities were: 3, 10, 10, 1, 7, 8, 11, 13, 6, 9, 13, 13, 15, 1, 6, 8. On June 18, a committee appointed to investigate alleged scandals in the Customs Department presented its report. The Conservatives were not satisfied with the report, and one of them, Mr. H. H. Stevens, on June 22, moved an amendment which, among other things, described the conduct of "the Prime Minister and the government" as "wholly indefensible" and the "conduct of the present Minister of Customs in the case of Moses Aziz" as "utterly unjustifiable". On June 23, Mr. Woodsworth (Labour) moved what Keith calls a "non-partisan" sub-amendment which would have struck out the condemnation of the Prime Minister, the Government, and the Minister of Customs, and added a condemnation of various persons on both sides of politics and in the Civil Service and provided for a judicial commission to continue the investigation. The Government accepted this sub-amendment; the Conservatives opposed it. On June 25 it was defeated by a majority of two. Mr. Fansher (Progressive) then moved a second sub-amendment, which would have left in the Stevens amendment the condemnation of the Prime Minister, the Government and the

---

* From *The Royal Power of Dissolution of Parliament in the British Commonwealth*, Toronto, Oxford University Press, 1943, pp. 131-140. By permission of the author and publisher.

Minister of Customs, and added Mr. Woodsworth's proposed condemnation of other persons, and provision for a judicial commission. The Speaker ruled this out of order. His ruling was challenged, and overruled by a majority of two. A motion to adjourn the debate, supported by the Government, was lost by one; somewhat later, at 5:15 a.m., Saturday, June 26, a second motion to adjourn the debate, also supported by the Government, carried by one. The Fansher sub-amendment had meanwhile been carried without a division, but the Stevens amendment had not been voted on.

During the week-end Mr. King asked for dissolution. The Governor General, Lord Byng, refused. Mr. King thereupon resigned. He announced his resignation to the House, Monday, June 28, saying that he believed that "under British practice" he was "entitled" to a dissolution. He declared that there was "no Prime Minister", "no Government"; declined to take part in a conference on the means of winding up the session; and moved that the House adjourn, which it did, at 2:15 p.m. The Governor General at once sent for Mr. Meighen, and asked him "if he could command a majority in the House to get the work of the session concluded in orderly manner." Mr. Meighen replied that he could having received informal promises from a number of the Progressives to the effect that they would vote with the Conservatives to get these all-important Bills through, pass Supply, and prorogue. The Governor General then requested Mr. Meighen to form a government, and in the evening he undertook to do so. Next day, during a conference of the Progressives, the Governor General sent for the Progressive leader, Mr. Forke. The Progressives thereupon drew up and gave to Mr. Forke "a confidential memorandum for his guidance". . . . The memorandum was as follows:

> That we assist the new administration in completing the business of the session. That we are in agreement on the necessity of continuing the investigation into the customs and excise department by a judicial commission. . . . That no dissolution should take place until the . . . commission has finished its investigation . . . and that Parliament be summoned to deal with the reports.

Mr. Meighen had accepted office as Prime Minister, but the formation of his Cabinet presented unusual difficulties. Mr. King and his colleagues had not followed the customary practice of holding office till their successors were appointed. They had left the Crown without a ministry, the country without a government, an action which appears to be without precedent in the history of the Empire. Mr. King had refused to engage in a conference on the question of finishing the session's business. The session was almost at an end; but Supply had not been voted; bills to amend the Special War Revenue Act and the Canada Evidence Act, thirteen divorce bills and eight other private bills had passed both Houses and awaited the royal assent. The important Long Term Farm Mortgage Credit Bill was still before the Senate. Under the law as it then stood, if Mr. Meighen formed a government in the ordinary way, every one of the 15 or so ministers with portfolio from the Commons, upon accepting office, would automatically have vacated his seat. This would have left the Conservatives and Liberals about equal. The government would have had to seek an adjournment or prorogation of about six weeks to allow time for ministerial by-election. [Later, the Act of 1931, 21-22 George V, c. 52, did away with the necessity for such by-elections.] Mr. King's attitude on the question of a conference suggests that he might have opposed an adjournment. . . . If he had opposed adjournment, it is by no means impossible that, with the Conservative strength reduced by 15 or 16, he could have carried with him enough Progressives to succeed. Mr. Meighen might have got prorogation for six weeks. But either adjournment or prorogation would have involved a long delay, highly inconvenient to the members of Parliament, especially the farmer members at that time of year; prorogation would have killed the Long Term Farm Mortgage Credit Bill, the Montreal Harbour Commission Loan Bill and two private bills; and either adjournment or prorogation would have involved carrying on for six weeks without Supply, which would have been possible but not desirable.

Mr. Meighen therefore announced that, to bring the session to an end promptly, he had "decided to constitute . . . a temporary Ministry . . . of seven members, who would be sworn in without portfolio, and . . . would have responsibility as acting Ministers of the several departments." After prorogation, he would "immediately address himself to the task of constituting a Government in the method established by custom. The present plan is merely to meet an unusual if not unprecedented situation."

The new Government met the House June 29, and proceeded to deal with the business on the Order Paper. The first main item was of course the still unfinished debate on the Stevens amendment. Mr. Rinfret, Liberal, now moved a fresh sub-amendment, which the Speaker declared to be in order. Mr. Geary, Conservative, challenged the Speaker's ruling, which was sustained by a majority of one. On a vote on the sub-amendment itself, the new Government received a majority of 12. A further new sub-amendment was then carried by agreement, the Stevens amendment so amended was carried by a majority of 10, and the report of the Committee, as amended, was also carried by 10.

On June 30, the Liberal Opposition moved a vote of want of confidence in the new Government on the ground of its fiscal policy. This was defeated by a majority of seven.

Mr. King followed this up in Committee of Supply by an elaborate cross-examination of the Ministers, designed to show that they were not validly appointed and were therefore not ministers at all. Mr. Lapointe, Liberal ex-Minister of Justice, then raised a question of privilege; that the acting ministers of departments, having really (so he alleged) accepted offices of profit under the Crown, had vacated their seats and had no right to appear in the House. These two propositions, as Mr. Bury, Conservative M.P. for Edmonton East pointed out, are of course mutually exclusive. If the acting ministers of departments were really *Ministers* of departments, there could be no question of the validity of their appointments; if they had not been validly appointed, and were not ministers of departments, then they had not vacated their seats. The two propositions, however, were ingeniously combined in a motion of Mr. Robb, Liberal ex-Minister of Finance:

That the actions in this House of the Honourable Members who have acted as Ministers of the Crown since the 29th of June, 1926, namely the Honourable Members for West York, Fort William, Vancouver Centre, Argenteuil, Wellington South, and the Honourable senior Member for Halifax, are a violation and an infringement of the privileges of this House for the following reasons: —That the said Honourable gentlemen have no right to sit in this House and should have vacated their seats therein if they legally hold office as administrators of the various departments assigned to them by Orders-in-Council; that if they do not hold such office legally, they have no right to control the business of Government in this House and ask for supply for the Departments of which they state they are acting Ministers.

After debate, this motion was put. Mr. Meighen's seat was of course vacant, which reduced the Conservative strength by one. Mr. Bird, Progressive member for Nelson, broke his pair and voted with the Liberals. As a result, the Government was defeated by one vote. The House then adjourned. Next day, July 2, before it could meet again, Mr. Meighen advised the Governor General to dissolve Parliament. Lord Byng accepted the advice, and Parliament was accordingly dissolved, without prorogation and without royal assent being given to any of the bills which were awaiting it.

These events raised no fewer than eight constitutional questions.

1. Was Lord Byng's refusal of dissolution to Mr. King constitutional in the light of the circumstances as they stood on the morning of June 28?

2. Did the constitutionality of that refusal depend on Mr. Meighen's actually being able to carry on with the existing House of Commons?

3. Did the constitutionality of the refusal depend on the constitutionality of the government of ministers without portfolio?

4. Was the Government constitutional?

5. Was the grant of dissolution to Mr. Meighen constitutional?

6. Was the constitutionality of refusing dissolution to Mr. King on June 28 affected by the grant of dissolution to Mr. Meighen on July 2?

7. Was the manner of dissolution of July 2 constitutional?

8. Did Lord Byng's action relegate Canada to a status inferior to that of Great Britain?

THE ROYAL PREROGATIVE IN CANADA: THE SELECTION OF SUCCESSORS TO MR. DUPLESSIS AND MR. SAUVE*

J. R. MALLORY

Every country subconsciously modifies its constitution in response to a changing set of assumptions about society. In Canada it can hardly cause surprise if the assumptions about the royal prerogative have altered considerably over the years. In particular, deference to the prior right of political parties to choose their own leaders is steadily eroding the discretionary prerogatives of the Crown.

The problem is essentially this: it is the responsibility of the representative of the Crown to designate a first minister. Canadians have become so accustomed to the sedulously cultivated notion that democracy and "responsible government" have transferred all executive power to the prime minister and the cabinet that it comes as a nasty shock to discover that the formal head of state actually has the constitutional right, in this case, to act on his own responsibility. The shock is even greater when the duty falls upon a lieutenant-governor, because in the provinces this officer has become, according to the conventional wisdom, a mere cypher.

Nevertheless the settled constitutional practice is perfectly clear. "The selection of a new Prime Minister," stated a memorandum issued to the press by Sir Robert Borden on his retirement, "is one of the few personal acts which, under the British constitution, a Sovereign (in Canada the representative of the Sovereign) is required to perform." The task becomes all the more necessary and important when a prime minister dies in office, because it is the action of the Crown in bringing about the formation of a new government which confers legitimacy and authority on the political leaders of the state without undue delay. The simplicity of this arrangement is in marked contrast with the uncertainty which surrounds the rules which enable government to be carried on in the United States in the event of presidential incapacity, and the somewhat arbitrary line of succession in the event of the death of a president. The essence of the constitutional arrangements which govern these matters in Canada is that the governor acts on his own authority and with complete freedom in finding a prime minister who can govern and who is capable of claiming the allegiance of a body of disciplined followers within the legislature. . . .

It is however, becoming increasingly clear that this straightforward doctrine of the prerogative is now being eroded by practice and modified by an unwillingness on the part of the public either to understand or to admit that the discretionary prerogative does exist. This is not all a matter of ignorance and misinformation. There are those who think that the head of state should never exercise any but

* From *The Canadian Journal of Economics and Political Science*, Vol. XXVI, No. 2, May, 1960. By permission of the author and publisher.

automatic functions, because the discretionary prerogative is inconsistent with democratic government. This case is lucidly argued by Professor Edward McWhinney, who argues that the governor is really choosing the next party leader and (whether he chooses the right man or not) becomes necessarily involved in "partisan political issues." He thinks that the succession to the office of prime minister should be automatic by recognizing the rule that the office should go to the next senior minister as a "caretaker," until the party has chosen its own new leader. This, he thinks, would be "in line with the contemporary constitutional trend towards the limitation or elimination of discretionary powers in non-elective organs of government."

The most convincing method of supporting this argument is to convince oneself that elected persons somehow possess a *mana* not given to those who have been merely appointed. History, as Dr. Forsey has pointed out, suggests certain practical objections. If this rule had been followed on the death of Sir John A. Macdonald in 1891, the succession would have fallen upon Sir Hector Langevin, and it was Sir Mackenzie Bowell, the senior surviving minister, who was such a disastrous choice in 1894. Since Canadian political parties normally choose their leaders in party conventions a delay of several months could elapse in which we were in the hands of a caretaker government. On balance it is clearly better, in the rare cases where the succession is not clear, to recognize that the initiative of the head of state is a necessary and useful device for bringing about the transfer of power.

The circumstances surrounding the choice of a prime minister in Quebec following the deaths of Maurice Duplessis and Paul Sauvé suggest, however, that history is on the side of Professor McWhinney. Briefly, the sequence of events was as follows.

In 1959 Mr. Duplessis was touring mining developments in the Ungava region when, on September 3, he had a stroke which left him paralyzed and without the power of speech. Further seizures followed but he lingered on until the early hours of September 7. Characteristically, he had been careful not to give any clear indication of his choice as a successor. Nevertheless Mr. Sauvé had begun to emerge as the logical successor. He combined experience and ability with comparative youth, and he had acted as leader in the House during Mr. Duplessis' absence in the 1958-9 session of the legislature.

As is usual in such circumstances, the mortal illness of the Premier led to a great deal of ill-informed speculation concerning the precise constitutional position. There seemed to be a widespread belief that it was the duty of the cabinet to choose a successor. This notion was rightly rejected by the *Montreal Star,* which asserted in an editorial (September 10) that "the choice rests with the Lieutenant-Governor alone as representative of the Crown. He may, if he chooses, consult widely and take advice. He is not bound to do so. Lieutenant-Governor Gagnon, according to reports, will receive a petition from the National Union caucus, asking him to appoint a cabinet minister as Premier. He is not obliged to do so, although in all likelihood, he will." . . .

In point of fact, the constitutional situation is precisely the same in Quebec on this matter as in the federal government. In both cases the death of a prime minister dissolves the *cabinet*. This, however, does not terminate the appointments of ministers, nor does it terminate their membership in, respectively, the Executive Council and the Privy Council. The mistake here is to confuse the cabinet (a wholly informal body with no legal basis) with the Council (which is the legal agency through which ministers collectively—as the Governor in Council—exercise powers). Of course the lieutenant-governor appoints ministers to the Executive Council: he does so on the premier's advice. Under responsible government, the cabinet cannot meet unless there is a prime minister. He need not be present, but he must be alive in order to give them constitutional life. Hence, while ministers might meet informally after Mr. Duplessis' death, there could not be a meeting of the cabinet because there was no premier. In fact several such meetings took place. On September 8 there was a meeting of ministers—described in the press as "a caucus of cabinet ministers"—in Mr. Sauvé's suite in the Château Frontenac. There was also, it appears, another meeting of ministers to plan arrangements for the funeral. Mr. Sauvé quite properly stated that these meetings "were not of an administrative character." However, the press continued to describe them as meetings of cabinet.

On the evening of September 10, after the funeral of the late Premier in Three Rivers, the ministers met at seven o'clock in the Parliament Buildings. There they signed a petition addressed to the Lieutenant-Governor asking him to call upon Mr. Sauvé to form a government. Meanwhile, in the Private Bills Committee Room, the Union Nationale caucus, composed of legislative councillors and members of the Legislative Assembly, was meeting. The caucus was then asked by the ministers to approve the petition.

"Submission of the petition to a caucus of party members was only a matter of courtesy, as the private members do not have a say in recommending the selection of a government leader to the Lieutenant-Governor," added the Montreal *Gazette's* Quebec correspondent. Nor, it should be remarked, does anyone else. In this case the governor acts on his own discretion, although he is free to consult anyone he chooses in order to arrive at a correct assessment of the political situation. However, such counsel as the governor receives is not "advice" in the strict constitutional sense, because it is not advice for which the adviser can be held politically responsible to the legislature. In this case, had Mr. Gagnon indicated to ministers that he would like their advice, the procedure would have appeared to be more in accordance with established usage. The method actually adopted has the appearance of denying the prerogative altogether.

The petition was then taken to the Lieutenant-Governor by the Minister of Finance, the Minister of Colonization (who also happened to be the chief party organizer), and the Chief Party Whip. Then the Lieutenant-Governor sent for Mr. Sauvé and commissioned him to form a government. On the following day the new administration was sworn in.

Paul Sauvé was destined to be Premier of Quebec for little over one hundred days. In this brief period he brought about a complete transformation in the atmosphere of Quebec politics and spectacular changes in the policies of the Union Nationale party. In the midst of this bracing atmosphere of change he was stricken, on January 2, 1960, with a fatal heart attack.

This time the stages of constitutional action were painfully familiar to his ministers, but the task of finding a successor infinitely more difficult. When Mr. Duplessis died there was little doubt about the identity of his successor, and Mr. Sauvé had moved with sure skill to remove what doubts there were. As soon as they received news of Mr. Sauvé's death, ministers rushed to Montreal. Their first objective was to pay their respects to the dead; their second to consider the anxious problem of the succession. There were signs of strain and bad temper in the refusals to make statements after their meeting in Montreal. Rumour had already placed in the field the names of Messrs. Yves Prévost, Provincial Secretary; Antoine Rivard, Attorney General; Antonio Barrette, Minister of Labour; and Daniel Johnson, Minister of Hydraulic Resources. There was talk of an interim premier and a caretaker government pending a party convention, but it is likely that this merely reflected the difficulty of agreeing on any but a compromise candidate. A parliamentary caucus was called for Thursday, January 7. . . .

On the eve of the caucus all of the candidates except Mr. Barrette had made it clear that they had withdrawn from the race. It was thus possible for the ministers to carry to the caucus a unanimous recommendation. This was endorsed without visible signs of disunity, and later in the day the Lieutenant-Governor sent for Mr. Barrette. It is not known what discussions and manoeuvres took place to achieve party unity, but the federal M.P. for Bellechasse, Noël Dorion, found it necessary to deny that he had intervened in the discussions that preceded the caucus. Whether there was intervention from federal Conservative leaders is uncertain, but certainly the threat of a party split was a genuine danger. Some of the difficulties were later exposed by the action of a party back-bencher, Dr. Lizotte of l'Islet, who announced on January 13 that he was giving up political life because "at the recent party caucus we did not have the freedom to choose the man we wanted for premier." In a subsequent statement the Chief Whip of the party described Dr. Lizotte as "a very tired man." On February 1, Dr. Lizotte, still a member of the legislature and the party, was *en route* for New York for "medical consultations," after stating that he had faith in Mr. Barrette because he was "an honest man."

Undoubtedly the strain of preserving a façade of unity was considerable, but except for Dr. Lizotte, it was preserved. A statement by the Chief Whip of the party, which appeared in *Le Devoir* on January 14, described the proceedings at the caucus, which had hitherto been kept private because of a "gentleman's agreement" not to discuss them publicly. The caucus had been presided over by the Minister of Colonization and Chief Organizer of the party. This discussion, as he reported it, gave an impression of well-organized restraint. The Attorney General, Mr. Rivard (himself one of the leading candidates for the leadership), had spoken early and made it clear that while all could express their views he was authorized to say that all members of the Executive Council had agreed that the only one of their number whose name would be put forward was that of Mr. Barrette. In the face of this it would have been rather difficult to force a contest for the leadership.

It is clear that in the matter of choosing a leader the Union Nationale has strong similarities with the British Conservative party whose habit is described by Robert McKenzie as follows: "There can be no question of forcing a contest. . . . Convention requires that on that occasion all potential rivals should affirm their unswerving allegiance to the tribal chief. The tribe then speaks with one voice and the new Leader has 'emerged'."

The only conclusion one can draw from these events is that in Canada the discretionary prerogative in choosing a prime minister has in practice been displaced by a system of selection by organs of the political party. This may prove to be highly embarrassing in the future when the preservation of prerogative discretion might be highly desirable in cleaning up a situation in which the struggle for the succession might completely disrupt party unity.

One of the most interesting aspects of the whole situation is that such reverence for "democratic" forms and such a complete rejection of the idea of the dis- cretionary prerogative should happen in Quebec and in particular to the Union Nationale party which in the past has shown no particular objection in principle to executive discretion of any sort. There was some speculation that there ought to be a party convention to pick a successor to Mr. Duplessis and, later, to Mr. Sauvé, but the absurdity of this idea for the Union Nationale soon became apparent. It would appear that the idea was rejected not so much on the grounds of its obvious inconvenience, but because such a procedure would be too incongruous in the Union Nationale. Nevertheless the procedure that was followed was striking enough. The party leaders were careful to secure the acquiescence of the parlia- mentary caucus, and the choice of a leader by the parliamentary group, elsewhere outmoded by the convention with rank-and-file participation, is more in accord with the nature of the party.

The use of the "petition" to the Lieutenant-Governor is a novelty. It is clear that what was intended was to create the impression of a unanimous "draft" of Mr. Sauvé, and it was a handy precedent in ensuring unity behind Mr. Barrette. It has greater similarities with the manoeuvres of the American convention than with anything in Canadian politics. It shows, no doubt, that Quebec's appetite for the American way of life extends further into the area of political machinery than had previously been suspected.

THE LIEUTENANT-GOVERNOR'S DISCRETIONARY POWERS: THE RESERVATION OF BILL 56 IN SASKATCHEWAN*

J. R. MALLORY

Before proroguing the legislative session on April 8, 1961, the Lieutenant-Governor of Saskatchewan, Frank L. Bastedo, intimated that he was reserving Bill 56 for the signification of the pleasure of the Governor General. This bill, entitled "An Act to Provide for the Alteration of Certain Mineral Contracts," would have given to the lieutenant-governor in council the power to modify existing mineral contracts, and contained the provision that it would expire on December 31, 1961. After prorogation Mr. Bastedo issued a statement to the press, which said in part, "this is a very important bill affecting hundreds of mineral contracts. It raises implications which throw grave doubts of the legislation being in the public interest. There is grave doubt as to its validity." These doubts were not shared by his constitutional advisers, who informed him that in their view the bill was within the powers of the legislature and advised him to assent to it.

The royal veto—even a suspensive veto, which is what in effect reservation is— is deemed to be dead in most jurisdictions where the British cabinet system operates. No British sovereign since Queen Anne has refused to give assent to a bill, and the exercise of the power to reserve or withhold assent is generally regarded as a relic of colonial thraldom which disappeared when the fetters of Downing Street control were removed. How then can it continue to exist in a Canadian province?

Under the powers conferred upon him by section 90 of the British North America Act, a lieutenant-governor may do one of three things with a bill which has passed through all its stages in the legislature and is presented to him for royal assent so that it is transformed into an Act of the legislature: he may signify that he assents to the bill in the Queen's name; he may withhold his assent; or he may reserve the bill so that it may be considered by the governor general. The first of these three courses is the normal one, and requires no comment. The second is a simple veto; the bill is dead and can be revived only by introducing it again into the legislature, passing it through all its stages, and presenting it again for assent at a subsequent session of the legislature. The third is not a withholding of assent (that is, there is no veto), but the decision as to whether assent will be given or withheld is passed back to the governor general, acting on the advice of his ministers in Ottawa.

Seventy bills have been reserved by lieutenant-governors since Confederation. However, fifty-nine of these were reserved before 1900, most of them in the early

* From *The Canadian Journal of Economics and Political Science,* Vol. XXVIII, No. 4, November, 1961. By permission of the author and publisher.

days of provincial government. Since 1920 there have been four: three in Alberta in 1937, and the one here considered. The use of these wide discretionary powers of the lieutenant-governor was characteristic of the period of almost colonial status of the provinces (particularly the western provinces) in relation to the dominion. The revival of the power in Alberta in 1937 caused general surprise. It had become widely believed that the power had become constitutionally obsolete in the same way that the position of the governor general as an imperial officer had disappeared as a result of the achievement of Canadian autonomy. So general was the uncertainty that the federal government referred the whole question of the scope and validity of the powers of disallowance, reservation, and withholding assent to the Supreme Court in the autumn of 1937.

The Supreme Court had no difficulty in finding that these powers continued to subsist, unaffected by changes in constitutional conventions, and the powers were equally valid, whether the legislation was *intra vires* the provincial legislature or not, and that the only limitations on the discretion of the lieutenant-governor were instructions from the governor general.

While the power of the lieutenant-governor is unrestricted in law, it was intended to operate as one of the means by which the federal government could intervene in a province to prevent the enactment of legislation which threatened some wider interest which required protection in the national interest. In other words, the reservation of bills was intended to be a power exercised by the lieutenant-governor acting in his capacity as a Dominion officer. . . .

Sir John A. Macdonald, when minister of justice, caused a minute of council to be adopted in Ottawa in 1882 and communicated to lieutenant-governors in order to make clear to them that they should exercise their powers of reservation only when instructed to do so. "It is only in a case of extreme necessity that a Lieutenant-Governor should without such instructions exercise his discretion as a Dominion Officer in reserving a bill. In fact, with the facility of communication between the Dominion and provincial governments, such a necessity can seldom if ever arise."

In other words, a lieutenant-governor who reserves a bill on his own authority is acting within the scope of his legal powers, but not within the spirit of the constitution.

Was Mr. Bastedo acting, directly or indirectly, on instruction from Ottawa? The present instructions of lieutenant-governors do not specify any classes of bills which may, or should be reserved. Prime Minister Diefenbaker, when asked in the House of Commons on April 10 whether the bill has been reserved, replied:

> . . . The first information the government received on this matter was on Saturday, when the lieutenant governor telephoned the under secretary of state that he had reserved a bill of the Saskatchewan legislature for the signification of the Governor General's pleasure. . . . We have no other information on the matter. There was no consultation in advance in any way, and any action in this regard would be taken by the lieutenant governor himself.

Two days later, in answer to another question in the House, the Prime Minister made a further statement in which he said:

> . . . The reservation by lieutenant governors have [*sic*] been generally accepted as dependent on a request from the governor in council. There was no discussion in this regard, as I have already pointed out. We had no knowledge of the action to be taken by the lieutenant governor. However, the action was taken, and as yet the reasons which the lieutenant governor is required to transmit to the Governor General for the course he followed have not come to hand. As soon as they do the governor in council will take such action as is deemed proper, with full regard to the fact that this government has consistently taken the attitude that if legislation is within the legislative competence of the provinces, except constitutionally in extra-ordinary circumstances there should be no interference with provincial jurisdiction.

Finally, on May 5th, Mr. Diefenbaker tabled in the House the order in council "in which His Excellency the Governor General by and with the advice of Her Majesty the Queen's privy council for Canada declares his assent to Bill No. 56 of the legislature of Saskatchewan passed during the present year and which was reserved by the lieutenant governor of Saskatchewan for the signification of the pleasure of the Governor General in accordance with the terms of the British North America Act." The order in council dealt with the two grounds upon which the Lieutenant-Governor had acted noting that in the opinion of the Minister of Justice the bill was *intra vires* the Saskatchewan legislature, and that "the expression 'conflict with national policy or interest' does not relate solely to a difference of principle or point of view, but must include matters of practical or physical effect, and that in this sense the bill is not in conflict with national policy or interest."

In his statement to the House, the Prime Minister reminded members that the Lieutenant-Governor's action had not been preceded by consultation with the federal government. "I have no hesitation in saying," he said, "that had there been such consultation my colleagues and I would have recommended to the Governor General that the lieutenant governor be instructed not to reserve the bill."

He referred to Macdonald's minute of council of 1882 and noted that "in view of the development of communications since" there should be ample opportunity for consultation before reservation. He then said, "I should point out that while no formal instructions have yet been given to lieutenant governors [never] to reserve a bill unless upon specific instructions, my colleagues and I are now considering whether such formal instructions should be given." Unfortunately, the *Hansard* reporters omitted that "never," here inserted in brackets, which was in the typewritten text of the Prime Minister's statement. The instructions to lieutenant-governors referred to above seem, however, not to have been issued.

Mr. Bastedo seems to have felt impelled to reserve the bill for two reasons: he thought, contrary to the advice of his own Attorney-General and cabinet, that it was *ultra vires,* and he doubted if the bill was in the public interest. The federal government was unable to subscribe to either of these views. However, even had the Lieutenant-Governor been right, there are other remedies in the constitution which are less reminiscent of the prerogative powers of the Crown as they existed in the days of the Stuart kings. The proper body to decide the question of *vires* is the courts, and there can be little doubt that the interests adversely affected by the bill are able to afford recourse to litigation. Should the bill be regarded as gravely affecting the public interest of the country, then the responsibility for disallowing it—after due deliberation—rested on the federal government. Instead they were dragged into the issue without being given any choice in the matter.

The action of Mr. Bastedo furnishes sufficient reason, if any more is needed, for removing the power of reservation from the constitution. The Lieutenant-Governor acted with complete legality, but his action was wholly alien to the spirit of the constitution. A peculiarity of the British constitutional system is that behaviour which may be legally correct can nevertheless be wholly unconstitutional. This is particularly true in the realm of the prerogative, where wide discretionary powers exist but are in fact strictly confined by a number of conventions of the constitution which Dicey defined as "rules for determining the mode in which the discretionary powers of the Crown (or of the Ministers as servants of the Crown) ought to be exercised."

In Canada, we cannot safely assume that even lieutenant-governors have read Dicey or understand the constitution. In this matter it has now become necessary to bring the law of the constitution closer to political and constitutional realities. At the Constitutional Conference in 1950 the premiers of Quebec, Manitoba, Saskatchewan, and Alberta advocated the amendment of the BNA Act so as to abolish the power of reservation. No dissenting voice was heard. Perhaps now is the time to press again for abolition.

Reservation has one particularly objectionable feature, in that it contains within it a sort of "pocket veto." The federal government is not obliged to do anything at all about a reserved bill. If no action is taken at all, then the bill has been effectively vetoed. Since the bill under consideration would expire in any event on December 31, 1961, inaction would have destroyed its effect completely. Such a course of action is not without precedent, and could be justified by the argument that any action would be interference with provincial jurisdiction. As long as the disallowance power remains in existence, reservation is in any event an unnecessary prop to the federal power. The continuance of reservation merely makes it possible for the federal government to be involved by inadvertence in local issues in which it may have no direct interest.

HONOURS IN CANADA*

For some years after Confederation awards were made of a few hereditary honours and some knighthoods and companionships in orders of chivalry, and this policy continued until the end of the first Great War.

On May 22, 1919, during the premiership of the Rt. Hon. Robert L. Borden, a resolution adopted by the House of Commons requested His Majesty to refrain from granting titular honours to Canadian citizens in the future. This policy was reversed in 1933 when, during the premiership of the Rt. Hon. R. B. Bennett, the Canadian Government recommended a number of such awards, which were duly granted on New Year's Day, 1934. Although titular honours were again conferred in 1935, the new administration which took office later that year under the premiership of the Rt. Hon. Mackenzie King revived the previous policy of the Government of 1919, and no titular honours have been recommended or awarded since that time.

On July 24, 1942, a Special Committee on Honours and Decorations reported to the House as follows:

> As a result of their deliberations your Committee desire to make the following recommendations:
> (1) That His Majesty's subjects domiciled or ordinarily resident in Canada be eligible for the award of Honours and Decorations, including awards in the Orders of Chivalry, which do not involve titles.
> (2) That His Majesty's Government in Canada consider a submission to His Majesty the King, of proposals for the establishment of an Order limited in number but not involving a title, for which His Majesty's subjects domiciled or ordinarily resident in Canada shall alone be eligible.

During the second Great War a large number of decorations were awarded to members of the armed forces and to civilians for war service. On July 1, 1946, the last Canadian honours list terminated decorations for war service for civilians. No awards in orders of chivalry have since been given to Canadian civilians. Recommendations are made from time to time for the award to civilians of decorations in recognition of exceptional bravery.

In 1967 Prime Minister Lester B. Pearson announced the creation of the Order of Canada.

* From *Canadian Almanac and Directory for 1970*, Toronto, Copp Clark, 1970, p. 654. By permission of the publisher.

BIBLIOGRAPHY

Lieutenant-Governor

Forsey, E. A., "The Extension of the Life of Legislatures," *C.J.E.P.S.*, Vol. XXVI, No. 4, November, 1960.

Hendry, J. McL., *Memorandum on the Office of Lieutenant-Governor of a Province: Its Constitutional Character and Functions*, Ottawa, Department of Justice, 1955.

La Forest, G. V., *Disallowance and Reservation of Provincial Legislation*, Ottawa, Department of Justice, 1955.

McGregor, D. A., *They Gave Royal Assent: The Lieutenant-Governors of British Columbia*, Vancouver, Mitchell Press, 1967.

Mallory, J. R., "Disallowance and the National Interest: The Alberta Social Credit Legislation of 1937," *C.J.E.P.S.*, Vol. XIV, No. 3, August, 1943.

Mallory, J. R., *Social Credit and the Federal Power in Canada*, Toronto, University of Toronto Press, 1954.

Mallory, J. R., "The Lieutenant-Governor as a Dominion Officer: The Reservation of the Three Alberta Bills in 1937," *C.J.E.P.S.*, Vol. XIV, No. 4, November, 1948.

Saywell, J. T., *The Office of Lieutenant-Governor*, Toronto, University of Toronto Press, 1957.

Governor General

Cobham Viscount, "The Governor General's Constitutional Role," *Political Science*, Vol. XV, No. 2, September, 1963.

Franck, T., "The Governor General and the Head of State Functions," *Canadian Bar Review*, Vol. XXXII, No. 10, December, 1954.

Graham, Roger, (ed.), *The King-Byng Affair, 1926: A Question of Responsible Government*, Toronto, Copp Clark, 1967.

Kennedy, W. P. M., "The Office of Governor General of Canada," *Canadian Bar Review*, Vol. XXXI, No. 9, November, 1953.

Mallory, J. R., "Canada's Role in the Appointment of the Governor General," *C.J.E.P.S.*, Vol. XXVI, No. 1, February, 1960.

Mallory, J. R., "Seals and Symbols: From Substance to Form in Commonwealth Equality," *C.J.E.P.S.*, Vol. XXII, No. 3, August, 1956.

Mallory, J. R., "The Election and the Constitution," *Q.Q.*, Vol. LXIV, No. 4, Winter, 1957.

McWhinney, E., Mallory, J. R., Forsey, E. A., "Prerogative Powers of the Head of State (The Queen or Governor General)," *Canadian Bar Review*, Vol. XXXV, Numbers 1, 2, 3, January, February, March, 1957.

Morton, W. L., "Meaning of Monarchy in Confederation," *Royal Society of Canada, Transactions*, Fourth Series, Vol. I, 1963.

Saywell, J. T., "The Crown and the Politicians: The Canadian Succession Question, 1891-1896," *Canadian Historical Review*, Vol. XXXVII, No. 4, December, 1956.

Stanley, G. F. G., "A 'Constitutional Crisis' in British Columbia," *C.J.E.P.S.*, Vol. XXI, No. 3, August, 1955.

Willis-O'Connor, H., *Inside Government House*, Toronto, Ryerson Press, 1954.

TWELVE
THE EXECUTIVE PROCESS: CABINET

This chapter and the one which follows reflect the great interest Canadians have displayed recently in the fundamental problem of the balance of power struck between the cabinet and the House of Commons. Since Mr. Trudeau became prime minister in April, 1968, there has been a growing concern on the part of many observers with the increase in the power of the executive, as represented by the cabinet, and the decrease in the prestige of the legislature, as represented by the House of Commons. Even for those who have not shared the alarm, it is true to say that most of them have been fascinated by the style of the new prime minister and by the structures he has built up for exercising power.

This chapter begins appropriately, therefore, with selections from a five-part series of articles by Anthony Westell which examines the style of Prime Minister Trudeau, the growth of the prime minister's personal office, the reorganization of the privy council office, and Mr. Trudeau's responses to Parliament. Two charts, originally prepared by Professor Ronald Blair and somewhat revised by the editor, present graphically the organizational structure of the cabinet, including its new committees, introduced by Mr. Trudeau, and the pattern of organization of the prime minister's office (PMO) and the privy council office (PCO) inaugurated recently. An extract from a speech by the Hon. Donald S. Macdonald, who is the government leader in the House of Commons, outlines the burdens of being a minister and how the new cabinet committees assist in lightening the load.

With one exception the rest of the chapter contains items from the second edition which seemed worth repeating because of their pertinence. The editor's article documents the acquaintance most Canadians have with the representative nature of the Canadian cabinet by illustrating the familiar principle with a comparative analysis of our four most recent cabinets. An examination of the Trudeau cabinet, which has been added to the article that appeared in the second edition, shows that with minor departures the present government's composition merely confirms the important unwritten conventions of our constitution which require that any federal cabinet should include representatives of the major geographical, religious, linguistic, and occupational elements that compose the country. The extract from Sir George Foster's diary, though dated, is still one of the best depictions available of the hectic competitive struggle that ensues to get into the centre of power. A. D. P. Heeney's classic essay on developments in the Canadian cabinet system from 1939 to 1945 appeared in the first edition of this book, pp. 145-159. The appendix to it, outlining the functions of the prime minister, is reprinted again here, as is the interesting statement to the Commons by a previous prime minister of the policy governing the disclosure of cabinet papers. The item from the privy council office stating the salaries and allowances of ministers has been checked and is repeated also here. A portion of a recent article by Professor Alan Alexander outlining the political and constitutional position of Canadian parliamentary secretaries has been added to this edition. It supplements the article by Professor Denis Stairs which was an original study of the statistics of the rates of promotion of parliamentary secretaries to cabinet ministers. Professor Stairs has brought his article up to date for this third edition. Although the Hon. Mitchell Sharp is no longer minister of finance, his explanation of how the budget and estimates are prepared which appeared in the second edition is still well worth reproducing again in this edition.

The bibliography refers to a good deal of valuable literature on the cabinet, on the power structure, and on decision-making at the executive level.

TRUDEAU — NEW STYLE PM, POWER AND POLITICS*

ANTHONY WESTELL

Two years after being sworn into office Pierre Trudeau has gathered more power into his own hands than any previous prime minister.

He has built a personal political staff on a scale never before seen in Ottawa and centralized control of the federal bureaucracy in his own executive suite.

Trudeau tells his cabinet, "I shan't be around long," so that his ministers keep in line for the succession, and he stands above their battles so that they vie for his support.

His backbenchers regard his intellect with awe and sometimes fear the lash of his sarcasm when they question his policies.

He refuses to play Parliament's game of petty politics and his relations with the Governor-General are no closer than correct, as his compelling personality upstages a vice-regal couple who have made little impact on the public.

Trudeau's skill at communication overcomes normal political liabilities, and he easily tops the polls.

His frustrated opponents cry "president," meaning it as a protest against his power. Trudeau smiles, and his image-makers accept it as a compliment because

* From the *Toronto Daily Star*, April 11-17, 1970. By permission of the publisher.

they believe Canadians are conditioned by the memory of U.S. president John F. Kennedy to want a presidential leader.

But Trudeau's political philosophy is to create counterweights to power. The checks and balances to his own authority are appearing, sometimes with his encouragement . . . Parliament changes its role and new political forms emerge to challenge the presidential power.

POWER CENTRE — THE PMO

The command post of every Canadian government is in the towered, turretted and gargoyled East Block on Parliament Hill.

Here the Prime Minister has his offices and gathers his chosen political staff around him in high-ceilinged Victorian chambers behind anonymous green baize doors.

At the north end of the block, where there is rug underfoot and red plush set into the door panels, the mandarins of the Privy Council Office extend their influence into all the departments of state as they plan and co-ordinate government programs and exercise strategic control over the flow of paper through the cabinet machine.

The Prime Minister's Office and the Privy Council Office today occupy almost half the building erected a century ago to house all the principal ministries of Canada at Confederation, and they long ago overflowed into a warren of offices in the attic storage space.

The East Block, in fact, is the closest Canadian equivalent to Washington's White House as the headquarters of the executive arm of government.

Prime Minister Pierre Elliott Trudeau has accepted this more readily than his predecessors and enlarged his personal staff to give him greater effective power and control over the entire operations of government.

NUMBER ON STAFF

His office establishment is 77 persons, including confidential aides on private contract down to $5,000-a-year civil service stenos. At the most recent count, 73 posts were filled.

This compares with Lester Pearson's establishment of 44 in 1967, his last year as prime minister, and far fewer in the time of John Diefenbaker.

The fact that Trudeau's staff is larger than that of his predecessors is not necessarily a criticism.

Pearson's aides were grossly overworked and hardly knew what it meant to take a day off at weekends. They fired decisions from the hip and the office was sometimes in a state of barely controlled chaos which was reflected in the image of the government.

Diefenbaker was destroyed partly by the absence of an effective machine for making decisions and exercising executive authority.

Trudeau has learned the lesson of these mistakes because his staff is based on veterans of the Pearson years, and even earlier.

Contrary to widespread impression, he has not brought in a whole new team, but taken over the existing East Block establishment and enlarged it by recruiting, in the main, young men who were already working around the government.

PRINCIPAL AIDES

His principal aide, for example, is Marc Lalonde, who first came to Ottawa to work for Conservative minister Davie Fulton in the Diefenbaker era and later returned as policy secretary to Pearson. One of Lalonde's first pieces of advice to Trudeau was to enlarge the private staff so that aides would have time to think and to organize.

Among the new aides, executive assistant Gordon Gibson, chief speech writer Tim Porteous, special assistant Michel Vennat and regional desk supervisor Dave Thomson, to mention only some examples, all worked previously for Liberal ministers.

They are all familiar faces on Parliament Hill, and when observers talk in a worried way about the new men and new ways in the East Block, they are probably thinking chiefly of Jim Davey, 40-year-old program secretary, a slightly mysterious figure because he does not fit any of the conventional Ottawa patterns.

A slim figure, with thin fair hair and an anxious pointed face, Davey is a scientist by training and a planner and programmer by vocation.

He worked on market research in Montreal and experimented with techniques of organization and analysis in local riding politics before going to work for Trudeau in the leadership campaign.

Now he lives in the heart of civil service Ottawa—his neighbors include External Affairs Minister Mitchell Sharp and retiring Deputy Finance Minister Bob Bryce—goes jogging every morning, and walks to work in the East Block, where he tries hard to obey Trudeau's injunction to all his staff to stay out of controversy by keeping a low profile.

As program secretary and resident systems expert, Davey analyzed the PM's responsibilities in his different roles as head of government, parliamentary leader, public personality, chief of the Liberal party and private man.

Flow charts and other techniques of business organization ration the PM's time and attempt to keep him on top of all his jobs.

Davey also tries to keep the over-all government political program on a four-year time track, intervening in policy decisions when they seem to be lagging, and keeps in touch with U.S. think-tanks to try to give the administration a perspective on Canada through to the year 2000.

This passion for planning, this professionalism in the East Block, is deeply suspicious to politicians and observers raised in the tradition of gentlemanly amateurism.

Many of the people who regularly deplored the disasters and crises of the

Pearson and Diefenbaker years now look back upon them with affection as somehow more reassuring and comfortable than the smooth hum of Trudeau's computer.

But the fact is that Trudeau is running a different style of government and of politics.

The speed and pressure of government administration is constantly increasing. To use only one East Block index, the number of papers going before the cabinet doubled from an average of 383 a year in 1957-59 to about 800 a year 10 years later. . . .

Trudeau also uses his personal staff to develop information and advice from outside the cabinet and the regular channels of civil service organization, so that he has policy options before him when he makes final decisions.

While all this explains why Trudeau has increased his private staff, it does not change the fact that, for better or for worse, he has drawn more of the reins of power into his own hands than any recent prime minister.

THE MAIL FLOWS IN — AND OUT

In the TV age, when the Prime Minister talks directly to the people, more and more Canadians want to communicate back to him. They write to Pierre Trudeau in unprecedented and increasing numbers.

The Prime Minister's office received 17,000 pieces of mail during February, but the average is 450 a day. This compares with 185 letters a day when Lester Pearson was prime minister.

The flow of answers has risen even more dramatically. While previous prime ministers were content merely to acknowledge many communications, Trudeau and his staff provide long informative answers.

During the Pearson period there were 21 employees in his correspondence section. Trudeau now has 37.

The increase of 16 accounts for more than half the total and much-criticized increase in the Prime Minister's personal establishment.

When Trudeau came to office and the mail began to pour in, attracted by his power of communication, government management experts and IBM experts helped set up a system to handle it.

Mail from ministers, members of Parliament, provincial premiers, heads of federal agencies, Liberal party leaders and other VIPs is routed to Trudeau's desk.

Other letters which are for any reason distinguished—they may be wise or witty or of special human interest—are submitted to Trudeau together with a reply ready for his approval and personal signature.

The mass of the mail, some 300 pieces a day, is handled by the correspondence office. A research unit provides standard answers to standard queries, and these are coded into special cards.

By selecting the right combination of cards, a letter writer can compose an appropriate answer to most correspondents seeking information from the Prime Minister.

The cards activate an automatic typewriter which produces an individualized reply, leaving space for the name and any additional information to be typed in.

Correspondence Secretary Henry Lawless, an intense and precise young man who was formerly director of the Canadian Federation of Mayors and Municipalities, signs this mail.

He also provides Trudeau each month with a detailed statistical analysis of the mail, complete with a narrative commentary and a selection of typical letters.

The correspondence division and its enlarged staff is an increasingly important channel of communication between Trudeau and the public. He takes in a broad sample of public opinion which yields a sophisticated understanding of the moods and concerns of the nation, and he sends out his personal explanations to tens of thousands of Canadians every year.

REGIONAL DESK MEN

Another way in which Trudeau has increased his staff and his personal political reach is by the appointment of four regional desk officers.

Prime ministers who come to office after long political experience have friends and contacts to call in Halifax or Vancouver or Toronto when they need private intelligence. But Trudeau's roots in the Liberal party are shallow and his political background limited to Quebec.

(A current and possibly apocryphal story relates that when Denison mine owner Steve Roman opened a recent talk with Trudeau with the familiar refrain of favor seekers, "I've been a Liberal for years . . .", Trudeau put him down by saying pointedly, "I haven't been.")

The desk officers partly make up for this deficiency by keeping Trudeau alert to issues and opinion in the West, the Maritimes and Quebec. They also serve as a direct channel to provincial premiers and community leaders, supplementing and sometimes bypassing the provincial representation offered by cabinet ministers and members of Parliament.

Ontario Liberals originally refused to approve the idea of a staff officer reporting directly to the PM on their province. Recently they came around to the view that the right man—Colin Kenny, former director of the Ontario Liberal party—could serve both the PM and the Ontario caucus.

Trudeau likes to make maximum use of every trip out of Ottawa and his regional officers move ahead of him, programming every minute of his time. . . . ALL the implications of an invitation are weighed in advance, and one or more staff officers go ahead to inspect the ground and lay out the program to obtain the maximum benefit.

When Trudeau went to Winnipeg recently, for example, primarily to speak at a fund-raising dinner, he also met leaders of the grain industry, received a deputation of Mennonites and looked in at the Selkirk by-election.

It was all programmed by West deskman Dave Thomson.

APPOINTMENTS MADE FROM 'TALENT BANK'

A third area in which Trudeau has extended personal control is in making several hundred senior appointments each year to the Senate, crown corporations, federal agencies and departments, and so on. Choosing the right men is a vital part of administration—and of patronage.

Most prime ministers have relied on personal knowledge or on recommendations from ministers and bureaucrats. Trudeau insists on an alternative source of advice and information in his own office.

Francis Fox, who formerly worked as an aide to Consumer and Corporate Affairs Minister Ron Basford, is now in charge of Trudeau's talent bank, directing the compiling and checking of names and recommendations.

The big job at the moment is filling Senate vacancies and Trudeau is being presented with lists of suitable political and non-political names.

The British Columbia list, for example, includes the names of vetern Liberal workers George Van Roggen and Lawrence Jolivet, and writer-naturalist-judge Roderick Haig-Brown.

Another function of the talent scouts is to keep an eye on local political problems.

In Manitoba, former provincial Liberal leader Gil Molgat has first party claim to a Senate seat. But if he resigns from the legislature and the Liberals lose the by-election, their strength would fall below the minimum level for a recognized opposition party. This would mean the present party leader would no longer be eligible for the $6,000 salary paid to the leader of a recognized opposition party.

The problem has to be negotiated by the PM's staff with the Manitoba Liberals before Molgat can be offered a Senate post.

Trudeau's increased staff help him to do a better job, but also to extend his personal political reach.

THE PCO — ADMINISTRATIVE CENTRE

When Prime Minister Mackenzie King sat down with his ministers for a cabinet meeting, he had two boxes before him on the table.

In the first box, the cabinet secretary placed papers requiring attention, and then discreetly withdrew. He returned after the private meeting to see which papers had been shifted into the second box, meaning they were approved for action.

The cabinet gave no explanations, had no written agenda and kept no minutes.

That was just 30 years ago when government was smaller and problems less complex.

The cabinet secretariat in the Privy Council Office has been growing steadily ever since, and today it is an elite staff encouraged by Prime Minister Pierre Trudeau to exercise a subtle, centralizing influence over the entire federal administration.

While the Prime Minister's private office staff is his political arm, the Privy Council Office is his agency for controlling the public administration.

Its mandarins are little known to the public but widely respected and sometimes feared in the federal service. They are credited by admirers with bringing a new cohesion to government policy-making, and accused by critics of destroying such outside initiatives as Paul Hellyer's housing task force.

Wise ministers seek the understanding and support of the Privy Council Office before taking proposals to cabinet, and cabinet secretary Gordon Robertson has laid down the doctrine: "Any civil servant above clerical or stenographic grades who has spent any substantial time in a job without contributing to some degree to the policy he administers should be fired. . . ."

Trudeau has enlarged the staff and the influence of the Privy Council Office as part of the process of centralizing power around his own person.

During Lester Pearson's last year as prime minister, 1967-68, the Privy Council Office establishment was 150. Now it is 210, made up of a cabinet secretariat of 82, federal-provincial secretariat of 26, science secretariat 20, and 82 administrative and support staff.

The big increase of 47 jobs came when Trudeau, in effect, added a priorities and planning division to the cabinet staff.

Pearson realized in his last months of office that failure to foresee the mounting costs of new programs and make tough decisions had edged his government and the country into deep financial difficulties. He set up a cabinet committee on fiscal priorities, and the Privy Council Office staffed it.

When Trudeau took over, he broadened the committee mandate to setting priorities for all programs, not just fiscal commitments. The new Privy Council Office division was set up to serve the committee, and placed under Michael Pitfield, 32-year-old deputy cabinet secretary and an occasional travelling companion for the Prime Minister.

The planning staff has become an important instrument for controlling the government machine, standing between finance department and Treasury Board and sometimes competing for power with both.

With the cabinet committee which Trudeau chairs, it is now working on next year's program of government activity—a long way from the old, free-and-easy, play-it-off-the-cuff style of administration.

This programming function adds to the traditional sources of Privy Council Office power and influence.

INFLUENCE OF MANDARINS

The first source is access to the Prime Minister, Cabinet secretary Robertson, Ottawa's senior mandarin and a reserved but pleasant man with graying hair and the deep tanned face of a skier, who attends Trudeau's morning staff meetings and supplies him with all the official information and briefings he requires.

The second source of influence is control of the cabinet agenda and paperwork. When a departmental minister wants to take a proposal to cabinet, the Privy Council Office decides which committee to send it to, if the supporting documents are in order and, occasionally, when to bring it forward to the full cabinet.

Since Trudeau reorganized and rationalized the system of cabinet committees, this control of routine has become more rigid and important.

After the housing task force proposals were rejected a year ago, and Hellyer resigned, his aides bitterly laid the blame on Privy Council Office influence. They said that the task force took the precaution of inviting Robertson to dinner before forwarding the report, and sensed at once that he was uneasy about the constitutional implications of making federal grants to cities.

Trudeau was in Europe at the time. Before Hellyer got to see him on the day of his return to Ottawa, he had been fully briefed on the dangers of the task force proposals, which were subsequently buried in cabinet committees.

Ministers complain that Privy Council Office men and members of the Prime Minister's private office staff are intervening more in the deliberations of cabinet committees. They are never quite sure whether the officials are speaking for themselves or for Trudeau, who often prefers to reserve his own opinion and try out ideas through other mouths.

The Privy Council Office deliberately seeks to stay small and free of administrative responsibilities so that it can be an objective elite, co-ordinating the policies of operating departments and chairing inter-departmental meetings to resolve conflicts.

Occasionally it sets up a new secretariat to co-ordinate action on problems for which responsibility is shared by several departments. There is current talk of a Privy Council Office secretariat on pollution.

One revealing measure of Privy Council Office influence is to read a paper given by Robertson at the annual conference of the Institute of Public Administration of Canada in 1967, before Trudeau became prime minister. He analyzed many of the problems of cabinet and Parliament and suggested the solutions which Trudeau later adopted: Freeing ministers from daily attendance at question period to give them more time at their desks; shorter parliamentary sessions with planned allocation of time; more use of Commons committees, particularly to handle spending estimates; more effective organization of cabinet committees; appointment of more ministers.

Robertson added another idea: "The American system (of government) may be better suited in some respects to these times than the British. It may be that we will have to accept compromises to make the principle of ministerial responsibility flexible enough to work today."

"Perhaps one of these is the development of a doctrine by which changes in legislation in committee can be regarded as not matters of confidence unless the government so decides."

That would encourage the opposition and strengthen independence of government backbenchers, but Trudeau hasn't adopted it yet.

USING TV TO CAPTURE PUBLIC OPINION

The Liberals discovered that television is more potent than Parliament in February, 1968. That was the time when prime minister Lester Pearson went to the people, on TV, to appeal against the verdict of the Commons, and won.

His government had been defeated, more by accident than opposition design, in a vote on a tax bill in the Commons, and was immediately faced with a demand for resignation, echoed almost unanimously by the press.

Pearson hurried back from holiday to deal with the last of his many crises in office. He accepted the tactical advice of his press secretary, Romeo Leblanc, formerly CBC French-language TV correspondent in Washington, to use the networks to put his arguments for a reprieve directly to the nation.

The nation listened and then sent its instructions in a flood of mail to the opposition: End the crisis so that the government could get on with the budget intended to shore up the dollar and hold its party leadership convention.

The opposition bowed to public opinion and backed down, allowing the government to continue. The strategists on both sides began to draw the thoughtful conclusion that there had been a decisive change in the attitude of the people to Parliament.

They had discovered in fact, before Pierre Trudeau became Prime Minister, that the people were no longer awed by Parliament and its dusty traditions, and certainly did not accept its decisions as final.

DECLINE OF PARLIAMENT

The decline of the Commons had been apparent for years, of course, and the subject of much anxious comment. . . . Instead of a national forum, the Commons had become for many Canadians a theatre of the absurd in which mock battles were fought with wooden swords, the members were all actors, and nothing really changed.

As the backdrop to disenchantment, there was the intuitive understanding—still only half-formed today and of uncertain final shape—that representative democracy may be of passing relevance.

. . . Now that the people are in constant communication with the PM and the government, they are less willing to delegate their judgment to MPs. . . .

Trudeau . . . is a poor performer in the Commons and controls largely by refusing to recognize it as very important.

This is not to say he is autocratic or contemptuous. . . . Trudeau himself is a more faithful attender at the question time than most prime ministers have been, and reasonable queries usually get courteous replies. . . .

But the Commons is not primarily for the serious business of eliciting information or engaging in constructive comparison of ideas. It is for scoring party points, and Trudeau can hardly be bothered with that sort of battle, in which he is not very good anyway.

He answers partisan points with a quip or shrugs them off with disdain. Then, when he chooses, he strolls out of the House to make his case directly to the public by TV.

In the House debate, Trudeau is often put down by Opposition Leader Robert Stanfield, who has trained himself to be an effective parliamentarian.

On TV, Trudeau is, in a CBC man's admiring phrase, "better than Laugh-In," while Stanfield, "looks like yesterday."

Stanfield can only express his frustration by attacking Trudeau for arrogance and blaming him for the decline of Parliament. But having said that, the Tory leader has to face reality by being absent more and more from the Commons as he goes out into the country to make public speeches.

"If we stay in the House we're dead," he remarked recently to an aide.

TRUDEAU STRENGTHENING PARLIAMENT

Prime Minister Pierre Trudeau may scandalize the critics by preferring television to the Commons as a channel of communication to the public, and by showing more interest in dialogue with students and farmers and protest groups than in answering opposition members at question time.

But he is also encouraging Parliament to be a more effective auditor and scrutineer of his government, and he has done more than any prime minister for years to assist his backbenchers.

The centre of parliamentary activity has shifted from the Commons chamber to the committees which are flourishing as never before.

INCREASED COMMITTEE WORK

The parliamentary staff is growing by over 100 this year, an increase of almost 10 percent at a time when government payrolls are frozen. Seventy-two of the new jobs are to support the work of the committees, reflecting the startling growth in output.

In the 1964-65 session, Commons committees reported on 36 matters, in the last session there were 122 reports.

Last year, committees held 339 meetings and spent 451 hours reviewing spending estimates, far more time than the full House could have devoted to the task.

This session, the committees have heard 397 witnesses so far, an unprecedented input of information and expertise from outside the government.

Last week, the verbatim record of the committees totalled 9,029 pages, compared with 5,268 pages in the Hansard record of the full House.

Nobody claims the committee system is anywhere near perfect. MPs who can lurk in decent obscurity in the full Commons are exposed as incompetents by the less formal, more demanding work of small committees.

There are probably too many committee sessions, particularly for members of minor parties who have to spread time and expertise too thin.

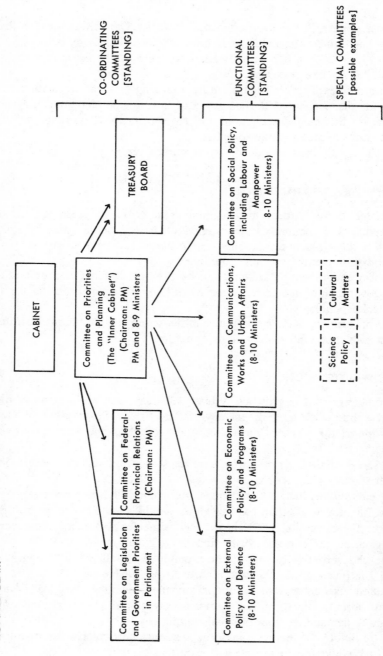

ORGANIZATION OF TRUDEAU CABINET*
RONALD BLAIR

* From a chart drawn up in May, 1968. By courtesy of the author.

ORGANIZATION OF PMO AND PCO*

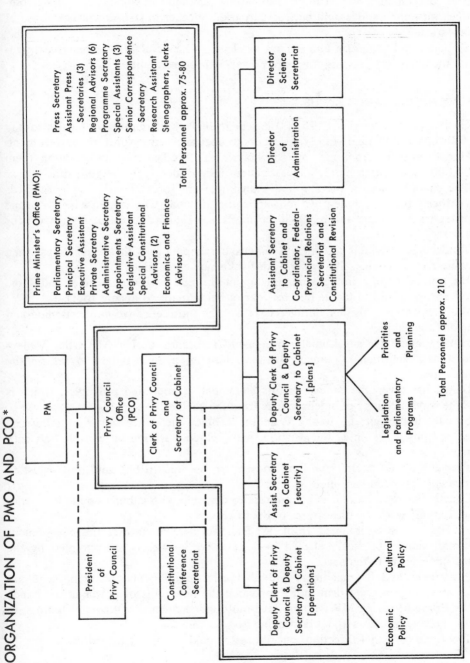

Prime Minister's Office (PMO):

Parliamentary Secretary
Principal Secretary
Executive Assistant
Private Secretary
Administrative Secretary
Appointments Secretary
Legislative Assistant
Special Constitutional
    Advisors (2)
Economics and Finance
    Advisor

Press Secretary
Assistant Press
    Secretaries (3)
Regional Advisors (6)
Programme Secretary
Special Assistants (3)
Senior Correspondence
    Secretary
Research Assistant
Stenographers, clerks

Total Personnel approx. 75-80

PM

President
of
Privy Council

Privy Council
Office
(PCO)

Constitutional
Conference
Secretariat

Clerk of Privy Council
and
Secretary of Cabinet

Deputy Clerk of Privy
Council & Deputy
Secretary to Cabinet
[operations]

Economic
Policy

Cultural
Policy

Assist. Secretary
to Cabinet
[security]

Deputy Clerk of Privy
Council & Deputy
Secretary to Cabinet
[plans]

Legislation
and Parliamentary
Programs

Priorities
and
Planning

Assistant Secretary
to Cabinet and
Co-ordinator, Federal-
Provincial Relations
Secretariat and
Constitutional Revision

Director
of
Administration

Director
Science
Secretariat

Total Personnel approx. 210

* From a chart drawn up by R. S. Blair in February, 1969, and revised by the editor in July, 1970.

The government's own attitude is sometimes ambiguous; while encouraging committees with one hand, it will occasionally use the other to slap down their sense of independence.

But the trend to reform and renewal is clear, and Liberal MPs as much as opposition members are pressing for more power and responsibility. . . .

RESEARCH FUNDS AND CAUCUS

He has [also] provided $195,000 a year to leaders of opposition parties to pay 22 full-time and five part-time researchers to document criticism of the government.

Under pressure from his own backbenchers, Trudeau is now granting them $130,000 for research by the Liberal caucus independently of the government.

The caucus meets in private and is an important forum in which Liberal MPs can criticize the government without appearing disloyal. The way in which a prime minister treats caucus and reacts to criticism is a significant test of his respect for democracy.

Trudeau is a regular attender at caucus but impatient with the meetings when they are merely steam-valve sessions for backbench complaints.

He can be cutting in his summing up at the end of each meeting, and some members are afraid to tackle him for fear of being made to appear fools.

But Trudeau has also encouraged caucus to be more effective in questioning and checking the cabinet.

Having made Gerald Laniel, 45-year-old insurance broker MP from Valleyfield, Que., chairman of caucus, he gave him an open mandate to reform the organization.

Laniel has given the caucus its first statement of operating principles, which is in some ways a charter of independence from the cabinet.

Equally important, he wrung from the cabinet the concession that ministers, when opening a file on new legislation, will include a section on consultation with caucus.

Trudeau agreed not to give final consent to the finished bill until he is satisfied that caucus has been consulted.

Caucus has reorganized its committees to coincide with cabinet committees, and they alternate weekly with sessions of the full body.

. . . [Laniel] also obtained from Trudeau his agreement that the next caucus chairman should be freely elected by Liberal MPs, instead of appointed by the prime minister, as in the past.

Parliament and its machinery are obviously adapting and changing, and are going to change a great deal more, to match the new tools of power in the hands of the Prime Minister. MPs should have more independence and greater latitude to check the government without destroying it.

The trend is in that direction, but not fast enough to satisfy the critics.

THE BURDEN OF BEING A MINISTER — LIGHTENED BY CABINET COMMITTEES*

DONALD S. MACDONALD

In 1970, while Ministers may get the occasional opportunity to return to their constituencies for weekends, they will be very fortunate indeed to get so much as ten days' holidays each.

A Minister, of course, is a member of the principal executive committee of the nation, the Cabinet. In the year from July 1st, 1968, to June 30th, 1969, the full Cabinet met 70 times, while there were 378 meetings of Cabinet Committees. A total of 1,315 Cabinet Documents were considered and the whole process resulted in 601 recorded decisions. With the exceptions of the Prime Minister, who is the Chairman of our Executive Committee, and of Senator Martin and myself, who have special Parliamentary duties, every Minister acts in some capacity as administrator of a Government Department with annual expenditures of millions of dollars. In the case of the Department of Transport, for instance, the budget for the Department for 1969-70 is $307,606,800 and there are budgets exceeding $200,000,000 voted to the various Crown Corporations and Agencies for which the Minister of Transport happens to be responsible.

Like any executive, a Cabinet Minister must report to meetings of the shareholders. In this case, he normally reports to their representatives in Parliament. His reports must be regular and must be thorough, for their examination will be complete and any weaknesses are certain to be caught.

In addition to the administrative and parliamentary duties, a Minister has political responsibilities. He must be a representative of his province or a region of his province in its dealings with the Federal Government. He is also required to represent his own constituency and, through public addresses, tours, public and private meetings, press conferences, television programs, radio talks and even printed articles, it is a responsibility of Ministers to publicize the problems of government and their possible solutions.

With so heavy a load on every Minister and on the Cabinet as a whole, it was quite clear to this Government, when it came into office, that additional means had to be found to enable Ministers to discharge all of these functions effectively. Just as the work of the House of Commons was decentralized into committees, so has the work of the Cabinet been decentralized. Five committees have been established on the basis of subject material. These are Cabinet Committees on External Policy and Defence, Economic Policy and Programs, Science Policy and Technology,

* From a speech by the Hon. Donald S. Macdonald, President of the Privy Council and Government Leader in the House of Commons, given in September, 1969. By permission of the author.

Social Policy, and Cultural Affairs and Information. In addition, there are four co-ordinating Committees of the Cabinet. The first is a traditional committee, the Treasury Board, which oversees the expenditures by the Federal Government. The other three are more recent; they are Committees on Priorities and Planning, Legislation and House Planning, and Federal-Provincial Relations.

The results of the formation of this committee system for the Cabinet have been noteworthy. While the Committees of the Cabinet have been able to attend to the mass of administrative detail facing any large organization, the Cabinet as a whole has been able to devote itself more and more to the broader principles of planning and policy for which the Cabinet was originally intended in our system of government.

In addition to the reorganization of the Cabinet, the required appearances of Ministers in Parliament are better planned. . . . Until last year, Ministers were expected to appear five times a week, to answer questions of which they had almost never received notice. For each Minister, this usually meant one hour of preparation each day and in excess of another hour of questions, or, to be more accurate, waiting for questions. During the 1960's, usually fewer than a dozen Ministers were asked questions each day. This meant that on the average, more than half the Cabinet — indeed, often two-thirds of the Cabinet — devoted up to two hours a day for questions that never came. In the last session and in the present session, we have altered this routine by reducing each Minister's appearance in the House of Commons to three times a week. While there still is no notice of questions, there is now a more predictable timetable for Ministers. Since this system was initiated, the average number of Ministers asked questions each day has remained virtually the same, that is, eight or nine each day. However, the number of Ministers required to attend the House for Question Period has been reduced by one-third. In other words, while formerly 60 percent of the Cabinet had to waste its time preparing for Question Period when they did not receive questions, the new system has reduced this figure to 30 percent. Needless to say, this has given Members of the Cabinet invaluable additional time to administer the affairs of their Departments and to carry on their other important functions as Ministers.

. . . As the problems facing government grow in number and in complexity, Ministers are likely to have less and less time to deal with each problem. . . . It is . . . likely that the number of Ministers will be increased and, as has been done already in some Departments such as Finance or the Secretary of State's Department, Ministers without Portfolio may be appointed to assist other Ministers with particularly onerous responsibilities. Nevertheless, time for Ministers and time for Parliament will remain in the same category as time for executives everywhere: their most precious commodity.

THE REPRESENTATIVE NATURE OF THE CANADIAN CABINET*

PAUL FOX

Since the cabinet is the centre of power in the Canadian system of government, many different interest groups will seek to be represented in it. Provinces such as Quebec, for instance, will be much more concerned about protecting their minority position by means of representation in the cabinet than in the Senate, which was intended originally to be the organ for guaranteeing the provinces a voice at Ottawa. The same will hold true for minority religious and ethnic groups, or for occupational and professional organizations.

A prime minister will be prepared to listen to such pleas not only because he wishes to secure the allegiance of all these different factions but also because, by means of well-chosen cabinet ministers, he can establish across the country pillars of party strength responsible to him. In each province a federal cabinet minister may well be the chief power in the local party, the link between it and Ottawa, and the channel through which flows influence, patronage, and party loyalty.

Thus, by virtue of the federal and party systems in Canada, certain definite customs have grown up governing the construction of cabinets which no prime minister, whatever his party, would dare to flout. First, he must make sure that he has tried to give representation to each of the ten provinces (with the possible exception of the smallest, Prince Edward Island). The largest provinces of Ontario and Quebec will believe themselves entitled to more than one member, the quota having been raised progressively through the years to at last six each, while British Columbia, as third in order of size, will claim two or three seats. Even within these provinces there will be such strong feelings of regional identity that eastern Quebec, including Quebec City, will have to receive recognition as well as western Quebec, including Montreal. The eastern townships in Quebec will also probably try to get representation. In Ontario it will be impossible to select all the ministers from the central area around Toronto, since eastern, western, and northern Ontario will expect representation too. Careful attention must also be given to achieving a proper distribution of posts amongst the religious faiths in the country. Protestants and Roman Catholics and perhaps others, will receive appointments in proportion to their numerical strength in the country. Catholic appointments will have to be subdivided between Anglo-Irish Roman Catholics and French Roman Catholics and Protestant appointments amongst the various Protestant churches, if possible in proportion to their sizes. Members of the Ukrainian Orthodox faith, Jews and others will feel that they should be recognized as well. Moreover, some of these groups located in certain provinces will demand specific representation, for example, the English-speaking Protestants in Montreal and Roman Catholics in Ontario.

* From an article by the author which was revised in May, 1966, and June, 1970.

Various economic groups will also press their claims, often to particular port-folios. Prairie wheat farmers will expect the minister of agriculture to be chosen from amongst their numbers or, at least, from the west. The department of fisheries will have to go to someone from either the east or west coast. Business and financial circles will seek a minister of finance who is sympathetic to their views, trade unions a minister of labour who understands their problems, and veterans a minister of veterans' affairs who has been a serviceman and will listen to them.

Special interests will also make their voices heard. Women's associations may argue that there should be more women in the cabinet, young people's groups that there should be more youthful ministers, Indians that there should be an Indian member, and French-speaking Acadians that there ought to be an Acadian in the government.

The result is that every Canadian cabinet becomes highly federalized, a mirror of the various forces that compose the country. This is well illustrated by a comparative analysis of the Liberal government of Mr. St. Laurent at the beginning of 1957, the Conservative government of Mr. Diefenbaker which replaced it later that year, the Liberal government of Mr. Pearson that in turn succeeded it in 1963, and the Trudeau government of June 10, 1970.

The St. Laurent Liberal cabinet contained one member of parliament from every province except Prince Edward Island, which received a parliamentary assistant. British Columbia had two representatives in the cabinet, Ontario six, and Quebec five (formerly six, one was recently deceased). The Ontario members were apportioned judiciously in the ratio of two to northern Ontario, one to western, one to eastern and two to central Ontario. In Quebec three ministers were chosen from the province's eastern region in the neighbourhood of Quebec city and two from Montreal in the west.

There were 13 Protestants in the cabinet, of whom eight belonged to the largest Protestant denomination, the United Church, and two to each of the Anglican and Baptist churches, while one called himself simply a "Protestant." Of the six Roman Catholic ministers, four were primarily French-speaking, one was Anglo-Irish, and one was of English-speaking and French-speaking parentage. Ontario's group of six ministers was composed quite fairly of four Protestants and two Catholics and Quebec's five included one representative of the Protestant English-speaking enclave in Montreal.

Occupationally, this cabinet contained nine lawyers (the most numerous occupational group in the Commons), one notary, three engineers, two former civil servants, one farmer, one educator, one medical doctor, and one businessman. The farmer was the minister of agriculture, the minister of fisheries was from the west coast, and the minister of trade and commerce was a prominent former businessman and engineer.

In addition, the group of 13 parliamentary assistants of the day showed much the same sort of proportional distribution in terms of geography, religious faith, and occupation.

The Conservative government that succeeded this Liberal administration illustrated that the same principles of federalism were at work. Every province received at least one seat in the new cabinet while Ontario was given seven members, Quebec three (later increased to five with one more "promised"), British Columbia three, Saskatchewan two, and Manitoba two. In these provinces with plural membership the appointments were distributed fairly equitably throughout each province.

There were 17 Protestants in the cabinet, their grouping by denominations corresponding exactly, by happy coincidence or design, to the order of size of the various Protestant faiths: six members of the United Church, five Anglicans, three Presbyterians, two Baptists, and one "Protestant". With later additions from Quebec, there were six Roman Catholics, four of whom were primarily French-speaking, and two of whom were Anglo-Irish. There was also one member of the Ukrainian Orthodox faith, who as a Ukrainian represented what was then the fourth largest ethnic group in Canada. He came from Ontario, while Quebec's contingent included one English-speaking Protestant from Montreal.

The Conservative cabinet contained nine lawyers, four educators, four businessmen, two chartered accountants, two farmers, and one army officer. The ministry of finance went to a member from Toronto, the department of agriculture to a member from Alberta, and the portfolio of fisheries to an MP from Prince Edward Island. A former army colonel was appointed minister of veterans' affairs, and a distinguished army general with the Victoria Cross became minister of national defence. (The Liberals had also had a minister with the Victoria Cross. He had held the portfolio of veterans' affairs.)

The 13 parliamentary assistantships were also distributed amongst various provinces, faiths, and occupations.

The Liberal cabinet appointed by Mr. Pearson after his electoral victory in April, 1963 reflected the continuation of the representative principle. Its 26 members (the largest number to date) contained 10 representatives of Ontario, eight of Quebec, two of British Columbia, and one of each of the other provinces except Saskatchewan, which had not seen fit to elect any Liberals to Parliament. The 10 Ontario appointments were distributed so that five went to central Ontario (including three to Toronto), three to northern Ontario, and one each to western and eastern Ontario. Eastern Quebec received only one minister but the Eastern Townships and the Anglo-Saxon bastion in Westmount were not overlooked.

The cabinet was balanced neatly with an even split between Protestants and Roman Catholics, 13 each. The Protestants included eight members of the United Church, three Presbyterians, one Anglican, and one "Protestant", while the Roman Catholics were subdivided into nine predominantly French-speaking members, three Anglo-Saxons, and one of mixed parentage.

Mr. Pearson's first cabinet contained 10 lawyers, six businessmen, four former civil servants, two ex-professors, two agriculturalists, and one economist. The ministries of finance and trade and commerce went to Toronto, justice to Quebec, northern affairs and forestry to British Columbia, fisheries to New Brunswick, veterans' affairs to a former prisoner-of-war, and agriculture to Alberta.

The 16 parliamentary secretaryships were distributed in such a way that they reflected the representative principle also. Ontario received six, Quebec five, British Columbia two, and Nova Scotia, New Brunswick, and Newfoundland one each. Nine of the secretaries were Protestants and seven Roman Catholics. Balance within the top echelon of departments was achieved by frequently appointing as a parliamentary secretary to a minister an MP of a different provincial and religious affiliation from the minister, for instance, an Ontario, English-speaking, Protestant secretary to a Quebec, French-speaking, Roman Catholic minister, or a Quebec, French-speaking, Roman Catholic secretary to an Ontario, English-speaking, Protestant minister.

When Mr. Trudeau became prime minister in April, 1968, it might have been expected that his more unconventional approach to politics would result in a major departure from observing the traditional representative principle in the Canadian cabinet. But an examination in detail of the appointments to his first cabinet, as modified by changes up to the time of revising this article on June 10, 1970, reveals that there was no substantial alteration in adherence to the long-standing customs regarding representation in the cabinet.

The body continued to grow in size, acquiring 30 members in place of Mr. Pearson's 26 ministers and in sharp contrast to the 13 members with which Sir John A. Macdonald began in 1867. Ontario and Quebec still received the lion's share of nominations, the former obtaining 11 and the latter 10, but with the exception of British Columbia which captured three awards and Prince Edward Island which received none (having failed to elect any Liberals), the rest of the provinces each got one cabinet minister. In Ontario and Quebec the prizes were distributed throughout each province with reasonable judiciousness, although some Torontonians, including one leading newspaper, complained about the under-representation of Toronto in comparison to Montreal since after Paul Hellyer's resignation the score was only two to six. Perhaps because of such criticism, the prime minister promoted a parliamentary secretary from Toronto, Robert Stanbury, to cabinet rank shortly thereafter. This appointment brought the number of ministers without portfolio in Mr. Trudeau's government to the unusually large total of four, which did mark a minor departure from form.

Despite the fact that Prime Minister Trudeau implied he was putting more emphasis on quality than had some of his predecessors, his cabinet nevertheless emerged with much the same complexion in religious and occupational respects as prior administrations. It contained 15 Protestants, 14 Roman Catholics, and one Hebrew, the last being an innovation since the Hon. Herb Gray is the first Jew ever to be appointed to a Canadian cabinet. Occupationally, however, the familiar pattern was repeated with 11 lawyers leading the pack accompanied by eight businessmen, four academics, two agriculturalists and two labour figures, and one former civil servant, one journalist, and one chartered accountant. The average age of ministers was about 45 years, not all that much less than in previous governments.

In one respect Mr. Trudeau's cabinet did differ from its predecessors. While the prime minister has not increased the proportion of ministers of French maternal tongue beyond the customary one-third of the total, he has tried consciously to give a greater number of senior posts to French-speaking members, in keeping with his policy of fostering genuine equality between the two official language groups. He also has drawn heavily on French-speaking colleagues, as one might expect, for "confidents" in what becomes inevitably in practice if not in proclamation "the inner cabinet." An article by Walter Stewart in *Maclean's* magazine in October, 1969, entitled "The 30 Men Trudeau Trusts" alleges that this group includes the Hon. Jean Marchand, the Hon. Gérard Pelletier, Marc Lalonde, who is the prime minister's principal secretary, and Gordon Robertson, the clerk of the privy council and secretary of the cabinet. What is disturbing is not that both colleagues are French-speaking but that the inner circle contains two individuals who are not cabinet ministers. Perhaps this arrangement is Mr. Trudeau's most significant departure from custom in cabinet-making.

As for the 16 parliamentary secretaries appointed to the Trudeau ministry, their characteristics differ little from the traditional pattern of representing the various geographical, denominational, linguistic, and occupational components of Canadian federal politics.

Such a striking similarity in the elements represented in four different cabinets is a good indication of the strength of the representative principle that lies behind cabinet-making in Canada. In addition to this, of course, a prime minister must consider the desire of friends and party supporters (for themselves or others), the claims of the "grand old men" of the party, who may have been ministers in previous regimes, and the need to blend into a harmonious team conflicting and antipathetic personalities and points of view. Thus, it is not surprising that one British prime minister said that the business of drawing up a cabinet "resembled nothing so much as the zoological gardens at feeding time." The wonder is that any cabinet contains as much ability as it does since capacity is frequently a minor consideration.

GETTING INTO THE CABINET*

SIR GEORGE FOSTER

[The scramble for a position in the cabinet which occurs when a new government is being formed is well illustrated by excerpts from the diary of Sir George Foster during the cabinet-making period that followed the Conservative victory in the 1911 election. Having served as minister of finance in five previous Conservative

* From W. S. Wallace, *The Memoirs of the Rt. Hon. Sir George Foster, P.C., G.C.M.G.*, Toronto, Macmillan, 1933, pp. 155-156, as corrected from the original diary in the National Archives, Ottawa. By permission of the Estate.

administrations, Foster believed himself entitled to the same post again, and he did not hesitate to let the new prime minister, R. L. Borden, know. The anxieties of the aspirant, the pressures applied to the prime minister, and the inner forces at work are all clearly revealed in a few brief entries.]

Sept. 22. The govt. defeat is a decisive and general one. . . .

Sept. 23. General congratulations pour in from all sides. Left for Ottawa.

Sept. 24. At home in peace and quietness again. Borden came in at noon. Telephoned him, but he was being protected by wife—no communication.

Sept. 25. Now the cabinet-making begins, in the papers and in the clubs. B. keeps to his house and sees those he calls for. No communication.

Sept. 26. Taylor as a middleman suggests Ch. Tariff Comm., with $10,000, as a nice thing, I told him I was not out for office, and would accept none. No other communication.

Sept. 27. Certain parties are in tow. Perley appears to be the manager. Davis-Shaughnessy in evidence. Reporters (Hamilton) at old business. No communication.

Sept. 28. To-night Osler sees me. Financial interests opposed to my being F.M. Would relieve situation if I would remain out. *Globe* criticism feared. I told him plainly I would not commit suicide. No communication from Borden. Rogers says a portfolio, but not F.M. or Trade and Commerce, seat in Senate.

Sept. 29. The interests seem to be dominant, and Borden doesn't know his mind from day to day. I have advised my friends, and they are at work. No communication.

Sept. 30. To-night at 9 p.m. B. asks me to come up. He skated all around, and finally suggested Sec'y of State. I told him I wouldn't consider it. My old position was what I wanted.

Oct. 1. A quiet day, rest and reading. Hazen is here, and Rogers seems in charge. The Kemp Gooderham-McNab-Graham crowd make up the financial int.

Oct. 2. Fine. More people here. More excitement. Saw Hazen, McLeod, Crockett, Roach, etc. All are strong for me in old position. McGrath had peculiar conference.

Oct. 3. No further word from B. Letter from Clouston, and conference with Dobie. Financial interests not adverse. My friends are making things hot.

Oct. 4. More people. More wire-pulling. Deputations galore, and general suspense. B. seems helpless on the surf.

Oct. 5. Called by Chief, and offered Trade and Commerce. Ask why F.M. not given. Ans.: reasons of high politics. My capabilities, honesty and service fully recognized.

Oct. 6. A bothersome day. Backing and filling. Irresolute and fearful. He is an odd man.

Oct. 7. No word from Borden to-day. Saw Boyce and Smith, who are raging at the outsiders, especially White.

Oct. 8. The day fine. Rested without outside disturbance. . . .

Oct. 9. No announcement yet, and no word from Borden since Friday night. I hear Toronto is bombarding him. Hazen is here—what others I know not.

Oct. 10. This morning the announcement of new govt. The unseemly squabble is ended. Some weak links in the chain. There will be deep dissatisfaction with White. Sworn in at 11 a.m. except Burrell.

[Foster was appointed minister of trade and commerce.]

FUNCTIONS OF THE PRIME MINISTER*

A. D. P. HEENEY

The most recent minute of Council on this subject is P.C. 3374 of October 25, 1935, which reads as follows:

"The Committee of the Privy Council, on the recommendation of the Right Honourable W. L. Mackenzie King, the Prime Minister, submit the following Memorandum regarding certain of the functions of the Prime Minister—

1. A Meeting of a Committee of the Privy Council is at the call of the Minister and, in his absence, of that of the senior Privy Councillor, if the President of the Council be absent;
2. A quorum of the Council being four, no submission, for approval to the Governor General, can be made with a less number than the quorum;
3. A Minister cannot make recommendations to Council affecting the discipline of the Department of another Minister;
4. The following recommendations are the special prerogative of the Prime Minister:

Dissolution and Convocation of Parliament: Appointment of—
>> Privy Councillors;
>> Cabinet Ministers;
>> Lieutenant-Governors;
>>> (including leave of absence to same);
>> Provincial Administrators;
>> Speaker of the Senate;
>> Chief Justices of all Courts;
>> Senators;
>> Sub-Committees of Council;
>> Treasury Board;

* Quoted in "Cabinet Government in Canada: Developments in the Machinery of the Central Executive," *The Canadian Journal of Economics and Political Science,* Vol. XII, No. 3, August, 1946. By permission of the author and publisher.

> Committee of Internal Economy, House of Commons;
> Deputy Heads of Departments;
> Librarians of Parliament;
> Crown Appointments in both Houses of Parliament;
> Governor General's Secretary's Staff;

Recommendations in any Department.

The Committee advise that this Minute be issued under the Privy Seal, and that a certified copy thereof be attached, under the Great Seal of Canada, to the Commission of each Minister."

CABINET PAPERS NOT DISCLOSED TO SUCCESSORS*

Right Hon. L. B. Pearson (Prime Minister): . . . I want to say a word now about a question that has been raised . . . about the propriety of the use by one government of reports and information bearing on the operations of a previous government. There are many reports and documents and, indeed, the great majority of reports, documents and records are quite proper to be brought to the attention of a government even if they concern activities during a previous administration. This is done and has been done since Confederation as a normal aspect of governmental administration. Administration records, including inquiries and investigations and reports, can be used in this way except, and the exception is a very important one, memoranda to the cabinet, to cabinet committees, and records of discussions of the cabinet or cabinet committees: they cannot be properly used. These cabinet papers may not even be seen by the successor government. Letters of understanding to this effect were exchanged when governments changed in Canada in 1957 and again in 1963. Cabinet and cabinet committee material will not be produced for a successor government by the secretary of the cabinet even if, which is inconceivable, a minister or prime minister should ask for it.

* From *House of Commons Debates,* May 3, 1966, p. 4627. By permission of the Queen's Printer.

SALARIES AND ALLOWANCES OF MINISTERS*

	Prime Minister	Ministers in Charge of Departments, including Solicitor General	Minister without Portfolio
The Salaries Act (C.21, 1953-4)	$25,000	$15,000	
Sessional Indemnity (C.14, 1963) Taxable as Income	12,000	12,000	$12,000
Expense Allowance (C.14, 1963) (Tax free)	6,000	6,000	6,000
Motor Car Allowance (C.14, 1963) (Tax free)	2,000	2,000	2,000
Vote Appropria- tion Act No. 5, 1961			7,500
Totals	$45,000	$35,000	$27,500

* From the Privy Council Office, courtesy of H. B. Stewart, July 23, 1970.

THE POLITICAL AND CONSTITUTIONAL POSITION OF PARLIAMENTARY SECRETARIES*

ALAN ALEXANDER

. . . The purpose of this article is to examine the constitutional position of a peripheral group in Canadian national administration and to examine the possibility that Canadian politicians may soon have to accept the existence of cabinet and subcabinet levels within the government. The peripheral group is the Parliamentary Secretaries, holders of offices which were legally established as recently as 1959, but whose historical development can be traced back to the latter part of the First World War.

The first instances of political appointments from within the House of Commons at a level below that of cabinet minister came in 1916 and 1917 when there were appointed a Parliamentary Secretary of the Department of Militia and Defence, a Parliamentary Under-Secretary of State for External Affairs and a Parliamentary Secretary of the Department of Soldiers Civil Re-establishment. It seems obvious that in making these appointments, the Prime Minister, Sir Robert Borden, envisaged the development of a ministry along British lines, for the Canada Year Book lists these appointees as "ministers not in the cabinet." It would appear that the notion of Parliamentary Secretaries as being non-ministerial assistants, having a position somewhere between that of the British Parliamentary Secretary and the Parliamentary Private Secretary, appeared much later in history of the development of the system.

Borden's experiment with a system closely modelled on that of Britain was short-lived and these positions were dispensed with almost as soon as the war was over. The end of Borden's ministry was followed by the Mackenzie King era of Canadian politics which lasted, with a few breaks, until 1948. Mackenzie King was personally attracted by the idea of appointing what he called "Parliamentary Assistants" and the intention of introducing such appointments was intimated in the Speech from the Throne in 1936. The proposal, however, was stillborn, and the necessary legislation was not brought before the House. In 1943, however, the Speech from the Throne contained the statement that "You will be asked to make provision for the appointment of parliamentary assistants to those of my ministers whose duties have become particularly onerous because of the demands of war." This proposal sparked off the first detailed examination of the system as it might be applied to

* From an article revised and updated in November, 1969, by the author, who is a member of the Department of Political Science, Lakehead University. The original article was published in *Parliamentary Affairs,* Vol. XX, No. 3, Summer, 1967. By permission of the author and publisher.

Canada, and it is significant that many speeches during the Debate on the Address discussed the suggestion with reference to the British model. . . .

Throughout the Debate, Mackenzie King was reluctant to accord the new appointees the status of junior ministers, although at one point he did use the phrase "assistant ministers." . . . [However,] the Prime Minister seems to have been unable to decide whether, in British terminology, he was introducing Parliamentary Private Secretaries or junior ministers. . . .

King's reluctance was merely the public expression of the unwillingness of Canadian politicians to move away from the single-level governmental structure and it is this rigidity of attitude which requires explanation. . . . The real danger for Canadian politicians is that if the Secretaries were given junior ministerial status there might arise a situation where appointment to a subcabinet position might be thought to satisfy the provincial claim to ministerial representation and preferment. This fear, has, I think, ruled out the idea of full ministers outside the Cabinet and has so far prevented the full realization of the administrative potential of the system of Parliamentary Assistants. . . .

. . . It is, I think, fair to assume that these Assistants [appointed during and after the Second World War] were considered an integral part of the departmental organisation if not of the ministerial structure. On the side of those who say that these appointments are not junior ministerial in nature, the major piece of evidence is Mackenzie King's statement . . . which excluded the Parliamentary Assistants from adherence to the doctrine of collective ministerial responsibility and left them free to express their own views. This assertion, however, is surely negatived by the payment of a salary to these Assistants. A politician who receives a salary by virtue of his appointment to a position by the Prime Minister must find his freedom of action circumscribed. . . .

The informal, non-statutory system of Parliamentary Assistants continued until 1958 when the Conservative Government of John Diefenbaker . . . [enacted] in 1959 the Parliamentary Secretaries Act. . . . Mr. Diefenbaker said that ". . . the system is one that will bring about a degree of apprenticeship for members who are chosen to occupy this high and important position (of cabinet minister)." The Prime Minister, in this statement, implied that the tasks of the Parliamentary Secretaries would be ministerial in character and that appointment was the first step in the ladder to the Cabinet.

This refreshing whiff of realism was, however, nullified by a statement made by Mr. Diefenbaker during the Second Reading Debate—a statement upon which the present ambiguous position of the Parliamentary Secretaries is based. In answer to a question from an opposition member, the Prime Minister said: "The Hon. Member from Kootenay West asked whether the parliamentary secretaries are to be given the status of junior ministers, and without any qualification in this regard I say that they are not." Thus Mr. Diefenbaker condemned his new statutory appointees to the same political limbo which had contained Mackenzie King's less formal Parliamentary Assistants. The influence of the political and structural considerations mentioned above had prevented another Prime Minister from giving official recognition to what was to become a fact of political life—that Canadian administration is moving inexorably toward a two-tier ministerial system somewhat akin to the British model.

•   •   •

Now that ten years have passed since the first appointments of Parliamentary Secretaries under the 1959 Act, it is perhaps possible to draw some conclusions about how the system has developed, both in the light of the duties which Parliamentary Secretaries have discharged and by looking at the way in which Prime Ministers have used the system and the effect which this has had on the Canadian ministerial structure. . . .

. . . It must be concluded that the attitude of the Prime Minister to these appointments, as well as the attitude of provincial politicians, is based on the same criteria [regional representation] as govern appointment to the Cabinet, and that both sides are increasingly coming to regard the secretaryships as in some way "ministerial" in character. It is unlikely that provincial representation would be as important a selection factor if the Parliamentary Secretaries were no more than non-governmental, personal assistants to ministers. Neither Prime Ministers nor provinces regard the Parliamentary Secretaries as the glorified errand boys which they would be if all official statements of their position were accepted as being strictly accurate. . . .

A study of the Canadian House of Commons debates for these years reveals that Parliamentary Secretaries regularly answered questions in the House on behalf of their departments, or, more accurately, their Ministers' departments, and none of these answers gives the impression of being given simply to save the Minister time or effort. Almost all of them give the impression of being delivered by someone with detailed knowledge of the department concerned, an impression which is strengthened by the responses of the Secretaries to frequent supplementary questions. Even in such a sensitive area of government policy as External Affairs there is ample evidence of the deep involvement of the Parliamentary Secretary in the business of the department. . . . These examples serve merely to illustrate the kind of responsibilities given to Parliamentary Secretaries by their ministers. The fact that most of the Parliamentary Secretaries were given comparable duties by their departmental heads seems to suggest that withholding of the title of junior ministers from these officials is nothing short of fatuous. . . . Canada's Parliamentary Secretaries have duties which are indistinguishable from those of British junior ministers. . . .

In April of 1967, moreover, there took place in the House a debate on a private member's bill which would have upgraded the status of the Parliamentary Secretaries so that they would have become junior ministers (a proposal which had been mentioned in the House on many previous occasions and which was advanced this time by a former Parliamentary Secretary), while at the same time reverting to the old title, Parliamentary Assistant, and removing the provision that they be appointed annually. During the debate it was clear that members regarded the duties of the Secretaries as being ministerial in nature and that there was some feeling in favour of the introduction of a two-tier ministerial structure of which the Parliamentary Secretaries would constitute the second tier. The government was sympathetic to the bill but due to the objection of one member . . . [the bill was] talked out during its committee stage. . . .

The situation of Canada's Parliamentary Secretaries is, therefore, highly anomalous. Theoretically they are non-ministerial assistants to Cabinet Ministers, but in practice they perform tasks which would be performed in Britain by the junior ministers rather than by the Parliamentary Private Secretaries. They are paid a salary for their services, they may not hold company directorships, and yet they are supposedly not subject to the doctrine of collective responsibility, and their freedom of speech and action is not affected by their tenure of their positions. Given all of these factors, Prof. Dawson's description of the Parliamentary Secretaries as being "quasi-ministers" is very close to the truth. . . .

With a Cabinet of thirty members it should be possible to introduce some measure of reform which would maintain a fair representation for all provinces in the Cabinet while at the same time providing a more flexible method of filling the less prestigious ministerial positions and the Parliamentary Secretaryships, the latter becoming officially recognised as junior ministerial appointments. Even if the idea of full ministers outside the Cabinet is not adopted, and even if, as at present, the Parliamentary Secretaryships are apportioned provincially, it is difficult to see how giving them junior ministerial status would materially affect the position and influence of provincial representatives in the Cabinet.

The rewards in administrative efficiency which would flow from the establishment of a two or even three-tier government structure do not yet seem to outweigh the supposed political advantages of the present system. Perhaps if Canadian politicians can be convinced that they can have their cake and eat it too, that increased efficiency and the preservation of equitable provincial representation in the Cabinet are not mutually exclusive, and that the single-level structure which has characterised Canadian government since Confederation is neither immutable nor indispensable to the federal system, they will become more enthusiastic about a British governmental practice which has not yet been adapted for Canadian use.

PARLIAMENTARY SECRETARIES — ONWARD TO THE CABINET*

DENIS STAIRS

Parliamentary assistants to ministers, or parliamentary secretaries as they have been termed since 1960, were first appointed in Canada on a salaried basis by Prime Minister Mackenzie King in April 1943. Since then the number of appointees provided for in government appropriations has increased from seven to sixteen, and thus far secretaries have been assigned regularly to every cabinet except for an interval of more than a year and a half following the general election of March, 1958.

When the first appointments were announced in 1943, there was considerable discussion of the possibility that the new position would prove to be a stepping stone to higher places, and particularly to the cabinet. The experience of nearly 27 years can now shed some light on this issue.

Of the 118 parliamentary secretaries designated up to and including those of October 20, 1969, 38 received their initial appointments under the Liberals between 1943 and 1957, 36 during the "Diefenbaker Years," 29 under Prime Minister Pearson, and 15 during the administration of Mr. Trudeau. (Mr. Trudeau has actually made a total of 18 appointments, but of the 18 MPs concerned, three—Jean-Charles Cantin, Stanley Haidasz, and James E. Walker—had already served as parliamentary secretaries under Mr. Pearson.) During the period as a whole, 41 of this group of 118 at some time or other achieved cabinet rank.

To determine more accurately the proportion of those who were promoted, however, it seems reasonable at the time of this writing (November 1969) to exclude from the calculations the 15 new appointments made by Mr. Trudeau, on the ground that his government has not been in office sufficiently long for many promotions from this group to have occurred; (thus far there have been only two). This would then leave a total of 103 original appointments, of which 39, or about 38 percent, were of men who were eventually to enter the cabinet. The percentage might increase very slightly if the Progressive Conservative party were returned to power at the next general election, and if further cabinet appointments were made from the ranks of former Conservative parliamentary secretaries, but this possibility now appears rather remote. The figure will also rise slightly if any of the three men who retained their secretaryships through the changeover from the Pearson administration to that of Mr. Trudeau are admitted on some future occasion to ministerial rank. The political careers of the 38 secretaries appointed under the Liberals from 1943 to 1957 can now be regarded, of course, as having reached or

* A revision in November, 1969, of an article published originally in the second edition of this book. The author, who is a member of the Department of Political Science, Dalhousie University, wishes to acknowledge with gratitude the assistance of his colleague, Professor Murray Beck, for his assistance in providing important additional data.

passed their respective peaks, and of this group, 19, or 50 percent, subsequently became members of the federal cabinet.

Even the smaller result of 38 percent, however, indicates a much higher "success-index" than that of the House of Commons as a whole, and this impression is reinforced if the figures are examined from another perspective. By 1948 five members of the Liberal government had had previous experience as parliamentary secretaries; by 1949 the number had increased to seven, and by 1950 to nine. In 1951, 11 of the 23 men who at some time during the course of that year held a cabinet post were former parliamentary secretaries, and the number stayed within one or two points of that figure until the end of the Liberal administration. In the period from 1943 to 1957 as a whole, the Liberals promoted a total of 14 parliamentary secretaries to cabinet office. Similarly, by the final year of the Diefenbaker government, a total of seven parliamentary secretaries had been appointed to the cabinet, indicating a rate of advancement which, on the average, was the same (about one promotion per year) as that in evidence under King and St. Laurent.

The figures for recent years, moreover, show that the significance of the office of parliamentary secretary as a stepping-stone to the cabinet has been increasing. Mr. Pearson's *first* cabinet included seven former parliamentary secretaries, of whom only two had held ministerial posts in previous Liberal administrations. Furthermore, of the 29 MPs who were appointed as parliamentary secretaries for the first time during the period of the Pearson government, as many as 10 (on average, about two per year) were promoted to the cabinet before Mr. Pearson retired, and three more became ministers under Mr. Trudeau. Of the 29 members of the cabinet appointed by Mr. Trudeau in July 1968, 14 (including the Prime Minister himself) had served at one time or other as parliamentary secretaries.

To determine the fate of those parliamentary secretaries who did *not* succeed in acquiring cabinet posts, it seems convenient once again to select for consideration only those included in the group of 103 who were given their initial appointments before the advent of the Trudeau government. Of these, 39 eventually reached cabinet office, leaving 64 "failures," including 19 "King-St. Laurent" Liberals, 29 Conservatives, and 16 "Pearsonites." Among the King-St. Laurent Liberals, three were appointed to the bench and one to the Senate, four retired from federal politics, one died, and 10 were electoral casualties. Of the Conservatives, four retired from federal politics, 12 were electoral casualties, and 13 were still in the House of Commons when Mr. Pearson formed his first government. Among the Pearson appointments, three are still parliamentary secretaries, three were returned to the back benches during Mr. Pearson's tenure of office, one was returned to the back benches and subsequently appointed to the Senate, one was fired as a result of the Rivard affair and later resigned from the House of Commons, four were defeated in the 1968 general election, three lost their secretaryships during the changeover from the Pearson government to that of Mr. Trudeau, and one retired from federal politics.

Taking the group of 64 as a whole, 26 were electoral casualties, 16 lost their positions as a result of changes in government leadership, nine retired from federal politics, three were returned to the back benches by the Prime Minister who had appointed them in the first place, three were appointed to the bench and two more to the Senate, one died, another was fired, and three were still in harness in November 1969. From these figures it is clear that general elections are by far the most formidable hazard confronting parliamentary secretaries who aspire to cabinet office. In fact, if all those who lost their opportunity for promotion because they or their party were defeated at the polls (39 in all) are excluded from the pre-Trudeau total of 103, then of the 64 remaining, as many as 60 percent (39 in all) eventually entered the federal cabinet.

In addition to the investigation into the secretaries' career patterns, a comparison was made of the socio-economic characteristics of the groups appointed respectively by the two major parties. Taking the *ethnic variable* first, and using the father's heritage as the deciding factor in the few cases in which the parents were ethnically mixed, it was found that of the 36 Conservatives, 28 (about 77.8 percent) were Canadians of British (including Irish) descent, six (16.7 percent) were Canadians of French descent, and two belonged to other groups (one Italian, one Scandinavian). In the case of the 82 Liberals, the distribution between "British" and "French" Canadians was more even and reflected more accurately the distribution of the two groups in the population at large: of these, 49 (59.8 percent) were Canadians of British descent, 28 (34.1 percent) were of French descent, and five came from other groups (two Italian, one Scandinavian, one Polish, and one Jewish). Interestingly, the proportion of French-Canadian appointments has increased under each Liberal regime—from 31.6 percent in the King-St. Laurent period, through 34.5 percent under Mr. Pearson, to 40 percent in the government of Mr. Trudeau. In all the periods, of course, ethnic groups other than British or French have been underrepresented.

An attempt to discover whether there was any significant difference in the *age-distribution* of Conservative and Liberal secretaries produced negative results. The pattern was similar for both parties, with most of the appointments (66.1 percent) falling between the ages of 36 and 50. Of the 118 total, 10 were less than 36 when they were first appointed, 33 were between 36 and 40, 25 between 41 and 45, 20 between 46 and 50, 14 between 51 and 55, eight between 56 and 60, and eight more were 61 or older. The Trudeau appointments were somewhat atypical in that they were concentrated almost entirely in the middle-age category: 14 of Mr. Trudeau's 15 appointments, or 93.3 percent, fell within the 36-50 age bracket. (The fifteenth was 53.)

The distribution of the secretaryships among the various *religious denominations* proved more interesting. Of the 36 Conservatives, 41.7 percent were Roman Catholics (including six of French descent, and nine of descent other than French), 25 percent were Anglicans, and 33.3 percent belonged to other Protestant denominations (mainly United and Presbyterian). Among the 82 Liberals, however, as many as 52.4 percent were Roman Catholics (including 28 of French descent and 15 of descent other than French), only 8.5 percent were Anglicans, and 39 percent belonged to other denominations (mainly United, Presbyterian and Baptist, but including one Jew and one unstated). The figures thus support the common assertion that the Liberal party is a more "Roman Catholic" party than is the Conservative, and that Anglicans tend to be more common among Conservatives than among Liberals.

The large representation of Roman Catholics among the Liberal appointments was partly, of course, a reflection of Liberal strength in French Canada. Nevertheless, the proportion of Roman Catholics among Liberal appointments has been increasing in *both* the "French" *and* "non-French" categories under each successive Liberal government. Thus, while Roman Catholics of French descent constituted 31.6 percent of the appointments under King and St. Laurent, 34.5 percent under Mr. Pearson, and 40 percent under Prime Minister Trudeau, at the same time the proportion of "non-French" Roman Catholic appointees increased also— from 7.9 percent in the King-St. Laurent period, through 24.1 percent during the Pearson regime, to 33.3 percent (thus far) under the government of Mr. Trudeau.

A study was also made of the *educational qualifications* of the 118 appointees. It was found that of the 82 Liberals, 15 (18.3 percent) had high school training or less, 14 (17.1 percent) held Bachelor's degrees, teaching diplomas or some approximate equivalent, and 53 (64.6 percent) possessed post-graduate or professional qualifications. Among the 36 Conservatives the average level of education was a little lower, with nine (25 percent) having high school or less, an additional nine (25 percent) holding Bachelor's degrees or approximate equivalents, and 18 (50 percent) carrying post-graduate or professional qualifications.

Clearly the level of education in the group as a whole was very high, with 94 (79.7 percent) of the 118 appointees having a university degree or equivalent. Less encouraging from some points of view, however, is the fact that of the 71 secretaries having post-graduate or professional training, 53 (74.6 percent) were lawyers. More generally, 44.9 percent of the parliamentary secretaries appointed between 1943 and the autumn of 1969 came from the legal profession. The remainder were distributed more or less at random among farmers, teachers (various levels), businessmen, civil engineers, and physicians.

Finally, since it is often suggested that secretarial appointments may be used by prime ministers to assist them in allocating executive offices among the various provinces, their *geographical distribution* was also examined. The results are given in Table I:

TABLE I: Provincial Distribution of Parliamentary Secretaries
In Recent Governments

Party	Ont.	P.Q.	B.C.	Alta.	Sask.	Man.	P.E.I.	N.S.	N.B.	Nfld.	NWT	Total
King-St. Laurent Liberals	8	13	4	1	2	3	2	5	—	—	—	38
Conservatives	16	8	1	2	1	2	1	3	1	1	—	36
Pearsonites	9	12	2	—	—	—	—	1	2	3	—	29
Trudeau Liberals	7	6	1	—	—	—	—	—	—	—	1	15
TOTAL	40	39	8	3	3	5	3	9	3	4	1	118

It is difficult to draw definite conclusions from these figures without also taking into account the distribution of cabinet seats, and in any case the data inevitably reflect to some extent, although not entirely, the distribution of electoral support for the various governments in the country at large. A thorough analysis would require a study of the distribution of cabinet and secretarial posts taken together and at different points in time. Regarded at face value, however, the figures suggest that, where possible, attempts have been made to represent all the provinces, although the weakness of the Liberals on the prairies under Mr. Pearson and Mr. Trudeau, and in the Atlantic provinces since 1968, has also been reflected in the distribution pattern. The data tend in addition to reflect the strength of the Liberals in Quebec, and of the Conservatives in Ontario.

HOW THE BUDGET AND ESTIMATES ARE PREPARED*

MITCHELL SHARP

Needless to say, the budget-making process does not begin or end with budget night.

The budget speech is the culmination of a continuous process of economic analysis and appraisal. This is carried on not only in the Department of Finance, but in other departments and agencies including the Department of Trade and Commerce, the Dominion Bureau of Statistics, and the Bank of Canada.

Moreover, in considering the budget speech in the context of the government's financial operations, it is important to understand that the main decisions announced in the budget speech deal with the money-raising side.

The other side, of course, is that of expenditures. The amount and direction of government spending can be just as important as revenues and taxation in helping to shape national economic policy. The total size of government expenditures can have an appreciable effect on the economy.

THE ESTIMATES

The preparation of the government's expenditure program is governed to a large extent by the Parliamentary tradition that the House of Commons controls the Crown's purse strings. During the late months of every year, each department of government prepares its spending budget for the following fiscal year beginning the next April 1st. The departmental programs come under the control of the Treasury

---

* From a speech given on April 21, 1966, by the Hon. Mitchell Sharp, who was then Minister of Finance and who is now the Secretary of State for External Affairs. By permission of the author.

Board—probably the most important and powerful committee of the cabinet. Each department and its minister feel, quite naturally, that his operations and plans for new programs are absolutely essential. Most of these new programs are interesting and almost always commendable and worthwhile. But their total cost is usually excessive. So there follows a time of trial within the Treasury Board. There is a careful, critical appraisal and preliminary weeding-out process by the Treasury Board staff. Even after that, it is almost inevitable that when the spending plans of all departments as a whole come before the Board late in the year, the final pruning — the final establishment of priorities — remains to be completed.

Perhaps I should draw a discreet curtain of silence over the subsequent discussions. It boils down to a question of priorities, and the final decisions are based on a mixture of economic, social and political considerations.

The end product of all this work is a bulky blue book, entitled *Main Estimates,* which is presented to Parliament usually around the end of January. This book contains more than 600 individual items, each of which must receive individual approval in Parliament.

Understandably, the *Main Estimates* are not the final work on government expenditures for the year. They are compiled four to six months before the new fiscal year begins, and 16 to 18 months before the year ends. Therefore, as the year progresses, it is customary for the government to submit Supplementary Estimates to Parliament, to cover new or unforeseen expenditures.

The House of Commons spends a good deal of time in Standing Committees and in Committee of the Whole considering the spending Estimates. In the normal year, the Estimates receive approval on the last day of the Parliamentary session. But the Government requires funds to meet its month-to-month requirements. Civil Servants, contractors and suppliers, for example, cannot be expected to wait months for payment. Therefore, the Government has to ask Parliament on several occasions during the year to pass interim supply bills. . . .

BUDGET PREPARATION

The other side of the budgetary process is the question of revenues. And here we come to the central issue of the budget presentation.

Governments hear all sorts of demands for increased spending and all sorts of urgings for tax reductions—and sometimes both from the same proponent. Few who urge the adoption of costly new programs are prepared to suggest how they should be financed. Those who call for lower taxes rarely make concrete proposals for matching cuts in expenditures. A Finance Minister's life is not an easy one.

As I indicated earlier, the government's basic expenditures program is pretty well settled by the beginning of January. The Minister of Finance must then turn to the central issues of the budget speech: tax and revenue policy, and general economic policy for the year ahead.

Working with his senior economic advisers, including the Governor of the Bank of Canada, the Minister must forecast the economic weather ahead. At the same time, he is receiving lots of free advice on tax changes from two or three dozen delegations, representing a variety of industrial, trade, labour and farm organizations. Letters shower in from other organizations and individuals urging specific tax reductions. All of these specific proposals, together with the department's comments and analysis, are assembled in a loose-leaf book that has come to be known, rather ominously, as "the Black Book". Very rapidly, it swells into a very bulky volume of 200 to 300 pages. In a series of meetings with government officials, the Black Book is considered page by page. Each request is studied on its merit—and some have a good deal of merit. It has been said that the Black Book is a mixture of interest, amusement, and boredom.

It must be apparent by now that the Minister of Finance is a pretty busy man during the first couple of months each year. It is a time of decisions, and in reaching these decisions the Minister must weigh them against a number of major questions.

Let me list some of these questions, in order to indicate the nature of the budget process. Does the year ahead call for a budgetary surplus or deficit—and how much of a surplus or deficit? How will the budget decisions affect economic growth and employment and efficiency? What will be the impact on prices? Will a new policy have helpful or adverse effects on the balance of payments? How can fiscal policies be co-ordinated effectively with monetary policy? How do they measure up to the long-run growth projections of the Economic Council of Canada? I shall be frank and add that decisions must also be weighed against another question as well: what will their political effect be? This criterion inevitably looms large in a House of Commons where the government does not have a majority.

All of these questions must be answered and decisions reached on the main pattern of the budget by around mid-February.

Then follows another busy period when detailed questions are settled—when decisions are made on scores of specific proposals in order to translate the broad economic and fiscal decisions into practical results.

Finally, in the last two weeks or so before the budget date, the budget speech itself takes shape — the words which announce and explain budget policy, and the former tax and tariff resolutions which precede the budget legislation.

This, then, is the document which Parliament and the country wait for so expectantly on budget night.

BUDGET SECRECY

Preparation of the budget is hedged about with the most careful secrecy precautions. Preliminary drafts of the speech, for example, are numbered and recorded. The typing is done by a small group of trusted secretaries. Only a handful of people have access in advance to the complete text. Even in Cabinet the Minister of Finance has traditionally been reluctant to reveal his plans to his colleagues too far in advance of the event.

In Britain, the strict rules of secrecy have required the resignation of two

Cabinet Ministers. One was just before the Second World War when a minister— not the Chancellor of the Exchequer—made a comment at a private dinner party about one somewhat broad aspect of anticipated budget policy. The other resignation occurred just after the war when the Chancellor of the Exchequer, on his way into the Commons chamber to deliver a budget speech, made a joking remark to a press reporter of a change in the tobacco tax. The Chancellor had expected to start his speech within 15 minutes. But House business delayed him for almost an hour and before he could announce the tax changes a newspaper appeared with headlines about the tobacco tax. . . .

Up until 1941, the Canadian practice was to present the budget in the afternoon. That year, the budget speech announced a new excise tax on sugar, to become effective that midnight. The news came out shortly after three o'clock in Ottawa— which was just after noon in Vancouver. A tremendous amount of sugar was sold and delivered free of tax in Vancouver that day. As a result, subsequent budgets have been presented in the evening, with tax changes made known well after all security and commodity markets have closed.

●   ●   ●

BIBLIOGRAPHY

Privy Council, Cabinet, Prime Minister

Banks, M. A., "Privy Council, Cabinet, and Ministry in Britain and Canada: A Story of Confusion," *C.J.E.P.S.,* Vol. XXXI, No. 2, May, 1965. (See also "Comments," *ibid.,* Vol. XXXI, No. 4, November, 1965 and Vol. XXXII, No. 1, February, 1966.)

Burke, Sister T. A., "Mackenzie and His Cabinet, 1873-1878," *Canadian Historical Review,* Vol. XLI, No. 2, June, 1960.

Dawson, R. M., *William Lyon Mackenzie King: A Political Biography,* Vol. 1, *1874-1923,* Toronto, University of Toronto Press, 1958, Chapter 13.

Forsey, E. A., "Government Defeats in the Canadian House of Commons 1867-73," *C.J.E.P.S.,* Vol. XXIX, No. 3, August, 1963.

Forsey, E. A., "Meetings of the Queen's Privy Council for Canada, 1867-1882," Address to the 38th Annual Meeting of the Canadian Political Science Association, Sherbrooke, P.Q., June 8, 1966.

Fraser, B., "Your Guide to the New Split-Level Cabinet," *Maclean's,* April 4, 1964.

Gibson, F. W., (ed.), *Cabinet Formation and Bicultural Relations: Seven Case Studies,* Studies of the Royal Commission on Bilingualism and Biculturalism, No. 6, Ottawa, Queen's Printer, 1970.

Halliday, W. E. D., "The Executive of the Government of Canada," *C.P.A.,* Vol. II, No. 4, December, 1959.

Halliday, W. E. D., "The Privy Council and Cabinet Secretariat in relation to the Development of Cabinet Government," *Canada Year Book, 1956,* Ottawa, Dominion Bureau of Statistics, 1956.

Jones, G. W., "The Prime Minister's Powers," *Parliamentary Affairs,* Vol. 18, No. 2, Spring, 1965.

MacQuarrie, H. N., "The Formation of Borden's First Cabinet," *C.J.E.P.S.,* Vol. XXIII, No. 1; February, 1957.

Morton, W. L., "The Formation of the First Federal Cabinet," *Canadian Historical Review*, Vol. XXXVI, No. 2, June, 1955.

O'Leary, D., "The Cabinet Revolt — How They Tried to Get Rid of Diefenbaker," *Canadian Commentator*, July-August, 1963.

Ondaatje, C., Swainson, D., *The Prime Ministers of Canada, 1867-1968: Macdonald to Trudeau*, Don Mills, General Publishing, 1967.

Public Archives, *Guide to Canadian Ministries Since Confederation, July 1, 1867, January 1, 1957*, Ottawa, 1957; *Supplement, January 1, 1957-August 1, 1965*, Ottawa, 1966.

The Political Process, Power Structure, and Decision-Making

Bourassa, G., "Les élites politiques de Montréal: de l'aristocratie à la démocratie," *C.J.E.P.S.*, Vol. XXXI, No. 1, February, 1965.

Corbett, D., *Politics and the Airlines*, Toronto, University of Toronto Press, 1966.

Crispo, J. H. G., *International Unionism in Canada: A Canadian-American Experiment*, Toronto, McGraw-Hill, 1966.

Eayrs, J., *In Defence of Canada: Vol. I, From The Great War to the Great Depression, Vol. II, Appeasement and Rearmament*, Toronto, University of Toronto Press, 1961 and 1965 respectively.

Farrell, B., *The Making of Canadian Foreign Policy*, Toronto, Prentice-Hall, 1969.

Newman, P. C., "The Ottawa Establishment," *Maclean's*, August 22, 1964.

Peers, F. W., *The Politics of Canadian Broadcasting 1920-51*, Toronto, University of Toronto Press, 1966.

Porter, J., *The Vertical Mosaic: An Analysis of Social Class and Power in Canada*, Toronto, University of Toronto Press, 1965.

Schindeler, F. F., *Responsible Government in Ontario*, Toronto, University of Toronto Press, 1969.

Stewart, W., "The Powerful Ottawa Politicians You Don't Elect," (Executive Assistants to Ministers), *Canadian Weekly*, July 31, 1965.

THIRTEEN

THE LEGISLATIVE PROCESS: HOUSE OF COMMONS

An introduction to this chapter in the third edition might well begin with the same words that were used in the second edition: "A number of steps have been taken recently to improve the functioning of the House of Commons but most of the traditional problems remain, in particular the basic inherent conflict between the government and the private members, especially those on the opposition side of the House."

Since 1966 further efforts have been made to improve House procedure but the fundamental problem has not been solved — that of reconciling the government's ambition to have the Commons operate efficiently in passing its legislative program each year with the opposition parties' desire, and duty, to criticize it, hamstring it, and if possible, to destroy the government. *Plus ça change, plus c'est la même chose.* Like the war between the sexes, the conflict will never be ended because it is the essence of the situation. The most that can be hoped for in our system of democratic, cabinet-parliamentary government is that some reasonable and fair balance will be struck between the two counter-vailing forces of government and the representatives of the governed.

Whether or not this has been achieved in the changes that have been made in House procedure since the Trudeau government came to power in 1968 is the subject of the first two articles, in particular, in this chapter. The first selection by Professor Denis Smith is an attack upon what he believes to be an excessive increase in power by the government. The author alleges it has been carried to the point where our parliamentary system is being transformed into a presidential system. A contrary view defending the government and explaining the recent changes in House procedure is contained in an excerpt from a speech by the Hon. Donald S. Macdonald, who is an ideal spokesman for the view since he has been the government's House Leader and has ben instrumental in introducing the changes.

All of the other items in this chapter bear on the same subject but they explore additional basic facets of the life process of the Commons. Mark MacGuigan, who is the Liberal MP from Windsor-Walkerville, describes the problems of backbenchers and the functioning of the new committee system and of the party caucus in the House. Largely as a result of complaints such as Mr. MacGuigan's emanating from its own members, the Liberal government reformed its caucus procedures in 1969. The Liberals continue to hold a caucus every Wednesday morning, as do the other parties, but on alternate weeks they break it up into committees which meet with ministers. An actual schedule of such a caucus is reproduced here as an example of the new procedure. These items are especially valuable since little has been written in Canada on the subject of the operation of Parliament itself, let alone on the caucus about which there is scarcely a word in print.

George Bain's article on private members' legislation has been carried over from the second edition, as has Peter Dempson's account of an MP performing a function other than the traditional role of a legislator. Both cast considerable light on seldom-illumined subjects. Using the Dempson example as an illustration, the editor notes in his article the various roles that MPs can play and argues that despite the recent changes which have provided more research assistance for MPs, such as the introduction of the Canadian Political Science Association's "internist" program, the members' greatest need is still for more extensive help in research.

The question of providing an ombudsman (or ombudsmen) for Canada is included in this chapter because of the connection between this office and Parliament. Professor Rowat's article makes this connection clear but that is only one of its minor virtues. The excerpt from his testimony before a Parliamentary committee is one of the best brief explanations of the office available and also one of the most convincing arguments for its establishment, as might be expected from Canada's leading authority on the subject. Moreover, his remarks are still pertinent because although several provinces have appointed an ombudsman since his comments were reprinted in the second edition — notably New Brunswick, Alberta, Quebec, and Manitoba — the federal government has not yet seen fit to follow suit. The chapter concludes with a delightful personal account of how an ombudsman performs his job, written by the first Canadian ombudsman to be appointed, Mr. George B. McClellan in Alberta.

For an earlier article by Douglas Fisher on committees in the House of Commons in the 24th Parliament, see the first edition of this book, pp. 206-216; similarly for an item explaining Manitoba's Standing Committee on Statutory Regulations and Orders (pp. 217-218) and for Pierre Berton's article on the problem of conflicting interests of elected representatives (pp. 203-205).

The bibliography, which has been brought up to date, lists a number of important works, some of which might well have been included here but for lack of space. Professor Denis Smith's report on the office of Speaker of the House of Commons is a good example.

THE TRANSFORMATION OF PARLIAMENTARY GOVERNMENT IN CANADA*

DENIS SMITH

In the last five years, the Canadian House of Commons has gone through the first thorough and comprehensive reform of its procedures since 1867. The process of reform that was begun in 1964 came to a stormy climax last July with the adoption under closure of the Government's proposal for a regular time-limitation (or guillotine) rule. While the Government has agreed that there should be a review this autumn of the House's experience under the new rules, and while certain adjustments and refinements are likely, the body of the reformed rules will probably stand for a few sessions at least, while the House learns new habits and absorbs the effects of the changes that have occurred. These changes have been substantial ones, and it will take some time before their full implications become clear. . . .

Members of the Canadian House of Commons have intermittently criticized aspects of the House's rules and practices since Confederation; and there have been desultory attempts to alter the rules in this century, especially in 1906, 1913, 1927, 1947, and 1955. . . .

The measures of reform adopted from time to time in this century have all tended to restrict unlimited debate in the House, by limiting acceptable motions and debatable motions (1906, 1913); by providing for the possibility of closure (1913); by limiting the length of speeches (1927, 1955, 1960); and by restricting the number of days devoted to major general debates on the Speech from the Throne, the Budget, and Supply (1955). But the most severe restrictive measure, the closure, has rarely been used, because of its clumsiness and the likelihood of public criticism; and the other measures have done little to make the House's operations more orderly or more subject to the efficient leadership of the Government. . . .

•   •   •

Big government [has] overtaken both Cabinet and Parliament. In Canada as elsewhere in the industrialized world over the last half century, the size, responsibilities and opportunities for initiative of the permanent administration have expanded enormously. While departments have multiplied and divided, while independent agencies and crown corporations have been born and grown prematurely

* Extract from a paper presented to the Progressive Conservative Party's Priorities for Canada Conference, Niagara Falls, Ontario, October 10, 1969. By permission of the author, who wishes to express gratitude to the Canada Council for a grant to assist research on the condition of Parliamentary government in Canada, of which the paper was a reflection.

into monsters, the instruments of Cabinet and Parliamentary control of the leviathan have remained negligible. . . .

What may be equally as important as the growing burdens of government is the mythology of Parliamentary government. For the mythology has disguised the reality. We are still bemused by the classic models of Parliamentary government presented with such grace and clarity by Walter Bagehot and John Stuart Mill to an English audience in the mid-nineteenth century. . . . We have, we are told, a system of responsible parliamentary government, in which the public elects individual Members to the House of Commons and the House of Commons, in turn, chooses a Government. Thereafter, while the Cabinet governs, the House holds it responsible for all the actions of the administration, and in the event of parliamentary disapproval, can overthrow the ministry, or force it to seek a fresh mandate from the electorate. The Prime Minister is chairman of the Cabinet; the public service is the loyal and anonymous servant of the Cabinet; the Cabinet is the servant of the House of Commons and only indirectly of the electorate. The theory puts the House of Commons close to the centre of the system, where it is meant to act as "the grand inquest of the nation," influencing, supervising and controlling the actions of the executive.

While the Canadian literature of politics points out that parliamentary control may not be quite up to the theory, the theory is maintained as the ideal. As a result, many of the real forces at work in Canadian politics are underrated or ignored. The tendency is, when describing forces and practices which contradict the model, to see them as aberrations pulling the system away from the Victorian ideal, but rarely as primary forces in their own right which may be basically shaping the system.

. . . But a point may come, in adding up the distortions and aberrations from the norm, when it becomes more comprehensible to abandon the original description and try to put together another one which accommodates the evidence more completely and satisfactorily. I think this point has been reached in understanding how the Canadian system works.

•   •   •

The best short reassessment of the British model — and now a familiar one — is Richard Crossman's introduction to the 1964 edition of Bagehot's *The English Constitution*. Here, Crossman argues that Bagehot's description of the Cabinet in Parliament was falsified soon after publication of *The English Constitution*. The emergence of highly disciplined mass parties took independent power from individual Members of Parliament; the immense new administrative bureaucracy took much ordinary decision-making power away from ministers; and an organized secretariat for the Cabinet, and especially for the Prime Minister, gave the Prime Minister the effective powers of a president. . . .

Does the story sound familiar in Canada? It does. The Canadian Prime Minister, indeed, may be further along the road to being a presidential leader than the British, for distinct Canadian reasons.

For one thing, the Canadian House of Commons has never possessed the reserve of aristocratic prestige which once gave the British House of Commons some leverage alongside or against the Prime Minister. For most of its life the Canadian House has been a popular chamber, based on wide popular suffrage; Canadian Prime Ministers have always made their primary appeal for support not *in* the House of Commons, but outside, to the electorate. . . .

The House of Commons is diminished in importance, as compared to the British House in the period from 1832 to 1867, because it is the electorate, not the House of Commons, which chooses and deposes Prime Ministers. The essential influence upon government is the sovereign public, not a sovereign Parliament. Prime Ministers keep their eyes upon the Gallup Polls, and not normally upon readings of the House of Commons' temperature. And the public sees the Government as one man's Government. This public assumption gives the Prime Minister great power over his colleagues.

The fact is a commonplace in Canadian understanding, and yet it is not satisfactorily integrated into the normal liberal model of the parliamentary constitution. We know that general elections are competitions between party leaders for the Prime Minister's office; we concentrate our attention upon the leaders, and the parties encourage us to do so; once in office, we see that Prime Ministers exercise almost tyrannical power over their ministers and backbenchers; Prime Ministers frequently ignore the House of Commons, or treat it with disdain, unless they perceive that the public is watching (which it only occasionally is); and our Prime Ministers freely admit their own predominance over the House of Commons and the necessity of it. . . .

These events [the replacement of Mackenzie King as Prime Minister by Arthur Meighen in 1926 and the defeat of the Diefenbaker Government in the House in 1963] illustrate Richard Crossman's claim that a Prime Minister can no longer be replaced by public and constitutional means if he does not wish to go. They illustrate more than that: given an alert Prime Minister, it is virtually impossible to replace him even by "undercover intrigue and sudden unpredicted *coup d'état.*" He has too many weapons of influence and patronage in his hands, and his adversaries have too few. He is virtually as immovable as an American President during his term of office.

The five years of minority government under Mr. Pearson emphasized the same point. Even without a majority in Parliament, a Canadian Prime Minister is normally secure in office, and scarcely faces the danger of defeat in the House, because one or another of the opposition parties is almost certain to vote with the Government on any division to assure its own survival. . . .

In both the United Kingdom and Canada, the Prime Minister gains his predominance over his colleagues and the House of Commons by winning general elections and exercising the power of dissolution at his own discretion. But in Canada the Prime Minister possesses still more authority granted him from outside Parliament which brings him closer to the American President. He is chosen by a popular convention. The Canadian conventions have increasingly come to duplicate the effects of the American presidential conventions. Under the open embrace of gavel-to-gavel television, the conventions have become as central a part of national political life as the campaigns, and perhaps more central, because of their concentrated drama and intense TV coverage. In the conventions the political process is almost entirely personalized, issues fade away, and the winner is the only one to walk away alive. . . . If anything has accelerated the trend to presidential politics in Canada, it has been the enthusiastic adoption of televised national leadership conventions. . . .

Set against the overwhelming power and public prestige of the Prime Minister are the traditional duties of the legislature. Even if one admits that the power of *overthrowing* governments has been surrendered, the House of Commons is supposed to retain the power and responsibility to provide a public forum of discussion on national issues, to scrutinize spending and legislation, and to safeguard the rights and freedoms of citizens by its vigilant criticism. These are worthy goals; but even *they* fade on closer examination. . . . In its less spectacular, day-to-day performances, the House of Commons normally, if grudgingly, does the work the Government directs it to do, and does so without making much critical impression on Government measures or on the public. This is so because the Government wishes it to be so, and because, until the December, 1968 reforms, the House was the victim of its own diffuse rules, which did not lend themselves to sharp, critical investigation of Government measures.

• • •

The reforms of December, 1968, while extending some of the principles first outlined in 1965, were notably more radical. They reorganized and simplified the manner of passing legislation in the House; they diverted detailed debate on all estimates and virtually all legislation from the floor of the House to the specialised committees; they established an annual timetable for the consideration of spending estimates; they created a Special Committee on Statutory Instruments; and they reduced to twenty-eight the number of days in an annual session controlled by the Opposition for debate on topics of its choice. Again, the nice balancing of concessions to the House against concessions to the Government brought the agreement of all parties to the proposals. . . .

The new Procedure Committee went to work again this year [1969] and the Government brought its revised guillotine proposal, rule 75, to the House in July. The opposition — and the Government — had worked conscientiously to make the rule less objectionable to the House than [former proposed rule] 16A, and it was less objectionable. But it still contained too much sting for the combined opposition, in section 75C, which gave the Government, in the absence of agreement by the other parties, the power to timetable discussion on the stages of individual bills by Government resolution, following notice and a short debate. The provision meant that if necessary a determined Government could guide a piece of controversial legislation through the House in a minimum of four days of debate over a period of ten sitting days, against the protests of the minority.

The persistence of the Trudeau Government in pressing for the guillotine made its impression on the opposition and the press, and during July negotiations went on among the parties to compromise on a measure which would grant the Government's wish but extend the minimum period of ten days to something longer. When the opposition seemed hopeful of reaching agreement with the Government, the Cabinet suddenly broke off discussion, closure was imposed, and the measure was adopted on division in its original form.

The sudden reversal by the Government was curious: it can probably be explained by the Prime Minister's unerring presidential instincts. As in December, the Prime Minister was watching public reaction to the debate more closely than the House's reaction. He apparently found that the public, this time, was not unduly concerned. In mid-July, he commented on the debate that it was a "stupid fili-buster," and said that no one outside Parliament cared what was going on in the House. In his speech before the closure, he remarked that "In a democracy the ballot box, not the filibuster, is the ultimate and appropriate technique of assessment." And in the adjournment debate the next day he let fall his testy comments about the inconsequence of parliamentary debate to the public that elects Prime Ministers:

> The opposition seems to think it has nothing else to do but talk . . . That is all they have to do. They do not have to govern, they have only to talk. The best place in which to talk, if they want a forum, is, of course parliament. When they get home, when they get out of parliament, when they are 50 yards from Parliament Hill, they are no longer hon. members — they are just nobodys, Mr. Speaker.

Judging that Members of Parliament are political nobodies, the Prime Minister felt it prudent to ignore the real possibility of agreement within the House on a compromise rule acceptable to the other Parliamentary parties, turned his back on the discussions, and imposed his will on the House in a matter of its own procedure. This was as clear an indication as there has ever been that the Canadian Prime Minister is inclined to think of himself as a crypto-president, responsible directly to the people and not to the House of Commons. But Lyndon Johnson would never have spoken this way of Everett Dirksen!

CONCLUSION

We seem to have created in Canada a presidential system without its congressional advantages. Before the accession of Pierre Trudeau, our presidential system, however, was diffuse and ill-organized. But Pierre Trudeau is extraordinarily clear-headed and realistic about the sources of political power in Canada. On the one hand, he has recognized the immense power of initiative and guidance that exists in the federal bureaucracy; and he has seen that this great instrument of power lacked effective centralized political leadership. He has created that coordinated leadership by organizing around him a presidential office, and by bringing order and discipline to the Cabinet's operations. He has made brilliant use of the public opportunities of a party leader, in convention, in the general election, and in his continuing encounters outside Parliament. He has recognized that the public responds first to personalities, not to issues, and so he campaigns for the most generalized mandate. And now, finally, he has successfully altered the procedures of the House of Commons so that it may serve the legislative purposes of an efficient presidential administration.

In doing all these things he has taken advantage of trends and opportunities that already existed. *All* Prime Ministers have been moving — under pressure — in the same direction, but none so determinedly as Prime Minister Trudeau; he has taken the system further, faster, more self-consciously, than it would otherwise have gone. Are we now to be left with this completed edifice of presidential-parliamentary government, in which the House serves the minor purpose of making presidential programs law without much fuss?

Probably not, because the system still contains some fundamental inconsistencies. How clearly the Prime Minister and Members of Parliament see these inconsistencies, I cannot be sure; but they exist, and they will create difficulties. As we have seen, the changes in the rules and practices of the House have *not only* served the *Government's* purposes; they have also, in many ways, benefited individual Members and the opposition parties.

In the course of achieving rules of procedure much more tractable for the Government's purposes, the reforms and the reforming atmosphere have also created a more intractable *membership* of the House, with new and potentially powerful instruments of leverage *against* the Government in their hands. The opposition parties are better equipped by their research funds and their role in legislative committees to criticize the administration from a basis of knowledge. The restrictions of time allocation in the House give these parties an incentive to organize their attacks with more precision and directness than before. Government backbenchers, long silent and frustrated by party discipline, permitted only to express their opinions freely in secret caucus, have been given the taste of greater freedom in the new committees of the House. . . . For the moment, the Government may hold the reins tightly, but the pressures in the House are likely to mount.

One result may be that the Government will find itself more frequently embarrassed by independent backbenchers. They will probably continue to demand *their own* research assistance, and increasingly the rights to speak critically and to vote against Government measures: first in committee, and then, by extension, in the House. (But always more and more in public, where they can be heard.) The party discipline of the majority will be put under increasing strain, and the Opposition will take every chance to encourage the tension. If we have a President, they will be saying, in effect, then why shouldn't we also have an independent Congress?

The Government, in response to such pressures, may put on the screws in private, but it will have difficulty withdrawing the public machinery of criticism that it has now acquiesced in. The House will never agree to return to its fumbling and disorganized pattern of pre-1965. With the taste of influence, and facing a more efficient executive, it will be more inclined, not less, to be independent and sometimes intransigent. If we believe, as the parliamentary myth leads us to believe, in the virtues of *public* policy making and strong *public* criticism of Government, this will surely be a salutary development. The Prime Minister will be challenged by the kind of countervailing force that he believes in.

The other possible response of Governments may be to accept the logic of these Parliamentary pressures, and to move more surely to a system of congressional checks and balances. This would involve the granting of independent powers to Parliamentary committees to choose their own chairmen, hire their own substantial staffs, pursue their own independent investigations, initiate their own legislative proposals, and freely amend and reject the Government's measures. It would involve the provision of administrative assistance for MPs comparable to that available to Senators and Congressmen, and salaries matching their new responsibilities. It would involve, undoubtedly, the admission of television cameras to committees and to the House floor, to bring the House closer to the public. It would involve, finally, and probably gradually, the abandonment of the convention of confidence, so that Governments could expect to stay in office for full terms in spite of regular defeats in the House. . . .

A GOVERNMENT LOOK AT THE NEW RULES*

DONALD S. MACDONALD

Parliament . . . was originally intended to be a leisurely body. When Sir Winston Churchill described the House of Commons as being "the best club in the Empire," he was really referring to the glorious and comfortable past. Parliament was not intended to last very long; sessions were kept as short as possible, and the Opposition was always very bitter in its complaints when it appeared that the Government was taking too long to put legislation through the House. . . . A Member of Parliament considered his position in public life as merely a part-time venture. In the early years after Confederation, even Ministers of the Crown spent most of the year outside of Ottawa attending to private business. How things have changed in less than a century! . . .

You may be interested as an illustration in a comparison between [the 1870] session and the recently completed 1968-69 session of Parliament. There were 198 sittings of the House of Commons in 1968-69, as compared to 62 in 1870. Thus a Member of Parliament now is faced with a full-time job and there is no likeli-

---

* A version prepared by the editor of extracts from two speeches given by the Hon. Donald S. Macdonald, President of the Privy Council and Government Leader in the House, on September 5, 1969, and November 4, 1969. The first address was published in more extensive form in *Canadian Public Administration*, Vol. XIII, No. 1, Spring, 1970. The version presented here is published with permission of the author.

hood that Parliament will be summoned on the basis of what time is "convenient" for Members. A total of 51 Public Bills, 5 Supply Bills, and 13 Private Bills were passed this year, as contrasted to 31 Public Bills, 1 Supply Bill, and 18 Private Bills in 1870. As far as written Questions are concerned, in 1870 there were 61; in 1968-69, there were 2,723, all of which, by the way, were either answered or withdrawn by the questioner during this past session. . . . In 1870, oral questions were few and far between; in the 1968-69 session, however, roughly 40 minutes were spent almost every day on all questions. In 1870, virtually every bill put before the House of Commons was passed. Because of the pressure of time in the 1968-69 session of Parliament, a total of 12 Government bills expired on the Order Paper at the prorogation of the session. A number of other items which the Government had intended to put before the session had to be postponed until 1969-70, because of the pressure of time.

Parliament in 1870 had to sit for only three months, but, for the present session just begun, the Parliamentary year had to be advanced to the end of October of 1969 and will go on until at least the end of June. Even so, experience in the past ten years had shown that it was still necessary to find a way in which to accomplish more business and to provide for more profound examination of Government activities in this very limited period of time.

•   •   •

. . . From the very beginning the House of Commons has been called together to consider business put before it by the Government. It is true, of course, that Private Members may and do originate Bills and Motions; but the House expects almost all its work to be initiated by the Ministers. It has made provision for this by allocating about 19 hours out of the 27 hours in the normal week to Government Business. In other words, the Government initiates. It submits bills to the House of Commons. It submits spending programmes, with estimates of costs, to the House. In turn, the House of Commons acts as a board of auditors checking, testing, and passing judgment on the Government's proposals.

How well has the House done its work in recent years? That is a question that I cannot presume to answer. Instead, let me put before you the criticisms of the House that have concerned me most. The first of those criticisms is that the House has not done its work thoroughly, that it has been more zealous in politicking than in the careful and disinterested study of bills and spending estimates. The second is that the House, despite its lack of thoroughness, has been slow. . . . And the third criticism is that the House, by reason of long, tedious sessions, bores good Members on both sides and attracts, not admiration, but contemptuous indifference, even hostility, from the public.

These criticisms have worried most Members. Our problem has not been self-righteousness, but rather how to find cures for our confessed weaknesses.

Perhaps I should say here that almost inevitably the Government party and those in opposition tend to have different attitudes toward parliamentary reform. The Ministers worry about how they will ever find time to run their departments, to think through policies, and to shape the estimates and bills for the next Session. The Opposition, realizing that once the House has adjourned, they, unlike the Ministers, must go back to their private activities, activities which normally attract little publicity, may want year-round, or, at least ten-month sessions. Ministers, therefore, will talk about the waste of time. The Opposition, in contrast, will expatiate on the dangers of trying to make the trains run on time.

Moreover, the Government party has a selfish interest in trying to make the House function better: the better things go, the more likely is the electorate to re-elect the Government. In contrast, the Opposition has a short-run interest in resisting reform; but this they must not do too obviously.

Despite these differences, as the ills of the House were diagnosed again and again over the past four or five years agreement developed on two points. The first of these was that we were trying to do certain kinds of very important business in highly unsuitable forums or theatres. We were trying to examine, [for instance], the spending estimates for each fiscal year, department by department, vote by vote, in the Committee of Supply, a committee composed of all the Members of the House. . . .The second point in the diagnosis was that because the House had not prescribed dead-lines for much of its work, even when there was no filibustering, the House procrastinated. . . .

NEW RULES OF PROCEDURE

Let me now come to the changes in the procedures of the House that we made during the present session. . . .

First, the Speaker's rulings on points of order were made final. Under the old rules, a Member against whom the Speaker had ruled on a point of order always could appeal to the House. . . . It is our hope that the abolition of appeals from the Speaker will be an effective step towards the achievement of a truly independent Speaker.

The second change relates to financial resolutions. It was a rule formerly that no bill entailing expenditure of money was to pass the House unless the Members had resolved in committee that that expenditure should be made. . . . Last December, the House agreed to eliminate completely the need for financial resolutions. It was the opinion of the House that the cost entailed by a bill could be discussed better on second-reading motion after the bill had been made public. This one change, by eliminating repetition, probably will save from ten to fifteen days each year.

This may not seem much of a saving. But let us remember that the number of sitting days in a session rarely exceeds 160. For example, the House is to meet again this year on October twenty-second. With the standard adjournments at Christmas and Easter, there will be a total of 155 sitting days before the first of July. From that total, we must subtract the 10 days required for the Speech from the Throne and the consequent debate, the 6 days required for the budget debate, and the 25 days reserved for the Opposition. That would leave 114 days for ordinary government business. In this context, a saving of 10 to 15 days looms large.

The third change relates to the business of supply, the granting of funds to Government. . . . [These lengthy and numerous requests by departments were considered by the Committee of Supply, composed of the whole House. . . .] Moreover, the motions that the Speaker leave the Chair for the House to resolve itself into the Committee of Supply were amendable and debatable on six occasions [lasting two days each]; and these amendments and debates inevitably entailed the question whether the Government continued to enjoy the confidence of the House. . . . Under the old system, the House of Commons would sometimes talk almost endlessly on a few items, often leaving the Government temporarily short of funds, and then at the end of the session, the House would vote millions and millions of dollars without the least bit of scrutiny.

Under the new procedures, the President of the Treasury Board presents the Government's estimates of spending for each department in about mid-winter. These estimates of expenses are then referred to the relevant Standing Committees of the House of Commons. The members of these Committees, which also deal with the legislation coming from the departments involved, make themselves familiar with the operations of the agencies and departments which they are studying and are able to examine thoroughly the estimates and therefore the programs of the Government for the coming fiscal year. The Committees are required to report on the estimates to the whole House before the end of the spring, so that the supply bill resulting from estimates is passed before the summer recess. . . .

Instead of the 12 days spent on the six "Supply Motion" debates, there are now 25 days on which the Opposition decides what will be debated by the House. Five of those days come in the autumn, seven before the end of the fiscal year, and thirteen before the end of June. At the end of the allotted days in each of these three periods, the House deals definitively with whatever requests for supply and appropriation are then before it. For example, at the end of the second period, in March, the House will deal with the request for money to cover the final supplementary estimates and with the request for interim supply to begin the new fiscal year.

This new arrangement means that before the Government can get supplies of money from the House, the Opposition has a chance to reveal to the House and to the country all the shortcomings which, it believes, it has detected in the conduct and the policies of the Government. Only after this revelation does the House deal with supply business. . . .

The results of the new method of dealing with the business of supply are numerous. The estimates now are being examined by elected representatives of the taxpayers before or immediately after the new fiscal year begins. They are examined in small specialist committees where a Member has a chance to get explanations from the Minister, or the Parliamentary Secretary on policy, and from the nonpolitical servants of the Crown on data and technical matters. The Opposition has opportunities throughout the session to show why the Government should be thrown out of office. The Government, in its turn, knows that on certain dates, it will be told by the House whether or not its bills can be paid. And, perhaps, most important, a basic framework has been provided for annual sessions of Parliament starting in the autumn and ending about the first of July.

Another giant step was the elimination of debate on the budget resolutions. Under the old rules, the Minister of Finance tabled proposed resolutions relating to tax changes in the course of his budget statement. These would be debated during the six-day budget debate. Then each proposed resolution would be debated in the Committee of Ways and Means. And after each proposed resolution had been carried, a bill based on it would be introduced in the House and passed through all the normal stages in the legislative process. This meant that tax changes were discussed in three different contexts: collectively during the budget debate, individually at the resolution stage, and again, individually, during the passing of each bill. There was general agreement in the House that nothing much, other than the spending of time, was achieved by separate debates on each of the proposed resolutions. Under the new procedure, the tax changes advocated by the Minister of Finance can be discussed during the budget debate and then as each bill goes through all its stages.

The final major change made last December was in the process by which a bill passes the House of Commons. At first reading, a draft of a bill is put before the House. The second-reading motion asks the House whether or not it wants to pass a bill directed to the ends or purposes of that draft. If the House decides affirmatively, the text of the Bill must be prepared. What the House has before it is only a draft text submitted by one of its Members. The House has not yet touched that text.

It is fully recognized by the House that it is not a body suitable for writing bills even when a draft has been provided. What the House has done for generations in Britain and Canada is to give this job, the job of approving the details of a text, to a committee. However, in Canada, that committee always consisted of all the Members. In short, nothing was gained by sending the bill to committee other than an important degree of informality.

Under the new Standing Orders adopted last December, almost all draft bills go to one of the Standing Committees after second reading in the House. There the clauses are examined and are improved or approved. When the Standing Committee has completed its work, it reports back to the House the text of the bill as adopted and recommended by the committee.

The obvious shortcoming of this procedure is that only those Members who are on a Standing Committee — the standard number now is twenty — have a chance to work directly on the text. To overcome this defect, the report stage has been made debatable. Any Member who wishes to have a change made in a bill as reported back from a Standing Committee may give written notice to the House of the change he wishes to propose; and when the House considers the report of the committee, the Member may move his amendment. [The other great advantage in the new system is that seven or eight discussions on different subjects may go on simultaneously.]

•   •   •

The House of Commons has thus organized its time to provide for a greater quantity of business. To aid in putting more quality into those hours, the Government decided to provide a sum of almost $200,000 a year for research assistance to the Opposition and it hopes to provide a comparable amount to the private Members on the Government side. Research assistance has also been afforded to some Parliamentary Committees, so that the deliberations of those committees might be better informed. The Government has always had at its disposal the entire public service to provide the information required to defend its proposals. It seemed appropriate to provide the private Members of Parliament with assistance in an effort to equalize the "information gap," as it were, and to assist them in the scrutiny of the administration and the legislation put before Parliament.

Unfortunately, this streamlined legislative process and the improved process of granting supply did not prove to be enough. The principal obstacle to public business did not prove to be isolated individual time wasting. It was rather the conscious wasting of time as a party decision. An effort by the Opposition to defeat parts of a program, not by logic nor by vote, but through the mere wasting of time, left the Government a hard choice between continuing with the contentious bill or losing the rest of the program. The use of the filibuster is, in effect, a form of closure, since it prevents the House from considering other matters concerned with the nation's welfare. This happened during the last session with the Criminal Code amendments. It was to overcome this veto by the minority that the time allocation rules were evolved. They were intended to permit the House to arrive at a decision after a bill had received reasonable study, but before a filibuster had prejudiced the work of Parliament. . . .

The new Standing Orders 75A, 75B, and 75C were adopted. . . . Standing Order 75A provides that when all the parties agree to a timetable for a bill, a motion incorporating that timetable may be put to the House for immediate decision. . . . Standing Order 75B provides that when the majority of the parties agree as to when the debate on one stage of a bill is to end, a motion incorporating that agreement may be put to the House for decision after two hours of debate. This rule is highly favourable to minor parties, for it puts them in a position to unite with the Government against the Official Opposition. My own impression is that neither the Government nor the Official Opposition could have accepted Standing Order 75B unless a means of overcoming minor party dominance had been provided.

Standing Order 75C allows the Government—when either 75A or 75B has been tried unsuccessfully—to propose to the House, for decision by the House, when the debate on a stage of a bill is to end. Numerous safeguards are provided. First, the debate on that stage must be in progress. The Government must let it become clear that there is a jam. Second, the Government must give a day's notice before proposing the time-limit motion to the House. Third, the time-limit motion itself is debatable for two hours. Fourth, the time limit prescribed by that motion must provide for at least one full additional day of debate. Fifth, if the procedure has to be used on all stages of a bill, it must be used three different times, that is on the second-reading stage separately, on the committee stage separately, and finally on the report and third-reading stages.

In my view, this is not a crude rule. In fact, its defect may be that it contains so many safeguards, so much due process, that it will not be effective against obdurate opposition. . . .

The people have a right to expect the Ministers to administer their departments well, to think through their policies, and to prepare sound bills; but the Ministers cannot do these things if they are busy ten or eleven months of the year in Parliament. Similarly, the people have a right to expect the Members of the House of Commons to examine the conduct of the Government—its administration, its policies, and its bills—with infinite care and to recognize that infinite speech is not the outward and visible sign of infinite care. In 1968 and 1969, the House took giant steps to move forward from its colonial origins and to bring itself into step not only with the Mother of Parliaments, but, what is more important, with the needs of our country as it enters upon its second century.

BACKBENCHERS, THE NEW COMMITTEE SYSTEM, AND THE CAUCUS*

MARK MacGUIGAN

BACKBENCHERS

Members of Parliament may walk the corridors of power but they do not yet have access to the executive suites where the important decisions of government are made. Ours is still an executive-run system in which the decisions that matter most are made, not by Parliament, nor even by the parliamentary caucus of the majority, but by cabinet ministers and senior government officials.

But the power of the decision-making elite is far from absolute. Backbenchers sometimes rebel, at least in the privacy of caucus, and they are not unacquainted with lesser ways of making ministers' lives uncomfortable. More important, the complexity of the whole governmental system defies absolute control by any man or any group, however highly placed. To some degree the system itself is the master, limiting the options of both government and caucus.

Perhaps this is because the system does not have a military-like chain of command. Rather it has a number of power centers: cabinet ministers (not necessarily

* From a series of three articles written by Mark MacGuigan, Liberal Member of Parliament for Windsor-Walkerville, who was Chairman of the Special Committee of the House of Statutory Instruments. The articles were published in the *Windsor Star* on June 11, June 18, and July 2, 1969. By permission of the author and publisher.

themselves all working in tandem), the mandarins of the civil service, the managerial group in Crown corporations and agencies, and in a small way members of Parliament and senators. The system is not easily put in motion, nor easily brought to a halt, by any power center.

Certainly what most clearly stands out in the view from the back bench is the system itself—not the control of the cabinet, nor the daily conflict with the opposition, but the systematic mass which is not readily converted into energy. The legislative mills appear to grind slowly, and not always exceedingly fine. The executive appears to have many of the same matters continually under consideration, without coming to a conclusion. The administrative mechanism appears to proceed on its own, sometimes blunting the sharp points of legislation by overly rigid interpretation, sometimes filling in the gaps through exaggerated powers of regulation-making. The very complexity of the system keeps both MPs and ministers so occupied that they have little time for critical reflection. It might seem to be a gigantic conspiracy, if there were any conspirators, or at least any conspirators apart from everyone in the system. But it is not a conspiracy so much as a common plight.

How is change possible? Cabinet ministers have the power to accomplish a great deal but are harried by administrative, legislative, and political duties which leave them with little opportunity for anything beyond their daily round. Obviously the civil servants have little incentive to attempt to change the system. They are more comfortable in it than any other group, and, if their wishes do not always prevail, at least they are not often thwarted. The backbenchers have the will, but neither the power, nor the time, nor the organization to carry out the reform of the system.

The principal reason for hope is the expressed determination to reform the system on the part of the one man with sufficient power to do it—the Prime Minister. In his first year of office he moved in many directions to change the system. In the House of Commons, for instance, the rules have been changed to allow Standing Committees to take over all the detailed work of scrutinizing estimates and legislation which was formerly done in Committee of the Whole in the House. . . .

On the administrative side the changes have been equally impressive. Although the details are shrouded in the secrecy characterizing all cabinet matters, important changes have been effected in cabinet procedures which have led to a more profitable use of cabinet time. In addition, a number of departments have been reorganized along more functional lines, and effective use has been made of ministers without portfolio in assisting more senior ministers. The institution of duty days for ministers' attendance during the oral question period in the House has made available more ministerial time to enable ministers to master their departments. Further, the establishment of a Special Committee on Statutory Instruments to study ways in which the House can exert some measure of control over the regulation-making process of government may succeed in increasing the real legislative power of the House.

. . . However, much more remains to be done than has yet been accomplished. . . .

At present the influence that members do have rests on their personality rather than on their status. MPs' working conditions and facilities are so inadequate that they impose a crushing burden on members who want to perform their legislative role effectively. The use made at present of Parliamentary Secretaries is minimal, and the cabinet needs to be further reorganized to make it possible for an inner core of principal ministers to have time for thought as well as for action. Finally, Parliament has yet, through its Special Committees, to devise means of keeping delegated legislation under proper control. . . .

THE NEW COMMITTEE SYSTEM

The Standing Orders of the House of Commons as adopted in 1962 provided for 14 standing committees, the more important of which consisted of 50 to 60 members. The size of these committees with quorums of 15 to 20 members imposed an impossible burden on a House of only 265 (now 264) members—or, more accurately, would have imposed such a burden if substantial use had been made of them.

There was, however, very little incentive for the Government to have matters referred to committees, because committee consideration of a bill or departmental estimates was extraneous to the legislative process and did not take the place of the committee-of-the-whole stage in the House. Every time it made such a referral to committee, therefore, the Government ran the risk of having the same debate twice, first in committee and again in the House. Nevertheless, despite this great disadvantage the Pearson Government made more use of committees than any previous Government.

It is probable that the principal motivating force in the Trudeau Government's decision to establish the committee system as an integral part of the legislative process was to save parliamentary time. A legislative committee system can save time on bills or estimates because a number of committees meeting simultaneously can accomplish a great deal more than a single Committee of the Whole. Paradoxically they can also give a more detailed and penetrating scrutiny to legislation or estimates; the division of labour enables certain members to specialize and available time allows more leisure for pursuit of subtle points.

Under the new system of procedure which came into effect on January 14, 1969, the Government undertook to send all bills to committee as a matter of course after second reading. Although the number of Standing Committees has been increased to 18, the membership has been reduced to 20 (with the exception of two committees of 30 members each). The Government takes one more than half of the places on each committee, and all committees except Public Accounts choose a Government member as chairman. Most MPs belong to two committees. Committees usually meet on Tuesday and Thursday mornings and afternoons, with occasional night and Friday morning meetings. Each committee is assigned a clerk, and all committee proceedings are conducted and published in both official languages.

Since the establishment of the new system, there has been considerable controversy, both public and private, over the role of the Government backbencher in it. While clearly the Government foresaw that greater participation by its backbenchers would result from the changes, it perhaps did not realize how greatly a taste of freedom would affect its backbenchers.

There have always been two controls which kept the backbenchers in line. The positive one was that of advancement, which does not need to be explicit in order to be real; while "yes" men are not necessarily promoted, "no" men almost never are (and hence there have been very few of them). The negative factor was effective where a sufficiently large number of backbenchers was involved as to make individual reprisals impracticable. A government's most potent weapon is to threaten dissolution of Parliament and a general election. Although the crisis of February, 1968, which resulted from the Government's defeat on third reading of a tax bill, finally made it clear that a Government is not compelled to regard a defeat on a particular measure as a vote of non-confidence unless it chooses to do so, the Government can always hold over the MPs' heads the threat that it will decide to interpret any adverse vote in the House that way.

The institution of the committee system completely removed the negative control over matters referred to committee, because a defeat for the Government in a committee vote cannot even theoretically be considered a vote of non-confidence. It also lessened the effectiveness of the positive control, because most matters on which the Government would be likely to be defeated in a committee by its own supporters (who, after all, accept the same basic philosophy) would usually be comparatively minor and therefore much less likely to prejudice a member's career.

The result of the new system was, therefore, predictable. Since it came into effect at the beginning of 1969, Liberal members have on several occasions themselves moved amendments to Government bills, or voted in support of Opposition motions or amendments. The most notable instance occurred in the Justice Committee on March 25, 1969, when an amendment to the breathalyzer sections of the Omnibus Criminal Code Bill was proposed by a Liberal MP and, despite the opposition of the Minister of Justice, was carried, with five Liberals and four Conservatives outvoting two New Democrats and the four Liberal members who voted for the Government version.

The significance of additional freedom for Government backbenchers on Standing Committees does not so much lie in the number of times they may actually reverse their own frontbenchers. Such occasions will undoubtedly remain rare. Rather what is important is that, once recognized as having this right, they can then effectively pressure ministers to make changes in legislation which they would not otherwise be likely to make but which do not actually impair the overall scheme of the legislation. There is no better example of a minister's accepting an unwanted change than in the case of the breathalyzer amendment. Despite the fact that he had the power to reverse the committee decision on report stage in the House when the committee reported the amended bill back to the House and the matter again became a question of confidence, the Minister decided not to do so.

No doubt ministers will have to learn to live with a good many such compromises in the future.

Whether or not the Government yet accepts the fact, it made a fundamental change in our system when it introduced the legislative committee. In my view, the change is a major improvement, because it enables the individual member to make a more creative contribution to the law-making process. At the same time it produces better legislation, because it is the product of a broader decision-making group. The only loss is in the power of the executive.

Some older parliamentarians feel that private debate in caucus achieved the same effect of modifying Government proposals without the disadvantage of embarrassing the Government, since it was removed from the ken of the outside world. But those who have sat in caucus know how easy it is for a Government to manage caucus, and even to ignore its views on any particular matter, unless the caucus is almost unanimous and prepared to press a matter strongly. Whatever the merits of the older system, (and I do not think they are great), the Government cannot now abolish the legislative committee because the new system is too much more efficient. And given the system, the new breed of backbenchers is not going to accept the role of mere ciphers in which the executive controls every parliamentary action.

. . . There are still too many committees and probably too many MPs on each committee. There are too few committee rooms, interpreters, transcribers, and clerks, and no experts to assist members in acquiring technical knowledge.

There is inadequate time allowed in the parliamentary schedule for meetings to take place. Committees have no budgets and no right to establish their own agendas. Finally, committee members have no guarantee of relative permanence of assignment and therefore have inadequate incentive to master particular fields of legislation. The legislative committee system has been well begun, but it will not achieve its great potential without time, money, and intelligent direction.

THE CAUCUS

A caucus is a private meeting of the elected members of a political party for the purpose of exchanging views on the political questions of the day. The word "caucus" probably comes from an Algonquin word, *kaw-kaw-was*, meaning to talk, and it first appeared in the English language in the early part of the eighteenth century as the name of a political club in Boston. . . .

The word made its first appearance in England in 1877 with a rather different meaning, when it was used by Joseph Chamberlain to describe a new system of party organization through constituency meetings which he was developing in Birmingham. Since Disraeli's colourful use of the term the next year to describe the Liberal political machine of the day, it has usually had in England the unflattering sense of a system of party organization with the sole purpose of election management. . . . The British political system still does not have a body which is equivalent to the Canadian understanding of a caucus. The 1922 Committee is the organized form of the backbench members of the Conservative Party in the House of Commons, but ministers do not attend its meetings unless specially summoned. The Parliamentary Labour Party more closely approximates a caucus since it theoretically includes the frontbenchers as well, but when the Labour party forms the Government, the relationship between the ministry and the backbenchers tends to follow the Conservative pattern.

The common attendance of ministers and backbenchers which characterizes the caucus in Commonwealth countries other than Britain is probably a legacy of their colonial past in which all elected members worked together against the executive officials appointed by the Mother Country. As the first British colony to achieve self-government, Canada had to develop a system of party solidarity in Parliament without the assistance of parliamentary precedents from anywhere else. The Canadian party caucus is therefore a uniquely Canadian institution, though now paralleled by similar structures in other Commonwealth countries.

There is a basic difference between the role of the caucus in a party which forms the Government and its place in a party which is in Opposition, resulting from the fact that opposition parties do not have responsibility for the presentation of a legislative program. An Opposition caucus may have internal difficulty in establishing a common position respecting Government legislation, but there is no difference in the responsibility which its various members bear either in the House or in caucus (except the unique responsibility of the leader of the official opposition)—all are equal in status. But within the Government caucus the members of the cabinet carry a special responsibility for the introduction of Government legislation, and therefore have a special status within the caucus just as they do within the House. The principal focus within a Government caucus is therefore always the relationship between the ministerial and non-ministerial members of the caucus.

Former Prime Minister Mackenzie King probably accurately expressed the general purpose of a Government caucus when he said in the House in 1923 that it "is the means whereby a government can ascertain through its following what the views and opinions of the public as represented by their various constituencies may be . . . a means of discovering the will of the people through their representatives in a manner which cannot be done under the formal procedure which is required in this chamber." The Government caucus exists for the purpose of consultation between ministers and backbenchers.

But to whose use is the consultation put? In other words, is the caucus a device by which the Government controls its members or is it rather a means through which the backbenchers control the cabinet? The history of Canadian politics leaves little doubt that the Government caucus is of greater utility to the ministry than to the members, and that it is, in effect the chief instrument of Government control of the House of Commons. Undoubtedly the years have seen a lessening in cabinet absolutism and a growth in caucus democracy, but even yet caucus control of cabinet is only weak and interstitial. A closer look at the operation of the Government caucus at present will explain why.

The Government caucus meeting usually runs from 10:30 to 12:15 on Wednesday mornings during a parliamentary session. Cabinet ministers are expected to attend and most backbenchers want to. The meeting opens with announcements of events or committee meetings, followed by reports from the regional caucuses (which have met earlier from 9:30 to 10:30). Sometimes these reports spark brief debates. Next there are reports from the House leader and from the Whip respecting the business of the House, which may provoke questions. Then, unless there is a special subject for discussion, the floor is thrown open for members to raise subjects of which they have given advance notice to the chairman.

On a typical morning the chairman will have had notice of perhaps six or eight subjects, on each of which there may be a number of speakers (without notice) depending on the degree of interest the subject arouses. If the subject concerns a particular cabinet minister, he may be one of the speakers. Even with the time limit of three minutes for each speaker except a minister, it may happen that only three or four subjects are reached before the chairman calls on the Prime Minister to reply at 12 o'clock. The Prime Minister normally takes about 15 or 20 minutes to comment on the views expressed earlier. When the Prime Minister has finished, the caucus immediately adjourns.

On rare occasions these regular weekly meetings are completely devoted to a single subject. Somewhat more often, a minister will give a report to the caucus on what he proposes to do with respect to some matter under his jurisdiction, though in very general terms, because our parliamentary tradition is that MPs other than ministers may not know the details of Government legislation until a bill has obtained first reading in Parliament.

In addition to these meetings of the full caucus, there are also many meetings of caucus committees, all of which are of an ad hoc character even when they meet frequently. There is no established procedure and the chairman is usually whichever member happened to call the group together. Sometimes the minister whose departmental responsibility is related to the subject under discussion may attend, but often he will not. When a minister attends, he will listen to the views of backbenchers on policy which has not yet been announced, or, where a bill has already been presented, explain its terms to those present.

In such a situation there are obviously many factors working in favor of Governmental control. The caucus is very loosely organized (its executive has only the power to recommend and seldom does even that), and consequently discussions in full caucus cover only a small part of the Government's total legislative program. Many of the letters raised by members are either local in nature or trivial in character. No motions are put in caucus and no votes taken, and the Government is therefore always free to interpret caucus opinion in its own way. There is no real dialogue with the Prime Minister since he always has the last word. Perhaps worst of all, most of the discussion is after the fact, when the Government has already announced its policy, or at least made up its mind as to what it will do.

It is hardly surprising that most Government MPs in the past have abandoned any attempt to work collectively through the caucus and have set about attempting to advance their ideas, and incidentally their careers, through individual action. If

SCHEDULE OF A CAUCUS MEETING
LIBERAL PARTY

LIBERAL CAUCUS COMMITTEE MEETINGS/REUNIONS DES COMITES DU CAUCUS

Hour/Heure: 10:00 a.m.   Date: February 4, 1970/4 février 1970

Number Numéro	Committee's Name Nom du comité	Chairman Président	Room Salle	Agenda	Minister Ministre Present	Remarks Remarques
1	SCIENCE—TECHNOLOGY & URBAN AFFAIRS / SCIENCE—TECHNOLOGIE & AFFAIRES URBAINES	K. Hymmen	208 WB / 208 E.O.	(a) Preliminary Discussion on Urban Affairs (b) Bill C-137 Motor Vehicle Safety Act AND Aircraft Pollution / (a) Discussion préliminaire sur affaires urbaines (b) Bill C-137 (Loi sur la sécurité des véhicules automobiles & Pollution (aviation))	Hon. D. Jamieson	(a) 10:00 a.m. (b) The Minister will be present from 11:00 a.m.
2A	ECONOMIC POLICY (Resources & Dev.) / POLITIQUE ECONOMIQUE (Ressources & Dev.)	E. Corbin	308 WB	Northern oil policy & Northern Development and associated question / Développement du Nord canadien, ressources huilières & autres questions se rapportant au Nord canadien	Hon. J. J. Greene / Hon. J. Chrétien	
2B	ECONOMIC POLICY (Finance-Trade-Ser.) / POLITIQUE ECONOMIQUE (Finance-Commerce-Services)	A. Gillespie	209 WB / 209 E.O.	Wages & Prices, restraints or controls? Anti-inflationary policies. / Salaires et Prix (contrôle & restrictions) Politiques anti-inflationnistes	Hon. E. J. Benson / Hon. R. Basford	
3	SOCIAL POLICY / POLITIQUE SOCIALE	J. Guilbault	307 WB / 307 EO	(a) The Federal Superior Court Act (b) Tax Appeal Board (c) National Law Reform Commission / (a) Loi sur la Cour Supérieure fédérale (b) Bureau d'appel sur la Taxation (c) Loi nationale sur la réforme pénale	Hon. J. Turner	
4	CULTURE INFORMATION COMMUNICATIONS	B. Howard	212 WB / 212 EO	Cultural Policy as related to Canadian identity. 1. Outline of the problem & the instruments available. / Politique culturelle en relation avec l'identité canadienne. 1. Le probleme & moyens disponibles	Hon. G. Pelletier / Hon. R. Stanbury	First of a three part series. Meeting held in 212 W.B. Cette étude sera divisée en trois étapes Réunion aura lieu dans la pièce 212 E.O. —
5	EXTERNAL AFFAIRS DEFENCE—FED. PROV. RELATIONS / AFF. EXTERIEURES DEFENSE—RELATIONS FED. PROV.	W. Allmand	207 WB / 207 EO.	(1) Foreign Policy Review (2) Francophonie Relations / (1) Révision de la politique extérieure (2) Relations avec la francophonie	Hon. M. Sharp	

the individual member's influence comes solely from his own gifts of intellect, personality, and persuasion, and in no way stems from his status as a member of the caucus, then he will normally lack the incentive to participate seriously in the caucus.

The most interesting fact about the present Government caucus is that it is composed of members who, rather than devoting all their efforts to individual achievement, appear to be determined to make the caucus work as a system, in company with a Prime Minister who has been encouraging the caucus to organize itself in such a way as to increase its influence and even its power. Certain achievements are already apparent: changes in the Post Office Bill, a major recasting of the Estate Tax Bill, a certain measure of independence of Standing Committees of the House — and a special weekend caucus at the end of the parliamentary session in June, 1969, on "The Role of the Backbencher." In the long run the special caucus is likely to be seen as the major achievement of the parliamentary year.

[Since these articles were written, further changes have been made within the Government caucus, partly as a result of the special caucus meeting referred to above. The Government has agreed to present proposed bills in outline to the caucus before the cabinet acts upon them. The Government caucus has also organized itself into committees which have designated chairmen. The entire caucus still meets every Wednesday morning, for the full period every second week but on alternate weeks for the period from 9:30 to 10 a.m., which is followed then by meetings of the caucus committees. An example of the latter kind of Government caucus meeting is given in the actual schedule on page 384, which was not provided by the author of the foregoing article.]

PRIVATE MEMBERS' LEGISLATION*

GEORGE BAIN

OTTAWA—There are about 20 pages at the beginning of each day's Routine Proceedings and Orders of the Day where are to be found, in wondrous profusion, the legislative schemes which individual members of Parliament hold near and dear to their hearts.

There are the pages on which are set down what are usually called private members' bills and are properly called public bills, and the resolutions in which MPs solicit the support of the House (for instance, No. 11, Reid Scott's motion which says "that, in the opinion of this House, the Divorce Act, 1930, should be amended. . .").

* From *The Globe and Mail,* Toronto, March 1, 1966. By permission. Revised by the editor in July, 1970.

A private member's bill, if passed, becomes law just as a government bill does; a resolution, since it seeks only an expression of opinion, has no effect except as it may cause the Government subsequently to take note of that opinion and bring in legislation to accommodate it.

It isn't very often that anything final comes of private members' bills and resolutions, largely because the time allotted to debate them is small—one hour a day, to a total of 40 times in a session. What happens is that a member's bill gets to the top of the heap, is debated for an hour—and is still being debated when time runs out, with the result that it goes to the bottom of the list again. The list is usually so long as to make it unlikely that any bill will rise to the top twice.

But the private members' bills and resolutions are instructive in that they show what the members as individuals are thinking about—and what the members are thinking about as individuals today may become tomorrow's legislation if enough of them get to thinking about the same things.

There were 113 private members' bills on the order paper at the end of last week and they dealt with such variety of subjects as the stabilization of hog and egg prices, abolition of capital punishment, abolition of the Senate, and something described as an "act to amend the Combines Investigations Act (floor penalties, criminal joint tortfeasors, and moieties)."

[Private MPs have also proposed 61 resolutions on various subjects that call for debate on such matters as the advisability of an inland waterway from Winnipeg to Edmonton and the study of automobile safety.]

A member may have only one resolution on the order paper at one time, but there is no such restriction as to bills. David Orlikow (NDP, Winnipeg North), the man with the concern about tortfeasors and moieties, is the sponsor of no fewer than eight.

One of them would permit the householder 72 hours to change his mind after he had been sold a 20-volume set of an encyclopaedia, or a new garage door, or a cupboardful of dishes by a door-to-door salesman; the deal would become final only after that time. Another would define the circumstances in which wire-tapping would and would not be permissible—and would provide penalties for misuse. A third would end the situation in which union organizers can be kept out of a company town by the company's declaring the whole town private property.

A member's pet projects may go marching on even after he has departed if they attract another member. Mr. Orlikow, for instance, admits that one or more of his eight probably originated with Hazen Argue, who subsequently left the NDP for the Liberal Party, was defeated in the last two general elections as a Liberal, and is now returning to Ottawa in the new glory of a senator.

Several members may (and often do) submit bills dealing with the same subject matter. For instance, there are four bills on the order paper relating to capital punishment. Three members—Ron Basford (L, Vancouver-Burard), A. B. Patterson (SC, Fraser Valley), and Fernand Leblanc (L, Laurier)—want the political affiliations of candidates shown on ballot papers at elections. At present, only name, address and occupation are provided.

Mr. Basford also has a bill which would provide that when an MP had reached the age of 75, his seat would be declared vacant, as if he had died. It would prohibit anyone from offering himself as a candidate beyond the age of 75.

There are bills on the order paper which would make various changes concerning elections—for instance, lowering the voting age to 18, placing restrictions on the amount of money that may be spent, and prohibiting the publication of opinion poll results before elections.

Two members—Maurice Allard (Ind. PC, Sherbrooke) and Perry Ryan (L, Toronto-Spadina)— have sponsored bills to provide for a Canadian national anthem. Mr. Ryan, in another bill, wants dates set for the beginning and end of each session of Parliament.

A GOOD MEMBER EARNS HIS PAY*

PETER DEMPSON

How valuable is a member of Parliament to his riding?

It depends.

An MP's personality has a lot to do with it. So does his persuasiveness. So, too, the makeup of the constituency. And, of course, it helps if the member is a supporter of the Government. . . .

One MP who has been giving a good account of himself in his relatively short time in the House of Commons is James Baskin, a quiet, affable, 38-year-old Renfrew lumberman. A Conservative, he won his seat—Renfrew South—in 1957. He was re-elected in March, 1958.

His win was all the more convincing because in June, 1957, he defeated former Revenue Minister J. J. McCann, who had represented the riding since 1935.

An indefatigable worker, Jim Baskin isn't happy unless he's doing something for his constituents. He's aggressive, untiring and he speaks out strongly on their behalf in Parliament.

"We like him," says Edward P. Enright, a Renfrew insurance agent. "He gets things done."

Mr. Baskin's accomplishment can't be measured in terms of new federal spending he's been able to attract to Renfrew South riding. But in that respect alone he's succeeded in getting Ottawa to loosen its pursestrings on more than $5,000,000 for housing, public works and other projects for the constituency.

He's done much more than that. He was instrumental in obtaining a 40-hour work week for employees at the Civil Defence College, Arnprior. He arranged to have a survey of pulpwood stands throughout the riding, preliminary to establish-

* From *The Telegram,* Toronto, January 28, 1959. By permission of the publisher.

ment of a pulp mill. He persuaded postal authorities to approve a twice-daily rural mail delivery out of Barry's Bay. He exerted pressure to have mail service generally improved throughout the constituency.

A huge electronics plant at Renfrew had indicated it might be forced to close, due to drop in orders. Mr. Baskin got busy and was able to talk the management into remaining open. Too, he was successful in rounding up some orders for a large aircraft-engineering firm in Renfrew, due to his influence on the government.

His list of achievements for Renfrew South is well known to his constituents. It goes on and on.

The Canadian National Railways had announced it intended to withdraw its passenger service from Ottawa to Barry's Bay because it was losing money. Jim Baskin listened to the protests of his people, then went to both CNR and the Government. The service is not only in operation today but it has been improved considerably.

Mr. Baskin has made representations to Ottawa on behalf of old age pensioners in his riding. He has spoken out for veterans, disabled, the blind. He has found jobs for 200 people, but admits unemployment is still a serious problem.

When a new seven-mile road was needed to the RCAF station Roymount, he was able to get the Federal Government to assume 50 percent of the cost. When a new wharf was required at Barry's Bay, Mr. Baskin saw to it that Ottawa built one.

At all times Mr. Baskin works closely with Mines Minister James A. Maloney, MPP for South Renfrew. Frequently on projects, provincial and federal, jurisdiction overlaps.

"He's a good member," says Mr. Enright. "He's always on call for speaking engagements, social functions and what have you."

Constituents generally agree. Some months ago when a new road was built from Arnprior to the Civil Defence College, they named it Baskin Drive.

OUR MPs — THEIR ROLES AND NEED*

PAUL FOX

. . . There is a great deal of misinformed opinion about the work our members of Parliament at Ottawa do. There is a widespread feeling, for instance, that MPs aren't earning their pay if they are not glued to their seats in the House of Commons. Editorial writers often complain bitterly about the sparse attendance in the House, and visitors to the Commons' galleries are frequently dismayed not to see their local representative of the people at his desk, or if he is there, to notice that he is reading a newspaper, writing a letter, or chatting to his neighbour. All this is

* From a revision of an address given by the author in Hamilton, Ontario, May 20, 1966. Revised further in July, 1970.

taken by the public—and by people who should know better—as a sign of the inadequacy of our politicians.

This criterion of judgment of our MPs is wide of the mark. The last way to estimate the value and effectiveness of an MP is to clock the number of hours he sits in the House of Commons. Any one can sit, and most people can even manage to look wise. Department stores use sophisticated mannequins to display their goods. But no one judges the intelligence and efficiency of a department store by the number of hours the inert forms spend sitting in the show windows.

Basically the House of Commons is one of the display windows of politics, presenting a tableau or a spectacle for the public to watch. Call it what you will, but the daily proceedings of the House are essentially one more scene from the great, never-ending Canadian Political Drama, a serial that runs continuously all about us, comprising the whole political cosmos of the state, of which only parts are visible to the people because they are acted out on the public stage.

The visible depiction of the world of politics is necessary to catch the public's attention, to give it a glimpse into current political issues, and to elicit its interest, identification, and participation in affairs by simplifying and dramatizing them. But this is only one side of the political firmament. Behind the public display lies most of the operating process of politics—the complex and involved invisible world of discussion, bargaining, policy- and decision-making, within the executive, administrative, and even legislative branches of government. Its nature precludes it from being exposed and explained clearly and simply to the public.

The MPs play a role in this invisible empire but it is not appreciated because it is off the public stage and harder to describe. The active MP can perform many worthwhile functions other than merely being a parliamentarian. He can be an assiduous committee man, for example, working quietly but effectively on House committees or on his party's caucus committees, a function that is very important, especially in relation to policy-making, though it is not likely to result in much publicity. Secondly, he can be a sort of hound-dog researcher, sniffling around in half-buried issues, digging up meaty bones for himself and the public to chew on. Thirdly, he may be an organization man, carrying out chores in his party, for instance, speaking, travelling, and propagandizing all over the country. Fourthly, he may decide to act as a business agent for his constituency, trying to promote its interests wherever and whenever possible, a function described in an article in POLITICS: CANADA entitled "A Good Member Earns His Pay." Legitimate activity of this kind can be, and should be, differentiated from mere patronage-seeking. Finally, the MP may be a social welfare officer, assisting citizens to thread their way through the increasingly complicated maze of the welfare state by acting as their personal representative in Ottawa (looking into complaints about pensions, immigration cases, and the like). A great deal could be said on this last function alone. . . .

Whatever the MP's function, one thing is clear. Although his emolument is now reasonable ($18,000 a year, $12,000 of which is paid as a stipened, and $6,000 as a tax-free expense allowance, bringing his real gross income to something like

$22,000), and though he now has such essential aids to his work as an office to himself, an allotment of stationery and a stenographer, a mailing franc, free long distance and local telephone calls, and the opportunity for a free return air trip to his constituency once a week plus a railway pass, the worthwhile MP still needs more research assistance. Most MPs have neither the time, the energy, or the money to get any serious research done for themselves.

The result is that they lack fresh and informed thinking to inject into the political process to advance the discussion of issues and to balance the government's strength based on its close relation to the civil service. The same old arguments are bandied back and forth time and time again. The MPs quote the newspapers, and the newspapers quote the MPs, and no one becomes much wiser in the process.

In Congress in the United States, by way of contrast, the facilities for research are plentiful. The Library of Congress has on its staff more than 200 research assistants. Congressmen and Senators may also hire research assistants out of their large expense allowances. The latter amounts vary since they are set by a complicated formula but they average about $50,000 a year per member, in addition to his annual salary which in March 1970, it was proposed by a bill in Congress, should be raised to $42,500. Some representatives hire as many as nine personal assistants. Some also have young post-graduate university students working for them as researchers under a plan for "internists" that the American Political Science Association has been running very successfully for more than a decade.

In Canada, however, the big breakthrough came only with two developments following the 1968 election. Prime Minister Trudeau's government decided to allocate $195,000 a year for research purposes to the opposition parties in the House, which were to share the amount and use their own discretion as to how to spend it on such a function. The Conservatives received $125,000 and subsequently employed a staff of nine research officers. The NDP and Créditistes received $35,000 each, the NDP using their allotment to hire three young research workers. In February 1970, under pressure from his own backbench Liberal MPs who felt they were neglected since they had access to neither the government's civil service research facilities nor to the opposition parties' funds, the prime minister allotted $130,000 a year to the Liberal caucus for research. In addition, the research service of the Parliamentary Library, which had been made available to all MPs since 1965, was extended so that by 1970 it employed 12 officers and six secretaries and clerks.

The second development was the establishment by the Canadian Political Science Association of an "internists" program quite similar to the APSA's model. Mr. Alfred Hales, Conservative MP for Wellington, had been sponsoring for some time in Parliament a private member's resolution recommending the creation of such a system but it was not until 1969 when Professor Donald Smiley was the President of the CPSA that the project was finally launched with the aid of funds obtained from a charitable foundation. The first batch of 10 young men and women, who are graduates in political science selected from universities in various parts of Canada, are coming to Ottawa in mid-1970 to go to work for MPs, primarily as research aides.

It is to be hoped that the number of such assistants can be increased in future years and that additional funds will be made available to all parties and to the Library of Parliament to improve research facilities further. It was reported early in 1970 that the volume of requests to the Library for such aid had grown in four years to such an extent that the interval between a request being received and a detailed reply prepared was stretching to between six weeks and three months.

One incidental benefit accruing from the American experience with "internists" is that it has introduced a number of bright young political scientists to the process of government, improving their professional training, leading them into productive research studies, and giving them a taste for political life. But all this has been in addition to their providing valuable research help to Congressmen and Senators. Apparently, such assistance is still our Canadian MPs' greatest need.

WHY WE NEED AN OMBUDSMAN*

D. C. ROWAT

I think there is a stronger case for a scheme of this nature in Canada than in some of the other democracies of the world, because we have not done quite so much in the way of providing remedies for a citizen against administrative action.

The basic reason why the scheme has become of great interests is that there has been a tremendous growth in the administrative side of the government, in the functions and activities, and in the discretionary powers granted to officials, while the existing remedies—in case there is an arbitrary, unfair, or unjust decision made against an individual by an officer of administration—are inadequate.

I think it would be worth reviewing this very briefly. First, in Canada you find that administrative procedure has not been laid down in many cases for departments or agencies of government to use in dealing with individual cases. On the other hand, the United States has an administrative procedures act which was passed in 1946. It has been proposed in this country by the bar association, but not adopted in any jurisdiction. Both the U.S. and Great Britain have had elaborate investigations of the problem by official bodies, and Britain has set up a council on administrative tribunals with functions somewhat paralleling those of an ombudsman; but in this country we have done very little about studying the problem.

* Oral testimony by Professor Donald C. Rowat, Department of Political Science, Carleton University, Ottawa, to the House of Commons Standing Committee on Privileges and Elections, as reprinted from the *Minutes of Proceedings and Evidence of the Committee,* No. 7, October 1, 1964. By permission of the Queen's Printer .

My second point is that the appeals available to a citizen in a case where he believes that an arbitrary decision has been made, or that he has a grievance against administrative action, are very limited. We have set up in this country a number of specialized appeal bodies such as the income tax appeal board, the appeal in connection with immigration, and so on, but there is no comprehensive system of administrative appeal as in many countries of Western Europe, where there is a complete and comprehensive system of administrative courts. The Council of State in France is perhaps the best known and the most comprehensive of the administrative courts in Western Europe. Similarly, there is an administrative court system in Western Germany, which has existed in Germany for many years; its jurisdiction was extended by the constitution of the new Western Germany.

My third point is that the opportunity for reviewing administrative decisions by the courts is seriously limited here as elsewhere in the English-speaking world. You are all familiar with the fact that many pieces of legislation include a privative clause stating that there shall be no appeal to the courts, particularly regarding decisions made by certain types of boards or commissions. But even where there is an opportunity for appeal, the way in which the appeal may get before the courts is very complicated. This is done by ancient writs, and often it takes a very skilled lawyer to know which kind of writ should be used; if he makes a mistake, the case may fail. So it is a complicated business getting an appeal before the courts.

Another factor is that the courts operate rather slowly; and it is likely to be very costly in relation to the importance of the issue or the money involved, and a citizen would hesitate, especially in minor cases, to appeal his case to the courts.

Another limitation is that the courts usually have taken the view that they will make a decision on the law only, and an appeal on the merits of the case cannot be brought before the courts. Where there is a discretion, the court feels that it should not substitute its judgment for that of the competent administrator who is an expert in his field.

My fourth point is one with which you are familiar: parliament itself is the traditional vehicle before which to bring complaints and grievances about the actions of administrators and the executive, yet parliament is seriously limited in what it can do. Members of parliament may find themselves very heavily loaded with cases brought before them by their constituents. I think that perhaps members of this committee would agree that they have plenty of work to do in their various capacities. If the number of complaints should become overwhelming, it tends to take their time away from other important functions of the legislator, such as consideration of policy and legislation, and keeping up with events that would be necessary as background for dealing with important proposals laid before parliament.

In this regard I think you would be interested in having the results of a questionnaire which . . . was sent to you by a student at our university who was writing his master's thesis on this subject . . . the results are based upon about 70 replies from members of the House of Commons. . . . Some received under 10 [complaints] per month; yet two members received as many as 65 per month. It was difficult to work from the ranges and to strike an average, but it appeared that the average number of complaints monthly numbered about 15; and if you take this average for all members of parliament, and multiply it by 12, you get what I think is a rather startling figure of about 50,000 complaints a year which members of parliament receive from constituents concerning some aspect of governmental administration.

Of course it may have been mainly the overburdened members of parliament most in favour of the ombudsman scheme who replied to this questionnaire. But even if the average for all members were reduced to, let us say, 10 complaints per month, you would still have a figure of over 30,000 complaints per year.

The members replying estimated that only about 70 percent of their complaints deal with federal matters, and about 30 percent deal with provincial and municipal matters. The members of parliament of course have to refer these to provincial or municipal authorities, or try to deal with them in some other way.

Now, . . . because the majority of the complaints deal with the substance of the decision, if an ombudsman were set up at the federal level in this country he would not deal with the whole range of complaints received by members of parliament. The argument frequently rises that an ombudsman would do the work that a member of parliament should be doing. I think it is pretty clear that he is not going to be able to deal with all these 30,000 complaints per year; but he would deal with those which have to do with procedure, with fairness, and with justice, without going into the merits of the decision which was made. . . .

You might be interested in the main areas of complaints. . . . The most popular area was complaints which had to do with pensions. . . . Income tax was the next most popular subject. Citizenship and immigration came next. Then the number went down rapidly to health and welfare, unemployment insurance, and veterans' affairs. These were the main areas of complaint.

It is interesting to note that in the first three areas we also have administrative appeal bodies. Even so these were the most popular areas of complaint. So this may mean that our appeal bodies are not working effectively. On the other hand, as one member of parliament said in his reply, it may mean that the constituent simply wants to enlist the support of his member of parliament in behalf of his case and perhaps no more than that.

The great majority of those who replied to the questionnaire said that they had had complaints that had been settled unsatisfactorily. That is perhaps not surprising, because members of parliament cannot always get at the facts. They may tend to side with the complainant and feel that his trouble has been settled unsatisfactorily because they could not get at the full facts of the case. They are not in a position to be an independent judge of the case. This is where the great advantage lies with an ombudsman, since he would have the power to investigate thoroughly and find out what the facts of the case are.

I would remind you that Sir Guy Powles mentioned that the great majority of the members of parliament in New Zealand felt that an ombudsman was a positive aid rather than a hindrance to them because of his aid in selecting cases which should legitimately be looked after. In any case the majority of those who replied to this questionnaire felt that the ombudsman would be a help to them; that is, about three fourths of those who replied felt that the ombudsman would be desirable and of assistance.

•   •   •

It doesn't surprise me that members of parliament find it difficult to deal with some of these complaints in a thoroughly satisfactory way. . . . This has to do with my fifth point about the difficulty of a citizen being able to secure redress, and that is the matter of secrecy of the administration under the commonwealth parliamentary system. It is a long tradition, and because of this tradition of conducting administrative matters on the executive side of government secretly, it is impossible for individual citizens, or in some cases even for members of parliament, to find out exactly what went on. In some cases it is even difficult for the citizen to establish a prima facie case that there is a suspicion that an abuse has been engaged in, because he cannot get at enough facts even to establish this.

Now, the great advantage of the ombudsman scheme it seems to me is that even those who may be afraid of administrative activities being laid open to publicity may be willing to grant to an officer of parliament the opportunity to have access to information on the administrative side of government.

My sixth point is . . . that the Canadian system of legal aid is inadequate. The fact is that many other countries of the world are far ahead of Canada in the provision of legal aid for citizens who cannot afford to pay counsel to appear in the courts on their behalf, or to lodge appeals on their behalf. I would draw attention to the eighty five hundred officers in Japan whose job it is to provide help to citizens in this matter. . . .

My seventh point is . . . that, psychologically, people need to know that there is some impartial body willing to act on their behalf. Psychologically, they need a "wailing wall"; they need to have some outlet to which they can go with their complaints. All of you as members of parliament are familiar with this; but it may be desirable to have one focal point that they know about. . . .

It is obvious to me that a federal ombudsman would not be enough to cover all administrative complaints. There must be also similar officers in the provinces of Canada. . . .

Now, another problem in Canada is that we have a party situation . . . if the ombudsman is appointed by the government he might come to be sympathetic with or identified with the government of the day. . . . The parliamentary commissioner [must be given] continuity of tenure.

Another requirement to make the office effective, I think, is to have the provision that one of the existing standing committees or a special committee of the House of Commons should receive the ombudsman's report, consider it, and ascertain whether something has been done about his recommendations. Otherwise they may fall on deaf ears if there is no provision to take them up and take action on them.

With regard to the appointment of a parliamentary commissioner, it seems to me that provision should probably be made for the political parties to agree on the appointment to make sure that he has the support of all parties, and that he is an independent officer. . . .

Canada is much bigger than any of the countries which now have the ombudsman system. There is a problem whether a single officer would be adequate to deal with complaints coming from such a very large population, so greatly separated geographically. This is one of the reasons why I have suggested that the ombudsman should be "plural"—that there should be a complaints commission of, let us say, three members. . . .

I think the powers of an ombudsman or parliamentary commissioner as he is called, in this country should be very wide . . . and should include the army, public corporations, commissions, boards, and agencies of all kinds. At the provincial level I think the office of provincial ombudsman should cover local government and magistrates' courts. . . .

By way of conclusion I would like to say that in my view the ombudsman scheme is one of those rare inventions in the machinery of government which is worthy of very serious consideration by all democracies. It is like the development of the parliamentary audit, which is one of the very important inventions in the machinery of democratic government, and is a system which has spread to all democratic countries. . . .

On the other hand, we must recognize that it is no cure-all for all of the problems or difficulties which I have mentioned with respect to securing redress against administrative action. I think that many other reforms are needed. For instance, we need much simpler judicial remedies. We need somewhat wider opportunities for appeal to the courts, especially on points of law. We need more provision for special administrative appeal bodies on the merits of a decision. Perhaps this system should be extended to resemble the situation in France and West Germany and some other countries, which have a comprehensive system of administrative courts. We also need a better system of legal aid. . . .

OUR FIRST OMBUDSMAN TELLS HOW THE OFFICE WORKS*

GEORGE B. McCLELLAN

The appointment in Canada of ombudsmen in Alberta, New Brunswick and Quebec is an excellent illustration of how government under the democratic system can set up additional safeguards against injustice and discrimination.

The same development is occurring in many other countries. The ombudsman for the state of Hawaii asumed office last July 1, the first state ombudsman in the United States.

•   •   •

* From the *Toronto Daily Star*, October 29, 1969. By permission of the publisher.

It is no wonder that the average citizen often finds himself faced with what he regards as an incomprehensive bureaucracy when he tries to deal with the giant complex of government and its agencies, on some problem which vitally affects his health, his home, his property or his income.

Think then how much worse off are the illiterate, the semi-literate, the partially educated, or those thousands of recent Canadians whose mother tongue is neither English nor French.

Let me cite you an example of what is a very common occurrence.

A man with a Grade 4, 5 or 6 education who has worked all his life at manual labor—coal miner—bush worker, or in some such field—has a problem with some government department and writes a letter to the department.

I see these letters every day—the effort of the man in a complex computerized society, trying to make himself understood and lacking, almost entirely, the essential tools with which to do it.

His letter arrives on the desk of some busy civil servant, who, quite understandably does not understand it, or what may be worse, misunderstands it.

He may not always have the time or he may not be sufficiently interested to try to find out the real nature of the problem. He writes his reply couched in the language of his occupation—sometimes referred to as civil servicese.

When it is received by the complainant, he does not understand it, and being a normal human being, he gets upset. He may write another letter, and he may well decide to use the language he is most used to, and which, depending upon his calling or avocation, may be extremely descriptive.

Public servants are human too, and inclined to take umbrage upon having their ancestry traced back three or four generations, with a particularly canine tinge.

The result is that you have an impasse, and unless the original complaint can get to someone higher up who has the necessary remedial authority, he is finished.

An injustice may have been done and this is where the ombudsman comes in.

I may make an investigation either on a complaint, which must be written, or I may make an investigation of my own volition.

Generally speaking, I am not authorized to investigate matters which lie entirely within the jurisdiction of local government, such as cities, municipalities, counties, or of course, the federal government.

I may not intervene in matters which are before the courts or in the decisions of courts, although I have on occasion taken an opinion expressed by a court and endeavored to have it implemented where no such action has already been taken, if it refers to a government agency.

One of the most difficult messages to get across to the public is that my office is not an office of initial complaint. I am not authorized to investigate where there is a right of appeal or objection or a right to apply for a review on the merits of the case to any court or tribunal—until after that right of appeal or objection, etc., has been exercised, or until after the time prescribed for the exercise of that right has expired.

Thus you will see that you should not come to the ombudsman with your initial complaint until you have exhausted all the existing avenues of review or appeal.

He is not a replacement for long-established appeal procedures. He follows after they have been found insufficient.

On the other hand, where any act or section of an act specifically provides that there shall be no appeal from a decision under that act or section, you may at once take your case to the ombudsman, and he has the authority to investigate it.

I have been asked to investigate cases 30 to 45 years old, where every witness was dead and the complainant usually old, had nursed his grievance through the years until it became an obsession. . . .

If the complaint is frivolous or vexatious, or is not in good faith, I may decline it or if a person has not sufficient personal interest in the subject matter of his complaint.

This helps me dispose of the man who simply wants to take a wide swipe at government right across the board and opens up by suggesting that I reduce the salaries of the premier, the members of the cabinet, members of the executive council and members of the entire legislative assembly.

Somewhere between 50 and 60 percent of the complaints I receive are completely out of my jurisdiction, dealing with business affairs, marital problems, neighborhood squabbles and so on.

If I had to take complaints orally, my whole staff and myself would be occupied seven days a week, 24 hours a day doing nothing but listening.

When they are received by letter, those matters outside my jurisdiction can be disposed of fairly quickly by a return letter.

Let me hasten to add however, that I accept almost any form of written communication from the uneducated and the semi-literate.

If we do not understand the letter, we will see the complainant personally. We will, and have, provided an interpreter where necessary, and stay with the complainant until we completely understand the nature of his complaint.

In my work I am provided with two particularly useful tools. One is the authority by which I may require that any government department or government agency file be produced for my scrutiny.

The other tool is the authority I have to get to whatever desk I need to get to, including that of the minister himself, to present my views and to make out a case for the complainant where I consider it justifiable.

I have a permanent solicitor, and I have the benefit of his legal advice, as does the complainant.

I consider the most fundamental requirement for the successful conclusion of a case, is a thorough investigation by competent and fully experienced investigators and in this respect I am well served.

I have in addition to the solicitor and two investigators, a Complaints Analyst, and a secretary and stenographic staff.

Keeping in mind that the complainant usually does not have the resources of the department to support his case, I commence my investigation in a completely impartial manner, until I reach a point where I consider the complaint is justified.

I then move over into a position of advocacy for the complainant and I become his representative, using all the authority which is given me by the legislature in an effort to have the injustice or discrimination rectified.

The majority of the cases which are rectified are done so as a result of informal discussions between myself and senior departmental officials.

The more informal the proceedings can be kept, the less danger there is in formal and delaying confrontation.

If the matter cannot be settled in this manner, I then submit my opinions and recommendations to the minister in writing, where I think the case is justified.

If we are unable to resolve the matter and I am still convinced of the justness of my cause, I may then submit my opinions and recommendations to the cabinet. I have only had to do this twice.

In the event that I fail to convince the cabinet and my views remain firm, I submit my opinion and recommendations to the speaker of the legislature.

A report is then tabled in the legislature and becomes a public document available to the news media. Furthermore, I may publish through the news media reports of general matters or on particular cases in the interests of a complainant or perhaps of a department.

This is an authority which I would be inclined to use if the legislature were not sitting and I had some complaint which I considered urgent and important, and was unable to have it remedied in any other way.

The first full year I was in office, 1968, we received a total of 535 complaints.

In 1969 that figure was exceeded by the end of September.

There is a fantastic variety in the types of complaints with which I deal.

Probably the one which created the most publicity was that of a man who spent 30 years in a mental hospital, the last 22 of which he was sane and was unable in any way to get an independent review of his mental condition.

Such a review is automatic for persons medically committed to a mental hospital.

This man was arrested for the murder of his infant son and another child. He was found not fit to stand trial by reason of insanity, and committed to a mental hospital.

Eight years later he was found sane and fit to stand his trial. The jury found him not guilty by reason of insanity at the time of the offence.

He was returned to the mental hospital and remained there for 22 years as a sane man, despite the fact that at no time had he exhibited anything but the utmost co-operation with the hospital authoriies.

Medical reports had been submitted to the attorney-general's department urging his release, but as he was committed under the Criminal Code, a federal act, he was not entitled to the obligatory review available to those persons committed under the provincial Mental Health Act.

He wrote me, and I secured a recommendation to the lieutenant-governor from the attorney-general for his release.

At my recommendation he was granted a lifetime pension and some additional funds to help him set up a modest apartment. He is approximately 60 years of age and with his background, practically unemployable.

I had two other contrasting cases.

In the first, three men working in a remote area came to the nearest town on payday and two of them became intoxicated. The third left them and they followed him, knocked him down and robbed him of $400.

They were arrested shortly after and all the money they had between them was removed by the police and submitted to the courts.

The amount was approximately $581 or $181 more than they had stolen. They were convicted and sentenced to 18 months and two years respectively.

In the meditative atmosphere provided by the prison, it dawned on one of them that he and his friend had received none of their own money back following the case.

He inquired, only to be told that the $581 had been paid out in restitution.

He wrote to the ombudsman. Investigations verified the fact that the clerk of the court had in fact paid in restitution $181 more than the men had been convicted of stealing.

I was able to obtain restitution for the two prisoners. . . .

It is from the area of the gut issues of human life in our society that I receive the great majority of my complaints, workmen's compensation, public welfare, child welfare, medicare, property rights, compensation for property used for public utilities.

Health, home and hunger are still the most fundamental human problems.

I face some hostility in certain quarters, but when I accepted this trust, I knew I was not entering a popularity contest.

If there are two qualities which I think are absolutes in the qualifications for an ombudsman, they are patience and a certain quiet obstinacy.

Once, in discussing what I considered a very serious injustice, with an official of a department, he, in justifying the action taken by his department, said: "But we did nothing unlawful."

Where such thinking exists, it becomes the duty of the ombudsman to make it clear that legal justice and natural justice are not always synonymous.

BIBLIOGRAPHY

Parliamentary Procedure

Beauchesne, A., (ed.), *Rules and Forms of the House of Commons,* Toronto, Carswell, 4th ed., 1958.

Bourinot, J. G., *Parliamentary Procedure and Practice in the Dominion of Canada,* Toronto, Canada Law Book Co., 3rd ed. 1903.

Canada, *Standing Orders of the House of Commons, October, 1969,* Ottawa, Queen's Printer, 1969.

Dawson, W. F., *Procedure in the Canadian House of Commons,* Toronto, University of Toronto Press, 1962.

Functioning of Parliament

Abel, A. S., "Administrative Secrecy," *C.P.A.*, Vol. XI, No. 4, 1968.

Aitchison, J. H., "The Speakership of the Canadian House of Commons," in Clark, R. M., (ed.), *Canadian Issues: Essays in Honour of Henry F. Angus*, Toronto, University of Toronto Press, 1961.

Anderson, S. V., *Canadian Ombudsman Proposals*, Berkeley, University of California, 1966.

Balls, H. R., "The Public Accounts Committee," *C.P.A.*, Vol. VI, No. 1, March, 1963.

Bishop, P. V., "Restoring Parliament to Power," *Q.Q.*, Vol. LXXVII, No. 2, Summer, 1970.

Blair, R. S., "What Happens to Parliament?" in Lloyd, T., and McLeod, J. T., (eds.), *Agenda: 1970*, Toronto, University of Toronto Press, 1968.

Brownstone, M., "The Canadian System of Government in the Face of Modern Demands," *C.P.A.*, Vol. XI, No. 4, Winter, 1968.

Burke, E., "Speech to the Electors of Bristol," in *Speeches and Letters on American Affairs*, London, Dent, Everyman's library, 1908.

Corry, J. A., "Adaptation of Parliamentary Processes to the Modern State," *C.J.E.P.S.*, Vol. XX, No. 1, February, 1954.

Dawson, W. F., "Parliamentary Privilege in the Canadian House of Commons," *C.J.E.P.S.*, Vol. XXV, No. 4, November, 1959.

Forsey, E. A., "The Extension of the Life of Legislatures," *C.J.E.P.S.*, Vol. XXVI, No. 4, November, 1960.

Forsey, E. A., "Parliament's Power to Advise," *C.J.E.P.S.*, Vol. XXIX, No. 2, May, 1963.

Forsey, E. A., "The Problem of 'Minority' Government in Canada," *C.J.E.P.S.*, Vol. XXX, No. 1, February, 1964.

Hawkins, G., (ed.), *Order and Good Government*, Proceedings of 33rd Couchiching Conference, Toronto, Canadian Institute on Public Affairs, 1965.

Hockin, T. A., "The Advance of Standing Committees in Canada's House of Commons: 1965 to 1970," *C.P.A.*, Vol. XIII, No. 2, Summer, 1970.

Hoffman, D., and Ward, N., *Bilingualism and Biculturalism in the Canadian House of Commons*, Document 3 of the Royal Commission on Bilingualism and Biculturalism, Ottawa, Queen's Printer, 1970.

Hopkins, E. R., "Streamlining Parliament," *Canadian Banker*, Vol. LX, No. 2, Spring, 1953.

Jewett, P., "The Reform of Parliament," *Journal of Canadian Studies*, Vol. 1, No. 3, November, 1966.

Johnson, J. K., (ed.), *The Canadian Directory of Parliament, 1867-1967*, Ottawa, Public Archives of Canada, 1968.

Kersell, J. E., *Parliamentary Supervision of Delegated Legislation*, London, Stevens and Sons, 1960.

Knowles, Stanley, *The Role of the Opposition in Parliament*, Toronto, Ontario Woodsworth Memorial Foundation, 1957, (pamphlet).

Kornberg, A., "The Social Bases of Leadership in a Canadian House of Commons," *The Australian Journal of Politics and History*, Vol. XI, No. 3, December, 1965.

Kornberg, A., "Caucus and Cohesion in Canadian Parliamentary Parties," *The American Political Science Review*, Vol. LX, No. 1, March 1966.

Kornberg, A., *Canadian Legislative Behaviour: A Study of the 25th Parliament*, New York, Holt, Rinehart and Winston, 1967.

Kornberg, A., and Thomas, N., "The Purposive Roles of Canadian and American Legislators: Some Comparisons," *Political Science*, Vol. XVIII, No. 2, September, 1965.

Kornberg, A., and Thomas, N., "Representative Democracy and Political Elites in

Canada and the United States," *Parliamentary Affairs,* Vol. XIX, No. 1, Winter, 1965-66.

Lamontagne, M., "The Influence of the Politician," *C.P.A.,* Vol. XI, No. 3, Fall, 1968.

Laundy, P., "Procedural Reform in the Canadian House of Commons," in Lankster, R. S., and Dewor, D., (eds.), *The Table Being the Journal of the Society of Clerks-at-the-Table in Commonwealth Parliaments for 1965,* London, Butterworth, Vol. XXXIV, 1966.

Lloyd, T., "The Reform of Parliamentary Proceedings," in Rotsein, A., (ed.), *The Prospect of Change,* Toronto, McGraw-Hill, 1965.

Macdonald, Donald S., "Change in the House of Commons—New Rules," *C.P.A.,* Vol. XIII, No. 1, Spring, 1970.

Mallory, J. R., "Delegated Legislation in Canada: Recent Changes in Machinery," *C.J.E.P.S.,* Vol. XIX, No. 4, November, 1953.

Mallory, J. R., "The Uses of Legislative Committees," *C.P.A.,* Vol. VI, No. 1, March, 1963.

Mallory, J. R., "Vacation of Seats in the House of Commons: The Problem of Burnaby-Coquitlam," *C.J.E.P.S.,* Vol. XXX, No. 1, February, 1964.

Normandin, P. G., (ed), *The Canadian Parliamentary Guide, 1966,* Ottawa, 1966, (annual).

Power, C. G., Michener, D. R., *et al.,* "Focus on Parliament," [A collection of articles written on various aspects of Parliament], *Q.Q.,* Vol. XLIII, No. 4, Winter, 1957.

Premont, J., "Publicité de documents officiels," *C.P.A.,* Vol. XI, No. 4, Winter, 1968.

Robertson, R. G., "The Canadian Parliament and Cabinet in the Face of Modern Demands," *C.P.A.,* Vol. XI, No. 3, Fall, 1968.

Rowat, D. C., "An Ombudsman Scheme for Canada," *C.J.E.P.S.,* Vol. XXVII, No. 4, November, 1963.

Rowat, D. C., "How Much Administrative Secrecy?," *C.J.E.P.S.,* Vol. XXXI, No. 4, November, 1965. (See also "Comments," *ibid.,* Vol. XXXII, No. 1, February, 1966.)

Rowat, D. C., *The Ombudsman: Citizen's Defender,* Toronto, University of Toronto Press, 1965.

Rowat, D. C., "Recent Developments in Ombudsmanship," *C.P.A.,* Vol. X, No. 1, March, 1967.

Schindeler, F., "The Role of the Opposition in Ontario," Address to the 38th Annual Meeting of the Canadian Political Science Association, Sherbrooke, P.Q., June 10, 1966.

Schindeler, F. F., *Responsible Government in Ontario,* Toronto, University of Toronto Press, 1969.

Smith, D., *The Speakership of the Canadian House of Commons: Some Proposals,* A paper prepared for the House of Commons' Special Committee on Procedure and Organization, Ottawa, Queen's Printer, 1965.

Thorburn, H. G., "Parliament and Policy-Making," *C.J.E.P.S.,* Vol. XXIII, No. 4, November, 1957.

Turner, J., *Politics of Purpose,* Toronto, McClelland and Stewart, 1968, especially chap. 2, "The Member of Parliament."

Ward, N., "Called to the Bar of the House of Commons," *Canadian Bar Review,* Vol. XXXV, No. 5, May, 1957.

Ward, N., *The Canadian House of Commons: Representation,* Toronto, University of Toronto Press, 1950.

Ward, N., "The Committee on Estimates," *C.P.A.,* Vol. VI, No. 1, March, 1963.

Ward, N., *The Public Purse: A Study in Canadian Democracy,* Toronto, University of Toronto Press, 1962.

FOURTEEN

THE LEGISLATIVE PROCESS: SENATE

The Senate continues to be affected by the wave of change and the proposals for change that have been so evident in the Canadian political system in recent years. In the second edition of this book it was noted that between 1962 and 1966 the Senate had been altered in two respects. An amendment to the British North America Act in 1965 (14 Eliz. II, C.4) required senators appointed thereafter to retire at 75 years of age rather than to hold office for life and it offered generous retirement pensions to encourage former appointees to choose to retire voluntarily if they were 75 years of age or more. The relevant sections of this statute may be found in the second edition of *Politics: Canada*, pp. 290-293. (The second edition also noted in passing that this amendment was one of the few enacted by the Canadian Parliament under the authority of the amending power conferred on it by Amendment No. 2 in 1949.) The second change effected in the period from 1962 to 1966 created a Divorce Commissioner to assist the Senate's Divorce Committee in performing its role. For an article explaining that change, see the second edition, pp. 293-295.

The new retirement provision still holds, of course, but since the second edition appeared the Senate has been deprived entirely of its remaining function in granting divorces by the Divorce Act which went into effect early in 1968. The Senate dealt with its last petition for divorce (most of which had originated from Quebec and Newfoundland) on November 26, 1969, when the courts in these two provinces assumed jurisdiction in this subject, completing the roster of provinces to do so.

Proposals for reform of the Senate have taken a spurt recently. The notion is anything but new since the Senate as an institution has been criticized continually almost from its inception in 1867. (See, for example, a good discussion of reform of the Senate by its own members in one of their debates in 1951, reprinted in part in the first edition of this book, pp. 227-246.) But the subject has been revived lately by the federal government which raised the possibility of reform in its white paper, *Federalism for the Future*, Ottawa, Queen's Printer, 1968, p. 26, presented to the first Federal-Provincial Constitutional Conference in February, 1968, and then offered some specific proposals for reform in its white paper, *The Constitution and the People of Canada*,

Ottawa, Queen's Printer, 1969, pp. 28-34 and 76-78, tabled at the Second Meeting of the Constitutional Conference in February, 1969.

The federal proposals are summarized and appraised in detail by Professor E. Donald Briggs in an excellent article which appears in an edited form in this chapter. The article by Anthony Westell which follows points out how reluctant the present prime minister has been to make the traditional sort of patronage appointments to the Senate, in the hope no doubt that the existing institution might be reformed, although he has not been able to hold back on all occasions. The chapter concludes with a pair of extracts from the *House of Commons Debates* which exemplify two familiar approaches to the problem of the Senate. Stanley Knowles, NDP MP, argues for the total abolition of the Senate while a former government spokesman defends the maintenance of the institution for traditional reasons.

The bibliography lists the few recent books and articles that have appeared on the Senate.

REFORM OF THE SENATE: A COMMENTARY ON RECENT GOVERNMENT PROPOSALS*

E. DONALD BRIGGS

The perennial, time-worn question of Senate reform has again come to the fore in Canada. Like many of his predecessors, Prime Minister Trudeau promised reform of the upper house when he first took office. Since that time Senate Government Leader Paul Martin has on several occasions indicated that he is anxious to see its role in government recognized and extended. Moreover, some official suggestions for reform have already been put forward. These are contained in the white paper, *The Constitution and the People of Canada*, published in February 1969. [See *ibid.*, pp. 28-34.]

The suggestions are of two sorts. First, on the organizational side, it is proposed that a review of the distribution of Senate membership be undertaken; that the term of office for Senators be reduced to a set number of years, (perhaps six, with a possibility of reappointment); and, probably most important, that Senators be "partly appointed" by the provincial governments. Second, on the functional side, it is suggested that the Senate's powers be curtailed in some respects and extended in others. The curtailment would result from providing that "in the general legislative process" the House of Commons would be enabled to over-rule rejection of a bill by the upper house (p. 32). The extension would come from giving the latter

* From an article by the author in the *Queen's Quarterly*, Vol. LXXVII, No. 1, Spring, 1970. By permission of the author. The author wishes to thank his colleagues, Professor K. G. Pryke and C. L. Brown-John, for helpful suggestions during the preparation of this article.

"special responsibility" in dealing with legislative measures concerning human rights and the official languages, as well as the right to approve appointments to the Supreme Court, ambassadorial positions, and the chairmanships of cultural agencies. Over these specific matters it is proposed that the Senate should have an absolute veto.

These proposals are under consideration. . . . [But] so far, little public comment of any kind has been made on them.

In putting the proposals forward the Government has been motivated by more than the desire to "improve" the Senate. Senate reform and the revitalization of Canadian federalism are apparently seen as closely linked, and the purpose of the suggested changes is stated to be to enable the Senate "to play a more vital role in reflecting the federal character of our country" (p. 28). In these and other suggestions for constitutional change, however, the Government was also concerned with maintaining the customary responsibility of the cabinet to the House of Commons alone—hence the rejection of such ideas as that for a directly-elected Senate. The proposed Senate changes are consequently described as providing "the best balance between the principles of responsible and representative government and the need in a federal state for the adequate protection of regional and cultural interests" (p. 32).

There are, however, a number of things about these proposals which are both surprising and puzzling. In the first place, it is not entirely obvious that changes in the method of handling many of the matters over which it is proposed to give the Senate special power are either necessary or desirable in and of themselves. To most Canadians the manner in which ambassadors, for instance, have been appointed has been unobjectionable. It is not easy to see, either, how these proposals are related to, or can be expected to solve, the principal problems of federalism, or what value there may be in them if they do not tend in this direction. Finally, the extent to which they would be effective in reforming or upgrading the Senate may also be questioned, particularly since the new duties proposed for the upper house are plainly of no great significance in terms of the general governmental burden of the central administration.

These considerations are not equally relevant to the organizational proposals, of course, but it may be argued that the latter are unlikely to be effective in improving the position or reputation of the Senate either, unless the functional changes succeed in transforming it into an obviously important body. Each of the proposals has its own weaknesses, however, and they are consequently better discussed individually than collectively.

ORGANIZATIONAL REFORM

The proposal which by itself seems likely to cause least difficulty is that of a specific term of office for Senators. Sinecures for life or even to age seventy-five have only one thing to recommend them: they ensure that once Senators are appointed they will be relatively immune from pressure by the appointing authority. That this is a principle of paramount importance with respect to judicial and perhaps some other offices is obvious, but its applicability to legislators is considerably more doubtful. It may be argued, in fact, that if the Senate is to become even partly a provincial or regional instrument, then Senators should be to some degree responsive to the wishes or policies of their provincial governments. In general, too, a less static membership for the upper house would probably be advantageous. Whether it would prove to be equally desirable to have federally-appointed Senators subject to pressure from the federal cabinet is more problematic, but this problem will be taken up more fully below.

In much the same way, the proposal to review the distribution of Senate seats seems, on the face of it, reasonable enough. As the white paper points out, no such review has been undertaken since confederation, though the original regional balance was upset by assigning Newfoundland an extra six seats when it became a province in 1949. There are admitted inequalities—or at least peculiarities—in the present distribution. Not only does the Atlantic region have thirty seats as compared with twenty-four for each of the other regions, but there are inconsistencies as between individual provinces, particularly between those in the east on the one hand and those in the west on the other. It is difficult, for instance, to reconcile New Brunswick's ten senatorial seats with British Columbia's six when the former has fewer than seven hundred thousand people and the latter close to two million.

It may be argued that since representation in the Senate has always been on a regional basis, comparisons of individual provinces in this way are not relevant. Once the possibility of redistribution is raised, however, such inequalities become a legitimate subject for consideration, particularly as the Government in this case has not revealed the basis on which it thinks redistribution should be undertaken. The fact that some Senators are to be appointed by the provinces also promises to make provincial as against regional representation more important than in the past.

Representation in second legislative chambers, of course, especially in federal systems, is not normally on the basis of population; witness the fact that each state in the United States has two Senators when they vary in population from Alaska's two hundred and fifty thousand to New York's seventeen million. Rather, the idea is that interested blocs or geographical areas should be represented to provide a balance with the population-based representation in the lower house. The simplest and perhaps the most logical way of accomplishing this is to give equal representation to each of the federated units, as has been done in the United States. A Canadian Senate composed of ten representatives from each province would therefore be logical, were it not for the fact that this would mean reducing Quebec's share of the total seats from approximately 23.5 percent to a mere 10 percent at precisely the time that province is demanding recognition of its special linguistic and cultural position within confederation. Granting, then, that Quebec should be accorded special recognition, other difficulties also appear. The west, for example, and perhaps the Maritimes as well, would be less than happy if their strength were to decline in relation to Quebec's. Ontario might also be a problem, but might feel less strongly about it than the west provided a reasonable balance were maintained between French and English Canada as a whole.

Given such difficulties, however, one is tempted to suggest that it might be better to leave things as they are. In view of the Government's declared intention of making the Senate the guardian of regional and cultural interests, however, this would not be without difficulties either. To date, the Senate has not been of any great importance to any of the provinces, and hence the distribution of its seats has not been of much importance in their eyes either. But, obviously, if it is to be rededicated to their use, this will no longer be the case, and redistribution will almost inevitably be demanded by one or more of them. It was undoubtedly recognition of this fact that led to the Government's somewhat tentative inclusion of such a review in its proposals. Needless to say, the same factors which are likely to make review necessary will also intensify the difficulties of achieving it.

With a minimum of good will on all sides, however, a solution should not be beyond the ingenuity of our collective political leadership. Two formulas might be suggested as containing at least some of the elements out of which a solution might be constructed. The first would be to provide for a ninety-seat house in which Quebec would be given one-third, or thirty seats, with the remaining two-thirds being divided equally among the other three regions (twenty seats each). The second, and perhaps from the aesthetic point of view the better, formula would again allow Quebec thirty seats, but out of a total of one hundred and twenty, with each of the other nine provinces having ten. In the first case all three "English" regions would lose strength relative to Quebec, but provided the blocks were equally distributed among the eastern and western provinces (five each) the most glaring inequalities between the provinces of these regions would be eliminated. Under the second formula, Quebec would retain approximately the same proportion of the total seats as she has now (actually a gain of 1.5 percent), while relative to her the east would make a slight gain and the west a considerable one. Ontario would obviously be the big loser relative to all the other regions, but it may be doubted whether there is any good reason for treating her differently from the other largely English provinces. Either of these formulas, or some variation thereon, would be more logical and would reflect existing political realities more precisely than present arrangements.

Theoretically, therefore, redistribution presents no great problem, and it would certainly seem to be desirable from a number of points of view. Of the organizational proposals, however, both the most substantive and the most uncertain in result is that of making appointments partly provincial. Two obvious and interrelated questions arise from this proposal. First, what does, or should, "partly" mean? Second, why, when the declared object of Senate reform is to create a house which will reflect more precisely "the federal character of our country," are the provinces to be allowed to appoint only some of the Senators but not all of them?

The white paper gives no indication whatever of what the Government may have in mind by "partly," but it does indicate the Government's feeling that while it is necessary to give expression to provincial interests, "the interests of the country as a whole should continue to find expression in the Senate to maintain there an influence for the unity of Canada" (p. 30). Presumably it is that portion of the Senate which will continue to be appointed by the federal cabinet which is expected to be such an influence.

One may sympathize with the objective of giving expression to the interests of the country as a whole, but whether the federal appointment of some Senators is necessary to achieve this, or whether Senators so appointed would actually constitute an influence for unity is questionable. The Government appears to anticipate that provincially appointed Senators will be so preoccupied with parochial interests that unless some counter-balance is provided chaos or deadlock or some such catastrophe will result. It should not be forgotten, however, that the Senate is and will continue to be only the second legislative chamber, with no independent existence or mandate of its own. Legislation will continue to be initiated largely by the cabinet and discussed by the Commons from a predominantly national viewpoint, and it will be the duty of the Senate to take the traditional "sober, second look" at what is passed to it from the lower house or directly from the cabinet. As long as cabinet and Commons do their work effectively, therefore, there is little chance that "the interests of the country as a whole" will be neglected or that these interests could be ignored by even the most parochially-minded Senate. It is true that provincially-oriented Senators may be inclined to be more critical of federal legislative proposals, and critical from a different point of view, than present ones, but this would seem to be precisely the purpose and value of having them in the Senate in the first place; they would bring a new and different perspective to the work of the central government, and hopefully by so doing would pave the way for better understanding and more co-operation between the different levels of government.

What the Government means by unity, and what the connection is between it, the presence of federal appointees in the Senate, and the expression of "national" interests, is far from clear in any case. Is it unity within the Senate which is sought? Or concurrence of the Senate with the "national" view of the federal cabinet? One might be excused for suspecting that it is the latter which concerns the Government most, since there seems little reason to assume that the provincial or regional orientation of its members would necessarily mean inability to achieve at least sufficient unity to reach decisions in the upper house. Apart from anything else it is reasonable to suppose that voting would ultimately resolve differences in a provincially-oriented Senate as elsewhere in democratic institutions.

The degree to which federal appointees might be able to act as catalysts in reconciling conflicting provincial viewpoints is also doubtful. Federal no less than provincial appointees must be from somewhere, and even if they should in theory be selected at large rather than on a regional or provincial basis, a reasonable distribution over the country would be necessary. When and if federal and provincial views should conflict, minority groups of federal appointees would likely to find themselves caught between two pressures: to act in accordance with their provinces' interests or views on the one hand, or to conform to the central government's view on the other. If they should tend to lean to the latter, they would be less likely to exert influence in the direction of unity than to form simply another faction within the chamber—a "they" group against which opposition might even solidify. If they should tend to "go provincial" on the other hand, any advantage of federal appointment, except that of patronage, would be lost. In neither case would they contribute to Senate unity in any obvious way.

Assuming the validity of this line of reasoning, and assuming that it could not have been overlooked by the drafters of the reform proposals, it follows that the provision for the continued appointment of some Senators by the federal government is likely to have been intended not only to provide patronage but also a means of preventing or discouraging excessive divergence between the Senate and the cabinet. However, both the need for and the wisdom of attempting to "build in" unity in this fashion must be questioned. Undoubtedly the primary responsibility for governing the country must continue to rest on the federal cabinet and the directly elected representatives in the House of Commons and consequently the forceful expression of their views must be guaranteed. But as it was pointed out above, there is little danger that this would cease to be the case even if the Senate were entirely devoid of "national" spokesmen. Moreover, it must be remembered in this context that except with regard to a very few, not very significant matters, the "new" Senate is not to have a deciding voice in any case: the Commons is to be given power to overrule it in all "general legislative matters." While this is not a power which should be resorted to on any regular basis, it would provide a means whereby the government could, if necessary, ensure that its view of the country's interests would prevail.

Use of this procedure, furthermore, would at least be honest. It would bring differences between federal and provincial authorities into the open and provide an issue upon which voters could ultimately pass judgement. This would be less true if federally appointed Senators, either because of their numerical superiority (we are not told that they will not be numerically superior, though we might hope that the Government's intentions are more honourable than that) or for some other reason, were able to circumvent differences within the Senate itself. An "arranged" unity, however, would obviously be no unity at all, and a Senate so constituted as to provide an appearance of unity would, from the point of view of federalism, be no advance over present arrangements. Unfortunately, indications are that the Government is not yet ready to face that fact. But since the Government does not propose giving the Senate sufficiently important functions to cause the provinces to take a very active interest in its deliberations or the performance of its members, all of this becomes somewhat beside the point. The "new" Senate, as it materializes from the present proposals, is simply never likely to be sufficiently concerned with, or important in relation to, the major issues of federalism to make federal-provincial confrontations within it a serious threat to harmony on Parliament Hill. This, of course, makes the Government's concern for unity even more unnecessary.

These factors are of immediate and practical as well as long-term and theoretical importance. Apart from anything else, if the proposed changes in the Senate are to be successful at all, it is essential that the provincial governments should be satisfied that they, or their appointees, will have a real and significant role to play in the new institution. If they are not convinced of this from the outset they are unlikely to take seriously such appointive responsibilities as they are finally accorded, and as a result the quality of Senate membership is likely to give far more legitimate cause for concern than it has to date. The white paper obliquely recognized the importance of this when it expressed the hope that federal and provincial governments "would engage in healthy competition" to ensure that the best men available would be appointed to the upper house (p. 34).

Provincial attitudes are likely to be determined largely by two factors: the proportion of Senate membership to be appointed by them, and the importance of the functions to be performed by the house. The first is self-explanatory in that there is a direct relationship between the number of representatives and the importance of their role. On the other hand, numbers alone mean little if the functions of the house are unimportant. We must consequently turn now to an analysis of the proposals for functional reform. These, unfortunately, are perhaps even more open to criticism than the organizational ones.

FUNCTIONAL REFORM

The proposal to accord the Senate "special responsibility" with respect to legislation affecting civil rights and the official languages may seem unobjectionable and natural given the special interest which Quebec in particular has in some of these matters. In terms of the extent of the national government's powers and legislative responsibilities, however, it cannot be said to be particularly significant, nor are civil and language rights matters with which the provinces, with the exception of Quebec, are either especially concerned or especially competent to deal.

Moreover, in view of the Government's intention to entrench a comprehensive Charter of Fundamental Rights in the constitution, it may be questioned whether legislative safeguards are necessary even from Quebec's point of view. The proposed Charter is to contain guarantees of linguistic as well as the customary legal and human rights, and once it has been enacted all of these matters will presumably be protected by the courts against legislative encroachments. . . .

Much the same can be said for the confirmation powers which are proposed. On the one hand they seem unlikely to elate the provinces with the opportunities they present for participation in the essentials of the governing process at the national level, and on the other their inherent value also seems open to question.

The proposal to have ambassadorial appointments, for instance, approved by the Senate will almost certainly come as a surprise to most Canadians. Many, it seems safe to say, will find the reasons behind the proposal puzzling, and the benefits to be derived from such a procedure—for the Senate, the provinces, the country, or the diplomatic corps—perhaps even more so. . . . Moreover, . . . there are cabinet prerogatives of far greater potential danger than the right to appoint ambassadors or, for that matter, judges of the Supreme Court, and these proposals would therefore be of comparatively little significance in that connection. . . .

One would not have thought, either, that the provinces would have any great interest in participating in the appointment process. With the possible exception of one, in fact, it seems safe to say that they have not. Quebec, however, has in recent years developed a well-publicized penchant for dabbling in international affairs. . . . While it is by no means clear that Quebec would consider indirect participation in the appointment of ambassadors (and/or, for that matter, the heads of cultural agencies) a satisfactory substitute for the freedom of action which, as a "nation," she claims as her necessary right, it is clearly something of this kind that the Government hopes to achieve. . . . Nevertheless, to institutionalize provincial participation in even such a relatively minor matter as the appointment of ambassadors is surely to concede that the provinces have some legitimate interest in the international field, and such a concession could make additional encroachments more difficult to resist.

The proposal that appointments to the Supreme Court also be subject to confirmation by the Senate has a similar origin and is undoubtedly expected to yield similar advantages. Quebec has also long contested the competence of the Supreme Court to decide constitutional issues between the provinces and the central government. . . . What the Government is now proposing is a compromise, which, as in the case of ambassadors and cultural agencies, concedes the principle but refuses to go the distance. It seems clear, in fact, that the Government's whole design for Senate reform has been motivated primarily by, and is aimed primarily at providing a solution to, the "Quebec problem." . . .

It may equally be argued that the Government has shown little real interest in Senate reform *per se*. . . . What is more important, however, is that the proposed changes, organizational and functional, collectively constitute only very minor surgery which is at best, calculated to cure some peripheral ills rather than the inherent feebleness of the patient.

By far the most serious and insistent criticism of the present Senate is that it serves no useful function. Unfair as this criticism is in a number of respects, it may be argued that it is the first problem with which reform measures should deal, and that measures which fall short of this goal are not reform in any real sense at all. Since the special tasks visualized for the new Senate are largely ritualistic, and since its power is to be largely confined to these tasks, it seems unlikely that the position or the reputation of the upper house will be substantially improved by the proposed changes.

Both these problems could, at least in principle, be fairly simply solved, and without making the Senate into a rival of the Commons in any significant sense. All that would be necessary would be to convert the Senate into what I have elsewhere called a "House of Provinces," [see bibliography for reference] which would be composed of representatives of the provincial governments, and which would be given the power of approving all measures falling within the area of joint federal-provincial responsibility. Such an arrangement would give the Senate the obvious *raison d'être* it has always lacked, and at the same time ensure the continuing interest of more than one province in its operations.

. . . At the constitutional conference of June 1969, the federal government agreed that the provinces should have the power to block federal spending in provincial areas of jurisdiction (i.e., cost-sharing programmes). The means, however, by which the provinces would exercise this power was not spelled out. According to press reports, Prime Minister Trudeau had suggested an arrangement under which any two of the four senatorial districts could veto federal spending in areas of provincial jurisdiction, but this, along with alternative formulas proposed by the provinces, was referred for further study. . . .

There seems to be here an obvious opportunity to combine the search for appropriate machinery for federal-provincial co-operation with the movement to make the Senate an instrument of federalism. Why should the upper house not become the continuing federal-provincial conference which could thresh out such matters as well as take responsibility for such specific tasks as are contained in the proposals under discussion here? . . .

. . . The key would be to ensure senatorial responsiveness to provincial policies, and this could be accomplished by seconding members of provincial governments to the Senate on whatever basis individual provinces might think desirable. There would thus be no specific term of office for Senators at all (except perhaps for federal appointees, if these should still be regarded as necessary), and perhaps no specific membership as such. This would provide the maximum of flexibility from the provincial point of view, while the importance of the senatorial responsibilities would at the same time ensure that careful consideration would at all times be given to selecting suitable representatives. From the federal point of view such a Senate would be powerful, but with a provision that the Commons could overrule except with regard to matters designated as of legitimate provincial concern, its effective strength would be sufficiently channelled so that the authority of the House of Commons and the cabinet's primary responsibility to it would also be preserved.

Nevertheless, there is no doubt that this would be a radical departure from the traditional concept of the Senate and of second chambers generally, and it is not easy to predict all the consequences which might follow if it were adopted. While it would almost certainly bring the Senate publicity and recognition of the kind it has never before enjoyed, it would not be the type of recognition which Senator Martin and some others have been urging and it is perhaps not even certain that a "House of Provinces" of this type could to the same extent carry on the kind of work for which these spokesmen consider it to deserve recognition. As they have rightly pointed out, the Senate at present makes a considerable contribution to the governing process by its extensive committee work, and by giving detailed and in some cases first-instance study to legislative proposals, thus saving much time for the hard-pressed House of Commons. They believe that these functions could and should be extended still further, and it would undoubtedly be useful if they were. Would a House composed largely or entirely of untenured ambassadors of the provinces be able to perform such functions?

The answer is not clear one way or the other, but whether this is the most important consideration may be questioned in any case. The point is that because of a variety of pressures from a variety of sources means have to be found to institute a new kind of federalism. At the same time, for equally varied reasons, Senate reform seems to have been accepted as desirable and necessary. . . .

. . . Is it to be reformed, or is it, in a phrase recently used by Senator Keith Davey on the CBC, merely to be "tinkered with?" Is it to be made a genuine instrument of federalism and protector of provincial and regional interests, or merely a device for spiking the guns of Quebec? The white paper does not give much ground for encouragement on either score. Certainly if the "reforms" are instituted as proposed the result will be that the Senate will be far worse off than before. Its effective power will have been curtailed and confined to a few largely ritualistic tasks, a fact which will not fail to impress the public as confirmation of its inherent uselessness. The quality of its membership is likely to decline since provincial regimes can hardly be expected to devote much energy or care to the selection of people to perform tasks of little direct importance to them, and since political debts at the provincial level are unlikely to be owed to individuals who are very familiar with or interested in federal affairs. Consequently, not even the traditional functions of the Senate referred to above could be expected to be performed as well as at present. Neither, of course, is all this likely to do anything whatever for the state of Canadian federalism in any general sense.

Real Senate reform cannot be accomplished without giving it something of obvious importance to do. Neither can the real needs of Canadian federalism be accommodated by the Senate without giving it authority over matters of substance. Both mean making the Senate powerful in at least some respects. If that is not a prospect which the Government can accept, it would perhaps be better to leave the Senate as it is, concentrate on extending and publicizing its traditional functions, and look elsewhere for solutions to the problems of federalism. It will certainly be unfortunate however, if some more serious attempt is not made to solve both problems with one blow by turning the Senate into something approaching a "House of Provinces."

TRUDEAU'S LONG DELAY SHOWS NAMING SENATORS IS AN AGONIZING TASK*

ANTHONY WESTELL

Prime Minister Pierre Elliott Trudeau has on his desk a long list of nominees to fill 13 vacant seats in the Senate, and is expected soon to make his choices from among them.

* From the *Toronto Daily Star*, November 18, 1969. By permission of the publisher.

He has already delayed too long. One of the vacancies dates back to 1966, another to 1967, and several to last year. At a time when the upper house is increasing it investigative and legislative activities, the shortage of members makes it difficult to man all the committees.

It was generally expected that Trudeau would recommend the appointments before the new session of Parliament began last month. But he pleaded the priority of other, more urgent problems demanding his attention.

Such procrastination is more the rule than the exception in the appointment of senators. Prime Minister R. B. Bennett, who held office 1930-35, began the bad habit by allowing 19 vacancies to accumulate. Mackenzie King juggled at one time with 18 empty seats. Louis St. Laurent was so undecided that at one time 23 places, almost a quarter of the total, were empty.

The truth is that making appointments to the upper house is one of the most delicate and unrewarding tasks to confront every prime minister. Candidates are pressed on them from every side and when they make their choices, they upset far more people than they please.

It is not only the unsuccessful candidates who are disgruntled, but also, very often, the powerful political figures who have nominated them. . . .

The task is steadily becoming more difficult. From the early days of Confederation, it was assumed that appointments would be partisan; that is, a Grit PM would appoint Grit senators and a Tory PM would appoint Tory senators, with no argument of quibbling.

The first prime minister, Sir John A. Macdonald, appointed 117 senators, all Conservatives except two who were personal friends. Sir Wilfrid Laurier appointed 81 Liberals.

There was no real problem about partisanship as long as the office of prime minister changed hands between the parties, and the balance in the Senate could be restored from time to time. But during the 22 years of Liberal government prior to 1957, the number of Tory senators dwindled to five, and there was rising agitation for a better, less partisan balance of appointments.

The basic reason that Louis St. Laurent allowed 23 vacanies to accumulate was that he could not see his way through this problem. He was under the usual pressure to reward his own supporters, but he could hardly appoint a new flock of Liberals when there were so few sitting Tories. So, like other PMs before and since, he procrastinated.

When St. Laurent finally made four non-partisan appointments in 1955 he received an inordinate amount of praise for such statesmanship. But even that did not really solve his problem, and he went out of office in 1957 with 14 Senate seats empty—a fact bitterly resented by the Liberal party and its hopeful nominees.

John Diefenbaker was able to appoint Tories without much criticism because there was clear need to build up the Conservative ranks in the Senate.

But nothing did more to undermine Lester Pearson's claim to be a New Politician than his partisan record of Senate appointments. His motives and his integrity were impugned every time he appointed a Liberal, regardless of the man's merits and the sanction of tradition.

This is what makes Trudeau's task so difficult. He has to cope not only with the competing pressures upon him from within the Liberal party, but also with the public expectation that he will rise above patronage.

His list of nominees is made up from several sources. The senior minister from each province in which vacancies occur is expected to propose candidates.

Thus Arthur Laing, public works minister, has a say in filling the four vacant seats from British Columbia; Jim Richardson, supply and services minister, puts up names for three seats from Manitoba; Allan MacEachen, manpower and immigration minister, nominates candidates for two seats from Nova Scotia; and so on.

Influential Liberals from outside Parliament, provincial premiers, for example, also submit recommendations, and some people call attention to their own claims.

The government leader in the Senate, oddly enough, is not always consulted. But the present leader, Paul Martin, is making such vigorous efforts to improve the image of the upper house that it is reasonable to assume he is pressing the Prime Minister for distinguished appointments.

Trudeau himself is approaching the problem in the organized and rational way which characterizes his administration. His staff have been making extensive inquiries about possible candidates to give the Prime Minister plenty of material on which to work when he makes his choice.

They are hopeful that he will resist fierce party and patronage pressures to set a new, high standard in the selection of members of the upper house.

ABOLISH THE SENATE*

Mr. Stanley Knowles (Winnipeg North Centre) moved the second reading of Bill No. C-15, to amend the British North America Act, 1867 (abolition of the Senate).

He said: Mr. Speaker, the purpose of this bill is to abolish the Senate. . . .

The bill itself, Mr. Speaker, is one which most hon. members have seen on previous occasions, because this is not the first time I have introduced it. Indeed, my arguing for the abolition of the Senate goes back over a period of many years.

●   ●   ●

* From *House of Commons Debates*, April 1, 1966, pp. 3758-3765. By permission of the Queen's Printer.

May I say, Mr. Speaker, that this bill is not being presented in the context of recent appointments to the other place. Public opinion about those appointments already has expressed itself in various ways. It is not presented out of special concern over the amount of money which it costs to maintain the upper house; neither is it presented in relation to anything the Senate has done or failed to do in recent months. I present it, if I may do so, in an academic sense; I present it on the basis of an appeal to the common sense of Canadians.

May I put it this way: if we in this House of Commons, or we as Canadians who happen to be here in this House of Commons, were called upon to draft a constitution for democratic government for the people of Canada, I do not know the details of the constitution we might produce, but I am reasonably certain we would start with the principle of democracy. I am reasonably certain we would stick with that principle; we would say that the main thing we should provide would be that the people who would govern the country would be elected by the people themselves.

I submit that, if we worked out provisions for election machinery, somehow bringing together in this capital city 200 or 300 members to represent the people, formulate their laws and provide for their government, having done so we would not then take the further step of providing for some one man to appoint a body of another 100 people, non-elected, who would have the authority to veto the decisions of the elected representatives. Is that not precisely what we have in the kind of parliament we have now?

●   ●   ●

Mr. Grant Deachman (Vancouver-Quadra): Mr. Speaker, I am delighted to have the opportunity of talking out this bill this evening because had I not risen in my place to see this bill through six o'clock, the Senate I am sure would no longer have existed on the morrow. I certainly hope that my party and my Prime Minister will see fit to reward me for this service to the other place in a way in which they would not otherwise be able to reward me had I chosen to stay in my place.

I want to say that the argument of my hon. friend, the hon. member for Winnipeg North Centre (Mr. Knowles) was ably presented in this house, but being an abolitionist, it appears he also wishes to abolish the Senate. I commend to him that he look again at the old institution, so that when this bill is again reached in the order of public bills, we can debate this question perhaps a little differently. . . .

An hon. Member: Six o'clock.

Mr. Deachman: Had I been going to speak longer on the subject I should have brought with me stories going back to 1926 with which to regale the hon. member.

Mr. Speaker: Order, please. The hour for consideration of private members business has now expired.

At six o'clock the house adjourned without question put, pursuant to standing order.

NO — NOT YET*

Mr. John R. Matheson (Parliamentary Secretary to Prime Minister): Mr. Speaker,
. . . I would remind hon. members, before we talk in terms of destroying a constituent part of parliament, that there was much reason and logic to the creation of this particular institution, the Senate, by the founding fathers.

This evening I spent some time reading the address given by the then Attorney General, John A. Macdonald, on February 6, 1865, in the parliamentary debates on the subject of the confederation of the British North American provinces. One cannot read this lengthy address by this constitutional authority of the day without appreciating that many of the problems facing the colonies of those days still continue to exist in Canada.

Actually, though my experience in this house is very limited in comparison with that of the hon. member for Winnipeg North Centre (Mr. Knowles), I remember vividly the year 1961 when on two occasions, in the case of class and kind legislation and in the Coyne affair, many Canadians were grateful for the existence of the other place. Sir, economic life today is governed by a mixture of private decisions taken in the corporate sector of the economy and of public decisions taken by governments, with the latter constantly assuming greater importance.

I do not think there is any argument that in the post-war years there has been a profound change in distribution of income and in economic organization, and this is to the good. But to do this soundly and well there have to be certain constitutional safeguards. It is a fact that government action brings more and more aspects of life and affairs within its orbit. Perhaps one can even say that the citizen is progressively stripped of effective influence on certain directions of government. Perhaps it is the Senate in certain particulars which becomes the great safeguard of the liberties of the public. I think of some of the persons presently holding seats in the other place whose wisdom, judgment and experience in matters of civil liberties and in matters of welfare and economic change are significant and important to the future growth and well-being of this country.

Mr. Deputy Speaker: Order, please. The time allotted to the hon. gentleman has expired.

Mr. Knowles: The Senate is saved by the bell.

* From *House of Commons Debates*, May 17, 1966, p. 5258. By permission of the Queen's Printer.

BIBLIOGRAPHY

Albinski, H. S., "The Canadian Senate: Politics and the Constitution," *American Political Science Review,* Vol. LVII, No. 2, June, 1963.

Briggs, E. D., "The Senate: Reform or Reconstruction?" *Q.Q.,* Vol. LXXV, No. 1, Spring, 1968.

Canada, *Rules of the Senate of Canada,* Ottawa, Queen's Printer, 1964.

Dawson, W. F., "Parliamentary Privilege in the Senate of Canada," Address to the 38th Annual Meeting of the Canadian Political Science Association, Sherbrooke, P.Q., June 8, 1966.

Hopkins, E. R., "Financial Legislation in the Senate," *Canadian Tax Journal,* Vol. VI, No. 5, September-October, 1958.

Kunz, F. A., *The Modern Senate of Canada, 1925-1963, A Re-appraisal,* Toronto, University of Toronto Press, 1965.

Lambert, N., "Reform of the Senate," *Winnipeg Free Press,* Pamphlet No. 30, April, 1950.

Lee, B., "Age and Criticism Do Not Weary Them," *The Globe and Mail,* Toronto, February 7, 1966.

Lyon, P. V., "A New Idea for Senate Reform," *Canadian Commentator,* July-August, 1962.

MacKay, R. A., "How to Reform the Senate," *Canadian Commentator,* May, 1963.

MacKay, R. A., *The Unreformed Senate of Canada,* Toronto, McClelland and Stewart, revised edition, 1963.

MacKay, R. A., "To End or Mend the Senate," *Q.Q.,* Vol. LXXI, No. 3, Autumn, 1964.

MacNeill, J. F., "Memorandum for Senator Robertson, re the Senate, Reasons Given by Proponents of Confederation for Constituting a Second Chamber," Ottawa, Senate, February 16, 1950.

Morin, J. Y., "Un nouveau rôle pour un Sénat moribund," *Cité libre,* Vol. XV, juin-juillet, 1964.

Newman, P. C., "Pearson's Senate Choices—Odd Kind of 'New' Politics," *Toronto Daily Star,* November 17, 1964.

Orban, E., *Le Conseil législatif de Québec,* Montréal, Bellarmin, 1967.

Turner, J. N., "The Senate of Canada—Political Conundrum," in Clark, R. M., (ed.), *Canadian Issues: Essays in Honour of Henry F. Angus,* Toronto, University of Toronto Press, 1961.

FIFTEEN
THE ADMINISTRATIVE PROCESS

This chapter takes a broader approach to the administrative side of government than did the comparable chapter in the second edition. The change is indicated by the alteration of the title from the "Civil Service" in the second edition to "The Administrative Process" in the present edition. Thus, this section deals less with specific issues within the civil service than with more general but probably also more important problems emanating from the existence of a huge bureaucracy in our midst in the modern democratic, collectivist state.

One justification for this shift in emphasis, if any is needed, is that many of the major changes which were being introduced into the public service of Canada when the second edition went to press and which seemed novel then are now operating almost routinely. Hence, for example, there is little need to repeat the essence of the Civil Service Act of 1961, which was described by Mr. S. H. S. Hughes in an article that can be found in the first edition on pp. 164-172, or the recommendations of the Glassco Royal Commission on Government Organization, which proposed overhauling the structure of the civil service and which were reprinted in the second edition, pp. 226-230. Collective bargaining also has been implemented in the public service since the second edition appeared. Thus, this edition contains an article giving a brief, factual account of its introduction and an extract from a speech reflecting on how the process has been working, given by the man who ought to know, the Hon. C. M. Drury, who as President of the Treasury Board is in charge of collective bargaining.

Since bilingualism in the civil service has become a goal towards which the present government is working with a specific policy whose essence has been set down in the *Official Languages Act* which has been reproduced in Chapter 4 *supra*, it is unnecessary to repeat here the selections from the *House of Commons Debates* which appeared in the second edition outlining the policy (pp. 238-240) and weighing its advantages and disadvantages (pp. 241-242). However, it should be noted that the latter discussion concerning the extent to which bilingualism imperils the merit principle in the civil service is still a major part of the continuing debate over the wisdom of seeking to have a bilingual public service.

The chapter moves to broader considerations with the inclusion of an extract from

Professor Rowat's now famous article attacking the amount of administrative secrecy that is adhered to in Canada today. His article will be popular with the growing body of citizens who resent and deplore the tendency of bureaucracies and governments to wrap every issue in a mystery within an enigma stamped "confidential." They undoubtedly will applaud also his solution, which is to shift to the more open Swedish system. The House of Commons' Special Committee on Statutory Instruments was of much the same mind as Professor Rowat when it submitted its Third Report recommending that certain steps be taken to cope with the evils that have accompanied the recent swelling tide of delegated legislation in Canada. These recommendations are reprinted in full in this chapter.

Not all is gloom in the administrative process, however. An article by the editor notes that there is a new trend by governments in Canada to grant to their civil servants greater freedom to participate actively in politics. The Hon. Mitchell Sharp, who has had experience as both a senior civil servant and an elected politician, discusses this facet of the relationship between the expert and the politician as well as some other interesting aspects of the administrative process.

The bibliography at the end of the chapter is divided into three sub-sections that deal with various aspects of administration, including problems of crown corporations. Undoubtedly the best consistent source of scholarly and professional discussion of administrative issues in Canada is the quarterly journal of the Institute of Public Administration of Canada, *Canadian Public Administration*. Several books of readings dealing with this area have appeared recently. For references to them, see the bibliography.

THE INTRODUCTION OF COLLECTIVE BARGAINING IN THE PUBLIC SERVICE*

The Public Service Staff Relations Act came into force on March 13, 1967. Introducing collective bargaining into the Public Service, it represents one of the most important developments in the history of the relations between the Canadian Government and its employees.

For many decades, Public Servants had virtually no say in determining the terms and conditions of their employment. Indeed, their role has been compared to that of a petitioner, occasionally successful in presenting a brief. By the mid 1950s, however, a clear consensus had developed among the Public Service employee associations in favour of collective bargaining and, for the next ten years, the Government of Canada was under growing pressure to make it available to its employees. . . .

* From *External Affairs*, Monthly Bulletin of the Department of External Affairs, Vol. XIX, No. 5, May, 1967, pp. 184-186. By permission of the Queen's Printer.

It was clear . . . that, if collective bargaining was to function effectively, a new and simpler system of job classification and pay would have to be introduced. The old system, introduced in 1919, was too cumbersome to provide a logical framework for bargaining rights or the negotiation of pay-rates. It did not enable the Government to respond flexibly to changes in outside rates of pay while retaining the necessary relation of rates between jobs within the Service. . . .

In order that collective bargaining may function effectively, it has also been necessary to establish a central management agency. The Treasury Board was chosen for this role, and has been given the necessary powers by the Financial Administration Act, which also came into effect on March 13. Under the terms of this legislation, the Board will be authorized to act for the Government, subject, of course, to the Government's direction, on all matters relating to personnel and financial management, general administrative policy and the organization of the Public Service. It will also serve as the principle agent of the Government in the collective bargaining process and will be authorized to establish rates of pay, hours of work and other conditions of employment.

Certain of the powers granted to the Treasury Board by the Financial Administration Act were exercised previously by the Civil Service Commission. Consequently, a third bill, called the Public Service Employment Act, providing for their transfer to the Board, was passed and came into force on March 13 to replace the old Civil Service Act. Under its terms, the Public Service Commission, as it is now called, will be responsible for staffing the Public Service with qualified personnel. Other responsibilities include the creation of a variety of training and development programmes and the provision of certain advisory services.

Taken together, the reclassification programme and the three measures, which have some roots in the recommendations of the [Glassco] Royal Commission on Government Organization as well, represent one of the most dramatic changes ever to take place in the legislation governing the Public Service.

The introduction of collective bargaining into the Public Service is also making increasing demands on employee associations. To meet the challenge, two of the largest—the Civil Service Association of Canada and the Civil Service Federation of Canada—merged in January of this year to form the Public Service Alliance of Canada. Other associations also have stepped up their activities. [For example], Foreign Service Officers from the Department of External Affairs and the Department of Trade and Commerce have responded by forming their own organization—the Professional Association of Foreign Service Officers. . . .

Under collective bargaining, Public Servants, through their associations, will have a much greater say in determining the terms and conditions of their employment. The grievance procedure, which the Act requires each Department and Agency to set up, will ensure that employees' complaints receive a full hearing, if they wish, at the highest level. Disputes concerning the interpretation of collective agreements and arbitral awards or disciplinary actions by the employer may in certain instances be referred to arbitration or adjudication, an arrangement which provides a further guarantee that the rights of employees and their associations will be fully protected. The independent Public Service Staff Relations Board, established by the Act, is responsible for seeing that both parties to collective bargaining comply with the requirements of the Act. . . .

SOME REFLECTIONS ON COLLECTIVE BARGAINING IN THE PUBLIC SERVICE*

C. M. DRURY

. . . In the short period of 2½ years since the Public Service Staff Relations Act was proclaimed, the Treasury Board as the employer has dealt with no less than 79 bargaining units covering almost 190,000 employees in the first round of collective agreements alone. Already 71 of these units—covering close to 180,000 employees—have signed first round agreements and second round agreements for 2 units covering some 3,500 employees have been signed. Second round negotiations are presently underway for an additional 24 bargaining units which cover close to 80,000 employees and we hope to have second round agreements completed with these groups very shortly.

Many common problems have been aired over the past few years, and many specific objections raised to collective bargaining in the Public Service. . . .

A common objection is that, insofar as the Treasury Board is concerned, the decisions are pre-ordained. It is said that we know in advance how much money we are prepared to give, how many holidays we are prepared to accept, what fringe benefits, what hours of work, what kinds and extent of leave we are prepared to grant and that the negotiations leading up to these decisions are completely meaningless.

I should like to state once and for all that such is not the case. I do not mean by this that the Treasury Board goes into collective bargaining with a completely clean slate. Like any employer, we calculate pretty closely in advance how much we can afford to give and where we have to put on the brakes. . . . Settlements arrived at in the Public Service tend [also] to be taken as indicators in the private sector and we cannot, therefore, if we wish to keep inflationary trends under control, agree to wage increments that are particularly inflationary. . . .

The introduction of collective bargaining brought many new concepts and many new ideas into the Public Service. A good example of this new thinking was demonstrated in the manpower adjustment program which . . . [involved layoffs]. There is absolutely no doubt in our mind that management has the right and the responsibility to make the decisions regarding layoff policy. However we do have

* From a speech given on October 1, 1969, by the Hon. C. M. Drury, President of the Treasury Board. By permission of the author.

a moral and legal responsibility to consult with the unions on this subject. And this we did. Through the convenient form of the National Joint Council—a body consisting of representatives of both the staff side and the official side—we raised the problem of manpower adjustment and solicited the opinions of the staff associations concerned. We got plenty of suggestions in reply. We formed a smaller committee and worked with the staff side to develop the guidelines which were subsequently published. . . .

Another example is in the contentious issue of Medicare. Once again, through the National Joint Council, we had developed an understanding with the staff associations concerning the payment of Medicare premiums. . . .

Consultation carries over beyond the point at which an agreement is signed between the Federal Government as an employer and the unions which represent its employees. In fact, the whole complex business of the administration of contracts poses some of the most difficult problems we have to cope with in this modern area of collective bargaining. This is particularly so during the first years when we are negotiating and setting up contracts covering long periods of retroactive pay, when new unions are being certified, when new bargaining positions are being developed, and when whole new concepts are being introduced in the government service. . . .

When it faces the possibility of a major strike, the Government as an employer must necessarily tend to think in terms beyond its immediate responsibility as an employer. We must, in fact, weigh the cost of the settlement against the cost of the strike. . . .

We have had a major strike and we have had some wild cat strikes in the Public Service since collective bargaining came to pass. We undoubtedly shall have some more. There will undoubtedly be many Canadians who will decide that collective bargaining in the Public Service is a mistake and should be eliminated. I submit that this has not been proven. I submit that collective bargaining has, by and large, been successful in the Public Service and will become a greater success as we gain experience in the use of this important part of the democratic process.

HOW MUCH ADMINISTRATIVE SECRECY DO WE NEED?*

DONALD C. ROWAT

To question the principle of administrative secrecy is to question a long-cherished tradition of the British parliamentary system. Yet when one explores the full range of its adverse effects one cannot help but ask whether it conforms with the requirements of modern democracy. . . .

* From *The Canadian Journal of Economics and Political Science*, Vol. XXXI, No. 4, November, 1965. By permission.

In Canada, several professional groups have been complaining about the effects of administrative secrecy upon their own particular realm of activity without realizing that it is a more general and basic problem. First, there are the newspapermen and broadcasters. They complain that because of civil service anonymity they must work in a crazy world of illicit purveyors of official information who, like gossipers, give them a story but insist that they must not tell anybody, or that if they publish it, they must not give its source. They also object to the many meetings of boards, commissions, and local councils which are closed to the press and public. Scientists complain that the wall of military secrecy prevents the free flow of information essential to scientific development. Historians and other scholars find that they have no right of access to public documents. No rules exist regarding types or ages of documents which they may see, and the granting of access is entirely at the discretion of the department concerned. Lawyers complain about the tradition of Crown privilege, a tradition so extreme that the Government has a right to refuse an official document to a court even though it may contain essential evidence.

To the average citizen, "the administration" is anonymous, faceless, and impervious. He has no right of access to official information, even if he has a personal interest in a case. He may get so little information about a decision against him that he has no way of knowing whether it was made by unfair procedures or for improper reasons. Such a situation is an irresistible temptation to arbitrary action.

There is so much evidence of the undesirable effects of administrative secrecy that I believe the time has come to question the entire tradition. After all, it is based on an earlier system of royal rule in Britain that is unsuited to a modern democracy in which the people must be fully informed about the activities of their government. Has not this tradition been preserved by politicians and officials mainly for their own convenience? Is it absolutely necessary? I wonder whether we have ever really faced these questions.

It is important to realize that any large measure of government secrecy is incompatible with democracy. This is true for two reasons. First, secrecy leads to distrust and fear on the part of the public. If one does not have full access to the facts one can easily imagine the worst. Yet the decisions made by party caucuses, cabinets, and federal-provincial conferences at the very apex of our political system, are made in secret. Much of the political process is hidden from the people, and they can hardly be blamed if they imagine the worst. . . . Second, the people cannot control their government without knowledge. Yet the means available to the opposition parties and to the public for obtaining information about administrative activities are woefully inadequate. Opposition MP's usually have to dig vital information out of a reluctant Government. Often they do not know what to ask for because they do not know what is really going on behind the clouds surrounding Mount Olympus. Our system is based on the premise that we must trust the Government and hope for the best. This is entirely too paternalistic a concept for a democracy. Parliament and the public cannot hope to call the Government to account without an adequate knowledge of what is going on; nor can they hope to participate in the decision-making process and contribute their talents to the formation of policy and legislation if that process is hidden from view.

. . . Since the principle of secrecy in the British parliamentary system has been imbibed with our mother's milk, so to speak, we find it hard to believe that a country can get along without it. . . . [Yet] it is indeed true that for almost two hundred years the Swedish Constitution has provided for open access to official documents and full information to any citizen about administrative activities.

This provision is so unusual, perhaps unique in the world, that one immediately thinks of the many circumstances under which secrecy is desirable. How can such a provision work successfully in practice? Are there not serious limitations upon its application? The answer is that of course there are limitations, and these are provided for in the Constitution itself. But the important point is that the *principle* has been reversed: whereas in most countries all documents are secret unless a specific authority is given for their release, in Sweden they are all public unless legal provision has been made for them to be withheld. . . . In general the right of free access is to prevail, and this right shall be subject *only* to the exceptions listed. The Constitution goes on to say that the specific cases in which official documents are to be kept secret shall be "closely defined" in a special statute. As one might expect in a modern welfare state, this law, called the Secrecy Act, spells out an impressive list of matters that must be kept secret. . . .

A full appreciation of the impact of the principle of open access can be gained only by giving some examples of the extensiveness of its operation. It applies, for example, to public documents kept by all sorts of administrative agencies, from government departments to police officers, administrative tribunals, and local governments. Even Parliament is under the rule; for instance, a citizen can demand to see the minutes of its committees. Moreover, anybody is entitled to ask for documents; he does not have to show that he has a legal interest in seeing them nor is he obliged to say for what purpose he wants them. To make sure that agencies do not purposely delay in answering a request, the Constitution provides that a requested document shall be "made available immediately or as soon as possible," and the courts in their judgments have taken this rule seriously. The definition of "public document" includes not only those prepared but also those received by a public authority. And their availability to the newspapers has been organized as a routine service. . . .

I believe that the Swedes are right. The principle of open access to administrative information is essential to the full development of democracy. The Commonwealth countries have inherited the tradition of secrecy from an earlier era of absolute monarchy, and have not yet succeeded in throwing off this tradition because it has suited the convenience of modern governments. In spite of the enhanced need for secrecy in certain areas resulting from the Cold War, the logic of democracy demands that the long-term trend be in the direction of the principle of publicity. This trend may be seen in the growth of vast public information services for modern democracies, in the relaxation of the fifty-year rule, and in the steady development of legislation in the United States towards the Swedish principle of open access. My recommendation for Canadians, then, is that we should prepare to abandon the principle of secrecy.

Barry Mather has recognized the writing on the wall by presenting at this session of Parliament a private member's bill designed to establish the publicity principle. [Bill C-39; first reading, April 8, 1965.] Though the bill is only one page long, it contains the main elements of the Swedish scheme. . . .

An important benefit of open access is the participation of the public in the formation of policy. The public have a chance to criticize and discuss proposals *before* decisions are made. One of the disabilities of our present system is that the Government has no easy way of testing public reaction to a measure before it is presented in almost final form to Parliament. Hence, the Government must resort to royal commissions to stir up interest and form a public opinion on proposed measures. In Sweden and other parliamentary countries of Western Europe, draft bills are made public and widely discussed with all interested groups *before* being presented to the legislature.

There is no doubt that cabinet responsibility would work somewhat differently under the principle of publicity. But this may be all to the good: it may make the cabinet *more* responsible. . . . There are good grounds for the belief that, under the Commonwealth parliamentary system, the cabinet is too dominant. Being in a position to accept or reject proposed reforms, Governments naturally tend to reject proposals that would limit their own powers. . . .

INTERIM PROPOSALS

. . . I should like to make a number of [interim] proposals designed to overcome some of the worst disadvantages of administrative secrecy. First, the Government should be far less "hush-hush" about its security screening and secrecy classification procedures. . . .

Immediate steps should also be taken to make documents more readily available to scholars. Until now the Canadian Government has followed the unsatisfactory practice of departmental discretion, trusted favourites, and no rules except meticulous adherence to the rules of other countries where Canadian documents contain information from these countries. . . . A much shorter period, say twelve years, should be adopted as the norm, with clear authority required to keep sensitive documents longer than this, and discretion to release non-sensitive documents earlier. . . .

Another valuable step towards the necessary disclosure of administrative information would be the establishment of Ombudsmen for the federal and provincial governments. The main argument for an Ombudsman, or independent parliamentary commissioner to hear complaints against the administration, is that he could investigate a decision on behalf of the citizen and find out exactly why it was made. . . .

CONCLUSIONS

By now it will be clear, I hope, that all of these proposals should be considered only as interim measures. The outright adoption of the principle of free access to government documents should be our ultimate objective. This does not mean there will be no administrative secrecy. There will always be the problem of drawing a line between the Government's need to deliberate confidentially and the public's need for information. It is simply a question of emphasis. In the past we have been stating the principle the wrong way around: "Everything is secret unless it's made public," instead of, "Everything is public unless it's made secret." . . .

RECOMMENDATIONS FOR CONTROLLING DELEGATED LEGISLATION*

. . . Your Committee wishes to confine itself solely to the area of delegated legislation. Your Committee's contention is . . . that there should be, as a general rule, public knowledge of the processes of delegated legislation before, during, and after the making of regulations, and that any derogation by government from this rule requires justification. . . .

Four hundred and twenty of the 601 Acts of Parliament examined by the Committee (constituting substantially all of the statutes now in force) provide for delegated legislation. Moreover, . . . statutory powers to make regulations have been used very extensively. The following statistics confirm this impression: 6,892 regulations covering 19,972 pages were published in the *Canada Gazette* during the period from January 1, 1956, to December 31, 1968, an average of 530 regulations a year. This does not take into account those regulations which are expressly exempted from publication and also some documents which are perhaps in fact of a legislative nature but are not officially considered to be so by the regulation-making authority. . . .

Your Committee believes that the controls its recommends will provide the safeguards necessary to limit the executive power of law-making without interfering unduly with its exercise.

●   ●   ●

* From the *Third Report of the Special Committee on Statutory Instruments*, Ottawa, Queen's Printer, 1969. (This Committee of the House of Commons met under the Chairmanship of Mr. Mark MacGuigan, MP, and issued its Third Report, containing its recommendations, following the Session 1968-69.) By permission of the Queen's Printer.

SUMMARY OF RECOMMENDATIONS

The following is a summary of your Committee's recommendations:
1. Regulations made in the exercise of the prerogative power of the Governor in Council, insofar as they are of a legislative character, should be subject to

the same procedures and requirements as other regulations of a legislative character.

2. Except in the interests of national security, there should be no exemptions from the requirements of the *Regulations Act* other than as to publication.

3. Rules governing practice or procedure in judicial proceedings should not be excluded from the requirements of the *Regulations Act*.

4. The *Regulations Act* should be amended to provide a more inclusive definition of the word "regulation."

5. The Minister of Justice should be charged with the responsibility of deciding for all regulation-making authorities which documents should be classified as regulations.

6. All departmental directives and guidelines as to the exercise of discretion under a statute or regulation where the public is directly affected by such discretion should be published and also subjected to parliamentary scrutiny.

7. All enabling acts for regulation-making authorities should accord with the following principles:

   (*a*) The precise limits of the law-making power which Parliament intends to confer should be defined in clear language.

   (*b*) There should be no power to make regulations having a retrospective effect.

   (*c*) Statutes should not exempt regulations from judicial review.

   (*d*) Regulations made by independent bodies, which do not require governmental approval before they become effective, should be subject to disallowance by the Governor in Council or a Minister.

   (*e*) Only the Governor in Council should be given authority to make regulations having substantial policy implications.

   (*f*) There should be no authority to amend statutes by regulation.

   (*g*) There should be no authority to impose by regulation anything in the nature of a tax (as distinct from the fixing of the amount of a license fee or the like). Where the power to charge fees to be fixed by regulations is conferred, the purpose for which the fees are to be charged should be clearly expressed.

   (*h*) The penalty for breach of a prohibitory regulation should be fixed, or at least limited by the statute authorizing the regulation.

   (*i*) The authority to make regulations should be granted in subjective terms.

   (*j*) Judicial or administrative tribunals with powers of decision on policy grounds should not be established by regulations.

8. The Minister of Justice should, where he deems it appropriate, refer the enabling clauses in any Government bill to the proposed Standing Committee on Regulations at the same time as the bill is referred to the relevant Standing Committee for Committee consideration.

9. Before making regulations, regulation-making authorities should engage in the widest feasible consultation, not only with the most directly affected persons, but also with the public at large where this would be relevant. Where a large

body of new regulations is contemplated, the Government should consider submitting a White Paper, stating its views as to the substance of the regulations, to the appropriate Standing Committee. When enabling provisions and statutes are being drawn, consideration should be given to providing some type of formalized hearings on consultation procedures where appropriate.

10. The Government should take all necessary steps to facilitate the expansion of the Legislative Section of the Department of Justice and to provide thorough training for legal officers in the Department, including those seconded to other departments, in the drafting of regulations.

11. The present examination of regulations by the Privy Council Office as to form and draftsmanship and by the Department of Justice as to conformity with the *Canadian Bill of Rights* should be continued, and the scrutiny by the Department of Justice should also take into account the other criteria for regulations proposed in this Report.

12. The *Regulations Act* should provide, as a general rule, that a regulation shall not come into force until the date on which it is transmitted to the Clerk of the Privy Council. In cases of emergency a regulation might come into effect at the time of making.

13. Section 9 of the *Regulations Act,* which allows exemptions from the provisions of the Act, should be amended to provide for exemptions from publication and time of publication only.

14. All regulations, regardless of the regulation-making authority, should be available for public inspection.

15. The statutes should resort more than they do now to the use of provisions stating that the regulations made thereunder, or under specified sections thereof, do not become effective until published on some specified period thereafter.

16. Regulations should be consolidated on a much more regular and frequent basis than has been the practice in the past, and at least once every five years.

17. The present quarterly consolidated index and table of Statutory Orders and Regulations should include reference to all regulations which have been exempted from publication.

18. All regulations should be laid before Parliament forthwith after their transmittal to the Clerk of the Privy Council and their recording and numbering by him. *Votes and Proceedings* should list under "Returns and Reports Deposited with the Clerk of the House" the title of each regulation (which should be as descriptive as possible) the Act under which it is made, its date and the date of its transmittal.

19. A new Committee on Regulations should be established, with the following particulars:
    (1) It should be a Standing Committee of the House of Commons.
    (2) All regulations should stand permanently referred to it.
    (3) It should strive to operate in an objective and non-partisan way.
    (4) It should have a small membership to enable it to operate effectively.

(5) To make the objectivity of the Committee apparent, there should be some rotation among parties in the chairmanship.
(6) It should normally sit in public session.
(7) It should be empowered to sit while Parliament is not sitting.
(8) It should have adequate staff.
(9) It should examine regulations on the basis of six criteria:
    (*a*) Whether they are authorized by the terms of the enabling statute.
    (*b*) Whether they appear to make some unusual or unexpected use of the powers conferred by the statute under which it is made.
    (*c*) Whether they trespass unduly on personal rights and liberties.
    (*d*) Whether they have complied with the provisions of the *Regulations Act* with respect to transmittal, certification, recording, numbering, publication or laying before Parliament.
    (*e*) Whether they
        (i) represent an abuse of the power to provide that they shall come into force before they are transmitted to the Clerk of the Privy Council or
        (ii) unjustifiably fail to provide that they shall not come into force until published or until some later date.
    (*f*) Whether for any special reason their form or purport calls for elucidation.
(10) It should have the usual investigative powers of a Standing Committee.
(11) It should have the same power as other Standing Committees to report to the House.
20. The Scrutiny Committee should have the power, in its discretion, to refer regulations to other Standing Committees and that they should then stand referred to such Committees for consideration.
21. Normally Parliament should exercise its power to review by a resolution that a questionable regulation be referred to the Government for reconsideration but Parliament should continue to provide, where appropriate in individual statutes, for a procedure by way of affirmative or negative resolution.
22. The Scrutiny Committee should have the power to report at any time on general matters affecting the law or practice with respect to regulations.
23. Your Committee should be reconstituted in the next session to allow further consideration of certain matters referred to in this Report. . . .

GIVING POLITICAL RIGHTS TO CIVIL SERVANTS

PAUL FOX

. . . For many years it was conventional wisdom that it was best to keep civil servants out of active, partisan politics, that is, from doing anything more daring than voting, such as being a candidate or openly campaigning for a party. The prevailing view was that this sort of restriction was necessary not only to improve the quality of administration but to protect the public servants themselves against accusations of political partisanship. No doubt this attitude was the product of the patronage, office-seeking, venality, inefficiency, and blatant partisanship that pockmarked earlier experience with public employment in Canada, the United States, and elsewhere.

However, most of these evils have now been eliminated from, or at least minimized in, our public service. Indeed, we seem to have succeeded so well in neutralizing our civil servants that the current image of them is of good, gray political eunuchs, harmless to the point of impotence.

Perhaps that explains why the pendulum seems to be swinging back now to favour giving our bureaucrats the right to be politically active if they so choose. Perhaps the reversion in attitude is also the result of the intensified democratic spirit which is abroad in this age and which manifests itself in this respect in urging that civil servants should have the same political rights as other citizens.

Whatever the explanation for the change in attitude and whatever the merits of either view, there certainly has been a pronounced movement recently in Canada towards liberalizing the regulations governing the political activity of public servants. In discussing this subject, Professor T. H. Qualter has pointed out in his book in this Series, *The Electoral Process in Canada,* that:

> In Saskatchewan, under provisions first enacted in 1947, a member of the provincial public service who wishes to be a candidate for public office (presumably this would apply to federal as well as provincial politics) is entitled to leave of absence for the thirty days prior to the date of the election. [See the *Revised Statutes of Saskatchewan, 1965,* C.9, s.62(2).] If the candidate is elected, "he shall be deemed to have resigned his office or place of profit under the Government or his employment in the public service of the province on the day immediately prior to the day on which he was elected." The position of the civil servant is even further protected by the provisions that if he is apparently elected, and resigns, and his election is subsequently set aside or invalidated for any reason, his resignation is automatically withdrawn and he is deemed to have been on leave until such time as the election is finally determined. In an age when so many competent people are in government employment, these are eminently reasonable propositions.

Other jurisdictions in Canada have also loosened their restrictions on public servants engaging in political activity. For instance, the Ontario government sets out in its *Manual of Administration,* published in 1966, in Section IV re Personnel, H-4, the more tolerant policy to be pursued in allowing provincial employees to participate in political activity, as well as in public appearances on radio and television. At the federal level, the Public Service Employment Act [see *Statutes of Canada,* 1966-67, C. 71, s. 32] now permits grants of leave to civil servants to enable them to run for office. According to a report by The Canadian Press on May 28, 1968, at least seven federal government employees had taken advantage of the new opportunity to secure leaves of absence and were running as candidates in the June election. In October, 1969, a press report stated that the new NDP government in Manitoba was considering adopting the former Saskatchewan CCF's policy of allowing civil servants to run for political office without resigning their jobs unless they were to win. These few examples may be a sign of the times and of the change in attitude towards civil servants engaging in politics. . . .

THE EXPERT, THE POLITICIAN, AND THE PUBLIC*

MITCHELL SHARP

I have never felt that my long experience as a senior official [in the civil service] has been a handicap, either in winning a seat or engaging in any other form of political activity—except perhaps with one exception. I must admit that my experience as an advisor and administrator has made me cautious. I have an irresistible urge to understatement, which is not a common characteristic of most politicians and is not always compatible with party propaganda. . . .

So the conclusions that I have reached, based on my own experience and the experience of some of my colleagues, is that professional experience in Parliament, that is, as a professional civil servant, does not unfit a man or a woman for politics; but neither is it likely to induce many officials to forsake their interesting and useful careers to venture forth on to these stormy and unpredictable waters. I do not think that anyone need fear that government is going to be taken over by experts who happened to have served in the public service.

But may I suggest for your consideration that politics is improved by the presence of a few people who have had professional experience in the business of government. There need not be concern either that the presence of former public servants in politics reflects upon the impartiality of the public servants. We should note that in Canada civil servants have the vote; they are not a political unit, and they are not permitted to engage in partisan political activity. Their responsibility

* From *Order and Good Government,* edited by G. Hawkins, Proceedings of the 33rd Couchiching Conference, Toronto, Canadian Institute on Public Affairs, 1965. By permission of the author and publisher.

and their interest is to serve the government of the day to the best of their ability, and this, from my observation, they do. I noted, for example, that I have in my Department today many public servants who had the full confidence of the government that was defeated last year, and I can detect no difference in their attitude towards me from the attitude that I had towards my Minister when I was a civil servant serving under both the Liberal and the Conservative governments. I was not particularly enamoured of the political parties that happened to be in power when I was the civil servant—neither the Liberals nor the Conservatives—and I am certain that civil servants retain that healthy scepticism.

I think it is quite clear that senior civil servants in Canada are people of considerable influence. The efficiency of government depends very much upon them, and that is why their selection and their training is of such vital importance to the nation. I believe, for example, that it is almost as important to be sure that you get men and women of ability into the public service as that you get men of ability and integrity into Parliament. It is true that civil servants are appointed. They have to be appointed by someone. In our system of government, they are appointed by the Civil Service Commission, with the exception of the Deputy Minister; but even in this field the tradition is well established that they are appointed from the ranks of the civil servants. These civil servants enjoy security of tenure and, generally speaking, are beyond the reach of the elected representative of the people. I am inclined to look upon this as a virtue of our system of government.

As a Minister, I want independent advisers around me, advisers who will tell me the facts and who will give me their advice without fear or favour. . . . I do not think it would serve the public interest or our democratic form of government if I had to depend upon advisers whom I had appointed or who had been appointed by the political party of which I happen to be a member, and who would feel they had to please me in their advice. . . .

Permanent civil servants, while they are important people, cannot frustrate the will of government. They do, however, have a powerful influence upon the decisions of government. I suggest that this influence is more often than not for the better, because the civil servants are experienced, and because they have no political axes to grind. The Ministers make the decisions; they have to come before Parliament to defend their decisions. They are not privileged to "pass the buck" to their permanent advisers. Any Minister who got up in the House of Commons and said under criticism that "this is the view of my Deputy Minister, and that's why I did it," would have a very short life as a Minister. . . .

Perhaps this permanent and expert civil service does give the government of the day a great advantage over the opposition in Parliament; to some extent this is inevitable and indeed desirable. The government has the responsibility for governing, and it is in the best interests of the country that it should be able to discharge that responsibility well. . . . The Minister who comes in without experience is more at the mercy of the civil service than is the Minister who has had some experience. I do not believe, however, that the presence of this kind of Minister is essential for the functioning of our parliamentary democracy. I do feel, however, that whether or not in the future there are in the government people who have served as civil servants, the general level of Cabinet Minister qualifications in a professional way are going to rise. As our society becomes better educated, there are going to be more men with professional capacity in the arts that are important to government and who will find their way into politics and into government itself. . . .

. . . There will have to be improvements in the functioning of parliamentary institutions themselves, in order to balance the influence of the expert in the government. In other words, Parliament itself must be able to probe and be prepared to probe very much more deeply into the functioning of government itself. . . . I really am disappointed in the level of probing and debate that goes on in Parliament on many of the issues that are before it, and this arises for many reasons. It is not very popular in the country to spend time trying to understand the intricacies of the problems that face government today; these do not make many headlines. The newspapers are, of course, more inclined to give headlines and space to the Member of Parliament who talks about something that the public readily understands. Unless Parliamentary institutions are improved along the lines I have suggested, it is quite possible that effective control would tend to get out of the hands of Parliament itself. But this need not happen, and I am confident that it will not happen. We shall find ways of coping with it. . . .

Members of Parliament, it seems to me, are rather diffident about approaching civil servants, and often unnecessarily so. I had, when I was a Deputy Minister, a number of Members of Parliament from the opposition who used to come to me and ask for information, and make their submissions on matters in which I had some interest and concern. I found this was perfectly proper; I would not of course give them advice in the sense of advice on policy or anything of that kind, but I was quite happy to give them any information that could be given to them publicly. They were also privileged, of course, to ask questions in Parliament and to obtain the information in that way. I have a feeling that the opposition does not realize that it could get more help from the public service without in any way contravening the proprieties. . . .

. . . If I may speak now as a former civil servant, I was always disappointed when the Minister did not have to use all the material that I had prepared for the ensuing debate, when the opposition failed to raise the points which I was quite sure they would raise. And I think that generally speaking, in the professional civil service, debate is welcomed. The civil servant would like to see the issues of government debated in public. It does not concern him, since he is not committed to do more than serve the government, what the outcome would be. His job is to support the government by advice, by information, and by his administration, and I know, looking back on my own experience, that the debate on the issues with which I would be concerned was welcomed by me; I was very disappointed when the opposition failed to see the chink in the government's armour. . . .

. . . At the end of the war, or at least during the war, there was a great influx of civil servants to Ottawa to handle the very complex problems that arose out of the war and the post-war period of reconstruction. During that time, there were attracted to the public service of Canada people from all walks of life. . . . Now, as our civil service has matured, more and more of the senior officials are those who were recruited from the universities after graduation, and there is less and less of this variety of experience. I have felt, and I think there have been others who have also felt the same way, that it might be desirable if it were possible to introduce into the public service, in order to get a more rounded and varied experience, people who had been in business or had taught at a university, and so on. . . .

BIBLIOGRAPHY

Civil Service

Armstrong, R., "Some Aspects of Policy Determination in the Development of the Collective Bargaining Legislation in the Public Service of Canada," *C.P.A.*, Vol. XI, No. 4, Winter, 1968.

Blackburn, G. A., "A Bilingual and Bicultural Public Service," *C.P.A.*, Vol. XII, No. 1, Spring, 1969.

Callard, K. B., *Advanced Training in the Public Service*, Governmental Studies Number 1, Toronto, The Institute of Public Administration of Canada, 1958.

Carson, J. J., "The Changing Scope of the Public Servant," *C.P.A.*, Vol. XI, No. 4, Winter, 1968.

Civil Service Commission, *Personnel Administration in the Public Service*, Report of the Civil Service Commisson of Canada (Heeney Report), 1958.

Cloutier, S., "Le Statut de la Fonction publique du Canada: Son histoire," *C.P.A.*, Vol. X, No. 4, December, 1967.

Cloutier, S., "Senior Public Service Officials in a Bicultural Society," *C.P.A.*, Vol. XI, No. 4, Winter, 1968.

Cole, Taylor, *The Canadian Bureaucracy, 1939-1947*, Durham, N. C., Duke University Press, 1949.

Cole, Taylor, *The Canadian Bureaucracy and Federalism, 1947-1965*, Denver, University of Denver, 1966.

Côté, E. A., "The Public Services in a Bicultural Community," *C.P.A.*, Vol. XI, No. 3, Fall, 1968.

Department of Public Printing and Stationary, *Organization of the Government of Canada*, Ottawa, Queen's Printer, 1965 (annual).

Deutsch, J. J., "Some Thoughts on the Public Service," *C.J.E.P.S.*, Vol. XXIII, No. 1, February, 1957.

Deutsch, J. J., "The Public Services in a Changing Society," *C.P.A.*, Vol. XI, No. 1, Spring, 1968.

Frankel, S. J., *A Model for Negotiation and Arbitration between the Canadian Government and Its Civil Servants*, Montreal, McGill University Press, 1962.

Frankel, S. J., *Staff Relations in the Civil Service: The Canadian Experience*, Montreal, McGill University Press, 1962.

Gosselin, E., Lalande, G., Dozois, G., Boyd, R., "L'administration publique dans un pays bilingue et biculturel: actualités et propos," *C.P.A.*, Vol. VI, No. 4, December, 1963.

Heeney, A. D. P., "Civil Service Reform, 1958," *C.J.E.P.S.*, Vol. XXV, No. 1, February, 1959.

Hodgetts, J. E., *Pioneer Public Service: An Administrative History of the United Canadas, 1841-1867*, Toronto, University of Toronto Press, 1955.

Hodgetts, J. E., "The Civil Service and Policy Formation," *C.J.E.P.S.*, Vol. XXIII, No. 4, November, 1957.

Hodgetts, J. E., "Challenge and Response: A Retrospective View of the Public Service of Canada," *C.P.A.*, Vol. VII, No. 4, December, 1964.

Hodgetts, J. E., and Duivendi, O. P., "The Growth of Government Employment in Canada," *C.P.A.*, Vol. XII, No. 2, Summer, 1969.

House of Commons, *Minutes of Proceedings and Evidence, Special Committee on the Civil Service Act,* March 20—June 23, 1961, Ottawa, Queen's Printer, 1961.

Kwavnick, D., "French Canadians and the Civil Service of Canada," *C.P.A.*, Vol. XI, No. 1, Spring, 1968.

Tunnoch, G. V., "The Bureau of Government Organization," *C.P.A.*, Vol. VIII, No. 4, December, 1965.

Vaison, R. A., "Collective Bargaining in the Federal Public Service: The Achievement of a Milestone in Personnel Relations," *C.P.A.*, Vol. XII, No. 1, 1969.

Administration

Baker, W. A., "Management by Objectives: A Philosophy and Style of Management for the Public Sector," *C.P.A.*, Vol. XII, N. 3, Fall, 1969.

Balls, H. R., "Financial Administration of the Government of Canada," *Canada Year Book, 1956,* Ottawa, Dominion Bureau of Statistics, 1956.

Balls, H. R., "Improving Performance of Public Enterprise through Financial Management and Control," *C.P.A.*, Vol. XIII, No. 1, Spring, 1970.

Barr, J. J., "A Despotism of Boards Choking Alberta," *The Edmonton Journal,* Feb. 21-22-23, 1966 (in three parts).

Bieler, J. H., Burns, R. M., Johnson, A. W., "The Role of the Deputy Minister," *C.P.A.*, Vol. IV, No. 4, December, 1961.

Bridges, The Rt. Hon. Lord, "The Relationship Between Ministers and the Permanent Departmental Head," *C.P.A.*, Vol. VII, No 3, September, 1964.

Bryden, M., and Gurney, M., "Royal Commission Costs," *Canadian Tax Journal,* Vol. XIV, No. 2, March-April, 1966.

Canada, *Report of the Royal Commission on Government Organization* (Glassco Report), Ottawa, Queen's Printer, 1962-3, 5 vols.

Courtney, J. C., "In Defence of Royal Commissions," *C.P.A.*, Vol. XII, No. 2, Summer, 1969.

DesRoches, J. M., "The Evolution of the Organization of Federal Government in Canada," *C.P.A.*, Vol. V, No. 4, December, 1962.

Doern, G. B., "The Role of Royal Commissions in the General Policy Process and the Federal-Provincial Relations," *C.P.A.*, Vol. X, No. 4, December, 1967.

Donnelly, M. S., *et al.*, "Aspects of Municipal Administration: A Symposium," *C.P.A.*, Vol. XI, No. 1, Spring, 1968.

Forrest, D. G., "Performance Appraisal in Government Services," *C.P.A.*, Vol. XII, No. 3, Fall, 1969.

Hanson, H. R., "Inside Royal Commissions," *C.P.A.*, Vol. XII, No. 3, Fall, 1969.

Henderson, G. F., *Federal Royal Commissions in Canada 1867-1966: A Checklist,* Toronto, University of Toronto Press, 1967.

Hodgetts, J. E., "The Role of Royal Commissions in Canadian Government," *Proceedings of the Third Annual Conference,* The Institute of Public Administration of Canada, Toronto, 1951.

Hodgetts, J. E., "Should Canada Be De-Commissioned? A Commoner's View on Royal Commissions," *Q.Q., Vol.* LXX, No. 4, Winter, 1964.

Kernaghan, W. D. K., "An Overview of Public Administration in Canada Today," *C.P.A.*, Vol. XI, No. 3, Fall, 1968.

Kernaghan, W. D. K., (ed.), *Bureaucracy in Canadian Government,* Toronto, Methuen, 1969.

Lyngseth, D. M., "The Use of Organization and Methods in Canadian Government," *C.P.A.,* Vol. V, No. 4, December, 1962.

Mallory, J. R., "The Minister's Office Staff: An Unreformed Part of the Public Service," *C.P.A.,* Vol. X, No. 1, March, 1967.

McKeough, W. Darcy, "The Relations of Ministers and Civil Servants," *C.P.A.,* Vol. XII, No. 1, Spring, 1969.

McLeod, T. H., "Glassco Commission Report," *C.P.A.,* Vol. VI, No. 4, December, 1963.

Mitchell, H., *et al.,* "To Commission or Not to Commission," *C.P.A.,* Vol. V, No. 3, September, 1962.

Rea, K. J., and McLeod, J. T., (eds.), *Business and Government in Canada: Selected Readings,* Toronto, Methuen, 1969.

Ritchie, R. S., Heeney, A. D. P., MacKenzie, M. W., Taylor, M. G., "The Glassco Commission Report," *C.P.A.,* Vol. V, No. 4, December, 1962.

Santos, C. R., "Public Administration as Politics," *C.P.A.,* Vol. XII, No. 2, Summer, 1969.

Shoyama, T. K., "Advisory Committees in Administration," *Proceedings of the Ninth Annual Conference,* The Institute of Public Administration of Canada, Toronto, 1957.

Stead, G. W., "The Treasury Board of Canada," *Proceedings of the Seventh Annual Conference,* The Institute of Public Administration of Canada, Toronto, 1955.

Steele, G. G. E., "The Treasury Board as a Control Agency," *C.P.A.,* Vol. IV, No. 2, June, 1961.

Steele, G. G. E., "The Role of the Treasury Board," *Canadian Chartered Accountant,* November, 1961.

Tunnoch, G. V., "The Glassco Commission: Did It Cost More Than It Was Worth?" *C.P.A.,* Vol. VII, No. 3, September, 1964.

Tellier, P. M., "Pour une réforme des cabinets de ministres fédéraux," *C.P.A.,* Vol. XI, No. 4, Winter, 1968.

Walls, C. E. S., "Royal Commissions — Their Influence on Public Policy," *C.P.A.,* Vol. XII, No. 3, Fall, 1969.

White, W. L. and Strick, J. C., "The Treasury Board and Parliament," *C.P.A.,* Vol. X, No. 2, June, 1967.

Willis, J., Eades, J. E., Angus, H. F., *et al.,* "The Administrator as Judge," *Proceedings of the Eighth Annual Conference,* The Institute of Public Administration of Canada, Toronto, 1956.

Willms, A. M., "The Administration of Research on Administration in the Government of Canada," *C.P.A.,* Vol. X, No. 4, December, 1967.

Willms, A. M., and Kernaghan, W. D. K., (eds.), *Public Administration in Canada: Selected Readings,* Toronto, Methuen, 1968.

Crown Corporations

Ashley, C. A., *The First Twenty-five Years: A Study of Trans-Canada Air Lines,* Toronto, Macmillan, 1963.

Ashley, C. A., and Smails, R. G. H., *Canadian Crown Corporations,* Toronto, Macmillan, 1965.

Barbe, R. P., "Le contrôle parlementaire des enterprises au Canada," *C.P.A.,* Vol. XII, No. 4, Winter, 1969.

Black, E. R., "Canadian Public Policy and the Mass Media," Address to the 38th Annual Meeting of the Canadian Political Science Association, Sherbrooke, P.Q., June 9, 1966.

Bridges, The Rt. Hon. Lord, "The Relationship Between Government and Government-Controlled Corporations," *C.P.A.*, Vol. VII, No. 3, September, 1964.

Canada, *Report of the Committee on Broadcasting*, (The Fowler Report), Ottawa, Queen's Printer, 1965.

Corbett, D., *Politics and the Airlines*, Toronto, University of Toronto Press, 1965.

Friedman, W., (ed.), *The Public Corporation: A Comparative Symposium*, Toronto, Carswell, 1954.

Hull, W. H. N., "The Public Control of Broadcasting: The Canadian and Australian Experiences," *C.J.E.P.S.*, Vol. XXVIII, No. 1, February, 1962.

Hull, W. H. N., "The Fowler Reports Revisited: A Broadcasting Policy for Canada," Address to the 38th Annual Meeting of the Canadian Political Science Association, Sherbrooke, P.Q., June 9, 1966.

Kristjanson, K., "Crown Corporations: Administrative Responsibility and Public Accountability," *C.P.A.*, Vol. XI, No. 4, Winter, 1968.

Shea, A. A., *Broadcasting, The Canadian Way*, Montreal, Harvest House, 1963.

Spry, G., "The Decline and Fall of Canadian Broadcasting," *Q.Q.*, Vol. LXVIII, No. 2, Summer, 1961.

Weir, E. A., *The Struggle for National Broadcasting in Canada*, Toronto, McClelland and Stewart, 1965.

SIXTEEN

THE JUDICIAL PROCESS

The judiciary has attracted more public attention in recent years than it has previously, although political scientists still tend to discuss it less than many other aspects of Canadian government. However, in part because of the public's aroused interest in justice in general and no doubt because of Prime Minister Trudeau's own long-standing personal and professional concern with the law, including his recent term as minister of justice, the judicial process has been given more attention recently, for example, at federal-provincial constitutional conferences and in the press.

One positive result of this new interest has been the improvement of the administration of justice by the federal government and a number of provinces. Sufficient progress has been made in this regard that it did not seem fair or accurate to repeat in this edition of *Politics: Canada* the scathing criticisms of the judicial process that were levelled against it by Sidney Katz in his article which appeared in the second edition (pp. 247-255), although it is too much to believe that some of his strictures do not still apply to some jurisdictions.

The chapter begins with Professor Peter Russell's original article on the Supreme Court's interpretation of the written Canadian constitution, the British North America Act, since the Court became the final appellate tribunal in 1949. The three judgments that appeared in the first edition have been omitted. The decisions by the Judicial Committee of the Privy Council in the three leading cases of Russell vs the Queen (1882), Toronto Electric Commissioners vs Snider (1925) and Re Weekly Rest, Minimum Wages and Hours of Labour Acts (1937) are now readily available, along with other leading cases, in Professor Russell's paperback, *Leading Constitutional Decisions*. See the bibliography for details, and also for other references to the subject of judicial interpretation, especially Professor W. R. Lederman's useful paperback, *The Courts and the Canadian Constitution*.

The tenor of current discussion of judicial reform is represented here by the reproduction of the proposals for reform of the Supreme Court offered by the federal government under the name of Prime Minister Trudeau in the white paper presented to the second meeting of the Federal-Provincial Constitutional Conference in February, 1969. While few judges have ever had to be removed from the bench in Canada, the next item in the chapter describes one famous instance, which is included less because of its importance than its colourfulness and because it is a rare illustration of the procedure laid down. Martin Knelman's article raises the recurring issue of political appointments to the bench and gives the points of view of several prominent members of the Canadian Bar Association. A recent debate in the House of Commons, reprinted in part here, brought a number of MPs to their feet in defence of the present system. The last item in the chapter indicates that the former government was not prepared to alter tradition by appointing an independent commission to recommend judicial nominations. It should be noted that although the present government has not yet created such a body officially, it has moved in that direction by relying increasingly on the advice of the bar association and its members before making appointments to the bench. The present administration also has improved the quality of the judicial process by discouraging judges from digressing from their duties in court. It has favoured raising the salaries of federal judges appreciably and at the same time has frowned upon their taking on such additional tasks as being royal commissioners or arbitrators in labour disputes. The salaries which were paid to the members of the several different levels of federal courts in Canada in 1963, following an increase in that year, are itemized in a footnote in the second edition, p. 250. Additional sizable increases were approved in 1967 for judges in certain courts; for example, superior and appellate court judges were advanced to $26,000 per annum and county court judges to $19,000. In April, 1970, the Hon. John Turner, minister of justice, told the House of Commons Justice Committee that the need to raise salaries and to improve the pensions of about 425 federally appointed judges was "urgent." He said, "It is becoming increasingly difficult for me to persuade leading practitioners to accept appointments because salaries aren't in line." (According to federal statistics for 1967, self-employed lawyers ranked third highest in income among occupational groups, their reported average being $22,064 a year.)

The bibliography in this chapter includes references to judicial interpretation and to the judiciary in general, but the bibliography on civil liberties has been transferred to the end of Chapter 18.

THE SUPREME COURT'S INTERPRETATION OF THE CONSTITUTION SINCE 1949*

PETER H. RUSSELL

In December, 1949 the Supreme Court of Canada became the final court of appeal for Canada. This was accomplished by the simple expedient of an Act of the Dominion Parliament, the constitutional validity of which had been previously established by a 1947 decision of the Privy Council. With the exception of cases

* Published originally in this book with permission of the author, who is a member of the Department of Political Economy, University of Toronto.

in which the litigation had begun prior to December, 1949, no longer could aggrieved litigants carry their case across the Atlantic and plead before the Judicial Committee of the Privy Council that the decision of a Canadian court be reversed. Now a Canadian court, appointed by the Canadian Government, staffed by Canadian jurists, was Canada's highest judicial organ. Canada had passed another — almost the final—milestone on her road to nationhood.

At the time this change was effected it was only logical that interest in it was focussed primarily on the area of constitutional law. In a federal state with a written constitution defining the boundaries of the national and regional legislatures, the court of last resort, through the process of judicial review, can have an enormous influence on the legislative policies pursued by both levels of government. As Professor Kelsen has said, "A court which has the power to annul laws is consequently an organ of legislative power." Indeed, it was as the arbiter of our Constitution—the British North America Act—that the Judicial Committee had become a centre of controversy in Canada. Now, with that tribunal giving way to the Supreme Court of Canada, there was a great deal of speculation as to how this transition would affect the interpretation of the B.N.A. Act.

Looking forward to the new era of judicial autonomy, two rival patterns of hopes and fears were evident. By far the most vociferous viewpoint was expressed by the Privy Council's critics. They had attacked the Judicial Committee for what they regarded as its unjustified and unwise reduction of Dominion power and they now hoped that an indigenous highest court would emancipate Canada from the stultifying effects of their Lordships' constitutional conceptions. On the other hand, there were those, mainly in French-speaking Canada, who cherished the Privy Council's constitutional handiwork as a vital bulwark of provincial autonomy against the onslaught of centralizing forces. To these, the abolition of appeals looked ominous. The inclusion of a provision in the Supreme Court Amendment Act of 1949, which guaranteed that three of the nine Supreme Court judges would always come from Quebec, did little to offset their fears. They were more impressed by the fact that the Dominion executive appointed all the judges. Hence, those who subscribed to this school of thought were inclined to heed the warnings of those theoreticians of federalism who insisted that to permit one level of government the exclusive power of appointing the umpire of the federal system constituted a serious deviation from "pure federalism."

It is against this background of speculations that we shall examine the Supreme Court's record of constitutional adjudication from the abolition of appeals in 1949 until the end of 1960. The cases discussed deal only with questions concerning the division of legislative powers. With each of the major issues some attempt has been made to indicate the major contrasts, if any, between the Supreme Court's approach and that of the Privy Council.

The most serious charge in the traditional indictment of the Privy Council's interpretation of the B.N.A. Act was that it had reduced Parliament's power to legislate for "the peace, order and good government of Canada" from the position of a residual clause in the division of powers to the status of an emergency power. For those centralists who pressed for a reinstatement of the Dominion's General power, Lord Simon's judgment in the *Canadian Temperance Federation case* of 1946 had provided a new ray of hope. There, Lord Simon, in maintaining the validity of what was virtually the same statute as was involved in Russell v. The Queen, had gone a long way towards undermining the authority of the emergency doctrine. The true test, he stated, of whether the Dominion's General power could be invoked to uphold legislation was not the existence of an emergency but "the real subject matter of the legislation: if it is such that it goes beyond local or provincial concern or interests and must from its inherent nature be the concern of the Dominion as a whole. . . ." The impact of this dictum was partially offset by two later decisions of the Privy Council which returned to the emergency doctrine as the justification for bringing legislation under the General power. Nevertheless, Lord Simon's words were now part of the record, so that, even if the newly emancipated Supreme Court were to assume the yoke of *stare decisis* and consider itself bound by its predecessor's decisions, this opinion could provide the necessary support for extending the scope of the Peace, Order, and Good Government clause beyond emergency situations.

Despite the apparent centrality of "Peace, Order, and Good Government," it has been a key issue in only two of the constitutional cases that have been before the Supreme Court in the past decade. In the first of these cases, *Reference re. Validity of Wartime Leasehold Regulation* (1950), the court was asked to pass on the constitutionality of the Federal Government's rent-control regulations. These orders-in-council had been made under the authority of the National Emergency Transitional Powers Act, which continued those provisions of the War Measures Act that Parliament had deemed necessary for dealing with the economic dislocations arising out of the war. Although the court referred to the Peace, Order, and Good Government clause as the constitutional support for the regulations, in doing so it did not have to go beyond the emergency doctrine. Even this was significant in as much as a number of the judges stated that unless there was "clear and immutable" evidence to the contrary, they would not question Parliament's declaration (in the preamble to the Act) that an emergency exists. This policy in the context of an enduring "cold war" situation might well make even the emergency conception of the General power a more fertile source of legislative capacity. It is worth noting that during the 1950s two of the statutes which entailed the widest extension of Dominion power were the Defence Production Act and the Emergency Powers Act.

It was the case of *Johannesson v. West St. Paul* (1952) that provided a more revealing test of the Supreme Court's treatment of "Peace, Order, and Good Government." Here, the constitutional issue revolved around the competing claims of the Dominion Parliament and the Manitoba Legislature to make laws regulating the location of aerodromes. The court was unanimous in sustaining the Dominion's Aeronautics Act and in finding the Manitoba legislation and regulations *ultra vires*. Certainly the most significant aspect of this decision was the test that the court used to determine whether the regulation of civil aviation was a subject-matter of legislation embraced by the "Peace, Order, and Good Government" clause. On this point, four of the five judges who wrote opinions explicitly accepted Lord Simon's test of national importance. Mr. Justice Kellock used these words: "Once the decision is made that a matter is of national importance, so as to fall within the peace, order and good government clause, the provinces cease to have any legitimate jurisdiction with regard thereto and the Dominion jurisdiction is exclusive." Of course the court could dress up this approach in the cautious language of *stare decisis* by referring to Lord Simon's formulation of the national aspect test and Lord Sanky's allusion to the national importance of Aeronautics in the Aeronautics Reference of 1932. But this cannot disguise the fact that in selecting these cases a choice was exercised between contrasting judicial traditions. *Stare decisis* might just as easily have permitted resort to the 1937 Reference cases in which national importance, aside from emergency situations, was rejected as a proper test for invoking the General power.

But it would be a mistake to accept the Johannesson case as a decisive breakthrough. It must be pointed out that the court's validation of the Dominion's Aeronautics Act did not, in itself, constitute an expansion of the central legislature's powers. The Aeronautics Act had been validated previously by the Privy Council in 1932 (although on that occasion Section 132—the treaty implementing power— rather than the General power had been singled out as the basis of the Act's constitutionality). The effect of the national importance test in the Johannesson case was essentially negative; it prevented a province from encroaching upon a field of legislation already occupied by the Dominion. It may well be that the Supreme Court would be less prepared to adopt Lord Simon's conception of "Peace, Order, and Good Government" if it was required to support the entry of Parliament into an activity already subject to provincial law.

Supreme Court cases since Johannesson v. West St. Paul throw no light on this conjecture. Thus, for the centralist cause, the Johannesson case represents encouragement but hardly victory. The enumerated powers of Section 91, far more than "the residuary power," have served as the vehicle for judicial initiatives. These initiatives, as we shall now see, have generally leaned towards the expansion of the Dominion's powers.

The Judicial Committee's attenuation of the Dominion's Trade and Commerce power had come in for almost as much criticism as its treatment of the General power. There had never been much quarrel with the assumption that some limits would have to be set to Section 91 (2) if a reasonable measure of provincial autonomy were to be preserved. But the restrictive nature of those limits and the inflexible way in which they had been delineated by the judiciary had been the source of much discontent. Although the Trade and Commerce power was occasionally employed by the Privy Council to circumscribe the provinces' powers of trade regulation and as one of a number of supports for Dominion legislation, its emasculation had proceeded so far that as an independent source of constitutional power for significant legislation in the field of economic regulation it had been rendered very nearly useless. Further, for the purpose of drawing a clear line between those forms of trade which could be regulated by the Dominion and those which could be regulated by the provinces, the Privy Council had adopted the categories of inter-provincial and intra-provincial trade. These categories when applied uncritically to the activities of an interdependent economy resulted in a division of jurisdiction which precluded efficacious legislation by either the Dominion or the Provinces. The debilitating effects of this approach were felt most severely in connection with marketing legislation. Where produce at the point at which regulation was desirable could not be segregated into that destined for the provincial market and that destined for the extra-provincial market, and where delegation of legislative powers between Parliament and provincial legislatures was precluded, it appeared that judicial construction of the B.N.A. Act had produced a constitutional hiatus.

Since 1949 the Supreme Court has delivered two judgments that cast some light upon its treatment of the Trade and Commerce power. While neither case marks a revolutionary approach, taken together they suggest, to use Professor Laskin's words, "a decided thaw in the hitherto frozen federal commerce power." In the first of these cases, *Reference re. (Ontario) Farm Products Marketing Act* (1957), the court was asked to answer eight questions concerning certain provisions of and regulations under an Ontario marketing Act. Since it was provincial legislation whose validity was being examined, the Dominion's Trade and Commerce power was referred to only negatively as limiting the application of Ontario's marketing schemes to intra-provincial trade. Even so, the way in which a majority of the judges elucidated the distinction between intra-provincial trade (subject to provincial jurisdiction) and inter-provincial or export trade (subject to Dominion jurisdiction) suggested a large area in which Head No. 2 of Section 91 could serve as a constitutional foundation for national economic policies. The court's relatively liberal appraisal of Section 91 (2) did not have any direct bearing upon the outcome of the case: all the judges accepted at face value the wording of the opening question of the Reference Order, to the effect that the "Act applies only in the case of intra-provincial transactions." The significance of this case, then, is to be measured not in terms of its substantive results but in terms of the pragmatic approach to constitutional adjudication which it implies. This approach was most evident in Mr. Justice Rand's opinion from which the following passage is quoted:

> Trade arrangements reaching the dimensions of world agreements are now a commonplace; interprovincial trade, in which the Dominion is a single market, is of similar importance, and equally vital to the economic functioning of the country as a whole. The Dominion power implies responsibility for promoting and maintaining the vigour and growth of trade beyond provincial confines, and the discharge of this function must remain unembarrassed by local trade impediments.

What stands out here by way of contrast with earlier judicial efforts to divide jurisdiction over trading activities is that the point of departure is not fixed categories of Dominion and Provincial economic responsibility but rather judicial notice of the evolving requirements of a national economy.

In the second case, *Murphy v. C. P. R. and A.-G. Canada* (1958), the Trade and Commerce power was invoked as the basis for the constitutionality of the Canadian Wheat Board Act. Here, the court showed that it was prepared to regard the federal commerce power as an independent source of legislative authority broad enough to sustain a Dominion marketing Act, which is of crucial importance to the national economy. However, the facts of this case were such as to qualify the significance of the court's use of Section 91 (2). The impugned provisions of the Act came clearly under the heading "Regulation of international and inter-provincial trade in wheat" and the plaintiff, Murphy, who was challenging the C.P.R.'s refusal to handle his wheat because he had failed to comply with the pro-visions of the Act, was clearly shipping wheat across provincial boundaries.

The implications of this decision appeared of much greater consequence when the Manitoba Court of Appeal referred to it in the case of *Regina v. Klassen* (1959). Here, in contrast to the Murphy case, the facts posed a more severe chal-lenge to the traditional bifurcation of legislative authority over trade into intra-provincial and extra-provincial compartments. The issue in the Klassen case was whether regulations made under the Canadian Wheat Board Act could be applied to a feed-mill whose business was carried on entirely within a province. Drawing upon the Supreme Court's decision in the Murphy case, the Manitoba court upheld this application of the Dominion statute to *intra-provincial* transactions on the pragmatic grounds that, if the intra-provincial market was severed from the scope of the Act, the whole attempt to create an orderly scheme for marketing the annual wheat crop would be rendered impossible. Considerations of economic policy took precedence over legalistic categories.

From the above cases it seems fair to conclude that if since 1949 there has not been a positive expansion of the scope of the federal commerce power, the Supreme Court has at least demonstrated a more pragmatic and less legalistic approach to the general problem of adjusting national and local interests in marketing matters. Even so, much of the court's work in this area may now be rendered largely academic by its treatment of the delegation question.

During the 1930s and 1940s many of those who viewed the Privy Council's "watertight compartments" treatment of the division of powers as a frustrating obstacle to the effective handling of some of Canada's major social and economic problems looked to the delegation device as the most likely way of hurdling the constitutional barrier. If the Judicial Committee in the course of interpreting the B.N.A. Act had effected a division of authority inappropriate to the needs and resources of the provinces and the Dominion, then, it was argued, at least the legis-latures and Parliament should be free to delegate their powers to one another. As for the constitutionality of the delegation device, this question, prior to 1949, had not been canvassed by either the Privy Council or the Supreme Court. The Privy Council's only pronouncement on the subject was made by Lord Watson in 1899, and this was to the effect that delegation by a provincial legislature to Parliament or vice versa was invalid. However, this was simply a remark thrown out in the course of argument and was not central to the case. In his Appendix to the Sirois Commission Report, J. A. Corry, after a thorough examination of the issue, had concluded that it was still an open question.

Thus, when the Supreme Court in 1951 and 1952 was directly faced with the delegation issue, it was breaking rather new and significant ground. The net result of these two cases was paradoxical: first, direct delegation was banned, and, then, indirect delegation was approved. In the first case, the *Nova Scotia Inter-delegation* case (1951), the court declared Nova Scotia's Bill 136 *ultra vires*. This Bill constituted an attempt by the Nova Scotia legislature to delegate part of its law-making authority (in this case in the field of labour law) directly to the Parliament of Canada. In addition, the Bill looked forward to Parliament delegating part of its legislative authority to the Nova Scotia legislature. The judges based their decision on the "watertight compartments" view of federalism. In Mr. Justice Rand's words, this type of delegation was "utterly foreign to the conception of a federal organization."

If the advocates of flexible federalism were at all dismayed by this decision, their anguish was short-lived. The following year, in the case of *P.E.I. Potato Marketing Board v. H. B. Willis Inc.,* the Supreme Court designed an escape from its doctrine of the Nova Scotia Inter-delegation case. Here the issue concerned an attempt by the Dominion in the Agricultural Products Marketing Act (1949) to delegate to provincial marketing boards the power of regulating inter-provincial and export trade in agricultural products. The court ruled that this manner of delegation was constitutionally valid. In order to reach this decision the court distinguished the Nova Scotia case on the grounds that, there, legislative power was being delegated to other legislatures, whereas, in this case, the recipient of the delegated power was the subordinate agency of another legislature. The latter was justified because it involved merely an attempt by Parliament "to employ as its own a Board, or agency, for the purpose of carrying out its own legislation."

Whether or not one agrees with the logic of this distinction, it must be acknowledged that the decision in the Willis case opened a significant chink in the dike which separates Section 91 of the B.N.A. Act from Section 92. Indeed, on at least two occasions since then the Provinces and the Dominion have resorted to this device of "indirect delegation" to circumvent the effects of other judicial decisions. The most striking example of this occurred after the Privy Council brought down its decision in the case of *A.-G. Ont. v. Winner* (1954). Since the original litigation in the Winner case had begun prior to the abolition of appeals, it was possible to appeal the Supreme Court's decision to the Privy Council. The outcome of this appeal was a victory for the Dominion: the Judicial Committee amended the Supreme Court's judgment and found that the Dominion alone had the power to regulate the operations of inter-provincial bus lines. Within two months representatives of the Federal Government and nine Provinces met to consider the implications of the Winner case. As a result of this meeting the Dominion Parliament passed the Motor Vehicle Transport Act, which was designed to delegate back to provincial licensing boards any of the powers over extra-provincial motor carriers that the Dominion might have won in the Winner case.

Parliament used the same technique again in 1957 to overcome the consequences of another judicial decision. This time, the ruling to be circumvented was part of the decision in Reference re. Ontario Farm Products Marketing Act (see above).

In answer to one of the questions in this Reference, the court found that Ontario's incorporation of licensing fees, in its marketing regulations, which were designed to equalize the returns of producers, constituted indirect taxation and was therefore *ultra vires*. Following this, the Dominion Parliament, working on the assumption that a legislative power denied to the Provinces is within the Dominion's orbit, amended its Agricultural Products Marketing Act and delegated the power of imposing equalization levies to provincial marketing agencies. The ironic finale to this episode occurred four years later, when the Supreme Court in the case of *Crawford & Hillside Farm Dairy Ltd., et al. v. A.-G. B.C.* (1960) apparently reversed its position on provincial marketing levies. In this case the court ruled that where a provincial marketing scheme attempts to equalize the returns of producers this is still legislation in relation to trade and not indirect taxation. Consequently, provincial marketing levies such as had been declared *ultra vires* were now valid so long as they applied only to intra-provincial trade. This decision thus rendered superfluous Parliament's earlier amendment to the Agricultural Products Marketing Act.

The Supreme Court's validation of the "indirect delegation" device has undoubtedly opened up another channel of legislative co-operation in the Canadian federal system. This device, when both levels of government are willing to use it, makes it much easier for the national and local legislatures to overcome the difficulties of divided jurisdiction or, as the aftermath to the Winner case suggests, enables them to accommodate political pressures which are not recognized by the courts. In a word, where it is applicable, this device removes the sense of finality from the process of constitutional adjudication.

One of the major laments of the centralist critics of the Privy Council was that tribunal's invalidation of the Dominion's Industrial Disputes Investigation Act (the Lemieux Act) in the Snider case of 1925. The basic purpose of the Lemieux Act was to establish collective bargaining machinery that would be applicable to all mines, transportation and communication agencies, and public service utilities. By finding this statute *ultra vires,* the Privy Council had apparently disqualified the Dominion's efforts to provide a procedure for handling industrial disputes that were national in scope.

In 1955 the Supreme Court in yet another Reference case was confronted with the task of delineating legislative authority in relation to collective bargaining arrangements. In this *Reference re. Validity of Industrial Relations and Disputes Investigation Act* the court unanimously found the federal statute *intra vires*. The decisive difference between this Act and the Lemieux Act which it had replaced was that it applied only to those activities that were within the legislative authority of Parliament. Consequently, this judgment confirmed the bifurcation of power in the field of labour relations. Whether labour relations in a particular industry are subject to federal or provincial law depends on whether that industry is one that can generally be brought under one of the heads of Section 91 or of Section 92. For instance, in the 1955 Reference, the court was also asked to decide whether employees of a Toronto stevedoring company were subject to the Dominion's

Industrial Relations and Disputes Investigations Act. A majority of the court answered this question in the affirmative on the grounds that, since the Company serviced only boats engaged in foreign trade, its activities were subject to Head 10 (Navigation and Shipping) of Section 91.

Mr. V. C. MacDonald has described the Supreme Court's treatment of the labour relations question as "a truly gigantic step from the conclusions of the Privy Council in Snider's case. . . ." This perhaps overstates the case. Certainly the 1955 Reference contrasts with the Snider case to the extent that it denies provincial jurisdiction over collective bargaining in *some* industries. But it must also be noticed that the Supreme Court judgment does not uphold the argument that had prevailed in the lower courts in Canada prior to the appeal of the Snider case to the Privy Council; namely, that the settlement of major industrial disputes was a distinct and independent area of legislative activity and as such was subject to the Dominion's power to legislate for the Peace, Order, and Good Government of Canada. The principal way in which the 1955 decision might lead to an expansion of Federal jurisdiction over labour relations is through the judiciary adopting a generous construction of those industrial activities that are subject to Dominion authority. This has already happened on more than one occasion. In the *Pronto Uranium case,* for example, Judge McLennan of the Ontario Supreme Court ruled that labour relations in uranium mines were subject to the Dominion's legislation because activities related to the production of atomic energy came under the Peace, Order, and Good Government clause.

In the B.N.A. Act there is, of course, nothing comparable to the American Bill of Rights, which explicitly prohibits local and federal legislatures from violating certain basic rights. However, judicial review can affect civil liberties by determining whether the Dominion or the Provinces have the power to restrict fundamental freedom. Prior to 1949 this issue had not been explored in a definitive way by the Privy Council. Consequently, the three constitutional cases in the 1950s which raised civil liberty questions provided rather fertile soil for indigenous judicial seeds.

The three leading cases in this area are also of special interest to the political scientist because they tended to push the Supreme Court into a definite posture in regard to one of the most significant areas of conflicting values in Canadian life. On the surface the three cases would appear admirably suited to play such a role. They all concerned provincial legislation that curtailed some aspect of religious or political freedom; in all three cases it was the Province of Quebec whose legislation was under attack; in all three cases that province's Court of Appeal had upheld the legislation; in all three cases the Supreme Court reversed the decision of the lower court.

Saumur v. Quebec (1953) was the most perplexing of the three. In this case, Saumur, a Jehovah's Witness, challenged a Quebec City by-law forbidding the distribution in the streets of any book, pamphlet, or tract without the permission of the Chief of Police. In a narrow sense Saumur won his case. The Supreme Court on a five to four vote found that the by-law did not prohibit the Jehovah's Witnesses from distributing their literature in the streets. In a broader and more significant sense Saumur and those who view with alarm provincial laws authorizing the police to control the dissemination of opinions lost their case. In the opinions of five of the judges, including the three from Quebec, it was within provincial competence to limit freedom of religious expression. The other four, rejecting the view that the phrase "civil rights" in Section 92 (13) refers to liberties such as freedom of religion, ruled against provincial competence in this matter. Saumur's victory, then, did not turn upon constitutional grounds but upon the much narrower opinion of Mr. Justice Kerwin. The latter conceded the constitutional validity of the by-law but reasoned that it did not apply to the Jehovah's Witnesses because it had to give way to the Quebec Freedom of Worship Act. Given the narrow basis of Kerwin's judgment, the Quebec legislature made quick work of the Saumur decision by amending the Freedom of Worship Act so that Jehovah's Witness publications would be clearly classified under the exceptions to the Act.

In contrast to the Saumur case, the case of *Birks & Sons v. Montreal* (1955) was more productive of solid constitutional fruit. The Quebec statute attacked in this case by Henry Birks & Co. required that storekeepers should close their shops on six Catholic Holy days. In a surprising display of unanimity all nine members of the court found the legislation *ultra vires*. Two elements of this decision stand out. In the first place, the court's basic point of departure from the Quebec Court of Queen's Bench lay in classifying the Act as one whose main concern was religious observance and not the regulation of working hours. Second, and this is the important constitutional doctrine, the court ruled that such legislation, which makes the failure to observe a certain religious practice a crime, falls under Parliament's power to enact criminal law (Section (91)).

Certainly the court's most prominent treatment of political freedoms arose in the case of *Switzman v. Elbling and A.-G. Quebec* (1957), which invalidated Quebec's Communist Propaganda Act. This Act, popularly known as the "Padlock Law," prohibited the use of houses for Communist meetings and banned the printing and publication of literature propagating the Communist ideology. The Supreme Court's decision here was in line with its earlier decision in the Birks case. With only Mr. Justice Taschereau dissenting, the court determined that the "pith and substance" of the Act was the suppression of Communism and, as such, it was beyond provincial jurisdiction. Once again it was the Dominion's power to legislate in relation to Criminal Law to which the majority referred as the constitutional basis for legislation restricting civil liberty. But, more spectacular and potentially of greater importance to the question of civil liberties in the Canadian Constitution was the doctrine formulated by Mr. Justice Rand and supported by two of his fellow judges, Kellock and Abbott.

Mr. Justice Rand, who has been described by Professor Laskin as the "greatest expositor of a democratic public law which Canada has known," throughout these cases attempted to discover within the B.N.A. Act an implicit Bill of Rights that would at least protect fundamental liberties from abridgement by provincial legislatures. In the Winner case of 1951, Rand first brought up the notion of the

"Rights of a Canadian Citizen." According to this doctrine, the institution of a common Canadian citizenship was an essential by-product of the nation created by the constitutional Act of 1867. This "citizenship" bears in its wake certain fundamental rights which all Canadians must enjoy and which are constitutionally beyond the range of provincial power. In this case, the particular "Right of a Canadian Citizen," which Rand elucidated as grounds for limiting the scope of New Brunswick's Motor Carrier Act, was the right to the use of highways. In the Saumur case, Rand referred to the phrase "a constitution similar in principle to that of the United Kingdom," which appears in the preamble to the B.N.A. Act, as the constitutional support of fundamental freedoms. This phrase, he reasoned, implies government by parliamentary institutions, a necessary condition of which is freedom of the press and freedom of public discussion. Rand developed this thesis further in the Padlock Law case. Again, he saw in the preamble to the B.N.A. Act a political theory that demands free speech and a free press as essential conditions of a Parliamentary Democracy. Mr. Justice Abbott went one step further than Rand and suggested that this implicit guarantee of free speech meant that "Parliament itself could not abrogate this right of discussion and debate."

Impressive as Rand's ideas may be as exercises in political philosophy, it must be noted that they are still some way from becoming a settled part of our Constitutional Law. In none of the cases in which Rand enunciated his thesis was it either endorsed by a majority or the turning point in the decision. Indeed, the late Chief Justice Mr. Kerwin in the Saumur case explicitly disavowed Rand's use of the preamble to the B.N.A. Act. Nevertheless, while the court as a whole may have declined to be as adventurous as Mr. Justice Rand, it has still partially clarified the constitutional position of civil liberties. After the Birks case and the Padlock Law case, the Dominion's Criminal Law power looms as an effective constitutional restraint on provincial laws that aim at circumscribing political and religious liberties.

Thus far we have examined Supreme Court decisions in those areas of constitutional interpretation which have traditionally attracted the attention of students of Canadian federalism. But these cases by no means give a full picture of the Supreme Court's performance as the umpire of the federal system. In addition to the 12 cases mentioned above, there were 26 other constitutional cases before the Supreme Court in the period under review. While these cases may not have raised what have come to be regarded as the classic issues of judicial review, in many instances they did result in decisions that had a significant impact on the legislative capacities of the Provinces and the Dominion. In the past, political scientists have often been so dazzled by the court's treatment of the General power and Property and Civil Rights that they have been somewhat blind to the importance of some of the other enumerated powers as sources of legislative authority and issues of judicial review.

Two of these rather neglected issues which were prominent in the 1950s were the Dominion's Criminal Law power (Section 91 (27)) and the question of taxation. We have already seen in the Civil Liberties cases how Parliament's Criminal

Law power was invoked against provincial attempts to legislate with respect to religious practice and political freedoms. In nine other cases the Criminal Law power was at the centre of the constitutional dispute. In two of these cases the court invoked Section 91 (27) to uphold Dominion statutes. The most important of these was *Goodyear Tire & Rubber Co. v. the Queen* (1956) in which the court used Head 27 of Section 91 to sustain provisions of the Combines Investigation Act. This judgment served as a reminder of the extent to which 91 (27) can support legislation pursuing economic policy goals. Mr. Justice Rand declared that "it is accepted that head (27) of Section 91 . . . is to be interpreted in its widest sense. . . ." Against this broad interpretation of the Criminal Law power must be balanced the court's tendency to uphold provincial legislation that was being attacked as an infringement of Head 27 of Section 91. This was the basic question in the seven other "criminal law" cases, and in all but one the court found the impugned provincial legislation *intra vires*.

The constitutional prohibition of indirect provincial taxation was the central issue in five cases. It is beyond the scope of this article to examine these cases in any detail, but two cases are significant enough to merit some comment. In *Cairns Construction Ltd. v. Government of Saskatchewan* (1960) the court ruled that Saskatchewan's Education & Hospitalization Tax was *intra vires*. This was a retail sales tax, so that the court's decision provided a further constitutional underpinning for what has become an increasingly important source of provincial revenue. On the other hand, in *Texeda Mines Ltd. v. A.-G. B.C.*, by invalidating British Columbia's Mineral Property Tax, the Court, through Mr. Justice Locke, indicated a severe limitation to the province's powers of taxation. In this instance, although the B.C. tax in form resembled a Saskatchewan tax that had been found valid by the court in 1952, in substance it was ten times higher than the Saskatchewan tax and, consequently, it was distinguished and invalidated.

When the Privy Council was Canada's final court of appeal, the method it employed in constitutional adjudication came in for almost as much discussion as the substance of its decisions. Most of the Privy Council's English-speaking critics were advocates of judicial activism. According to this conception of judicial review, the court's function in a country with a written constitution was to adjust the terms of the constitutional text to the rapidly changing requirements of a dynamic environment. These judicial activists singled out the Privy Council's apparently strict adherence to the principle of *stare decisis* and its literalistic interpretation of the B.N.A. Act as the aspects of its method which precluded the kind of judicial statesmanship they advocated. While the Privy Council's critics looked forward with some optimism to the Supreme Court's emancipation, there were others, not surprisingly associated with the provincial rights view of federalism, who were alarmed at the prospect of any major deviation by the Supreme Court from the Privy Council's traditions. Parliamentary spokesmen of this school of thought went so far as to move, unsuccessfully, an amendment to the Act abolishing appeals which would have made previous Privy Council decisions binding on the Supreme Court.

It is extremely difficult to summarize with any degree of precision the Supreme

Court's record with regard to these matters of method. As far as *stare decisis* is concerned, it is clear that the court is under no statutory compulsion to adopt the earlier rulings of the Privy Council as the bases for its own judgements. At the same time it is also clear that *in practice* the Supreme Court since 1949 has never explicitly overruled a Privy Council decision or, indeed, any of its own previous judgments. Thus, the court appears to be somewhere between the position of the United States Supreme Court and its own position prior to the abolition of appeals: unlike its American counterpart it has not officially declared its readiness to discard old judicial precedents when they no longer seem suitable but, in contrast to its own pre-1949 position, it is relatively free to work out its own policy of interpreting and applying Privy Council precedents. This rather ambiguous position becomes, perhaps, more comprehensible if we acknowledge that even when a court formally follows a practice of *stare decisis* this does not necessarily result in as inflexible and predictable a course of decisions as is sometimes suggested. Given rival precedents on the same general question and the art of distinguishing previous cases as different from the one at hand, it is entirely possible for a court, while looking exclusively to past cases for the premises of its reasoning, in fact so to select, ignore, and distinguish cases that it is able to evolve its own doctrines of constitutional Law.

Stare decisis is naturally linked to that other controversial aspect of judicial review—the unimaginative, literalistic interpretation of the B.N.A. Act as opposed to the statesmanlike adaptation of the constitutional text. Which of these alternative approaches has the Supreme Court tended to follow? Again it is impossible to give a simple answer. It would be misleading to brand the Supreme Court's approach as either distinctively literal or distinctively liberal. If any contrast can be drawn here between the Supreme Court's record and that of its predecessor, it would be in terms of an increasing degree of pragmatism in the court's interpretation of the division of powers, especially in areas affecting economic welfare. In a number of cases, individual judges have based their reasonings not so much on the words of the B.N.A. Act as on the adverse practical consequences they felt would flow from an alternative decision to the one they were giving. For instance, Mr. Justice Locke, in the Johannesson case, based his opinion against provincial regulation of aerodromes partly on his estimation of the "intolerable" state of affairs that would result if the national development of airlines was obstructed by local regulations. Similarly, the court's examination of the concepts of intra-provincial and extra-provincial trade in the Ontario Farm Products Marketing Reference was much more concerned with elaborating a workable scheme for the division of legislative authority than with a close textual scrutiny of the B.N.A. Act. Of course, these are only isolated examples, but still it is in these occasional outbursts of functionalism that we are apt to find some vindication of Edward Blake's opinion that the great merit of a Canadian Course of last resort would be in its possession of "the daily learning and experience with Canadians, living under the Canadian Constitution, acquire . . . and which can be given only by residence on the spot."

There is one other aspect of the Supreme Court's method that calls for some comment; that is its practice of having a number of judges write opinions in each case—even in cases where all the judges reach the same result. This is in marked contrast to the Judicial Committee's custom of publishing only one opinion for every case. No matter how divided their Lordships may have been in private, their public face was always one of unanimity. In contrast to this, the Supreme Court, in the 37 constitutional cases it handled in the period under review, on the average included four opinions in each case.

This rather different practice has been a mixed blessing. The inclusion of the minority's opinion, when the court is split, has the undoubted advantage of displaying the alternative principles of interpretation upon which the case hinged. Also, we know from American experience that the minority opinion of today can become the majority opinion of tomorrow. But, unfortunately, the Canadian Supreme Court has failed to combine this practice of multi-opinion writing with any procedure for co-ordinating the separate opinions. Unlike the United States Supreme Court, the Canadian court does not present a majority opinion which at least indicates the common ingredients of those judgments that determined the outcome of the case. This means that when several judges, constituting the majority in a given case, all write separate opinions, it is extremely difficult to ascertain the common grounds of their disparate arguments and, hence, the basic principles established by the case. For example, in the Saumur case, the five judges who made up the majority all wrote separate opinions and, while they all agreed to allow the appeal, their opinions represented at least three different viewpoints on the central constitutional issue. This disjointed system of opinion writing not only might make it perplexing for the professional lawyer who must somehow determine the net effect of the different opinions, but also, in many cases, it prevents the court from performing what should surely be a necessary adjunct of the process of constitutional adjudication; namely, the clarification of constitutional principles for the public at large.

PROPOSALS FOR REFORMING THE SUPREME COURT*

PIERRE ELLIOTT TRUDEAU

The first question that naturally arises relates to the means for providing the structure of the Court. At present the Constitution makes no provision for a Supreme Court other than to give to Parliament a power to establish one and to define its jurisdiction. The structure and jurisdiction of the Court are therefore provided by legislative act of the central government. The Government of Canada feels that it would now be more appropriate that the Constitution itself provide for the exist-

* From *The Constitution and The People of Canada*, Ottawa, Queen's Printer, 1969, pp. 40-44 and 82-86. By permission of the Queen's Printer.

ence, the appointment and tenure of judges, and the major powers of the Supreme Court. This would be more consistent with the Court's role as the final interpreter of the Constitution of a federal state.

The structure of the Court also raises a problem as to the size of its membership. In considering this matter the Government of Canada, while not wishing to foreclose the issue, has been guided by two objectives: first, to ensure that various interests (defined by legal system and region) are represented; and secondly, to ensure that the Court is of a sufficient size to allow it adequately to handle the work load imposed upon it without at the same time becoming unwieldy. Consequently, we have proposed that the current size of the Bench of the Supreme Court of Canada, nine judges, be retained at least for the present.

As to the jurisdiction of the Court, two main theses have been advanced in various quarters. The first is that there should be a constitutional court dealing only with constitutional matters on appeal from all courts in Canada. This thesis has as its corollary that there would be a federal appeal court to deal with other matters on appeal, more particularly questions of strictly federal law and, possibly, matters of provincial law. The second thesis is that the ultimate tribunal should have a complete or integral jurisdiction so that constitutional questions could be dealt with in the normal course of litigation and in the context of all the relevant circumstances including those relating to the other legal questions that almost always are involved in such matters.

The Government of Canada has felt that a body of integral jurisdiction would be more in keeping with our traditions and with a sound appreciation of how our law works in practice. Artificial divisions in the interpretative process would not assist in the second development of constitutional law. This is not to say that the Government has rejected the possibility of some flexible structures within the Court that would provide, such as at present, for a panel to hear civil law cases or for a panel to hear common law or federal law questions but this could be worked out within the Court in relation to the exigencies as they may arise.

In considering the manner of selection of the members of the Court, the Government of Canada has been concerned that this body must exercise a judicial, not an arbitral, function. Judges should not be regarded as representatives of several different governments which could conceivably be allowed to appoint them. For this reason, a single system of appointment is to be preferred. It is recognized, however, that to ensure continued confidence in the Court it would be preferable that there be some form of participation on behalf of the provinces in the appointing process. It is therefore proposed that nominations of potential appointees be submitted by the federal government to the Senate for approval. If the proposals for the revision of the Senate are adopted, provincial viewpoints could be effectively expressd by this means. This system would not, of course, apply to those who were already members of the Court at such time as it might be reconstituted under the Constitution and with a new system of appointment. . . .

At the same time, it is assumed that the provincial courts would continue to administer provincial laws and many federal laws. . . . We do not at this time propose any change in the structure, jurisdiction, or method of appointment of judges of these courts. . . .

[From the Appendix, *ibid.*, pp. 82-86.]

SUPREME COURT

1.   The Constitution should establish a general Court of Appeal for Canada to be known as the Supreme Court of Canada consisting of nine judicial offices, including the office of Chief Justice of Canada, of whom at least three shall be appointed from the bench or bar of Quebec.

2.   The general provisions of the present Constitution respecting appointment, tenure and independence of the judiciary should be made applicable to the Court.

3.   Nominations of persons to the Supreme Court of Canada could be placed before the Senate for approval prior to appointment.

4.   The Constitution should authorize the Supreme Court of Canada to depart from a previous decision when it appears right to do so.

It was thought important to accord the Supreme Court the freedom necessary to interpret the Constitution as a living document. Thus, it should be authorized to depart from precedent where, in its opinion, circumstances demand it. . . .

5.   Persons appointed judges of the Court should have at least ten years' standing at the bar of the province from which they are appointed or a combined standing at the bar and on the bench of at least ten years.

6.   Provision should be made in the Constitution that the Court will enjoy ultimate appellate jurisdiction in any action or other proceeding in which any validity of any Act or enactment of the Parliament of Canada or of a legislature is in issue and that the remainder of the Court's jurisdiction, whether appellate or advisory, and its remaining constitution, powers and procedure will be prescribed by Act of the Parliament of Canada. . . .

7.   Provision should also be made that five judges of the Court shall constitute a quorum for the hearing and determination of appeals except in cases where the constitutional validity of an Act of Parliament or of a legislature is in issue in which case the quorum shall be seven judges; and when dealing with appeals from the Province of Quebec, the three judges appointed from that province shall sit on and act in the determination of those appeals.

8.   In the event that one or more of the three judges appointed from the Province of Quebec is unable to act in the disposition of appeals from that province, the Chief Justice or, in his absence, the senior puisne judge, shall have authority to designate one or more members of the superior courts of Quebec to sit as ad hoc judges of the Court by way of replacement. . . .

OTHER COURTS

9. The Constitution should continue to provide that the Parliament of Canada has jurisdiction to establish a national court or courts for the better administration of the laws of Canada, and it should further provide that the general provisions of the Constitution respecting the appointment, tenure and independence of the judiciary should be applicable to the judges of any court or courts so established.

This proposition is submitted to provide for the continuation and modification of existing federal courts.

APPOINTMENT OF JUDGES OF SUPERIOR, COUNTY AND DISTRICT COURTS

10. The Constitution should continue to provide for the appointment of judges of Superior, County and District Courts by the central executive.

LEWIS ST. G. STUBBS, JUDICIAL REBEL*

Lewis St. George Stubbs, 79, removed from the bench in 1933 in the course of a legal and political career that made his name known across Canada, died last night.

His dramatic removal from the bench was due mainly to charges concerning his actions in 1929 and 1930 as Manitoba Surrogate Court judge. He had refused to grant letters of administration in the estate of Alexander Macdonald, millionaire Winnipeg merchant, to Mr. Macdonald's daughter, Mrs. Grace Anne Forlong, and her husband.

The Manitoba Court of Appeal granted the letters over his head and, he charged, clandestinely. He held a public meeting in a Winnipeg theatre and a resolution was passed asking the Legislature to invalidate the Appeal Court action.

Superior Court judges asked the federal justice minister to remove Judge Stubbs from the bench and Mr. Justice Frank Ford was appointed Royal Commissioner to investigate.

The 24-day hearing created intense interest across the country. Judge Stubbs suggested that the inquiry be held in the Winnipeg auditorium and that admission be charged.

After hearing 600,000 words of evidence, Mr. Justice Ford found him guilty of judicial misconduct.

Testimony included the fact that Judge Stubbs often had said that "there is one law for the rich and another for the poor." One commission attorney described him as a judicial rebel.

In his own defense, Judge Stubbs said: "I would much rather have done what

* From *The Canadian Press*, May 13, 1958. By permission.

I did and go off the bench, than not to have done what I did and stay on the bench."

He topped the poll in Winnipeg in 1936 when 21 candidates were seeking 10 seats in the Manitoba Legislature. He sat as Independent member of the provincial House until 1949.

CAN POLITICS AND THE BENCH BE SEPARATED*

MARTIN KNELMAN

How can political affiliation be made less important and qualifications more important in the federal Government's appointment of judges? And how can incompetent judges be removed from the bench?

These were two of the problems considered Saturday by a panel at the midwinter meeting of the Ontario section of the Canadian Bar Association.

"There must be some check on the executive (the Cabinet) on making these appointments to the bench," said Stanley E. Fennell of Cornwall, former president of the Canadian association. "It must come from some organization of the bar prepared to stand up and say: 'These people are qualified and these people are not'."

One of the most important criteria must be integrity, Mr. Fennell said. And he made it clear that by this he meant much more than a record without criminal conviction. "How low can we get?" he asked.

E. C. Leslie of Regina, who was unable to appear on the panel, suggested in a statement read to the session that provincial patronage would be reduced if the British North America Act were amended to make the federal Justice Minister directly responsible for the appointment of judges.

But Walter Owen of Vancouver and L. P. Pigeon of Quebec contended that this change would not make appointments less political.

Two delegates disagreed about what role the association should play. W. S. Montgomery of Toronto said the matter was outside the scope of the association. Gordon Ford of Toronto replied: "There's nothing we're more vitally interested in than the appointment of judges." Mr. Ford asked the panelists whether the association should prepare lists of qualified candidates for the Government.

Mr. Fennell said the association should not try to impose lists on the Government but instead should classify candidates listed by the Government as qualified or unqualified.

Arthur Patillo of Toronto, chairman of the committee, asked the panel at the

* From *The Globe and Mail*, Toronto, February 7, 1966. By permission.

beginning of the discussion to keep personalities out of the debate. No names were mentioned.

(On Jan. 19, Justice Minister Lucien Cardin appointed Ivan Rand, a former judge of the Supreme Court of Canada, as a commission of inquiry to investigate allegations that Mr. Justice Leo Landreville of the Ontario Supreme Court should be removed from the bench.)

On the problem of removing judges, Mr. Fennell said there should be a quiet, proper judicial procedure, the results of which would be binding. "The retirement of a judge should not carry a stigma. He should be able to bow out gracefully."

Under the present system, he said, the bar association is sometimes able to press a judge who has become incapable to resign. But in some cases, the judge balks and the problem is: "How are you going to get rid of him?"

Since 1867, only four cases involving judges have been considered by committees of Parliament, Mr. Fennell noted, adding that there must have been more judges whose competence has been questioned than that.

The occasional judge who refuses to bow to pressure "has had too much of the bottle or is too far gone mentally," Mr. Fennell said.

The qualities Mr. Fennell thinks should count most in the appointment of judges:

—The person must have unquestionable integrity;

—He must be courteous and seem to be courteous;

—He must be in good mental and physical health;

—He must, above all, have the capacity to appreciate and resolve the problems of litigants before him.

"Some of our worst judges were some of our best trial lawyers. Some of our best judges had never been in court before in their lives. If the man knows a little law, so much the better."

POLITICAL APPOINTMENTS NOT BAD*

Mr. Prittie (Burnaby-Richmond): . . . The bar association resolutions are all of a similar type. They suggest that the government consult a committee of the bar association of the particular province in which the appointment is to be made and select from nominees of the association in the making of appointments to the bench. This is not to say that persons who are supporters of the government in power should not be considered; certainly they should be. Some of the best people in this country are engaged in politics. I have to say that because I am surrounded by them.

One thing is true. We have to look beyond the rather narrow field of supporters of the political party in power for appointments to the bench. . . .

* From *House of Commons Debates,* March 30, 1966, pp. 3621-3631. By permission of the Queen's Printer.

Mr. Asselin (Charlevoix): . . . Mr. Chairman, it has too often been said in this house that the political appointment of our judges in the superior courts or courts of appeal was questionable. As a member of the bar, I wish to protest against that tendency to let the people think that the political appointment of judges is not a good thing.

In my humble opinion, and by experience, when judges are appointed to the superior court or to the court of appeal, in short, to any court, they retain, I am happy to say, that feeling of impartiality about the ordinary man. Just because a man is appointed by a Liberal government or a Conservative government or any other, it does not mean that he does not assume his responsibilities when he becomes a judge. . . .

I think our governments appoint judges mainly because of the appointee's experience and legal knowledge. I also believe that in addition to that knowledge, a judge must equally be aware of the problems facing our taxpayers. He must have been in touch with the people and, in my opinion, a former member of parliament and government member surely has greater competence, because in addition to his awareness of the people's problems, he knows the problems of the parties involved, which would prove useful to him when called upon to administer justice. . . .

I also wish to point out to the minister that he might consider the possibility of changing the method of removing a judge from office.

At the present time, the act provides that, to dismiss a judge, a petition has to be approved unanimously by both houses, that is, the House of Commons and the Senate. Now, such procedure is extremely difficult and complicated. I do not think it has been used very often in the political history of our country. . . . I should like to see the act amended so that the bar of a province could present to the governor in council a petition, signed by the majority of its members, for the removal of a judge who had committed acts not in keeping with his functions and so that the governor in council could be empowered to deal with such a petition. . . .

•   •   •

Mr. Bell (Carleton): . . . I say to you, sir, that the independence, the impartiality, and the ability of the judiciary of this nation compare exceedingly favourably with the judiciary of any other nation. I know of no other place in the world where you will find a better judiciary than we have here in Canada. . . .

I want to add that I never have believed a man should be disqualified from any office because he engages in public service, and I say there is no higher degree of public service than service to a political party because service to a political party is the bedrock of our democracy. If you do not have people of ability who are prepared to serve in our political parties and give a spirit of enthusiasm to political parties, then we will not have democracy in this country.

I think the last thing in the world we should have is the elimination from appointment to the bench of men and women who have sought to give public service through our political parties. . . .

Mr. Pennell: Mr. Chairman, I am somewhat surprised that this . . . measure should arouse so much intellectual shot and shell in this chamber. However, I appreciate both the motive and the point of the hon. member for Burnaby-Richmond. At the same time I should add that I must support the proposition eloquently advanced by the hon. member for Carleton. . . .

In conclusion let me say that during my 20 years at the bar I have never heard the slightest suggestion that the prior political activities of a judge in any way influenced his judgment. I say this at the same time recognizing the point made by the hon. member for Burnaby-Richmond. . . .

•   •   •

Hon. Lucien Cardin (Minister of Justice): Mr. Speaker, first, I should like to thank hon. members who took part in this debate which I found most interesting because suggestions were made that will prove quite useful to me, in my capacity as Minister of Justice, and could make my task easier. . . .

One problem which has arisen and is causing some difficulty to the Chief Justices and the Attorneys General of the different provinces is the increasing number of inquiries and commissions which require the presence of sitting judges. This disorganizes the arrangement of the work by the Chief Justices for the different court terms. I and my predecessors have in the past been trying to work with the Chief Justices and Attorneys General in order to work out a plan whereby these inquiries can be carried out without disrupting too much the work organized and planned by the Chief Justices, and these arrangements are working out fairly well.

I was rather surprised that more stress was not placed by hon. members on the salaries of judges. Every one who has spoken has mentioned the need for the best possible calibre of judge available and I think that the salaries of judges are one important aspect which members of the house should consider. . . .

Personally, and I think I can say this very sincerely, I have been very much concerned about the appointment of judges. I have very carefully read the briefs prepared by the Canadian Bar Association and many other organizations which have spoken about the method of appointing judges. I have also spoken to my colleagues about it and many of them have had long discussions on the whole problem of appointing judges . . . but I must say that most suggestions and recommendations I have heard have not convinced me that by the utilization of any of these suggested methods we would in fact have better judges. . . .

IMPROVING THE METHOD OF APPOINTMENT*

Question No. 556—**Mr. Faulkner:**
1. Has the government considered the question of appointing a commission, composed of members of the legal profession and others, to make recommendations to the Minister of Justice respecting appointments of judges to the superior, district and county courts of Canada?
2. If so, what decision has been reached in this regard?

Hon. Lucien Cardin (Minister of Justice):

1. Yes.

2. The government has decided not to make any changes for the present in the methods or procedures for the appointment of judges.

BIBLIOGRAPHY

Browne, G. P., *The Judicial Committee and the British North America Act,* Toronto, University of Toronto Press, 1967.

Cheffins, R. I., "The Supreme Court of Canada: The Quiet Court in an Unquiet Country," *Osgoode Hall Law Journal,* Vol. IV, No. 2, September, 1966.

Joanes, A., "Stare Decisis in the Supreme Court of Canada," *Canadian Bar Review,* Vol. XXXVI, No. 2, May, 1958.

Laskin, B., *Canadian Constitutional Law: Cases, Text and Notes on Distribution of Legislative Power,* Toronto, Carswell, 3rd ed., 1966.

Laskin, B., "The Supreme Court of Canada: A final Court of and for Canadians," *Canadian Bar Review,* Vol. XXIX, No. 10, December, 1951.

Lederman, W. R., *The Courts and the Canadian Constitution,* Toronto, McClelland and Stewart, 1964.

Logan, G. R., "Historical Sketch of the Supreme Court of Canada," *Osgoode Hall Law Journal,* Vol. III, 1964.

MacDonald, V. C., "The Privy Council and the Canadian Constitution," *Canadian Bar Review,* Vol. XXIX, No. 10, December, 1951.

MacDonald, V. C., *Legislative Power and the Supreme Court in the Fifties,* Toronto, Butterworth, 1961.

MacKinnon, F., "The Establishment of the Supreme Court of Canada," *Canadian Historical Review,* Vol. XXVII, 1946.

McWhinney, E., "A Supreme Court in a Bicultural Society: The Future Role of the Canadian Supreme Court," in Ontario Advisory Committee on Confederation, *Background Papers and Reports,* Toronto, Queen's Printer, Vol. I, 1967.

McWhinney, E., "The new, Pluralistic Federalism in Canada," *La Revue Juridique Thémis,* Vol. II, 1967.

McWhinney, E., *Judicial Review in the English-Speaking World,* Toronto, University of Toronto Press, 4th ed., 1969.

Morin, J.-Y., "A Constitutional Court for Canada," *Canadian Bar Review,* Vol. XLIII, 1965.

Olmsted, R. A., *Decisions relating to the BNA Act, 1867, and the Canadian Constitution, 1867-1954,* Ottawa, Queen's Printer, 1954, 3 vols.

* From *House of Commons Debates,* May 25, 1966, p. 5493. By permission of the Queen's Printer.

Peck, S. R., "A Behavioural Approach to the Judicial Process: Scalogram Analysis," *Osgoode Hall Law Journal,* Vol. V, No. 1, April, 1967.

Peck, S. R., "The Supreme Court of Canada, 1958-1966: A search for Policy through Scalogram Analysis," *The Canadian Bar Review,* Vol. XLV, December, 1967.

Read, H., "The Judicial Process in Common Law Canada," *Canadian Bar Review,* Vol. XXXVII, 1959.

Russell, P., *Leading Constitutional Decisions,* Toronto, McClelland and Stewart, 1965.

Russell, P. H., "The Jurisdiction of the Supreme Court of Canada: Present Policies and a Programme for Reform," *Osgoode Hall Law Journal,* Vol. VI, No. 1, October, 1968.

Russell, P. H., *Bilingualism and Biculturalism in the Supreme Court of Canada,* Document of the Royal Commission on Bilingualism and Biculturalism, Ottawa, Queen's Printer, 1970.

Strayer, B. L., *Judicial Review of Legislation in Canada,* Toronto, University of Toronto Press, 1969.

Scott, F. R., "Centralization and Decentralization in Canadian Federalism," *Canadian Bar Review,* Vol. XXIX, No. 10, December, 1951.

Senate of Canada, *Report to the Honourable the Speaker Relating to the Enactment of the British North America Act, 1867,* (O'Connor Report), Ottawa, Queen's Printer, 1939.

Judiciary

Angus, W. H., "Judicial Selection in Canada,—The Historical Perspective," Address to the Annual Meeting of the Association of Canadian Law Teachers, Sherbrooke, P.Q., June 10, 1966.

Clark, J. A., "Appointments to the Bench," *Canadian Bar Review,* Vol. XXX, No. 1, January, 1952.

Jaffary, S. K., *Sentencing of Adults in Canada,* Toronto, University of Toronto Press, 1963.

Kinnear, H., "The County Judge in Ontario," *Canadian Bar Review,* Vol. XXXII, No. 1, January, 1954, and No. 2, February, 1954.

Lederman, W. R., "The Independence of the Judiciary," *Canadian Bar Review,* Vol. XXXIV, No. 7, August-September, 1956 and No. 10, December, 1956.

Lederman, W. R., *The Courts and the Canadian Constitution,* Toronto, McClelland and Stewart, 1964.

Russell, P. H., "Constitutional Reform of the Canadian Judiciary," *Alberta Law Review,* Vol. VII, No. 1, January, 1969.

SEVENTEEN
AMENDING
THE CONSTITUTION

The problem of arriving at agreement on a method of formally amending the British North America Act by Canadians within Canada is still outstanding in mid-1970. Since the first edition of this book in 1962, which reprinted the proposed "Fulton Formula" for amendment and the objections to it by the government of Saskatchewan, the Hon. Guy Favreau, minister of justice in the Liberal government of 1963, introduced a revised formula, dubbed the "Fulton-Favreau Formula" because it altered the original formula in only a few, though significant, ways. Though the F-F Formula was agreed to by all the provinces, it was finally rejected by the Lesage government in early 1966.

For the background to the problem prior to 1960, see the first edition of this book, pp. 81-90. A selection from the federal government's White Paper on amendment, which appeared under the authorship of Mr. Favreau as minister of justice, outlines developments from the conferences in 1960 to the conferences in 1964 that resulted in the production of the "Fulton-Favreau Formula." The latter is reprinted here in its entirety, in the form of the draft bill in which it was presented to the public. The considerable criticism the formula elicited both within and outside Parliament is represented here by one of the more informed speeches on the subject that was given in the House of Commons. The exchange of correspondence between Prime Minister Lesage and Prime Minister Pearson in which Mr. Lesage withdrew Quebec's endorsation of the formula appeared in the second edition of this book, pp. 146-150.

The bibliography gives references to the standard works on the subject. The federal government's White Paper is a most useful comprehensive document reviewing the events of the past few years.

THE SEARCH FOR A NEW METHOD: CONFERENCES 1960-1961 AND 1964*

GUY FAVREAU

The Conference of Attorneys-General . . . met four times in the . . . 14 months, in October 1960, in November 1960, in January 1961 and in September 1961. A meeting of Deputy Attorneys-General was also held in November 1961.

The Hon. E. D. Fulton, Minister of Justice, suggested to the first session that the Conference might first consider—without writing an amending formula—the question of transferring authority to Canada to amend the Constitution in all respects in which it is not now amendable by any legislative authority in Canada. It was suggested that a United Kingdom statue should be obtained to authorize the Parliament of Canada, with the consent of the legislatures of all the provinces, to make any amendments to the Constitution. It was thought that this would at least transfer to Canada final amending authority. It was admitted that this authority might be too rigid in some respects, but it was felt that once such complete amending authority had been transferred to Canada, a suitable amending formula could be agreed upon and enacted under the authority that had been conferred. However, it was generally believed that the Conference could find an acceptable amending formula at once, and discussion proceeded on that basis.

An amending formula eventually emerged from these discussions. Briefly it was as follows: the Parliament of Canada could make laws repealing, amending or re-enacting any provision of the Constitution of Canada subject to the following conditions, as set out in the draft:

1. No law relating to the legislative powers of the provinces, to the rights or privileges granted or secured by the Constitution of Canada to the legislature or the government of a province, to the assets or property of a province, to the use of the English or French language, to the minimum representation or "Senatorial floor" of a province in the House of Commons (section 51A), or to the amendment procedure itself, was to go into effect unless it was concurred in by the legislatures of all the provinces.

2. No law relating to one or more but not all the provinces should come into force unless it was concurred in by the legislature of every province to which the provision referred.

3. No law made in respect to education should come into force unless it was concurred in by the legislatures of all the provinces other than Newfoundland, and no law affecting education in Newfoundland was to go into force unless it was consented to by the legislature of Newfoundland.

* From *The Amendment of the Constitution of Canada*, a White Paper published by the Hon. Guy Favreau, Minister of Justice, Ottawa, February, 1965, pp. 27-31. By permission.

4. No law affecting any other provision of the Constitution should come into force unless it was concurred in by the legislatures of at least two-thirds of the provinces representing at least 50% of the population.

To overcome the rigidity of the rule of unanimity set forth in condition (1) above, a "delegation" clause was included in the formula. It provided that under specified conditions, the provinces could delegate to Parliament authority to enact a particular law—in respect of a subject coming within the major categories of provincial matters—that would otherwise be within the exclusive jurisdiction of the provinces to enact; and that Parliament could similarly delegate to provincial legislatures authority to enact a particular law that would otherwise be within the exclusive jurisdiction of Parliament to enact. Such delegation would specifically require, in each case, an Act and the consent of both Parliament and at least four provincial legislatures.

. . . However, some differences of view remained and the plan [the "Fulton Formula"] was not carried through to completion.

In June 1964, the Prime Minister of Canada, the Right Honourable L. B. Pearson, indicated, in connection with the amendment of section 94A of the British North America Act to provide for benefits supplementary to Old Age Pensions, his intention of proposing to the provincial governments that the question of the procedure for amending the Constitution in Canada be placed on the agenda of the federal-provincial conference to be held in Charlottetown the following September. . . .

At the conclusion of the Conference on September 2nd, the Prime Minister and Premiers announced in a press communique that they had ". . . affirmed their unanimous decision to conclude the repatriation of the B.N.A. Act without delay". To this end, the communique added, "they decided to complete a procedure for amending the Constitution in Canada based on the draft legislation proposed at the Constitutional Conference of 1961, which they accept in principle". It was also agreed that an early meeting of the Attorneys-General of Canada and the provinces would be called, to complete the amending formula devised by the 1961 Conference, and to report to the Prime Minister and Premiers.

The Attorneys-General met in Ottawa on October 5th, 6th, 13th and 14th. Their main problem—as had been forecast at the 1950 Conference and recognized in Charlottetown—was to integrate the exclusive power of amendment conferred on Parliament in 1949 (section 91(1)) into the procedure of amendment proposed in 1961. The Attorney-General agreed that the provision of section 91(1), suitably adjusted, should form part of a general and comprehensive amending procedure— just as the corresponding provision of section 92(1), relating to the exclusive power of amendment of the provinces, would be included in such a procedure.

The problem posed by section 91(1) was that it defined Parliament's powers in broad general terms—broader, for example, than those that had been contemplated in 1935-36. The intention in 1949 was to give Parliament power to amend the Constitution of Canada in its purely federal aspects only, but to leave it to the Courts to determine precisely what matters were included in or excluded from the powers conferred. It was the generality and uncertainty of this provision that had been objected to by the provinces in 1949-50 and in 1960-61.

The Conference therefore defined Parliament's exclusive power of amendment with greater accuracy and precision, so as to ensure that Parliament's authority would not conflict with fundamental provincial rights or with the other provisions of the amendment procedure. Specifically, this power was defined as applying to "the Constitution of Canada in relation to the executive Government of Canada, and the Senate and House of Commons". Certain exceptions were added, notably those concerning the representation of the provinces in the Senate, and the principles of proportionate representation of the provinces in the House of Commons. Comparison of this definition of Parliament's exclusive power of amendment with the definition that was contemplated in 1935-36 illustrates a marked degree of consistency in the thinking and the approach to this subject at both the federal and the provincial levels.

In addition to the substantial changes that resulted from inclusion of section 91(1) as revised, and section 92(1), the Attorneys-General recommended four other technical changes in the 1961 amending formula. They also added a new Part, providing for a schedule that would give the French version of the Act to be submitted to the United Kingdom Parliament, thus making both English and French texts official.

The Conference of Attorneys-General unanimously recommended this amending procedure to the Conference of the Prime Minister and Premiers, which, in turn, unanimously accepted it on October 14th, 1964. . . .

[Quebec subsequently withdrew its assent. For the exchange of letters confirming this, and for the Fulton-Favreau Formula, see *infra*. For the Fulton Formula, see the first edition of *Politics: Canada*, pp. 91-94, where it is reprinted *verbatim*, in company with an abridgement of Saskatchewan's objections to it, *ibid.*, pp. 94-98.]

THE FULTON-FAVREAU FORMULA

AN ACT TO PROVIDE FOR THE AMENDMENT IN CANADA OF THE CONSTITUTION OF CANADA*

October 14, 1964.

WHEREAS the Senate and House of Commons of Canada in Parliament assembled have submitted Addresses to Her Majesty praying that Her Majesty may graciously be pleased to cause a measure to be laid before the Parliament of the United Kingdom for the enactment of the provisions hereinafter set forth:

Be it therefore enacted by the Queen's most Excellent Majesty, by and with the advice and consent of the Lords Spiritual and Temporal, and com-

---

* Final draft of bill approved by the Federal-Provincial Conference of the Prime Minister and Premiers, October 14, 1964.

mons, in this present Parliament assembled, and by the authority of the same, as follows:

PART I

POWER TO AMEND THE CONSTITUTION OF CANADA

1.   Subject to this Part, the Parliament of Canada may make laws repealing, amending or re-enacting any provision of the Constitution of Canada.

2.   No law made under the authority of this Part affecting any provision of this Act or section 51A of the British North America Act, 1867, or affecting any provision of the Constitution of Canada relating to

(a)   the powers of the legislature granted to a province to make laws,

(b)   the right or privileges granted or secured by the Constitution of Canada to the legislature or the government of a province,

(c)   the assets or property of a province,

(d)   the use of English or French language,

shall come into force unless it is concurred in by the legislatures of all the provinces.

3. (1)   No law made under the authority of this Part affecting any provision of the Constitution of Canada that refers to one or more, but not all, of the provinces, shall come into force unless it is concurred in by the legislature of every province to which the provision refers.

(2)   Section 2 of this Act does not extend to any provision of the Constitution of Canada referred to in subsection (1) of this section.

4. (1)   No law made under the authority of this Part affecting any provision of the Constitution of Canada relating to education in any province other than Newfoundland shall come into force unless it is concurred in by the legislatures of all the provinces other than Newfoundland.

(2)   No law made under the authority of this Part affecting any provision of the Constitution of Canada relating to education in the province of Newfoundland shall come into force unless it is concurred in by the legislature of the province of Newfoundland.

(3)   Sections 2 and 3 of this Act do not extend to any provision of the Constitution of Canada referred to in subsection (1) or (2) of this section.

5.   No law made under the authority of this Part affecting any provision of the Constitution of Canada not coming within section 2, 3 or 4 of this Act shall come into force unless it is concurred in by the legislatures of at least two-thirds of the provinces representing at least fifty percent of the population of Canada according to the latest general census.

6.   Notwithstanding anything in the Constitution of Canada, the Parliament of Canada may exclusively make laws from time to time amending the Constitution of Canada in relation to the executive Government of Canada, and the Senate and House of Commons, except as regards

(a) the functions of the Queen and the Governor General in relation to the Parliament or Government of Canada;

(b) the requirements of the Constitution of Canada respecting a yearly session of Parliament;

(c) the maximum period fixed by the Constitution of Canada for the duration of the House of Commons, except that the Parliament of Canada may, in time of real or apprehended war, invasion or insurrection, continue a House of Commons beyond such maximum period, if such continuation is not opposed by the votes of more than one-third of the members of such House;

(d) the number of members by which a province is entitled to be represented in the Senate;

(e) the residence qualification of Senators and the requirements of the Constitution of Canada for the summoning of persons to the Senate by the Governor General in the Queen's name;

(f) the right of a province to a number of members in the House of Commons not less than the number of Senators representing such province;

(g) the principles of proportionate representation of the provinces in the House of Commons prescribed by the Constitution of Canada; and

(h) the use of the English or French language.

7. Notwithstanding anything in the Constitution of Canada, in each province the legislature may exclusively make laws in relation to the amendment from time to time of the Constitution of the province, except as regards the office of Lieutenant-Governor.

8. Any law to repeal, amend or re-enact any provision of the Constitution of Canada that is not authorized to be made either by the Parliament of Canada under the authority of section 6 of this Act or by the legislature of a province under the authority of section 7 of this Act is subject to the provisions of sections 1 to 5 of this Act.

9. Nothing in this Part diminishes any power of the Parliament of Canada or of the legislature of a province, existing at the coming into force of this Act, to make laws in relation to any matter.

10. No Act of the Parliament of the United Kingdom passed after the coming into force of this Act shall extend or be deemed to extend to Canada or to any province or territory of Canada as part of the law thereof.

11. Without limiting the meaning of the expression "Constitution of Canada", in this Part that expression includes the following enactments and any order, rule or regulation thereunder, namely,

(a) the British North America Acts, 1867 to 1964;

(b) the Manitoba Act, 1870;

(c) the Parliament of Canada Act, 1875;

(d) the Canadian Speaker (Appointment of Deputy) Act, 1895;

(e) the Alberta Act;

(f) the Saskatchewan Act;

   (g)   the Statute of Westminister, 1931, in so far as it is part of the law of Canada; and

   (h)   this Act.

PART II

BRITISH NORTH AMERICA ACT, 1867, AMENDED

12.   Class 1 of section 91 of the British North America Act, 1867, as enacted by the British North America (No. 2) Act, 1949, and class 1 of section 92 of the British North America Act, 1867, are repealed.

13.   The British North America Act, 1867, is amended by re-numbering section 94A thereof as 94B and by adding thereto, immediately after section 94 thereof, the following heading and section:

DELEGATION OF LEGISLATIVE AUTHORITY

"94A. (1) Notwithstanding anything in this or in any other Act, the Parliament of Canada may make laws in relation to any matters coming within the classes of subjects enumerated in classes (6), (10), (13) and (16) of section 92 of this Act, but no statute enacted under the authority of this subsection shall have effect in any province unless the legislature of that province has consented to the operation of such a statute in that province.

    (2) The Parliament of Canada shall not have authority to enact a statute under subsection (1) of this section unless

   (a)   prior to the enactment thereof the legislatures of at least four of the provinces have consented to the operation of such a statute as provided in that subsection, or

   (b)   it is declared by the Parliament of Canada that the Government of Canada has consulted with the governments of all the provinces, and that the enactment of the statute is of concern to fewer than four of the provinces and the provinces so declared by the Parliament of Canada to be concerned have under the authority of their legislatures consented to the enactment of such a statute.

    (3) Notwithstanding anything in this or in any other Act, the legislature of a province may make laws in the province in relation to any matter coming within the legislative jurisdiction of the Parliament of Canada.

    (4) No statute enacted by a province under the authority of subsection (3) of this section shall have effect unless

   (a)   prior to the enactment thereof the Parliament of Canada has consented to the enactment of such a statute by the legislature of that province, and

   (b)   a similar statute has under the authority of subsection (3) of this section been enacted by the legislatures of at least three other provinces.

    (5) The Parliament of Canada or the legislature of a province may make

laws for the imposition of punishment by fine, penalty or imprisonment for enforcing any law made by it under the authority of this section.

(6) A consent given under this section may at any time be revoked, and

(a) if a consent given under subsection (1) or (2) of this section is revoked, any law made by the Parliament of Canada to which such consent relates that is operative in the province in which the consent is revoked shall thereupon cease to have effect in that province but the revocation of the consent does not affect the operation of that law in any other province, and

(b) if a consent given under subsection (4) of this section is revoked, any law made by the legislature of a province to which the consent relates shall thereupon cease to have effect.

(7) The Parliament of Canada may repeal any law made by it under the authority of this section, in so far as it is part of the law of one or more provinces, but if any repeal under the authority of this subsection does not relate to all of the provinces in which that law is operative, the repeal does not affect the operation of that law in any province to which the repeal does not relate.

(8) The legislature of a province may repeal any law made by it under the authority of this section, but the repeal under the authority of this subsection of any law does not affect the operation in any other province of any law enacted by that province under the authority of this section."

PART III

FRENCH VERSION

14.   The French version of this Act set forth in the Schedule to this Act shall form part of this Act.

PART IV

CITATION AND COMMENCEMENT

15.   This Act may be cited as the *Constitution of Canada Amendment Act.*
16.   This Act shall come into force on the...............day of................

CRITICISMS OF THE FORMULA*

Mr. Andrew Brewin (Greenwood): Mr. Speaker, I regret that we in this party are not able to join the mood of self congratulation which has surrounded the announcement of the agreement between the provincial premiers and the Prime Minister on a formula for repatriation or amendment within Canada of the Canadian constitution. In our opinion this occasion should not be one of national

* From *House of Commons Debates,* October 15, 1964, pp. 9069-9070. By permission of the Queen's Printer.

rejoicing but rather one of national mourning. . . . The truth as we see it is that the agreed formula and the draft act which accompanies it will be a monumental error. If I may borrow the expression used by Professor Bora Laskin, an acknowledged constitutional expert, the adoption of this formula would be an unmitigated constitutional disaster.

No one denies the desirability of working out a formula for constitutional amendment which would enable the constitution of Canada to be amended within Canada. We in this party have frequently urged that this course be followed. But it would be immature for Canadians to allow this legitimate national aspiration to obscure the fact that what we are going to be asked to do is to exchange the easy yoke of a relic of colonialism for the self imposed bondage of a constitutional straitjacket.

The Fulton-Favreau formula, as it must now be known, is a formula for constitutional futility and absolute rigidity. The form of the communique issued and of the draft act itself which was attached to this communique obscure this reality; because the announcement states that as a general rule amendments may be made to the constitution by the parliament of Canada, acting with the concurrence of the legislatures of at least two-thirds of the provinces representing at least 50 percent of the population.

If this statement were true it would of course represent a reasonable degree of flexibility. Unfortunately it is not true. The exceptions, so called, to this general rule are infinitely more important than the general rule itself; in fact it is very hard to imagine anything that would fall within the general rule. The exceptions specifically mentioned in this act include any change in the constitution affecting any provision of the constitution of Canada relating to the powers of the legislature of a province to make laws, and state that such amendments cannot be made unless concurred in by the legislatures of all the provinces. This exception, so-called, covers the distribution of powers between the provincial legislatures and the federal parliament set out in sections 91 and 92 of the British North America Act.

This, as any person with any knowledge in this field knows, represents the very core of our constitutional system, and the formula in effect hands an absolute veto to every individual province in respect of amendments to that constitutional core. Even the United Nations, which has been plagued by the veto, gives that power of veto only to the great powers. We propose by this formula to hand it to every individual province no matter how small.

It is not only the substance of the proposed amending formula but the way it has been arrived at which calls for the strongest comment. This formula has been presented to the Canadian people as the result of a closed conference between the Minister of Justice and the attorneys general. We say that this hole in the corner procedure is totally unsatisfactory. For one thing, this parliament is being practically bypassed. It is true that we were allowed one day to debate this matter, but on that one day the Minister of Justice carefully refrained from stating what the attitude of the government was, or from seeking to justify the restrictive formula which is apparently proposed by the government.

In that debate the hon. member for Royal, speaking for the official opposition, and I, speaking for my own party, both suggested the importance, which has been mentioned today by the right hon. Leader of the Opposition, of linking the amending formula with the entrenchment of basic individual rights, creating a constitutional bill of rights. Our suggestions made in this parliament appear to be totally ignored in favour of this closed conference. . . .

BIBLIOGRAPHY

Alexander, E. R., "A Constitutional Strait Jacket for Canada," *Canadian Bar Review,* Vol. XLIII, No. 3, March, 1965.

Angers, F. A., "Le problème du rapatriement de la constitution," *L'Action nationale,* Vol. LIV, novembre, 1964.

Brady, A., "Constitutional Amendment and the Federation," *C.J.E.P.S.,* Vol. XXIX, No. 4, November, 1963.

Cook, R., *Provincial Autonomy, Minority Rights and the Compact Theory, 1867-1921,* Studies of the Royal Commission on Bilingualism and Biculturalism, No. 4, Ottawa, Queen's Printer, 1969.

Gérin-Lajoie, P., *Constitutional Amendment in Canada,* Toronto, University of Toronto Press, 1950.

Laskin, B., "Amendment of the Constitution: Applying the Fulton-Favreau Formula," *McGill Law Journal,* Vol. XI, No. 1, January, 1965.

Marion, S., "Le pacte fédératif et les minorités françaises au Canada," *Cahiers des dix,* Vol. 29, 1964.

Morin, J. Y., "Le rapatriement de la constitution," *Cité libre,* Vol. XVI, No. 2, décembre, 1964.

Stanley, G. F. G., "Act or Pact? Another Look at Confederation," *Canadian Historical Association Annual Report,* Ottawa, 1956.

Rowat, D. C., "Recent Developments in Canadian Federalism," *C.J.E.P.S.,* Vol. XVIII, No. 1, February, 1952.

EIGHTEEN
PROTECTING CIVIL RIGHTS

The question of whether or not Canada should have a formal Bill or Charter of Human Rights has been under much discussion in recent years. The British North America Act of 1867 contained no such declaration of rights, which might be similar, for instance, to that found in the Bill of Rights attached as the first ten amendments to the American constitution. This omission from the B.N.A. Act reflected, of course, the British tradition that an individual's rights were protected more satisfactorily by judicial interpretation of common law and by specific legislative enactments than by their enshrinement in a formal, "written" constitution.

In Canada the argument has centred on two major questions: first, whether the conventional British approach should continue to hold sway over the example set by American practice, and second, if it were thought advisable to move in the latter direction, whether a bill of rights should be entrenched within a written constitution—for instance, within a revised B.N.A. Act—or whether it should be enacted merely as ordinary statutory law. The second question raises another consideration in a federal country such as Canada, namely, the thorny issue of divided jurisdiction. Since some of the subjects which would be included undoubtedly within either an entrenched, constitutional bill of rights or an ordinary statutory law would fall within the competence of the federal Parliament and others would fall within the jurisdiction of provincial legislatures, there would be a need for agreement on subject matter between the federal government and presumably all the provincial governments if one wished to achieve a uniform, pan-Canadian charter of rights. Such a bill of rights would entail also the additional difficulty of arriving at a method of amendment of the charter which was acceptable to all jurisdictions.

Because of problems of this sort, Mr. Diefenbaker, when he was prime minister, fulfilled his long-standing ambition to obtain a bill of right for Canada by settling for the enactment by Parliament of an ordinary statute. Thus, the "Diefenbaker" Canadian Bill of Rights came into being as a federal law in 1960. It is reprinted in its statutory form *infra*. For an excellent, extensive study of its history, contents, and the issues involved, see in particular the book by Professor Walter Tarnopolsky noted in the bibliography in this chapter.

The entire subject was raised again for active discussion in 1968 when Mr. Trudeau, who was then the minister of justice, presented vigorously to the first of the current series of federal-provincial constitutional conferences his arguments for a constitutionally-entrenched charter of rights, which he had long regarded as a superior form to a mere statute. His views were expressed in writing to the conference in a federal government position paper which appeared under his name and was entitled *A Canadian Charter of Human Rights*. An extract from this document giving the gist of his arguments and an outline of the rights which he suggested ought to be included in any bill of rights, follows in this chapter.

A number of the provincial governments have been cool to Mr. Trudeau's proposals but the most incisive critique yet available of both the general arguments for such a charter and the specific contents of the federal paper have come from Professor Donald Smiley. He presented his views in a major article which is reprinted here in a slightly reduced version.

Discussions about the advisability of entrenching rights in a constitution tended to be the focus of attention during the late nineteen-sixties. The "Diefenbaker" Bill of Rights was regarded as a dead letter by virtually all commentators because although it had been on the statute books since 1960, it had seldom been cited by counsel in pleading cases or been weighed heavily by courts in rendering decisions. Then, suddenly, in late 1969 it took a new lease on life when the Supreme Court of Canada made much of it in handing down what appears to be a leading civil libertarian decision in "the Drybones case." An account of this interesting case and its possible implications is contained in a lively newspaper article which concludes this chapter.

The Drybones case puts a large question mark over the course that is likely to be pursued now in protecting civil liberties in Canada. Will there be a continuation of the effort to entrench rights constitutionally, or will there be a tendency to return to reinforced interpretation of the existing Canadian Bill of Rights?

DIEFENBAKER'S CANADIAN BILL OF RIGHTS*

8 - 9 ELIZ. II, C. 44

[*Assented to 10th August, 1960*]

An act for the Recognition and Protection of Human Rights and Fundamental Freedoms

The Parliament of Canada, affirming that the Canadian Nation is founded upon principles that acknowledge the supremacy of God, the dignity and worth of the human person and the position of the family in a society of free men and free institutions;

* From *Statutes of Canada*, 1960, Vol. I, pp. 519-522. By permission of the Queen's Printer.

Affirming also that men and institutions remain free only when freedom is founded upon respect for moral and spiritual values and the rule of law;

And being desirous of enshrining these principles and the human rights and fundamental freedoms derived from them, in a Bill of Rights which shall reflect the respect of Parliament for its constitutional authority and which shall ensure the protection of these rights and freedoms in Canada.

Therefore Her Majesty, by and with the advice and consent of the Senate and House of Commons of Canada, enacts as follows:

PART I

Bill of Rights

1.   It is hereby recognized and declared that in Canada there have existed and shall continue to exist without discrimination by reason of race, national origin, color, religion or sex, the following human rights and fundamental freedoms, namely,

(a) The right of the individual to life, liberty, security of the person and enjoyment of property, and the right not to be deprived thereof except by due process of law;

(b) The right of the individual to equality before the law and the protection of the law;

(c) Freedom of religion;

(d) Freedom of speech;

(e) Freedom of assembly and association; and

(f) Freedom of the press.

2.   Every law of Canada shall, unless it is expressly declared by an Act of the Parliament of Canada that it shall operate notwithstanding the Canadian Bill of Rights, be so construed and applied as not to abrogate, abridge or infringe or to authorize the abrogation, abridgement or infringement of any of the rights or freedoms herein recognized and declared, and in particular, no law of Canada shall be construed or applied so as to

(a) Authorize or effect the arbitrary detention, imprisonment or exile of any person;

(b) Impose or authorize the imposition of cruel and unusual treatment or punishment;

(c) Deprive a person who has been arrested or detained
   (i) of the right to be informed promptly of the reason for his arrest or detention,
   (ii) of the right to retain and instruct counsel without delay, or
   (iii) of the remedy by way of habeas corpus for the determination of the validity of his detention and for his release if the detention is not lawful;

(d) Authorize a court, tribunal, commission, board or other authority to compel a person to give evidence if he is denied counsel, protection against self crimination or other constitutional safeguards;

(e) Deprive a person of the right to a fair hearing in accordance with the principles of fundamental justice for the determination of his rights and obligations;

(f) Deprive a person charged with a criminal offense of the right to be presumed innocent until proved guilty according to law in a fair and public hearing by an independent and impartial tribunal, or of the right to reasonable bail without just cause; or

(g) Deprive a person of the right to the assistance of an interpreter in any proceedings in which he is involved or in which he is a party or a witness, before a court, commission, board or other tribunal, if he does not understand or speak the language in which such proceedings are conducted.

3.   The Minister of Justice shall, in accordance with such regulations as may be prescribed by the Governor in Council, examine every proposed regulation submitted in draft form to the Clerk of the Privy Council pursuant to the Regulations Act and every Bill introduced in or presented to the House of Commons, in order to ascertain whether any of the provisions thereof are inconsistent with the purposes and provisions of this part and he shall report any such inconsistency to the House of Commons at the first convenient opportunity.

4.   The provisions of this part shall be known as the Canadian Bill of Rights.

PART II

5.   (1) Nothing in Part I shall be construed to abrogate or abridge any human right or fundamental freedom not enumerated therein that may have existed in Canada at the commencement of this Act.

(2) The expression "law of Canada" in Part I means an Act of the Parliament of Canada enacted before or after the coming into force of this Act, any order, rule or regulation thereunder, and any law in force in Canada or in any part of Canada at the commencement of this Act that is subject to be repealed, abolished or altered by the Parliament of Canada.

(3) The provisions of Part I shall be construed as extending only to matters coming within the legislative authority of the Parliament of Canada.

6.   Section 6 of the War Measures Act is repealed and the following substituted therefor:

"6.   (1) Sections 3, 4 and 5 shall come into force only upon the issue of a proclamation of the Governor in Council declaring that war, invasion or insurrection, real or apprehended, exists.

(2) A proclamation declaring that war, invasion or insurrection, real or apprehended, exists shall be laid before Parliament forthwith after its issue, or, if Parliament is then not sitting, within the first fifteen days next thereafter that Parliament is sitting.

(3) Where a proclamation has been laid before Parliament pursuant to subsection (2), a notice of motion in either House signed by ten members thereof and made in accordance with the rules of that House within ten days of the day the proclamation was laid before Parliament, praying that the proclamation be revoked, shall be debated in that House at the first convenient opportunity within the four sitting days next after the day the motion in that House was made.

(4) If both Houses of Parliament resolve that the proclamation be revoked, it shall cease to have effect, and Sections 3, 4 and 5 shall cease to be in force until those sections are again brought into force by a further proclamation but without prejudice to the previous operation of those sections or anything duly done or suffered thereunder or any offense committed or any penalty or forfeiture or punishment incurred.

(5) Any act or thing done or authorized or any order or regulation made under the authority of this Act, shall be deemed not to be an abrogation, abridgement or infringement of any right or freedom recognized by the Canadian Bill of Rights."

PROPOSAL FOR A CONSTITUTIONAL CHARTER OF HUMAN RIGHTS*

PIERRE ELLIOTT TRUDEAU

THE NEED

Canada's main constitutional documents—the British North America Act, 1867 and its amendments—contain few guarantees of specific liberties. The courts have from time to time been invited to find in the B.N.A. Act some implied guarantee that fundamental rights are constitutionally protected from either federal or provincial encroachment, but such an interpretation has never since been the basis of a majority judgment in the higher courts. At this time in their history, Canadians are not afforded any guarantees of fundamental rights which (a) limit governmental power *and* (b) possess a large measure of permanence because of the requirement that it be amended not by ordinary legislative process but only by the more rigorous means of constitutional amendment.

The 1960 Canadian Bill of Rights has served to inhibit Parliament from amending the terms of that Bill and from violating its principles, but this is not a constitutional limitation on Parliament, only an influence. Additionally, that Bill has in practice had a limited application because the Courts have held that it does not expressly over-ride any provisions inconsistent with it which may be

* From *A Canadian Charter of Human Rights,* Ottawa, Queen's Printer, 1968. By permission of the Queen's Printer.

contained in earlier federal statutes. . . . [However, see *infra,* Rae Corelli, "How An Indian Changed Canada's Civil Rights Laws."]

Nor can any other human rights legislation (federal or provincial) be considered truly "constitutional": all of it is subject to amendment or repeal by the enacting legislature; none of it attempts to affect the validity or effect of other conflicting laws. Such legislation, in addition, is generally directed against the invasion of human rights by individuals, not by governments or legislatures (though in some cases it does bind the Crown).

To overcome these shortcomings while preserving the essential purpose of the present Bill, a constitutionally entrenched Bill of Rights is required which will declare invalid any existing or future statute in conflict with it. Language in this form would possess a degree of permanence and would over-ride even unambiguous legislation purporting to violate the protected rights.

In addition to these considerations of permanency, there is an even more pressing reason why a bill of rights, in order to be effective, must assume a constitutional— rather than a merely legislative—form. This arises out of the Canadian constitutional division of legislative competence as between Parliament and the provincial legislatures. In Canada, authority to legislate with respect to some of the rights regarded as fundamental lies with the provinces, authority to legislate with respect to others of these rights lies with Parliament, and authority with respect to the balance is shared by the two. Only by a single constitutional enactment will the fundamental rights of all Canadians be guaranteed equal protection. A bill of rights so enacted would identify clearly the various rights to be protected, and remove them henceforth from governmental interference. Such an amendment, unlike most proposed constitutional amendments, would not involve a transfer of legislative power from one government to another. Instead, it would involve a common agreement to restrict the power of governments. The basic human values of all Canadians—political, legal, egalitarian, linguistic—would in this way be guaranteed throughout Canada in a way that the 1960 Canadian Bill of Rights, or any number of provincial bills of rights, is incapable of providing.

THE CONTENTS

. . . Existing human rights measures in Canada are limited in scope. The Canadian Bill of Rights emphasizes political freedoms (speech, assembly, religion) and legal rights (freedom from arbitrary deprivation of life, liberty or property, and equality before the law). Other federal legislation and most provincial legislation is confined to prohibitions against discrimination in employment, admission to trade union membership, or the provision of accommodation. Some do go further. The Saskatchewan Bill of Rights, for example, embraces political and legal rights as well as a wider range of egalitarian rights, and the old Freedom of Worship Act (enacted during the pre-Confederation Union and still in effect in Ontario and Quebec) gives some guarantee of freedom of religion.

It is now suggested that there be included in a constitutional bill those rights which have been legislatively protected in Canada, and to add to them those linguistic rights which are recommended by the Royal Commission on Bilingualism and Biculturalism in the first volume of the Commission's report.

Rights which may be included in a bill of the sort under consideration here fall into five broad categories: political, legal, egalitarian, linguistic, and economic. . . .

1. POLITICAL RIGHTS

This term is used in a broad sense to cover matters of belief, their expression and advocacy. The several political rights (here called "freedoms") are enumerated; following each there is a short discussion of the major legal considerations which attach thereto.

(a) Freedom of expression

These freedoms are presently protected legislatively in Section 1 of the Canadian Bill of Rights and in section 4 of the Saskatchewan Bill of Rights. The cases which have been decided to date indicate that these freedoms are largely subject to control by Parliament in the exercise of its criminal law power. There are, however, aspects of freedom of expression which may be subject to provincial limitation, as for example through the law of defamation, or through laws regulating advertising in provincial and municipal elections. For this reason adequate protection can only be offered in the form of a constitutional bill.

The means of definition of this freedom are of equal importance to its declaration. The question arises whether freedom of expression is best guaranteed in simple terms without qualification, or whether the limitations of this freedom ought to be specified. Opponents of an unconditional declaration fear that such wording might restrict the application of Criminal Code prohibitions against obscene or seditious publications, or provincial laws pertaining to defamation or film censorship. This is unlikely, however, for free speech as it developed in England was never equated with complete license. . . .

In Canada, existing federal laws against sedition and obscenity have been construed so narrowly that it is unlikely they would be held to conflict with a guarantee of free speech. The obscenity provisions of the Criminal Code have been applied since the enactment of the Canadian Bill of Rights without any conflict being recognized.

It is also unlikely that existing provincial laws against defamation would be upset by a free speech guarantee. As long as such legislation is confined to protecting long-recognized private rights of reputation there would be no conflict with the concept of "free speech." . . .

The alternative to a broad, unqualified description of "freedom of speech" is an enumeration of specific exceptions. An example of this more detailed type of language is found in Article 10 of the European Convention on Human Rights. . . .

A similar, detailed, approach has been taken in several constitutions patterned after the European Convention. By specifying the grounds for permissible limitations upon the right, possible uncertainties have been removed. The disadvantage of this technique, however, is its lack of flexibility and the difficulty of adapting the language to changed circumstances. For this reason the simple form of description is recommended.

(b) Freedom of conscience and religion

There is some legislative protection now. The Canadian Bill of Rights, section 1, recites "freedom of religion". The Saskatchewan Bill of Rights, section 3, declares the right to "freedom of conscience, opinion, and belief, and freedom of religious association, teaching, practice and worship". The Freedom of Worship Act (applicable in Ontario and Quebec) declares the right to "the free exercise and enjoyment of religious profession and worship". It is arguable, however, that a guarantee of "freedom of religion" does not protect the freedom of the person who chooses to have no religion. To protect such persons, consideration could be given to widening the guarantee to protect, for example, "freedom of conscience".

Freedom with respect to the individual's internal belief or conscience might well be considered absolute and not qualified in any way. It is the external manifestation of the exercise or furtherance of beliefs which may give rise to problems and the need for limitations in the interest of public safety and order.

In these areas, for example, no one would dispute that federal laws should be able to prevent acts in the exercise of religious beliefs which would constitute obscenity, sedition, bigamy, or homicide. It is more debatable, however, what further powers Parliament should possess to permit it to restrict other religiously-motivated acts. An example is the imposition of Sunday closing of businesses on Christians and non-Christians alike. . . .

(c) Freedom of assembly and association

These freedoms are now legislatively protected by section 1 of the Canadian Bill of Rights and by section 5 of the Saskatchewan Bill of Rights. They are closely related to freedom of expression and many of the comments made with respect to legislative jurisdiction over freedom of expression are equally applicable here. As with freedom of expression, they are not usually considered to be absolute but rather are subject to limitations in the interest of public order. Present federal limitations of this nature are mainly found in the Criminal Code relating to unlawful assembly, riot, conspiracy, watching and besetting, and disturbing the peace. Provincial limitations exist in laws dealing with the incorporation or regulation of commercial, educational, charitable and other organizations otherwise within provincial control, in the use of roads and parks for public assemblies, and the like. All these limitations appear to be consistent with freedom of assembly and association so long as they are clearly related to the preservation of public safety and order.

2. LEGAL RIGHTS

These rights go to the very root of the concept of the liberty of the individual, so highly prized in Canada. They are dealt with now, to a certain extent, in sections 1 and 2 of the Canadian Bill of Rights and in section 6 of The Saskatchewan Bill of Rights. They are recognized as well by other statutory provisions and by rules of statutory interpretation developed by the courts. There is not, however, any constitutional protection of the rights.

These rights and their protection fall within both federal and provincial jurisdiction, depending on the context. . . .

The Canadian Bill of Rights lists most of the legal rights which need protection; with modification its provisions could form the basis for similar guarantees in a constitutional bill. Using it as a frame of reference, it is suggested that the rights enumerated below should be guaranteed:

(a) *General security of life, liberty and property*
The Canadian Bill of Rights declares

> The right of the individual to life, liberty, security of the person and enjoyment of property, and the right not to be deprived thereof except by due process of law.

. . . The words "due process of law" have been given a double interpretation in the United States. The first of these is as a guarantee of procedural fairness. In this respect, similar words used in the Canadian Bill of Rights are intended to guarantee the specific requirements of fair procedure. The words "due process" have, in addition, been given a substantive interpretation in the United States' courts with the result that the words have been employed as a standard by which the propriety of all legislation is judged. At one time the words used in this latter sense resulted in the judicial invalidation of minimum wage legislation, laws against child labour, and hours-of-work statutes. . . .

In examining American experience with "due process", it appears that the guarantee as applied to protection of "life" and personal "liberty" has been generally satisfactory, whereas substantive due process as applied to "liberty" of contract and to "property" has created the most controversy. It might therefore be possible to apply the due process guarantee only to "life", personal "liberty" and "security of the person". The specific guarantees of procedural fairness set out elsewhere in the bill would continue to apply to any interference with contracts or property. In this fashion the possibility of any substantive "due process" problems would be avoided.

In the alternative, if "due process" is to remain applicable to "liberty" of contract and to "property", there should be spelled out in some detail what is involved. . . .

(b) *Equal protection of the law*
The Canadian Bill of Rights, section 1(b) declares "the right of the individual to equality before the law and the protection of the law".

It might be argued that this wording serves to overlap other provisions. . . . [But] because the basic concept is sound, it is desirable to retain some such guarantee. . . .

(c) Cruel punishment, etc.

Section 2(b) of the Canadian Bill of Rights now provides that no law of Canada is to be deemed to "impose or authorize the imposition of cruel and unusual treatment or punishment". This provision is similar to one in the English Bill of Rights of 1689. A guarantee against such treatment or punishment is also found in the Eighth Amendment to the U.S. Constitution, where it has caused few difficulties. While a court would likely be extremely reluctant to substitute its opinion of a proper punishment for that of the legislature, the power to do so could prove useful in extreme cases.

(d) Rights of an arrested person

Section 2(c) of the Canadian Bill of Rights states that no law of Canada shall be deemed to
> deprive a person who has been arrested or detained
>> (i) of the right to be informed promptly of the reason for his arrest or detention,
>> (ii) of the right to retain and instruct counsel without delay, or
>> (iii) of the remedy by way of *habeas corpus* for the determination of the validity of his detention and for his release if the detention is not lawful. . . .

It is recommended that the same rights be protected in a constitutional bill. . . .

(e) Right of a witness to counsel

Section 2(d) of the Canadian Bill of Rights provides that no law of Canada is to be deemed to
> authorize a court, tribunal, commission, board or other authority to compel a person to give evidence if he is denied counsel, protection against self-crimination or other constitutional safeguards . . .

and this right should appear in a constitutional bill.

(f) Fair hearing

Section 2(e) of the Canadian Bill of Rights provides that no law of Canada shall be deemed to
> deprive a person of the right to a fair hearing in accordance with the principles of fundamental justice for the determination of his rights and obligations . . .

This is a fundamental requirement which is already generally recognized in the public law of Canada. In a new constitutional bill of rights it might well be placed in association with the fundamental rights to life, liberty and property.

. . . Wider language may be needed if it is the intention that "fair hearing" requirements be extended to such activities as the granting or withdrawal of licences by government agencies, the certification or decertification of unions, or the conduct of a hearing in an investigation under the Income Tax Act or under a provincial Securities Act.

(g) Presumption of innocence

Section 2(f) of the Canadian Bill of Rights states that no law of Canada is to be deemed to

> deprive a person charged with a criminal offence of the right to be presumed innocent until proved guilty according to law in a fair and public hearing by and independent and impartial tribunal, or of the right to reasonable bail without just cause . . .

The presumption of innocence is a fundamental ingredient of Canadian criminal justice, and must be guaranteed. . . .

A constitutional bill of rights will assure that these provisions regarding presumption of innocence, and fair and public hearings will apply equally to prosecutions under provincial legislation as to prosecutions under federal law. Such protection is not afforded by the 1960 Canadian Bill of Rights.

(h) The right to an interpreter

Section 2(g) of the Canadian Bill of Rights states that no law of Canada is deemed to

> deprive a person of the right to the assistance of an interpreter. . . .

This is an important right, and should be retained.

(i) Other legal rights for possible inclusion

There are other legal rights which might be included in a constitutional bill of rights which were not included in the 1960 Canadian Bill. Following are some examples.

> (i) Guarantee against *ex post facto* laws creating crimes retroactively . . .
>
> (ii) Guarantee against unreasonable searches and seizures. . . . At the present time in Canada, evidence obtained not only by means of an unreasonable search but by actual illegal means (as, for example, by theft) is generally completely admissible in the Courts. It is suggested that this double standard of conduct should no longer be tolerated on the part of law enforcement agencies. Illegally obtained evidence should be as inadmissible as an illegally obtained confession.
>
> (iii) Guarantee of the right of a citizen not to be exiled. . . . It is suggested that any exile, whether arbitrary or not, should be prohibited. . . .

3. EGALITARIAN RIGHTS

. . . Existing legislation shows a widespread concern about racial and similar discrimination. The Canadian Bill of Rights declares that the rights listed in Section 1 . . . exist without discrimination by "race, national origin, colour, religion or sex". Federal legislation and legislation in eight provinces and both territories prohibit discrimination in employment. Seven provinces and the two territories also prohibit discrimination in public accommodation. The greater number of these statutory provisions, however, are designed to affect only private conduct. A constitutional bill of rights would serve to limit discriminatory activities on the part of governments as well.

The prohibited criteria of discrimination, as well as the areas of activity where discrimination is forbidden, should be considered in any anti-discrimination clauses:

(a) Prohibited criteria of discrimination

It is suggested that the bill should provide that the criteria listed in section 1 of the Canadian Bill of Rights—race, national origin, colour, religion, sex—should be retained as prohibited criteria for discrimination. Additional prohibited criteria might be considered, as for example, ethnic origin.

(b) Areas of activity where discrimination might be forbidden

  (i)   voting or the holding of public office;
  (ii) employment—here it is suggested that there be added a qualification to the effect that distinctions based on a *bona fide* occupational qualification are not prohibited. In this way, possible difficulties concerning, for example, provincial legislation authorizing the hiring of teachers for denominational schools on the basis of their religious belief will be avoided;
  (iii) admission to professions where admission is controlled by professional bodies acting under legislative authority;
  (iv) education—special provisions will be required here to avoid inconsistencies with the guarantees of separate or denominational schools contained in section 93 of the B.N.A. Act and corresponding sections in other constitutional statutes relating to other provinces. . . ;
  (v)   use of public accommodation, facilities and services;
  (vi) contracting with public agencies;
  (vii) acquiring of property and interests in property. . . .

4. LINGUISTIC RIGHTS

Section 133 of the British North America Act, 1867 provides as follows:

> Either the English or the French Language may be used by any Person in the Debates of the Houses of the Parliament of Canada and of the Houses of the Legislature of Quebec; and both those Languages shall be used in the respective Records and Journals of those Houses; and either of those Languages may be used by any Person or in any Pleading or Process in or issuing from any Court of Canada established under this Act, and in or from all or any of the Courts of Quebec.
>
> The Acts of the Parliament of Canada and of the Legislature of Quebec shall be printed and published in both those Languages.

Thus there already exists a constitutional guarantee of the use of both languages in governmental processes, but this extends only to the legislature and courts of Quebec and to the Parliament and courts of Canada. In matters of education, it has been held that the guarantees of separate or denominational schools do not include any guarantee of the right to use either language as a medium of instruction.

It is submitted that these language guarantees be extended to other institutions of government and to education as has been recommended by the Royal Commission on Bilingualism and Biculturalism. These guarantees would prove effective, it is suggested, if incorporated into a constitutional bill of rights. . . .

5. ECONOMIC RIGHTS

The kind of rights referred to here are those which seek to ensure some advantage to the individual and which require positive action by the state. The Universal Declaration of Human Rights, for example, included such rights as the right to work, the right to protection against unemployment, the right to form and join trade unions, the right to social security, the right to rest and leisure, the right to an adequate standard of living, the right to education, and the right to participate in the cultural life of the community. The United Nations Covenant on Economic, Social and Cultural Rights adopted by the General Assembly in 1966 included and elaborated upon these rights.

The guarantee of such economic rights is desirable and should be an ultimate objective for Canada. There are, however, good reasons for putting aside this issue at this stage and proceeding with the protection of political, legal, egalitarian and linguistic rights. It might take considerable time to reach agreement on the rights to be guaranteed and on the feasibility of implementation. The United Nations recognized these problems when it prepared two separate Covenants on Human Rights—one on Civil and Political Rights and one on Economic, Social and Cultural Rights, thus giving nations an opportunity to accede to them one at a time.

It is therefore suggested that it is advisable not to attempt to include economic rights in the constitutional bill of rights at this time.

THE CASE AGAINST THE CANADIAN CHARTER OF HUMAN RIGHTS*

DONALD V. SMILEY

. . . Proposals that there be the entrenchment in the Canadian constitution of what are variously regarded as fundamental human rights have come from several quarters since the Second World War. The scheme laid before the federal-provincial

* From the Presidential Address to the Canadian Political Science Association, 1969 published in the *Canadian Journal of Political Science/Revue Canadienne de Science politique*, Vol. II, No. 3, September, 1969. By permission of the author and the publisher.

constitutional conference by the government of Canada in February 1968 recommended an entrenched charter of what were classified as political, legal, egalitarian, and linguistic rights. . . .

It might plausibly be argued that the opposition of most of the provinces to the constitutional entrenchment of human rights as recommended by the federal authorities makes the adoption of such a measure very improbable in the foreseeable future. In terms of their positions as stated before and at the constitutional conference of February 1969 only Newfoundland, Prince Edward Island, and New Brunswick support the federal scheme. British Columbia, Alberta, and Manitoba are opposed to any entrenchment of individual rights. Ontario, Nova Scotia, and Saskatchewan have accepted the desirability of the charter with the major modification that it should extend only to fundamental political rights. Quebec has accepted the principle of entrenchment, but only under the conditions that far-reaching reforms are affected in the distribution of legislative powers and the establishment of a tribunal dealing exclusively with constitutional matters. Despite this lack of agreement, it is possible that the federal government will in the end sponsor some kind of "opting in" procedure as suggested by Prime Minister Pearson in respect to linguistic rights at the 1968 conference. If such an amendment were effected, rights within federal legislative jurisdiction would be constitutionally entrenched throughout Canada and in provincial matters subsequent to particular provincial governments or legislatures giving their agreement. Apart from such a procedure, the whole of the Canadian constitution is, in Mr. Trudeau's words, "up for grabs," and in the complex bargaining ahead it is possible that the federal government will put a high enough priority on the Charter to make the concessions necessary to overcome provincial objections.

In clearing the ground for my skirmish with supporters of the Charter, I may say that I agree that the protection of human rights is the final end of government and that the degree to which human rights are safeguarded is the final test by which any polity should be judged. . . .

My disagreement with the supporters of the Charter is thus not on the basis of final values but rather of evidence and the prudential political judgments based on such evidence. If and when the chips are down, I am a liberal rather than a democrat, but unlike Mr. Trudeau I find little in the contemporary situation in Canada which makes it necessary for me to choose between these two commitments.

Although human rights are primary, it is elemental to realize that at different times and under different circumstances humane societies recognize different rights and order those so recognized according to quite different priorities, and that the rights won in one generation often become in quite unintended ways the bastions of reaction and privilege in the next. . . .

Part of the processes of change to which we are being subjected is the assertion of new human rights and demands that we rank the existing ones differently. For purely illustrative purposes here are some of the areas where the reordering of human rights is occurring or may reasonably be expected in the near future:

First, we must redefine the permissible kinds of political participation and protest and the physical means that those charged with the security of the organized community may use against those persons who exceed such limits to protest and participation as are set by law. We have passed rapidly from the politics of pressure and influence to the politics of confrontation; confrontation in some cases going no further than to dramatize what protesters believe to be intolerable situations and in others going to subject all or part of the community to inconvenience, financial penalty, or danger. In defining these new limits there are some hard questions to be answered about whether these are to be the same for all or, alternatively, whether some can demonstrate that the normal workings of the political system are so unresponsive to their demands—or that these demands are so inherently righteous—that these people are allowed to press their interests in ways not permitted to others. The escalation in the intensity of domestic political conflict has led to new means of surveillance and coercion by those charged with maintaining internal order and security, and it seems inevitable that the increasing incidence of radical protest will lead to new and more restrictive definitions of loyalty and new ways of enforcing these limits. Increasingly sophisticated methods of crowd-control are now upon us, methods which both make such control more effective and allegedly do not subject those against whom they are used to more than temporary physical or psychological impotence. And if liberally minded people are successful in having fluorides put in the common water-supply perhaps the rest of us in the future will be able to think up convincing reasons for preventing the authorities from being granted permission to pour mild depressants into the same reservoirs to becalm communities inflamed by racial or other tensions!

Second, in the reordering of human rights we are experiencing changes in the way in which equality is defined. It has become accepted as universal morality that persons should not be discriminated against because of their race, ethnic origin, sex, or religion. From time to time the law adds new categories deemed to be irrelevant to how people are to be treated such as the age or marital circumstances of those seeking employment. But if people may not legitimately be disadvantaged because they fall in one of these categories, may public policies be designed to confer advantage on them? And if this is done cannot those not within such classifications validly complain of discrimination? In the United States, for example, judicial decision has brought about a "color-blind Constitution" just at the time when there are new demands that race be regarded as one of the most important categories for determining how people are to be treated. An increasing number of negroes define their blackness as their most important identification and assert that for the foreseeable future compensatory measures are needed to mitigate the effects of centuries of exploitation. . . .

In Canada we are locked in debate among contradictory definitions of linguistic and cultural equality. Various kinds of "two nations" formulations assert that the crucial equality is that between the historic French- and English-speaking communities. The major thrust of the recommendations of the Royal Commission on Bilingualism and Biculturalism is towards defining equality as the right of individuals to affiliate themselves with the linguistic community of their choice in such provinces or areas as have official language concentrations of significant size. In some areas of English-speaking Canada equality is understood to mean the right of French Canadians and members of other minority groups to assimilate into the Anglo-Saxon community without penalties because of their previous cultural and linguistic backgrounds. Problems both of theory and practice arise in the relation between the indigenous people and other Canadians. The Hawthorn-Tremblay Report of 1966 recommends that the Indian be treated as a "citizen plus," that he have the option to enter the wider society without discrimination or, alternatively, to retain his membership in a traditional community whose welfare and integrity are protected by public policy. As in the case of other historically disadvantaged groups, to begin to treat Canadian Indians today as if their background and affiliations were irrelevant is perhaps not equality.

Third, new measures are needed to redress the alarming imbalances in mutual information between citizens and bureaucracies. We are just now beginning to realize the frightening possibilities for surveillance in closed-circuit television and various electronic listening devices. We are becoming aware of the potentialities for social control in the increasingly more refined data-collection and data-retrieval procedures of public and private agencies. Radical protest leads almost inevitably to more widespread infiltration of organizations by those charged with internal security and the attendant invasions of privacy and corrosions of human relations. But as the dimensions of individual privacy are progressively restricted, governments continue to assert the privilege of carrying on many of their own most crucial processes in secret and to determine unilaterally, and in accord with their own convenience, the information about these processes to be made available to the public. In the period ahead, some of the most critical struggles for human freedom may revolve around the citizen's right to privacy on the one hand and his right to public information on the other. . . .

In the field of material needs, we are just beginning to recognize the urgency of consumer rights. Former societies did not have to worry about privacy and up to the present neither democratic theory nor democratic practice emphasized what has now become this compelling necessity of human dignity. Perhaps we are even being faced with the more basic question, "When is a human being?" The current controversy over abortion raises the old question of whether human life comes into existence at conception, at birth, or sometime between these two events. At the other end of the line, so to speak, perhaps a fundamental human right in the future will be an assurance to the individual that his carcass will not be used as a handy source of spare parts unless and until he has been pronounced dead by procedures less casual than those commonly now used. And when the geneticists and/or the computer scientists put together forms of existence having some, but likely not all, the distinctive characteristics of humans, in what ways will these creatures be granted the rights previously enjoyed only by those having their origins in the traditional process of human procreation?

In a period where there is a rapid reordering of human rights, the ways by which rights are finally and authoritatively defined are the most crucial activities of government. If the proposed Charter were enacted some or all of the following might happen:

First, certain provisions might be stated so unequivocally as not to permit any subsequent dispute or interpretation as to their meaning.

Second, the constitution might subsequently be amended so as to change the scope of entrenched human rights. On the whole, it is less likely that previously entrenched rights would be removed or restricted than that new rights would be given such protection. It is also likely that any acceptable amending procedure will make such amendments subject to unanimous provincial consent. Thus the entrenchment of human rights at any particular time imposes the formulations of that time on the future in the sense that a small minority can obstruct future changes.

Third, the Charter might be overridden by Parliament's emergency powers. One of the propositions submitted by the federal government to the 1969 conference [in *The Constitution and the People of Canada*] recommended that "where Parliament has declared a state of war, invasion or insurrection, real or apprehended, to exist, legislation enacted by Parliament which expressly provides therein that it shall operate notwithstanding this Charter, and any acts authorized by that legislation, shall not be invalid by reason only of conflict with the guarantees of rights and freedoms expressed in the Charter." Thus, unlike the American Bill of Rights and despite the absolutist claims made for the Charter, constitutionally entrenched rights in Canada are under emergency conditions to be subject to the will of the federal legislature.

Fourth, the generalized provisions of the Charter are given their meaning by judicial interpretation. This is the crucial feature of the proposal. Supporters of the Charter have been peculiarly reticent in explaining that its effect is to confer on the judiciary new and extended powers; in misleading language drawn from the French and American political traditions rather than our own this measure is alleged to transfer power not from legislatures to courts but rather to "the people" from governments. Mr. Trudeau as Minister of Justice attempted to minimize the radical nature of his proposal by arguing that parliamentary sovereignty in the Canadian Confederation had been qualified from the first by a constitutional division of legislative powers and judicial review. However, parliamentary sovereignty so qualified is very different in its practical results from a situation in which there is a wide range of constitutional prohibitions binding all levels of government, and quite new tasks are imposed on the courts of law.

In defining and ordering human rights the judicial method as it has developed in Canada suffers from major disabilities:

First, judicial review is sporadic. Unlike legislatures and executives, the courts have a narrow range of discretion in timing the decisions they make, either in the course of litigation or in giving advisory opinions when directed by the federal or provincial cabinets. Thus enactments which are later declared unconstitutional can and often do remain in effect for long periods before cases involving their validity come before the courts. Further, in interpreting the constitution the courts ordinarily decide only the issues in the particular case before them and leave for later decision the consequences for cases which are somewhat similar and, in denying the validity of laws, whether and in what ways the offending legislature could attain broadly the same objectives by enactments framed somewhat differently.

Second, under present circumstances most Canadians do not have the financial resources to undertake legal action to protect their rights. We have no national organizations corresponding to the American Civil Liberties Union or the National Association for the Advancement of Colored People which have at their disposal large resources of specialized legal talent to defend those whose constitutional rights are challenged. Provisions for legal aid to those without the funds to pay for such services are to a greater or lesser degree inadequate everywhere in Canada. There has been some limited progress here in the establishment of provincial and local civil liberties associations in some parts of Canada and in the development of programs of legal assistance. . . .

Third, in our judicial tradition the courts in coming to decisions take into explicit account a restricted range both of facts and values. For the most part, the courts apply to the constitution the same rules of interpretation that are used in determining the meaning and effect of other statutes. Although I am here oversimplifying, the raw materials of the decision are the facts of the case, the usual and accepted meaning of the words of the enactment and what courts at the same or at higher levels in the judicial hierarchy have decided in previous cases deemed to be similar. In some cases the courts proceed further and examine the intent of the legislature which enacted the statute and the surrounding circumstances, although whether this is appropriate is a matter of dispute both among members of the Canadian judiciary and legal scholars. There are of course Canadian constitutional decisions where broader considerations than those mentioned above have been taken into account, and many scholars argue that the usual rules of statutory interpretation are by themselves inadequate guides when questions involving the constitution are under review.

However, the broad thrust of Canadian constitutional interpretation is positivist. This is not good enough in our present circumstances. For example, if individual privacy is to be protected effectively decisions will have to be made largely on the basis of an up-to-date appreciation of the technology of surveillance devices. In ordering the relations between the Canadian Indian and the rest of the community the public authorities need the most sophisticated analyses that social scientists can provide. The Canadian judiciary is badly equipped both by its traditional procedures and by training and inclination to use scientific knowledge creatively in the making of public policy. The legal realists assert that the courts in coming to decisions do in fact take into account a broader range of factors than the canons of statutory interpretation imply. Particularly in a review of the constitution, where the range of judicial discretion is often wider than when other statutes are involved, it is inevitable that judges will be influenced by their formulations of the essential nature of the polity and their evaluations of the public consequences of their decisions. However, within the Canadian tradition these considerations are seldom made explicit and are concealed in decisions within a morass of legal verbiage unintelligible to the average interested citizen. Again this will not do. If our courts are given the task of making the final and authoritative definitions of human rights it is essential that they, along with other organs of government, enter into a continuing dialogue with the Canadian public about the premises of these decisions. It is my assumption that the ethos of democracy has so permeated the public consciousness that no public body which proceeds otherwise will have its powers regarded as legitimate.

Fourth, the courts have few resources to enforce their decisions. The proposed Charter implies that on occasion the judiciary will challenge elected bodies representing deeply felt sentiments in the national or provincial communities. Under contemporary circumstances the effective exercise of human rights often requires positive action from legislatures and executives. The American experience indicates that when the courts clash with other organs of government the implementation of judicial decisions is by no means automatic or certain.

The general disabilities of the judicial method in defining human rights are reinforced by the more specific characteristics of the Canadian legal culture. It is my impression that Canadian legal education and scholarship have been for the most part technical in nature and have not on the whole concerned themselves deeply with broader matters of public policy and political philosophy. Despite the very great advances that are reportedly being made in enhancing the quality of judicial appointments, I remain unconvinced that the Canadian courts are a sufficient repository of superior wisdom and statesmanship to entrust with the new functions. There is in the federal proposals a thinly disguised enthusiasm for the Supreme Court of the United States in the past generation. But the differences between the two experiences are vast. The United States constitution has developed a central and symbolic role in fostering allegiance to the polity as ours has not. The American political formula is a creedal one based on natural law foundations leading to the authoritative definition of consitutional orthodoxy by an authority removed from overt partisan influences. Much of the activity of the Supreme Court of the United States in defining human rights has been in the direction of a national system of criminal law, something Canadians have had from the first under the existing constitution. Perhaps most crucially, the Supreme Court of the United States works within the environment of an enormously rich and sophisticated tradition of legal-philosophical debate about the most fundamental matters, an environment largely absent in Canada.

Another of the many questions which the supporters of the Charter have not raised is the compatibility or otherwise between the new tasks being assigned to the courts and the effective performance of other judicial functions. The American experience—and I would argue that it is here relevant—is that a final court of review which makes important and controversial public policy decisions inevitably becomes the object of partisan political debate. The federal proposal of February 1969 that a reconstituted Senate approve appointments to the Supreme Court of Canada would, if enacted, provide an arena for such partisanship. A strong case can be made that the kind of judicial function implied by the charter will compromise the imputed impartiality of the courts, and in particular of the Supreme Court of Canada, in adjudicating private and public interests where conflicts of a narrower scope are involved. The Canadian judiciary has maintained a high reputation for impartiality, a reputation that persists even when judges leave their courtrooms and involve themselves in contentious matters where legal standards in the strict sense do not apply, as when they sit on labour conciliation boards, participate in redefining electoral districts, and become members of royal commissions and other inquiries dealing with controversial public issues. . . . These kinds of activities are already putting the reputation of judicial impartiality under strain, and the new and controversial tasks suggested for the courts by the Charter would almost inevitably contribute to these influences.

Supporters of the Charter might agree with much of the argument I have made but still maintain that, on balance, the constitutional entrenchment of rights was justified on the double grounds that it would introduce a measure of certainty into what rights are recognized in Canada and that, again on balance, courts can be expected to be more zealous than elected politicians in safeguarding human rights. It is undeniable that there are many uncertainties with respect to human rights in Canada. Part of these relate to the division of legislative powers—for example, how far might Parliament go in defining racial or religious discrimination as criminal offences? The question has never been resolved as to whether the preamble of the British North America Act constitutes the elements of an implied bill of rights limiting the powers of the provinces and perhaps of Parliament as well. In matters within federal jurisdiction the status of the 1960 Bill of Rights is unclear. Nearly a decade of experience indicates to me that the major difficulty with the bill is not, as its critics claim, that it can be amended or repealed by the ordinary legislative processes but rather that the courts have not found in it an unambiguous directive for interpreting and perhaps invalidating federal legislation. This is so even though the language of the bill appears clear to the effect that "Every law of Canada shall, unless it is expressly declared by an Act of Parliament of Canada that it shall operate notwithstanding the Canadian Bill of Rights, be so construed and applied as not to abrogate, abridge or infringe or to authorize the abrogation, abridgement or infringement of any of the rights and freedoms herein recognized and declared . . ." So far as legislative intent is concerned, the evidence indicates that the government of the day—and in particular the Prime Minister and his Minister of Justice—regarded the Bill of Rights as a constitutional statute by whose terms other federal enactments were to be judged and, if found wanting, invalidated by the courts. But if the proposed Charter resolved some or all of the existing uncertainties it would almost inevitably create even more serious ones in the several decades it would take for the new traditions of judicial interpretation to evolve. What could we expect in the meantime? Would the courts exercise a high degree of self-restraint in striking down legislation alleged to be contrary to the Charter? Or would judges come rampaging out to do battle for human rights? Or, alternatively, would they develop towards a presumption of constitutionality with respect to some provision of the Charter and put other provisions in a "preferred position"? Would judges in interpreting the Charter take into account the cultural duality of Canada? And in particular what recognition, if any, would they give to the circumstances that in some important respects the civil and common law systems define rights in quite different ways? As the Canadian constitution moved toward a definition of individual rights what doctrines of judicial standing would evolve, that is, what persons would be regarded as having a sufficiently direct interest in particular legislation or executive acts to challenge their validity in the courts? It is the goal of a democratic polity that individuals, at least with the assistance of normally competent lawyers, can at any time determine with some precision what their rights are under the law. However, the answer to existing uncertainties lies not with the Charter but in the clearer definition from time to time of human rights by Parliament and the provincial legislatures, preferably aided by some form of ongoing federal-provincial collaboration in such matters. The courts have, and will continue to have, a crucial role in the protection of human rights. But it seems to me that this role can best be fulfilled when the judiciary proceeds from the traditional protections of the two legal systems supplemented and extended from time to time by precise and detailed legislative enactments.

Is it reasonable to expect that Canadian courts will be more zealous than legislatures in the protection of human rights? The incumbent judiciary does not impress me in this respect. In the few cases when federal actions have been challenged as infringing upon the provisions of the 1960 Bill of Rights the higher courts have shown an extraordinary degree of self-restraint. But the pervasive major premise of those who support the charter is a distrust of legislatures, executives, voters, and the whole democratic political process. The federal proposal of 1968 nowhere recommends entrenching the right to vote — although almost parenthetically it suggests that where this right exists persons should not be discriminated against in its exercise because of race, religion, national origin, colour, or sex. (Significantly, those latter safeguards do not appear in the revised Charter as proposed by Mr. Trudeau in February 1969). It is revealing that the federal government did not see as desirable the extension in the Charter to the provinces of the existing provisions of the BNA Act which require an annual session of Parliament and, except under defined conditions of national emergency, a general election every five years. The proposed Charter recommends several important restrictions on the existing powers of the provinces. However, such restrictions do not include those governing the provincial franchise, annual legislative sessions, and periodic elections and these can be altered or amended by the usual legislative processes. Thus in the federal proposal the whole process of democratic political debate and political conflict are seen exclusively in the perspective of the hazards they contain for human rights rather than in their potentialities for protecting and extending these rights.

Whatever general dispositions toward human rights that elected bodies in Canada may be assumed to have, it is undeniable that in this decade there has been a legislative recognition of such rights unprecedented in Canadian history. Parliament and most of the provinces have enacted bills of rights and in some jurisdictions specialized administrative agencies have been established to implement these purposes. Both Ontario and Quebec have royal commissions at work inquiring in a detailed way into human rights and important legislative action is expected on the basis of their recommendations; in the latter province many of the "obstacles to democracy" which Mr. Trudeau so well analysed a decade ago have been removed and there is reportedly to be a bill of rights incorporated into the revised civil code. Alberta, New Brunswick, and now Quebec have appointed ombudsmen and it is likely that other Canadian jurisdictions will soon experiment with this institution. Parliament has liberalized Canadian law in respect to capital punishment, divorce, abortion, birth control, and homosexuality. In Ottawa and most of the provinces there has been a legislative and executive recognition of the French language that not even the most sanguine would have predicted as recently as, say, five years ago. There has been a belated and as yet insufficient effort toward bettering the circumstances of the Indian and Eskimo peoples. Perhaps the most dramatic victory for human rights in Canada during this decade occurred during March 1964 in Ontario when the Attorney General introduced into the legislature a bill to extend vastly the *in camera* investigatory powers of the Ontario Police Commission; the reaction of the public to this repressive measure was almost instantaneous and resulted in the quick withdrawal of the bill and the resignation of the cabinet minister responsible for it. In general, there can never be any reasonable complacency about human rights but *in toto* legislative and administrative action in Canada during this decade constitute significant achievements for freedom and dignity.

It is likely that a stronger case can be made for the Charter than its supporters have formulated. Such a reasoned argument might proceed along two lines: First, new and illiberal influences are upon us and it is probable that Canadian legislators will be less solicitous of human rights than in the recent past. Second, Canadian judges will respond, and quickly, to the challenge of the Charter and transform themselves into zealous and sophisticated libertarians. But such a case has not been made and the rationale of the Charter published under the name of Mr. Trudeau has been made in terms which are pretentious, misleading, and intellectually shoddy. . . .

First, in the document *A Canadian Charter of Human Rights* there is a pretentious three-and-a-half-page summary of the whole of the western tradition in politics. . . . Nowhere is the elementary analytical distinction made between natural and positive law. There is no substance in this pseudo-erudition except the assertion that in the western tradition there has been a continuing disposition toward the protection of human rights by law. So far as I know, there is no challenge to this principle in Canada, and the principle in itself gives no guidance in determining the appropriate "mix" of common or civil law safeguards, legislative enactments, and constitutional entrenchment in protecting human rights.

Second, in the document referred to above this sentence occurs: "An entrenched bill of rights would offer this constitutional protection [to human rights], although at the price of some restriction on the theory of legislative supremacy."

But who cares about the *theory* of legislative supremacy? The proposal is no more and no less than to transfer certain kinds of crucial policy decisions from legislatures to courts. What are the inhibitions against saying so clearly and without equivocation?

Third, here is a sentence from *The Constitution and the People of Canada*, published under Mr. Trudeau's name in February 1969. "A constitutional guarantee of human rights would thus represent a commitment by all governments to the people—a commitment that, whatever their legislative powers, they will not deny the fundamental values which make life meaningful for Canadians" (p. 16). On a personal basis, I find repugnant some of the values "which make life meaningful" for some Canadians. If there is one value in Canadian life which I cherish it is that no one has yet prescribed any set of values to which I am required to assent. I hope that all citizens of perverse and independent spirit will unite to put down the arrogance of politicians who would inflict this kind of creedal Canadianism—or un-Canadian creedalism—upon us. . . .

Fourth, in the 1969 document we find this sentence: "To enshrine a right in a constitutional charter is to make an important judgment, to give to the right of the individual a higher order of value than the right of government to infringe upon it." Nowhere is the superficiality of the case made for the Charter so clearly shown. No reasonable person believes that in all cases individual rights even though constitutionally entrenched, are to take precedence over other claims which have no such protection. Mr. Trudeau's argument proceeds on the assumption that encroachments on human rights are always unequivocal and that disinterested and liberal persons will be able to agree when such encroachments have been made. This is, of course, not so. In a society generally committed to liberal values—and this is the only kind of society where procedural safeguards of human rights are of more than marginal consequences—men sharing these values can and will weigh conflicting claims differently. When does a particular kind of expression become a "clear and present danger" to society? How far do constitutional prohibitions extend to private organizations operating under public regulation or with public financial assistance? How is the fine line to be drawn between *predicting* that certain conditions can be righted only by violence and *advocating* violence? What kinds of restrictions can a liberal community impose on aliens wanting to enter that community as visitors, residents, or citizens? How does freedom of expression relate to means of expression which are inherently quasi-monopolistic? What are the kinds of overt conduct that can be justified in the name of freedom of religion, and when privileges are granted in these directions, should they be extended only to members of organized religious groups? How does one strike a balance between the claims of procedural regularity and the need for speedy, expert, and inexpensive adjudication of disputes? There are manifold complexities in the delicate balancing of social priorities which is the essence of protecting human rights. Unfortunately, none of these yield to superficial sloganeering about the rights of individuals preceding those of governments.

In a time of turbulence when the things which we most value are under attack it is understandable that some will come forward to promise us certainty. Only such impulses can explain the misleading and absolutist language in which the Charter is presented. The rights which it is to recognize are "basic" and "fundamental" — although no serious attempt is made to demonstrate that these claims are more essential than others which are not to be so protected. So far as fundamental rights are concerned, we are to "guarantee" them, to "entrench" them, and finally to "enshrine" them. Perhaps the more accurate term is "entomb." For in the nature of things there is no sure and certain way to protect human rights — no certainty that courts will be more zealous than legislatures in meeting the future requirements of human freedom and dignity and no certainty, but rather the reverse, that a judiciary intent on defending such rights will long be able to restrain a community bent on their destruction. We can only say with Judge Learned Hand, "this much I think I do know—that a society so riven that a spirit of moderation is gone, no court *can* save, that a society where that spirit flourishes, no court *need* save, that in a society which evades its responsibility by thrusting upon courts the nature of that spirit, that spirit will in the end perish."

To end, one of the most intractable dilemmas confronting the responsible man is how to act prudently today without foreclosing the possibilities of tomorrow. Those who would enact a charter of human rights are confident enough of their own judgments to wish to press on future generations of Canadians—if there be such—a particular formulation of the requirements of human dignity. . . . But there is another way than that of the Charter. The master tradition of the British parliamentary system affirms that with one exception a legislature can enact as it chooses, either as sovereign or within the restrictions imposed by a federal division of legislative powers. That single exception is that it cannot bind future Parliaments. There is here elemental wisdom we would do well to ponder.

HOW AN INDIAN CHANGED CANADA'S CIVIL RIGHTS LAWS — THE DRYBONES CASE*

RAE CORELLI

It was a fateful moment for Canada when, early in the morning of April 10, 1967, Joe Drybones was convicted of having been drunk in a public place (viz., the lobby floor in the Old Stope Hotel in Yellowknife) and fined $10.

Because that was the first act in a 2½ year courtroom drama which was to propel Canada onto the threshold of a revolution in the field of law and civil rights.

The last act was performed six weeks ago by the Supreme Court of Canada

* From *Toronto Daily Star*, January 2, 1970. By permission of the publisher.

which ordered the conviction quashed and the fine refunded on the grounds that the 42-year-old bespectacled and illiterate Indian had been denied equality before the law.

The court's authority for that historic decision?

None other than the much-maligned and ridiculed Canadian Bill of Rights. From the day it was enacted by John Diefenbaker's Progressive Conservative government nearly 10 years ago, the bill had been so thoroughly shunned by the courts that it had virtually no force or effect in Canadian law.

Lawyers had despaired of ever winning a case on the strength of it even though its guarantees of human rights and fundamental freedoms were supposed to take precedence, or so it seemed, over all other federal laws.

The trouble was that no court had ever placed that interpretation on it — until six weeks ago, that is, when the Supreme Court of Canada said that's exactly what the words in the bill meant.

Legal scholars and constitutional law experts across the nation have been excitedly studying the 6-to-3 decision for weeks and now they say it may have an impact on the administration of justice in Canada far beyond their first impressions.

For instance, these experts say, by giving to the Bill of Rights the meaning it did, the Supreme Court of Canada has also given itself—and all other courts in the country — the unprecedented power to over-rule Parliament and throw out unjust federal laws. (The Bill of Rights doesn't apply to provincial law.)

The significance of that is that the day may come when you will be freed by a court — not because you are necessarily innocent but because the law under which you were charged has been found to be discriminatory or manifestly unjust or unduly restrictive.

Says Justice Minister John Turner: "This extremely important decision by the Supreme Court of Canada establishes the paramountcy in law of the Bill of Rights as it relates to federal legislation. . ."

To understand why the decision excites legal experts and where it may conceivably lead, let's examine the bizarre saga of Joe Drybones.

After the RCMP lugged the unconscious Indian away from the Old Stope Hotel (where owner Fred Rasche used to quell mutineers by raining blows on the splintered bar with a five-pound sledge-hammer), they charged him with violating a section of the Indian Act which makes it unlawful for Indians to be drunk off a reservation.

(Since there are no reservations in the Northwest Territories, it's impossible for an Indian to be legally drunk anywhere, including his own home.)

Joe Drybones was convicted, fined the statutory minimum of $10 and let go the following Monday morning (he got boiled on Saturday night). Later that day, lawyer Brian Purdy, a 27-year-old native of Toronto and a graduate of Halifax's Dalhousie University law school, noticed the record of Drybones' conviction in the Yellowknife court office.

It suddenly struck him, Purdy said afterward, that the Indian Act was discriminatory because it contained harsher penalties for drunkenness than those contained in the territorial liquor ordinance under which white men were prosecuted. (For one thing, the white man's law contains no minimum fines.)

Purdy went to see Drybones and explained through an interpreter the law as he saw it. Joe, who didn't have a lawyer at his trial, decided to appeal the conviction.

The appeal was heard June 5 at Yellowknife by Mr. Justice William G. Morrow of the Territorial Court. Purdy based his case largely on section 1 of the Bill of Rights which guarantees "the right of the individual to equality before the law."

Drybones, Purdy said, had enjoyed no such equality. Moreover, he argued, the Bill of Rights is supposed to take precedence over every other law of Canada unless Parliament explicitly decrees otherwise.

Since the Indian Act contained no such decree, Purdy said, the section had to give way to the Bill of Rights and the conviction against Drybones should therefore be set aside.

Morrow agreed. "This portion of the Indian Act is to me a case of discrimination of sufficient seriousness that I must hold that the intoxication sections of the Indian Act (violate) the Canadian Bill of Rights," he said in his judgment.

The crown appealed Morrow's decision to the Territorial Court of Appeal which comprised Chief Justice Sidney Bruce Smith of the Alberta Court of Appeal and two of his colleagues.

Drybones won again. The appeal court said that while it was Canadian government policy to treat Indians differently (often for their own protection) "one would have hoped that that could have been done without subjecting Indians to penalties and punishments different to those imposed on other races."

That judgment finally got the attention of the federal justice department in Ottawa and it launched last-ditch appeal proceedings before the Supreme Court of Canada.

On Oct. 28, 1968, G. Brian Purdy, three years at the bar, found himself in the panelled chambers of the highest court in the nation. Opposing him was a justice department team headed by Assistant Deputy Attorney-General Donald H. Christie.

Chief Justice John R. Cartwright, believing the issue had far-reaching implications for both the courts and the law of the country, had taken the unusual step of assembling all nine judges to hear the argument. Grave and attentive, they gazed down from the 35-foot-wide elevated bench ranged across the end of the chamber.

"It was enough to scare you right out of your socks," said Purdy.

Purdy's entire case was a single sentence 13 typewritten lines long. In it, he repeated his contention that because the Indian Act imposed a more severe penalty than the territorial liquor ordinance, it therefore violated the Bill of Rights and its offending sections should be declared "inoperative."

Then Christie presented the government's case, the court rose and everyone went home to await the decision.

On New Year's Day, 1969, the Old Stope Hotel caught fire and burned to the ground.

All over the Northwest Territories, drunk prosecutions under the Indian Act piled up but were not proceeded with because the crown was awaiting word on the fate of the law.

Joe Drybones, meanwhile, had long since got his $10 back and had lost interest in the whole affair. Purdy says he doubts whether Joe really comprehended what was going on or, for that matter, if he really knew or cared that there was such a thing as the Supreme Court of Canada.

(In January, 1968, Purdy and a bush pilot spent most of one day scouting the snow desert around Yellowknife by plane, looking for Joe so they could serve him with the notice of the crown's appeal to the Ottawa court. They finally found him by following his dog-team tracks. "Since he already had his 10 bucks back, I think he thought we were all nuts," said Purdy).

Then last Nov. 20, more than a year after the case was argued, the Supreme Court delivered its ruling. The 29 foolscap pages shot holes in the Indian Act and transformed the Bill of Rights from a dusty and half-forgotten relic into one of the most important laws in the country.

Mr. Justice Roland A. Ritchie, who wrote the majority opinion dismissing the crown's appeal, said "an individual is denied equality before the law if it is made an offence punishable at law, on account of his race, for him to do something which his fellow Canadians are free to do without having committed any offence. . . ."

The drunkenness section of the Indian Act, he said, created just that kind of offence and therefore it had to go. . . .

Mr. Justice Emmett M. Hall, agreeing with Ritchie, went so far as to liken the "philosophic concept" of the majority decision to the historic school desegregation order of the United States Supreme Court in 1954.

Said Hall:

> The Canadian Bill of Rights is not fulfilled if it merely equates Indians with Indians in terms of equality before the law, but can have validity and meaning only when . . . it is seen to repudiate discrimination in every law of Canada by reason of race, national origin, color, religion or sex . . . in whatever way that discrimination may manifest itself, not only as between Indian and Indian but as between all Canadians. . . .

A judge of a provincial Supreme Court, who asked that his name be withheld, says the Drybones decision is the first time in history that the Supreme Court of Canada has gone beyond its traditional constitutional role of settling arguments over legislative jurisdication between the provinces and the federal government.

"The court has added a new dimension," he said. "That dimension is that even though the federal government may pass legislation that is completely within its jurisdiction, that legislation shall not stand if its language is such as to create discrimination or the lack of equality before the law.

"The Supreme Court of Canada now employs its own test of a law. It superimposes the Bill of Rights on the statute at issue and if that statute offends, out it goes. It's the biggest decision we've had in years, perhaps ever. Any legislation that affects human rights will be fair game." . . .

Gerald LeDain, the dean of York University's Osgoode Hall Law School and an acknowledged expert in constitutional law, said it would be "politically impossible" for Parliament to enact legislation not subject to the bill because those exceptions would have to be "expressly stated."

Potentially, said LeDain, the Drybones decision could "open the way to a shift in the balance of power between Parliament and the judiciary." More power to the courts would produce an "effective limitation on the sovereignty of Parliament."

"The Supreme Court of Canada now has the capacity to affirm those values that have never been given judicial notice in this country," LeDain said. "We have always had 'technical protection' for those values but now the court can apply them freely without having to rely on legal technicalities."

However, he warned, Drybones is only one decision. The danger was that a flock of ill-conceived and frivolous appeals based on it would get short shrift and make the court increasingly reluctant to explore the whole concept any further. . . .

In the Commons Nov. 20, the day the judgment came down, Diefenbaker called it an "epochal judgment . . . which upheld the authority of the Canadian Bill of Rights in providing and assuring that all Canadians shall have equal rights." The decision, he said, supported "the Bill of Rights in its entirety so far as discrimination is concerned." And for the Chief, it was vindication for his efforts in ramming the bill through.

And what of G. Brian Purdy

Last week, he waded into a new kind of challenge—planning a defence for a citizen involved in the first arrest for possession of marijuana in the Northwest Territories.

FOOTNOTE: For taking the Drybones appeal to the Territorial Court and appearing as the defendant when the crown appealed first to the Alberta court and then the Supreme Court of Canada, Purdy got less than $1,500. All of it was paid out of the territorial legal aid plan. And that, ironically, is bankrolled by the federal government.

BIBLIOGRAPHY

MacGuigan, M., "The Development of Civil Liberties in Canada," *Q.Q.* Vol. LXXII, No. 2, Summer, 1965.
Russell, P. H., "A Democratic Approach to Civil Liberties," *University of Toronto Law Journal,* Vol. XIX, 1969.
Schmeiser, D. A., *Civil Liberties in Canada,* London, Oxford University Press, 1964.
Scott, F. R.; et al., "A collection of articles on the Canadian Bill of Rights," *Canadian Bar Review,* Vol. XXXVII, No. 1, March, 1959.
Scott, F. R., *Civil Liberties and Canadian Federalism,* Toronto, University of Toronto Press, 1959.
Tarnopolsky, W. S., *The Canadian Bill of Rights,* Toronto, Carswell, 1966.

NINETEEN
GOVERNMENT
PUBLICATIONS

Professor Land's article is self-explanatory. It is a very useful guide for those who wish to find material in the voluminous and confusing world of federal and provincial government publications. Mr. Land explains the origins of most major publications and the nature of their contents. He also lists bibliographical works that give additional information about governmental publications.

A DESCRIPTION AND GUIDE TO THE USE OF CANADIAN GOVERNMENT PUBLICATIONS*

BRIAN LAND

Government publications range in scope from the formal papers, debates and journals of our legislatures, and from the annual reports of the various departments, divisions, and branches, to the more popular periodicals and booklets for tourists, and to "how to do it" booklets for the handyman or housewife.

The following paragraphs describe some of the more important serial publications of the federal government such as the debates, journals, departmental reports, statutes, and gazettes, and review some of the guides, catalogues, indexes and checklists of government publications.

THE MAJOR SERIAL PUBLICATIONS

Debates of the House of Commons

The most familiar of the legislative publications are the debates which give a verbatim account of what is said in Parliament. The several volumes each session record the daily debates of the House, messages of the Governor-General and varying information such as lists of members of the House and of the Ministry. Like those of the British Parliament, the Canadian *Debates* are referred to as *Hansard* in honour of the printer, T. C. Hansard, who reported the British *Debates* in the early nineteenth century.

The only example of printed debates as we know them today which were published before Confederation are the *Parliamentary Debates on the Subject of the Confederation of the British North American Provinces,* published in 1865 and republished in 1951. This volume was indexed by the Public Archives at Ottawa under the title *Index to Parliamentary Debates on the Subject of the Confederation of the British North American Provinces,* compiled by M. A. Lapin and edited and revised by J. S. Patrick.

The debates of the early Canadian Parliaments, as in most countries, were not officially reported and the only records are, with a few exceptions, the so-called *"Scrapbook Debates"* which are in the Library of Parliament. These debates consist of clippings from the newspapers of the time, which have been mounted in scrapbooks and for which handwritten indexes have been made. The *"Scrapbook Debates"* cover the period from Confederation to 1874, and are now available on microfilm, published by the Canadian Library Association, Ottawa, 1954. From 1870 to 1872 three volumes of debates of both Houses were printed but were

---

* Revised in November, 1969, for this book by the author, who is the Director of the School of Library Science, University of Toronto.

unofficial in origin. These are referred to as the *"Cotton Debates"* after the name of the *Ottawa Times* reporter, John Cotton, who covered the sessions. Not until 1875 did the House of Commons itself begin reporting its debates. From 1875 to 1879 the contract for reporting these debates was awarded to private reporters, but from 1880 on, an official staff of reporters was appointed to secure permanency and uniformity.

As a Centennial project of the Parliament of Canada under the auspices of the Library of Parliament, the debates of the House of Commons and Senate covering the years 1867 to 1874 are being edited for publication by Professor Peter B. Waite of Dalhousie University, Halifax. The first volume of the House of Commons *Debates* in this series covers the first session of the first Parliament, November 6, 1867, to May 22, 1868, and was published in 1967. This edition is principally a collation by Professor Waite of the debates published in the *Ottawa Times* and in the Toronto *Globe,* during the period.

The daily edition of the *Debates* is issued during each session of Parliament on the morning following each day's sitting and contains the speeches in English as delivered and the English translation of speeches delivered in French. A daily edition of the *Debates* containing the speeches in French as delivered and the French translation of speeches delivered in English is also issued on the day following delivery. Following publication of the daily edition, proofs of their speeches or remarks are sent to members for suggested changes which must be confined to the correction of errors and essential minor alterations. At the end of each session, revised bound volumes are published. At the present time, each Wednesday's edition of the daily *Debates* includes an alphabetical list of members with their constituencies, party affiliations and addresses; a complete list of standing, joint and special committees with the membership of each; members of the Ministry according to precedence; and a list of parliamentary secretaries.

In recent years, a cumulative index to the daily *Debates* of the House of Commons has sometimes been issued in unbound form at intervals during the session. The complete index is included in the final bound volume of the *Debates* for the session.

Debates of the Senate

This series is also referred to as *Hansard* from its prototype, the parliamentary debates of Great Britain. The Senate began publishing its *Debates* in 1871. From 1871 to 1899 they were published in English only, and from 1871 to 1916 the contract for reporting was awarded to various persons, but in 1917 an official reporter was appointed. The *Debates* of the Senate covering the first session of the first Parliament, November 6, 1867 to May 22, 1868, have been edited by Professor Waite and were published in 1968 as part of the Centennial project of the Parliament of Canada referred to above.

The Senate *Debates* are, like those of the House of Commons, recorded and printed day by day and the same opportunity is afforded its members to amend or correct errors and omissions in the daily *Debates,* so that the bound volume at the end of the session can be complete and correct. The amount and extent of corrections in *Hansard* are subject to discussion and agreement in each House respectively. Whenever a change in membership of the Senate occurs, a revised roster is published in the Tuesday issue of the daily *Debates* listing the Senators according to seniority, alphabetically, and by province. Officers of the Senate are also listed.

In recent years, a cumulative index to the daily *Debates* of the Senate has sometimes been issued in unbound form at intervals during the session. The complex index is included in the final bound volume of the *Debates* for the session.

Votes and Proceedings and Journals of the House of Commons

The *Votes and Proceedings* of the House of Commons are published daily when the House is in session and constitute the official records of the House. The *Votes and Proceedings* include the daily transactions of the House, accounts of the introduction of bills, referral of questions to committees, resolutions amended or carried, votes taken, debates adjourned, proclamations and rosters of committee members. Everything printed above the Speaker's signature in the daily *Votes and Proceedings* appears at the end of each session in the bound *Journals* of the House of Commons, which then become the official records of the House. The *Journals* are so named because they provide a complete and concise record of the proceedings of the House in chronological order, day by day. Everything printed below the Speaker's signature in the *Votes and Proceedings* such as notices of committee meetings, are omitted from the *Journals*.

The bound *Journals* include a numerical "List of Appendices" consisting of reports of committees, most of which have usually been published separately. Occasionally, however, the reports of special joint committees of the House of Commons and the Senate are published in the bound *Journals*. An example is the *First and Final Report* of the Special Joint Committee on the National and Royal Anthems which was presented to the House on February 16, 1968. An index to the *Journals* is included in the final volume for each session.

Minutes of the Proceedings and Journals of the Senate

The *Minutes of the Proceedings of the Senate,* the official record of proceedings, are issued daily when the Senate is in session and correspond to the *Votes and Proceedings* published by the House of Commons. At the end of each session, the *Minutes of the Proceedings* are republished in full with an index as the *Journals* of the Senate. Since the 1964-65 session, the *Journals* of the Senate have been issued in two parts: Part I deals with all matters coming before the Senate with the exception of "Resolutions for Dissolution and Annulment of Marriages," which are contained in Part II. For the most part, "Appendixes" to the *Journals* of the Senate consist of committee reports published separately. As in the case of the House of Commons, committee reports occasionally are included in the bound *Journals*. A recent example is the *Final Report* of the Special Committee on Aging, presented to the Senate on February 2, 1966.

Routine Proceedings and Orders of the Day

The *Routine Proceedings and Orders of the Day,* issued daily by the House of Commons when it is in session, is the agenda for proceedings and includes all outstanding business before the House of Commons each day. It lists the order of business for the week and the routine of business for each day, including reports from standing and special committees, motions, introduction of bills, and government notices of motion. The *Routine Proceedings and Orders of the Day* are not cumulated or republished.

In the case of the Senate, sections dealing with "Routine Proceedings" and "Orders of the Day" appear each day in the *Minutes of the Proceedings.* These sections constitute the agenda for each day's business of the Senate, and are not subsequently published in the *Journals* of the Senate.

Sessional Papers, 1867/68-1925

This series included most of the reports that came before Parliament and were ordered printed, with the exception of the reports of committees which were printed as appendices to the *Journals* of each House. There were several volumes of sessional papers for each session, and each volume includes an alphabetical and numerical list of the papers for each session. They are not paged continuously and indexes refer to the number of each document rather than to pages. Much of the material published in the *Sessional Papers* was also published elsewhere, e.g., a branch report might appear in the *Sessional Papers,* be published separately, and published as part of a departmental report as well as being issued in both English and French. The government ceased publication of the *Sessional Papers* series in 1925 after having published some 923 volumes since Confederation, but the departmental reports formerly included were continued in the series of *Annual Departmental Reports.*

General Indexes to the Journals of the House and to Sessional Papers

In order to facilitate their use, a consolidated *General Index to the Journals of the House of Commons of Canada, and of the Sessional Papers of Parliament* was published on five occasions covering the following periods: 1867-1876; 1877-1890; 1891-1903; 1904-1915; and 1916-1930. General indexes to the *Journals* of the House of Commons are planned to cover the years 1930-1945, and 1946-1962.

Annual Departmental Reports, 1924/25-1929/30.

This series included reports of some commissions as well as continuing the departmental reports issued in *Sessional Papers* up to 1924. Since this series also duplicated material issued in other forms, it was dropped in 1930 as an economy measure.

Acts of Parliament

All *Bills* originating in the House of Commons or Senate are printed after first reading. *Bills* originating in the House are distinguished by the letter C and numbered chronologically; those of the Senate, by the letter S and numbered chronologically. If successful, *Bills* are printed after the third reading as passed. When Royal Assent has been given, these *Bills* become *Acts* and are assigned individual chapter numbers along with the name of the reigning sovereign and the year of reign, e.g., 18 Eliz. II, c. 33. *Acts* may be issued separately as well as being published in bound form in the *Acts of the Parliament of the Dominion of Canada* or, as they are more commonly known, as the *Statutes of Canada*. Since the first session of the twenty-eighth Parliament, which began in September, 1968, all *Bills* and *Statutes* have been printed in both the official languages of Canada, the English text in the left-hand column of each page and the French in the right-hand column.

Since 1875, the volumes of the *Statutes of Canada* have been divided into two parts, one devoted to Public General Acts, and the other to Local Private Acts. A preliminary section includes proclamations, despatches, appointments, etc. Formerly, orders-in-council were also included. The government issues no bound volume of bills which have failed to pass, and most libraries do not keep them beyond the session in which they were proposed. For special compilations and indexes to legislation of the federal government, one should consult Marion V. Higgins: *Canadian Government Publications,* described below.

Revised Statutes of Canada

The *Revised Statutes,* which bring legislation amended since its original passage up to date, have been issued four times since Confederation: 1886, 1906, 1927, and 1952. A new revision is planned.

Special Compilations of Statutes

From time to time, the government issues special compilations and consolidations of statutes for the convenience of court officials, lawyers, and the public generally. An example of a special compilation is the *Canadian Citizenship Act and the Regulations,* published in 1969.

Statutory Orders and Regulations

Orders-in-Council were first published in the *Statutes of Canada* for 1872. From 1874-1939, statutory orders and regulations having the force of law were published in the preliminary section of the *Statutes of Canada.* On two occasions during this period, consolidations were published by the federal government: *Orders-in-Council, Proclamations, Departmental Regulations, etc., having the force of Law in the Dominion of Canada* (1875), and *Consolidated Orders-in-Council of Canada* (1889).

Since 1939, there has been a steady increase in the number of statutes which confer power on the Minister to make orders and regulations. The systematic publication of statutory orders "of general or widespread interest or concern" is a fairly recent development. It began in 1940 with the publication of *Proclamations and Orders-in-Council* [*relating to the War*]. Eight volumes of this series were published covering the period from August 26, 1939 to September 30, 1942. During the period from 1940 to 1942, the federal government also published three volumes of the consolidated *Defence of Canada Regulations.* In October 1942, a new publication, *Canadian War Orders and Regulations* began. Its title changed to *Statutory Orders and Regulations* in October 1945 and it ceased publication in January 1947.

Since January 1, 1947, provision has been made for publication of statutory orders and regulations in *Part II* of the *Canada Gazette.* In 1950, a *Statutory Orders and Regulations Consolidation* was published bringing together all statutes which conferred the power to make orders or regulations, and all orders and regulations having a general effect. A later *Statutory Orders and Regulations Consolidation* was published in 1955. By consulting the *Statutory Orders and Regulations Consolidation,* the *Canada Gazette, Part II,* and its quarterly *Consolidated Index,* which are described below, one has a record of all current statutory orders and regulations published since January 1, 1955.

Canada Gazette

The *Canada Gazette,* now published in two parts in a bilingual format, is the official gazette of Canada. All proclamations issued by the Governor-General under the authority of the Governor-in-Council, and all official notices, orders-in-council, regulations, advertisements, and documents relating to the government of Canada, or matters under the control of Parliament thereof, and requiring publication, are published in the *Canada Gazette* unless some other mode of publication thereof is required by law. Some regulations are exempted from publication by Section 9 of the *Regulations Act.*

The *Canada Gazette, Part I,* is published every Saturday with an index, and there is an annual index at the end of December. *Part I* contains notices of a general character, proclamations, certain orders-in-council, divorce notices, and notices under the Bank, Bankruptcy, Insurance, Corporations, and Navigable Waters Protection acts, applications to Parliament for charters, and lists of successful candidates for various positions in the Public Service of Canada.

The *Canada Gazette, Part II,* is published every second and fourth Wednesday of the month and contains all orders, rules, regulations, and proclamations of a legislative or of an administrative character having a general effect or imposing a penalty as described above under statutory orders and regulations. Special editions are published, when required, at irregular intervals.

The *Consolidated Index to Statutory Orders and Regulations* is a quarterly publication which indexes all statutory orders and regulations made under statutory authority and published in the *Canada Gazette, Part II,* and in force at any time since January 1 of the current calendar year. For reference to statutory orders and regulations in force in any previous year, reference should be made to the December 31 index of the year in question.

REPORTS OF COMMISSIONS, TASK FORCES AND COMMITTEES

Reports of Royal Commissions

Royal commissions are appointed under the terms of the *Inquiries Act* by the executive arm of government, i.e., the cabinet, to carry out full and impartial investigations of specific problems and to report their findings so that decisions might be reached and appropriate action taken. When the cabinet has approved of the setting up of a royal commission, it issues an order-in-council which is published in the *Canada Gazette, Part I,* giving the terms of reference, powers and names of the commissioners. The Commission is usually empowered to call witnesses and to hold public hearings. When the Commission has completed its investigation and made its report to the Prime Minister, the report is subsequently published. There has been a recent trend towards the commissioning of special studies which are prepared as supplements to the main report; for example, 26 special studies were published by the Queen's Printer as supplements to the *Report* of the Royal Commission on Health Services. Usually royal commissions are popularly referred to by the names of their chairmen; hence, the so-called "Carter report" is the *Report* of the Royal Commission on Taxation, whose chairman was Kenneth LeM. Carter.

Each edition of the *Canada Year Book* carries a list of newly appointed royal commissions, both federal and provincial, indicating the date of their appointment and terms of reference. A useful reference list is *Federal Royal Commissions in Canada, 1867-1966; a Checklist,* by George F. Henderson, published by the University of Toronto Press.

Reports of Task Forces

The term "task force" became a common expression during World War II when it was used to describe a military force, frequently involving different services, assembled to undertake a specific task. In the jargon of government, the term is used to describe a group of experts gathered together to tackle a particular problem of public concern. In Canada, the use of task forces to help formulate government policy on such topics as labour relations, the government's role in sport, and housing, became fashionable in the late 1960s. In its composition and operation, the task force stands somewhere between a royal commission and a Parliamentary committee. Usually, the task force is made up of academics and other experts from outside government who work closely with senior civil servants. The task force may commission special studies, invite briefs and hold public hearings.

As in the case of royal commissions, reports published by task forces frequently are referred to by the name of their chairman. Thus, the *Report* of the Task Force on the Structure of Canadian Industry, whose chairman was Professor Melville H. Watkins, is often called the "Watkins report". *To Know and Be Known; the Report of the Task Force on Government Information,* published in 1969, contains valuable material on government publications and information agencies, including the Queen's Printer.

Reports of Parliamentary Committees

Unlike the royal commission, which is the creature of the executive, the parliamentary committee is a vital part of the legislative arm of government—the House of Commons and Senate. Parliamentary committees are of three kinds: the Committee of the Whole House, standing committees, and special committees.

The main function of the Committee of the Whole House is deliberation, rather than inquiry, and clause-by-clause discussion of the bills under consideration, which is facilitated by relaxation of the formal rules of debate and party discipline. The proceedings of the Committee of the Whole House are reported without a break in the *Debates* and in the *Journals* and there is no special problem in locating them.

The first session of the twenty-eighth Parliament, 1968-69, adopted major changes in the Standing Orders of the House concerning the business of supply and the business of ways and means formerly dealt with in the Committee of Supply and in the Committee of Ways and Means respectively. As a result of these changes, detailed scrutiny of government estimates and consideration of bills arising out of budget tax proposals are now given by the appropriate committees of the House of Commons. The effect of the 1969 changes in House procedure has been to extend significantly the functions of its standing committees and, as a consequence, their influence and importance.

The standing committees are permanently provided for in the Standing Orders, and are set up at the commencement of each session of Parliament to consider all subjects of a particular type arising or likely to arise in the course of the session, e.g., agriculture; broadcasting, films and assistance to the arts; external affairs and national defence; finance, trade and economic affairs; fisheries and forestry; health, welfare and social affairs; Indian affairs and northern development; justice and legal affairs; labour, manpower and immigration; national resources and public works; privileges and elections; procedure and organization; public accounts; regional development; transport and communications; and veterans affairs. The deliberations of standing committees are published as *Minutes of Proceedings and Evidence* as their meetings occur.

Special committees are frequently set up to consider and report on particular bills or upon special subjects. Recent examples include the Special Committee on Bill C-120, the Official Languages Bill, and the Special Committee on Statutory Instruments. The chief function of the special committee is to investigate, and it is the legislative prototype of the executive's royal commission except that its members must be members of Parliament. Deliberations of special committees are also published as they occur as *Minutes of Proceedings and Evidence*.

Occasionally, special committees have been converted into quasi-standing committees called "sessional committees" by enlarging their original orders of reference which provide them with a greater degree of permanence than ordinary special committees, e.g., the Sessional Committee on Railways, Air Lines and Shipping Owned and Controlled by the Government.

A "joint committee" is one appointed from the membership of both the Senate and House of Commons, e.g., the Joint Committee on the Library of Parliament, and may be either a standing or special committee.

A few committtee reports, such as those of the 1968-69 Special Committee on Procedure of the House, are published in the daily *Votes and Proceedings;* most, however, are published separately and are listed in the catalogues issued by the Queen's Printer.

INDEXES AND CATALOGUES OF GOVERNMENT PUBLICATIONS

Canadian Government Publications, by M. V. Higgins

Although in need of revision, the manual on *Canadian Government Publications,* compiled by Marion V. Higgins and published in 1935 by the American Library Association, remains the outstanding descriptive bibliography in its field. It includes federal publications beginning with the united Province of Canada, 1841-1867. Publications are arranged according to the issuing office, and brief histories of the various governmental agencies are supplied along with a list of their publications. These publications are divided into two large groups: serial publications and special publications. For serials, inclusive dates of publication are shown with a note as to whether or not the reports appeared in the *Sessional Papers* and *Annual Departmental Reports.* The section on special publications includes all those publications issued by each governmental agency which were not published in the *Journals* or *Sessional Papers.* There is a general subject index.

Government Catalogues Issued Before 1953

For federal government publications issued prior to 1953, the indexes and catalogues available were incomplete, spasmodic, and originated from many different sources. From 1890 to 1934, the *Annual Report* of the Department of Public Printing and Stationery contained a list of government publications issued during the fiscal year arranged according to the issuing agency. No bibliographical details were given except paging. This department also issued a *Price List of Government Publications* which was superseded in 1928 by the catalogue of *Official Publications of the Parliament and Government of Canada.* This latter publication was issued from 1928 to 1948 in different forms, later being known as the *Annual Catalogue.* It was simply a list of titles and prices of all official publications procurable from the King's Printer and no bibliographical details were supplied. It had supplements at intervals up to 1952, when it was replaced by the current series of daily, monthly and annual catalogues.

Government Catalogues Issued Since 1953

In 1953, the Queen's Printer published the *Canadian Government Publications Consolidated Annual Catalogue,* a basic work which superseded the old *Annual Catalogue* of 1948 and its supplements to 1952. The *Consolidated Annual Catalogue* attempted to include all federal government publications in print as of September, 1953. The *Annual Catalogue, 1954,* supplemented the *Consolidated*

Annual Catalogue, 1953, and listed federal government publications issued between October 1953 and December 1954. Both the 1953 and 1954 editions were also published in French. Since 1955, a bilingual *Annual Catalogue* has been published.

The *Annual Catalogue* supersedes issues of the bilingual *Monthly Catalogue* which in turn cumulates issues of the bilingual *Daily Checklist.* The purpose of these catalogues is to provide a comprehensive listing of all official publications, public documents and papers, not of a confidential nature, printed or processed at government expense by authority of Parliament or of a government agency, or bought at public expense for distribution to members of Parliament, public servants, or the public. These publications make it possible to check the bibliographic details, price and distribution policy of any current federal government publication. The *Monthly Catalogue* and the *Annual Catalogue* are indexed by personal author, title and subject. Since 1963, the *Monthly Catalogue* and the *Annual Catalogue* have also indexed about two dozen Canadian government periodicals by personal author, title and subject.

The Queen's Printer also publishes a series of *Sectional Catalogues* which provide a more detailed subject approach to the many thousands of government publications. To date, the following *Sectional Catalogues* have been published: Labour, Northern Affairs and National Resources, Mines Branch, Forestry, Dominion Bureau of Statistics, and Canada Treaty Series.

Certain other federal government agencies such as the Department of Agriculture, the Geological Survey and the National Research Council of Canada have issued excellent guides or indexes to their publications giving greater detail than is possible in the general catalogues mentioned above. The Dominion Bureau of Statistics has issued an *Historical Catalogue of Dominion Bureau of Statistics Publications, 1918-1960,* designed as a guide to its publications since its inception. In 1969, D.B.S. also published a *Catalogue* in two parts: Part I—Publications, lists approximately 1,100 publications grouped by subject areas; Part II—Data Files and Unpublished Information, includes information which may be useful to a limited number of individuals or organizations, but which is not published because interest in it is not considered to be sufficiently broad.

Canadiana

In 1951, the National Library of Canada (then known as the Canadian Bibliographic Centre) began issuing *Canadiana,* a national monthly bibliography listing books about Canada, published in Canada, or written by Canadians. Since 1952, one part of *Canadiana* has been devoted to federal government publications and all listings are in full bibliographic form giving author, title, edition, publisher, date and place of publication, paging, series notes and other pertinent information. Coverage of federal government publications in *Canadiana* is not as comprehensive nor are listings as quick to appear as is the case with the *Monthly Catalogue* issued by the Queen's Printer. Nevertheless, the bibliographical description for each item listed is considerably more complete, often supplying details about previous publications in the same series. Since 1953, one part of *Canadiana* has listed current publications of the ten provincial governments.

There are annual cumulations to the monthly issues of *Canadiana* for the years 1951 to 1966. Although there has been no such annual cumulation since 1966, an annual index has been published for the years 1967 and 1968. In 1968, quarterly, semi-annual and annual cumulations of the monthly index began. Federal and provincial government publications have been included in the index since 1964.

Provincial Government Publications

In general, publications of the provincial governments parallel the types issued by the federal government. Most provinces publish votes and proceedings, journals, sessional papers, annual departmental reports, statutes, and gazettes. A few also publish their debates. Because of a dearth of published catalogues or indexes, however, provincial government publications are much more difficult to locate than those of the federal government. For some provinces, retrospective bibliographies of their publications have been compiled:

Publications of the Government of the Province of Canada, 1841-1867, compiled by Olga B. Bishop, Ottawa, National Library of Canada, 1963.
Publications of the Government of British Columbia, 1871-1947, compiled by Marjorie C. Holmes, Victoria, King's Printer, 1950.
Publications of the Government of the North-West Territories, 1876-1905, and of the Province of Saskatchewan, 1905-1952, compiled by Christine MacDonald, Regina, Legislative Library, 1953.
Publications of the Government of Nova Scotia, Prince Edward Island, New Brunswick, 1758-1952, compiled by Olga B. Bishop, Ottawa, National Library of Canada, 1957.
Publications of the Government of Ontario, 1901-1955; a checklist compiled for the Ontario Library Association by Hazel I. MacTaggart, Toronto, University of Toronto Press, 1964.
Répertoire des Publications Gouvernementales du Québec de 1867 à 1964, compiled by André Beaulieu, Jean-Charles Bonenfant and Jean Hamelin, Québec, Imprimeur de la Reine, 1968.

For current provincial government publications, *Canadiana,* previously cited, provides the only comprehensive list in terms of coverage of all provinces. Some provinces do issue periodic lists of current government publications:

New Brunswick Government Documents is a checklist of New Brunswick documents received at the Legislative Library in Fredericton and has been issued annually since 1955.
Publications of the Province of Nova Scotia, is a checklist of Nova Scotia publications, compiled by the Legislative Library. The first issue covered the year 1967.
Significant Publications of the Government of Prince Edward Island covering

the years 1967-68 was published in 1968 by the Legislative Library of Prince Edward Island.

Bibliographie du Québec; Liste Trimestrielle des Publications Québécoises ou Relatives au Québec, which the Bibliothèque Nationale du Québec, Montreal, began publishing in 1969, contains a section on current publications of the government of Québec.

Publications, published from time to time since April 1966 by the Bureau de L'Editeur Officiel de Québec, lists legislative and departmental publications for sale by that office. Each current list supersedes the previous list.

Publications, published by the Queen's Printer and Publisher of Ontario, 1970. This is a list of Ontario publications in print, and supplements are planned.

BIBLIOGRAPHY

Archer, J. H., "Acquisition of Canadian Provincial Government Documents," *Library Resources and Technical Services,* Vol. 5, Winter, 1961, pp. 52-59.

Berry, P. L., "United States and Canadian Government Documents on Microforms," *Library Resources and Technical Services,* Vol. 5, Winter, 1961, pp. 60-67.

Gregory, W., (ed.), *List of Serial Publications of Foreign Governments, 1815-1931,* New York: H. W. Wilson Co., 1932. [Includes Canadian and provincial serial publications.] Reprint edition, New York, Kraus Reprint Co., 1967.

Murray, F. B., "Reference Use of Canadian Documents," *Library Resources and Technical Services,* Vol. 5, Winter, 1961, pp. 48-51.

Pross, C., "Bibliographies of Provincial Government Documents," *APLA Bulletin,* Vol. 32, December, 1968, pp. 100-104.